Engaging Language Learners through Technology Integration:

Theory, Applications, and Outcomes

Shuai Li
Georgia State University, USA

Peter Swanson
Georgia State University, USA

A volume in the Advances in Educational Technologies and Instructional Design (AETID) Book Series

Information Science REFERENCE
An Imprint of IGI Global

Managing Director:	Lindsay Johnston
Production Editor:	Jennifer Yoder
Development Editor:	Erin O'Dea
Acquisitions Editor:	Kayla Wolfe
Typesetter:	Michael Brehm
Cover Design:	Jason Mull

Published in the United States of America by
Information Science Reference (an imprint of IGI Global)
701 E. Chocolate Avenue
Hershey PA, USA 17033
Tel: 717-533-8845
Fax: 717-533-8661
E-mail: cust@igi-global.com
Web site: http://www.igi-global.com

Library of Congress Cataloging-in-Publication Data

Engaging language learners through technology integration : theory, applications and outcomes / Shuai Li and Peter Swanson, editors.
pages cm
Includes bibliographical references and index.
ISBN 978-1-4666-6174-5 (hardcover) -- ISBN 978-1-4666-6175-2 (ebook) -- ISBN 978-1-4666-6177-6 (print & perpetual access) 1. Language and languages--Study and teaching--Technological innovations. 2. Language and languages--Study and teaching--Computer network resources. 3. Educational technology.
I. Li, Shuai, 1982- editor of compilation. II. Swanson, Peter, 1964- editor of compilation.
P53.855.E54 2014
418.0078--dc23

2014013113

This book is published in the IGI Global book series Advances in Educational Technologies and Instructional Design (AETID) (ISSN: 2326-8905; eISSN: 2326-8913)

British Cataloguing in Publication Data
A Cataloguing in Publication record for this book is available from the British Library.

All work contributed to this book is new, previously-unpublished material. The views expressed in this book are those of the authors, but not necessarily of the publisher.

For electronic access to this publication, please contact: eresources@igi-global.com.

Advances in Educational Technologies and Instructional Design (AETID) Book Series

Lawrence A. Tomei
Robert Morris University, USA

ISSN: 2326-8905
EISSN: 2326-8913

Mission

Education has undergone, and continues to undergo, immense changes in the way it is enacted and distributed to both child and adult learners. From distance education, Massive-Open-Online-Courses (MOOCs), and electronic tablets in the classroom, technology is now an integral part of the educational experience and is also affecting the way educators communicate information to students.

The **Advances in Educational Technologies & Instructional Design (AETID) Book Series** is a resource where researchers, students, administrators, and educators alike can find the most updated research and theories regarding technology's integration within education and its effect on teaching as a practice.

Coverage

- Digital Divide in Education
- E-Learning
- Collaboration Tools
- Social Media Effects on Education
- Game-Based Learning
- Curriculum Development
- Classroom Response Systems
- Virtual School Environments
- Educational Telecommunications
- Online Media in Classrooms

IGI Global is currently accepting manuscripts for publication within this series. To submit a proposal for a volume in this series, please contact our Acquisition Editors at Acquisitions@igi-global.com or visit: http://www.igi-global.com/publish/.

The Advances in Educational Technologies and Instructional Design (AETID) Book Series (ISSN 2326-8905) is published by IGI Global, 701 E. Chocolate Avenue, Hershey, PA 17033-1240, USA, www.igi-global.com. This series is composed of titles available for purchase individually; each title is edited to be contextually exclusive from any other title within the series. For pricing and ordering information please visit http://www.igi-global.com/book-series/advances-educational-technologies-instructional-design/73678. Postmaster: Send all address changes to above address.

Titles in this Series

For a list of additional titles in this series, please visit: www.igi-global.com

Tablets in K-12 Education: Integrated Experiences and Implications
Heejung An (William Paterson University of New Jersey, USA) Sandra Alon (William Paterson University of New Jersey, USA) and David Fuentes (William Paterson University of New Jersey, USA)
Information Science Reference • copyright 2015 • 325pp • H/C (ISBN: 9781466663008) • US $175.00 (our price)

E-Learning as a Socio-Cultural System A Multidimensional Analysis
Vaiva Zuzevičiūtė (Mykolas Romeris University, Lithuania) Edita Butrimė (Lithuanian University of Health Sciences, Lithuania) Daiva Vitkutė-Adžgauskienė (Vytautas Magnus University, Lithuania) Vladislav Vladimirovich Fomin (Vytautas Magnus University, Lithuania) and Kathy Kikis-Papadakis (Foundation for Research and Technology, Greece)
Information Science Reference • copyright 2014 • 349pp • H/C (ISBN: 9781466661547) • US $195.00 (our price)

Effects of Information Capitalism and Globalization on Teaching and Learning
Blessing F. Adeoye (University of Lagos, Nigeria) and Lawrence Tomei (Robert Morris University, USA)
Information Science Reference • copyright 2014 • 300pp • H/C (ISBN: 9781466661622) • US $195.00 (our price)

Engaging Language Learners through Technology Integration Theory, Applications, and Outcomes
Shuai Li (Georgia State University, USA) and Peter Swanson (Georgia State University, USA)
Information Science Reference • copyright 2014 • 388pp • H/C (ISBN: 9781466661745) • US $185.00 (our price)

Handbook of Research on Education and Technology in a Changing Society
Victor C.X. Wang (Florida Atlantic University, USA)
Information Science Reference • copyright 2014 • 1217pp • H/C (ISBN: 9781466660465) • US $495.00 (our price)

Educational Technology Use and Design for Improved Learning Opportunities
Mehdi Khosrow-Pour (Information Resources Management Association, USA)
Information Science Reference • copyright 2014 • 359pp • H/C (ISBN: 9781466661028) • US $215.00 (our price)

Handbook of Research on Digital Tools for Writing Instruction in K-12 Settings
Rebecca S. Anderson (University of Memphis, USA) and Clif Mims (University of Memphis, USA)
Information Science Reference • copyright 2014 • 684pp • H/C (ISBN: 9781466659827) • US $325.00 (our price)

Cases on Teaching Critical Thinking through Visual Representation Strategies
Leonard J. Shedletsky (University of Southern Maine, USA) and Jeffrey S. Beaudry (University of Southern Maine, USA)
Information Science Reference • copyright 2014 • 568pp • H/C (ISBN: 9781466658165) • US $215.00 (our price)

IGI GLOBAL
DISSEMINATOR OF KNOWLEDGE
www.igi-global.com

701 E. Chocolate Ave., Hershey, PA 17033
Order online at www.igi-global.com or call 717-533-8845 x100
To place a standing order for titles released in this series, contact: cust@igi-global.com
Mon-Fri 8:00 am - 5:00 pm (est) or fax 24 hours a day 717-533-8661

Editorial Review Board

Table of Contents

Detailed Table of Contents

NKT groups both outperformed the control group, and there was no difference between the two instructed groups in terms of accuracy and speed of response for processing both general and idiosyncratic cues. Combining the data of the two instructed groups, the learning trajectories of general and idiosyncratic cues showed distinct patterns for measures of speed (i.e. response times) and accuracy.

Chapter 3 reports on a study that explored the pedagogical potential of Turnitin, a plagiarism detection program typically used for punitive purposes, for helping writers whose second language (L2) is English to develop their understanding of plagiarism in the context of a US university as well as their English writing skill. Three ESL learners enrolled in a composition course at a US university completed three writing projects throughout one ten-week academic term. The results showed several ways that Turnitin supported L2 academic writing development: Turnitin's matched-text function encouraged the learners to reflect upon whether sources were appropriately cited, whether a citation was needed, to what extent their sources were credible, and whether there was a balance of original ideas and information from sources. These learning processes resulted in improvement in the learners' skills and confidence in English academic writing.

Chapter 4 presents a study that examined the effectiveness of a computerized program for teaching and practicing zero anaphora inference skills in L2 Chinese. The researcher first referred to psycholinguistic theories of reference tracking to decompose zero anaphora inference skill into three sub-skills. The teaching and practicing of the three sub-skills were then computerized. The effectiveness of the computer program (CALL group) was compared with that of teacher-led instruction (Classroom group). The results showed that, while both CALL and Classroom groups showed significant improvement in accurate inference of zero anaphora from pre-test to immediately posttest, the CALL group retained the gain from immediate to delayed posttest but the Classroom group did not. Moreover, although both CALL and Classroom groups outperformed the Control group at both immediate and delayed posttests, the CALL group's scores were significantly higher than those of the Classroom group. The findings point to an edge of CALL-based over classroom-based instruction in teaching reference tracking skills in L2 Chinese.

Chapter 5 reports on a study that investigated to what extent an online instructional module promoted learning in L2 French culture. Thirteen American learners of French were guided to complete an online instructional module for teaching one aspect of French culture, that is, French family life. The instruction consisted of two phrases. During Phase One, the learners read authentic texts about French family life. During Phase Two, the learners viewed four videos showing interviews with French native speakers coming from diverse backgrounds. In both phases, the learners were asked to first post their reactions to the instructional materials online and then to engage in online discussion on the topic. The results based on analyses of the learner postings revealed a collective shift from a primary ethnorelative understanding of French family life in Phrase One to a more ethnocentric orientation in Phrase Two. After comparing the instructional materials used in this study and those used in a related earlier project, the author reported that this was attributed to a lack of explicit instruction on the target cultural phenomenon as well as the somewhat contradictory views on French family life expressed in the authentic texts and by the native interviewees.

Chapter 6 presents a study that explored how off-line peer collaborative dialogues among pre-service Japanese teachers conducted during asynchronous CMC activities with distant L2 Japanese learners could serve the purpose of teacher education. Seventeen pre-service Japanese language teachers were divided into small groups to complete three interactive tasks with learners of L2 Japanese through asynchronous CMC. During each CMC-mediated task, the teachers needed to work together (i.e., through off-line peer collaborative dialogues) to prepare response postings to those created by the learners. The results showed that the off-line peer collaborative dialogues served as reflective practices to promote the teachers' discussions on a variety of topics related to teaching Japanese (e.g., evaluating learners' language use, determining the sources of linguistic errors, considering optimal ways for providing feedback). Certain technological features afforded by asynchronous CMC facilitated the teachers' collaborative reflective practices. For example, the time flexibility afforded by the technology enabled in-depth discussions among the teachers. In addition, the author found that logs of online exchanges and texts promoted the construction of intersubjectivity among the teachers.

Chapter 7 reports on a study that investigated the role of blogging in mediating L2 learners' socialization process before and after studying abroad. Three American learners of Japanese blogged with Japanese native speakers before, during, and after their sojourn in Japan. The results revealed that blogging, when combined with classroom-based instruction, facilitated the learners' socialization into the target language community. A comparison of the content of the learners' blogging interactions before and after study abroad showed a shift from a primary focus on exchanging factual knowledge to a focus on critical analysis of cultural and societal issues related to Japan. Meanwhile, the learners' blogging-related interactions showed the use of a wider range of address terms, incorporation of regional dialects and Japanese emotion symbols, and employment of gender-specific sentence-final particles. Moreover, the learners developed their style shift strategies over time, gradually incorporating plain forms in addition to honorific forms. The learners' individualized socialization processes as reflected in their blogging-related interactions were also reported.

Chapter 8 presents a study that examined whether and how L2 learners of Chinese developed their awareness of Chinese Internet Language (CIL) by engaging in linguistic practices at an online social networking site and through routine daily communication in a study abroad context. The participants were two American learners enrolled in an advanced Chinese class in a semester study abroad program in Shanghai (China). As it turned out, both learners showed moderate gains in their awareness of Chinese CIL (as measured by the CIL questionnaire) over time, although their instructor intentionally introduced CIL in classroom and asked the learners to use Sina Weibo (a China-based online social networking site). Both learners remained largely peripheral participants of the online social networking community throughout their sojourn. Nevertheless, the two learners differed in their use of CIL forms in their Weibo postings and in their routine conversations. This difference was attributable to the characteristics of the learners' daily linguistics practices afforded by their respective living conditions.

Chapter 9 reports on a study that investigated the role of different Japanese lexical categories (i.e., noun, onomatopoeia) in affecting the type and frequency of Language Related Episodes (LREs) emerged during Skype-mediated telecollaboration. Twelve American learners were paired with Japanese native speakers to conduct two online decision-making tasks, during which participants needed to negotiate the meaning of 14 nouns (Task One) and 14 onomatopoeias (Task Two). Results showed that lexical category affected the occurrence and uptake of different types of LREs. Moreover, Skype's multimodal functions (e.g., text chat, webcam, image sharing) were found to play a facilitative role during meaning negotiation of the targeted nouns and onomatopoeias by providing written and visual aid: the image function was used more often during Task One (focusing on nouns) than during Task Two (focusing on onomatopoeias), and the reversed pattern was found for the webcam function; finally, the text chat function was used equally often for both tasks.

Chapter 10 presents a study that focused on understanding how the various functions (e.g., Discussion, Comments, History, and Edit) provided by Wikispaces mediated the learners' collaborative writing efforts (i.e., negation of writing tasks, and co-construction of writing products). Six intermediate-level EFL learners (in China) and six intermediate-level ESL learners (in the US) were divided into small groups of three and engaged in their respective collaborative writing tasks. The results showed that the Discussion and Comment functions allowed both EFL and ESL learners to actively engage in task negotiation processes such as content discussion, social talk, task management, technical communication, and language negotiation. Regarding text co-construction, the History and Edit functions enabled both EFL and ESL learners to collectively develop and revise their writing product through various editing processes such as addition, deletion, rephrasing, reordering, and correction.

Chapter 11 reports on a study that examined Singaporean elementary school teachers' attitudes toward integrating Information and Communication Technologies (ICT) into Chinese language instruction. The study adopted a mixed method approach combining large-scale questionnaire survey and focus group discussions. The participants were 311 primary school Chinese language teachers in Singapore who completed an online questionnaire survey soliciting four aspects of information regarding: (1) perceived competence for using ICT, (2) resources and support for ICT integration, (3) perceived usefulness of ICT for teaching and learning Chinese, and (4) pedagogical use of ICT. A subset of 128 teachers participated in additional focus group discussions. Quantitative results showed that the participants generally held positive attitudes toward ICT use in teaching Chinese, and that the teachers' pedagogical use of ICT was predicated by perceived ICT competence, perceived usefulness, and resource and support. Results of the focus group discussions showed that, while the teachers generally perceived ICT as effective means for Chinese teaching, they also voiced caution against excessive use of ICT. The four barriers of ICT integration into teaching practice were: (a) Lack of fully developed instructional resources, (b) amount of time invested, (c) technological inconveniences, and (d) the impact of high-stake examinations.

Chapter 12 focuses on understanding tutors' attitudes toward online L2 English writing consultations implemented in a university in Hong Kong. A survey questionnaire was administered to 10 tutors to assess their attitudes superficially toward the two online modes: a virtual mode (consultations conducted through an online text-based platform), and a hybrid mode (a combination of virtual and face-to-face consultations). The results showed that the tutors generally favored the online modes of writing consultation. However, the tutors also felt that the online modes did not encourage tutee-initiated interaction as much as tutor-initiated interaction, which made the learning process more passive in the online modes than in the face-to-face mode. Based on the results of the questionnaire survey, the author further discussed ways of improving certain features of the virtual mode (e.g., adding a synchronous communication feature to the asynchronous platform) as well as ways to better prepare tutors for the relatively new modes of online consultation.

Chapter 13 examines French EFL learners' perception of a research-informed computer platform for English vocabulary learning (i.e., VocPAL) at a French university. The chapter starts with a detailed description of the development of VocPAL, citing cognitive theories of L2 learning as well as empirical evidence in SLA (e.g., the effects of frequency, involvement load, and attention to form on L2 learning). Recognizing the importance of learner perception in influencing the effectiveness of this researcher-designed CALL platform, the author collected responses to a survey questionnaire from 115 French learners, followed by interviews with a subset of participants who were either most satisfied or least satisfied with VocPAL. The results showed that the learners generally held positive views toward the use of VocPAL for vocabulary learning. Meanwhile, they also expressed varied levels of satisfaction with the various activities/features offered through VocPAL.

Chapter 14 presents a review of research that focused on using CALL for teaching and learning vocabulary for young EFL/ESL learners. Twenty-two studies published between 2004 and 2013 were identified for further analysis. The studies were evaluated against four criteria: (a) relevance, (b) appropriateness, (c) trustworthiness, and (d) contribution. The results showed that regarding the first main review question (i.e., effectiveness of CALL), CALL programs informed by SLA theories and practices were found to be generally effective for vocabulary learning. Meanwhile, however, the author noted a need to improve the research methodology in a considerable portion of the reviewed studies (e.g., using standardized vocabulary tests rather than researcher self-developed outcome measures to enhance comparison of research findings across studies). Regarding the second main review question (i.e., the implications of existing research), the results showed that learners generally held positive views toward CALL-mediated vocabulary teaching and learning and that developing an individualized proficiency-adjusted CALL program could help foster and maintain learners' positive attitudes.

Foreword

No one can—or would—deny the reality that technology has become a pervasive aspect of our everyday lives, from the tools we use to gather news and information, to the tools we use to socialize, and everything in between. The realm of education has followed suit, so that students of all ages and all subjects have explored technological innovations in their classrooms for many years now. Language educators are no exception and, in fact, may have understood the value of incorporating various technologies into our language classes long before our colleagues in other fields. After all, what better way to connect learners with the target culture and language and to create communities of learners, even beyond the confines of the classroom?

The past few decades have witnessed an incredible growth in Computer-Assisted Language Learning (CALL) studies and practices, effectively and definitively moving us beyond the phase of studies that ask *if* we should incorporate technology into our learning and into the phase of publications that explore the *why* and the *how* of such integration. It seems we, as a field of researchers and educators, have finally come to accept that the technology tools we play with in our everyday lives are not only here to stay (or at least to rapidly evolve into a new but related tool on a regular basis!), but that they also add value to our lessons and curricula – if used appropriately.

In spite of this much needed and very welcome change in our approach, the field of CALL as a whole seems to still be lacking in a greater theoretical understanding of the interactions between various technologies and the language acquisition and learning processes. We have focused largely on student and teacher attitudes towards these new tools, and we have frequently limited our investigations to practical how-to approaches. Such research is necessary and informative, to be sure, but many deeper questions still remain to be explored. For example, what theoretical aspects of the second language acquisition process are relevant to our incorporation of new technologies? In what areas can various emerging tools benefit our understanding of the SLA process? Are certain aspects of teaching and learning new languages facilitated through the incorporation of new tools? And crucially, why and how?

This volume explores these very questions. There are questions that cannot be answered in a single study or a single volume, but the papers herein move the investigation forward a few significant steps. These chapters offer a valuable combination of empirical studies that address important theoretical issues, with reports on specific applications and outcomes of the incorporation of new technologies into language curricula. Dealing with topics such as morphosyntactic development, pragmatic and intercultural sensitivity, vocabulary learning, and teacher education and academic citations and borrowing. The studies reported here employ a wide range of tools and technologies ranging from wikis, blogs, and various CMC tools to Skype, social networking, and other tutoring or learning programs. As such, this volume offers the reader a valuable insight into the *why* and *how* of computer-assisted language learning, in addition to the *what*. Not only does the volume open these new doorways to begin to explore what is on the other side, but it also lays the foundation for future work in CALL to continue in these valuable lines of investigation.

Gillian Lord
University of Florida, USA

Gillian Lord *received a BS from Vanderbilt University, an MA in Hispanic Literatures from the University of Virginia, and a PhD in Hispanic Linguistics from Pennsylvania State University. She joined the faculty of the Department of Spanish and Portuguese Studies (formerly the Department of Romance Languages and Literatures) at the University of Florida in 2001, where she serves as Chair of the department. She also directed the Lower Division Spanish program for over a decade prior to serving as Chair. In her time at the University of Florida, Professor Lord has won the Teacher of the Year Award, the Service Learning Faculty of the Year Award, and the Doctoral Dissertation Advisor/Mentoring Award. Professor Lord's research explores language teaching and learning in both the classroom and immersion settings, focusing primarily on the acquisition of foreign language sound systems. She also works in pedagogy and teacher education with an emphasis on the role of technology in language acquisition and education. She has published articles in well-known journals such as Foreign Language Annals, Hispania, CALICO and System, among others, and co-edited a volume on web 2.0 tools in language teaching (2009, CALICO). She recently published a monograph dedicated to understanding and developing language programs entitled Language Program Direction: Theory and Practice (2013, Pearson). Professor Lord recently served on the Executive Committee of the Computer Assisted Language Instruction Consortium (CALICO) and is completing her term as Spanish Head of the American Association of University Supervisors and Coordinators (AAUSC).*

Preface

BACKGROUND

The field of Computer-Assisted Language Learning (CALL) has witnessed rapid development over the past five decades (for historical reviews see Chapelle, 2001; Fischer, 2008, 2013; Heift & Chapelle, 2012). This development is, in part, a result of the parallel development in computer technology and in Second Language Acquisition (SLA) theory and practice. On the one hand, the development of information and communication technology has provided CALL practitioners with increasingly refined and a wider range of technologies for language teaching and learning purposes. For example, the fast development and dissemination of Internet-based Web 2.0 technologies around the world has given rise to various types of Computer-Mediated Communication (CMC) activities that enable language teachers and learners to interact conveniently with each other globally. On the other hand, over the past three decades, the field of SLA has seen an increasingly wider range of perspectives for theorizing and researching second language (L2) learning (e.g., linguistic, psycholinguistic, cognitive, and sociocultural perspectives). For example, a recent edited volume by VanPatten and Williams (2007) features more than a dozen major SLA theories and their representative applications to second language teaching and learning.

The development in both computer technologies and SLA has motivated CALL researchers and practitioners to argue for closer connections between the two fields in order to better inform the theorization and practice of CALL. The interest and effort in this regard started in the 1980s and has continued to the present day. This is reflected in a series of position papers (e.g., Chapelle, 2009; Doughty, 1987; Fischer, 2013; Garrett, 1991, 2009; Thorne & Smith, 2011), monographs and/or edited volumes (e.g., Chapelle, 2001), and special editions of academic journals (e.g., the special editions of the 2009 *Modern Language Journal* and the 2011 *CALICO Journal*) published over the span of several decades.

To a certain extent, the existence of such a sustained line of arguments for better connecting CALL practices with SLA research reflects both opportunities and challenges involved in this endeavor. First, the considerable development in both CALL and SLA calls for renewed understanding of the relationship between the two. While the emphasis in the late 1980s and early 1990s was more about the necessity of utilizing SLA theories and research findings to justify CALL practices (Garrett, 1991; Doughty, 1987), a more recent conceptualization focuses on how CALL and SLA can be mutually reinforcing (e.g., Chapelle, 2009; Garrett, 2009). The evolving understanding of the relationship between CALL and SLA entails empirical research on the design, implementation, and evaluation of SLA-informed CALL practices. Second, making connections between CALL and SLA does not always occur automatically among CALL practitioners, especially when priority is placed on keeping updated on technological innovations. As Thorne and Smith (2011) observed: "...many CALL specialists have exhibited the understandable tendency to become focused on the technology while perhaps attending less assiduously to emerging trends and current findings in second language acquisition, and more broadly, from research on human development" (p. 268). Finally, a better connection between CALL and SLA requires a more balanced representation of SLA theories in CALL research. As Fischer (2013) noted, the current CALL literature, with its major focus on Computer-Mediated Communication (CMC), particularly favors the *social* approaches to SLA that emphasize learner-external factors, and more research is needed to examine the learner-internal processes/factors involved in CALL-based L2 teaching and learning.

The aforementioned issues clearly call for empirical research that not only presents the design and implementation of SLA-informed CALL programs/projects but also examines their effects and evaluates their impact from multiple and balanced theoretical perspectives. Moreover, as Garrett (2009) observed, just as SLA as a field has focused predominantly on English and on a few other Western languages, there is a need for CALL researchers and practitioners to attend to non-Western languages (e.g., Chinese and Japanese) as well. Empirical CALL research on these underrepresented languages can both test and add to the generalizability of the existing findings.

Echoing such an understanding, this book represents a collective effort to contribute to the current CALL literature with the following features. First, it presents a collection of empirical studies that investigate/evaluate the effectiveness of SLA-informed CALL programs/projects. A range of theoretical perspectives related to language learning are drawn on, including, for example, an interactionist approach to SLA, Bayesian knowledge tracing (based on skill acquisition theory), functional linguistics, language socialization, communities of practice, and a sociocultural approach to SLA. Second, these studies demonstrate how various technologies and their applications can be used for assisting L2 teaching and learning. These include *Skype*-based telecollaboration, blogging, online social networking sites, *Wiki*, experimental CALL (eCALL), plagiarism detection software *Turnitin*, online courseware and video, and various researcher developed platforms. Third, a range of linguistic features, languages skills, and language teaching and learning related processes and factors are examined in this book. These include Chinese characters, L2 writing skills, pragmatic competence, language-related episodes, language socialization process, English articles, reference tracking skills in Chinese reading comprehension, collaborative peer dialogue for L2 writing, and beliefs in and attitudes toward CALL. In relation to the various targeted linguistic features and skills, a number of less represented languages in CALL research, including Chinese, Japanese, and French, are also examined in the book. Finally, this book presents an international perspective on CALL research as the international contributors examine their respective CALL programs/projects in various cultural contexts (e.g., China, France, Japan, Singapore, and USA). In presenting this collection of empirical studies on SLA-informed CALL, we hope to construct an evidence base to inform CALL researchers and practitioners for their future endeavors. The next section presents a more detailed introduction of the sections/chapters of this book.

ORGANIZATION OF THE BOOK

The book is divided into 5 sections. The themes of the 5 sections are: "Technology Integration for Second Language Research" (Section 1), "Technology Integration for Second Language Teaching" (Section 2), "Technology-Mediated Second Language Learning Processes" (Section 3), "Beliefs and Attitudes toward Technology Integration" (Section 4), and "Systematic Review of CALL Research" (Section 5).

Section 1: Technology Integration for Second Language Research

Section 1 includes two studies that demonstrate how computer technologies can allow researchers to precisely implement and administer language learning activities as well as to collect rich data for theory testing. Chapter 1 (Xu and Chang) presents two experiments that respectively investigated the effects of computer-assisted stroke animation (i.e., showing stroke order in writing characters) and visual chunking (i.e., creating larger processing units than strokes for character learning) on the learning L2 Chinese characters. Both experiments were informed by the Dual Coding Theory from cognitive psychology. Experiment one focused on the role of stroke animation. In this experiment, 36 beginning-level learners of Chinese enrolled in a US university were assigned to three learning conditions: an *animation* condition (in which the learners viewed the animated stroke order through short video clips), a *reading* condition (in which the learners only viewed the targeted characters on computer screen), and a *writing* condition (in which the learners practicing writing the targeted characters three times). The effects of the three learning conditions were assessed by a character recognition task and a character production task. As it turned out, *animation* and *writing* both led to more accurate and faster character recognition than *reading*; meanwhile, *writing* resulted in better character production than both *animation* and *reading*. Experiment two addressed the effects of visual chunking. Forty-eight beginning-level Chinese learners recruited from a US university were divided into two learning groups to learn 48 targeted characters: *grouped* (G) and *distributed* (D). For the G group, each learning session introduced characters that share the same radical (i.e., semantic component of a Chinese character); for the D group, each learning session introduced characters with different radicals. A set of four learning conditions were designed for all learners, namely *chunking* (i.e., viewing a video clip showing the incremental construction of a character with its constituent components), *writing* (i.e., handwriting a target character from memory), *reading* (i.e. viewing a target character), and *stroke reporting* (i.e., mentally counting the number of strokes and writing down one stroke as instructed). As with Experiment one, a character recognition task and a character production were used to assess the effects of learning. The results showed that neither group status (i.e., G vs. D) nor learning conditions (i.e., *chunking*, *writing*, *reading*, and *stroke report*) affected speed and accuracy of character recognition. However, an interaction effect was found for the measure of character production. Specifically, for the G group, *chunking* led to better score than *writing* and *stroke-reporting*, although it did not perform *reading*; for the D group, *writing* resulted in higher scores than *stroke-reporting*, although it did not outperform *chunking* and *reading*. Overall, the findings of this study illustrate a nuance picture regarding the effects of computer-assisted stroke animation and visual chunking in facilitating L2 Chinese character learning, that is, the effectiveness of the two learning mechanisms need to be evaluated in consideration of concurrent learning conditions as well as outcome measures.

In Chapter 2, Zhao reports on a study that that examined the effectiveness of using Web-based experimental CALL (eCALL) for teaching English articles to EFL learners in China. Adopting the Bayesian knowledge-tracing model, Zhao's eCALL system provided individualized learning programs based on the system's moment-to-moment estimation of individual learners' mastery of the target linguistic cues (i.e., the form-function mappings of English articles), that is, providing more practice opportunities for weakly mastered cues than strongly developed ones. The eCALL system was also able to document detailed information regarding learners' engagement with learning, thereby providing valuable information of learning process. Ninety-five Chinese EFL learners recruited from a Chinese university were divided into three groups: a computerized Knowledge-Tracing group (KT), a computerized No-Knowledge-Tracing group (NKT), and a control group. Over four days, the KT and NKT groups received two one-hour training on English articles through the online eCALL system. The training sessions focused on teaching 34 English article cues divided into two categories based on a functional linguistic analysis: general (i.e., semantically transparent mappings with high frequency of usage, such as using *the* to refer to a previous mentioned entity) and idiosyncratic (i.e., semantically opaque mappings with low frequency of usage, such as *the-river* and *Ø-lake*). Meanwhile, the control group practiced English writing and did not receive instruction/training on English articles. The effects of training was assessed by a computerized sentence-level cloze test administered three times to the participants: shortly before the first training session, immediately after the second training session, and two weeks after the second training session. The data was analyzed in accuracy and speed of response. The results showed that, although the KT and NKT groups both outperformed the control group, there was no difference between the two instructed groups in terms of accuracy and speed of response for processing both general and idiosyncratic article cues. The lack of an advantage of the KT group over the NKT group was attributed to the short period of training (a total of two hours for practicing 34 English article cues). However, a post-hoc analysis on the distinct learning curves of two representative cues provided useful information for determining the appropriate amount of training in future research.

Combining the data of the two instructed groups, the learning trajectories of general and idiosyncratic cues showed interesting patterns. For the measure of accuracy, general cues received higher accuracy scores than idiosyncratic cues at pre-test, and this pattern remained unchanged over time. Moreover, while the accuracy scores of both general and idiosyncratic cues showed significant improvement from pre-test to immediate posttest, the pattern differed between the two categories afterwards, that is, increased accuracy was observed from immediate to delayed posttests for general cues but not for idiosyncratic cues. For the measure of speed, although there was no difference between the two cue types at pre-test, the learners processed idiosyncratic cues significantly faster than general cues at both immediate and delayed posttests. On the other hand, the processing of both general and idiosyncratic cues became faster after training (as reflected by the significantly reduced response time). Meanwhile, although the processing speed became significantly slower at delayed posttest than at immediate posttest for both general and idiosyncratic cues, the processing speed was nonetheless faster at delayed posttest than at the pre-test, suggesting retained effect of training. Overall, this study explored the potential of an eCALL system in implementing an innovative theory-based instructional program. The findings can serve as a valuable reference for future research investigating the potential of eCALL systems.

Section 2: Technology Integration for Second Language Teaching

Section 2 presents four chapters that report on empirical studies that showed how computer technology can be used for teaching a variety of linguistic features, skills, and constructs (e.g., L2 writing, reference tracking skill, intercultural sensitivity). Chapter 3 (Kostka and Ebsworth) addresses the issue of plagiarism in L2 writing, which has become a challenge for educators. This is partly because of the easy access to online resources, and partly because of L2 learners' relatively limited target language proficiency and their different cultural understanding of the concept of plagiarism in the target culture. To this end, Kostka and Ebsworth made a commendable effort that explored the potential of using *Turnitin*, a plagiarism detection software typically used for punitive purposes, for helping L2 English learners to develop their understanding of plagiarism in the context of a US university as well as their English writing skill. Taking a social view of learning academic writing, the authors examined how the use of *Turnitin*-mediated

L2 academic writing development. The focal participants were three ESL learners who completed three writing projects throughout one semester. *Turnitin* was introduced at the beginning of the semester and was used throughout the entire semester by both instructor and the learners in a variety of instructional and learning activities (e.g., submitting drafts to *Turnitin* to check the amount of matched text, in-class discussion of the matched texts, etc.). The data collected from a variety of sources (e.g., student writing products, class observations, student online blog entries, as well as interviews with the learners, the course instructor, and the program coordinator) showed several ways that *Turnitin* supported L2 academic writing development. For example, *Turnitin*'s matched-text function encouraged the learners to reflect upon whether their sources were appropriately cited, whether a citation was needed, to what extent their sources were credible, and whether there was a good balance between original ideas generated by themselves and information from sources. Moreover, the above-mentioned learning processes led to improvement in the learners' academic writing skills, as comparisons of their writing drafts showed.

Switching to learners of L2 Chinese, Chapter 4 (Li) presents a study that examined the effectiveness of a computerized program for teaching and practicing zero anaphora inference skills in Chinese. Zero anaphora as a language-specific linguistic feature refers to the use of empty grammatical slot for referring to a previously occurred entity in the discourse. Because this linguistic feature is pervasive in Chinese but rarely exists in English, its accurate comprehension constitutes major difficulty for English native speakers learning L2 Chinese. To address this issue, Li first referred to psycholinguistic theories of reference tracking to decompose zero anaphora inference skill into three sub-skills. The teaching and practicing of the three sub-skills were computerized to ensure precise implementation. Specifically, two computer modules were developed for each of the three sub-skills. Meanwhile, the computer program was also designed to promote scaffolding (e.g., by providing various types of feedback on demand), engagement (e.g., by providing exercises with varying levels of difficulty), and reflection (e.g., by providing information that can induce reflection on learning). The effectiveness of the computer program was compared with that of teacher-led instruction that covered exactly the same instructional content. In this study, 45 American learners of Chinese recruited from second-year Chinese classes in a US university were randomly assigned to one of the three groups, a computer-assisted group (CALL), a classroom instruction group (Classroom), and a control group. Over two weeks, the CALL and Classroom groups engaged in their respective learning activities, while the control group did not receive instruction on zero anaphora inference. A written test assessing the three sub-skills was administered three times to the participants: immediately before, immediately after, and four weeks after the instructional activities. After the delayed posttest, the CALL and Classroom groups also completed questionnaires examining learner autonomy and learning strategy. The analysis based on the overall inference skill (i.e., combining scores reflecting three sub-skills) revealed that, while both CALL and Classroom groups showed significant improvement in accurate inference of zero anaphora from pre-test to immediately posttest, the CALL group retained the gain from immediate to delayed posttest but the Classroom group did not. Moreover, although both CALL and Classroom groups outperformed the control group at both immediate and delayed posttests, the CALL group's scores were significantly higher than those of the Classroom group. Additional analyses on the three sub-skills showed similar patterns. That is, the CALL group generally performed better than the Classroom group, and both instructed groups outperformed the Control group. The edge of the CALL group over the Classroom group was attributed to the higher level of learner autonomy (as demonstrated by the results of the autonomy questionnaire survey), engagement in learning (as shown by the amount of extracurricular time spent on learning the targeted linguistic feature), and interest (as reflected in the post-instruction survey). A unique contribution of this study to the CALL literature is that the computer program focused on a discourse-level linguistic feature (i.e., zero anaphora), which broadened the range of linguistic features that can be effectively taught through computer technology. Moreover, different from traditional CALL vs. Non-CALL comparative studies, the design, development, and implementation of the computer program was well grounded in psycholinguistic and pedagogical theories. Computer technology enabled precise implementation of the theory-based instruction, and proved to be (overall) more effective than classroom-based instruction.

Shifting to learners of L2 French, Chapter 5 (Garret-Rucks) presents a study that investigated the extent to which an online instructional module promoted cultural learning in L2 French. The study was motivated by a need to explore pedagogical means to foster cultural instruction in foreign language education in the US, as well as by the potential of Computer-Mediated Communication (CMC) in promoting intercultural exchanges. The participants were learners ($N = 13$) enrolled in an elementary French course in the US. Over a period of five weeks, the participants were guided to complete an online instructional module (jointly supported by the courseware Blackboard and YouTube) for teaching one aspect of French culture, that is, French family life. The instruction consisted of two phrases. During Phase One, the learners read authentic texts (written by native French speakers) about French family life. During Phase Two, the learners viewed four videos showing interviews with French native speakers coming from diverse background. These interviewees presented varied perspectives on French family life. In both phases, the learners were asked to first post their reactions to the instructional materials online and then to engage in online discussion on the topic. The learners' postings made during the two phrases were subjected to theme analyses, and were then compared in terms of their ethnorelative (i.e., acceptance, adaptation, and integration of target cultural norms) and ethnocentric (i.e., denial, defense, and minimization of target cultural norms) orientations. The results revealed a collective shift from a primary ethnorelative understanding of French family life in Phrase One to a more ethnocentric orientation in Phrase Two. This finding contracted that of a related project that demonstrated a revised pattern of development of the learners' intercultural orientation. After comparing instructional materials used in this study and those used in Garret-Rucks (2013), the finding reported in this chapter was attributed to a lack of explicit instruction on the target cultural phenomenon as well as the somewhat contradictory views on French family life expressed in the authentic texts and by the native interviewees. The results of this study have clear pedagogical implications for L2 cultural instruction in a foreign language learning context, that is, exposing elementary-level L2 learners to diverse cultural perspectives without explicit instruction on target cultural norms may negatively affect their cultural understanding. By presenting a case detailing *what has not worked out well* and comparing it with *what has worked out well*, this study can contribute to our current theorization and practice L2 cultural instruction through technology.

While the previous chapters in this section focus on using computer technology for teaching specific linguistic features and skills, Chapter 6 (Kitade) presents a study that, informed by sociocultural theory, explored how off-line peer collaborative dialogues among pre-service Japanese teachers conducted during asynchronous CMC activities with distant L2 Japanese learners could serve the purpose of teacher education. The participants were 17 pre-service Japanese language teachers divided into small groups to complete three interactive tasks with learners of L2 Japanese through asynchronous CMC. Each CMC-mediated task lasted for about three weeks, during which the instructors needed to work together (i.e., in the format of off-line peer collaborative dialogues conducted in a language lab) to prepare response postings to those created by the learners. The results showed that the off-line peer collaborative dialogues served as reflective practices to promote the teachers' discussions on a variety of topics related to teaching Japanese, such as evaluating learners' language use, determining the sources of linguistic errors, considering optimal ways for providing feedback. Importantly, certain technological features afforded by asynchronous CMC facilitated the teachers' collaborative reflective practices. For example, the time flexibility afforded by the technology enabled in-depth discussions among the teachers. In addition, logs of online exchanges and texts promoted the construction of intersubjectivity among the teachers. Overall, the findings suggest that the hybrid model combining online learner-teacher interactions and off-line peer dialogues among teachers can be a viable component of the pedagogy for L2 teacher education.

Section 3: Technology-Mediated Second Language Learning Processes

Section 3 includes four chapters that examine various L2 learning processes mediated by Computer-Mediated Communication (CMC). Chapter 7 (Ishihara and Takamiya) reports on a study that, based on theories of language socialization, explored the role of blogging in mediating L2 learners' socialization process (with a special focus on the development of pragmatic competence) before and after studying abroad. The participants were three adult intermediate-level American learners of L2 Japanese. Over a period of 16 to 21 months, the learners blogged with Japanese native speakers in Japan before, during, and after their sojourn in Japan. During the same period, the learners were all enrolled in Japanese classes and received explicit instruction on Japanese pragmatics. The researchers focused on the learners' blogging-related activities before and after study abroad, and collected data through multiple sources (e.g., blog entries and responses, video recordings of learner presentations and writing conferences, survey questionnaires, etc.). The results demonstrated that blogging, when combined with classroom-based instruction, facilitated the learners' socialization into the target language community. A comparison of the content of the learners' blogging interactions before and after study abroad showed a shift from a primary informational focus (e.g., exchanging factual knowledge) to a focus on critical analysis of cultural and societal issues related to Japan. Parallel to this process, the learners' blogging-related interactions showed pragmatic development as reflected in their use of a wider range of address terms, incorporation of regional dialects and Japanese emotion symbols, and employment of gender-specific sentence-final particles. Moreover, the participants developed their style shift strategies over time, gradually incorporating plain forms in addition to honorific forms. In spite of these shared areas of pragmatic development, the documented blogging-related interactions also captured the individualized socialization processes of the learners as they negotiate their differential emerging identity over time.

Focusing on a different Web 2.0 technology, Chapter 8 (Diao) presents a study that examined whether and how L2 learners of Chinese developed their awareness of Chinese Internet Language (CIL) by engaging in linguistic practices at an online social networking site and through routine daily communication in a study abroad context. Drawing on theories of language socialization and community of practice, and adopting a case study approach, Diao focused on two adult American learners (Yun and Ellen) enrolled in an advanced Chinese class in a semester study abroad program in Shanghai (China). The data were collected longitudinally from a variety of sources, including CIL questionnaire (administered at the beginning and toward the end of the study abroad period), field notes, interviews, recordings of learners' natural conversations with their immediate conversation partners (e.g., roommate, tutors, host family member), and learners' postings and digital profiles on the largest China-based social networking site (i.e., Sina Weibo). As it turned out, although the instructor of the study abroad program intentionally introduced CIL in classroom instruction and asked the learners to use Sina Weibo, both learners showed moderate gain in their awareness of Chinese CIL (as measured by the CIL questionnaire) over time. An examination of the learners' Sina Weibo postings showed that both Yun and Ellen remained largely peripheral participants of the online social networking community throughout their sojourn. On the one hand, the number of their postings was small (i.e., 14 for Ellen and 5 for Yun); on the other hand, the content of their postings mainly reflected the topics discussed in their language classes. Moreover, neither Ellen nor Yun attempted to connect to Weibo users other than their instructor and classmates. Nevertheless, the two learners differed in their use of CIL forms in their Weibo postings and in their routine conversations: While Yun never used any CIL (in these two venues) during her sojourn, Ellen occasionally employed CILs. According to the author, this difference was attributable to the characteristics of the learners' daily linguistics practices afforded by their respective living conditions. Ellen lived on campus and shared a room with a young Chinese college student who was an active user of Weibo and provided considerable input and modeling on the use of CIL; on their other hand, Yun lived with a host family who provided scarce opportunity for learning CIL. By illustrating the two learners' limited engagement in online linguistic practice through a major Chinese social networking site and their moderate gain in CIL over time, the study points to the challenges of utilizing this technology for language teaching/learning in a study abroad context. The author's discussion of the findings can also serve as a valuable reference for future instructors to design an effective pedagogy in incorporating this technology (i.e., online social networking) into L2 instruction.

Turing to Skype-mediated communication, Chapter 9 (Akiyama) reports on a study that adopted an interactionist approach to SLA to investigate the role of different Japanese lexical categories (i.e., noun, onomatopoeia) in affecting the type and frequency of Language-Related Episodes (LREs) emerging during telecollaboration. In this study, 12 beginning-level adult American learners recruited from an intensive Japanese class were paired with Japanese native speakers to conduct two online decision-making tasks. During the tasks, the participants needed to negotiate the meaning of 14 nouns (Task One) and 14 onomatopoeias (Task Two). In the first part of the analysis, the participants' Skype-mediated conversations were analyzed in terms of different types of LREs (e.g., preemptive and reactive LREs). The results showed that lexical category affected the occurrence and uptake of different types of LREs. For example, significantly more preemptive LREs with a lexical focus were found during Task One (focusing on nouns) than during Task Two (focusing on onomatopoeia); significantly more reactive LREs with a phonological focus emerged during Task Two than during Task One; finally, significantly more uptakes of reactive LREs were found during Task Two than during Task One. In the second part of the analysis, Skype's multimodal functions (e.g., text chat, Webcam, image sharing) were found to play a facilitative role during meaning negotiation of the targeted nouns and onomatopoeias by providing written and visual aid. Regarding the effects of lexical category on the use of the three multimodal functions afforded by Skype, the results showed that the image function was used more often during Task One (focusing on nouns) than during Task Two (focusing on onomatopoeias), and the reversed pattern was found for the Webcam function; finally, the text chat function was used equally often for both tasks. Overall, this study illustrates how Skype-mediated telecollaboration can facilitate a wide range of LREs, which are critical processes for L2 acquisition. The design of the learning tasks and the findings of this study can also inform instructors interested in incorporating Skype into L2 instruction.

In the last chapter in this section (Chapter 10), Li and Dell-Jones focused on wiki-based collaborative writing processes among EFL and ESL learners. Conceptualizing collaborative writing from the perspective of sociocultural theories, the authors explored how the various functions (e.g., *Discussion*, *Comments*, *History*, and *Edit*) provided by *Wikispace* mediated the learners' collaborative writing efforts (i.e., negation of writing tasks and co-construction of writing products). The participants were six intermediate-level EFL learners in China and six intermediate-level ESL learners in the US. The EFL and ESL learners were divided into small groups of three, and they engaged in their respective collaborative writing tasks. The results showed that the *Discussion* and *Comment* functions allowed both EFL and ESL learners to actively engage in task negotiation processes such as content discussion, social talk, task management, technical communication, and language negotiation. Different patterns of task negotiation, namely collectively contributing pattern (i.e., equal contribution of participants) and authoritative/responsive pattern (i.e., dominant contribution of one participant), emerged in both EFL and ESL groups' interactions. Regarding text co-construction, the *History* and *Edit* functions enabled both EFL and ESL learners to collectively develop and revise their writing product through various editing processes such as addition, deletion, rephrasing, reordering, and correction. An analysis of the content of the editing processes revealed differential foci of EFL and ESL groups (e.g., the EFL groups focused more on coherence and accuracy while the ESL group mainly attended to genre development), which appeared to reflect the differences in the nature of writing tasks, the degree of homogeneity/diversity of L1 background, and the amount of extracurricular language exposure. The findings of this study suggest that a wiki can be a useful technological medium for developing L2 writing skills through learner collaboration.

Section 4: Beliefs and Attitudes toward Technology Integration

Section 4 contains three chapters that examine beliefs and attitudes toward technology integration among stakeholders (language learners and instructors) in three different cultural contexts, namely Singapore, Hong Kong, and France. The study reported in Chapter 11 (Zhang, Zhao, and Li) was contextualized in a unique sociolinguistic landscape of Singapore where Chinese is one of the three mother tongues yet of less social prominence than English. The authors examined Singaporean elementary school teachers' attitudes toward and practice of integrating Information and Communication Technologies (ICTs) into Chinese language instruction. The study was guided by Ertmer's two-tier framework for understanding teacher-external and teacher-internal factors that affect ICT integration into education (e.g., Ertmer, 1999, 2005) and adopted a mixed-method approach combining large-scale questionnaire surveys and focus group discussions. The participants were 311 primary school Chinese language teachers in Singapore who completed an online questionnaire survey soliciting four aspect of information regarding (1) perceived competence for using ICT, (2) resources and support for ICT integration, (3) perceived usefulness of ICT for teaching and learning Chinese, and (4) pedagogical use of ICT. A subset of 128 teachers participated in additional focus group discussions. Quantitative results showed that the participants generally held positive attitudes toward ICT use in teaching Chinese. A series of regression analyses showed that the teachers' pedagogical use of ICT was predicated by perceived ICT competence, perceived usefulness, and resource and support. Results of the focus group discussion further showed that, while the teachers generally perceived ICT as effective means for Chinese teaching, they also voiced caution against excessive use of ICT. Moreover, the teachers mentioned four barriers for ICT integration into their teaching practice: (a) lack of fully developed instructional resources, (b) amount of time invested, (c) technological inconveniences, and (d) the impact of high-stake examinations. While these findings bear direct relevance to policy development in Singapore, the research method of this study can also be used to investigate beliefs and attitudes toward ICT use for language-teaching purposes in other countries/regions around the world.

Switching to a different geographic region (Hong Kong), Chapter 12 (Lee) focuses on understanding tutors' attitudes toward online L2 English writing consultations implemented in a university in Hong Kong. The university offers three modes of writing consultations, namely a virtual mode (consultations conducted through an online text-based platform), a face-to-face mode, and a hybrid mode (a combination of virtual and face-to-face consultations). A survey questionnaire was administered to 10 tutors to assess their attitudes superficially toward the two online modes. The results showed that, on the positive side, the tutors generally favored the online modes of writing consultation (e.g., flexibility in scheduling, playing a complementary role for regular face-to-face interaction, and providing an alternative consultation experience for both tutors and tutees). On the other hand, the tutors also felt that the online modes did not encourage tutee-initiated interaction as much as tutor-initiated interaction, which made the learning process more passive in the online modes than in the face-to-face mode. As such, the tutors generally expressed reservation regarding replacing the face-to-face mode with the virtual mode (i.e., online-only mode). Based on the results of the questionnaire survey, the author further discussed ways of improving certain features of the virtual mode (e.g., adding a synchronous communication feature to the asynchronous platform) as well as ways to better prepare tutors for the relatively new modes of online consultation. Although this study is based on a specific project in a specific university, the reflections by the in-service tutors on the advantages and issues of online writing consultations can inform future researchers and educators to design and implement similar projects.

While the previous two chapters focus on teachers' and tutors' views toward technology integration, Chapter 13 (Prince) examines French EFL learners' perception of a research-informed computer platform for English vocabulary learning (i.e., VocPAL) at a French university. The chapter starts with a detailed description of the development of VocPAL, citing cognitive theories of L2 learning as well as empirical evidence in SLA (e.g., the effects of frequency, involvement load, and attention to form on L2 learning). The key design feature of VocPAL is to promote the processing of form-meaning mappings through integrative use of sound, pictures, and various form-meaning association activities (e.g., translation, association exercise, and exposure to the targeted vocabulary items presented in stories). Recognizing the importance of learner perception in influencing the effectiveness of this researcher-designed CALL platform, the author collected responses to a survey questionnaire from 115 French learners, followed by interviews with a subset of participants who were either most satisfied or least satisfied with VocPAL. The results showed that the learners generally held positive views toward the use of VocPAL for vocabulary learning. Meanwhile, they expressed varied levels of satisfaction with the various activities/features offered through VocPAL. The association exercise and the use of pictures were considered to be useful for learning; however, the story feature (i.e., creating stories to string targeted vocabulary items together) was perceived to be not very motivating. This, according to the author, was attributed to the ways that the stories were structured and presented. These findings thus highlight the importance of careful design and implementation in the process of translating research-informed instructional proposals into practice.

Section 5: Systematic Review of CALL Research

The last section consists of one chapter (Chapter 14) that presents a review of research that focused on using CALL for teaching and learning vocabulary for young EFL/ESL learners. Highlighting the importance of connection CALL practice with SLA theory and research, Handley first outlined major findings in SLA regarding vocabulary acquisition (e.g., the role of intentional and incidental learning, the role of repetition, etc.). Then, she proposed four review questions with the following two as the foci of her study:

(1) What evidence is there that digital technologies facilitate vocabulary acquisition? (i.e., effectiveness of CALL) and (2) What insights can be gleaned regarding the use of digital technologies in vocabulary teaching in EFL/ESL? (i.e., implications). After several rounds of searching and screening, the author identified 22 studies published between 2004 and 2013 for further analysis. The studies were evaluated against four criteria: (a) relevance (to what extent is the study relevant to the research questions), (b) appropriateness (to what extent is the study's research design appropriate), (c) trustworthiness (to what extent is the study's overall methodology sound), and (d) contribution (a holistic evaluation based on the above three criteria). The results showed that regarding the first main review question (i.e., effectiveness of CALL), CALL programs informed by SLA theories and practices were found to be generally effective for vocabulary learning. Meanwhile, however, the author noted a need to improve the research methodology of a considerable portion of the reviewed studies (e.g., using standardized vocabulary test rather than researcher self-developed outcome measures to enhance comparison of research findings across studies). Regarding the second main review question (i.e., implication), the results showed that learners generally held positive views toward CALL-mediated vocabulary teaching and learning and that developing individualized proficiency-adjusted CALL programs could help foster and maintain learners' positive attitudes.

Shuai Li
Georgia State University, USA

Pete Swanson
Georgia State University, USA

REFERENCES

Chapelle, C. (2009). The relationship between second language acquisition theory and computer-assisted language learning. *Modern Language Journal*, *93*, 741–753. doi:10.1111/j.1540-4781.2009.00970.x

Chapelle, C. A. (2001). *Computer applications in second language acquisition*. Cambridge, UK: Cambridge University Press. doi:10.1017/CBO9781139524681

Doughty, C. (1987). Relating second-language acquisition theory to CALL research and application. In W. F. Smith (Ed.), *Modern media in foreign language education: Theory and implementation* (pp. 133–167). Lincolnwood, IL: National Textbook Company.

Ertmer, P. A. (1999). Addressing first- and second-order barriers to change: Strategies for technology integration. *Educational Technology Research and Development*, *47*(4), 47–61. doi:10.1007/BF02299597

Ertmer, P. A. (2005). Teacher pedagogical beliefs: The final frontier in our quest for technology integration? *Educational Technology Research and Development*, *53*(4), 25–39. doi:10.1007/BF02504683

Fischer, R. (2008). Introduction to the special issue. *CALICO Journal*, *25*, 377–384.

Fischer, R. (2013). A conceptual overview of the history of the CALICO journal: The phases of CALL. *CALICO Journal*, *30*(1), 1–9. doi:10.11139/cj.30.1.1-9

Garrett, N. (1991). Technology in the service of language learning: Trends and issues. *Modern Language Journal, 75*(1), 74–101. doi:10.1111/j.1540-4781.1991.tb01085.x

Garrett, N. (2009). Computer-assisted language learning trends and issues revisited: Integrating innovation. *Modern Language Journal, 93*, 719–740. doi:10.1111/j.1540-4781.2009.00969.x

Heift, T., & Chapelle, C. A. (2012). Language learning through technology. In S. M. Gass, & A. Mackey (Eds.), *The Routledge handbook of second language acquisition* (pp. 555–569). New York, NY: Routledge.

Thorne, S., & Smith, B. (2011). Second language development theories and technology-mediated language learning. *CALICO Journal, 28*(2), 268–277. doi:10.11139/cj.28.2.268-277

VanPatten, B., & Williams, J. (Eds.). (2007). *Theories in second language acquisition: An introduction.* Mahwah, NJ: Lawrence Erlbaum Associates Publishers.

Section 1
Technology Integration for Second Language Research

Chapter 1
Computer-Assisted Character Learning Using Animation and Visual Chunking

Yi Xu
University of Pittsburgh, USA

Li-Yun Chang
University of Pittsburgh, USA

ABSTRACT

This chapter examines the effects of computerized stroke order animation and visual chunking on character recognition and production. Through two experiments, the authors found that both computer-assisted presentation methods were effective, and their impact was comparable to or surpassed the traditional way of character learning through reading and writing. Specifically, animation was comparable to writing and more effective than reading in facilitating form recognition. Visual chunking produced better results in character production than writing when characters were presented in radical-based groups.

INTRODUCTION

It has been four decades since researchers first attempted to integrate computer-assisted language learning (CALL) in Chinese teaching, and these efforts started with the emergence of programs teaching Chinese characters (Yao, 2009). In many Chinese CALL software programs today, character or orthography learning remains a core component (e.g., *Multimedia Learning Suite*; *Chinese Character Tutor*).[1] The design features in these programs have developed in sophistication, offering a range of possibilities such as integrating sound, verbal information, colorful or dynamic images, and interactive feedback into learning. Despite the growing availability and popularity of the learning software, only a few empirical studies (e.g., Jin, 2003; Lu, 2011; Zhu, Fung, & Wang, 2012) have examined the effectiveness of using multimedia in comparison to the traditional rote memorization of reading and writing. Such direct comparisons shall allow Chinese as a Foreign Language (CFL) practitioners to make informed decisions regarding whether and what

DOI: 10.4018/978-1-4666-6174-5.ch001

types of multimedia should be used to facilitate students' character learning. In this study we are interested in exploring whether and how different multimedia presentation modes promote Chinese orthography learning among CFL learners, and we specifically focus on two widely-used presentation modes in computer-assisted character instruction: animation and visual chunking.

BACKGROUND

Due to the lack of systematic grapheme-phoneme correspondence in Chinese (e.g., DeFrancis, 1989), character learning is frequently identified as one of the greatest challenges for CFL learners (Everson, 1998). Learning how to write by rote repetition can be tedious (Allen, 2008), and it was suggested that character learning should be practiced individually by learners (Wang, 1998). Z. Zhang (1998) asserted that the computer is best suited for the time-consuming task of teaching students how to write, as the multimedia is not only instructional but also entertaining. The potential effect of multimedia learning is predicted by the Dual Coding Theory (DCT) (Clark & Paivio, 1991), which claims that the association of verbal and nonverbal representations enhances learning and memory retention. Nonverbal representations are nonlinguistic objects or events including shapes, sounds, and actions such as drawing lines. In the cognitive theory of multimedia learning, Mayer (1999, 2003) builds on the DCT and suggests that multimedia enables the combination of processing through the visual channel and verbal channel, which supports long-term memory. The impact of the DCT has been tested in previous character animation studies, although not always with positive findings (e.g., Jin, 2003; c.f., Zhu & Hong, 2005; Zhu et al., 2012). In the current project, we are interested in the roles of two particular visual encoding methods enabled by multimedia: stroke sequence animation, referred to as *animation* below, and character chunk presentation, or *chunking*. We selected these two encoding methods because animation and chunking are commonly-used features in character learning software (e.g., *eStroke*) and in on-line character learning platforms (Chen et al., 2011; Chen, Chien, & Chang, 2013). These two methods also respectively address two key characteristics of Chinese character composition, namely, stroke sequence and structural regularity.

Stroke Sequence and Animation

Images can encode spatial transformations and help students to visualize the dynamic process of events (Clark & Paivio, 1991). Stroke sequence animation programs take advantage of continuous animation of imagery stimuli to teach characters. Traditionally, learning how to write in Chinese is conducted by imitation, with teachers illustrating how a character is to be written on the board stroke by stroke and students imitating the movement in the air (Packard et al., 2006). Such a practice focusing on stroke movement and sequence is grounded in the psychomotor basis of drawing and handwriting (Law, Ki, Chung, Ko, & Lam, 1998). For instance, research on motor aspects of graphic productions shows that there are preferred as well as very difficult directions when it comes to people's drawing (Van Sommers, 1984), and the basic stroke types in Chinese character writing coincide with the preferred directions of drawing. While imitating a teacher's handwriting movement in the classroom is costly in terms of various resources, stroke sequence animation programs afford a potentially viable alternative that is unrestricted by time and space.

Animated pictures can have a facilitating and enabling effect on learners, in that it helps them to construct a mental model by explicitly showing the micro-steps of those phenomena that are impossible to realize from static images (Schnotz & Rasch, 2005). For instance, in studies on teaching non-language disciplines such as geometry, the positive effect of continuous animation in comparison to static graphic or discrete animation (two static graphics) has been reported (Schnotz, Böckheler, & Grzondziel, 1999; Thompson & Riding, 1990). The expansion of writing over time is specified as a typical phenomenon that can be best captured by computer animation (Bétrancourt, 2005). In the current project, one of our hypotheses is that with the complex Chinese writing system, computer animation illustrating how characters are to be written should facilitate orthographic learning.

Structural Regularity and Chunking

In addition to stroke sequence animation, another computer-enabled visual encoding method explored in this chapter is *visual chunking*. A chunk is "a meaningful unit of information built from smaller pieces of information" (Gobet & Lane, 2012, p. 541). The idea that *chunking* should facilitate verbal learning and language acquisition (Gobet et al., 2001) originates from Miller's (1956) seminal work, which demonstrates that short-term memory is limited to about seven items. Based on that, Chase and Simon (1973) postulates that memory can be enhanced if small pieces of information are grouped into larger units, thus allowing information to be recorded with a small number of chunks. The process of creating such large units is referred to as *chunking*. The chunking theory has been applied to studies on alphabetic language word recognition and learning. Words were decomposed into perceptual units such as syllables and morphemes in these studies, but the exact effect of learning through chunking remains indeterminate (e.g., Rastle, Davis, Marslen-Wilson, & Tyler, 2000; Rubin & Becker, 1979; Taft & Forster, 1975).

The chunking theory is applicable to Chinese character learning. Instead of being composed of a pile of random strokes, a character can be decomposed into radicals and chunks. Radicals are the smallest semantically or phonetically functional orthographic unit, and chunks are the smallest visually integrated unit unconstrained by a particular function (Shen & Ke, 2007). That is, while both radicals and chunks are recurring subcharacter components exhibiting regularity, they are not the same. For instance, the character 婚 (*hūn*, wedding) is composed of the semantic radical of 女 (*nǚ*, female) and the phonetic radical of 昏 (*hūn*, dusk). At the same time, the character has three chunks, including 女, which is coincidentally a radical, as well as 氏 and 日, which do not serve semantic or phonetic functions in this compound character. Thus, when it comes to Chinese characters, *chunking* is the process of decomposing characters into these subcomponents. Note that chunks are often lower-level components than radicals, as in the case of 日, which is a chunk and a subcomponent of 昏, a phonetic radical.

Several existing studies on computer-assisted Chinese learning utilized recurring radicals in character learning (Chen et al., 2013; Ki et al., 2003; Lam et al., 2004). But only a few studies examined character decomposition into chunks. Among them, Xu and Padilla (2013) illustrated that chunking through teachers' instruction promoted character learning and retention among CFL learners. Cao, Rickles, et al.'s (2013) study used visual chunking on computers, but it did not find significant behavioral differences between the *chunking* group and the reading and writing group. The current study intends to further the investigations on character learning through chunking presentation on computers.

The rest of this chapter is organized as follows: The next section summarizes research on stroke sequence animation in CFL, and reports our first experiment. Then, after reviewing relevant literature, we report a second experiment focusing on chunking presentation. A general discussion follows afterwards, and a conclusion is offered in the end.

ANIMATION: EXPERIMENT 1

Existing Studies

According to earlier research, animation as a multimedia presentation method enables learners to construct a dynamic mental model and is especially helpful for one to comprehend specific dynamic processes (Schnotz & Rasch 2005). Learning how to decompose and reconstruct characters is a case in point. Through animation, a viewer is exposed to the dynamic information of how a character is created in micro-steps in one's writing. Thus, animation might achieve a similar effect to handwriting practice in character learning.

In studies on reading skill development, handwriting was found to help learners with character recognition through orienting one's attention to the internal visual-spatial features in a character and through leaving a motor-related memory trace that can be activated during recognition. Learning through animation might achieve similar benefits. However, results from existing studies on using animation in character learning are not exactly conclusive. Jin (2003) compared three types of multimedia presentations: radical formation with etymology and orthographic rules, stroke sequence, and *pinyin* with a sound playback. Jin used accuracy in a multiple-choice recall task as the outcome measure and found that stroke sequence was less effective than radical formation but was more beneficial than *pinyin* presentation. In a different study, Shi (2012) used a custom-made animation program and reported that students who learned through animation had higher accuracy in answering stroke sequence related questions than the control group. On the other hand, some studies have shown that a multimedia character presentation was not always helpful. For instance, Zhu and Hong (2005) compared four learning conditions on computer media crossing two variables: with or without stroke animation, and with or without voice. They found that, in character production, voice had no significant effect, while animation had a significantly negative effect. Additionally, those who received the with-voice-with-animation treatment performed the worst among the four groups. The negative effect of animation was replicated in Zhu et al. (2012).

These mixed findings might be partly due to the inconsistency of the outcome measures employed in the previous studies, i.e., Jin (2003) used a multiple-choice task, Shi (2012) used a written test with various tasks on stroke sequence reporting, and Zhu and Hong (2005) as well as Zhu et al. (2012) used written *pinyin*/meaning productions and character writing tasks. More importantly, the animation program used in those studies differed in their user interface. Jin (2003) used animation together with sound playback, Shi (2012) used animation with sound and meaning display and participants were able to pause and replay animation, and Zhu and his colleagues displayed the character's form, *pinyin*, meaning, as well as a mnemonic paragraph in English. Zhu and Hong (2005) admitted that the negative effect of animation in their study might be caused by the fact that learners were overwhelmed by the amount of visual input that they had to process at the same time. It should be noted that in all these studies, learners were presented with multiple types of information simultaneously, i.e., visual animation plus sound, or animation plus mnemonics, etc. As Zhu et al. (2012) explained, simultaneous presentations of different information may cause a split attention effect, due to the restriction in the human subject's cognitive resources (Mayer & Moreno, 1998). Therefore, to truthfully reveal the effect of animation, it would be helpful to carry out an experiment in which the presentation of form, sound, and meaning is sequential instead of simultaneous, thus ensuring that participants' attention would be fully directed to only one modality (e.g., visual) and one type of input (e.g., stroke animation, no other text) at one time.

In our first experiment, we focus on investigating the effect of animation in comparison with these traditional methods of character learning. In addition to using a sequential presentation and excluding confounding factors from other visual stimuli, the present experiment has the advantage over the above-mentioned studies in using a within-subject design, and in controlling the participants' learning time, which varied across different conditions in some earlier studies (e.g., Shi, 2012). Because a fully specific orthographic representation is needed before one can access a character's sound and meaning in reading (Perfetti & Tan, 1998, 1999; Tan & Perfetti, 1998), we consider orthography processing to be the first step in character learning. The two research questions of this experiment were:

1. How do different types of character learning methods, namely, animation, reading, and handwriting, affect the speed and accuracy in character recognition?
2. How do animation, reading, and handwriting respectively affect the accuracy in character production?

Method

Participants

Thirty-six students enrolled in a first-year CFL class at a university in the northeastern United States participated in this study. All were adult native speakers of English and were not heritage students. Before participating, the students had received 20 weeks of classroom instruction within the regular Chinese language curriculum. They had knowledge of *pinyin*, knew the general rules of stroke sequence, and had a vocabulary of about 450 characters.

Stimuli

A larger database, the Chinese Orthography Database Explorer (CODE) (Chen, Chang, Chou, Sung, & Chang, 2011), was used to determine experiment materials. This database systematically analyzes relationships between 439 radicals and 6,097 characters, and is constructed as an auxiliary tool for organizing and determining characters as learning materials. The experiment materials were sixty Chinese characters that have identical forms in the traditional and the simplified systems; those characters had not been taught to the participants prior to the experiment. We selected those characters from the CODE database and divided them into three groups, with 20 characters each, based on the following criteria: characters in each group had approximately the same number of strokes (average: 10 strokes), the same number of chunks (average: 3.03 chunks), similar rankings in English translation frequencies (Brysbaert & New, 2009), and each group consists of 10 characters with the left-right structure and 10 with the top-down structure.

Design

A within-subject design using encoding method (e.g., *animation*, *reading*, and *writing*) as the independent variable was conducted. Participants were randomly assigned to one of three groups. Depending on the groups that the participants were in, they learned different sets of 20 characters in each encoding condition. Data collection took place in a behavioral lab equipped with computers; E-prime software (Schneider, Eschman, & Zuccolotto, 2002) was used to control stimuli display and to record participants' responses.

Procedure

A paper-and-pencil pre-test asking participants to write *pinyin* and meaning for each character confirmed that all learning materials were unknown to all participants. In all cases, the correct responses were less than 1%.

Participants then learned characters on computers. For every character, participants had a three-second exposure: one second to see the character form, one second to see the *pinyin* and hear the pronunciation, and one second to see the English translation on the computer. They then had 15 seconds to encode the character form with different methods. In these 15 seconds, in the *animation* condition, participants saw a video clip showing how the character was written stroke by stroke, and the movie played three times within 15 seconds. Participants were instructed not to have any kind of hand movement but to simply watch the movie. In the *reading* condition, participants viewed a static character form on the screen, and they were instructed to refrain from any hand movement. In the *writing* condition, participants were asked to write the character from memory three times. In each of the three conditions, this process of the initial three-second exposure plus the 15-second encoding, which summed to 18 seconds, was repeated three times in one learning session. For each encoding condition, there were three sessions, with two sessions in the first day and one session in the second day, so the participants had about three minutes in total to learn a character. All participants first experienced the *reading* condition, as it is unlikely that learning through *reading* would affect the participants' learning strategies when experiencing the other two conditions. Then, the sequences in which a participant experienced the *writing* and the *animation* conditions were counter-balanced.

Outcome Measures

Participants' learning outcome was assessed through a computerized *lexical decision* task and a paper-and-pencil *character production* task, conducted in this order immediately after the third learning session in each encoding condition. For each task, all 20 characters learned through that encoding condition were included as test materials.

The *lexical decision* task was designed to assess learners' visual-orthographic representation of character form and was commonly used in reading studies (e.g., Peng, Li, & Yang, 1997; Taft, Zhu, & Peng, 1999, among others). Participants saw one orthographic symbol on the screen and were asked to decide, as quickly and as accurately as possible, if the symbol was a real character or not. Faster reaction time (RT) and higher accuracy indicate more robust orthographic form representation. In this study, each *lexical decision* task was composed of 40 characters in total, including 20 learned characters (i.e., experiment materials) in that encoding condition, 10 familiar characters (i.e., characters learned by participants in their regular course curriculum prior to the experiment), and 10 unfamiliar characters (i.e., characters that were never exposed to participants either in their curriculum or any of the experiment learning sessions); half of the stimuli in each of the above-mentioned type were real characters, while the other half were not. The unreal characters were created by adding, deleting, or moving one stroke from one location to another within a character. This subtle difference ensured that the task tapped into refined orthographic representation.

In the *character production* task, participants were instructed to write the characters from memory based on given clues of *pinyin* and English translations. This task assesses participants' orthographic representation at a productive level.

Data Analysis

In the *lexical decision* task, E-prime assigned a score of 1 to each item that participants responded to correctly and a score of 0 to each item responded to incorrectly; E-prime also recorded participants' RT for each item. Accuracy rate on the 20 learned characters (in each condition) and RT on those correctly responded learned characters were analyzed.

In scoring the production task, we gave one point to a character written correctly in full, and gave 0.5 point if (1) participants produced at least 50% of the total number of chunks in the correct way, or (2) if the response could be recognized as the character intended and deviated from the correct form with no more than two strokes. Zero point was given to response that did not fulfill any of the criteria listed above. Two researchers independently scored the data and inter-rater reliability was 97.70%. In this study, we report percentage accuracies, which were calculated by dividing participants' achieved score by the maximum score that they could get (i.e., 20 points) and multiplying the result by 100.

Results

We performed a one-way repeated-measures analysis of variance (ANOVA) with encoding method as an independent variable. We set the significance level at .05 and report partial eta-squared (η_p^2) as an effect size. Pair-wise comparisons with Bonferroni adjustment were performed for any difference that reached significance. Table 1 shows the descriptive statistics for both tasks.

For *lexical decision*, there was a significant difference among encoding methods, $F(2, 70) = 16.30$, $p < .01$, $\eta_p^2 = 0.32$. *Reading* led to longer RTs than *animation* and *writing* ($p < .01$ for both), and there was no significant difference between *animation* and *writing*. Although there was no significant difference on accuracy, $F(2, 70) = 2.22$, $p = .12$, numerical results suggest a mirrored ordering of *writing*, *animation*, and *reading*, with *writing* and *animation* producing higher accuracy rates than *reading*, echoing the results of RTs. As for *character production*, we found a significant difference among encoding methods, $F(2, 70) = 6.24$, $p < .01$, $\eta_p^2 = .15$. Pairwise comparisons revealed that *writing* outperformed *animation* ($p = .01$) as well as *reading* ($p = .02$), while there was no difference between *animation* and *reading*.

To summarize, for the measure of character recognition speed, *animation* and *writing* were more beneficial than *reading* in leading to more rapid identification; for character recognition accuracy, *writing* and *animation* both led to a numerically higher accuracy rate than *reading*; for the measure of character production accuracy, *writing* outperformed both *animation* and *reading*.

CHUNKING: EXPERIMENT 2

Existing Studies

While animation programs draw learners' attention to the lowest-level component in a character, namely the strokes, some software programs emphasize the role of radicals and chunks in characters. Both radicals and chunks can be con-

Table 1. Means and Standard Deviations (in parentheses) in Recognition and Production Tasks in Each Condition (n = 36)

	Animation	Writing	Reading
Lexical Decision			
Accuracy (%)	80.42 (12.67)	83.61 (10.11)	77.36 (12.10)
Reaction time (ms.)	1252.25 (306.46)	1190.56 (223.01)	1449.53 (304.55)
Character Production (%)	53.89 (22.15)	64.79 (22.68)	55.42 (23.24)

Note. Reaction time is in milliseconds (ms.). The percentage of character production accuracy reflects the proportion of target-like responses out of all 20 items in each condition.

sidered as intermediate-level orthographic units higher on the hierarchy than strokes and features and lower than the whole character (Taft & Zhu, 1997)[2]. The position-specific feature of radicals and the recurring nature of chunks contribute to the structural regularity of characters. According to the literature, about 4,000 commonly-used compound characters are formed by 200 radicals (Feldman & Siok, 1999), and 80% of characters are composed by 118 chunks (W. X. Zhang, 1990)[3]. If learners can perceive characters as the composition of those orthographic units instead of a compilation of unrelated strokes, the burden to memorize thousands of characters can be reduced to the processing of a few hundreds of chunks (Shen & Ke, 2007). In addition, since radicals have interpretations that are generally consistent with the meaning of the whole character (Feldman & Siok, 1999; Shu & Anderson, 1999), the semantic information of the radical provides useful cues for efficient learning.

To underscore the structural regularity of characters, some software programs were designed with radical-sharing characters sequenced in clusters. For instance, in Lam et al. (2001), one type of material used was a set of rhymes containing characters with the same phonetic component, e.g., 青, 清, 晴, 请, 情, which share the component of 青 and all pronounced as *qing*, with different tones. The authors reasoned that grouping those characters together enabled students to recognize the similarities and differences among them. Another set of materials in the software, called *morphological component*, asked students to differentiate two sets of characters with different semantic radicals, e.g., a set with 妹, 姊, 妈, 她, which all shared the 女 (female) radical, and a second set with 伯, 你, 他, 们, which all shared the 亻 (person) radical. Lam et al. reported that teachers in Chinese primary schools were able to creatively use the software to conduct classes. Ki et al. (2003) also used software that enhanced students' awareness of radicals, and in their *Dragonwise* project that was carried out in 20 schools, they emphasized that characters should be embedded in meaningful contexts. The effect of radical-based character grouping in CALL has not been extensively explored in the CFL context, but a recent attempt was made by Chen et al (2013). In their study, Chen et al. compared traditional word-based classroom teaching with explicit orthography instruction using groups of radical-sharing characters as E-learning materials. The authors concluded that the E-learning group, in comparison with the traditional group, achieved better orthography knowledge development, including better radical form recognition and radical semantic and phonetic awareness.

Aside from radicals, chunks also function as frequently-recurring subcharacter components. Although studies on reading suggest that L1 Chinese adults decompose characters into chunks in visual word recognition (Zhu & Taft, 1994), studies on character instruction using chunks are scarce. Pak et al. (2005) found that L1 children were able to apply visual chunking strategies to process characters and that their ability to perceive chunks is correlated with reading proficiency. Cao, Rickles, et al. (2013) was the first study to examine whether chunking presentations on computers facilitate orthographic recognition among L2 Chinese learners; they found that the amplitude of N170, an early visuo-orthographic brain response, was greater when students learned characters through chunking than through reading or writing, suggesting that chunking drew learners' attention to local features of character component and helped learners to develop a more fully-specific orthographic representation system of characters. At the same time, Cao, Rickles, et al.'s behavioral data did not reach statistical significance, making it difficult to interpret to what extent learning through chunking helps learners in character recognition.

While the above-mentioned studies either confirmed the feasibility of using character grouping in e-materials or suggested the potential benefit of chunking, it is acknowledged that only data from experiments that specifically measure the grouping and chunking features in those software programs can provide convincing evidence (Ki et al. 2003). Our second experiment was carried out to tackle this question, that is, to examine the effects of character grouping in material sequencing and the multimedia presentation of chunking in E-learning among CFL learners. In addition, we integrated multimedia learning with traditional teaching in real language classrooms to enhance the ecological validity of this experiment. Specifically, we asked two research questions:

1. Does material sequencing in learning, i.e., presenting characters in clusters according to their radicals versus distributing these characters into different learning sessions, affect character form recognition and production?
2. Do different types of encoding methods, including visual chunking, reading, writing, and stroke-reporting (as a control condition), affect character form recognition and production?

Method

Participants

Forty-eight non-heritage English-speaking students enrolled in a first-year Chinese class at a university in the northeastern United States participated in this study. Half of the participants were assigned to learn characters that share the same radical in a grouped sequence (G), and the other half were exposed to these characters in a distributed sequence (D). Before data collection, students had received eight weeks of classroom instruction. To ensure that participants' Chinese proficiency levels were equivalent between the G and the D groups, the participants' Chinese overall course scores were used to match their proficiency, and there was no difference in their Chinese proficiencies, $t\,(46) = -1.50, p = .14$.

Stimuli

Forty-eight characters, deriving from eight semantic radicals (女 'female', 饣 'food', 日 'sun', 火 'fire', 木 'wood', 心 'heart', 贝 'money', and 钅 'metal'), with six characters each, were selected from the CODE, the same database used in Experiment 1. These eight sets of characters were matched with number of strokes (average: 10.11 strokes), number of chunks (average: 2.98 chunks), structures, and English translation frequencies (Brysbaert & New, 2009). None of these characters had been taught in class before the study. These 48 characters formed two sets of eight texts, used respectively in the G and the D groups. For the G group, the six characters sharing the same radical were embedded in one text, whereas for the D group, a text contained six target characters (from the same 48-character pool) that do not share the same radicals. See Appendix A for details of how learning materials were organized differently in the two groups and how they were integrated into a meaningful context. In the pretest, no participant gave correct responses for writing *pinyin* or identifying meaning for any of the 48 characters.

Design

A 2 × 4 mixed design was carried out with character presentation sequencing (G vs. D) as a between-subject variable and encoding method (*chunking*, *writing*, *reading*, and *stroke-reporting*) as a within-subject variable.

Procedure

All experiment sessions took place in regular class periods in four consecutive days in a language lab equipped with personal computers. In each class period, participants learned two texts in their respective conditions. For instance, on Day 1, for participants in the G group, they learned texts G1 and G2 and the 12 target characters (with 饣 'food' or 女 'female' radicals) embedded in those two texts. For participants in the D group, they learned text D1 and D2 and the two sets of non-radical sharing characters embedded in those two texts. Each class period consisted of a 20-minute traditional classroom learning part, which provided an ecological context for our experiment, and a self-learning part on computers.

In the traditional classroom learning part, the participants' regular instructors used PowerPoint presentation software to teach new words with *pinyin*, meaning, and picture, and led students to read and comprehend texts as well as practice language use. (All words containing target characters were the same in both sequencing conditions). Note that this part of the teaching was word-based instead of character-based, and the instructors did not give any etymological or orthographic explanations for any characters.

In the self-learning part on computers, participants learned twelve characters with one encoding method per day, and the sequence of encoding conditions was balanced by a Latin-square arrangement. To learn a character, participants had a three-second initial exposure, with one second each for form, sound, and meaning. Then participants used one of the four encoding methods to learn the character's form. Specifically, in the *chunking* condition, participants saw a video displaying two times how a character was built with chunks. Figure 1 gives an example of the screen display for 婚 (*hūn*, marriage) in the chunking condition. The addition of each chunk took 800 milliseconds (ms.), so that in the case of 婚, the encoding time was 4,800 ms., which is also the average encoding time for all characters. (Encoding time ranged from 3,200 ms. to 9,600 ms. for different characters depending on how many chunks the character has). Note that this encoding time for a given character remained the same when the character appeared in different encoding conditions. That is, when 婚 was presented in the *reading*, *writing*, and *stroke-reporting* conditions, the participants also had 4,800 ms. to read, write, or count, before the screen refreshed into another round of three-second initial exposure. In the *writing* condition, participants were asked to write the character from memory as completely and as many times as possible within the encoding time. In the *reading* condition, participants saw a static character image on the screen. Finally, in the *stroke-reporting* condition, participants did not see any image on the screen, and were asked to count from memory the number of strokes of a character and write down a specific stroke according to an assigned number on the screen. The *stroke-reporting* condition, creating a similar learning situation but adding burden to learners' processing cost, was used as a control group to determine the true learning effects of other encoding methods. The procedure of three-second initial exposure plus encoding time was repeated three times for each character. Taking the inter-stimulus interval into consideration, the total length of time that participants spent on learning a character was about 30 seconds on average. (see Figure 1)

Outcome Measures

Learning outcome was assessed through a *lexical decision* task and a *character production* task. The *lexical decision* task was implemented immediately after each day's learning session. There were 24 characters, including 12 target characters learned in that particular day, six familiar characters, and six unfamiliar characters. Half of these materials were real characters, and the other half were not.

The *character production* task was conducted on the fifth day. Before the assessment, participants first received a rehearsal, in which they reviewed all 48 characters one at a time with the same display sequences in their learning phase.[4] In the rehearsal, participants had six seconds to review each character, including viewing the form, *pinyin*, and meaning information of characters again. In the *character production* task, participants were asked to write a character based on its English

Figure 1. Chunking procedure

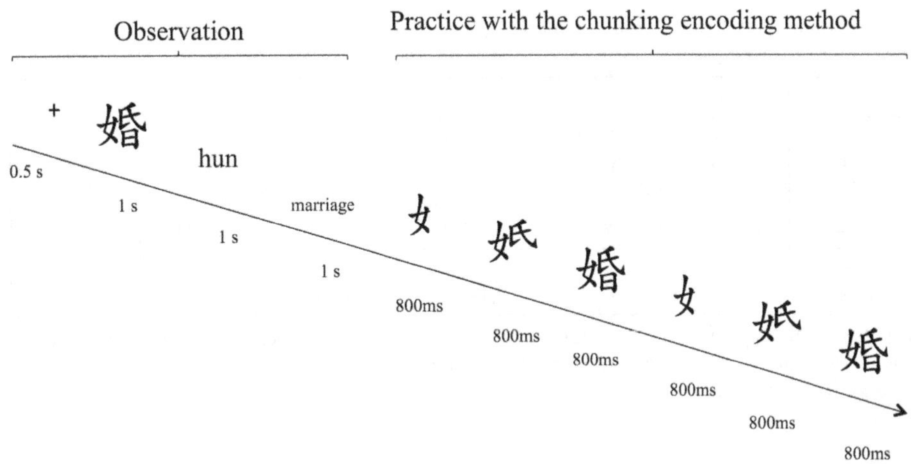

translation. The orders of the 48 characters were counterbalanced for different participants to avoid fatigue effects.

Data Analysis

For the *lexical decision* task, participants' accuracy rate and RT on the target characters were analyzed. For the *character production* task, we used a composite score that calculated the total of the attained scores in these four schemes: a full character score, in which the attained score was either 1 or 0, a layout score that assessed whether the production had the correct left-right or up-down structures, a chunk score based on the percentage of correct chunks produced, and a stroke score based on the percentage of correct strokes produced. We used this scoring method because it would sensitively reflect participants' orthographic awareness at different levels of character composition, including the character's strokes, chunks, layout and the character as a complete unit. In reporting results, we used percentage accuracies, which were calculated by dividing participants' achieved score by the maximum value that they could get and multiplying it by 100. Two researchers independently coded all data, and inter-rater reliability was 99.70%.

Results

We performed a two-way mixed ANOVA with sequencing condition as a between-subject variable and encoding method as a within-subject variable. Table 2 shows the descriptive statistics for both measures for the two sequencing conditions. For *lexical decision* accuracy rate, there was no significant two-way interaction, $F < 1$. There was also no significant main effect for either sequencing condition, $F(1, 46) = .42$, $p = .52$, $\eta_p^2 = .01$, or encoding method, $F(3, 138) = 1.62$, $p = .19$, $\eta_p^2 = .03$. Similarly, for *lexical decision* reaction time, there was also no two-way interaction, $F(3, 138) = 1.60$, $p = .19$, $\eta_p^2 = .03$. There was no significant difference either between sequencing condition averaged across encoding methods, $F(1, 46) = 3.87$, $p = .06$, $\eta_p^2 = .08$, or among encoding methods averaged across sequencing conditions, $F(3, 138) = 1.23$, $p = .30$, $\eta_p^2 = .03$.

As for the measure of *character production* accuracy, we found a two-way interaction, $F(3, 138) = 4.47$, $p < .01$, $\eta_p^2 = .09$. There was no significant difference on production accuracy between sequencing conditions averaged across encoding methods, $F(1, 46) = .26$, $p = .61$, $\eta_p^2 = .01$. However, there was a significant difference on production accuracy among encoding methods

Table 2. Means and Standard deviations (in parentheses) in Recognition and Production Tasks in Each Condition (G: n = 24; D: n = 24)

	Characters-in-group (G)				Characters-distributed (D)			
	C	W	R	S	C	W	R	S
LD %	72.48 (16.17)	71.15 (12.54)	71.88 (17.17)	76.04 (11.61)	68.40 (19.50)	69.26 (18.30)	69.98 (19.93)	74.31 (18.70)
LD RT	1161.52 (264.44)	1171.87 (269.45)	1186.90 (284.80)	1220.44 (265.58)	1322.16 (286.98)	1323.22 (289.39)	1231.19 (232.78)	1318.19 (301.04)
CP %	36.06 (19.86)	20.18 (12.26)	29.02 (17.58)	22.99 (18.52)	23.55 (20.01)	26.73 (16.31)	22.97 (17.51)	19.22 (14.51)

Note. LD refers to *lexical decision* task; % refers to accuracy rate; RT refers to reaction time; CP refers to *character production* task. The letters each stand for the following: G for grouped sequencing, D for distributed sequencing, C for visual *chunking*, R for *reading*, W for *writing*, and S for *stroke-reporting*.

averaged across sequencing conditions, $F(3, 138) = 3.32, p = .02, \eta_p^2 = .07$. To determine the pattern of differences of encoding methods on character production, we performed a simple main effect test of encoding for each of the two sequencing groups and, when results reached significance, we then used simple pair-wise comparisons with a Bonferroni adjustment to identify which pairs were significantly different. For the G group, the simple main effect of encoding was significant, $F(3, 69) = 3.74, p = .02, \eta_p^2 = .14$. Numerically, *chunking* led to the highest accuracy rate in production among the four conditions: it significantly outperformed *stroke-reporting* ($p = .03$) and marginally outperformed *writing* ($p = .07$). No other significant difference was detected. For the D group, the simple main effect of encoding was also significant, $F(3, 69) = 4.21, p = .01, \eta_p^2 = .15$. *Writing* significantly outperformed *stroke-reporting* ($p < .01$), and no other significant difference was found.

To summarize, in character recognition accuracy and speed (measured by reaction times), neither sequencing conditions nor encoding conditions affected the outcome. In character production accuracy, under the distributed condition, *writing* was more effective than *stroke-reporting* (but not *reading* or *chunking*); under the grouped condition, *chunking* was more effective than *stroke-reporting* and *writing* (but not *reading*).

DISCUSSION

As characters differ from one another in terms of strokes, chunks, and radicals, as well as structural configurations, visual-orthographic skills can be more important in character learning than learning words in an alphabetic language (Huang & Hanley, 1994; Leck, Weekes, & Chen, 1995). In addition, compared to L1 children, CFL learners might rely more on the visual form of characters to access the lexicon, since their linguistic knowledge of form-sound and sound-meaning links is weak (Wang, Perfetti, & Liu, 2003). In this study, we aimed to uncover the role of technology in supporting the development of orthographic processing skills and character writing skills.

In Experiment 1, after learning through *writing* and through *animation*, learners could differentiate target characters from illegal characters more quickly than learning through *reading*. They also had numerically higher accuracy rate in judging whether the stimuli were real characters or not when they learned characters through *animation* and *writing* rather than through *reading*. Both the RT and accuracy data suggested that *animation* and *writing* both led to a more refined orthographic representation than *reading*. In both animation and writing, learners pay close attention to the internal visual-spatial features of the character. Writing requires learners to decompose characters and reproduce an orthographically complete form by reconstructing each stroke correctly according to their spatial arrangement. Animation illustrates the visual features of each stroke and gives explicit instructions on how they position together to form a character. Since characters may appear like a square-shaped pack of strokes with no clear initial positions, these processes help learners to establish an accurate representation of the character's form with its detailed configural properties specified. This is helpful because a primary factor that differentiates characters from one another is the stroke, including the strokes' features, shape, number, spatial position, and compositional relations (Ching & Ching, 1975; W. W. Zhang, 2012).

However, although *animation* and *writing* led to similar results in recognition measures, *writing* outperformed both *animation* and *reading* in production. After learning under the *animation* condition, although learners had a refined orthographic representation, that did not transfer into productive skills. That is, animation is not necessarily more beneficial than studying a static image, if the instructional goal is to enable learners to write characters from memory rather than reading or recognition. This might be so because the passive viewing of an animation provides less support for sensory-motor components that function in actual writing.

In Experiment 2, we found a significant interaction effect between sequencing conditions and encoding methods for the measure of character production accuracy. First, under the distributed condition, *writing*, but not other methods, proved effective because it led to higher accuracy than *stroke-reporting*, the baseline condition. The *writing* effect replicates previous studies such as Guan et al. (2011) and Cao, Vu, et al. (2013). It should be noted that in those previous studies, characters were typically chosen from different radical groups without frequent radical overlap. Hence, these results from previous studies show the advantage of writing when learning materials are not derived from specific radical groups. In such a distributed way of sequencing, chunking did not appear to be particularly helpful, since there was no significant difference between *chunking* and *stroke-reporting* (the baseline condition).

In Experiment 2, under the grouped condition, *chunking* led to higher accuracy in character production than both *stroke-reporting* and *writing*. This means that the effect of chunking is evident only when material sequencing accentuates the recurring nature of subcharacter components. It can be suggested that radical-based sequencing encouraged learners to perceive characters as the composition of larger subcomponents instead of the compilation of strokes or a holistic grapheme. Thus, in the grouped sequencing condition, visual chunking further developed learners' sensitivity towards those intermediate-level orthographic units. Through the combination of radical-based sequencing and chunking, the visual-orthographic representation of a character can be built on the radical and chunk level, instead of directly on the stroke level. Learners who develop the orthographic awareness that chunks and radicals are useful subunits in character formation have fewer subunits to memorize than those who process characters as the composite of numerous strokes. In other words, when learners are asked to reproduce characters from memory, the larger the subunits, the easier the task (Taft & Chung, 1999).

The results indicate that highlighting subcharacter components through the combination of radical-based sequencing and chunking presentation helps learners to memorize a character's form by enhancing their orthographic structural awareness. Note that technology is an excellent tool to organize materials in different ways to realize different learning modes or teaching methods. For instance, Wang (1998) identified that grouping based on radicals and other cues can be a useful strategy in character learning, yet 80% of the students surveyed responded that they did not categorize characters into groups in self-learning. Implementing different kinds of character grouping in E-materials can easily help learners who lack systematic orthographic knowledge to categorize characters effectively.

In character recognition, unlike in Experiment 1, neither *writing* nor *chunking* led to higher accuracy scores than the other two conditions. Note that we could not attribute the lack of significant results in the recognition measures and the effect in production measure as a reflection of differences in the nature of the tasks, because the two tasks (i.e., character recognition and character production) were performed at different times. Instead, the lack of significant learning effect in character recognition is likely a result of the limited amount of practice afforded in this experiment. Whereas learners typically had about three minutes to study each character in previous studies (e.g., Guan et al. 2011), the 30-second time on task in this experiment proved to be insufficient to lead to significant results. Interpreting the results together with findings in Experiment 1 and previous studies, we suggest that time on task needs to reach a certain threshold for the effectiveness of any encoding methods to be realized.

The results from the two experiments confirmed that both *animation* and *chunking* can be highly effective CALL methods for character learning. Meanwhile, the effectiveness of *animation* and *chunking* seems dependent on specific pedagogical goals (i.e., recognition or production) and character sequencing (with radical-sharing characters presented in a cluster, or distributed). Specifically, for receptive skill development in reading, using animation software can be a viable alternative to handwriting practice, since its presentation is dynamic and gives explicit instructions on stroke features. Moreover, when materials are sequenced based on their shared structural components, as in the grouped sequence in Experiment 2, learners' attention is drawn to the systematic structural features of characters, and visual chunking can lead to a more economical way of memorization.

The above also suggests that the effectiveness of CALL depends on different ways of utilizing multimedia (i.e., animation or chunking), as well as several other instructional variables. For instance, the lack of significant results in character recognition in Experiment 2 indicates that practice time must reach a threshold for learning to be effective, regardless of the encoding methods. On the other hand, in the same experiment, the observed effect in character production after rehearsal suggests that knowledge recycling enhances memory. Thus, sufficient practice time and effective review schedules are factors that should be considered in learning.

In Experiment 2, we also verified the possibility of integrating orthography learning with communicative language and traditional classroom teaching. This approach has been implemented in Chinese children's classrooms. In both the *Dragonwise* project and our Experiment 2, texts were "deliberately written to contain [...] structurally related characters" (Ki et al., 2003, p.69). Whereas Ki et al. reported teachers' positive feedback to support this integrative approach, we provided evidence of actual learning effect that confirmed that orthography learning can be embedded within meaningful language context, and be conducted as a supplement to traditional classroom instruction which often focuses on word-based learning and grammar practice.

CONCLUSION AND FUTURE DIRECTIONS

This study investigated the effects of computer-assisted *animation* and *chunking*, in comparison with the traditional character learning methods of *reading* and *writing* on character recognition and production. We found that these types of dynamic presentations support CFL learners' orthography learning, with animation achieving beneficial effect in character form recognition, and chunking in radical-based character sequencing leading to beneficial outcome in helping learners to reproduce characters from memory. The degree of success in using these methods in establishing orthographic representations should be discussed in relation to the skills assessed (i.e., production, recognition), and in consideration with the character sequencing condition (distributed, grouped).

Some features of the animation and chunking technologies in this study should be noted. First, the animation technology used in this study avoids the split attention effect cautioned by Zhu et al. (2012). By presenting the form, sound, and meaning of the character consecutively in the initial exposure, and allowing learners to focus on character form decomposition and reconstruction during the stroke sequence animation, the animation program in this study ensured that learners were not overwhelmed by different types of input all at once, and still received both verbal information and visual (i.e., nonverbal) information to support their memory. The separation of audio, visual and verbal information is relatively easy to achieve in multimedia. For instance, *HyperChinese* allows delays in presenting the audio or the written form in vocabulary drilling, so that different types of information can be presented one by one. In the chunking presentation, we combined it with radical-based character grouping. Grouping, sorting, and listing characters based on their recurring subcharacter components is a feature recently utilized in some E-learning platforms (Chen et al., 2013).

The current study also has some limitations in the scope of multimedia features that it addresses. A potentially useful feature in character presentation not directly addressed is radical/chunk color-coding. In some software such as *eStroke*, different components in a character such as semantic and phonetic radicals are coded with different colors. While a black-and-white screen was used in the animation and chunking technology in this study, color-coding might achieve a similar effect to presenting chunks one by one in our Experiment 2, and this technology can be combined with stroke sequence animation, as done in *eStroke*. Further, in our experiments, practice time was controlled precisely across different learning conditions, but for learning purposes, it is beneficial to allow learners flexible practice schedules. Such features of *rewind*, *stop*, and *advance* are provided in some programs such as the one used in Shi (2012). How such individualized practice schedules facilitates learning should be investigated in future studies. Finally, the technology used in the project did not involve feedback during the learning stage, and we did not investigate character sound and meaning learning. For many computer programs that use character flashcards, interactive feedback is available (e.g., *Wenlin*) to help learners to connect the character's form with its sound and meaning. Future research could investigate how form-sound and form-meaning links can be strengthened through immediate feedback in multimedia software.

ACKNOWLEDGMENT

The two experiments reported in this chapter are part of two bigger projects, funded by the *Jiede Empirical Research Grant* for Chinese Pedagogy/Chinese Applied Linguistics from the Chinese Language Teachers Association and the FY12 Small Grant from University of Pittsburgh's Office of Research, both to the first author. Part of the data in Experiment 1 appears in the following article discussing character form, sound, and meaning learning: Xu, Y., Chang, L.-Y., Zhang, J., & Perfetti, C. A. (2013). The comparative effectiveness of reading, writing, and animation in Chinese as a foreign language character learning. *Foreign Language Annals, 46*(3), 423-444.

REFERENCES

Allen, J. R. (2008). Why learning to write Chinese is a waste of time: A modest proposal. *Foreign Language Annals, 41*(2), 237–251. doi:10.1111/j.1944-9720.2008.tb03291.x

Bétrancourt, M. (2005). The animation and interactivity principles in multimedia learning. In R. E. Mayer (Ed.), *The Cambridge handbook of multimedia learning* (pp. 287–296). New York, NY: Cambridge University Press. doi:10.1017/CBO9780511816819.019

Brysbaert, M., & New, B. (2009). Moving beyond Kucera and Francis: A critical evaluation current word frequency norms and the introduction of a new and improved word frequency measure for American English. *Behavior Research Methods, 41*, 488–496. doi:10.3758/BRM.41.4.977 PMID:19897807

Cao, F., Rickles, B., Vu, M., Zhu, Z., Chan, H., & Harris, L. et al. (2013). Early-stage visual processing predicts retention in second language learning. *Journal of Neurolinguistics, 26*, 440–461. doi:10.1016/j.jneuroling.2013.01.003 PMID:23798804

Cao, F., Vu, M., Chan, D. H. L., Lawrence, J. M., Harris, L. N., & Guan, Q. et al. (2013). Writing affects the brain network of reading in Chinese: A functional magnetic resonance imaging study. *Human Brain Mapping, 34*, 1670–1684. doi:10.1002/hbm.22017 PMID:22378588

Chase, W. G., & Simon, H. A. (1973). Perception in chess. *Cognitive Psychology, 4*, 55–81. doi:10.1016/0010-0285(73)90004-2

Chen, H. C., Chang, L. Y., Chou, Y. S., Sung, Y. T., & Chang, K. E. (2011). Construction of Chinese Orthographic Database for Chinese Character Instruction. *Bulletin of Educational Psychology, 43*, 269–290.

Chen, H. C., Chien, H. Y., & Chang, S. P. (2013). *Chinese radical-based character-family E-learning platform*. Retrieved from http://coolch.sce.ntnu.edu.tw/chinese2

Chen, H. C., Hsu, C. C., Chang, L. Y., Lin, Y. C., Chang, K. E., & Sung, Y. T. (2013). Using a radical-derived character E-learning platform to increase learner knowledge of Chinese characters. *Language Learning & Technology, 17*(1), 89–106.

Chen, H. C., Lin, Y. C., Xyue, J. Y., Chang, L. Y., Sung, Y. T., & Chang, K. E. (2011). *Development of Radical-Based Character-Family E-Learning Platform*. Paper presented at The Asia-Pacific Conference on Technology Enhanced Learning. Xi'an, China.

Chinese radical position frequency dictionary. (1984). Hunan, China: Hunan Institute of Computer Science.

Ching, N., & Ching, E. (1975). Teaching the writing of Chinese characters. *Journal of the Chinese Language Teachers Association, 10*(1), 20–24.

Clark, J. M., & Paivio, A. (1991). Dual coding theory and education. *Educational Psychology Review, 3*(3), 149–209. doi:10.1007/BF01320076

DeFrancis, J. (1989). *Visible speech: the diverse oneness of writing systems Honolulu*. HI: University of Hawaii Press.

Everson, M. E. (1998). Word Recognition among Learners of Chinese as a Foreign Language: Investigating the Relationship between Naming and Knowing. *Modern Language Journal, 82*(2), 194–204. doi:10.1111/j.1540-4781.1998.tb01192.x

Feldman, L. B., & Siok, W. W. T. (1999). Semantic radicals in phonetic compounds: Implications for visual character recognition in Chinese. In J. Wang, A. W. Inhoff, & H.-C. Chen (Eds.), *Reading Chinese script: A cognitive analysis* (pp. 19–35). Mahwah, NJ: Lawrence Erlbaum Associates.

Gobet, F., & Lane, P. C. R. (2012). Chunking mechanisms and learning. In Encyclopedia of the Sciences of Learning (pp. 541-544). Springer.

Gobet, F., Lane, P. C. R., Croker, S., Cheng, P. C.-H., Jones, G., Oliver, I., & Pine, J. M. (2001). Chunking mechanisms in human learning. *Trends in Cognitive Sciences*, *5*(6), 236–243. doi:10.1016/S1364-6613(00)01662-4 PMID:11390294

Guan, C. Q., Liu, Y., Chan, D. H. L., Ye, F., & Perfetti, C. A. (2011). Writing strengthens orthography and alphabetic-coding strengthens phonology in learning to read Chinese. *Journal of Educational Psychology*, *103*(3), 509–522. doi:10.1037/a0023730

Huang, H., & Hanley, R. (1994). Phonological awareness and visual skills in learning to read Chinese and English. *Cognition*, *54*, 73–98. doi:10.1016/0010-0277(94)00641-W PMID:7851080

Jin, H. G. (2003). Empirical evidence on character recognition in multimedia Chinese tasks. *Concentric: Studies in English Literature and Linguistics*, *29*(2), 36–58.

Ki, W. W., Lam, H. C., Chung, A. L. S., Tse, S. K., Ko, P. Y., Lau, E. C. C., …Lai, S. M. S. (2003). Structural awareness, variation theory and ICT support. *L1-Educational Studies in Language and Literature, 3*, 53–78.

Lam, H. C., Ki, W. W., Chung, A. L. S., Ko, P. Y., Lai, A. C. Y., & Lai, S. M. S. et al. (2004). Designing learning objects that afford learners the experience of important variations in Chinese characters. *Journal of Computer Assisted Learning*, *20*, 114–123. doi:10.1111/j.1365-2729.2004.00071.x

Lam, H. C., Ki, W. W., Law, N., Chung, A. L. S., Ko, P. Y., Ho, A. H. S., & Pun, S. W. (2001). Designing CALL for learning Chinese characters. *Journal of Computer Assisted Learning*, *17*, 115–128. doi:10.1046/j.1365-2729.2001.00164.x

Law, N., Ki, W. W., Chung, A. L. S., Ko, P. Y., & Lam, H. C. (1998). Children's stroke sequence errors in writing Chinese characters. *Reading and Writing*, *10*, 267–292. doi:10.1023/A:1008091730338

Leck, K. J., Weekes, B. S., & Chen, M. J. (1995). Visual and phonological pathways to the lexicon: Evidence from Chinese readers. *Memory & Cognition*, *23*, 468–476. doi:10.3758/BF03197248 PMID:7666760

Lu, M. T. P. (2011). *The effect of instructional embodiment designs on Chinese language learning: The use of embodied animation for beginning learners of Chinese characters*. (Doctoral dissertation). Retrieved from ProQuest Dissertations and Theses database.

Mayer, R., & Moreno, R. (1998). A split-attention effect in multimedia learning: Evidence for dual processing systems in working memory. *Journal of Educational Psychology*, *90*, 312–320. doi:10.1037/0022-0663.90.2.312

Mayer, R. E. (1999). Multimedia aids to problem-solving transfer. *International Journal of Educational Research*, *31*, 611–623. doi:10.1016/S0883-0355(99)00027-0

Mayer, R. E. (2003). The promise of multimedia learning: using the same instructional design methods across different media. *Learning and Instruction*, *13*, 125–139. doi:10.1016/S0959-4752(02)00016-6

Miller, G. A. (1956). The magical number seven, plus or minus two: Some limits on our capacity for processing information. *Psychological Review*, *63*, 81–97. doi:10.1037/h0043158 PMID:13310704

Packard, J., Chen, X., Li, W., Wu, X., Gaffney, J., Li, H., & Anderson, R. C. (2006). Explicit instruction in orthographic structure and word morphology helps Chinese children learn to write characters. *Reading and Writing*, *19*, 457–487. doi:10.1007/s11145-006-9003-4

Pak, A. K. H., Cheng-Lai, A., Tso, I. F., Hua, S., Wenling, L., & Anderson, R. C. (2005). Visual chunking skills of Hong Kong children. *Reading and Writing*, *18*, 437–454. doi:10.1007/s11145-005-6575-3

Peng, D. L., Li, Y. P., & Yang, H. (1997). Orthographic processing in the identification of Chinese characters. In H.-C. Chen (Ed.), *Cognitive processing of Chinese and related Asian languages* (pp. 85–108). Hong Kong: The Chinese University Press.

Perfetti, C. A., & Tan, L. H. (1998). The time course of graphic, phonological, and semantic activation in Chinese character identification. *Journal of Experimental Psychology. Learning, Memory, and Cognition*, *24*, 101–118. doi:10.1037/0278-7393.24.1.101

Perfetti, C. A., & Tan, L. H. (1999). The constituency model of Chinese word identification. In J. Wang, A. W. Inhoff, & H. C. Chen (Eds.), *Reading Chinese script: A cognitive analysis* (pp. 115–134). Mahwah, NJ: Lawrence Erlbaum Associates, Inc.

Rastle, K., Davis, M. H., Marslen-Wilson, W. D., & Tyler, L. K. (2000). Morphological and semantic effects in visual word recognition: A time course study. *Language and Cognitive Processes*, *15*, 507–538. doi:10.1080/01690960050119689

Rubin, G. S., & Becker, G. A. (1979). Morphological structure and its effect on visual word recognition. *Journal of Verbal Learning and Verbal Behavior*, *18*, 757–767. doi:10.1016/S0022-5371(79)90467-5

Schneider, W., Eschman, A., & Zuccolotto, A. (2002). *E-Prime user's guide*. Pittsburgh, PA: Psychology Software Tools, Inc.

Schnotz, W., Böckheler, J., & Grzondziel, H. (1999). Individual and co-operative learning with animated pictures. *European Journal of Psychology of Education*, *14*(2), 245–265. doi:10.1007/BF03172968

Schnotz, W., & Rasch, T. (2005). Enabling, facilitating and inhibiting effects of animations in multimedia learning: Why reduction of cognitive load can have negative results on learning. *Educational Technology Research and Development*, *53*(3), 47–58. doi:10.1007/BF02504797

Shen, H. H., & Ke, C. (2007). Radical awareness and word acquisition among nonnative learners of Chinese. *Modern Language Journal*, *91*, 97–111. doi:10.1111/j.1540-4781.2007.00511.x

Shi, L. (2012). *The effects of a custom-designed animation program on learning Chinese characters*. (Doctoral dissertation). Retrieved from ProQuest Dissertations and Theses database.

Shu, H., & Anderson, R. C. (1999). Learning to read Chinese: the development of metalinguistic awareness. In J. Wang, A. W. Inhoff, & H.-C. Chen (Eds.), *Reading Chinese script: A cognitive analysis* (pp. 1–18). Mahwah, NJ: Lawrence Erlbaum Associates.

Taft, M., & Chung, K. (1999). Using radicals in teaching Chinese characters to second language learners. *Psychologia*, *42*, 234–251.

Taft, M., & Forster, K. I. (1975). Lexical storage and retrieval for pre.xed words. *Journal of Verbal Learning and Verbal Behavior*, *14*, 638–647. doi:10.1016/S0022-5371(75)80051-X

Taft, M., & Zhu, X. (1997). Submorphemic processing in reading Chinese. *Journal of Experimental Psychology. Learning, Memory, and Cognition*, *23*, 761–775. doi:10.1037/0278-7393.23.3.761

Taft, M., Zhu, X., & Peng, D. (1999). Positional specificity of radical in Chinese character recognition. *Journal of Memory and Language*, *40*, 498–519. doi:10.1006/jmla.1998.2625

Tan, L. H., & Perfetti, C. (1998). Phonological codes as early sources of constraint in Chinese word identification: A review of current discoveries and theoretical accounts. *Reading and Writing*, *10*, 105–200. doi:10.1023/A:1008086231343

Thompson, S. V., & Riding, R., J. (1990). The effect of animated diagrams on the understanding of a mathematical demonstration in 11 to 14 years-old pupils. *The British Journal of Educational Psychology, 60*, 93–98. doi:10.1111/j.2044-8279.1990.tb00925.x PMID:1693087

Van Sommers, P. (1984). *Drawing and cognition: Descriptive and experimental studies of graphic production processes*. Cambridge: Cambridge University Press. doi:10.1017/CBO9780511897672

Wang, M., Perfetti, C. A., & Liu, Y. (2003). Alphabetic readers quickly acquire orthographic structure in learning to read Chinese. *Scientific Studies of Reading, 7*(2), 183–208. doi:10.1207/S1532799XSSR0702_4

Wang, S. C. (1998). A study on the learning and teaching of hanzi-Chinese characters. *Working Papers in Educational Linguistics, 14*(1), 69–101.

Xu, X., & Padilla, A. M. (2013). Using meaningful interpretation and chunking to enhance memory: The case of Chinese character learning. *Foreign Language Annals, 14*(3), 402–422.

Yao, T. C. (2009). The Current Status of Chinese CALL in the United States. *Journal of the Chinese Language Teachers Association, 44*(1), 1–23.

Zhang, W. W. [章文文] (2012). *A research into the orthographically similar radicals and characters in Chinese as a foreign language education.* [对外汉语教学中的近似偏旁及形近字研究]. (Master's thesis). Retrieved from CNKI database.

Zhang, W. X. (1990). From character chunks to character structure in Chinese as a foreign language teaching. *Teaching Chinese in the World, 2*, 112–120.

Zhang, Z. (1998). CALL for Chinese – Issues and Practice. *Journal of Chinese Language Teachers Association, 33*(1), 51–82. Available at http://www.csulb.edu/~txie/learn_online/issues.htm

Zhu, X., & Taft, M. (1994). *Complexity effects in Chinese character processing*. Paper presented to the Asian–Australian Workshop on Cognitive Processing of Asian Languages. Beijing, China.

Zhu, Y., Fung, A. S. L., & Wang, H. Y. (2012). Memorization effects of pronunciation and stroke order animation in digital flashcards. *CALICO Journal, 29*(3), 563–577. doi:10.11139/cj.29.3.563-577

Zhu, Y., & Hong, W. (2005). Effects of Digital Voiced Pronunciation and Stroke Sequence Animation on Character Memorization of CFL Learners. *Journal of the Chinese Language Teachers Association, 40*(3), 49–70.

ADDITIONAL READING

Bai, J. (2003). Making multimedia an integral part of curricular innovation. *Journal of the Chinese Language Teachers Association, 38*(2), 1–16.

Chen, H. C., Hsu, C. C., Chang, L. Y., Lin, Y. C., Chang, K. E., & Sung, Y. T. (2013). Using a radical-derived character E-learning platform to increase learner knowledge of Chinese characters. *Language Learning & Technology, 17*(1), 89–106.

Chuang, H. Y., & Ku, H. Y. (2011). The effect of computer-based multimedia instruction with Chinese character recognition. *Educational Media International, 48*(1), 27–41.

Everson, M. E. (2011). Best practices in teaching logographic and non-Roman writing systems to L2 learners. *Annual Review of Applied Linguistics, 31*, 249–274.

Jin, H. G. (2003). Empirical evidence on character recognition in multimedia Chinese tasks. *Concentric: Studies in English Literature and Linguistics, 29*(2), 36–58.

Li, X. (1996). HyperCharacters: A pilot study in computerized learning of Chinese characters. *CALICO Journal*, *14*(1), 77–94.

Shen, H. H. (2010). Imagery and verbal coding approaches in Chinese vocabulary instruction. *Language Teaching Research*, *14*(4), 485–499.

Shen, H. H., & Ke, C. (2007). Radical awareness and word acquisition among nonnative learners of Chinese. *Modern Language Journal*, *91*, 97–111.

Tsai, C. H., Kuo, C. H., Horng, W. B., & Chen, C. W. (2012). Effects on learning logographic character formation in computer-assisted handwriting instruction. *Language Learning & Technology*, *16*(1), 110–130.

Wang, J., Inhoff, A. W., & Chen, H. C. (Eds.). (1999). *Reading Chinese script: A cognitive analysis*. Mahwah, NJ: Lawrence Erlbaum Associates.

Xie, T. (1999). Using computers in Chinese language teaching. In M. Chu (Ed.), *Mapping the Course of the Chinese Language Field*. Chinese Language Teachers Association Monograph Series, Volume III (pp. 255–284). Kalamazoo, Michigan. Retrieved from <http://www.csulb.edu/~txie/papers/Using_computers.htm>

Xie, T., & Yao, T. C. (2009). Technology in Chinese Language Teaching and Learning. In M. Everson, & Y. Xiao (Eds.), *Teaching Chinese as a Foreign Language: Theories and Applications* (pp. 151–172). Boston: Cheng & Tsui.

Zhang, P., Xie, T., & Xu, J. (Eds.). (2004). *The studies on the theory and methodology of the digitalized Chinese teaching to foreigners* [数字化对外汉语教学理论与方法研究]. Beijing: Tsinghua University Press.

Zheng, Y. (2008). *Computer technology and teaching Chinese in the world*. Beijing: Foreign Language Teaching and Research Press.

Zhu, Y., Fung, S. L., & Wang, H. (2012). Revisiting the effects of pronunciation and stroke order animation in digital flashcards on memorization of Chines new words: Towards an adapted dual coding theory. *CALICO*, *29*(3), 563–577.

KEY TERMS AND DEFINITIONS

Chunk: *Bùjiàn*, a basic orthographic unit composed of interwoven strokes. A chunk may have as few as one stroke, although it usually has more. It is a graphic component of characters and can be differentiated from *radicals* because, unlike radicals, it is a recurring subcharacter component that is unrestricted by function.

Grapheme-phoneme correspondence (GPC): The transparency between letters and phonemes. This term usually applies to alphabetic languages. In the alphabetic writing system, orthographies vary in the transparency of mappings between letters and phonemes. For example, Finnish orthography is shallow (or transparent), because it has direct and consistent one-to-one mapping between grapheme and phoneme, whereas English orthography is relatively deep (or opaque), because it has less consistent GPC (e.g., < c > maps to phoneme /k/ in CAT, to phoneme /s/ in CITE, and /ch/ in SEARCH, a one-to-many mapping). Following this definition, Chinese does not have systematic GPC.

Lexical Decision Task: An online reaction time task performed with the assistance of computers. Participants decide whether a stimulus shown on the screen is a real character/word or not. Typically, participants are instructed to make a decision as quickly and accurately as possible, and press one of the keys on a keyboard or buttons on a response box to indicate their decision. The stimuli would include a mixture of real characters/words and unreal or pseudo characters/words. Reaction time is the time needed for participants to make a judgment from the onset of the stimulus to their responses. Faster reaction time and higher accuracy indicate better orthographic form representation.

Orthography: A normative aspect of writing systems. Simply put, it is the correct way to write a particular language. For a given language, an orthography is the implementation of the mapping principles between a visual script and its spoken language. In alphabetic writing system, orthography refers to the rules of spelling. In Chinese writing system, orthography refers to the logical spatial relationships among strokes, chunks, and radicals in a square-like space.

Radical: *Bùshǒu*, orthographic components of characters that provide either semantic or phonetic cues to the whole character. An integral character has only one radical, but most Chinese characters are compound characters that are formed by at least two radicals. In some literature, the term *radical* is used restrictively for semantic radicals. Some radicals can be further decomposed into smaller chunks, while others may coincide with chunks.

Stroke Sequence Animation: The display of animated character writing on the computer screen. It is a sequence of continuous images showing how a character would be written with the correct stroke sequence and direction of movement. The display creates an optical illusion as if the character is being handwritten by someone. Typically, such animation programs only show how the character is created stroke by stroke, without showing the image of a pen or a person's hand.

Visual Chunking: A sequence of screen display showing how several chunks are positioned together to construct a complete character. For instance, for a character that has a left-right structure with one chunk on the left side and two chunks on the right, the first screen shows the left-side chunk in an imaginary two-dimensional square, the second screen shows two chunks, with the second chunk at the top-right corner of the square, and a third screen shows the image of a complete character, with three chunks.

(Visual-)orthographic representation: The way that the grapheme of a character is perceived and mentally stored. In a high-quality representation, a character is perceived as having the logic composition of radicals, chunks, and strokes to their full specification.

ENDNOTES

1 The following is a list of software programs mentioned in the paper: *Chinese Character Tutor*. Liberty Township, OH: Flashware Int'l. (http://www.bridgetochina.com); *eStroke Animated Chinese* (v1.39). Hong Kong: Econ Media Ltd. (www.eon.com.hk/estroke/); *Multimedia Learning Suite: Chinese Characters*. LearnLift. (http://www.memorylifter.com/); *Wenlin 4.1*. Wenlin Institute, Inc. (http://wenlin.com).

2 In Taft and Zhu (1997), radicals refer ambiguously to semantic/phonetic radicals as well as chunks (p. 761-762).

3 The counting of chunks varies slightly in different studies. According to the *Chinese radical position frequency dictionary* (1984), there are 541 chunks. According to W. C. Zhang (1990), there are 560 chunks. In this study, we use *chunks* defined by the Chinese Orthography Database (Chen et al., 2011).

4 A rehearsal was scheduled before the production task because character production is presumably more challenging than recognition, and since participants had only about 30 seconds to learn each character in the learning session, we consider a rehearsal to be necessary for the production task to be meaningful. Because the rehearsal procedure was exactly the same for both sequencing conditions and on all characters, the different timing should not affect the comparative effectiveness of different encoding methods or sequencing conditions. At the same time, potential patterns in the recognition task should be interpreted as an immediate effect, while results in the production task should be interpreted as effects after rehearsal.

APPENDIX A: LEARNING MATERIALS IN EXPERIMENT 2

1. Table 3 shows the distribution of 48 characters appearing in different material sequencing conditions and their sample texts. G stands for grouped sequencing and D distributed sequencing. For instance, G1 refers to the first text learned under the grouped sequencing.

Table 3.

Day	Characters in texts in the G sequence	Characters in texts in the D sequence
1	G1: 蚀 饱 饶 馅 馋 馒	D1: 姑 银 概 蚀 赔 晌
	G2: 姑 娇 娃 婚 嫁 媳	D2: 旷 忍 败 钥 娃 烛
2	G3: 忍 忌 忽 急 患 愁	D3: 钓 账 饶 晒 桶 患
	G4:财 败 账 贩 贼 赔	D4: 饱 婚 烟 钻 忽 棚
3	G5: 钓 钥 钞 钻 银 锁	D5: 炮 急 贼 梯 锁 暗
	G6: 旷 晒 晌 晾 暄 暗	D6: 贩 钞 烘 馅 晾 嫁
4	G7: 炉 炮 烘 烟 烛 焰	D7: 材 炉 媳 愁 暄 馒
	G8: 材 板 桶 梯 棚 概	D8: 忌 财 板 娇 焰 馋

2. Sample text in the grouped sequencing (Text G1). Target characters are underlined. 小高的哥哥卖馒头和肉馅包子。小高很馋,吃十个才饱。哥哥说,你这样吃,要是我的店蚀本了,我不饶你。 (English translation of G1: Xiaogao's elder brother sells steamed buns and meat stuffed buns. Xiaogao is gluttonous. He does not feel full until he has had ten buns. His elder brother said, "If you eat buns like this and my restaurant loses capital, I would not forgive you.")
3. Sample text in the distributed sequencing (Text D1) 小高的姑姑在银器店工作,她每天大概从上午忙到晌午。做生意不蚀本,也不赔钱。她是一个很聪明的生意人。 (English translation of D1: Xiaogao's father's sister works in a silverware shop. She is busy approximately from morning to noon every day. She does not lose capital or suffer any loss when doing business. She is a very smart business person.)

Chapter 2
Enhancing Grammatical Accuracy and Linguistic Fluency:
English Article Tutor

Helen Zhao
The Chinese University of Hong Kong, Hong Kong

ABSTRACT

This chapter introduces a new paradigm of Web-based language learning, experimental Computer-Assisted Language Learning (eCALL) and its application in ESL and EFL grammar instruction. eCALL methods provide online training that complements classroom practice, while integrating second language acquisition theories and models. The authors introduce an eCALL tutor that teaches the correct use of the English article system. The authors examined the effectiveness of the tutor in an experimental study with 78 Chinese intermediate-advanced EFL learners. The tutor incorporated Bayesian knowledge tracing and provided individualized and adaptive training of English article usage. Learners' performance was measured by accuracy and response time. The results show that the tutor led to significant learning gains after three hours of tutor training, with gains retained two weeks later. The robust learning effects were documented by a significant improvement in accuracy and fluency of using the article.

INTRODUCTION

Recent advances in computer technology have stimulated approaches of computer-assisted language learning (CALL). These improvements are made possible with the growth of online resources such as games, dictionaries, grammars, translators, multilingual media, wiki pages, and social networking sites (Barr, 2008; Warschauer, 1995; Zhang & Barbar, 2008). Integrating these new functions with traditional classroom language teaching poses new challenges for researchers, as well as for teachers, developers, and learners. Nagata (1993), for example, pointed out that some CALL systems possess "limited capabilities for analyzing learners' responses, diagnosing their errors, and providing feedback" (p. 330). Garrett (1987) addressed similar concerns with existing

DOI: 10.4018/978-1-4666-6174-5.ch002

CALL systems: "Most students learn no more from grammar on the computer than they do from grammar in the workbooks, because much of the commercially available offerings are of the 'wrong, try again' model, which only indicates whether student-produced bits of language match the target language model stored in computer memory (sometimes also showing the correct answer) without indicating how or why the student input does not match" (p. 174). These problems prevented CALL systems from performing at their full potential in promoting effective learning.

This chapter introduces a new approach of CALL that addresses the above problems. This new approach is called experimentalized computer-based language learning or eCALL (Presson, Davy, & MacWhinney, 2013). eCALL systems incorporate experimental methodology as well as methods in dynamic assessment (Cen, Koedinger, & Junker, 2006) to produce demonstrable improvements in language learning. The eCALL system introduced in this chapter is a computer-based tutorial system (referred to as 'the Article Tutor') that provides English article instruction to second language (L2) learners. The article tutor has been tested in multiple experimental studies in which we explored the effectiveness of different instructional interventions in article instruction (Zhao, 2012; Zhao, Koedinger, & Kowalski, 2013). The main feature of article instruction in the current study is the incorporation of Bayesian knowledge tracing that provides adaptive and individualized training to L2 learners. The primary goal of this research is to develop an adaptive vehicle for testing the efficacy of Bayesian knowledge tracing in the domain of second language learning. A secondary goal is to capture the efficacy of instruction through dynamic assessment. The tutor documents detailed information on learner performance in the form of computer logs. A data repository and analysis tool called Datashop (Koedinger et al., 2010) codes and analyzes the logs in order to generate learning curves that reflect learners' dynamic changes in performance over time.

This chapter begins with an introduction of eCALL systems and their applications in cognitive language tutors. We will then introduce Bayesian knowledge tracing and how it functions in cognitive tutors. Next, we will provide a functional linguistic analysis of the English article system. We will introduce two types of article usages, *general* and *idiosyncratic*, which explain why the English article has been difficult for L2 learners to acquire. Next we will present the details of the experimental study, including its methodology, results, and discussions of its implications.

BACKGROUND

eCALL Systems

eCALL systems provide instruction grounded on theories of second language (L2) acquisition, psycholinguistics, human-computer interaction, and educational psychology. eCALL systems have been implemented in experimental or quasi-experimental studies. Such systems make it easier to assess learning. It can also provide detailed data, collected systematically online, that permit the formulation of more precise accounts of the language learning processes (Cen, Koedinger, & Junker, 2006; Presson, Davy, & MacWhinney, 2013).

There are several reasons for administering experimental instructions through an eCALL system. First, feedback provided through the computer is highly salient (Sagarra, 2007; Sauro, 2009). Computerized feedback helps enhance the visual saliency of grammatical forms that are typically low in perceptual saliency in oral interaction. In addition, the greater processing time required by computerized feedback than that afforded by face-to-face oral feedback leads to more attention to form and better memorization.

Second, eCALL systems are effective for controlling extraneous variables. In an eCALL environment, students in the same instructional condition are guaranteed to receive the same amount and type of training, feedback, and assessment. Student activities in the system can be carefully controlled and monitored. Moreover, researchers can easily achieve the type of random assignment that is much harder to implement in classroom-based research.

Third, an eCALL system offers advantages in terms of data storage and analysis. Data obtained from eCALL systems can be collected in the form of computer logs. These logs keep record of practically all the information researchers and teachers would like to collect such as the date and the response time (in milliseconds) of each learning trial, the question(s) given to the learner, the correct answer to the question, the answer(s) given by the learner, and the nature of tasks (pretest, immediate posttest, delayed posttest, training, questionnaire), etc. Logs document the entire learning process so that researchers and teachers can track the learner's performance at each stage of the learning process. Even in studies with large sample size, researchers and teachers can quickly obtain information regarding all learners' performance in a relatively small amount of time.

Last but not least, researchers can also administer computer-based instruction outside the classroom. Most eCALL practice can be assigned to students as independent learning homework. Such systems complement the shortage of class hours while encouraging students' autonomous learning.

Bayesian Knowledge Tracing

Since the mid-1990s, Corbett and Anderson's (1995) Bayesian knowledge tracing model has been widely used to model student knowledge in learning systems of various domains, including tutors for mathematics, computer programming, and reading skills (Baker, Corbett, Gowda, Wagner, MacLaren, Kauffman, Mitchell, & Giguere, 2010). This model is based on a cognitive model of skill acquisition with the goal of mastery learning. It attempts to monitor students' dynamic knowledge development as they practice a complex cognitive skill, to individualize the practice sequence to enable students to master the skill efficiently, and to accurately predict students' performance. It has its theoretical roots in John Andersen's research (Andersen, 1993; Andersen & Corbett, 1992; Andersen & Matessa, 1992) on student modeling and individualized instruction in intelligent tutors at Carnegie Mellon University (CMU).

According to Corbett and Andersen (1995), Bayesian knowledge tracing assumes that at any given opportunity to use a rule within a cognitive tutor, there exists a probability that a student knows the rule and may either give a correct or incorrect response. A student who does not know the rule generally will give an incorrect response, but there is a certain probability (called $p(G)$, the Guess parameter) that the student will give a correct response. Correspondingly, a student who does know the rule generally will give a correct response, but there is a certain probability (called $p(S)$, the Slip parameter) that the student will give an incorrect response. Each rule has an initial probability ($p(L_0)$) of being known by the student, and at each opportunity to practice a rule, the student has a certain probability ($p(T)$) of learning the rule. Once these four parameters are set, the model can be used to predict student performance. Figure 1 illustrates the relationship between the four parameters in the Bayesian Knowledge Tracing Model.

The four parameters in Bayesian knowledge tracing are customized for each rule, using data from students practicing that rule within the same tutor. The goal during parameter fitting is to figure out which combination of parameters best predicts the pattern of correct and incorrect responses in the existing data. That model is then used to make predictions about students' knowledge as they use the tutor.

Figure 1. Bayesian knowledge tracing model (Corbett and Anderson, 1995)

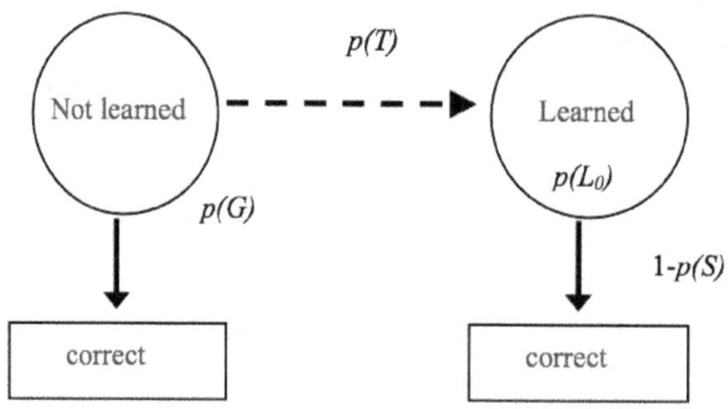

An equation:

$$P(L_n \,/\, Action_n) = P(L_{n-1} \,/\, Action_n) + ((1 - P(L_{n-1} \,/\, Action_n)) * P(T))$$

is used in Bayesian knowledge tracing to update the estimate of the student's knowledge state. The tutor system's estimate that a student knows a rule at time *n* ($P(L_n)$) is continually updated every time the student responds (correctly or incorrectly) to a question targeting the rule. First, the system calculates the probability that the student knew the rule before making the attempt, using the evidence from the current step. Then, taking this into account, it computes the probability that the student learned the rule during the problem step. According to Corbett and Andersen (1995), such algorithms lead to higher performance levels than random selection of practice stimuli or student selection of practice stimuli.

One of the earliest tutors adopting Bayesian knowledge tracing was the online learning environment in which CMU college students practiced writing short computer programs (Andersen & Corbett, 1993). The self-paced tutor was constructed around a cognitive model of the underlying skill that allowed the tutor to complete the exercises along with the students and provide feedback on students' actions. In each section of the tutor curriculum, students read an accompanying text that introduced a set of programming rules. The tutor followed with a set of exercises that provided practice on the rules. The students continued practicing exercises in a section until reaching a mastery criterion which was set to be 0.95 in the tutor. In other words, when the Bayesian model estimated a student's $P(L_n)$ of the programming rules to be above 0.95, the tutor would remind the student that he/she had successfully completed the session.

One of the best merits of the Bayesian model is that assessment is continuously integrated with practice. In classroom teaching or in most CALL systems, practice and tests are usually treated as individual modules of learning. Students work through study/test cycles to reach a higher level of performance. In knowledge tracing, practicing on the current step of using a rule is also assessing the student's current state of knowing the rule. Students simply continue practicing until reaching a hypothetical knowledge state of mastery. From this perspective, the Bayesian model implements the concept of dynamic assessment (Lantolf & Poehner, 2011) in cognitive tutors. In recent years, there has been an emergence of tutoring systems designed to facilitate L2 learning (MacWhinney, 1995; Pavlik & Anderson, 2005). Among them we rarely find learning systems adopting Bayesian knowledge tracing to promote L2 learning (Koedinger, Corbett, & Perfetti, 2012). This paper is one of the earlier endeavors of such an attempt.

The English Article System: A Functional Linguistics Analysis

The English articles such as *a(n)* and *the* are the most commonly used words in English, and yet their usage is surprisingly complex. This complexity poses a number of challenges for learners of L2 English. This is true even for advanced learners who have studied English for many years. The problem is particularly serious for learners whose first languages (e.g., Japanese, Chinese, Korean, Russian, Croatian) do not contain a similar article system (Celce-Murcia & Larsen-Freeman, 1999). Teachers of English as a second language find it difficult to understand how or why their students choose to use the English articles in the ways they do. As a result, teaching the article rule system effectively in the classroom often remains an elusive goal.

Both generativists (Ionin, Ko, & Wexler, 2004) and functionalists (Huebner, 1983) have expressed a substantial amount of interest in the article system. The generative approach of studying article acquisition is very difficult to apply to teaching (see discussion in Zhao, 2012). This study adopts a functional linguistic approach to analyze the English article system. A functional linguistics view of language acquisition understands the linguistic sign as a set of mappings between forms and functions (MacWhinney, 1987). *Forms* are the external phonological and word order patterns that are used in words and syntactic constructions. *Functions* are the communicative intentions or meanings that underlie language usage. Each lexical item or syntactic construction can be understood as a form-to-function mapping.

In the context of discussing the English article system, there are four forms: *the*, *a*, *an*, and the zero article (*0*). The form *the* specifies the definite article; the forms *a* and *an* encode the indefinite article (*a* is followed by noun phrases starting with consonants; *an* is followed by noun phrases starting with vowels); the form *0* is commonly known as the zero article or null article.

Compared with other grammatical structures (e.g., negation, passive voice, relative clause), article forms (*the*, *a*, *an*, zero article) are not salient structures that are easy to notice. Language learners cannot process target language input for both form and function at the same time (Robinson, 2005; Skehan, 1998; Tomasello, 1998). Learners must notice target forms in input, otherwise they process input for meaning only and fail to notice even important target forms. Because of the low saliency of article forms, learners often fail to process them and subsequently acquire them. Over time, the incorrect usages of articles tend to become fossilized in learners' interlanguage systems.

Switching to the functions in the English article system, Zhao (2012) reported that the four article forms are mapped with approximately 90 different functions or usages. Some of these functions are syntactic and semantic properties (e.g., countability, singularity, plurality); some are discourse-based properties (e.g., first mention, second mention, immediate situation); many are idiosyncratic surface features whose usage is highly conventional (e.g., names of rivers, lakes, malls, parks, bridges, theatres); and some combine syntactic and idiosyncratic properties (e.g., names of singular mountains or plural mountains). Zhao's study showed that quite a few functions are mapped onto four article forms. In another words, the English article system has a complex of form-function mapping.

Following MacWhinney (1987), one form-function mapping is defined as a unit or a *cue*. For example, the tag "*the – river names*" represents a cue since it maps the association between the form '*the*' and the semantic property of names of rivers (*the Mississippi River*). But the tag "*the – river names and second mention in the discourse*" is not a valid cue because one form is associated with two functions. In this case, the form-function mapping needs to be broken down to the smallest unit. Corresponding to the 90 functions of the article system (Zhao, 2012), there are approximately

90 article cues in the English language, each of which informs a form-function mapping.

Not all article cues are born equal due to their inherent properties. Drawing on the strength of corpus linguistics, Zhao (2012) found two types of article cues: *general cues* and *idiosyncratic cues*. Their major distinctions lie in frequency of usage and inherent semantic transparency. But both types include cues with the four article forms (*the*, *a*, *an*, *0*).

General cues (e.g., *0* – noncountable alone) have a much higher token frequency in the English language. In fact, they account for roughly 70% of article usages (Zhao, 2012). Meanwhile, they are semantically transparent cues; learners can use metalanguage to reason their logical meanings. For example, learners can refer to syntactic information such as modification structures (e.g., relative clause, prepositional phrase), categories of the head noun phrases (e.g., non-countable, plural), and discourse information (e.g., a reference previously mentioned, a reference uniquely identifiable in the immediate situation of the utterance "*can you pass me the salt*") to verbalize the explicit rules of general cues.

Idiosyncratic cues (e.g., *the* – river, *0* – lake), on the other hand, are far less frequent than general cues, and they only represent less than 10% of article usages in the English language in term of token frequency (Zhao, 2012). Low frequency of such cues is often accompanied by their semantic opaqueness. Learners find it difficult or almost impossible to rely on logical reasoning to interpret form-function mappings of these cues. For example, learners (and native speakers) are most likely to get stuck when being asked why river names (e.g., *the Mississippi River*) are used with the definite article *the,* but why lake names (e.g., *0 Lake Michigan*) are used with the zero article in English. Therefore, idiosyncratic cues are much less transparent compared with general cues in terms of articulation of metalinguistic explanation.

In summary, this chapter presents findings regarding the effectiveness of an eCALL system that teaches English article usage with the Bayesian knowledge tracing model. eCALL systems provide an ideal platform for testing the effectiveness of knowledge tracing that cannot be offered by traditional CALL systems. Knowledge tracing requires the instructional system to have a clear specification of the rules to be trained. More importantly, knowledge tracing demands that the system document and assess each step that the individual learner takes (or each problem that the learner solves). eCALL systems that collect detailed information of student performance in the form of computer logs provide such a platform where we can test the instructional effects of knowledge tracing in an experimental study. L2 English article learning, which involves complex process of rule learning, is also a good testing ground for the Bayesian model. Given the different natures of cues (general vs. idiosyncratic; definite vs. indefinite), we may also wonder whether they respond to article training and, in particular, to the Bayesian model in different ways. Therefore, in the current study we addressed the following research questions:

1. Does the Bayesian knowledge tracing model outperform a no-knowledge-tracing model in promoting accuracy and fluency development in article acquisition?
2. Does the Bayesian knowledge tracing model promote the same instructional effects (in terms of accuracy and fluency development) on different types of article cues (general vs. idiosyncratic; definite vs. indefinite)?
3. Does the English article tutor promote comparable amount of learning as well as pattern of learning for general and idiosyncratic cues?

METHOD

Participants

The 95 participants (36 males, 55 females) were Chinese intermediate-advanced EFL learners at a university in Beijing. The university is known for its foreign language education and research programs. The participants were freshmen and sophomores majoring in Spanish, Japanese, Italian, French, and Arabic. Their average age was 18.4 years. The average number of years of formal English language education was 7.8 years. None had participated in any research similar to this study before. All participants claimed to have learnt English grammar in the traditional grammar instruction method (explicit rule explanation followed by grammar drills). We consulted their English instructors and confirmed that their current English curriculum did not include any component of article instruction.

Materials and Design

The participants were randomly assigned by the computer program of the article tutor to one of the three conditions in the experiment: two article training groups (n = 80) and a control group (n = 15). As the main instructional manipulation of the current study was Bayesian knowledge tracing, the two article training groups were a knowledge-tracing condition (n = 36) and a no-knowledge-tracing one (n = 44). Both received article training from the tutor. The distinctions between the two conditions are discussed in the next section. The control group took the same pretest, posttest, and delayed posttests as the article training groups, but they practiced English writing during training and did not receive any form of feedback. They spent roughly the same amount of training time as the article training groups.

Within the article training groups, a 2 (training type: knowledge-tracing vs. no-knowledge-tracing) × 2 (Cue type: general vs. idiosyncratic) mixed factorial design was adopted. Both groups received training on thirty-three article cues: ten general cues and twenty-three idiosyncratic cues. This distribution actually simulates the natural distribution of the two types of cues in English: As discussed earlier, idiosyncratic cues were large in number but small in terms of token frequency; general cues were relatively small in number but had a high token frequency. We maintained this distribution in the tutor. We selected cues that were predicted to be of some difficulty to learners. We avoided cues that were commonly taught in the English grammar exercise books in China. For example, we avoided cues such as the anaphoric use of second mention (e.g., *I bought a book. The book was interesting*) which was acquired at the earlier stages (Stehle, 2009). Instead, we included the cue "second mention with variation" (e.g., *I saw a peacock at the zoo. The bird had beautiful feathers*). We also avoided cues that appear in expressions such as "*the* same as", "*the* next day" "in *the* morning" "*0* next month", etc. In another words, we wanted to choose cues that were not too familiar to the participants.

Article training was provided in the format of a sentence-level cloze task. The test items were developed from the Corpus of Contemporary American English (COCA). We selected sentences from COCA that belonged to the thirty-three article cues. We modified them by simplifying the sentence structures and replacing sophisticated vocabularies. The sentences had an average word count of 10.42 words.

The participants in the knowledge-tracing and no-knowledge-tracing conditions were given the same amount of training sentences (k = 660). In the no-knowledge-tracing condition, the number of training sentences (k = 20) was balanced for each cue. In the knowledge-tracing condition, the number of training sentence for each cue varied for different participants. This was because knowledge tracing provided individualized training to learners. Though the participants in the current study shared similar English learning backgrounds, their performances on individual cues still varied. The knowledge tracing mechanism in the tutor diagnosed the weaker cues for an individual learner and provided more training sentences on those cues. But the total number of training sentences remained the same for the two article training conditions. The amounts of training time of the two conditions that we calculated after the experiment were also not significantly different ($p = .171$).

Figure 2 exemplifies the tutor interface for the two article training groups. The interfaces for the knowledge-tracing and the no-knowledge-tracing groups were identical. There were two training sentences on each screen. The participants used a drop-down menu to make article choices. They could decide on which sentence to do first on a screen. They were given feedback (both metalinguistic and exemplar feedback) immediately after they made a choice. And they were given feedback regardless of whether the choice was correct or incorrect. The metalinguistic feedback provided the metalinguistic rule description for the trained cues, whereas the exemplar feedback presented several examples to illustrate the cues. For example, for the cue "*0*-parks, squares, stations", the tutor provided both the metalinguistic feedback "use the zero article with names of parks, squares, and stations" and the exemplar feedback "*0* Yellowstone Park, *0* Central Park, *0* Times Square, *0* Red Square, *0* Victoria Station, *0* Waterloo Station".

The participants were not allowed to move to the next screen unless they made both choices correctly. The tutor did not include any hint function.

Figure 2. A training page of the two article training groups

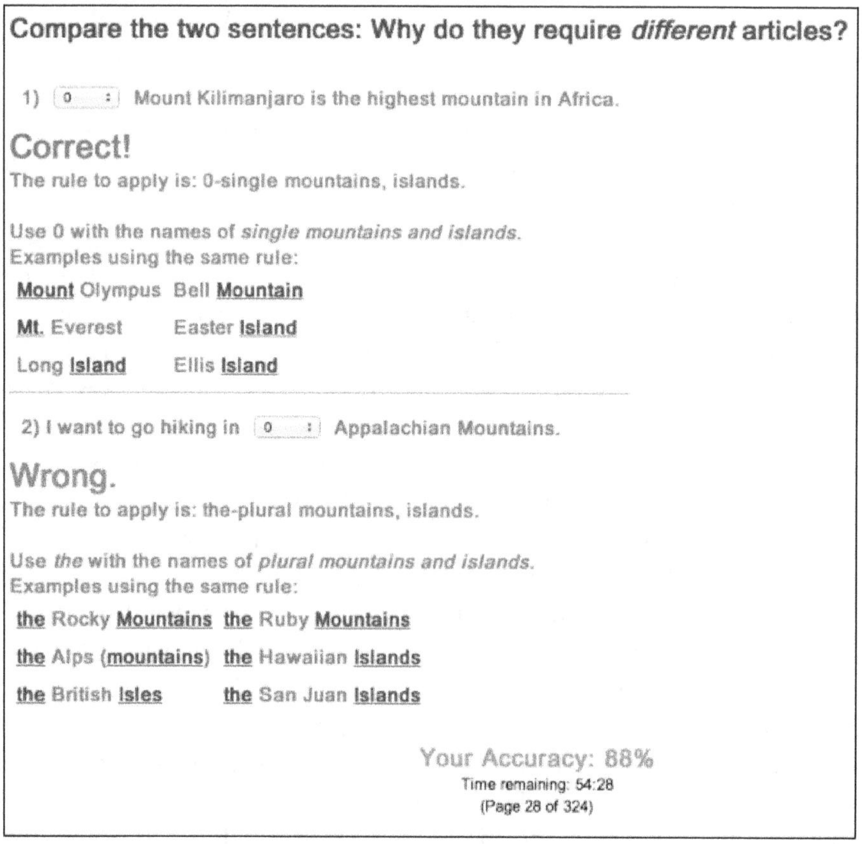

The participants could keep track of their accuracy of performance at the bottom of the tutor screen. To create a sense of time pressure, a countdown clock was placed at the bottom of the training screens. The clock started to count down from 25 minutes in the pretest and posttest and from 60 minutes in each training session.

Knowledge-Tracing and No-Knowledge-Tracing Conditions

The first step in implementing Corbett and Anderson's (1995) Bayesian knowledge tracing algorithm was to set the initial *P(S)*, *P(G)*, *P(T)*, and $P(L_0)$ parameters for each article cue. We used Baker et al.'s (2010) approach to train the parameters using student data from a previous but similar article tutor experiment (Zhao, 2012). The participants in this previous study were comparable to those in this study in terms of English proficiency. During this previous study, we collected 10,523 student attempts at choosing the correct article, with each attempt labeled with the article cue applied. We used Baker et al.'s (2010) method to utilize this data and arrived at the most likely parameter values. This approach allowed us to predict the probability of how the article cues were acquired by the participants in Zhao's (2012) study. Since the participants in the current study had similar language proficiencies and language learning backgrounds as in this previous study, we predicted that the current group of participants would show similar probabilities of acquiring the target article cues. These probabilities were programmed into the knowledge tracing mechanism of the tutor. In this way, the tutor already 'knew' how well a potential learner of a similar background had acquired the target article cues before the training started. The tutor also 'knew' the poorly acquired cues that deserved more training and the better acquired ones that needed less time and practice.

As we implemented this study, these probabilities began to be updated immediately after individual learners started their first practice trials. The knowledge tracing algorism was automatically updated $P(L_n)$ (the estimate that a student knows a rule at time *n*) after observing each correct/incorrect attempts made by individual learners. The tutor used the updated $P(L_n)$ for the item selection criteria. The item with the lowest $P(L_n)$ had the highest probability of being selected as the training item. Different learners had their own *worst* items. So the training items they received varied but also overlapped due to their similar backgrounds and proficiencies.

In addition to selecting the 'worst' item, the tutor was also programmed with another selection criterion. If we simply chose the next item to present with the lowest $P(L_n)$, the tutor would present the same item back-to-back. To introduce some variety while still giving more practice on the items least learned, we used $P(L_n)$ to set the selection criteria of training items as: random selection in proportion to percent unlearned. Percent unlearned for a cue was calculated by taking the probability the cue was "unlearned": $(1–P(L_n))$, divided by the sum of the probabilities each other cue was "unlearned". Thus, a difficult cue would have a higher percent unlearned compared to other cues and would thus be more likely to be chosen next. But it was still possible (but less likely) that a better-acquired cue would be chosen next. This selection criterion avoided over-training of unlearned cues and under-training of better-acquired cues.

Ideally, the knowledge tracing mechanism will not stop working unless a learner reaches the 95% accuracy rate of all the cues. The amount of training time needed to achieve this ultimate goal would exceed the time we were logistically allowed for data collection. So we set a limit to the number of training sentences (see Materials and Design). In contrast, the no-knowledge tracing group did not receive individualized training. They received a fixed set of training sentences presented to them in a random order. We estimated the number of training stimuli needed for a two-hour training based on the previous experiment (Zhao, 2012).

Procedure

The study was composed of three sessions. Session I included a pretest (25-min) and the first training session (1 hour). Session II (2 days later) included the second training session (1 hour) and an immediate posttest (25-min). Session III (2 weeks after Session 2) included a delayed posttest (25-min). We set these time limits by referring to the previous article tutor experiment (Zhao, 2012). All sessions were administered online.

All participants finished the initial login procedure at a computer lab on campus. They applied for a username, filled out an online background questionnaire, and tried with one practice screen to get used to the drop-down menu. Then their English instructor, whom we trained, described to them the procedure of the study and informed them of the URLs they needed to access the three tutor sessions. The whole process took less than 10 minutes. The three sessions were assigned to participants as individual homework. They were instructed to finish the first session by midnight of the second day after the login orientation, to complete the second session two days later, and to complete the third session 14 days later. Reminder emails were sent to them on the deadline days. They were specifically instructed not to stop in the middle of a session due to the recording of their response time. They were also told not to consult grammar books or other resources while doing the tutor homework.

Outcome Measures

The format of the pretest, the posttest, and the delayed posttest was computerized sentence-level cloze tests. Students made a choice out of three possibilities: *the*, *a/an*, and *0*. The entire test pool included 495 sentences: 33 article cues × 15 items for each cue. The test items came from the same pool of revised COCA sentences as the training sentences. But there was no overlap between the test items and the training items. The 495 test sentences were distributed into the three tests through the counter-balancing method. As a result, each cue was tested on 5 items per test. There were no repeating items on the three tests.

All tests were administered online. The screen design of the three tests was identical. There were four sentence items on each test screen. Participants were not allowed to move to the next screen unless they made all four choices. They were reminded of the time limit at the bottom of each screen. If they exceeded the time limit, they were told to continue until they finished the test. At the end of the test, they were informed of their average accuracy scores for the session.

The test data were automatically saved to the TalkBank Database (http://www.talkbank.org) in the form of computer logs. The two dependent variables of this experiment were accuracy and response time (in seconds). Following Jiang (2012), only the response time of correct responses was analyzed. The computer logs also documented other information for analysis, such as: (1) the response time of each click, (2) username, (3) task (pretest, or posttest, or training), (4) experiment condition, (5) session number, (6) the sentence number on a test screen, (7) the choice made by the learner, (8) the correct choice, (9) whether the learner is correct or wrong, (10) the cue name of the sentence, and (11) the test sentence item.

Data Analysis

The data collected from the pretest, immediate and the posttests were subjected to a data trimming procedure. Data trimming is a critical step in eCALL studies. This is because most eCALL experiments are assigned to students as homework. Because students choose when and where they complete the assignments, and because researchers have little control of students' engagement with the tutor, there is a high chance that students get distracted in the middle of a session which leads to exceptionally long response time between trials. On the other hand, it is also possible that some students carelessly do the training for the sake of finishing the assignment, so their response times between trials tend to be exceptionally short. Data trimming allows researchers to remove the data of careless participants and to adjust exceptionally long data points. In this study, we trimmed the data separately for the knowledge-tracing and the no-knowledge tracing group by removing the participants whose average response time was 2.5 standard deviations above or below the mean. We adjusted exceptionally long data points by calculating group averages for each rule and replacing all outliers (the mean plus/minus a coefficient [2.5] times the standard deviation) (Miller, 1991). After data trimming, 78 participants remained in the pool: the knowledge-tracing condition (n = 29), the no-knowledge-tracing condition (n = 34), and the control group (n = 15).

In addition to comparing the pre-, post-, and delayed posttests, the participants' learning curves during the training sessions were also analyzed. The learning curve analysis was supported by Datashop, the world's largest open data repository of transactional educational data collected from online learning courses, intelligent tutors, cognitive tutors, educational games, and simulations (Koedinger et al., 2010). In Datashop, a learning curve visualizes changes in student performance over time. The line graph displays trials across the x-axis, and a measure of student performance along the y-axis (Koedinger & Nathan, 2004). Datashop learning curves include several measures of student performance: (1) error rate (100% - accuracy rate); (2) number of incorrect answers; (3) step duration (the elapsed time of a trial in seconds); (4) correct step duration (the duration of a correct answer); and (5) error step duration (the step duration if the step was wrong). Since the dependent variables for the current study were accuracy and response time for correct responses, we used two measures to index Datashop learning curves: error rate and correct step duration. We found that delving into the training session gives us more in-depth information that cannot be obtained from the three tests. In particular, it allowed us to compare and contrast the learning trajectories of individual article cues.

To answer RQ1, we only analyzed the data of the two instructed groups (knowledge-tracing and no-knowledge-tracing groups). We performed independent samples t tests on accuracy and response time to compare the two groups at the pre-, post-, and delayed posttests. For RQ2, we wanted to explore whether knowledge tracing (and no knowledge tracing) would particularly favor any type of article cues. We used two-way repeated measures ANOVAs to investigate any interaction effects between knowledge tracing and cue types (i.e., general vs. idiosyncratic). For RQ3, we aimed to examine whether the article cues were learned in the same way or not in the tutor. Our focus was on the within-subject variables. So we merged the two instructed groups when comparing the two cue types. We performed 2 (cue type) x 3 (time) repeated measures ANOVAs to examine whether there was any interaction effect between time and cue type. The dependent variable of this statistical procedure was the gain scores (posttest mean minus pretest mean) and retained scores (delayed posttest mean minus posttest mean) on accuracy and response time.

RESULTS

RQ1: Comparing Knowledge-Tracing and No-Knowledge-Tracing Conditions

Descriptive statistics showed that the mean accuracy of the knowledge tracing condition changed from 0.592 at the pretest to 0.723 at the posttest and 0.703 at the delayed posttest. Similarly, the mean accuracy of the no-knowledge-tracing condition changed from 0.589 at the pretest to 0.761 at the posttest and 0.729 at the delayed posttest. In terms of response time, the knowledge tracing condition started with the pretest mean of 6.159 seconds per second per cue to 3.808 at the posttest and 4.669 at the delayed posttest. Also similarly, the no-knowledge-tracing condition dropped its mean time from 6.359 at the pretest to 3.744 at the posttest and 4.246 at the delayed posttest.

An independent samples t test showed no significant difference of accuracy ($t = 0.17, p = .86$) and response time ($t = -0.64, p = .53$) between the knowledge-tracing and the no-knowledge-tracing groups at the pretest. An independent samples t test again showed no significant difference in accuracy at the posttest ($t = -1.56, p = .12$) and at the delayed posttest ($t = -1.05, p = .30$). Similarly, the two groups did not show significant difference in response time at the posttest ($t = 0.27, p = .79$) and at the delayed posttest ($t = 1.40, p = .17$).

RQ2: Interaction between Knowledge-Tracing and Cue Types

Table 1 presents the descriptive statistics of general and idiosyncratic cues in terms of gained accuracy/time at the posttest and retained accuracy/time at the delayed posttest. A two-way repeated measures ANOVA showed no significant interactional effects between instruction type (i.e., knowledge-tracing vs. no-knowledge tracing) and cue type (i.e., general vs. idiosyncratic) in terms of gained accuracy ($F = 2.10, p = .15$) and gained response time ($F = 0.10, p = .75$) at the posttest. Similarly, no interactional effect was found in terms of retained accuracy ($F = 0.66, p = .42$) and retained response time ($F = 0.39, p = .53$) in the delayed posttest. Knowledge tracing, therefore, did not favor the learning of either general or idiosyncratic cues.

Similarly, a two-way repeated measures ANOVA showed no significant interaction between instruction type and cue type at the posttest in terms of gained accuracy ($F = 0.73, p = .51$) and gained response time ($F = 0.06, p = .98$). No significant interaction was found at the delayed posttest in terms of both retained accuracy ($F = 0.17, p = .90$) and retained response time ($F = 1.65, p = .18$). In short, knowledge tracing did not favor any specific types of cues; rather, it enhanced the overall learning of all types of cues.

RQ3: General vs. Idiosyncratic: Amount and Patterns of Learning

Table 2 presents the mean accuracy and response time of general and idiosyncratic cues at the pre-, post-, and delayed posttests.

A paired samples t test showed that general cues had significantly higher accuracy scores than idiosyncratic cues at the pretest ($t = 15.61, p < .001$). In terms of mean response time, a paired samples t test showed no significant difference between general and idiosyncratic cues ($t = 1.86, p = .07$) at the pretest. In short, general cues were better acquired than idiosyncratic cues in terms of mean accuracy but not in terms of mean response time before the training began.

Table 1. Gained accuracy and response time (in seconds) of cue types of the two instructed groups

	General cues				Idiosyncratic cues			
	Knowledge Tracing		No Knowledge Tracing		Knowledge Tracing		No Knowledge Tracing	
	Accuracy	Time	Accuracy	Time	Accuracy	Time	Accuracy	Time
Gained	0.08	-2.17	0.09	-2.37	0.16	-2.46	0.22	-2.75
Retained	0.02	0.76	0.02	0.47	-0.05	0.92	-0.07	0.523

Table 2. Mean accuracy and response time (in seconds) of cue types based on the two instructed groups

	General cues				Idiosyncratic cues			
	Mean Accuracy	SD	Mean Time	SD	Mean Accuracy	SD	Mean Time	SD
Pretest	0.70	0.10	6.42	1.32	0.53	0.05	6.31	1.41
Posttest	0.78	0.09	4.14	1.05	0.72	0.12	3.56	0.91
Delayed	0.80	0.09	4.74	1.32	0.67	0.11	4.27	1.23

In addition to pretest analyses, we also investigated the instructional effects on general and idiosyncratic cues. We first focused on accuracy as the dependent variable. A 3 (time) x 2 (cue type) repeated measures ANOVA showed that there was a significant time x cue type interaction effect ($F = 24.41, p < .001$). Considering this significant interaction effect, we went on to examine: (a) whether there was any significant difference between the two cue types at the posttest and delayed posttest, and (b) whether each cue type showed significant improvement over time.

We then conducted paired samples t tests at posttest and delayed posttest to determine whether there was any significant difference between general and idiosyncratic cues. We found that there were significant differences on mean accuracy between general and idiosyncratic cues at the posttest ($t = 4.29, p < .001$) and delayed posttest ($t = 12.24, p < .001$). Then we conducted separate one-way repeated measures ANOVAs to determine whether general and idiosyncratic cues demonstrated any improvement from pretest to posttest and from posttest to delayed posttest. We found that general cues showed significant improvements from pretest to posttest ($F = 45.82, p < .001$) and from posttest to delayed posttest ($F = 6.14, p = .02$). Idiosyncratic cues also showed significant improvement from pretest to posttest ($F = 237.05, p < .001$) but showed significant accuracy decrease from posttest to delayed posttest ($F = 36.40, p < .001$). In other words, despite the significant improvements of idiosyncratic cues from pre- to posttest, they still lagged behind the general cues at the posttest and delayed posttest.

Switching to the measure of response time, we performed the same sets of inferential statistical analyses. A 3 (time) x 2 (cue type) repeated measures ANOVA showed that there was a significant time x cue type interaction effect ($F = 4.10, p = .02$). Paired samples t tests at posttest and delayed posttest showed that there were significant differences on mean response time between general and idiosyncratic cues at posttest ($t = 7.74, p < .001$) and at delayed posttest ($t = 4.71, p < .001$). Referring to descriptive statistics, we can see that the learners processed idiosyncratic cues significantly more fluently than general cues at the posttest and delayed posttests. One-way ANOVAs showed that both general cues ($F = 354.26, p < .001$) and idiosyncratic cues ($F = 340.71, p < .001$) had significant response time decrease from pretest to posttest. One-way ANOVAs showed a reverse trend at the delayed posttest: both general and idiosyncratic cues had significant time increase from posttest to delayed posttest (general: $F = 33.53, p < .001$; idiosyncratic: $F = 36.02, p < .001$). Nonetheless, their mean response time at the delayed posttest was still significantly less than their pretest level (general: $F = 135.61, p < .001$; idiosyncratic: $F = 141.46, p < .001$).

One interesting finding that was generated from this research question is the significant difference in accuracy between general and idiosyncratic cues at the delayed posttest. The difference was due to the continuing accuracy increase of the general cues and the decrease of the idiosyncratic cues. In another word, while learners showed deteriorating performance on idiosyncratic cues after they completed training, they continued to improve their performance on general cues. One can also say that there seemed to be a delay in the learning of general cues. Learners put a great deal of attention on the learning of idiosyncratic cues during training. General cues did not seem to be 'prioritized' compared to idiosyncratic cues. But learners seemed to remember what they learned about general cues from the tutor two weeks after training was completed. Their accuracy scores increased to a significantly higher level compared to the pretest and the posttest.

Summary of Results

In summary, we found that the eCALL system in the current study promoted significant accuracy and fluency development in L2 article learning. The Bayesian knowledge tracing model did not outperform the no-knowledge-tracing model. The Bayesian model did not generate significantly different instructional effects on different types of article cues (general vs. idiosyncratic; definite vs. indefinite). In another words, knowledge tracing did not particularly favor any types of article cues. It functioned to boost the learning of all cues. But that does not mean that all cues were learnt in the same way. In terms of accuracy development, general cues outperformed idiosyncratic cues from pretest to delayed posttest; in term of fluency development (response time), the two types started at the same entry level but idiosyncratic cues outperformed general cues at the posttest and delayed posttest.

DISCUSSION

The intermediate-advanced students in this study were given a difficult task of learning thirty-three article cues within two hours of training. The article training groups managed to show significant effects of learning in the immediate posttest and retained learning two weeks later. Our study clearly demonstrated that given a difficult learning task, students would learn when they are given a large number of practice trials and accurate and explicit feedback.

Regarding RQ1, the results showed knowledge tracing to be the most important instructional mechanism in successfully promoting article learning in the tutor. But it failed to outperform the no-knowledge-tracing group. The results of RQ2 showed that the no-knowledge-tracing group did equally as well as the knowledge tracing group in learning all the types of article cues examined. This was not within our expectation. Knowledge tracing has been shown to be successful in promoting robust learning of knowledge components in mathematics, physics, chemistry, and foreign language (Baker et al., 2010). But perhaps the duration of training sessions in this study was not long enough for knowledge tracing to operate optimally, particularly when there were a relatively large number of article cues to be learned. In Corbett and Andersen's (1995) study, their tutor trained twenty-one computer programming rules in an average of fourteen sessions. Programming rules are more sophisticated and involve step-by-step analysis. The thirty-three article cues in our study are less complex and more straightforward than programming rules. But two sessions were not enough for students to master all the cues. The posttest mean accuracy (.744) of the article training groups was far from the mastery level (.950). This signals that perhaps a longer training time with more practice trials is necessary for knowledge tracing to be more effective.

But how long is enough? In addition to referring to accuracy scores at the posttests, we can also make use of the information provided by the Datashop learning curves to make predictions. Learning curves tell us how much is learned and more importantly how stable the learning has been. Cues with more rocky learning curves probably need more training time. For example, consider the following two learning curves (Figure 3). Both cues start at a 40% error rate when entering the tutor and land at almost 0% error rate at the end of the tutor. But the two cues show distinct learning trajectories. Obviously, the curve on the right is rockier despite the overall trend of falling down. We can predict that this cue needs more training time than the one on the left because we do not have consistent evidence that suggests the mastery of this cue. There is still a high probability that learners get it correct because of guessing rather than because of knowing. Traditional classroom-based or lab-based instructional studies without incorporating such a computer-based tool of dynamic assessment cannot capture this source of information and make predictions from it. eCALL

Figure 3. Smooth and rocky learning curves

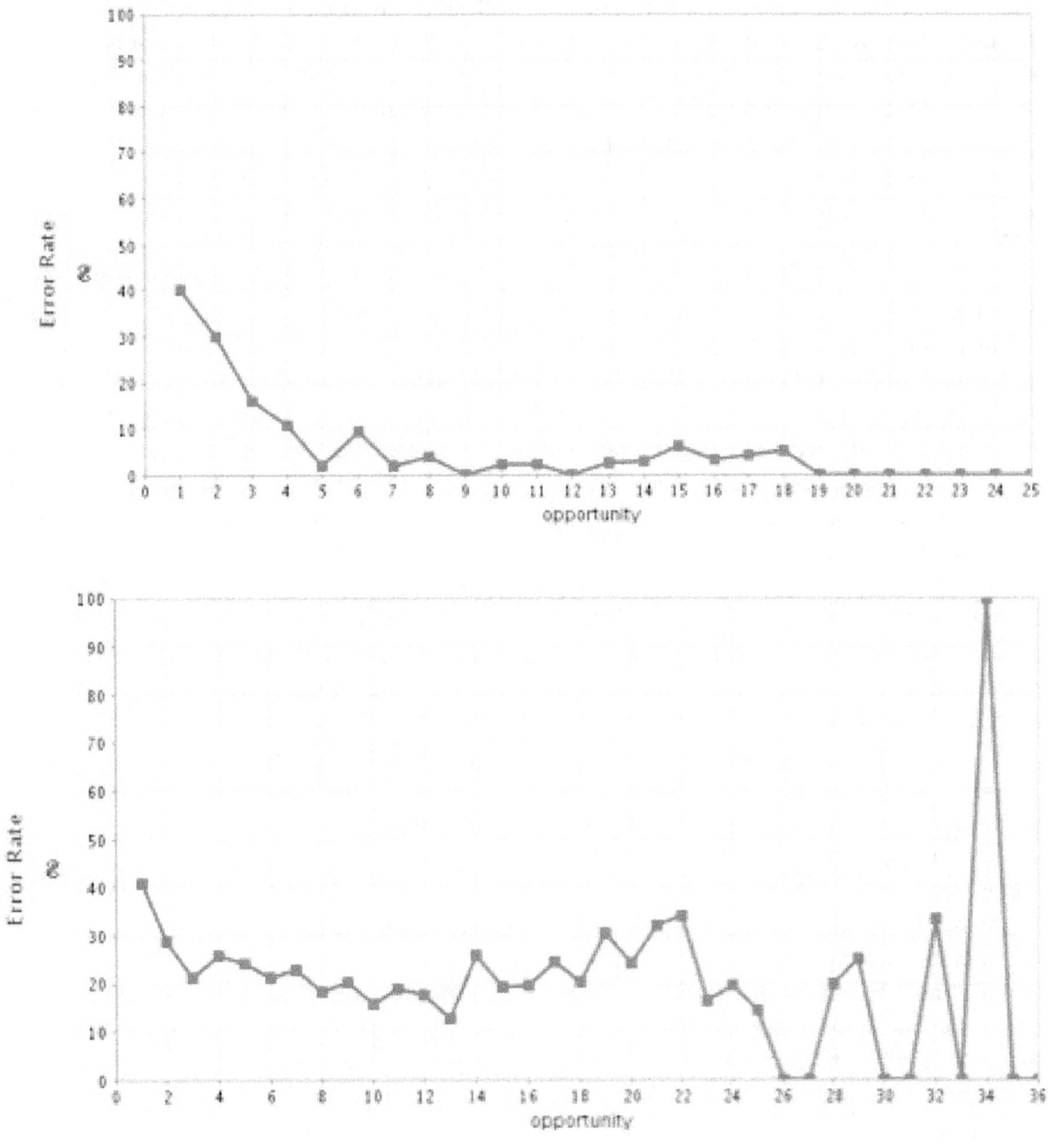

studies can easily document the entire training process in an instructional study regardless of the number of participants and/or where and when participants access eCALL systems.

Another important contribution of the study that we found regarding RQ3 is that the article tutor promoted significant learning on idiosyncratic cues. Idiosyncratic cues are particularly difficult to acquire by L2 learners. Because of their low frequency in natural discourse, learners have much less experience in learning and using them. Also due to their semantic opaqueness, learners did not understand why some idiosyncratic cues require the definite article whereas some do not. The students who used the article tutor showed significant learning of twenty-three idiosyncratic cues within only two hours of training.

This was an impressive instructional effect given the large number of cues and the limited amount of training time, but we did not find such a result surprising. Certain characteristics of idiosyncratic cues can enable successful learning. The first is that they are highly reliable cues. Most idiosyncratic cues have reliability higher than .90 (Zhao, 2012), that is, there are less than 10% of cases when a semantic feature (e.g., river or lake) is associated with more than one article form. Their form-to-function mappings are straightforward and reliable. In addition, rules of idiosyncratic cues are simple to understand and remember. For instance, the "river" cue says "Use *the* with names of river". It does not involve abstract thinking or logical reasoning in order to comprehend and memorize this usage. Once learners are given enough input with explicit feedback, idiosyncratic cues can quickly catch up. The feedback loop is shorter because of easy comprehension.

Another interesting finding that we generated from RQ3 was that the general cues showed a delayed learning effect, that is, general cues showed a significant accuracy gain after training. One possible explanation is that general cues have high semantic transparency. The metalinguistic information of general cues is analyzable and easier to verbalize, and hence easier to be stored in long-term memory. Two weeks after the training, learners could still retrieve the stored metalinguistic information at the delayed posttest. Another reason is that participants might have applied the knowledge of general cues that they learned from the tutor to real life usage. As we discussed earlier, general cues have significantly higher frequency than idiosyncratic cues in the English language. The three cues that have the highest availabilities in the English language (Zhao, 2012) are "*0*-plural" (*0 books*), "*0*-noncountable/mass nouns" (*0 passion*), and "*a/an*-singular countable" (*I bought 0 a book*), all of which are general cues. After the posttest, participants applied what they learned about these cues from the tutor to real life usage, and this contributed to their continuing increase in accuracy shown at the delayed posttest.

Idiosyncratic cues, however, perhaps required longer training time for such a robust learning effect to occur. Idiosyncratic cues required heavier memory load than general cues. The metalinguistic information of idiosyncratic cues is not analyzable and cannot be easily formulated. Learners almost have to rely purely on rote memorization to learn the form-function mapping. Within a relatively short period of intensive training, learners kept practicing these form-functions mappings and were able to store them in their short-term memory. They could quickly retrieve the information at the posttest. But at the delayed posttest two weeks later, they forgot a lot of these form-function mappings. Hence idiosyncratic cues had led to a significant deterioration of performance at the delayed posttest.

CONCLUSION

In conclusion, this chapter introduced a study on eCALL. It demonstrated a successful application of cognitive psychology and human-computer interaction theories in second language grammar instruction. We found that eCALL systems were naturally compatible with the Bayesian knowledge tracing model. The integration of the two generated effective instructional effects on L2 article learning. We found that the Bayesian model did not particularly favor the learning of certain types of cues over others. It functioned to achieve an overall learning effect.

Meanwhile, we realized the importance of a sufficient amount of training time for Bayesian eCALL systems. Due to logistic reasons, the current study could not afford to offer the learners a longer period of training hours. The Bayesian model could not achieve the ideal goal of mastery learning as defined by Corbett and Anderson (1995). But the fortunate side is that we have data storage and analytic tools such as Datashop that helps us make inferences about the extension of training hours for different types of cues to reach the mastery level. Future studies should try to clarify this question.

Finally, we need more eCALL studies, whether incorporating Bayesian knowledge tracing or not, that cover a wider variety of language structures in different L2s. This innovative language learning system can be linked to classroom teaching to provide deeper support for second language learning. As Presson, Davy, and MacWhinney (2013) put it, eCALL systems "can lead to a revolution in SLA research and theory, as we automatically log data, adapt student feedback, and conduct large-scale experiments with relatively low cost. Ideally these advances in theory, experimentation, training can be coordinated with best practices from classroom pedagogy to lead to breakthroughs in the learning of second languages" (p. 159).

ACKNOWLEDGMENT

We thank Brian MacWhinney, Kenneth Koedinger, Naoko Taguchi, Yasuhiro Shirai, Like Li, and Howard Seltman for their help in conducting this research. This work is supported by the Pittsburgh Science of Learning Center which is funded by the National Science Foundation award number SBE-0836012.

REFERENCES

Anderson, J. R. (1993). *Rules of the mind*. Hillsdale, NJ: Erlbaum.

Anderson, J. R., & Corbett, A. T. (1992). Acquisition of LISP Programming Skill. In S. Chipman, & A. Meyrowitz (Eds.), *Foundations of knowledge acquisition: Cognitive models of complex learning* (pp. 1–24). Hingham, MA: Kluwer.

Anderson, J. R., & Matessa, M. (1992). Explorations of an incremental, Bayesian algorithm for categorization. *Machine Learning*, *9*, 275–308. doi:10.1007/BF00994109

Baker, R. S. J. d., Corbett, A. T., Gowda, S. M., Wagner, A. Z., MacLaren, B. M., & Kauffman, L. R. et al. (2010). Contextual slip and prediction of student performance after use of an intelligent tutor. In P. D. Bra, A. Kobsa, & D. Chin (Eds.), *User modeling, adaptation, and personalization* (pp. 52–63). Germany: Springer. doi:10.1007/978-3-642-13470-8_7

Barr, D. (2008). Computer-enhanced grammar teaching. In F. Zhang, & B. Barbar (Eds.), *Handbook of research on computer-enhanced language acquisition and learning* (pp. 101–115). Hershey: Information Science Reference. doi:10.4018/978-1-59904-895-6.ch007

Celce-Murcia, M., & Larsen-Freeman, D. (1999). *The grammar book: An ESL/EFL teacher's course* (2nd ed.). Boston, MA: Heinle & Heinle Publishers.

Cen, H., Koedinger, K., & Junker, B. (2006). A general method for cognitive model evaluation and improvement. *Intelligent Tutoring Systems*, *4053*, 164–175. doi:10.1007/11774303_17

Corbett, A. T., & Anderson, J. R. (1995). Knowledge tracing: Modeling the acquisition of procedural knowledge. *User Modeling and User-Adapted Interaction, 4*, 253–278. doi:10.1007/BF01099821

Garrett, N. (1987). A psycholinguistic perspective on grammar and CALL. In W.F. Smith (Ed.), Modern media in foreign language education (pp. 169–196). Lincolnwood: National Textbook.

Huebner, T. (1983). *A longitudinal analysis of the acquisition of English*. Ann Arbor, MI: Karoma Publishers, Inc.

Ionin, T., Ko, H., & Wexler, K. (2004). Article semantics in L2-acquisition: the role of specificity. *Language Acquisition, 12*(1), 3–69. doi:10.1207/s15327817la1201_2

Jiang, N. (2012). *Conducting reaction time research in second language studies*. London: Routledge.

Koedinger, K. R., Baker, R. S. J. d., Cunningham, K., Skogsholm, A., Leber, B., & Stamper, J. (2010). A data repository for the edm community: The PSLC DataShop. In C. Romero, S. Ventura, M. Pechenizkiy, & R. S. J. d. Baker (Eds.), *Handbook of educational data mining* (pp. 43–56). Boca Raton, FL: CRC Press. doi:10.1201/b10274-6

Koedinger, K. R., Corbett, A. C., & Perfetti, C. (2012). The knowledge-learning-instruction (kli) framework: Bridging the science-practice chasm to enhance robust student learning. *Cognitive Science, 36*, 757–798. doi:10.1111/j.1551-6709.2012.01245.x PMID:22486653

Koedinger, K. R., & Nathan, M. J. (2004). The real story behind story problems: Effects of representations on quantitative reasoning. *Journal of the Learning Sciences, 13*(2), 129–164. doi:10.1207/s15327809jls1302_1

Lantolf, J. P., & Poehner, M. E. (2011). Dynamic assessment in the classroom: Vygostkian praxis for second language development. *Language Teaching Research, 15*(1), 11–33. doi:10.1177/1362168810383328

MacWhinney. (1987). The competition model. In B. MacWhinney (Ed.), *Mechanisms of language acquisition* (pp. 249–308). New York: Psychology Press.

MacWhinney, B. (1995). Evaluating foreign language tutoring systems. In V. M. Holland, J. D. Kaplan, & M. R. Sams (Eds.), *Intelligent language tutors: Theory shaping technology* (pp. 317–326). Mahwah, NJ: Lawrence Erlbaum.

Miller, J. (1991). Short report: Reaction time analysis with outlier exclusion: Bias varies with sample size. *The Quarterly Journal of Experimental Psychology, 43*, 907–912. doi:10.1080/14640749108400962 PMID:1775668

Nagata, N. (1993). Intelligent computer feedback for second language instruction. *Modern Language Journal, 77*, 330–339. doi:10.1111/j.1540-4781.1993.tb01980.x

Pavlik, P. I. Jr, & Anderson, J. R. (2005). Practice and forgetting effects on vocabulary memory: An activation-based model of the spacing effect. *Cognitive Science, 29*, 559–586. doi:10.1207/s15516709cog0000_14 PMID:21702785

Presson, N., Davy, C., & MacWhinney, B. (2013). Experimentalized CALL for adult second language learners. In J. W. Schwieter (Ed.), *Innovative research and practices in second language acquisition and bilingualism* (pp. 139–164). Amsterdam, the Netherlands: John Benjamins. doi:10.1075/lllt.38.10pre

Robinson, P. (2005). Cognitive complexity and task sequencing: Studies in a componential framework of second language task design. *IRAL, 43*, 1–32. doi:10.1515/iral.2005.43.1.1

Sagarra, N. (2007). From CALL to face-to-face communication: The effect of computer-delivered recasts and working memory on L2 development. In A. Mackey (Ed.), *Conversational interaction in second language acquisition* (pp. 229–248). New York: Oxford University Press.

Sauro, S. (2009). Computer-mediated corrective feedback and the development of L2 grammar. *Language Learning & Technology*, *13*, 96–120.

Stehle, M. (2009). *The interlanguage development of articles in English as a second language: A longitudinal study*. (Unpublished MA thesis). University of Pittsburgh, Pittsburgh, PA.

Tomasello, M. (1998). Introduction: A cognitive-functional perspective on language structure. In M. Tomasello (Ed.), *The new psychology of language: Cognitive and functional approaches to language structure* (pp. vii–xxiii). Mahwah, NJ: Erlbaum.

Warschauer, M. (1995). *E-mail for English teaching: Bringing the Internet and computer learning networks into the language classroom*. Alexandria, Virginia: TESOL Publications.

Zhang, F., & Barber, B. (2008). *Handbook of research on computer-enhanced language acquisition and learning*. Hershey: Information Science Reference. doi:10.4018/978-1-59904-895-6

Zhao, H. (2012). *Explicitness, cue competition, and knowledge tracing: A tutorial system for second language learning of English article usage*. (Unpublished Ph.D. Dissertation). Carnegie Mellon University, Pittsburgh, PA.

Zhao, H., Koedinger, K., & Kowalski, J. (2013). Knowledge tracing and cue contrast: Second language English grammar. In M. Knauff, M. Pauen, N. Sebanz, & I. Wachsmuth (Eds.), *Proceedings of the 35th Annual Conference of the Cognitive Science Society* (pp. 1653–1658). Austin, TX: Cognitive Science Society.

ADDITIONAL READING

Holland, V. M., Kaplan, J. D., & Sams, M. R. (1995). Intelligent language tutors: Theory shaping technology (Eds.). Mahwah, NJ: Lawrence Erlbaum.

Huddleston, R., & Pullum, G. (2002). *The cambridge grammar of the English language*. Cambridge: Cambridge University Press.

Koedinger, K. R., & Corbett, A. T. (2006). Cognitive tutors: Technology bringing learning sciences to the classroom. In R. L. Sawyer (Ed.), *The cambridge handbook of the learning sciences* (pp. 61–77). New York: Cambridge University Press.

Lyons, C. (1999). *Definiteness*. Cambridge: Cambridge University Press. doi:10.1017/CBO9780511605789

MacWhinney, B. (1985). Grammatical devices for sharing points. In R. Schiefelbusch (Ed.), *Communicative competence: Acquisition and intervention* (pp. 325–374). Baltimore, MD: University Park Press.

MacWhinney, B. (1987). Mechanisms of language acquisition (Ed.). New York: Psychology Press.

MacWhinney, B. (1997). Second language acquisition and the Competition Model. In J. Kroll, & A. De Groot (Eds.), *Tutorials in bilingualism* (pp. 113–142). Mahwah, NJ: Lawrence Erlbaum.

Master, P. (2002). Information structure and English article pedagogy. *System*, *30*, 331–348. doi:10.1016/S0346-251X(02)00018-0

Nassaji, H., & Fotos, S. (2011). *Teaching grammar in second language classrooms: Integrating form-focused instruction in communicative context*. New York: Routledge.

Quirk, R., Greenbaum, S., Leech, G., & Svartvik, J. (1985). *A comprehensive grammar of the English language*. Longman.

Sawyer, R. L. (2006). The cambridge handbook of the learning sciences (Ed.). New York: Cambridge University Press.

Schwieter, J. W. (2013). Innovative research and practices in second language acquisition and bilingualism (Ed.). Amsterdam, the Netherlands: John Benjamins.

KEY TERMS AND DEFINITIONS

Article Cues: In the English article system one cue informs one form-function mapping.

Bayesian Knowledge Tracing: This model with its application in cognitive tutors attempts to monitor students' dynamic knowledge development as they practice a complex cognitive skill, to individualize the practice sequence to enable students to master the skill efficiently, and to accurately predict students' performance.

eCALL Systems: Experimental Computer Assisted Language Learning systems.

General Article Cues: They are semantically transparent cues; second language learners can use metalanguage to reason their logical meanings. They have high frequency in the English language.

Idiosyncratic Article Cues: Their usages are idiosyncratic in nature. A lot of these usages can only be accounted for by historical conventions. Because of high idiosyncrasy, they are more opaque cues. Second language learners find it difficult or almost impossible to rely on logical reasoning to interpret form-function mappings of these cues. They have low frequency in the English language.

Linguistic Forms: Forms are the external phonological and word order patterns that are used in words and syntactic constructions.

Linguistic Functions: Functions are the communicative intentions or meanings that underlie language usage.

Section 2

Technology Integration for Second Language Teaching

Chapter 3
Using *Turnitin* to Support Students' Understanding of Textual Borrowing in Academic Writing: A Case Study

Ilka Kostka
Northeastern University, USA

Miriam Eisenstein Ebsworth
New York University, USA

ABSTRACT

Concerns about plagiarism are salient for the academic writing of second language (L2) writers of English, who face several challenges while learning academic discourse and proper citation conventions. Effective instruction is crucial in helping them learn to avoid plagiarism and borrow from sources appropriately. In this chapter, the authors present a case study of an English as a Second Language (ESL) composition class at a Midwestern university in the United States. This study is framed by a social view of learning that draws from Lave and Wenger's (1991) notion of a community of practice. Data included weekly classroom observations, interviews at the beginning, middle, and end of the 10-week academic term, surveys, and student participants' online blogs. Findings illustrate how Turnitin, an Internet-based matched-text detection program, was used to support academic writing instruction and help socialize learners into an American academic discourse community.

DOI: 10.4018/978-1-4666-6174-5.ch003

INTRODUCTION

Plagiarism is making us crazy... Collectively, as a professoriate, we're obsessed with it (Jenkins, 2011).

While plagiarism is hardly a novel phenomenon in higher education, the availability of the Internet and the proliferation of electronic texts have changed the ways students access information and weave outside sources into their academic texts. In response to these changes and to the fears that administrators and educators have about plagiarism, numerous software programs have been developed which can detect plagiarism in students' texts. Companies such as iParadigms, which produces the Internet-based software program *Turnitin*, have achieved enormous worldwide success in licensing their product to high schools and universities. *Turnitin* is one of many packages that attempt to offer a solution to the plagiarism problem.

Plagiarism is a particularly difficult issue for students whose second language (L2) is English. L2 writers may not fully appreciate the seriousness of plagiarism in the U.S. context, encounter the notion of plagiarism for the first time upon arrival in the United States or other English dominant countries, or have limited experience with academic writing. L2 writers' cultural backgrounds may also affect their understanding of plagiarism (Bloch, 2001; Deckert, 1993; Dryden, 1999; Pennycook, 1996; Scollon, 1995; Shi, 2006). They might not fully comprehend the notion of authorship and have difficulty viewing themselves as authors (Abasi, Akbari, & Graves, 2006). They also may be unable to distinguish between what is common knowledge and information from sources that require a citation (Emerson, 2008; Shi, 2008, 2011), which is critical for producing academic texts. Furthermore, L2 writers may have insufficient conceptual knowledge of academic discourse conventions that transcend sentence-level skills such as citing, paraphrasing, and summarizing (Gu & Brooks, 2008). Finally, they may have inadequate command of the academic language and vocabulary they need to paraphrase, summarize, and cite sources appropriately (Currie, 1998; Howard, 1995; Keck, 2006; Li & Casanave, 2012; Pecorari, 2008) and lack the confidence needed to produce original academic texts (Bloch, 2001).

As a result of these factors, ESL college instructors face several challenges as they prepare their students for the rigors of academic writing in students' mainstream composition classes and in their majors of study. While significant scholarship in literature for native and non-native English students (English L1 and L2 writers) has addressed many of these areas, few in-depth case studies have considered how plagiarism detection software may be used to teach students about proper citation and textual borrowing from a pedagogical perspective rather than to merely detect plagiarism. Given that numerous institutions worldwide already have licenses for these kinds of programs, it is worth considering how such software can be successfully incorporated into academic writing instruction.

In this chapter, we report on a case study of a post-secondary English as a Second Language (ESL) composition course that focuses on helping international students develop an understanding and command of English academic writing. We examine the use of plagiarism detection software in the class, with the aim of contributing to growing scholarly attention on effective plagiarism pedagogy that incorporates a digital detection component (*Turnitin*). We illustrate how L2 writers learn to avoid plagiarism by appropriately borrowing from sources and strengthening their academic writing skills.

BACKGROUND

What is Plagiarism?

While modern technology has afforded educators the opportunity to detect matched text more easily, the concept of "plagiarism" is not as easy to define. Buranen (1999) aptly notes that the term plagiarism has become "a kind of wastebasket into which we toss anything we do not know what to do with" (p. 64). Buranen goes on to say that plagiarism can include intentional cheating, purchasing a paper and submitting it as if it were written by the student, citing sources inaccurately, or incorrectly paraphrasing from a source. Plagiarism includes a wide range of behaviors that are placed in the same category, and as scholarship in this area has shown, plagiarism is a complex and culturally-bound concept.

Bloch (2012) discusses the use of metaphors to educate second language learners about plagiarism. He notes that the comparison of plagiarism to theft is not uncommon, but finds that it creates an unnecessary barrier between the learner and teacher. Instead, he considers how the rules of proper citation in academic writing can be likened to the rules of a game, a much less controversial comparison that focuses on processes, students' conscious decision-making, and pedagogy. While crediting Fish (2010) with comparing the rules of plagiarism to those of golf, Bloch makes a cogent argument for decriminalizing the way plagiarism is framed in academia and shifting the metaphors used to educate students to more neutral ones. Other scholars have redefined plagiarism to reflect its complexity and to illustrate that plagiarism is not a clearly "black-and-white" issue (Pennycook, 1996, p. 201). For instance, Howard (1993, 1995) distinguishes between plagiarism and "patchwriting." The latter term refers to a stage that may be present in a beginner writer's development and includes "copying from a source text and then deleting some words, altering grammatical structures, or plugging in one-for-one synonym substitutes" (Howard, 1993, p. 233). Howard's notion of patchwriting has helped draw attention to students' strategies in dealing with the challenge of academic writing, rather than their intent to cheat.

Because plagiarism is difficult to define succinctly (Buranen, 1999; Pennycook, 1996), we operationalize the term here to include a wide spectrum of writing-related behavior, including patchwriting (Howard, 1993) as well as direct copying and pasting from sources. In this study, we wanted to explore how students learned about all dimensions of plagiarism because they need to fully understand the wide range of behaviors that may be considered "plagiarism." In addition, we feel that definitions of plagiarism that are limited solely to purposeful challenges of academic integrity may not reflect the multitude of skills that are involved in avoiding it.

The Impact of Technology on Plagiarism

As noted above, the introduction and development of the Internet has added an additional layer of complexity to the plagiarism issue. First, there is debate as to whether or not the Internet has caused an increase in students' plagiarism. Some scholars have asserted that the Internet is associated with an increase in plagiarism in higher education (Atkins & Nelson, 2001; DeVoss & Rosati, 2002; Kitalong, 1998; Marsh, 2004; Szabo & Underwood, 2004), while others suggest that the Internet has not necessarily contributed to an increase in plagiarism (Park, 2003; Scanlon & Neumann, 2002; Pecorari, 2008). In either case, it must be acknowledged that irrespective of their intent, students can now copy and paste electronic texts more easily (McCabe, 2005).

Another challenge created by the Internet is that it provides a platform for "paper mills" to flourish. Although entities that sell or provide academic papers to students existed long before the advent of the Internet (Groark, Oblinger, & Choa, 2001), few would dispute that the Internet has provided convenient and ubiquitous access to them. A quick search on any major search engine brings one to numerous paper mill sites that offer essays on virtually any topic. Ritter (2005) argues that paper mills commodify academic discourse and appeal to students who may have mixed feelings about what kinds of text may be shared and taken, may have trouble using and reporting sources properly, and may not fully understand the notion of authorship. Ritter also notes that these sites "negate the academic value of authorship...changing that innocent eighteen-year-old in one's composition class from an author to a plagiarist, or, in the rhetoric of paper-mill sites, from a student to a *consumer*" (Ritter, 2005, p. 603). Similarly, "contract cheating" sites are also gaining popularity, where a student places a needed assignment on a website and asks writers to place bids on the paper to write it in his/her place (Chakrabarti, 2012; Clarke & Lancaster, 2006; Walker & Townley, 2012).

TURNITIN

As Pousada (2011) notes, the same technology that makes it easier for students to plagiarize now also makes it easier for instructors to detect. In recent years, the development of software that detects matched text, often referred to as anti-plagiarism software, has proliferated. According to a report by the Campus Computing Project (2011), 50% out of 523 American public and private research universities, public and private four-year colleges, and community colleges held licenses for anti-plagiarism software in the Fall 2010 semester. Many such programs and websites exist (i.e., Plagium, Copyscape, Article Checker, SafeAssign, and EVE 2, among others), the most popular of which is *Turnitin*.

Turnitin, which is marketed as a matched text detection software program, is currently licensed to 9,000 high schools and colleges and supported by 15 languages (*Turnitin*, n.d.). According to *Turnitin*'s homepage, the program checked over 80 million papers in 2012 alone and serves 1 million instructors, 20 million licensed students, and 10,000 educational institutions (*Turnitin*, n.d.). *Turnitin* works by matching text in a student's paper with text found in the software's enormous databases that include 24 billion webpages and 300 million papers previously submitted by students (*Turnitin*, n.d.). Results are shown as a percentage (or "similarity index") in an "originality report," the results of which are interpreted by the instructor. The originality report presents matched text using several different colors and links the matched text directly to the original electronic source. The side by side presentation of matched texts allows users to view original text next to the matched text. In Figure 1, we provide a screenshot of a sample *Turnitin* originality report (Turnitin, n.d.).

Although there is some scholarship in both English L1 and L2 literature regarding *Turnitin,* research on the program in higher education remains scarce. Some studies have investigated students' and instructors' perspectives of *Turnitin*. In a study of 116 first-year psychology students (71 of whom evaluated *Turnitin*), Betts, Bostock, Elder, and Trueman (2012) found that 68% of students felt reassured that they had written in their own words and 58% agreed or strongly agreed that *Turnitin* helped them understand plagiarism. In addition, Sutherland-Smith and Carr (2005) interviewed seven teachers from arts, business, law, education, and science and technology departments at an Australian university to examine their views of the program and whether they felt *Turnitin* would be an effective educational tool. Overall, teachers found *Turnitin* to be easy to use and agreed that the program would be more effective than they were in locating matched electronic text; however, four instructors raised concerns about the use of the program for punitive measures.

Figure 1. Screenshot of a Turnitin originality report (© 2014, iParadigms LLC. Used with permission

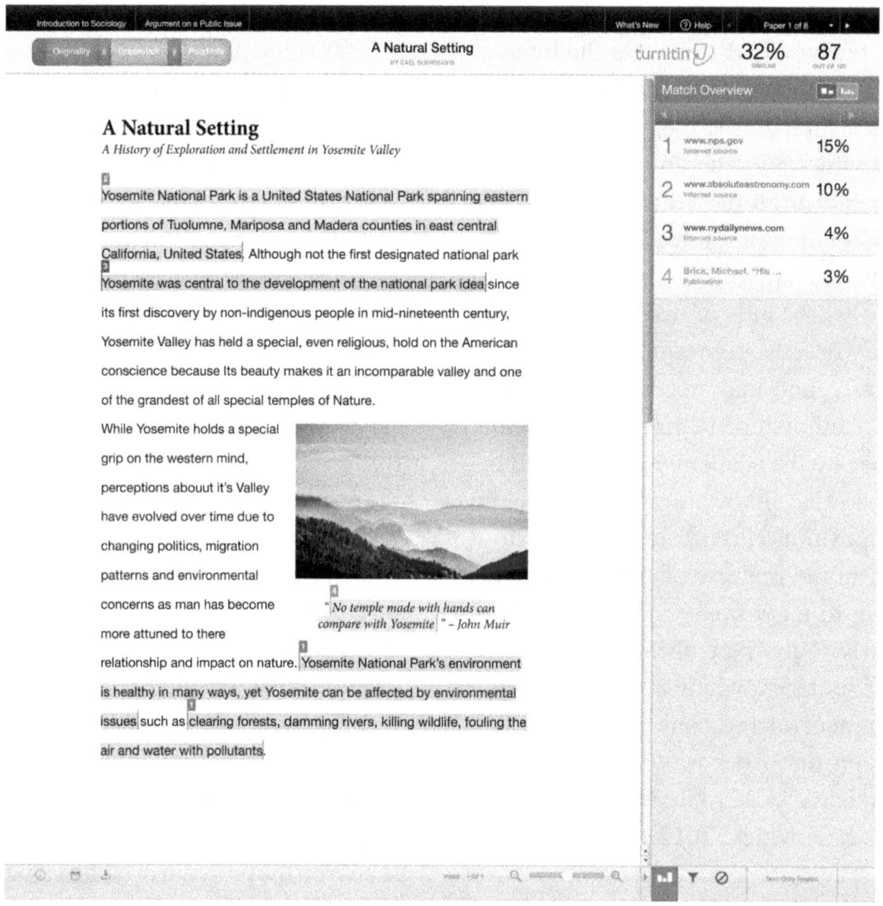

Other scholars have considered how *Turnitin* may be used to support learning. For instance, Rolfe (2011) examined the potential of the program for providing formative feedback on undergraduate students' writing. She found that participants used *Turnitin*'s originality reports to revise their work and reflect on their citation use. All students held positive opinions of the program and believed that the program was useful in helping them improve their academic texts. Although Rolfe's study was conducted with English L1 writers, her conclusion that "*Turnitin* is useful in that it highlights areas that need rewriting, and this is an important step in the development of literacy" also applies to the literacy development of L2 writers (p. 707). Stappenbelt and Rowles (2009) also support the use of *Turnitin* in helping students learn academic writing; the authors investigated first-year engineering students' perceptions of the program to self-correct their writing. Similar to Rolfe's (2011) findings, the majority of participants in Stappenbelt and Rowles' study held positive views of the program to support learning and believed that *Turnitin* helped them improve their paraphrasing skills and avoid plagiarism.

Finally, some scholarship has examined the effectiveness of *Turnitin* as a deterrent to plagiarism (Ali, 2013; Ledwith & Rísquez, 2008) and as a tool to measure the amount of students' plagiarism (Walker, 2010). Youmans (2011) examined the potential of matched text detection software in deterring plagiarism. In a study of undergraduate students at California State University, Youmans looked at whether knowledge that papers would be submitted to *Turnitin* would deter students from plagiarism and if students would plagiarize from their classmates. Youmans also examined whether the students would plagiarize less if they were asked to complete an assignment in which they chose whether to use citations. Results showed that students' knowledge of *Turnitin* did not affect the percentages of matched text. Interestingly, results also showed that the percentages of matched text were higher for students who were required to cite sources. Youmans suggests that students may have underestimated the program's ability to match text or they may have been "desperate" to succeed at any cost. Finally, *Turnitin* (2014) published a report this year which examined the effectiveness of the software on reducing plagiarism. Data included over 55 million papers submitted to *Turnitin* over a five-year period in more than 1,000 institutions of higher education. Results indicate that the amount of unoriginal text decreased overall by 39%.

Nevertheless, to date, research on the use of *Turnitin* with L2 writers is limited. Stapleton (2012) examined two groups of L2 graduate writers (one group had knowledge that their work would be submitted to *Turnitin* and the other did not). The first part of the study examined whether students would be deterred from plagiarizing, how percentages from the program's originality reports represented plagiarism, and how participants' grades were affected by plagiarism and/or originality report percentages. Results showed that although *Turnitin* did not provide information about students' intentions, the group of participants who had knowledge that their work would be submitted to *Turnitin* were deterred from plagiarizing. Nevertheless, Stapleton reminds us that originality reports must always be subject to interpretation, as a high percentage of matched text does not necessarily equal plagiarism.

While the positive role of *Turnitin* and similar detection programs has been reported in the literature reviewed above, criticism of such programs has also been voiced. At the 2013 Conference on College Composition and Communication (CCCC) in Las Vegas, Nevada, members passed a resolution stating that the organization does not endorse plagiarism detection services (Conference on College Composition and Communication, 2013). Yet, although they renounce plagiarism detection services (PDS) for creating distrust between students and teachers, and threatening students' privacy and rights to their own work, the CCCC "commends institutions who offer sound pedagogical alternatives to the use of PDSs and encourages institutions who use PDSs to implement practices that are in the best interest of their students."

The CCCC's resolution echoes the concerns of other scholars who have questioned the ethical basis of programs and software like *Turnitin* (Cochrane, 2006; Foster, 2002; Marsh, 2004; Purdy, 2005, 2009). For instance, Howard (2007) states that "in place of the pedagogy that joins teachers and students in the educational enterprise, plagiarism-detection software offers a machine that will separate them" (p. 12). Vanacker (2011) highlights several ethical concerns about *Turnitin*, that the teacher interprets and decides on a student's text, that students are "guilty-until-proven innocent," and that in some settings students' papers are submitted to the *Turnitin* database automatically unless the teacher opts out of doing so (p. 329). Scholars have also highlighted the technical limitations of the software itself (Heather, 2010; Royce, 2003).

Despite these criticisms, the sheer number of *Turnitin* licenses held by institutions worldwide demonstrates that the program remains popular and very much in use. Whether part of a holistic approach (Macdonald & Carroll, 2006; Shi & Casanave, 2012) or used in addition to teachers' eyes (McKeever, 2006), a better understanding of the pedagogical potential of *Turnitin* may greatly benefit students. Nevertheless, we know of only one study that has considered the potential of *Turnitin* for L2 writing instruction (Stapleton, 2012). Howard (2007) suggests that because readers and writers share access to the same digital resources, students need effective pedagogy and an understanding of new media that addresses the deep intertextual nature of textual borrowing. Hunt (2002) believes that fears over plagiarism and the Internet may even result in positive educational outcomes. Hunt goes on to say that Internet access can challenge teachers to think critically about the types of writing assignments given to students and how such assignments are graded; it encourages educators and students to think about how information is processed and organized, and pushes instructors to reflect on how students are taught about scholarship.

Because *Turnitin* and similar programs will remain as long as "they effectively address the problem of students engaging in extensive 'copy-and-paste' behavior, using the Internet as a convenient resource" (Ledwith & Risquez, 2008, p. 373), it is worth considering the value of the program for educational use. In the literature, there is an increasing call for pedagogy to address and prevent plagiarism (Howard & Davies, 2009; Li & Casanave, 2012; Pecorari, 2013); *Turnitin* may have the potential to support this process. As Emerson (2008) aptly states:

If Turnitin could be used by teachers committed to teaching academic writing skills, who could (and would) sensitively read the reports, and who understood the distinction between fraud and incorrect or inadequate use of sources, and if this tool was used in conjunction with an effective educational package that addressed process and voice and personal conferences with tutors, then we might make a strong case for Turnitin (p. 190).

A Social View of Learning Academic Writing

Our study is framed by a social view of learning, which considers learning as doing, becoming, experiencing, and belonging (Wenger, 1998); in other words, learning is the result of social participation in the world. As Valentine (2006) reminds us, "plagiarism becomes plagiarism as part of a practice that involves participants' values, attitudes, and feelings, as well as their social relationships to each other and to the institutions in which they work" (p. 89). For this reason, we believe that examining how students use *Turnitin* to learn about plagiarism and textual borrowing within their academic setting can shed light onto how students become members of these academic communities.

A social view of learning also aligns with one of the three schools of genre theory, English for Academic Purposes (EAP), which focuses on the teaching and learning of English in academic settings. As Hyland and Hamp-Lyons (2002) note, "An EAP perspective takes practitioners beyond preparing learners for study in English to developing new kinds of literacy: equipping students with the communicative skills to participate in particular academic and cultural contexts" (p. 2). Genres, or "abstract, socially recognized ways of using language" (Hyland, 2003, p.149), are used by members in these communities to maintain and develop social relationships. In academic settings, genres may include essays, research articles, textbooks, and peer feedback, among others (Hyland, 2006), all of which are used for particular purposes and for a particular audience.

At most institutions, ESL composition classes typically aim to prepare students for using academic discourse in their majors of study. If we consider Wenger's (1998) assertion, that "learning is an issue of engaging in and contributing to the practices of their communities" (p. 7), then we should examine how learners engage in and contribute to the practices of their academic communities. In our study, we consider how an ESL composition course functioned as a community of practice, which is defined as "a set of relations among persons, activity, and world, over time and in relation with other tangential and overlapping communities of practice" (Lave & Wenger, 1991, p. 98).

Present Study

Our study addresses the following question: What impact does *Turnitin* have on L2 writers' understandings of textual borrowing in English academic writing? A case study design suits our work because it allows us to deeply examine the role of *Turnitin* in developing students' academic writing skills (Stake, 2003) and to gain further insight into L2 academic writing instruction practices for a particular population. A case study approach is also appropriate for the questions we ask because we wanted to explore *how* the program supports academic writing instruction in its real-life classroom context (Yin, 2009). As Seliger and Shohamy (1989) note, "the ultimate goal of qualitative research is to discover phenomena, such as patterns of second language behavior not previously described, and to understand those phenomena from the perspective of participants in the activity" (p. 120).

METHODS

The Research Setting

We conducted a case study of a post-secondary English writing course that serves as a bridge between intensive English study and required mainstream composition courses. The study was conducted at Dunbar University (pseudonym), a medium-sized public institution in the Midwestern part of the United States. The course is housed in the Department of English Language and Literatures, which offers an M.A., a graduate endorsement, a graduate certificate in TESOL, and a graduate certificate in TEFL (Teaching English as a Foreign Language). The English Intensive Program (EIP) is also located in the Department of English and prepares international students for academic study in the United States. At the time this study was conducted, Dunbar operated on ten-week academic terms called quarters.

As the syllabus states, the main objective of this course is to help students become better readers and writers, learn to identify their strengths and weaknesses as writers, read critically, and increase their confidence and ability to write in a variety of situations. The course met twice each week in a computer lab, which provided students with their own computers and Internet access. In the lab, there was also a large screen in front of the classroom that the instructor used to project materials.

Students can either pass or fail the course and need at least a 70% to pass. Final course grades included completion of work done in class and major assignments, a final writing portfolio, and a timed essay exam. Because a critical component of the course included in-class writing and research, students could not pass the course if they had not attended class regularly. Upon successful completion, students have the option of taking English 101, a required composition course that is intended for native speakers, or enrolling in a specific section of English 101, which is intended for non-native English speakers.

Students completed three major assignments during the academic quarter which were all weighted equally in their final portfolios. The first assignment was a two-page summary and response paper based on a news article students chose; the first draft was due during the fifth week of the quarter. For the second assignment, students had to rhetorically analyze a text of their choice, which could have included a news article, painting, song, short story, editorial, or video. The first draft of the text analysis was due during the seventh week of classes and was three to four pages long. The third assignment, a four to six-page research paper, required students to research a topic of their choice in depth and use at least four credible sources to support their ideas. The first draft of the research paper was due during the ninth week of classes. On every draft, students received feedback from their peers and the instructor and while Alexandra (teacher pseudonym) assigned a letter grade to each final draft, students were given the choice either to keep their grade or revise their work by the end of the quarter. This allowed students the opportunity to work with *Turnitin* while revising their papers. Additionally, all students were asked to visit the University Writing Center (UWC) at least seven times over the course of the quarter to discuss their work with a peer tutor.

All students in the course received training in *Turnitin* at the beginning of the quarter; the instructor helped students log in to the program during class and explained exactly what they needed to do to upload their work and interpret their originality reports. We would like to point out that instructors in the English Department of Dunbar University are not required to submit students' work to *Turnitin*. The Department had held a license for approximately eight years when this study was conducted, and instructors could choose whether to use the program or not. The instructor of this course had used *Turnitin* several times in her English and ESL classes and was an experienced user of the program. She chose to use it in the course, but reminded students that *Turnitin* would not be the only mode of assessment. Rather, *Turnitin* would be used in conjunction with other resources to support students' academic writing growth.

Participants

Six students had registered for the course; however, only four students attended regularly and passed. Of these four students, three agreed to participate in the study; the fourth student declined to participate due to her other obligations that quarter. Carina, a pharmacy major from Brazil, had been in the United States for four months at the time the study was conducted. She had taken a listening and speaking course at Dunbar and was enrolled in the ESL composition course for the second time since the subsequent course (English 101) was full and she wanted to continue to improve her academic literacy skills. Ahn, an accounting major from Vietnam, had been at Dunbar for one year when she participated in the study. She had completed two advanced ESL courses in the EIP at Dunbar and had studied English in Vietnam for five years prior to arriving in the United States. Kumar, a computer science major from India, came to the United States with his family in ninth grade. He had to repeat this course because he did not pass the first time he took the course.

Alexandra, the course instructor, is an experienced ESL teacher and had been teaching at Dunbar for 12 years at the time the study was conducted. She holds a master's degree in English with a specialization in Teaching English to Speakers of Other Languages (TESOL), and has taught both mainstream and ESL composition courses at Dunbar. The final participant was Professor Miller (pseudonym), Director of Writing Programs in the English Department, with whom one interview was conducted. Professor Miller helped us gain a better sense of the department's stance on *Turnitin* and plagiarism, as he was able to describe the department's policies and procedures regarding plagiarism.

Data Collection and Analysis

Data included semi-structured interviews with the instructor and students at the beginning, middle, and end of the course, a brief background questionnaire for student participants completed at the beginning of the quarter, bi-weekly observations of each class, course documents (i.e., supplemental handouts, worksheets, and sample assignments), and students' *Turnitin* originality reports. Semi-structured interview questions provided the opportunity for participants to describe their experiences and perspectives regarding the course and their responses to the use of *Turnitin*, and encouraged them to add any additional information they considered relevant while insuring that key issues were addressed (see Appendix A for a list of all interview questions). All interviews were audio recorded then transcribed for analysis; each interview lasted approximately one hour.

In 19 class observations, we took field notes of the physical setting of the classroom, participants' interactions as they reviewed and discussed their work and *Turnitin* originality reports with each other and with the instructor, the course content and major topics of each lesson, and the researchers' reactions to the course. The observer's personal observations were also recorded in a separate column in the notebook, and all field notes were transcribed into a Microsoft Word document. In addition, participants were asked to keep an online journal (blog) at least once per week to record any thoughts they had about the course, *Turnitin*, or their progress in the course. The blogs were password protected and accessible only by the researchers; participants could not read each other's blogs. Both Carina and Ahn submitted entries every week but Kumar did not submit any; he reported in the second interview that he had trouble finding the time to write in his blog.

Data were analyzed using Wolcott's (1994) three-stage process of "transforming data," which involves data description, analysis, and interpretation. In the first stage, we described what was learned and observed as objectively as possible. In the second analysis stage, we systematically and recursively looked for patterns and themes and organized data into categories. In the final interpretation, we aimed to make sense of the data and form conclusions. Wolcott (1994) notes that although these three stages are fluid, "identifying and distinguishing among the three may serve a useful purpose, especially if the categories can be regarded as varying emphases that qualitative researchers employ to organize and present data (p. 11). At this stage, we also triangulated our data with the course instructor and an L2 writing expert who has published widely on plagiarism and was not affiliated with Dunbar University.

RESULTS

Using a community of practice framework allowed us to examine how participants and the course instructor used *Turnitin* to construct knowledge about several important components of academic writing (Lave & Wenger, 1991). While *Turnitin* is often used to detect matched text, the role of the program in this course was to increase students' understandings of the structural and conceptual notions relevant to academic writing. Professor Miller stated that *Turnitin* was used in the English Department to support instruction for English L1 and L2 writers, as he strongly believed that plagiarism was mostly a pedagogical issue. Throughout the academic term, students had substantial opportunities to construct knowledge about academic writing openly and collaboratively. *Turnitin* helped participants generate dialogue about avoiding plagiarism and about academic writing more broadly, and allowed students to construct their roles as members of the discourse community they were learning to become a part of (Price, 2002).

While this course focused on helping students become stronger readers and writers of academic texts, and because textual borrowing plays a critical role in those processes, we were pleased to find that *Turnitin* was never used for punitive purposes and that plagiarism was not a focal point of the course. The course instructor focused on helping students gain confidence and fully understand academic discourse conventions, and *Turnitin* was not used to intimidate students or enforce plagiarism policies and warnings. Instead, the instructor built a culture of trust in the classroom and told students that she did not expect them to buy a paper online, ask someone else to write a paper for them, reuse an old paper, or copy and paste text from another source, all of which assume an intent to be deceitful, or what Pecorari (2008) calls "prototypical plagiarism" (p. 4). Consistent with Professor Miller's perspective and that of the instructor, students knew that they could make mistakes, ask questions, help each other, and receive help from Alexandra and their peers at any time.

Our findings show that *Turnitin*, as used in this ESL writing class, helped students learn about textual borrowing in academic writing in various ways. First, the color-coding feature of matched text helped draw students' attention to the text and compel them to analyze why the text was matched. If students paraphrased information from a source, they had to check that their paraphrase did not match the original text too closely. If students quoted a text directly, they still had to ensure that they had included quotation marks and cited the source. Ahn reported that she appreciated the fact that she could submit drafts to the program first and make revisions accordingly. In Table 1, we show how she inaccurately introduced and quoted the original source in her first draft. *Turnitin* matched the text to the original source and because the text was highlighted, Ahn was able to see that she had two sets of quotation marks in a row. She then revised the text for her final draft to reflect the speaker's original quote accurately.

In the first interview, Alexandra discussed how the color-coding feature of *Turnitin* helped draw students' attention to the text and reinforce what she taught students in class. This feature of the program was useful in that regard because it created a concrete visual image for students to examine. Alexandra stated:

If we use that and they've taken an author's words, word-for-word, or if they have misunderstood paraphrasing, by simply changing an adjective and flipping a word or two around, Turnitin comes back with a big block of color, showing them that this writing came from another source. That works great for when what the student has written is exactly or very close to how it was written in the other document. So what I'll do is say you need to make this decision, now will you paraphrase it and put an in-text citation or will you keep it like this and put quotes around it and an in-text citation or will you let me consider this a plagiarized paper? Students are most often surprised by their big green or red block and are very happy to get in there and change it. (Interview 1)

Second, participants reported that they used *Turnitin* to help them evaluate the quality of their sources. Because the program provides a link to the original text it matches, students can simply click on the link and be directed to the original text. In the middle of the quarter, Carina reported that *Turnitin* helped draw her attention to the sources she cited in her summary and response

Table 1. Excerpt from Ahn's summary and response paper

Source	Content
Original source*	"We neglect these young people, especially those who are no longer in school, unable to find jobs, and are not being trained to be productive citizens," Rep. Rush continued, "but then we're left to wonder and pontificate on why a large percentage of unemployed and troubled youth resort to antisocial or violent behavior. There are few after-school programs and no jobs. EYADA seeks to address that."
Ahn's first draft	In the article, Rep. Rush continued to clarify his idea that "We neglect these young people, especially those who are no longer in school, unable to find jobs, and are not being trained to be productive citizens,","but then we're left to wonder and pontificate on why a large percentage of unemployed and troubled youth resort to antisocial or violent behavior. There are few after-school programs and no jobs. EYADA seeks to address that"...
Ahn's final draft	In the article, Rep. Rush continued to clarify his idea that "We neglect these young people, especially those who are no longer in school, unable to find jobs, and are not being trained to be productive citizens, but then we're left to wonder and pontificate on why a large percentage of unemployed and troubled youth resort to antisocial or violent behavior. There are few after-school programs and no jobs. EYADA seeks to address that"...

* from http://rush.house.gov

paper. Whenever *Turnitin* did not match text she quoted directly, she thought about the source she used and why the text was not matched. She stated, "The source wasn't academic that's why it didn't show in *Turnitin*, so I start thinking that it wasn't a good source and maybe I could find another thing in better sources" (Interview 2). If the source she cited was not reputable, *Turnitin* may not have found matched text. Of course, there are also perfectly appropriate texts that may not be captured by *Turnitin*, but raising the possibility of a problem was helpful for her.

Third, *Turnitin* helped participants reflect on whether information was common knowledge or needed a citation. Because the program color codes matched text, it draws students' attention to the text, where they can further analyze why the information was matched. The matched text allowed students to focus on the highlighted information and make decisions about what needed revising and if a citation was necessary. Ahn discussed how she evaluated matched text for this purpose:

It wasn't cited but it was matched. I didn't paraphrase. It's my idea but because it's general, not specific idea. I read it again and it's general idea that anybody can know. So I realize that that's the reason, it's not plagiarism. (Ahn, Interview 3)

In Table 2, we present data from a classroom observation conducted in the third week of the semester. In this class, students worked together to analyze a *Turnitin* originality report. Alexandra projected two sample originality reports on the large screen in front of the class, and the class spent 30 minutes discussing them. By this time in the academic quarter, students were working on choosing sources for their summary and response papers and were just learning about *Turnitin*. Alexandra showed students the various components of the program (e.g., the color-coded matches) and ensured that each student could log in with their Dunbar username and password.

Field notes recorded during the third week of the semester (as shown in Table 2) illustrate how the instructor and the class used *Turnitin* for learning purposes. First, the instructor led students through the program so they understood exactly how it worked. Students learned about how *Turnitin* links the matched text to the original source (e.g., npr.org). Second, the class discussed citation in two sample papers. In the first paper, the first match was highlighted in green and properly cited with quotation marks. Students then looked at the second source, which was matched in red, but noticed that there were no quotation marks. The instructor took the opportunity to tell students that the government website had to be cited and that the direct quotation needed quotation marks. Finally, students discussed the percentage that *Turnitin* provides in the originality report, which led to more general questions about academic writing. As the instructor noted, students' papers should be balanced between their own words and cited sources, which led to a discussion of what constitutes a "general sentence" (i.e., common knowledge that does not have to be cited) and what constitutes information that must be cited.

Finally, participants reported that *Turnitin* helped them learn to balance their ideas with other sources. They learned that they should not rely too heavily or too little on outside sources, and reported that the color-coding feature of *Turnitin* helped them see how much of their overall paper drew from other sources. Because *Turnitin* only provides a numerical percentage of matched text, and because there is not a particular percentage that would designate plagiarism, human eyes are always needed to interpret the total percentage of matched text in every originality report. Alexandra explained how she helped students interpret the scores:

A good writing teacher doesn't accept a paper that's mostly authors' words or mostly paraphrased without much interaction from the student writer. So I don't like to say "go for the numbers."

Table 2. Classroom observation field notes (Week Three)

Time	Activity	Personal Observations
11:40 am Orientation to *Turnitin*	• The teacher (T) announces that she will show students today how *Turnitin* works. T walks around to each student to make sure there are no problems finding the sample papers in the course management system. • T shows students what the various icons mean. • T asks students to practice submitting a sample paper and pulls up the paper on the large screen.	
11:45 am Analysis of Paper #1	• T pulls up the paper and says that 35% of the whole paper came from different sources. • T directs students' attention to a direct quote from npr.org, a source that was cited and matched in green (10%). T said the student cited this very well because the text is included in quotation marks and the author is giving credit to the original source. T clicks on the NPR website to show students that *Turnitin* links text to its original source. • Students look at red matched text. There's a 25% match to a government website. T asks students why we have to do this. One student responds that "we need to check the source to see where it came from." T agrees and says "Yes! If you have a good paper but forget to put quotation marks, it could either be a mistake or the work could be taken directly, but I know that nobody in this class will cheat." • A female student asks: "Why are there red and green colors?" • T answers that these colors help visually organize the matches. She thanks the student for the question.	
11:55 am Analysis of Paper #2	• T pulls up another paper that has a 4% match (from a local news website). • Students look at the paper and the matched text. • T said it was a great paper but the author didn't give any background information on the topic. T said a lot of beginning writers do that and it's okay. • T pulls up the original local news website and compares the matched text to the original. There are quotation marks so it's okay. • The class looks at another source that was cited in the paper but wasn't caught by *Turnitin.* T pulls up the source from Google. • T asks, "What does this tell you?" • One student answers that the program missed a source. • T says, "yes, it's not 100% foolproof. We need to check ourselves."	All students seem engaged; they are all paying attention and curious about the program.
12:05 Class wraps up	• One student asks what percentage of matched text is acceptable. • T says it's a great question; she says that a good paper is a balance of your own words and the words of others. 20% might be okay but you'll need more sources. 80% direct match means you need to use your own words more. • One student says the program also matches basic words. • T said this is "why we have to be smarter." • Another student asks if basic words are plagiarism. • T responds with an example, "The top reasons people eat so much junk food." She asks the class if this is plagiarism. • One student said we have to then worry about the main idea. • Another student said it was a "general sentence." • T said yes, that some words are so basic that anyone can say them. This is why we have to check every single instance of matched text in the report. • T asks if there are further questions and reminds the class that they will keep looking at originality reports. She said everyone must submit their first and final drafts to the program. • T collects HW and wishes students a good day.	I think the T uses the program not just to show source use, but to show students academic writing more generally?

However I do say, if (some students they want the numbers), if you can get about, say a research paper, an eight page research paper, if you can get about 25% to 20% of quoted material, whether they are partial quotes or whole quotes, but the rest a balance between your research and your own, at least half of it should be written from your own words. How you deal with the source use, break that down. (Interview 1)

Carina explained that whenever she received a very low percentage of matched text, she reflected on why the percentage would be low. She stated:

Turnitin showed me I didn't have enough sources to support response in summary/response task. Because it was always a low percentage I got. And I had to understand why I was always so low. And then the teacher always was showing me that it was low, that I need more sources and need to support my ideas, and then I got this. (Interview 3).

Similarly, Ahn reported that *Turnitin* helped draw her attention to her overall source use and stated, "If my essay have three source, and in the *Turnitin* I can know which source I use too much, I will revise it and make it less. Which one I use too little, like very few, I can use it more to balance it… because if I use quotation too much, I will paraphrase it and revise it in my own words" (Interview 2). In her summary and response paper, Ahn chose to respond to a news article about job prospects for African-American students in the United States. The *Turnitin* report for her first draft produced a 35% match from two different sources; 25% came from the main article she summarized and 10% was matched to another article that she used to support her ideas about the topic. All of the matched text was accurately cited and enclosed in quotation marks.

Nevertheless, Ahn felt that her own words and the direct quotations were not balanced because she had included too many of the latter. She revised her draft and when she submitted the final draft at the end of the quarter, the matched text percentage was the same as the first draft. In other words, Ahn did not reduce the amount of direct quotations in her paper. Instead, she further developed her ideas so the text was more balanced between direct quotations from the original article and her own response. In Table 3, we present sample text from Ahn's paper which illustrates how she used her own words to elaborate on the direct quotation she used at the beginning of the paragraph.

As this brief excerpt shows, Ahn expanded on her ideas considerably in the second draft. In the excerpt from the first draft, Ahn responded primarily to the author's directly quoted ideas. In the second draft, however, Ahn developed her own thoughts on the topic and provided additional support for the author's main argument (i.e., that unemployment increases crime for youths). She doubled the amount of words she used in this paragraph and expanded on other ideas, such as the personal fulfillment young people may receive by working.

Table 3. Sample text from Ahn's summary and response paper

First draft (107 words)	**Final draft (206 words)**
Yuki indicates that "the most effective and immediate way to address the problem is through job training and public works projects." I agree with him/her because his/her statement applies in my own experience. The children born to the unemployed teens could be unable to go to school, not being educated to be good citizens, hard to get communication with other people; however, when people do not have anything to do, they will find the ways to fill their time, and most of those ways are usually not good ways. So, troubled youth, destructive behavior will increase. In brief, we need to create more jobs for youth people.	Yuki indicates that "the most effective and immediate way to address the problem is through job training and public works projects." This is a great point because the children are born to the unemployed teens and could not go to school. Therefore they are not being educated to be good citizen. People who are being educated well will ignore them. From then, the society acts like two separate societies. Furthermore, when people do not have anything to do, they will find the ways to fill their time, and most of those ways are usually not good ways. So, destructive behaviors will increase in troubled youth. On the other hand, working will not only fill in young people's time, but also create experiences, joy, fun, or even bitterness that they need to pass through to be an adult. As a youth person, besides studying at school, I have a part time job which is related to my major. That helps me to focus more on my future career than join in anything else. Furthermore, the society needs young labor forces to inherit jobs from the labor forces who retire. In brief, we need to create more jobs for young people as well as a good educational environment.

DISCUSSION

Results from our study provide further support for scholarship that paints a positive picture of *Turnitin's* educational potential (Ali, 2013; Betts et al., 2012; Dahl, 2007; Ledwith & Rísquez, 2008; McKeever, 2006; Sutherland-Smith & Carr, 2005). The instructor and students held positive views of the program and stated that it was useful in supporting their learning processes (Stappenbelt & Rowles, 2009). In addition, students used the program to gain formative feedback on the effectiveness of their academic writing, reflect on their source use, and make revisions accordingly (Rolfe, 2011).

A community of practice framework allowed us to examine how participants and the course instructor used *Turnitin* to construct knowledge about academic writing together (Lave & Wenger, 1991). In this way, the course exhibited elements of Wenger's (1998) extended notion of a community of practice, which includes three fundamental components. First, there is a "mutual engagement" of doing things together. In this study, participants learned how to "do" academic writing as they were engaged in class and small group discussions, peer review, and in-class writing activities. Second, a "joint enterprise" involves negotiating meaning to create a shared identity. The participants were united by a common goal of learning English academic writing conventions to gain membership in an American discourse community (Swales, 1990). They also shared a common identity, which was that of international undergraduate students at Dunbar. Finally, members created a "shared repertoire" of common resources that was used in negotiating meaning. In our study, *Turnitin* originality reports, among other resources such as writing templates, course handouts, and sample papers from previous courses, provided a repertoire that helped students negotiate meaning about academic writing in class discussions, in small group sessions as students worked together in class, and individually with the instructor both in and out of class. All of these activities align with a social view of learning (Wenger, 1998) and provide insight into effective instruction on textual borrowing and *Turnitin*.

We also have tried to show how *Turnitin* was used to help create a "collaborative classroom" (Gergen, 2009), which also supports the notion of learning as a social activity. In a collaborative classroom, the instructor and students construct knowledge together and students' opinions are equally respected and valued. Collaboration played a major role in the L2 writing course examined in this study, as the course was very hands-on and students completed a lot of their work in class. Originality reports generated by *Turnitin* stimulated engaging dialogue about academic writing and textual borrowing, as we showed in Table 2. Throughout the quarter, the course instructor gave students many opportunities to work with each other and review each other's work. She effectively structured peer review sessions by providing students with specific questions (see Appendix B) that maximized the quality of feedback they gave and received. Students also made important decisions about their work and were given the freedom to choose their own topics, revise their work to obtain a higher grade if they wished, and gain control over their learning and progress in the course. The instructor's role was to give students the guidance and support they needed to become independent thinkers and writers, which in turn helped cultivate a "community of academic integrity" (Stappenbelt & Rowles, 2009, p. 1) within the course.

TURNITIN FOR L2 WRITING INSTRUCTION: AN EVALUATION

Our study indicates that *Turnitin* may be an effective learning tool when used for teaching and learning purposes, and we advocate that it be used in a manner similar to that reported in this study. In this study, *Turnitin* was used in conjunction with several other resources, including a project-based approach to writing instruction, substantial time for students to receive help and share their writing in class, continuous discussions of academic discourse, and consistent practice with paraphrasing, summarizing, and citing sources in each of the three assignments completed throughout the quarter. The curriculum of the course also helped learners participate in a shared history of learning *with* the instructor (Wenger, 1998), rather than as outsiders. Thus, we believe that *Turnitin* was effective in playing a critical role in involving students in their learning.

Overall, students in the course reported that they found *Turnitin* easy to use. All participants generally held a positive attitude towards *Turnitin* and found the program helpful. However, the results showed that not all students were comfortable with having their reports projected in class. For instance, Carina reported that she sometimes felt uncomfortable when the instructor projected her *Turnitin* originality report in front of the class, although the instructor had asked her permission beforehand. While Carina's concern does not reflect a limitation to the program itself, her insecurity in sharing her writing with the class before checking it herself reminds us that instructors must be sensitive to students' feelings. Carina preferred to have the time to view her report privately and check her percentage of matched text before her report was shared with the class. In her final blog entry, she wrote:

Every time I submit my text on "Turnitin", the teacher shows it to the classmates like an example in the opposite: do not write with such few sources and citations. I have no problem on showing my stuff, But I got upset at me, because my text never has enough citations. Teacher always complains that I give too much my opinion in the text and forget to cite works. And I know she is right.

If teachers opt to use *Turnitin* as a learner tool, we advise that they explain to students that they will not be penalized for a certain percentage of matched text. Instructors should also ask students if they feel comfortable sharing their originality reports with the class without having had the chance to view their reports first. Nonetheless, educators should be aware of the program's limitations. For instance, Kumar reported that *Turnitin* sometimes matched text to sources he had never used. This error appeared to be a function of the program, rather than an error made on his part. Although he found this frustrating, he asked Alexandra for help and used the opportunity to check his source use.

In addition, the program may not always catch every instance of matched text. For instance, Kumar had closely paraphrased a sentence from an original source and it was not highlighted in the first draft he submitted to *Turnitin.* In Table 4, we present the original text, Kumar's paraphrase in his first draft, and the same paraphrase in his final draft; the text was matched in *Turnitin* only in his final draft. If the text had been matched in Kumar's first draft, he would have had the opportunity to revise his paraphrase for his final draft.

Another limitation to the program is that it cannot detect who has actually written an original text. While this is not a limitation of the software *per se*, we are reminded that *Turnitin* is not always a sure way to catch "cheaters." Many students complete their assignments at home, where it is possible for them to ask someone to write an entire paper in their place. *Turnitin* matches papers to other papers submitted in the *Turnitin* database; therefore, if a student submits another student's paper that had never been submitted in *Turnitin*, the program would not be able to find a match to the original text. In our study, the course instructor avoided this issue by supporting students' writing processes at each step and giving students plenty of time to write in class. Ahn appreciated the opportunities to write and stated:

Table 4. Samples of Matched Text from Kumar's Summary and Response Paper

Source	Content
Excerpt from the original source*	But what is the proper relation between Art and Science? Saying that one deals with the objective while the other with the subjective is too easy, especially considering the way Art and Science have played off each other across history.
Kumar's first draft paraphrase (no match in *Turnitin*)	*The proper relationship between art and science is that art is playing with...*
Kumar's final draft (bold words highlighted were matched to the original source by *Turnitin*)	***The proper*** *relationship* ***between art and science*** *is* ***that*** *art is playing* ***with...***

* Taken from www.npr.org

I prefer to do everything in class because that time is for my, like if it is for English class, it's the whole time for my English so I can do everything for English. If I go home, I don't think I can concentrate. (Interview 3)

CONCLUSION AND FUTURE RESEARCH

This case study aims to fill a gap in the plagiarism literature by investigating the use of *Turnitin* for educational purposes in a L2 academic writing classroom. Because intensive English programs and preparatory non-credit classes are often a starting point for many international students studying in English-speaking countries, future research should consider how students learn about plagiarism in those contexts. Little is known about how *Turnitin* is used in intensive programs and whether educators in this context are using the software for punitive or pedagogical purposes, or both.

This study was limited by a small sample size of three participants. Carina and Kumar had also taken the course once before and were repeating the class for different reasons. In addition, we did not conduct a textual analysis of students' papers and only considered their perspectives and experiences with *Turnitin*. Because the course was very hands-on and because students had many opportunities to revise their work in class, with the Writing Center tutor, and in multiple drafts, we feel that a text analysis may not have provided a clear sense of how students made decisions about source use. We also needed to be careful with reference to publishing students' writing as their work is saved in *Turnitin's* database and thus, their confidentiality could be jeopardized.

Future studies might examine ESL instructors' views of *Turnitin* and the perspectives of students from other linguistic and cultural backgrounds at varying levels of proficiency in L2 writing. Much research has centered on English-speaking countries and Asia, and less is known about how students learn to avoid plagiarism in Central and South American, European, and African contexts. As enrollment of international students increases in English-speaking universities across the globe, educators who understand their students' linguistic and cultural backgrounds will be better prepared to teach them. Future research might also consider the perspectives of teachers and examine the discourse they use to discuss plagiarism. As we learned in this study, the instructor's approach to plagiarism and classroom discourse significantly affected students' learning. Finally, additional research is needed to provide insight into how *Turnitin* is used in ESL classrooms, how students and ESL teachers feel about the software, and how *Turnitin* may be used to support other components of academic writing. Future research might also investigate the effectiveness of other matched text detection software programs in helping students learn about textual borrowing.

Based on the insight we have gained in this study, we suggest a reconceptualization of the objective of matched text detection software. When used to support learning in a course that strives to create a community of academic learners, programs such as *Turnitin* may be beneficial for helping L2 writers gain a deeper and more nuanced understanding of textual borrowing and citation, develop confidence in their writing and self-editing skills, and feel comfortable weaving digital sources into their texts. However, we do not feel that it should be used solely to "catch" students' plagiarism, especially when originality reports are not carefully examined.

As we discovered in our study, learning to become a member of an academic discourse community was very much a shared experience among participants. Students discussed textual borrowing openly in an engaging and safe classroom atmosphere and had the freedom to make mistakes, ask questions, and collaborate. For this reason, we suggest that effective academic writing instruction is first and foremost the most important factor for helping students learn to avoid plagiarism. By focusing on instruction, we can shift attention from morality and punishment to teaching and learning.

ACKNOWLEDGMENT

The authors would like to thank the editors and anonymous reviewers for their insightful feedback on our drafts. We would also like to thank the course instructor for her enthusiasm and dedication to our project.

REFERENCES

Abasi, A., Akbari, N., & Graves, B. (2006). Discourse appropriation, construction of identities, and the complex issue of plagiarism: ESL students writing in graduate school. *Journal of Second Language Writing*, *15*, 102–117. doi:10.1016/j.jslw.2006.05.001

Ali, H. I. (2013). Minimizing cyber-plagiarism through Turnitin: Faculty's and students' perspectives. *International Journal of Applied Linguistics & English Literature*, *2*(2), 33–42. doi:10.7575/aiac.ijalel.v.2n.2p.33

Atkins, T., & Nelson, G. (2001). Plagiarism and the Internet: Turning the tables. *English Journal*, *90*(4), 101–104. doi:10.2307/821911

Betts, L. R., Bostock, S. J., Elder, T. J., & Trueman, M. (2012). Encouraging good writing practice in first-year psychology students: An intervention using *Turnitin*. *Psychology Teaching Review*, *18*(2), 74–81.

Bloch, J. (2001). Plagiarism and the ESL student: From printed to electronic texts. In D. Belcher & A. Hirvela (Eds.), Linking Literacies: Perspectives on L2 reading-writing connections (pp. 209–228). Ann Arbor, MI: University of Michigan Press.

Bloch, J. (2012). *Plagiarism, intellectual property and the teaching of L2 writing*. Bristol, UK: Multilingual Matters.

Buranen, L. (1999). But I wasn't cheating: Plagiarism and cross-cultural mythology. In L. Buranen, & A. Roy (Eds.), *Perspectives on plagiarism and intellectual property in a postmodern world* (pp. 63–74). Albany, NY: State University of New York Press.

Campus Computing Project. (2011). The 2010 National Survey of Information Technology in U.S. Higher Education. Retrieved from http://www.campuscomputing.net/

Chakrabarti, R. (2012). When essays for sale become contract cheating. *BBC News*. Available from, http://www.bbc.co.uk/news/education-20298237

Clarke, R., & Lancaster, T. (2006, June). *Eliminating the successor to plagiarism? Identifying the usage of contract cheating sites*. Paper presented at the meeting of the International Plagiarism Conference. Newcastle upon Tyne, UK.

Cochrane, M. (2006). *Does plagiarism-detection service violate student privacy?*. Available from, http://www.buffalo.edu/ubreporter/archive/vol38/vol38n7/articles/FSEC.html

Conference on College Composition and Communication. (2013). *2013 Resolutions & Sense of the House Motions.* Available from, http://www.ncte.org/cccc

Currie, P. (1998). Staying out of trouble: Apparent plagiarism and academic survival. *Journal of Second Language Writing*, *7*(1), 1–18. doi:10.1016/S1060-3743(98)90003-0

Dahl, S. (2007). The student perspective on using plagiarism detection software. *Active Learning in Higher Education*, *8*(2), 173–191. doi:10.1177/1469787407074110

Deckert, G. (1993). Perspectives on plagiarism from EFL students in Hong Kong. *Journal of Second Language Writing*, *2*(2), 131–148. doi:10.1016/1060-3743(93)90014-T

DeVoss, D., & Rosati, A. (2002). "It wasn't me, was it?" Plagiarism and the web. *Computers and Composition*, *19*(2), 191–203. doi:10.1016/S8755-4615(02)00112-3

Dryden, L. M. (1999). A distant mirror or through the looking glass? Plagiarism and intellectual property in Japanese education. In L. Buranen, & A. Roy (Eds.), *Perspectives on plagiarism and intellectual property in a postmodern world* (pp. 75–85). Albany, NY: State University of New York Press.

Emerson, L. (2008). Plagiarism, a *Turnitin* trial, and an experience of cultural disorientation. In C. Eisner, & M. Vicinus (Eds.), *Originality, imitation, and plagiarism: Teaching writing in the digital age* (pp. 183–194). Ann Arbor, MI: University of Michigan Press.

Fish, S. (2010). Plagiarism is not a big moral deal. *New York Times.* Available from, http://opinionator.blogs.nytimes.com/2010/08/09/plagiarism-is-not-a-big-moral-deal/

Foster, A. L. (2002). *Plagiarism-detection tool creates legal quandary.* Available from, http://chronicle.com

Gergen, K. (2009). *An invitation to social construction* (2nd ed.). London: Sage.

Groark, M., Oblinger, D., & Choa, M. (2001). Term paper mills, anti-plagiarism tools, and academic integrity. *EDUCAUSE Review*, *36*(5), 40–48.

Gu, Q., & Brooks, J. (2008). Beyond the accusation of plagiarism. *System*, *36*, 337–352. doi:10.1016/j.system.2008.01.004

Heather, J. (2010). Turnitoff: identifying and fixing a hole in current plagiarism detection software. *Assessment & Evaluation in Higher Education*, *35*(6), 647–660. doi:10.1080/02602938.2010.486471

Howard, R. M. (1993). A plagiarism pentimento. *Journal of Teaching Writing*, *11*(2), 233–246.

Howard, R. M. (1995). Plagiarisms, authorships, and the academic death penalty. *College English*, *57*(7), 788–806. doi:10.2307/378403

Howard, R. M. (2007). Understanding "internet plagiarism.". *Computers and Composition*, *24*, 3–15. doi:10.1016/j.compcom.2006.12.005

Howard, R. M., & Davies, L. J. (2009). Plagiarism in the internet age. *Literacy 2.0*, *66*(6), 64–67.

Hunt, R. (2002). *Four reasons to be happy about Internet plagiarism.* Available from, http://www.stu.ca/~hunt/plagiary.htm

Hyland, K. (2003). Genre-based pedagogies: A social response to process. *Journal of Second Language Writing*, *12*, 17–29. doi:10.1016/S1060-3743(02)00124-8

Hyland, K. (2006). *English for academic purposes: An advanced resource book.* London: Routledge.

Hyland, K., & Hamp-Lyons, L. (2002). EAP: Issues and directions. *Journal of English for Academic Purposes*, *1*, 1–12. doi:10.1016/S1475-1585(02)00002-4

Jenkins, R. (2011, August 14). Toward a rational response to plagiarism. *The Chronicle of Higher Education.* Available from, http://chronicle.com

Keck, C. (2006). The use of paraphrase in summary writing: A comparison of L1 and L2 writers. *Journal of Second Language Writing, 15*, 261–278. doi:10.1016/j.jslw.2006.09.006

Kitalong, K. (1998). A web of symbolic violence. *Computers and Composition, 15*, 253–263. doi:10.1016/S8755-4615(98)90058-5

Lave, J., & Wenger, E. (1991). *Situated learning: Legitimate peripheral participation*. Cambridge: Cambridge University Press. doi:10.1017/CBO9780511815355

Ledwith, A., & Rísquez, A. (2008). Using anti-plagiarism software to promote academic honesty in the context of peer reviewed assignments. *Studies in Higher Education, 33*(4), 371–384. doi:10.1080/03075070802211562

Li, Y., & Casanave, C. P. (2012). Two first-year students' strategies for writing from sources: Patchwriting or plagiarism? *Journal of Second Language Writing, 21*, 165–180. doi:10.1016/j.jslw.2012.03.002

Macdonald, R., & Carroll, J. (2006). Plagiarism- a complex issue requiring a holistic institutional approach. *Assessment & Evaluation in Higher Education, 31*(3), 233–245. doi:10.1080/02602930500262536

Marsh, B. (2004). *Turnitin*.com and the scriptural enterprise of plagiarism detection. *Computers and Composition, 21*, 427–438. doi:10.1016/j.compcom.2004.08.002

McCabe, D. L. (2005). Cheating among college and university students: A North American perspective. . *International Journal of Educational Integrity, 1*(1), 1–11.

McKeever, L. (2006). Online plagiarism detection services- saviour or scourge? *Assessment & Evaluation in Higher Education, 31*(2), 155–165. doi:10.1080/02602930500262460

Park, C. (2003). In other (people's) words: Plagiarism by university students--literature and lessons. *Assessment & Evaluation in Higher Education, 28*(5), 471–489. doi:10.1080/02602930301677

Pecorari, D. (2008). *Academic writing and plagiarism: A linguistic analysis*. London: Continuum.

Pecorari, D. (2013). *Teaching to avoid plagiarism: How to promote good source use*. Berkshire, England: Open University Press.

Pennycook, A. (1996). Borrowing others' words: Text, ownership, memory, and plagiarism. *TESOL Quarterly, 30*(2), 201–230. doi:10.2307/3588141

Pousada, A. (2011, November). *Cultivating respect for intellectual property in the English Class*. Paper presented at the meeting of Puerto Rico TESOL. San Juan, Puerto Rico.

Price, M. (2002). Beyond "gotcha!": Situating plagiarism in policy and pedagogy. *College Composition and Communication, 54*(1), 88–115. doi:10.2307/1512103

Purdy, J. (2005). Calling off the hounds: Technology and the visibility of plagiarism. *Pedagogy, 5*(2), 275–296.

Purdy, J. (2009). Anxiety and the archive: Understanding plagiarism detection services as digital archives. *Computers and Composition, 26*, 65–77. doi:10.1016/j.compcom.2008.09.002

Ritter, K. (2005). The economics of authorship: Paper mills, student writers, and first-year composition. *College Composition and Communication, 56*(4), 601–631.

Rolfe, V. (2011). Can *Turnitin* be used to provide instant formative feedback? *British Journal of Educational Technology, 42*(4), 701–710. doi:10.1111/j.1467-8535.2010.01091.x

Royce, J. (2003). Has *Turnitin*.com got it all wrapped up? *Teacher Librarian, 30*(4), 26–30.

Scanlon, P., & Neumann, D. (2002). Internet plagiarism among college students. *Journal of College Student Development, 43*(3), 374–382.

Scollon, R. (1995). Plagiarism and ideology: Identity in intercultural discourse. *Language in Society, 24*(1), 1–8. doi:10.1017/S0047404500018388

Seliger, H. W., & Shohamy, E. (1989). *Second language research methods*. Oxford: Oxford University Press.

Shi, L. (2006). Cultural backgrounds and textual appropriation. *Language Awareness, 15*, 264–282. doi:10.2167/la406.0

Shi, L. (2008). Textual appropriation and citing behaviors of university undergraduates. *Applied Linguistics, 31*(1), 1–24. doi:10.1093/applin/amn045

Shi, L. (2011). Common knowledge, learning, and citation practices in university writing. *Research in the Teaching of English, 45*(3), 308–334.

Stake, R. E. (2003). Case studies. In N. Denzin, & Y. Lincoln (Eds.), *Strategies of qualitative research* (pp. 134–164). Thousand Oaks, CA: Sage.

Stapleton, P. (2012). Gauging the effectiveness of anti-plagiarism software: An empirical study of second language graduate writers. *Journal of English for Academic Purposes, 10*, 125–133. doi:10.1016/j.jeap.2011.10.003

Stappenbelt, B., & Rowles, C. (2009, September). *The effectiveness of plagiarism detection software as a learning tool in academic writing education*. Paper presented at the meeting of the Asia Pacific Conference on Educational Integrity. Wollongong, Australia.

Sutherland-Smith, W., & Carr, R. (2005). *Turnitin*.com: Teachers' perspectives of anti-plagiarism software in raising issues of educational integrity. *Journal of University Teaching and Learning Practice, 2*(3), 93–101.

Swales, J. M. (1990). *Genre analysis: English in academic and research settings*. Cambridge: Cambridge University Press.

Szabo, A., & Underwood, J. (2004). Cyber cheats: Is information and communication technology fueling academic dishonesty? *Active Learning in Higher Education, 5*(2), 180–199. doi:10.1177/1469787404043815

Turnitin. (2014, February 5). *Turnitin study shows impact of plagiarism prevention and online grading at higher education institutions*. Available from, http://turnitin.com/en_us/about-us/press/turnitin-study-shows-impact-of-plagiarism-prevention-and-online-grading-at-higher-education-institutions

Valentine, K. (2006). Plagiarism as literacy practice: Recognizing and rethinking ethical binaries. *College Composition and Communication, 58*(1), 89–110.

Vanacker, B. (2011). Returning students' right to access, choice and notice: a proposed code of ethics for instructors using *Turnitin*. *Ethics and Information Technology, 13*(4), 327–338. doi:10.1007/s10676-011-9277-3

Walker, J. (2010). Measuring plagiarism: researching what students do, not what they say they do. *Studies in Higher Education, 35*, 41–59. doi:10.1080/03075070902912994

Walker, M., & Townley, C. (2012). Contract cheating: a new challenge for academic honesty? *Journal of Academic Ethics, 10*, 27–44. doi:10.1007/s10805-012-9150-y

Wenger, E. (1998). *Communities of practice: Learning, meaning, and identity*. Cambridge: Cambridge University Press. doi:10.1017/CBO9780511803932

Wette, R. (2010). Evaluating student learning in a university-level EAP unit on writing using sources. *Journal of Second Language Writing, 19*, 158–177. doi:10.1016/j.jslw.2010.06.002

Wolcott, H. F. (1994). *Transforming qualitative data: Description, analysis, and interpretation*. Thousand Oaks, CA: Sage.

Yin, R. K. (2009). *Case study research: Design and methods* (4th ed.). Thousand Oaks, CA: Sage.

Youmans, R. J. (2011). Does the adoption of plagiarism-detection software in higher education reduce plagiarism? *Studies in Higher Education, 36*(7), 749–761. doi:10.1080/03075079.2010.523457

ADDITIONAL READING

Abasi, A., & Akbari, N. (2008). Are we encouraging patchwriting? Reconsidering the role of the pedagogical context in ESL student writers' transgressive intertextuality. *English for Specific Purposes, 27*, 267–284.

Ali, H. (2013). Minimizing cyber-plagiarism through Turnitin: Faculty's & students' perspectives. *International Journal of Applied Linguistics & English Literature, 2*(2), 33–42.

Beltrán, E. V., Abbott, C., & Jones, J. (2013). *Inclusive language education and digital technology*. Bristol, UK: Multilingual Matters.

Blake, R. J. (2008). *Brave new digital classroom: Technology and foreign language learning*. Washington, DC: Georgetown University Press.

Bloch, J. (2007). Abdullah's blogging: A generation 1.5 student enters the blogosphere. *Language Learning & Technology, 11*(2), 128–141.

Blum, S. (2009). *My word! Plagiarism and college culture*. Ithaca, NY: Cornell University Press.

Brown, V., & Rubin, N. (2011). The ethics of Turnitin from a faculty's perspective. *National Teacher Education Journal, 4*(1), 47–52.

Campbell, C. (1990). Writing with others' words: Using background reading text in academic compositions. In B. Kroll (Ed.), *Second language writing: Research insights for the classroom* (pp. 211–230). Cambridge: Cambridge University Press.

Casanave, C. P. (2004). *Controversies in second language writing: Dilemmas and decisions in research and instruction*. Ann Arbor, MI: The University of Michigan Press.

Deckert, G. (1993). Perspectives on plagiarism from EFL students in Hong Kong. *Journal of Second Language Writing, 2*(2), 131–148.

Dong, Y. R. (1996). Learning how to use citations for knowledge transformation: Non-native doctoral students' dissertation writing in science. *Research in the Teaching of English, 30*, 428–457.

Ellery, K. (2008). An investigation into electronic-source plagiarism in a first-year essay assignment. *Assessment & Evaluation in Higher Education, 33*(6), 607–617.

Ferris, D. R., & Hedgcock, J. S. (2005). *Teaching ESL composition: Purpose, process, and practice* (2nd ed.). Mahwah, NJ: Erlbaum.

Flowerdew, J., & Li, Y. (2007a). Language re-use among Chinese apprentice scientists writing for publication. *Applied Linguistics, 28*(3), 440–465.

Flowerdew, J., & Li, Y. (2007b). Plagiarism and second language writing in an electronic age. *Annual Review of Applied Linguistics, 27*, 161–183.

Grohe, B., Schroeder, J., & Davis, S. R. B. (2013). Using online resources to improve writing skills and attitudes about writing and plagiarism of criminal justice students. *Journal on Excellence in College Teaching*, *24*(1), 23–45.

Harwood, N., & Petrić, B. (2012). Performance in the citing behavior of two student writers. *Written Communication*, *29*, 55–103.

Hirvela, A. (2005). Computer-based reading and writing across the curriculum: Two case studies of L2 writers. *Computers and Composition*, *22*, 337–356.

Hull, G., & Rose, M. (1989). Rethinking remediation: Toward a social-cognitive understanding of problematic reading and writing. *Written Communication*, *6*, 139–154.

Hyland, F. (2001). Dealing with plagiarism when giving feedback. *ELT Journal*, *55*, 375–381.

Hyland, K. (1999). Academic attribution: Citation and the construction of disciplinary knowledge. *Applied Linguistics*, *20*(3), 341-367.

Hyland, T. A. (2009). Drawing a line in the sand: Identifying the borderline between self and other in EL1 and EL2 citation practices. *Assessing Writing*, *14*, 62–74.

Keck, C. (2010). How do university students attempt to avoid plagiarism? A grammatical analysis of undergraduate paraphrasing strategies. *Writing & Pedagogy*, *2*(2), 193–222.

Liu, D. (2005). Plagiarism in ESOL students: Is cultural conditioning truly the major culprit? *ELT Journal*, *59*(3), 234–241.

Lyon, A. (2009). "You Fail": Plagiarism, the ownership of writing, and transnational conflicts. *College Composition and Communication*, *61*(2), 222–239.

Maxwell, A., Curtis, G., & Vardanega, L. (2008). Does culture influence understanding and perceived seriousness of plagiarism? *International Journal for Educational Integrity*, *4*(2), 25–40.

Mott-Smith, J. (2011). Establishing textual authority and separating voices: A new approach to teaching referencing. *English Teaching Forum*, *49*(2), 16–25.

Pecoari, D. (2001). Plagiarism and international students: How the English-speaking university responds. In D. Belcher, & A. Hirvela (Eds.), *Linking literacies: Perspectives on l2 reading-writing connections* (pp. 229–245). Ann Arbor, MI: The University of Michigan Press.

Petrić, B. (2012). Legitimate textual borrowing: Direct quotation in L2 student writing. *Journal of Second Language Writing*, *21*(2), 102–117.

Rees, M., & Emerson, L. (2009). The impact that Turnitin has had on text-based assessment practice. *International Journal for Educational Integrity.*, *5*(1), 20–29.

Rinnert, C., & Kobayashi, H. (2005). Borrowing words and ideas: Insights from Japanese l1 writers. *Journal of Asian Pacific Communication*, *15*(1), 31–56.

Roig, M. (1997). Can undergraduate students determine whether text has been plagiarised? *The Psychological Record*, *47*, 113–123.

Rolfe, V. (2011). Can Turnitin be used to provide instant formative feedback? *British Journal of Educational Technology*, *42*(4), 701–710.

Scollon, R. (1994). As a matter of fact: The changing ideology of authorship and responsibility in discourse. *World Englishes*, *13*, 33–46.

Shi, L. (2004). Textual borrowing in second-language writing. *Written Communication*, *21*, 171–200.

Shi, L. (2012). Rewriting and paraphrasing source texts in second language writing. *Journal of Second Language Writing*, *21*, 134–148.

Stapleton, P. (2010). Writing in an electronic age: A case study of L2 composing processes. *Journal of English for Academic Purposes*, *9*, 295–307.

Tardy, C. M. (2010). Writing for the world: Wikipedia as an introduction to academic writing. *English Teaching Forum, 48*(1), 12–27.

Tomaš, Z. (2010). Addressing writing instructors' needs for effective pedagogical resources on avoiding plagiarism. *Journal of Writing and Pedagogy*, *2*, 223–250.

Warschauer, M., & Grimes, D. (2007). Audience, authorship, and artifact: The emergent semiotics of Web 2.0. *Annual Review of Applied Linguistics*, *27*, 1–23.

Wheeler, G. (2009). Plagiarism in the Japanese universities: Truly a cultural matter? *Journal of Second Language Writing*, *18*, 17–29.

KEY TERMS AND DEFINITIONS

Academic Writing: A specific kind of writing used in academic settings that includes its own rules, styles, and conventions.

Matched Text Detection Software: Any software that matches text in a student's paper to other electronic text.

Plagiarism: While plagiarism definitions vary, the term generally refers to the use of another author's words or ideas without attribution to the source.

Second Language (L2) Writers: A writer of English who has any first language other than English.

Textual Borrowing: A common feature of academic writing that refers to incorporating information from outside sources into a text and citing the information borrowed.

Turnitin: An Internet-based software program that matches electronic text to text found in its database.

APPENDIX A: INTERVIEW QUESTIONS

Students (Interview 1)

- When did you learn to read and write in English?
- Describe your experiences with English academic writing at home and in the U.S. Are there any similarities? Differences?
- Do you use any dictionaries, translators, websites, search engines, or other Internet tools to help you write academic papers?
- What is the difference between academic writing in your country and writing in the U.S.?
- What is your definition of plagiarism?
- Where did you first learn about plagiarism?
- What kinds of print sources do you use in your writing in the U.S.?
- What kinds of electronic sources do you use in your writing in the U.S.?
- How have you learned about plagiarism in your other courses?
- Define who you think an author is.
- What do you know about the program *Turnitin?*
- What has been the most difficult part of writing academic papers in the U.S.?
- What has been the easiest part of writing academic papers in the U.S.?
- How comfortable do you feel in using sources in your writing?
- Is there anything else you'd like to add?

Instructor (Interview 1)

- How long have you been teaching this course?
- Please describe the overall objectives of the course.
- Please explain your teaching materials. What do you use in the course to support your instruction?
- How many lessons are devoted to the issue of academic honesty?
- How many lessons are devoted to citation practices?
- Please explain how you define the term "plagiarism" for your students.
- Please describe how you explain "authorship" to your students. How is it presented?
- Do students talk about how authorship is defined in their home countries?
- Please describe your experiences with plagiarism and second language (L2) writers.
- Have you had previous students that have directly copied and pasted? How have you addressed the issue?
- Please describe the challenges that non-native English speakers face in academic writing.
- What is the role of *Turnitin* in your course?
- Please describe how students typically react to *Turnitin.*
- Please describe the teaching materials you use to teach students about Internet plagiarism.

Students (Interview 2)

- Which writing tasks have you performed in this class? Please describe any assignments or in-class activities.
- Please describe your understanding of plagiarism and its consequences.
- How does your instructor use *Turnitin* in class?
- How do you think using *Turnitin* is improving your citation practices?
- Describe any challenges you face while writing academic papers.
- Which writing assignments have been difficult this term?
- Which writing assignments have been easy?
- Is there anything you'd like to add?

Instructor (Interview 2)

- Please describe how you evaluate students' understanding of plagiarism and academic writing.
- What has changed since you've started teaching L2 writers about plagiarism and now?
- Have you taught at other universities?
- What were some of the challenges that students faced in this course?
- How do you think students' understandings of plagiarism have changed?
- Please describe any instances of blatant plagiarism that occurred in this class.
- How did you use *Turnitin* this semester?
- When did you introduce *Turnitin* this term?
- How long have you been using *Turnitin?*
- Have you used other matched text detection software programs?
- Please describe students' reactions to *Turnitin.*
- What is most effective about using *Turnitin* to teach students about source use?
- What is least effective about using *Turnitin*?
- Which activities or assignments were particularly helpful for helping L2 writers understand plagiarism?
- Are there any different approaches you would use to teach L2 writers about plagiarism based on their cultural backgrounds?
- How would you teach English L1 students about plagiarism?
- Is there anything else you'd like to add?

Students (Interview 3)

- Please describe how you evaluate students' understanding of plagiarism and academic writing.
- What has changed since you started teaching L2 writers about plagiarism and now?
- Have you taught at other universities?
- What were some of the challenges that students faced in this course?
- How do you think students' understanding of plagiarism has changed?
- Please describe any instances of blatant plagiarism that occurred in this class.
- How did you use *Turnitin* this quarter?

- When did you introduce *Turnitin* this term?
- How long have you been using *Turnitin?*
- Have you used other matched text detection software programs?
- Please describe students' reactions to *Turnitin.*
- What is most effective about using *Turnitin* to teach students about source use?
- What is least effective about using *Turnitin*?
- Which activities or assignments were particularly helpful for helping L2 writers understand plagiarism?
- Are there any different approaches you would use to teach L2 writers about plagiarism based on their cultural backgrounds?
- How would you teach English L1 students about plagiarism?
- Is there anything else you'd like to add?

Instructor (Interview 3)

- What are your thoughts on this class now that it's over? General comments?
- Have you faced any particular challenges this term? (e.g., teaching, students, etc.)
- What worked well this term in teaching students about plagiarism and citation?
- How do you think students' understanding of plagiarism has changed?
- Is there anything you would have done differently this term?
- Will you make any changes to the course structure in the future?
- Were there any instances of blatant plagiarism in this course?

Interview with Dr. Miller

- Could you please tell me about your educational background and experience? (teaching here, other schools)
- What led you to your current position?
- What are your general goals for students and teachers in this program?
- Could you please tell me about the writing program in your department in terms of objectives and history?
- What are the challenges involved in getting students to acquire academic writing skills?
- Are there special challenges for English language learners?
- Do you have any problems (that you are aware of) with plagiarism?
- What is the department-wide policy on plagiarism?
- What is your definition of plagiarism?
- I understand that the department uses *Turnitin.* How long has the English Department been using the program?
- How do you hope that English composition instructors will use *Turnitin?*
- Could you please describe any challenges you face when handling cases of academic integrity.
- How do you prepare teachers for facing these challenges?
- What do you think is effective for teaching ESL writers to use sources appropriately?

APPENDIX B: QUESTIONS FOR IN-CLASS PEER REVIEW SESSION

Revision Questionnaire: 1st draft of the research paper

Check to see if your partner's essay includes all these elements of a research essay. Use this worksheet to revise your essay too.

What is the focus of the paper?
What style of research question does the essay answer (effect, comparison, definition, classification, process, or argument)?
Does the writer introduce the name of the author and title of the sources used?
Does the writer include a brief summary of each article stating the main points?
Does the writer include a quote of the idea or ideas they have responded to in each of the sources?
Does the writer include his/her response to the idea(s) from the article?
Does the writer include examples and details about the chosen topic from the readings or from life?
How many sources are referenced in the essay (you need 4, at least 2 from the library database)?
______ 4-5 pages, clearly written and well organized, MLA format including in text citations and Works Cited page

Give suggestions and advice to your partner

Say something good about the essay:
Now, tell where it might need work. For example:

- Is any part of the essay unclear? If so, what should the writer do?
- Is the example clear? If not, what can the writer do?
- Anything else?

Chapter 4
Computer-Assisted vs. Classroom Instruction on Developing Reference Tracking Skills in L2 Chinese

Liu Li
Ball State University, USA

ABSTRACT

Computer-Assisted Language Learning (CALL) has been proven effective in facilitating low-level second language (L2) reading comprehension skills such as decoding and word recognition. However, little is known about whether discourse-level reading skills such as reference tracking skills can also be effectively taught through CALL. This chapter overviews a study that designed and implemented a CALL program for teaching Chinese reference tracking skills (i.e., the identification of zero anaphors and the matching of their antecedents). The effects of the CALL program were compared with that of teacher-directed classroom instruction. Forty-five learners of L2 Chinese were randomly assigned to one of the three groups: a CALL group, a teacher-directed classroom instruction group, and a control group. A pretest, an immediate posttest, and a delayed posttest measuring different aspects of Chinese zero anaphoric inference skills were administered. The results show that, although the Classroom group and the CALL group both made substantial progress compared with the control group, the CALL group made significantly more gain than the classroom instruction group in acquiring zero anaphoric inference skills.

INTRODUCTION

Throughout centuries much emphasis has been put on the development of reading skills in schools. Currently, technological advances are opening new doors and providing new possibilities for applied linguistics and foreign language pedagogy. Research findings support that CALL (Computer Assisted Language Learning) has a positive impact on Second Language (L2) reading achievement, especially on low-level reading skills such as word recognition and decoding (Park, Zheng, Lawrence & Warschauer, 2013). Yet little is known about whether CALL can play a more positive role than

DOI: 10.4018/978-1-4666-6174-5.ch004

teacher-directed classroom instruction in improving L2 readers' higher level reading skills, which play a crucial role in learners' reading comprehension ability.

The present study attempts to fill this gap by investigating the effects of computer-assisted instruction on L2 learners' development of Chinese reference tracking skills. Reading as a language skill consists of various sub-skills, which include the knowledge of discourse structure and the skills of building coherent mental representation of the text for comprehension (Grabe, 2004). This study focuses on one specific skill of constructing discourse structure, i.e., reference tracking. In some languages such as Chinese, discourse is abundant with zero anaphora, which is the use of an empty grammatical slot to refer to a previously mentioned entity in the discourse (Aoun, 1985). This special linguistic feature poses huge obstacles for learners in understanding the referential relations in Chinese texts, especially for those whose first language (L1) does not have this linguistic feature (i.e., zero anaphora). In response to this difficulty in learning, a CALL program was designed in this study to improve L2 learners' reference-tracking skills in reading Chinese texts with zero anaphors. The success of the CALL program in enhancing higher-level reading skills such as anaphoric inference skills can provide new insights into the benefit of technology for L2 reading education.

BACKGROUND

Reference-Tracking from a Psycholinguistic Perspective

Anaphora is the use of a type of expression whose reference depends upon another referential element (Aoun, 1985). For example, in the sentence "Harry preferred the company of himself", "himself" is an anaphoric expression in that it is co-referential with the expression "Harry" in the subject position. Anaphora plays an important role in reference systems, which is crucial for discourse comprehension (Aoun, 1985).

Reference tracking, also called anaphora tracking, is the process of identifying the antecedent to which an anaphor refers. This process has been crucial in investigating questions about the construction of mental representation of discourse and text comprehension in reading (Shake & Stine-Morrow, 2011). Discourse comprehension crucially depends on the ability to coherently connect current information to previously presented information. Anaphoric expressions play an important role in establishing these cohesive links: they help the reader to establish links between the things and actions mentioned back and forth in discourse. The question then becomes how the readers establish such links.

In response to linguistic classifications of reference systems in the world languages, researchers have categorized reference-tracking systems from a psycholinguistic perspective (Huang, 2003, LaPolla, 1990). The first full-scale typology of reference-tracking systems was proposed by Foley and Van Valin (1984), who listed four types of devices: (1) switch function (Comrie 1989; Foley & Van Valin 1984, Van Valin, 1987), (2) switch reference, (3) gender/number/noun class, and (4) inference. Among these four categories, two types are related to the current study: switch function and inference. Switch-function is where a referent is tracked though a discourse by referring to its syntactic function, often the subject. This is the system used (along with gender marking) in, for example, English, French and many other European languages. Under this category, anaphors usually occur in the form of pronouns, sometimes in the form of proper names. The inference type, on the other hand, includes languages such as Chinese and Japanese, in which the tracking of a referent is largely a matter of inference because grammatical or lexical marking is seldom involved. The term "inference" means connecting prior knowledge with discourse-based information to create meaning beyond what is directly stated in the discourse. In languages that mainly or exclusively use inference type of reference, the "most distinctive characteristic is the occurrence of extensive and grammatically unrestrained zero anaphora" (Van Valin, 1987, p.520).

In languages with an inference reference system (e.g., Chinese, Japanese, Italian, and Spanish), the anaphors in a sentence may be left out; however, in languages with a switch function reference system (e.g., English, French, and German), the anaphors usually are present in a sentence (Cook, 2004). English is considered a typical language with a switch function reference system. Even in some cases when a proposition has no referent at all, native speakers of English have to fill in the syntactic slot by inserting a dummy pronoun. For example, "*Rains" is not a correct sentence; a dummy "it" has to be added to say "It rains". Languages with an inference reference system deal naturally with such cases of null-subject: *Ø* rains. In these languages, the dropped pronouns are often referred to as zero anaphora, which is the use of a gap (in a phrase or clause) that has an anaphoric function similar to a pro-form. Such typological differences can lead to difficulty for English speakers in learning this particular reading skill in a second language like Chinese that is typically different from their native language.

Zero Anaphora and Chinese Discourse

Unlike English, Chinese is a typical "inference" language in terms of the reference system. Zero anaphora exists in Chinese discourse extensively (Li & Thompson, 1981; Pu, 1997). Based on Tao's classification (1993, 2001), zero anaphora in Chinese can occur in four discourse patterns: (a) the switch-reference pattern, (b) the embedded clause condition, (c) the direct object condition, and (d) the return-pop condition (Fox, 1987; Tao, 1993, 1996, 2001). The following example presents a switch-reference pattern in which the grammatical subject of the second clause is different from that of the first clause: "他买了只小狗,. 叫得大声极了。(He bought a small dog, Ø barked very loudly)." The expression is not acceptable in English because of the use of zero anaphora (as the subject for the verb "barked"). The pronoun "it" has to replace zero anaphora to make the expression acceptable in English. Second, the embedded clause condition in Chinese occurs when zero anaphora replaces the subject of a subordinate clause in a sentence (e.g., "我有个姐姐一口气买了三条裙子"。I have a sister Ø bought three skirts.). The occurrence of zero anaphora here is not acceptable in English (Tao, 1993). Third, zero anaphora often replaces the direct object of a verb when its referent has been mentioned before. So the "it" in the English expression "I bought it" is often omitted in Chinese like the third zero anaphor $Ø_3$ in the following mini-dialogue:

Example 1:

A: $Ø_1$ 买了机票了吗? [$Ø_1$ Bought the flight ticket?]

B: $Ø_2$ 买了 $Ø_3$。 [$Ø_2$ Bought $Ø_3$.]

Finally, the return-pop condition refers to the presentation of a previously mentioned referent by using a reduced anaphoric device when there is a change of discourse topic between the two mentions of the same referent. In English, the return-pop always involves a pronoun (Fox, 1987), whereas in Chinese it may involve either a pronoun or zero anaphora (Tao, 1996, 2001). The return-pop pronoun in discourse makes use of "discourse cues" (Fox, 1987; Tao, 1996, p. 505) to help the hearer/reader track the referent of the pronoun in a distant previous sentence. The discourse cues recur in Chinese in the case of a return-pop zero anaphora to help the Chinese track the referent of the zero anaphora.

Since Chinese is a typical example of inference language in which zero anaphora is used much more frequently than pronouns (Li & Thompson, 1981; Pu, 1997), special inference skills for zero anaphoric tracking are required for Chinese discourse comprehension. It has long been found that speakers of different languages pay attention to different linguistic cues in discourse processing (e.g., Bates & MacWhinny, 1989). Tao (1996) proposed that, in discourse processing, it is highly likely that the specific discourse pattern may have forced Chinese speakers to pay significantly more attention to local discourse cues for inference than speakers of non-zero anaphora languages do. These local discourse cues include: (1) prior discourse context; (2) specific semantic requirements of the verbs associated with the referents; (3) the specific nature of the referents presented by zero anaphora; (4) words, especially verbs, that are associated with the referents; (5) language users' general knowledge about the world, including their social, cultural and personal experience (Tao, 1996). Therefore, English native speakers learning L2 Chinese need to develop a set of special reference tracking skills to help them cope with the zero anaphora they encounter in comprehending Chinese texts.

Compared with Chinese, English operates on a noun/pronoun system for reference. Usually, an anaphoric expression is represented by a proform or some other kind of deictic, for instance, a pronoun referring to its antecedent. Compared with Chinese speakers, English speakers primarily depend on syntactic and morphological cues for reference tracking, which involve far less inference than Chinese (Yang, Gordon, Hendrix, & Wu, 1999). Jin (1994) commented that learners of Chinese with English as their L1 tended to overuse nouns and pronouns and seldom use zero anaphora. In order to find out an explanation for such a difference between learners with different L1 background, Tao and Healy (1996, 2005) conducted a series of psycholinguistic experiments on the comprehension of zero anaphora. They found that the learners' L1 literacy background had an impact on their reading comprehension of zero anaphora. For example, when reading English texts with manipulated zero anaphors created by deleting the subjects of the sentences, Chinese and Japanese speakers performed significantly better than English and Danish speakers, whose L1s contain very limited zero anaphora. In addition to these differences found in reading, learners with various L1 backgrounds also exhibit some differences in writing. Jing-Schmidt (2011) compared three groups of learners on the use of zero anaphor in their writing. The first group consisted of Chinese Heritage Learners (CCHL) who were born in China and immigrated to US at an early age. The second group consisted of American Chinese Heritage Learners (ACHL) who were born and raised in US. The third group was consisted of Non-Heritage Learner (NHL). She found that the CCHL group produced significantly more zero anaphoric expressions in their writing than the other two groups. The ACHL group was only slightly better than the NHL group in terms of production frequency of zero anaphoric expressions. The findings of these studies indicate that learners' L1 background can significantly influence their use of zero anaphora.

Several studies have examined how to improve learners' ability to understand and use zero anaphora correctly in Chinese discourse. Cui (2003) argued that learners' error on zero anaphora was caused by their lack of knowledge about Chinese discourse structures. He contended that more language structures at the discourse level, such as zero anaphoric expressions, should be taught explicitly to the students. Jing-Schmidt (2011) reported on a study on the effects of explicit instruction in Chinese personal anaphora. Four classes of about 52 students learning Chinese as a foreign language were assigned to two groups: an experimental group and a control group. Following five 20-25-minute lessons, students were tested to see whether they could successfully finish three tasks: (1) comprehend Chinese personal anaphora; (2) judge the grammaticality of personal anaphora given in the sentences and correct the errors if there are any; and (3) fill in the blanks with the appropriate forms of personal anaphora. The results showed that, although there was no evidence that the instruction enhanced students' personal anaphora comprehension in Task 1, the experiment group significantly outperformed the control group at post and delayed posttests for Tasks 2 and 3. Clearly, there was an immediate and delayed effect of personal anaphora instruction for form correction and production. Overall, the students with explicit instruction in Chinese personal anaphora demonstrated significant pre-test to post-test gains during the 14-week instructional period.

The studies reviewed above indicate the possibilities of using various pedagogical interventions to teach reference tracking skills in Chinese and the potential benefits of such interventions. With the development of technology and social media, CALL has been increasingly used in many areas of SLA and proven beneficial (e.g., Shei & Hsieh, 2012). Yet so far less than a handful of studies have been done to explore how to utilize CALL to improve L2 learners' anaphoric inference skills, and there is an urgent need for research in this regard (Li, 2004).

Reference Tracking and CALL

L2 reference tracking skills have been taught in classroom through teacher-directed activities. Many Chinese as a second language textbooks contain explanations about and exercises for this linguistic feature. However, some researchers found that a large number of CSL teachers rely heavily on their intuitions when they explain zero anaphora (Li, 2004). They argued that teaching of the reference system in L2 Chinese has been ignored for too long and becomes a weak link in Chinese pedagogy. She advocated enhancing the learners' awareness of the discourse structure as one of the solutions for the pedagogy. Li (2004) argued that because zero anaphors take no explicit linguistic forms, a reader needs to have good knowledge and skills in order to identify and match them with their antecedents. From the students' perspective, a well-developed systematic program based on SLA theories can be more convincing. This pedagogical discrepancy calls for building a learning aid that is specially designed for improving anaphoric tracking in L2 reading.

With the invention of the computer, reading activities have existed on screen for some time (Hubbard, 2009). However, most of the CALL research on L2 reading so far has focused on word recognition and decoding. In Chun's (2006) review of CALL reading research, most of the studies were about L2 word recognition. These studies, together with several more recent ones on decoding and word recognition (e.g., Macaruso & Rod, 2011) have shown several advantages of CALL over classroom instruction. The benefits of using CALL in L2 reading instruction, as identified by researchers, include individualized learning, flexibility of time and usage, variety of input, intensive exercises, and high-level motivation among learners.

Despite the advantages of CALL found in many areas of SLA, little research has been conducted to explore possible CALL pedagogy for teaching higher-level reading skills, such as reference tracking skills discussed above among L2 learners (Chun, 2006). Based on the benefits found in CALL research on low-level reading skills, it is reasonable for researchers to investigate whether these advantages and benefits are also applicable to the acquisition of reading skills at the higher level. In this regard, several CALL studies present introductions to the features of CALL programs designed for teaching zero anaphoric inference skills in L2 Japanese. For example, Yamura-Takei, Fujiwara and Aizawa (2001) developed a CALL program named "Zero Checker" for learners of Japanese as a Second Language, targeting the acquisition of zero anaphora in Japanese. The CALL system was designed to automatically detect and evaluate the appropriateness of zero anaphors in students' written production. The researchers compared the CALL system's evaluation with that of human judges. The results showed no significant differences between the two. The researchers, however, did not report the effectiveness of the program in teaching the targeted linguistic feature.

In another study, Kitajima (2002) developed and piloted computer-mediated reading materials designed to help learners improve anaphoric resolutions and backward inferences in reading expository texts. The reading materials used in this CALL program provided vocabulary annotations and exercises with immediate feedback. The reading exercise consisted of three sections: pre-reading, reading, and post-reading. Kitajima contended that the computer-assisted reading materials could create an environment in which students can become actively involved in the learning process. This is because the students could access information as needed by using this software. Such accessibility and flexibility can help enhance their understanding of the language texts with target zero anaphors. The exercises (such as semantic maps) in this CALL program helped readers organize information in relation to topics, which provides useful background and contextual information for zero anaphoric inference. In contrast to multiple choice exercises or true-false exercises, which usually examine learners' comprehension of partial information in a text, these exercises on the global structure of the text provided a more holistic picture of the information that students learned from the text. At the same time, immediate feedback encourages students to monitor their reading comprehension. The computer-based reading materials were piloted with eight learners in a fourth-year Japanese course. The participants commented that the exercises helped them see how each statement was connected with others at the inter-sentential and discourse levels and thereby enabled them to track the references, especially zero anaphors, more easily. In addition, Kitajima reported that the computer-mediated reading materials in the CALL program enabled instructors to use class time more efficiently by spending more class time on discussion and debate of the issues raised in the reading texts. However, the author admitted that because there was no strong empirical evidence in this study, the effects of computer-mediated reading materials on the development of learners' abilities in zero anaphoric inference, as compared to classroom-based presentations of reading materials, needed to be further examined, Similarly, it is unknown whether readers of expository texts in this study will develop effective strategies that can be transferred to other texts. Kitajima also pointed out that, as increasing numbers of students are exposed to computer-mediated reading materials, the future will hold much room for research on the comparative effects of CALL students and those engaged in teacher-directed classroom instruction.

The above studies demonstrate the possibilities of developing a CALL system for learners to acquire zero anaphoric inference skills more efficiently. This study thus attempted to seek appropriate pedagogical methods through CALL to teach reference tracking abilities. It also explored the possible advantages of computer-assisted instruction over teacher-directed classroom instruction in teaching Chinese zero anaphora inference skill. The research questions of this study are:

1. Is computer-based instruction (i.e., CALL group) more effective in teaching zero anaphoric inference skills than teacher-directed classroom instruction (i.e., Classroom group)?
2. What is the difference between the CALL and Classroom group in terms of the students' engagement in the learning process?

METHOD

Participants

Forty-five undergraduate students enrolled in a Chinese program at a university in Pennsylvania (US) participated in this study. The Chinese program offered four levels of Chinese language instruction (i.e., Level 1, 2, 3 and 4). The participants for this study were recruited from Level 2 classes. By the time of this study, they were in their fourth semester of formal Chinese language learning at the university. All participants spoke English as their first language and there were no heritage students. The participants' ages were between 18 and 25 years (*M*=20.5). There were 24 females and 21 males. The participants were randomly assigned to one of the three groups: a CALL group, a teacher-directed classroom instruction group, and a control group. Each group had 15 students.

Target Zero Anaphoric Inference Skills

Based on psycholinguistic research on reference tracking (Tao, 1996), zero anaphoric inference skill is defined as consisting of three sub-skills: (1) identifying zero anaphor; (2) matching antecedent; (3) integrating reference information with context to construct a coherent mental representation of the text. The first sub-skill (i.e., identifying zero anaphors) is the ability to locate zero anaphors in sentences (see Example 2):

Example 2:
田云知道,大刚这一去, $Ø_1$ 三年五载是回不来的, $Ø_2$ 不禁心中一阵发酸。

Tian Yun knew, after Dagang left, $Ø_1$ *wouldn't come back until a few years later,* $Ø_2$ *couldn't help feeling very sad.*

The second sub-skill is matching the antecedents. This sub-skill means being able to track the antecedents of the anaphors. In the above example, the reader should be able to know the first zero anaphor Ø1 refers to "Dagang (大刚)", whereas the second one Ø2 refers to "Tian Yun (田云)". The third sub-skill is integrating the information for comprehension. This means that the reader is able to incorporate the references to construct a coherent and meaningful representation of the text as a whole.

Pedagogical Design

This study adapted McCarthy's (1999) reading skill pedagogy to develop a three-element reading skill pedagogy, which, in turn, guided the development of a CALL program for teaching zero anaphoric inference skills in L2 Chinese. McCarthy's (1999) "reading skill pedagogy" states that four necessary elements need continual implementation: scaffolding, learner autonomy, active involvement and feedback. Specifically, this pedagogy first provides level-appropriate input and help learners to understand and digest the input through scaffolding. Then, the learners are encouraged to engage in various interactions with heightened autonomy. Finally, the students' output would be evaluated with feedback. Based on McCarthy's framework, we propose a three-element pedagogy for teaching reading skills through CALL programs: scaffolding, engaging, and reflecting. The first element, "scaffolding", is the same as in McCarthy's framework. However, the second element, "engagement", subsumes both "autonomy" and "active involvement" in McCarthy's framework. This is because we consider students with high autonomy to be highly motivated to get involved in the learning process. The term "engagement" includes both internal motivation and external involvement. The last element, "reflection", corresponds to McCarthy's "feedback". This is because the purpose of providing various feedbacks is to encourage learners to reflect on their learning processes and outcomes. These three elements in our study are detailed below.

Scaffolding

Scaffolding in this study is defined as the process of moving students beyond their current developmental stage or skill set into progressively more difficult tasks (Lantolf, 2000; Lantolf & Thorne, 2006; Van Lier, 2004; Verity, 2005). Scaffolding relies on cognitive learning where the student learns by observing a more competent being (the teacher or the CALL program in this study) solving a problem or completing a task. The teacher or the CALL program provides support and models strategies for the student. Therefore scaffolding in this study is operationalized as teaching the concepts of zero anaphora and the skills of reference tracking in Chinese.

Engagement

Engaging students in the learning process is to increase their attention and focus, motivate them to practice target skills, and promote meaningful learning experiences. In this study, "engagement" was operationalized as the methods to boost the learners' motivation, to satisfy their individual needs and to encourage their participation in the various activities during the learning process. In this study, it was measured through the length of the learning time, the learning activities learners got involved in and their learning autonomy.

The CALL program is designed to address the needs, motivation, and performance of individual learners. For example, it can provide various forms of input: audio, videoand written text. Students could choose the type most suitable for their needs and learning style. The CALL program can also respond to the learners' application of input and provide constructive feedback concerning the learners' exercises and achievement. For example, although all the exercises were based on authentic reading materials, there were three difficulty levels for the students to choose from: low, medium and high. The low difficulty level included simplified mini-passages consisting of three to four sentences, with two characters for reference tracking. Example 2 above belongs to this category. The medium level included short passages consisting of eight two nine sentences with three to four characters for reference tracking. The high level included unabridged passages of over 10 sentences in length with more than three characters for reference tracking. In terms of feedback, the students could choose to get immediate feedback after they finish each item or delayed feedback after they finish several items (in this way, their flow of thoughts would not be interrupted). Depending on their style of reflecting on the errors, learners could also choose from three types of feedback with explanation or one type without explanation. Activities for the CALL group were planned carefully to provide interaction, inducing comprehensible output and modifying problems the learners have encountered through interactive activities. For example, an online forum and discussion board were open to encourage interactions among peers and between the teacher and the learners.

Reflection

Reflection is meant to encourage learners to make sense of what they have learned, why they learned it, and how that particular increment of learning took place. Reflection can be seen as a method for promoting autonomous and deep learning through enquiry. In this study, "reflection" was operationalized as the methods to encourage learners to reflect upon his/her learning process and learning outcome.

The CALL program in this study can generate a report on the students' participation on a daily basis, including detailed information such as when each student was engaged in the online learning and exercises and for how much time. Reflection on their learning outcome was also provided through students' choice of feedback types, filling in their online homework progress chart. Before doing the online homework, the students could key in a score they expected. When the actual score came out, the student was encouraged to write down the reason why his expected score was higher or lower than the actual score.

Reflection also means encouraging students to ask questions about their learning. The CALL program was designed to answer a wide range of questions on zero anaphora. The questions were classified into six categories: (1) where is the zero anaphor in this sentence? (2) What is the referent/antecedent of this anaphora? (3) What type of zero anaphor is this in this sentence? (4) What are the cues in the context used to identify the antecedent of a specific anaphor? (5) What's the meaning of a specific sentence? (6) Why am I wrong? Students were instructed to make inquiries or seek assistance whenever he/she did not understand the teaching materials or the exercises. The two-way communication between the computer and the learner created interactive activities for reflection.

Summary of Pedagogical Design

In a word, with careful planning, the researcher of this study designed a CALL program that encourages comprehensible input, output, interaction, and negotiation of meaning. For example, the student could choose their pace of learning; they could choose to participate in the available types of interaction most suitable for their personality or schedule (e.g., anonymous online-chatting, posting and answering questions on the discussion board, chatting online through the forum, e-mailing the instructor for their questions). In this way, it was hoped that the learners would feel the CALL environment was a mini-community where individual differences were recognized, accepted and assisted during the learning process. Although they were learning through a computer program, they felt they were independent as well as connected social beings in the learning process.

The Intervention

CALL Group

All participants in the three groups attended regular class. In addition, the participants in the CALL group received computer-based instruction consisting of six modules. Each module included two parts: (1) online instruction materials in the form of audio, video and text files; and (2) online exercises and homework. In each module, there were six exercise items and 12 accompanying homework items (the completion of the homework assignment was not required). The details of the six modules are described below.

The first two modules focused on the definition of zero anaphor and how to identify it (i.e., the first sub-skill). The four types of zero anaphors identified in Tao's (1993, 2001) studies were taught. The exercises and homework included marking the zero anaphor in texts and identifying the types of the zero anaphors.

The next two modules were designed to train the second sub-skill, i.e., matching the zero anaphor with its appropriate antecedent. There were two steps in training. The first was to locate the zero anaphors by marking its location in the sentences. The second step was to identify the antecedents of targeted zero anaphors (which was done through multiple-choice questions).

The last two modules focused on the training of the third sub-skill, i.e., integrating the information for comprehension. This was realized through translation exercises and multiple-choice questions. These exercises were designed to assess the learners' global understanding of the targeted sentence. The translation exercise required the students to type the English translation on the computer. The computer then evaluated the translation and provided feedback. The learner could then choose to either go back to re-do it again until it is correct, or click a bottom to see the correct answer. The multiple-choice exercises included questions such as the following:

Figure 1. Screenshot of exercises

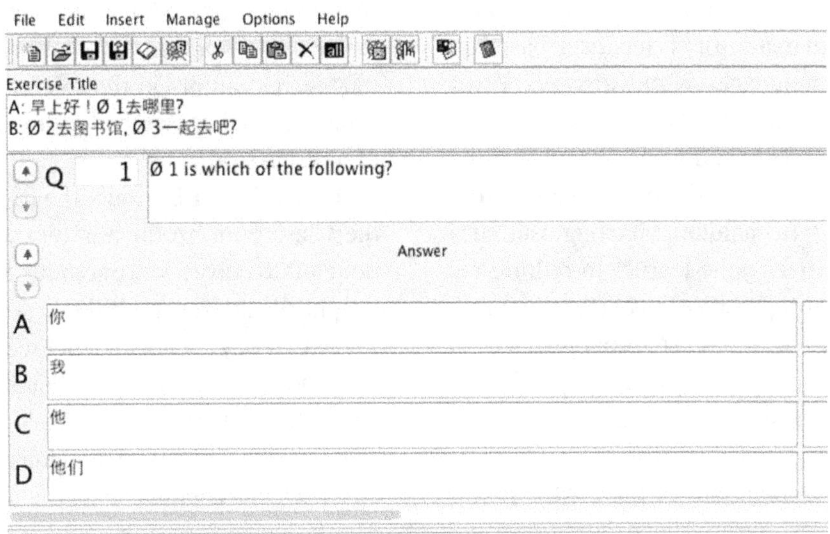

Example 3:

田云知道,大刚这一去,三年五载是回不来的,不禁心中一阵发酸。

Which is the true statement?

A. *Tian Yun was unhappy because she would be away for a long time.*

B. *Dagang was unhappy because he would be away for a long time.*

C. *Tian Yun was unhappy because Dagang would be away for a long time.*

D. *Dagang was unhappy because Tian Yun would be away for a long time.*

The correct answer is "C". If a learner's choice was incorrect, he could choose to see different types of feedback on the possible reasons. Like in the translation exercise, the learner could then choose to either go back to do it again until it is correct, or click a button to see the correct answer. The exercise and homework accompanying these two modules consisted of multiple-choices questions on antecedents and discourse cues that help match the appropriate antecedents. See the following example (Figure 1 presents the screenshot of a question similar to Example 4 below):

Example 4:

A: $\varnothing_1$ 去哪里?
B: $\varnothing_2$ 看电影, $\varnothing_3$ 一起去吧?

Question 1: $\varnothing_1$ is which of the following?
A. 你 B. 我 C. 他 D. 我们

Question 2: What is/are the discourse cue(s) for your matching in Question 1? (Choose as many as necessary)

A. Context, as it is a dialogue with another person.
B. Verb "去" which indicates an animated subject.
C. Topic chain.
D. The next sentence telling where to go.
E. The invitation from the second speaker.

Based on Garrett's proposal regarding CALL feedbacks (1995), four types of feedback were designed: (1) feedback that only indicates the answer is "correct" or "wrong"; (2) feedback that provides a linguistic explanation of why the answer is correct or wrong. For example: "This pronoun does not correspond to the topic chain in this paragraph."; (3) feedback that pinpoints the location of errors based on the computer's comparison of the student's input with the current answer and highlights the error (pattern markup); (4) feedback based on analysis of the anticipated wrong answers. Error messages associated with possible errors were stored in the computer and were presented if the student's response matched these possible errors (error-anticipation technique). Metalinguistic cues were provided to urge the learner to rethink his answer though group discussion or other learning activities. For example: "A zero pronoun needs to fit into the topic chain of this paragraph. Please reconsider your answer, or discuss your answer with the instructor and classmates."

The entire intervention for the CALL group lasted for two weeks during which the participants could access the CALL program online with their passwords. They could choose when to watch the instruction video delivered by the same instructor who taught the Classroom group (described below). They could finish all six videos in just one day if they chose to. Finally, the participants in the CALL group could chat online synchronously and/or post questions in the online discussion board – a function supported by the CALL program.

Classroom Group

Participants in the teacher-directed Classroom group were taught by the same teacher who filmed the video for the CALL group. All the teaching materials and instructional sequence in the Classroom group were the same as those in the CALL group. However, their classes were held in a room without computer equipment or other instructional technology. Students used the handouts and engaged in several types of activities emphasizing interactive and meaningful communication between the teacher and the students as well as among the students. Teacher-centered activity consisted of lecturing, explaining the target sub-skills on the board, having a whole-class discussion, choral drilling or asking individual students questions. Alternatively, students worked individually, in pairs or in groups on student-centered activities (e.g. discussion). Sometimes the teacher had the entire class working together on a project, with the teacher simply in the role of a facilitator. At times the teacher assigned a student to be in charge of a discussion.

Like the CALL group, the training period for the Classroom group was two weeks. The participants received six one-hour lectures on zero anaphoric inference skills. A lecture was held every two days. The students received a copy of the handout containing the content of each lecture before the lectures started. After each lecture, the students also received handouts of homework covering the content of the lecture on that day. The homework assignments for the classroom group were the same as those given to the CALL group. Like the CALL group, the homework for the Classroom group was optional. However, the Classroom group needed to report to their instructor on the amount the time they spent on studies after class and the amount of the homework they finished. The answers to the in-class exercises were checked and explained by the instructor. The keys to the homework were given to the students together with the handout of homework.

Control Group

The control group took the regular classes without any additional instruction on zero anaphora inferencing.

Test Battery

The test battery included three written tests: pretest, immediate posttest and delayed posttest. Each test included three parts: (1) 10 items for marking the positions of zero anaphors in texts (see Example 2 above), and identifying the types of the zero anaphors; (2) 10 items for matching the antecedents and identifying the discourse cue(s) for the matching (See Example 4 above); (3) 10 multiple-choice questions testing the reading comprehension of two texts (See Example 4 above). A pilot study was conducted to evaluate the quality of the test items. Two native Chinese speakers and the teachers in the Chinese program reviewed the tests for content validity and made suggestions for changes that were eventually incorporated into the final version of the tests.

In addition to analyzing participants' performance, the researcher administered a questionnaire (see Appendix A) to the CALL and Classroom groups after the delayed posttest was completed. The purpose of the questionnaire was to examine the learners' autonomy, and solicit students' views of the program and learning experience they had in the training.

In order to investigate the learners' autonomy, the researcher adapted and revised the questionnaire designed by Zhang and Li (2004), which consisted of 21 questions revised on the basis of the learning strategies classified by Oxford (1990), Wenden (1987) and O'Malley and Chamot (1990). Zhang & Li's questionnaire (2004) has been proved to have high content validity and high reliability. In our questionnaire, there were three parts. First, we incorporated the 21 questions about learning autonomy. Second, we asked the learners to rate their learning experience on a 5-point scale, with 1 as the "less enjoyable" and 5 as the "most enjoyable". Finally, the learners were asked to tell us the reasons why they liked and didn't like the learning experience.

Data Collection and Analysis

The pretests were administered to all three groups three days prior to the beginning of the intervention. Regarding the CALL group, the researcher administered the immediate and delayed posttests. The students in the CALL group could make individual appointments with the researcher to take the immediate posttest on the day they finished the training. Thirteen students out of 15 in the CALL group chose to take the test on the last day of the CALL training program, which was the same day as the Classroom group. The other two students chose to take the immediate tests two days earlier. The delayed posttest for the CALL group was also administered four weeks after the immediate posttest. For the Classroom group, the immediate posttests were administered on the last day of the two-week treatment period, and the delayed posttests four weeks after the posttests. The classroom teachers administered the pretests and delayed posttests to all students and the immediate posttests to the students in the teacher-directed groups.

As mentioned earlier, each test consisted of three sections. The scoring methods were: (1) for the 10 items for marking the positions of zero anaphors in texts and identifying the types of the zero anaphors, one point was given for marking a correct position, and another one point for correctly identifying the type of zero anaphor. The maximum score was 20 for this section. (2) for the 10 items for matching the antecedents and identifying the discourse cue(s) for the matching, one point was awarded for correctly matching the antecedent, and another one point for correctly identifying at least one discourse cue (for example, the use of connectives in the discourse, or the same topic chain, etc.) for the matching. The maximum score was 20 for this section. (3) For the 10 multiple-choice questions testing the reading comprehension of two texts, one point was given for each correct answer. For the entire test, the maximum score was 50. The researcher scored all the tests blindly, with no knowledge of participants' identity and/or group status. After the researcher scored the tests, two Chinese teachers at the university reviewed the students' answers. For all ambiguous answers, the researcher and the teachers discussed to reach consensus. The percentage of ambiguous answers was 2.7%

For the pretests, immediate posttests, and delayed posttests, the calculation of internal consistency was .90 for the identification task (i.e., section one), .71 for the multiple-choice task (i.e., section two), and .86 for the reading comprehension task (i.e., section three). To answer the research questions, repeated measures ANOVAs were used to compare the pretest, posttest, and delayed posttest results of the three groups.

The researcher administered the questionnaires in person on the day of the delayed posttest. The participants were required to finish the questions individually based on their own learning conditions. The answers to the multiple-choice questions were scored on a five-point scale. The answers to the open questions were collected and categorized.

RESULTS

Regarding Research Question One, Table 1 shows the descriptive statistics of the overall scores of the three tests. A 3 (group) x 3 (time) repeated measures ANOVA was performed on the test scores. There was a significant main effect of group, F (2, 42) = 12.832, $p < .001$. There was also a significant main effect of time, F (2, 42) = 13.304, $p < .001$. The group×time interaction effect was also significant F (2, 42) = 7.819, p = .014.

Following the significant interaction effect, analyses on the simple main effect of teaching methods was conducted. The CALL group showed significant differences among the three tests, F (2, 43) = 8.303, $p < .001$. Post Hoc simple comparisons showed that the scores of both the immediate posttest (F (1, 14) = 4.233, $p < .001$) and delayed posttest (F (1, 14) = 7.732, $p < .001$) were significantly higher than that of the pretest. There was no significant difference between immediate posttest and delayed posttest, F (1, 14) =13.118, p = .297. The Classroom group also showed significant differences among the three tests, F (2, 13) = 10.710, $p < .001$. The scores of both the immediate posttest (F (1, 14) = 2.03, $p < .001$) and the delayed posttest (F (1, 14) = 6.82, p = .035) were significantly higher than those of the pretest. Moreover, the score of the delayed posttest was significantly lower than that of the immediate posttest, F (1, 14) = 2.984, $p < .001$. The Control group showed no significant difference between the three tests, F (2, 13) = 32.231, p = 0.32.

Post hoc simple comparisons were also performed on the three tests among the groups. The control group's test scores at immediate and delayed posttest were both significantly lower than the CALL group, F (1, 29) = 15.978, $p < .001$ (for the immediate posttest), and F (1, 29) = 12.870, $p < .001$ (for the delayed posttest). The control group's test scores at immediate and delayed posttest were also significantly lower than the Classroom group, F (1, 29) = 5.278, $p < .001$ (for the immediate posttest), and F (1, 29) = 7.242, $p < .001$ (for the delayed posttest). For the two groups receiving the intervention, the Classroom group's test scores at immediate and delayed posttest were both significantly lower than the CALL group, F (1, 29) = 4.684, $p < .001$ (for the immediate posttest), and F (1, 29) = 9.825, $p < .001$ (for the delayed posttest). No interaction effect was found, F (2, 43) = 12.396, p = .083.

Table 2 shows the three groups' mean scores for each sub-skill task at the pretest, immediate and delayed posttests. Regarding Sub-skill One,

Table 1. Descriptive statistics of overall test scores

	Pretest		Immediate Posttest		Delayed Posttest	
Group	Mean	SD	Mean	SD	Mean	SD
CALL	11.80	3.72	40.20	4.69	39.33	4.64
Classroom	11.33	3.14	35.28	1.13	31.33	3.90
Control	11.88	4.48	11.24	3.02	11.70	3.34

Table 2. Mean scores for the three sub-skills

	Sub-skill One			Sub-skill Two			Sub-skill Three		
	Pre	Im	De	Pre	Im	De	Pre	Im	De
CALL	4.90	18.88	18.40	4.13	13.11	12.50	2.80	8.21	8.13
Classroom	4.61	18.39	17.57	4.13	9.33	8.24	2.63	7.59	7.51
Control	5.00	4.81	5.00	4.03	3.59	3.83	2.92	2.79	2.92

Note. Pre: Pretest; Im: Immediate posttest; De: Delayed posttest.

there was no significant difference between the three groups at the pretest, F (2, 43) = 7.978, p = .277, but there were significant differences at the immediate (F (2, 43) = 2.001, p = .029) and at the delayed posttest (F (2, 43) = 1.916, p = .011). Follow-up pairwise comparisons on immediate posttest scores showed that the CALL group outperformed the Control group, F (1, 29) = 1.929, p < .001, and that the Classroom group also scored significantly higher than the Control group, F (1, 29) = 2.824, p < .001. No difference was found between the CALL and Classroom groups, F (1, 29) = 11.380, p = .087. Regarding the delayed posttest, both the CALL group and the Classroom group significantly outperformed the Control group, F (1, 29) = 1.932, p < .001 (for CALL vs. Control) and F (1, 29) = 2.820, p < .001 (for Classroom vs. Control). Meanwhile, the CALL group also outperformed the Classroom group, F (1, 29) = 7.201, p = .048.

As for Sub-skill Two, there was no significant difference between the three groups at the pretest, F (2, 43) = 12.093, p = .831, but there were significant differences at the immediate (F (2, 43) = 4.891, p = .014) and at the delayed posttest (F (2, 43) = 4.101, p = .028). Follow-up pairwise comparisons on immediate posttest scores showed that the CALL group outperformed the Control group, F (1, 29) = 2.294, p < .001, and that the Classroom group also scored significantly higher than the Control group, F (1, 29) = 3.011, p < .001. The CALL scored significantly higher than the Classroom groups, F (1, 29) = 3.038, p < .001. In the delayed posttest, both the CALL group and the Classroom group significantly outperformed the Control group, F (1, 29) = 2.001, p < .001 (for CALL vs. Control) and F (1, 29) = 3.212, p < .001 (for Classroom vs. Control). At the same time, the CALL group also outperformed the Classroom group, F (1, 29) = 4.209, p = .046.

With regard to Sub-skill Three, there was no significant difference between the three groups at the pretest, F (2, 43) = 21.182, p = .782, but there were significant differences at the immediate (F (2, 43) = 3.904, p = .021) and at the delayed posttest (F (2, 43) = 2.412, p = .019). Follow-up pairwise comparisons on immediate posttest scores showed that the CALL group outperformed the Control group, F (1, 29) = 0.912, p < .001, and that the Classroom group also scored significantly higher than the Control group, F (1, 29) = 1.334, p < .001. The CALL group's score was significantly higher than the Classroom group, F (1, 29) = 1.824, p = .046. In the delayed posttest, both the CALL group and the Classroom group significantly outperformed the Control group, F (1, 29) = 1.013, p < .001 (for CALL vs. Control) and F (1, 29) = 1.822, p < .001 (for Classroom vs. Control). Meanwhile, the CALL group also outperformed the Classroom group, F (1, 29) = 4.001, p = .047.

Regarding Research Question Two, the results from the reports on the engagement in exercises were also different between the two experimental groups. The CALL group completed more homework than the classroom-instruction group: although all the participants were free to choose the amount of the homework, 11 participants in the CALL group finished all the homework assignments for all three difficulty levels; in contrast, only two participants in the Classroom group finished all homework assignments. In addition, all the participants in the CALL group participated in at least one type of online interaction (e.g., discussion-board, chat room, and email) with peers and/or with their instructor, whereas no participant in the Classroom group reported any interaction with peers or their instructor outside the classroom.

Regarding the scores from the autonomy questionnaires, the CALL group's mean score (M=62.40, SD=2.31) was significantly higher than that of the Classroom group (M=58.11, SD=1.02), $t(29) = 32.382, p = .045$. When asked to rate their learning experience of the program, the students in the two intervention groups had different opinions. The results of the questionnaire indicated that the CALL group (M=4.33, out of 5) enjoyed the learning experience more than the Classroom group (M=3.5, out of 5). When asked to tell which aspects they liked about their training program, the CALL group listed seven reasons: (1) flexibility, (2) variety of the teaching materials and activities, (3) fun, (4) feedbacks are helpful, (5) online discussion are fun, (6) self-monitoring the progress is more motivational, and (7) convenience (the participants could access the online program any time with their cell phone). The Classroom group listed four reasons: (1) face to face interaction with the teacher and other students, (2) systematic instruction, (3) class discussion, (4) attendance is required.

DISCUSSION

Research Question One asked whether there was any difference in learning zero anaphoric inference skills between CALL-based and classroom-based instruction. The results showed that, compared with the control group, the CALL group and the Classroom group both made significant progress from pretest to the immediate and delayed posttests, based on their composite scores. Although the gain of the Classroom group was somewhat not maintained at the delayed posttest (i.e., the delayed posttest score was lower than that of the immediate posttest), the improvement of the Classroom group was still significant even in the long run, when compared with the control group. These findings indicate that anaphoric inference skill is teachable through pedagogical intervention.

Traditionally, L2 decoding and grammar-construction in reading have been considered lower-level language skills, because these skills can be learned relatively quickly and easily for the majority of students, even during the course of early childhood. Higher-level reading skills, however, are much more difficult to learn because too many factors are involved during the higher-level reading processing. Our study addressed this thorny problem through targeting one specific inference skill: zero anaphoric inference. By analyzing the cognitive process of such a skill, we first decomposed it and identified three sub-skills from a psycholinguistic perspective: identifying the zero anaphor, matching the antecedent, and constructing a mental representation. Then, we developed explicit instructional materials and training exercises for training these sub-skills. The results of the study demonstrate that instruction based on psycholinguistic theories can be effective.

When we compared the performance of the CALL and Classroom group, the results showed that overall the CALL group significantly outperformed the Classroom group in the immediate posttests, based on their composite scores of the three sub-skills. Several reasons may have contributed to the CALL group's better performance over the Classroom group. The first might be the flexibility of learning in terms of time and style. For example, the CALL students could finish all the six video lectures in just one day if they chose to. Or they could break a module into several parts, and finish each part, wwhicheveris convenient for them. Such flexibility allowed participants to better manage time and take the course when they were in their best condition. Such flexibility also helped them address their individual differences in learning pace, that is, some students may learn a little bit faster than others. These students could proceed faster without getting bored, while others could take an more leisurely pace without feeling the pressure imposed by those fast learners. A self-paced learning schedule within a certain time span offered not only flexibility but also rigor. A progress report was generated by the CALL system and sent to the students email account. The students were also told to complete all the required learning materials before the deadline, and an immediate and a delayed test would be conducted after they finished the training. In this way, the flexibility was more like a "structured" freedom for the students. They could explore the learning method most suitable for them with some guidance set by the CALL program so as to finish their learning within a certain time frame.

The second reason might be a wide range of learning modes provided by the CALL program. The CALL program was designed to be adaptive to learners' personal interests and needs. It offered audio, visual, and interactive materials for learners with different learning styles to choose from. For instance, three modes of lectures were provided through the CALL program: audio, written and video. In the audio form, students could listen to the lecture. The written form of the lectures refers to the PowerPoint slides of the lecture. In the video form, students could watch a video of the lectures specifically filmed for the CALL group. The CALL instruction provided rich input in the form of integrated multimedia programs as well as explicit explanation of the discourse rules that can be viewed and reviewed at the learners' own pace. Such individualized instruction may better accommodate learners' individual progress along the path towards a common goal in the group. By providing various modes for learning materials and doing exercises, the CALL program was able to address the problem of different learning styles among students. For example, the students could choose one mode of lecture or a combination of two, depending on their preference. When doing the exercises or homework, the students could choose to get popped-out feedback immediately after they had finished each item, or wait until they finished everything. The feedback was provided in two modes: audio and written. The students could choose the mode they preferred or a combination of the two.

The overall scores of the students in the CALL group were also higher than the classroom instruction group in the delayed posttest. One of the reasons could be that the group developed a higher level of autonomy. It was found that the CALL group spent more time and did more homework than the Classroom group. This finding suggests, as Ellis (1993) has argued that the use of computer-based instruction can complement individualized structural syllabi and more effectively enable students to use the newly acquired structures to negotiate meaning through various method.

The results also show that the three sub-skills differentially benefited from the CALL-based instruction. The first sub-skill—the identification of zero anaphora—benefited equally from the classroom instruction and CALL program, as demonstrated in the immediate post-tests. However, the CALL group showed significantly more improvement in the second and third sub-skills. One possible explanation is that the first sub-skill is relatively easy. With a certain amount of training, either in classroom or through the CALL program, the students were able to accurately locate the position where a potential referential expression is needed. However, the second sub-skill—mapping the anaphor with its antecedent—seems more difficult, because the students had to choose from a number of referent candidates for the antecedent mapping. The process requires a lot of mental calculation based on the semantic, syntactical and discourse knowledge (Tao, 1996). In the same vein, the third sub-skill—integrating all the information for global comprehension—is also difficult for most of the students. In addition, the third skill is built upon the second sub-skill. If the students have difficulty in the second sub-skill, they won't be able to successfully accomplish tasks requiring the third sub-skill. In this study, the advantages of the CALL program over the classroom instruction on training more difficult sub-skills indicate that the features of the CALL program might be more effective in teaching difficult skills.

Our analyses showed that at the delayed post-test, the CALL group performed significantly better than the classroom-based group in the second and third sub-skill. This indicates that CALL is as effective as the classroom instruction on identification of zero anaphora, and more effective in matching antecedents and text comprehension. This suggests a better long-term effect of CALL-based teaching of zero anaphora inference skills than the classroom-based instruction. All these findings suggest that some elements of computer-based intervention support the development of zero anaphoric inference skill more effectively than classroom-based instruction.

Research Question Two asked whether there was any difference between the CALL group and Classroom group in terms of learning engagement. The questionnaire results indicated that the CALL group had significantly higher autonomy scores for learning than the Classroom group. The questionnaire results of the learners' learning experience indicated that the CALL group enjoyed the options and flexibilities the CALL program offered.

As mentioned earlier, higher autonomy among the learners of the CALL group might be one additional reason for the better achievement among the CALL group. Researchers have found that learners tend to be more engaged in learning activities when they have choice and control over their learning (Skinner & Belmont, 1993). Krashen (1996) argued that a non-threatening environment would facilitate language acquisition by lowering the affective filter to enhance learning for language learners. The use of multimedia through the CALL program likely provided additional support for comprehension and also accommodated the learners' different personalities. In doing so, it met the learners' various needs and reduced their anxiety level, which resulted in heightened learner autonomy of the CALL group.

CONCLUSION AND LIMITATIONS

The findings of this study clearly indicate that classroom-based and CALL-based instruction are both effective in teaching zero anaphoric inference skills to L2 learners of Chinese through careful pedagogical design and implementation. Moreover, CALL-based instruction was found to be more effective in helping learners develop this skill. Among the three-targeted sub-skills, the CALL program was particularly effective in developing two sub-skills: matching zero anaphors with their antecedents, and text comprehension. In addition, the CALL group better retained their gains than the Classroom group four weeks after the intervention ended. Finally, compared with the Classroom group, the CALL group showed a higher level autonomy for learning (i.e., spending more time on various learning activities).

The prevailing theme that emerged from this study is that theoretical guidance is essential in designing and implementing pedagogical plans. Teaching zero anaphoric inference skills through CALL is a brand-new area. Yet with proper application of relevant SLA theories, the CALL-based instruction turned out to be successful. This again proves the importance of integrating SLA theories into teaching practice (Chapelle, 2009; Garrett, 1991).

This study highlights the effectiveness of designing CALL programs based on sound pedagogical principles and linguistic/psycholinguistic theories can shed light on pedagogy development. There has been limited empirical evidence to support the existence of CALL pedagogy. The three-element pedagogy developed in this study proved effective in teaching a higher-level reading skill in a computer-based setting. When a CALL program is designed, it is important to take a pedagogy-based approach. This will force us to reconsider our assumptions, which may be based on intuition and observation. This study provides an example of how to conduct a research-based and research-oriented computer-based instruction. Although it is not a full-fledged course in online language teaching, the three-element pedagogy developed and employed here proves effective and convenient. It can be validated and improved through more research in future studies.

Despite some encouraging results of this study, improvement can be made for future research. First, some examples and exercises used in this study were chosen from authentic materials. A few students reported that these unabridged authentic materials were too long and sometimes too difficult to understand. Therefore, annotation of meaning and pronunciation should be better prepared in the future. Second, hypertexts can be introduced to the CALL program so that some gifted and more advanced students would have opportunities to learn additional and more challenging materials through the program. Third, the sample size of this study was relatively small to draw definitive conclusions. Despite these limitations, this study does present evidence of meaningful differences between the CALL-based and classroom-based groups' achievement scores. It shows that the potential of CALL programs goes beyond simply reinforcing grammar and discourse rules taught in the classroom through the provision of exercises. It is likely that the CALL program deepens the learners' understanding of the rules through a variety of options for learning and follow-up exercises. In addition, the flexibility of time management, the diversity of learning styles, and a variety of interaction methods provided in the CALL program would contribute to a successful enhancement of the learners' autonomy.

REFERENCES

Aoun, J. (1985). *A Grammar of Anaphora*. Cambridge, MA: MIT Press.

Bates, E., & MacWhinney, B. (1989). Functionalism and the Competition Model. In B. MacWhinney, & E. Bates (Eds.), *The cross-linguistic study of sentence processing* (pp. 3–73). New York: Cambridge University Press.

Chapelle, C. A. (2009). The Relationship Between Second Language Acquisition Theory and Computer-Assisted Language Learning. *Modern Language Journal*, *93*, 741–753. doi:10.1111/j.1540-4781.2009.00970.x

Chun, D. (2006). CALL technologies for L2 reading. In L. Ducate, & N. Arnold (Eds.), *Calling on CALL: From Theory and Research to New Directions in Foreign Language Teaching* (pp. 69–88). San Marcos, TX: CALICO.

Chun, D. M., & Plass, J. L. (1996). Effects of multimedia annotations on vocabulary acquisition. *Modern Language Journal*, *80*(2), 183–198. doi:10.1111/j.1540-4781.1996.tb01159.x

Comrie, B. (1989). Some general properties of reference-tracking systems. In D. Arnold, M. Atkinson, J. Durand, C. Grover, & L. Sadler (Eds.), *Essays on grammatical theory and universal grammar* (pp. 37–51). Oxford: Clarendon Press.

Cook, V. (2004). *The English Writing System*. London: Arnold.

Cui, S. (2003). 浅谈篇章语法的定义与教学问题 (On the definition of discourse grammar and pedagogy). *JCLTA*, *38*(1), 1–24.

Ellis, R. (1993). The structural syllabus and second language acquisition. *TESOL Quarterly*, *27*, 91–113. doi:10.2307/3586953

Foley, W. A., & Van Valin, R. (1984). *Functional Syntax and Universal Grammar*. Cambridge: Cambridge University Press.

Fox, B. (1987). *Discourse Structure and Anaphora*. Cambridge: Cambridge University Press. doi:10.1017/CBO9780511627767

Garrett, N. (1991). Technology in the service of language learning: Trends and issues. *Modern Language Journal*, *75*, 74–101. doi:10.1111/j.1540-4781.1991.tb01085.x

Garrett, N. (1995). ICALL and second language acquisition. In V. M. Holland, J. D. Kaplan, & M. R. Sams (Eds.), *Intelligent language tutors* (pp. 345–358). Mahwah: Lawrence Erlbaum.

Huang, Y. (2003). Switch-reference in Amele and logophoric verbal suffix in Gokana: A generalized neo-Gricean pragmatic analysis. In M. Georgiafentis, E. Haeberli, & S. Varlokosta (Eds.), Reading working papers in linguistics 7 (pp. 53–76). Reading, UK: University of Reading.

Hubbard, P. (2009). Introduction. In P. Hubbard (Ed.), Computer Assisted Language Learning (vol. 1, pp. 1–20). London: Routledge.

Jin, H. (1994). Topic-prominence and subject prominence in L2 acquisition: Evidence of English-to-Chinese typological transfer. *Language Learning*, *44*, 101–121.

Jing-Schmidt, Z. (2011). Zero anaphora in higher level Chinese writings across learner backgrounds. *Teaching Chinese in the World*, *25*(2), 258–267.

Kitajima, R. (2001). Enhancing higher order interpretation skills for Japanese reading. *CALICO Journal*, *19*, 571–581.

Krashen, S. (1996). *Under Attack: The case against bilingual education*. Culver City, CA: Language Education Associates.

Lantolf, J. (2000). Second language learning as a mediated process. *Language Teaching*, *33*, 79–96. doi:10.1017/S0261444800015329

Lantolf, J. P., & Thorne, S. (2006). *Sociocultural theory and the genesis of second language development*. Oxford: Oxford University Press.

LaPolla, R. J. (1990). *Grammatical Relations in Chinese: Synchronic and Diachronic Considerations*. Unpublished doctoral dissertation. University of California, Berkeley, U.S.A.

Li, C., & Thompson, S. A. (1981). *Mandarin Chinese: A functional reference grammar*. Berkeley: University of California Press.

Li, W. (2004). The discourse perspective in teaching Chinese grammar. *JCLTA*, *39*(1), 25–44.

McCarthy, C. P. (1999). Reading theory as a microcosm of the four skills. The Internet TESL Journal, 5(2). Retrieved from http://iteslj.org/Articles/McCarthy-Reading.html

Macaruso, P., & Rodman, A. (2011). Benefits of Computer-Assisted Instruction to Support. *Bilingual Research Journal*, *34*(2), 301–315. do i:10.1080/15235882.2011.622829

O'Malley, J. M., & Chamot, A. U. (1990). *Learning strategies in second language acquisition*. Cambridge, England: Cambridge University Press. doi:10.1017/CBO9781139524490

Oxford, R. L. (1990). *Language learning strategies: What every teacher should know*. New York: Newbury House.

Park, Y., Zheng, B., Lawrence, J., & Warschauer, M. (2013). Technology-enhanced reading environments. In M. Thomas, H. Reinders, & M. Warschauer (Eds.), *Contemporary computer-assisted language learning* (pp. 267–285). London: Continuum.

Pu, M.-M. (1997). Zero anaphora and grammatical relations in Mandarin. In T. Givón (Ed.), *Grammatical relations: Typological studies in language 35* (pp. 283–322). Amsterdam: John Benjamins Publishing Company. doi:10.1075/tsl.35.08pu

Shake, M. C., & Stine-Morrow, E. A. L. (2011). Age Differences in Resolving Anaphoric Expressions During Reading. *Neuropsychology, Development, and Cognition. Section B, Aging, Neuropsychology and Cognition, 18*(6), 678–707. doi:10.1080/13825585.2011.607228 PMID:21995819

Shei, C., & Hsieh, H. (2012). Linkit: a CALL system for learning Chinese characters, words, and phrases. *Computer Assisted Language Learning, 25*(4), 319–338. doi:10.1080/09588221.2011.589390

Skinner, E. A., & Belmont, M. J. (1993). Motivation in the classroom: Reciprocal effects of teacher behavior and student engagement across the school year. *Journal of Educational Psychology, 85*, 571–581. doi:10.1037/0022-0663.85.4.571

Tao, L. (1993). *Zero anaphora in Chinese: Cognitive strategies in discourse processing.* (Unpublished doctoral dissertation). University of Colorado, Boulder, CO.

Tao, L. (1996). Topic discontinuity and zero anaphora in Chinese discourse: Cognitive strategies in discourse processing. In B. Fox (Ed.), *Studies in Anaphora* (pp. 487–513). Amsterdam: John Benjamins Publishing Company. doi:10.1075/tsl.33.15tao

Tao, L. (2001). Switch reference and zero anaphora: Emergent reference in discourse processing. In A. Cienki, B. J. Luka, & M. B. Smith (Eds.), *Conceptual and discourse factors in linguistic structure* (pp. 253–267). Stanford, CA: CSLI Publications.

Tao, L., & Healy, A. F. (1996). Cognitive strategies in discourse processing: A comparison of Chinese and English speakers. *Journal of Psycholinguistic Research, 25*, 597–616. doi:10.1007/BF01712411

Tao, L. (2001). Switch reference and zero anaphora: Emergent reference in discourse processing. In A. Cienki, B. J. Luka, & M. B. Smith (Eds.), *Conceptual and discourse factors in linguistic structure* (pp. 253–267). Stanford: CSLI Publications.

Tao, L., & Healy, A. F. (2005). Zero anaphora: Transfer of reference tracking strategies from Chinese to English. *Journal of Psycholinguistic Research, 34*, 99–131. doi:10.1007/s10936-005-3634-5 PMID:15991875

Van Lier, L. (2004). *The ecology and semiotics of language learning*. Dordrecht: Kluwer Academic. doi:10.1007/1-4020-7912-5

Verity, D. (2005). Vygotskyan Concepts for teacher education. Pan-SIG Conference "Lifelong learning" proceedings. Retrieved from http://jalt.org/pansig/2005/HTML/Verity.htm

Van Valin, R. D., Jr. (1987). Aspects of the interaction of syntax and pragmatics: Discourse coreference mechanisms and the typology of grammatical systems. In *The pragmatic perspective: Selected papers from the 1985 international pragmatics conference 232* (pp. 513–531). Amsterdam: Benjamins Publishing Company.

Wenden, A., & Rubin, J. (Eds.). (1987). *Learner strategies in language learning*. Cambridge: Prentice-Hall.

Yang, C. L., Gordon, P. C., Hendrick, R., & Wu, J. T. (1999). Comprehension of referring expressions in Chinese. *Language and Cognitive Processes, 14*, 715–743. doi:10.1080/016909699386248

Ymura-Takei, M., Fujiwar, M., & Aizawa, T. (2001). Resolving and generation zero anaphor in Japanese: A language learning aid perspective. In *Proceedings of the 6th Natural Language Proceeding Pacific Rim Symposium* (pp. 557–562). New Delhi: Allied Publisher, Ltd.

Zhang, L. X., & Li, X. X. (2004). A comparative study on learner autonomy between Chinese students and west European students. *Foreign Language World, 4*, 15–23.

ADDITIONAL READING

Ariel, M. (1990). *Accessing NP antecedents*. London: Routledge.

Ariel, M. (1991). The function of accessibility in a theory of grammar. *Journal of Pragmatics, 16*, 443–463.

Breznitz, Z. (1987). Increasing first graders' reading accuracy and comprehension by accelerating their reading rates. *Journal of Educational Psychology, 79*(3), 236–242.

Carr, T., & Levy, B. (Eds.). (1990). *Reading and its development: Component skills approaches*. San Diego: Academic Press.

Chu, C. C. (1998). *A discourse grammar of Mandarin Chinese*. New York: Lang.

Chun, D. M., & Plass, J. L. (1996). Effects of multimedia annotations on vocabulary acquisition. *Modern Language Journal, 80*(2), 183–198.

Garrod, S., Freudenthal, D., & Boyle, E. (1994). The role of different types of anaphor in the on-line resolution of sentences in a discourse. *Journal of Memory and Language, 33*, 39–68.

Gass, S. M., & Selinker, L. (Eds.). (1992). *Language transfer in language learning*. Amsterdam: Benjamins.

Givon, T. (1983a). Topic continuity in discourse: The functional domain of switch-reference. In J. Haiman, & P. Munro (Eds.), *Switch-reference and universal grammar* (pp. 51–82). Philadelphia: John Benjamins Publishing Company.

Givon, T. (1983b). Topic continuity in discourse: An introduction. In T. Givon (Ed.), *Topic continuity in discourse: A quantitative cross-language study* (pp. 1–41). Amsterdam: John Benjamins Publishing Company.

Givon, T. (1990). *Syntax: A functional-typological introduction, II*. Amsterdam: John Benjamins Publishing Company.

Gordon, P. C., Grosz, B. J., & Gilliom, L. A. (1993). Pronouns, names, and the centering of attention in discourse. *Cognitive Science, 17*, 311–347.

Gordon, P. C., & Chan, D. (1995). Pronouns, passives, and discourse coherence. *Journal of Memory and Language, 34*, 216–231.

Gordon, P. C., & Hendrick, R. (1998). The representation and processing of co-reference in discourse. *Cognitive Science, 22*, 389–424.

Grosz, B. (1981). Focusing and description in natural language dialogues. In A. K. Joshi, I. A. Sag, & B. L. Webber (Eds.), *Elements of discourse understanding: Proceedings of a workshop on computational aspects of linguistic structure and discourse setting* (pp. 84–105). New York: Cambridge University Press.

Grosz, B., Jones, K. S., & Webber, B. L. (Eds.). (1986). *Readings in natural language processing*. Los Angeles: Morgan Kaufmann.

Koda, K. (2005). Learning to read across writing systems: Transfer, metalinguistic awareness and second-language reading development. In V. Cook, & B. Bassetti (Eds.), *Writing systems and second language learning* (pp. 311–334). Multilingual Matters.

Koda, K., & Reddy, P. (2008). Cross-linguistic transfer in second language reading. *Language Teaching, 41*(4), 497–508.

Li, C. N., & Thompson, S. (1979). Third-person pronouns and zero-anaphora in Chinese discourse. In T. Givon (Ed.), Syntax and semantics: Vol. 12. *Discourse and syntax* (pp. 311–335). New York: Academic.

Perfetti, C. A. (2003). The universal grammar of reading. *Scientific Studies of Reading, 7*(1), 3–24.

Perfetti, C. A., Liu, Y., & Tan, L. H. (2005). The Lexical Constituency Model: Some implications of research on Chinese for general theories of reading. *Psychological Review, 12*(11), 43–59.

Shi, D. (1992). *The nature of topic comment constructions and topic chain*. Unpublished doctoral dissertation. University of Southern California, Los Angeles, CA.

Tao, L. (1993). *Zero anaphora in Chinese: Cognitive strategies in discourse processing*. Unpublished doctoral dissertation. University of Colorado, Boulder, CO.

Tao, L. (1994) Topic choice, switch reference and zero anaphora: The on-line construction of grammar. In D. Ho & C. Tseng (Eds.) *ICLL-4 Proceedings* (pp.373–390). Taipei: Academia Sinica.

Tao, L. (1996). Topic discontinuity and zero anaphora in Chinese discourse: Cognitive strategies in discourse processing. In B. Fox (Ed.), *Studies in anaphora* (pp. 485–511). Amsterdam: John Benjamins Publishing Company.

Tao, L., & Healy, A. F. (1998). Anaphora in language processing: Transfer of cognitive strategies by native Chinese, Dutch, English, and Japanese speakers. In A. F. Healy, & L. E. Bourne Jr., (Eds.), *Foreign language learning: Psycholinguistic studies on training and retention* (pp. 193–211). Mahwah, NJ: Lawrence Erlbaum Associates.

Tsao, F. F. (1979). *A functional study of topic in Chinese: The first step towards discourse analysis*. Taipei: Student Book Co.

KEY TERMS AND DEFINITIONS

Anaphora: The use of a word as a regular grammatical substitute for a preceding word or group of words in discourse.

Higher-Level Reading Skills: Skills required to construct a coherent mental model of a text's meaning. Some common higher-level reading skills are inferencing, comprehension monitoring, and text structure knowledge.

Inference: In reading, inference is a conclusion a reader draws about the unsaid based on what is actually said. Drawing inferences while reading requires willingness to look at the evidence and come to a conclusion that has not been expressed in words. Only in reading, the evidence for the inference consists solely of words rather than actual events, expressions, or gestures.

Pedagogy: The method and practice of teaching, especially as an academic subject or theoretical concept. Pedagogy manifests itself through instructional theories, which guide instructors to develop conceptual knowledge and manage the content of learning activities in various educational settings.

Psycholinguistics: The studies of the psychological and neurobiological factors that enable and influence humans to acquire, use, comprehend and produce language.

Reference Tracking: (Readers or speakers) recognizing an anaphor in discourse, then correctly matching the anaphor with its antecedent mentioned in the previous discourse for the construction of local and global coherence.

Zero Anaphora: An empty grammatical slot referring to a previously mentioned entity in discourse.

APPENDIX A: LEARNER AUTONOMY QUESTIONNAIRE

Direction: In order to investigate the Learner autonomy, will you please circle the one answer to the following questions that best applies to you. Thank you very much for your help and patience!

Part I

Questionnaire Statements	Never	Rarely	Sometimes	Often	Always
1. I think I have the ability to learn Chinese well.					
2. I make good use of my free time in Chinese study.					
3. I preview before learning new materials.					
4. I find I can finish my task on time.					
5. I keep a record of my study, such as keeping a diary, writing review etc.					
6. I make self-examinations with the exam papers chosen by myself.					
7. I reward myself such as going shopping, playing etc. when I progress.					
8. I attend out of class activities to practice and learn the language.					
9. During the class/training, I try to take advantage of opportunities to take part in activities such as pair/group discussion, etc.					
10. I know my strengths and weaknesses in my Chinese study.					
11. I choose books and exercises which suit me, neither too difficult nor too easy.					

Part II

12. I study Chinese here due to:
    1) my parents' demand
    2) curiosity
    3) getting a good job, help for my major
    4) interest in Chinese culture, such as film, sports, music, etc.
    5) 3 and 4
13. I think the learner-teacher relationship is that of:
    1) receiver and giver
    2) raw material and maker
    3) customer and shopkeeper
    4) children and partners
    5) explorer and director
14. I think my success or failure in Chinese study is mainly due to:
    1) luck or fate
    2) Chinese studying environment
    3) studying facilities (aids)
    4) teachers
    5) myself

15. Whether students should design the teaching plan together with teachers or not, my opinion is:
    1) strongly agree
    2) agree
    3) neutral
    4) oppose
    5) strongly oppose
16. When the teacher asks questions for us to answer, I would mostly like to:
    1) wait for others' answers
    2) think and get ready to answer
    3) look up books, dictionaries
    4) clarify questions with teachers
    5) join a pair/group discussion
17. When I meet a word I don't know, I mainly:
    1) let it go
    2) ask others
    3) guess the meaning
    4) 2 and 5
    5) look up in the dictionary
18. When I make mistakes in study, I'd usually like the following ones to correct them:
    1) let them be
    2) teachers
    3) Classmates
    4) Others
    5) books or dictionaries
19. When I am asked to use technologies that I haven't used before (e. g. internet discussion),
    1) I resist using them
    2) I put it off or try to avoid it
    3) I feel worried, but use them anyway
    4) I learn them following others
    5) I usually try to learn new skills
20. The following way is most useful in my Chinese study:
    1) taking notes
    2) mechanical memory
    3) doing exercises of grammar, translation, words etc.
    4) classifying or grouping or comparing
    5) group discussion
21. I usually use materials selected:
    1) only by teachers
    2) mostly by teachers
    3) by teachers and by myself
    4) mostly by myself
    5) only by myself

22. I enjoy the training very much.
    1) strongly oppose
    2) oppose
    3) neutral
    4) agree
    5) strongly agree

Part III

23. Why did you enjoy the training?
24. Which aspects of the training do you think need improving?
25. On average, how much time did you spend on the training each day?
26. Did you still review the training materials and exercises after the training session was finished? If yes, how often did you review the materials and exercises?

Chapter 5
Investigating Optimal Computer-Mediated Cultural Instruction to Foster Intercultural Sensitivity in Online Peer Discussions

Paula Garrett-Rucks
Georgia State University, USA

ABSTRACT

Online classroom discussions in response to instruction about native speakers' cultural perspectives can foster learners' intercultural understanding (McBride & Wildner-Bassett, 2008). However, Garrett-Rucks (2013) found that varying the format of the cultural instruction prior to learners' online discussions can change learning outcomes. This chapter builds on Garrett-Rucks' previous finding—that native speaker informant videos promoted learners' intercultural sensitivity more than the combined use of authentic texts and explicit cultural instruction—by investigating the use of authentic texts in the absence of explicit cultural instruction. Specifically, the present study examines the ways in which 13 language learners enrolled in a Midwestern introductory French class in the United States (US) collectively mediated NS perspectives toward family practices presented in French informant videos compared to authentic texts in online peer discussions. A content analysis of the discussion transcripts detected collective shifts in learners' intercultural sensitivity—shifts from ethnorelative and ethnocentric stages of Bennett's (1993) Developmental Model of Intercultural Sensitivity—reflected in participants' postings. Findings from the analysis contribute to an understanding of ways to maximize learners' development of intercultural sensitivity in online peer discussions with optimal uses of computer-mediated cultural instruction outside of classroom instruction time.

DOI: 10.4018/978-1-4666-6174-5.ch005

INTRODUCTION

Fostering learners' *intercultural sensitivity*, the psychological ability to deal with cultural differences (Bennett, 1993), is increasingly important to prepare learners for success in multicultural industrialized societies and to become responsible global citizens (Kumaravadivelu, 2003). Over a decade ago, foreign language (FL) educators started responding to the need to prepare learners for intercultural understanding in the FL curriculum as evidenced in the addition of the *Cultures Standards (2.1* and *2.2)* (National Standards in Foreign Language Education Project, 2006). Despite the cultural turn in the field, there are still substantial issues to be addressed. Educators are often confused and anxious about the implementation and assessment of culture learning in FL instruction (Cutshall, 2012; Fantini, 2011; Fox & Diaz-Greenburg, 2006). In particular, instructors who follow the ACTFL position statement to maintain over 90% of their instruction in the target language (TL) struggle to foster meaningful cultural inquiry among learners with limited linguistic mastery, offering a possible explanation for why the *Culture Standards (2.1* and *2.2)* are neither taught nor assessed by a sizeable number of teachers (Phillips & Abbott, 2011, p. 7). Fortunately, advances in technology offer possibilities to meet the *Culture Standards* at beginning levels of instruction.

Previous research (Garrett-Rucks, 2013) demonstrated an effective use of computer-mediated cultural instruction used to foster adult beginning French language learners' intercultural sensitivity outside of the classroom while preserving TL use for classroom instruction time. The learners in Garrett-Rucks' (2013) study participated in two online classroom discussions that consisted of two phases over a five-week long discussion for each cultural topic—(1) Greetings and (2) Education. During Phase 1 of a discussion, learners discussed the cultural perspectives from *explicit cultural instruction* (written for US learners about French culture) and *authentic texts* (written by French speakers for French speakers), followed by French informant videos in Phase 2. The analysis of the discussion transcripts revealed that the explicit cultural instruction perpetuated ethnocentric thinking among learners, whereas the French informant videos fostered learners' development of intercultural sensitivity. Although the authentic texts were primarily ignored by the learners who relied more heavily on the explicit cultural information in their Phase 1 postings, the few learners whose postings drew from the authentic texts bore witness to the development of intercultural sensitivity. Accordingly, the present study investigates the influence of authentic texts and French informant videos in the absence of explicit cultural instruction. Findings from this study can contribute to an understanding of the optimal design of computer-mediated cultural instruction to prepare FL learners for meaningful online classroom discussions.

BACKGROUND

Foreign language education and intercultural communication are inextricably linked given their overlapping areas. However, the two fields have developed separately—FL education has existed for centuries whereas research on intercultural competence was formalized a little over 50 year ago in support of US Peace Corps training (Fantini, 2011). Yet, FL education that does not address culture learning risks producing "fluent fools" (Bennett, 1997, p. 16), that is second language (L2) speakers who lack intercultural depth. As a profession, FL educators have assumed the responsibility of fostering learners' intercultural understanding at the foundation of their practice. As noted in an earlier version of the National Standards for Foreign Language Learning (1996):

Even if students never speak the language after leaving school, for a lifetime they will retain the cross-cultural skills and knowledge, the insight, and the access to a world beyond traditional borders (p. 24).

In 1999, ACTFL stressed the need for FL learners to understand target culture members' perspectives toward their ways of life (practices) and their contributions to the world (products) as an outcome of their FL learning experience in the *Cultures Standards* as defined below:

- **Standard 2.1:** Students demonstrate an understanding of the relationship between the practices and perspectives of the culture studied.
- **Standard 2.2:** Students demonstrate an understanding of the relationship between the products and perspectives of the culture studied (National Standards in Foreign Language Education Project, 1999).

Although commonly referred to as the 3Ps—practices, products, and perspectives, one can clearly see that *perspectives* is fundamental to the understanding of the target culture, and as such it is given twice the emphasis of the other two Ps—practices and products. In the same vein, (Bennett, 1993) describes *intercultural sensitivity* as the ability to deal with diverse perspectives and complex worldviews. Bennett's influential assessment, the Developmental Model of Intercultural Sensitivity (DMIS) serves as a framework to explain six stages of increasing sensitivity toward cultural differences. The first three stages (Denial Stage, Defense Stage and Minimization Stage) are considered *ethnocentric* or monocultural in that one's own culture is seen as the only culture or the *better* culture. The second three DMIS stages are *ethnorelative* (Acceptance Stage, Adaptation Stage and Integration Stage) where the individual's culture is one of many equally valid worldviews.

Technology Use to Achieve the Cultures Standards

Advances in technology have provided a wealth of resources to support environments which facilitate the understanding of alternate perspectives in culture learning. Furthermore, the Internet has provided a tool to make accessing authentic texts and establishing contacts with native speakers easier than ever before. Several intercultural exchanges accomplished through tandem learning —exchanges between nonnative speakers (NNSs) and native speakers (NSs)—have been specifically designed to get students to take a step back from their own cultural beliefs with exposure to alternate perspectives from L2 speakers (Belz, 2002; Belz & Müller-Hartmann, 2003; Müller-Hartmann, 2000; O'Dowd, 2003). One of the most common and established projects in computer assisted FL learning environments is email exchanges (Warschauer, Shetzer, & Meloni, 2000). The aim of most email assignments is to foster personal connections between intercultural partners as students learn about one another and themselves. However, studies on synchronous communication have reported more advantages than email, such as the exchange of messages in real time with the goal of communicating quickly, and it has been considered a preferred method of communication for youth (Thorne, 2003) compared to the more traditional sense of email. Lomicka (2006) reviewed a large number of studies that examined NS and NNS pairs during virtual chat conversations, although they primarily focused on linguistic development such as scaffolding and negotiation of meaning rather than culture learning.

Intercultural projects which use synchronous or non-synchronous exchanges are categorized as telecollaborative when the added component of videoconferencing is used (Belz, 2002, 2005; Kinginger, 2004; O'Dowd, 2003; Thorne, 2003; Ware & Kramsch, 2005). Ware and Kramsch (2005) defined a telecollaborative project as *a technology-mediated language and culture exchange in which language learners write to one another in both their native and target languages … [that] involve the use of both synchronous (real-time) and asynchronous (delayed-time) writing, as well as teleconferencing functions that allow for the exchange of visual and aural communication. (p. 203)*

Telecollaborative projects are often characterized by collaborative work between classes as well as student-to-student partnerships affiliated with individual institutions. One influential and noteworthy telecollaborative project, *Cultura,* is still considered a forerunner in intercultural projects (McBride & Wildner-Bassett, 2008). *Cultura* was developed in the summer of 1997 at the Massachusetts Institute of Technology. The aim of the project was to get advanced language learners to work in tandem with other students who lived where their target language was spoken, and together they investigated the subtle differences between the two cultures. *Cultura* used a comparative approach that asked learners to observe, to compare and to analyze parallel materials juxtaposed from their respective cultures, fostering the development of learners' intercultural sensitivity.

This keystone project illustrates the potential for computer-mediated communication (CMC) to assist intercultural connections to help achieve the *Cultures Standards.* Unfortunately, however, few beginning FL classes have the infrastructure or time in their curriculum to integrate such elaborate projects. Furthermore, intercultural exchanges do not guarantee heightened intercultural understanding as an automatic outcome (Kern, Ware, & Warschauer, 2004). Several studies have reported difficulties which resulted in frustration (Belz, 2002; Belz & Müller-Hartmann, 2003), miscommunication (Ware, 2005; Ware & Kramsch, 2005) and worse, furthering of cultural stereotypes (Belz, 2002; Belz & Müller-Hartmann, 2003; O'Dowd, 2003; Ware, 2005). Reasons cited for these problems include unequal levels of technological or linguistic competence between the two groups of students (Belz, 2002); differences in university schedules and student motivations (Belz & Müller-Hartmann, 2003; Kramsch & Thorne, 2002); and issues of interpersonal communication and internet pragmatics (Belz & Müller-Hartmann, 2003; O'Dowd, 2003; Ware & Kramsch, 2005). Ware's (2005) research reported on "contextual tensions that arose from the different socially and culturally situated attitudes, beliefs, and expectations that informed students' communicative choices in the online discourse" (p. 1).

Although only a few studies have investigated CMC use between peers, referred to as *intracultural* communication (NNS-NNS), many benefits have been reported (Darhower, 2002; Kern, 1995; Meunier, 1998; Warschauer, 1996). Specifically, these researchers reported that intracultural CMC use can encourage students to interact with each other and reduce effects of shyness (Kern 1995; Warschauer, 1996) and increase participation, motivation, and attitudes towards writing (Meunier, 1998). CMC participants in Meunier's (1998) study claimed that they were "interested in their peers' ideas and thrilled by the authenticity of their exchanges" (p 177). Findings from Darhower's (2002) study also showed student interest to express their ideas and explore each other's perspectives in CMC sessions.

Although to date there is a paucity of studies which examine online cultural discussions between peers within a FL class (Abrahams, 2006), there is evidence that CMC facilitates cultural acquisition in NNS-NNS intracultural exchanges (Garrett-Rucks, 2013; McBride & Wildner-Bassett, 2008). Garrett-Rucks' (2013) study mentioned earlier offers empirical evidence to support the use of online discussions among peers in response to specific types of computer-mediated cultural instruction in English, outside of classroom instruction, in order to foster beginning learners' intercultural sensitivity while preserving TL use in the classroom. In particular, her study revealed how explicit cultural instruction perpetuated ethnocentric thinking in online classroom discussions until exposure to video recordings of French informant perspectives toward both French and US cultural practices fostered collective shifts in learners' intercultural sensitivity away from ethnocentric thinking. In an attempt to further identify the critical elements in computer-mediated cultural instruction to foster learners' intercultural sensitivity, the current study omits explicit cultural instruction and presents learners with authentic texts compared to French informant videos while asking the following research question:

What factors in the online discussions (the authentic texts and the French informant videos) appear to influence collective shifts—predominant shifts at the group level between learners' ethnocentric and ethnorelative thinking —in the learners' intercultural sensitivity toward an alternate cultural practice?

METHODS

Participants and Procedures

Thirteen students enrolled in a fall semester introductory French course at a Midwestern technical college participated in weekly online classroom discussions, in English, outside of the classroom, on *BlackBoard* course management system for course credit. There were seven females and six males between the ages of 19 and 60. No heritage learners were present. This communicative language course was taught primarily in the TL by a native French speaker. Outside of the classroom instruction, there were three online classroom discussions in English, centering on (1) French greetings, (2) French education and (3) French family life over the course of a 16-week semester. The present study investigates the third discussion for which the computer-mediated cultural instruction primarily differed from Discussions 1 and 2 in that it contained no explicit cultural instruction. The researcher provided participants with a 15-minute demonstration the first day of class to illustrate how to access the cultural instruction and the discussion threads found on *BlackBoard*. The learners were informed that the cultural instruction would count for 10% of their participation grade in the course and that the researcher would send the course instructor the students' participation grade, based solely on the word count of the postings. The instructor had no access to the online discussions, beyond weekly correspondence with the researcher pertaining to the discussion topics and learners' participation grade.

Each of the three discussions lasted for five weeks and consisted of two phases. For Phase 1, participants were required to access two sources; (1) online cultural instruction taken from the *univers culturel* portion of Carnegie Mellon's Open Learning Initiative (OLI) for French, and (2) authentic texts—those written by native French speakers for native French speakers—about these same cultural practices. For Phase 2, learners accessed pre-recorded interviews in English, between the researcher and four diverse French informants (see Appendix A for French informant profiles and Appendix B for interview question). What differed in Discussion 3, the focus of the present study, from Discussions 1 and 2 was the OLI instruction in Phase 1. The OLI instruction in Discussions 1 and 2 consisted of explicit cultural instruction—written explanations about French perspectives toward alternate cultural practices intended for US learners of French, whereas for Discussion 3 the OLI lesson consisted of an authentic text—descriptions about French culture written by French speakers, for French speakers. Therefore, the learners in the present study accessed two authentic texts—the OLI authentic text and an authentic text selected by the researcher—with no explicit cultural information in Phase 1 of Discussion 3. However, Phase 2 of Discussion 3 had the same French informants in video interviews as Discussions 1 and 2.

For all three discussions, students were required to post their reactions to the online cultural materials—the OLI lesson and authentic text—during Week 1 of the discussion and then to respond to two of their peers' postings on the discussion board during Week 2. For Phase 2 of each discussion, participants accessed French informant videos and then posted their reactions to the interviews on the discussion board for Week 3 and then responded to two of their peers' postings on the discussion board during Week 4. During Week 5 of each discussion, participants were instructed to reflect on all of the cultural materials and comments made on the discussion board and then to post their final impressions of the French cultural practices. Discussion prompts (Appendix C) instructed students how to make their weekly postings (where to find the cultural instruction, the posting word limit, and the discussion questions) over the course of each five-week discussion. The discussion prompts promoted students' exploration of the relationships between the practices and products of French culture and the perspectives of French people compared to their own culture, in adherence to the goals of the *Standards for FL Learning* (*Standards 2.1, 2.2*, and *4.2*).

The OLI cultural lesson selected for Discussion 3 presented different definitions of the family in France in an article called « Eight ways to create a family » (March 10th, 2002) in a French newspaper, *Le Monde*. This article presented statistics on the changes in marriage practices, such as couples choosing to live together prior to marriage, an increase in the average age at which people choose to get married, an increase in the divorce rate, and an increasing number of couples choosing to do a civil solidarity pact (a.k.a. PACS) over marriage. The OLI lesson stated specifically that only 8% of couples were choosing to do the PACS over a marriage in 2002. The authentic text selected by the researcher contained more recent (2008) demographic information concerning the PACS, life expectancy, and out of wedlock births taken from another French newspaper, *le Nouvel Observateur*. Specifically, this authentic text explained that the number of couples selecting the PACS over a traditional wedding had increased to nearly 50% in 2008, a continually increasing number since its creation in 1999. The learners contributed a total of 44 postings for Discussion 3, similar to the number of postings in the two previous discussions.

Data Analysis

The first step in identifying the influences of the two different types of cultural instruction on learners' development of intercultural sensitivity toward an alternate cultural practice was to identify the themes regarding family practices in the learner data. By using a line-by-line coding method (Charmaz, 2006), I identified learner comments about (1) birthrate/death rate, (2) children born out of wedlock and (3) the PACS (a civil solidarity pact in France). I then identified the most salient (most frequently discussed) theme, the PACS, in order to maximize the amount of available data that bore witness to learners' intercultural sensitivity toward a specific alternate cultural practice.

After identifying the PACS as the most salient alternate French cultural practice addressed in the discussions, I assessed the class's intercultural sensitivity toward the PACS as a whole in response to the authentic texts (Phase 1) compared to the French informant videos (Phase 2). To do so, I identified each posting concerning the PACS and evaluated the learners' comments within the evaluation criteria provided in Bennett's (1993) Developmental Model of Intercultural Sensitivity (DMIS). Bennett's DMIS consists of six stages grouped into three Ethnocentric Stages and three Ethnorelative stages. The three Ethnocentric

Stages (Denial Stage, Defense Stage and Minimization Stage) describe varying degrees in which the individual's culture is the central worldview. Each Ethnocentric Stage is defined as follows:

- **Stage 1—Denial:** The individual denies the difference or existence of other cultures by erecting psychological or physical barriers in the forms of isolation and separation from other cultures.
- **Stage 2—Defense:** The individual reacts against the threat of other cultures by denigrating the other cultures (negative stereotyping) and promoting the superiority of one's own culture. *Reversal Phase—In some cases, the individual undergoes a reversal phase, during which the worldview shifts from one's own culture to the other culture, and the own culture is subject to disparagement.
- **Stage 3—Minimization:** The individual acknowledges cultural differences on the surface but considers all cultures as fundamentally similar.

The three Ethnorelative Stages (Acceptance Stage, Adaptation Stage and Integration Stage) describe the individual's more complex worldviews in which cultures are understood relative to each other and actions are understood as culturally situated. Individuals in these stages are considered to exhibit intercultural sensitivity toward cultural differences. Bennett defines each Ethnorelative Stage as follows:

- **Stage 4—Acceptance:** The individual accepts and respects cultural differences with regard to behavior and values.
- **Stage 5—Adaptation:** The individual develops the ability to shift his frame of reference to other culturally diverse worldviews through empathy and pluralism.
- **Stage 6—Integration:** The individual expands and incorporates other worldviews into his own worldview.

In order to reduce the researcher's subjectivity in the assessment, a second rater also evaluated the learner statements independently. Although both raters agreed on the DMIS stages for the majority of the postings that addressed the salient cultural topic, both raters met to discuss and agree on the three (out of 44) postings where they initially disagreed. In order to investigate the influence of the pedagogical interventions in each discussion phase, the researcher calculated the percentage of ethnocentric (DMIS stages 1-3) postings and ethnorelative (DMIS stages 4-6) postings for each phase of the discussion—the authentic texts for Phase 1 and French informant interviews for Phase 2—with attention to learners' explicit comments about specific forms of cultural instruction on their thinking. Once the percentages of ethnocentric and ethnorelative postings were calculated for each phase of the discussion, a comparison was made to detect *collective shifts* from learners' ethnocentric thinking to enthorelative thinking (stages 4-6), or vice versa, between the two phases of the discussion.

RESULTS

There were 44 postings made over Discussion 3—21 for in Phase 1 and 23 in Phase 2. For Phase 1 of the discussion, 15 of the 21 postings concerned the PACS, the most frequently discussed cultural practice in Phase 1. The majority of postings (9/15) were made by individuals evaluated in ethnorelative stages (6 Acceptance, 3 Adaptation) of the DMIS and six postings were made by individuals assessed in ethnocentric stages (3 Defense, 3 Minimization) as illustrated in the following examples.

Examples of Ethnorelative Perspective Statement from Phase 1 of Discussion 3

Example 1: With divorce happening so often after marriage, it seems as though [French] people are just starting to commit to each other in their own way and avoiding marriage all together. (Acceptance Stage)

Example 2: The increase of PACS in France is interesting and reminds me of a common wealth union here in the States. Although "couple hood" isn't so celebrated here and I think the French are on to something. (Adaptation Stage)

Examples of Ethnocentric Perspective Statements from Phase 1 of Discussion 3

Example 3: Marriage just doesn't mean as much these days; it is too easily replaced [in France]. (Defense Stage)

Example 4: I think it's wicked interesting that France has a significantly lower divorce rate than the US despite the apparent popularity of cohabitation, having children out of wedlock, and civil partnerships that I keep hearing are going to 'destroy the sanctity of marriage.' (Reversal phase of Defense Stage)

Example 5: The idea of family life is changing and seems to be affected all around the world…. (Minimization Stage)

The participants evaluated in ethnocentric stages either contrasted French and American perspectives with evaluative statements, stating a preference for one cultural practice over the other (Examples 3-4), or minimized cultural differences, claiming all cultures are the same (Example 5).

For the second phase of the Discussion 3, students were instructed to access the French informant videos on YouTube. Three of the four French informants explained their disrespect for the PACS. Only one French informant described

Figure 1. A comparison of learners' intercultural sensistivity in Phase 1 to Phase 2

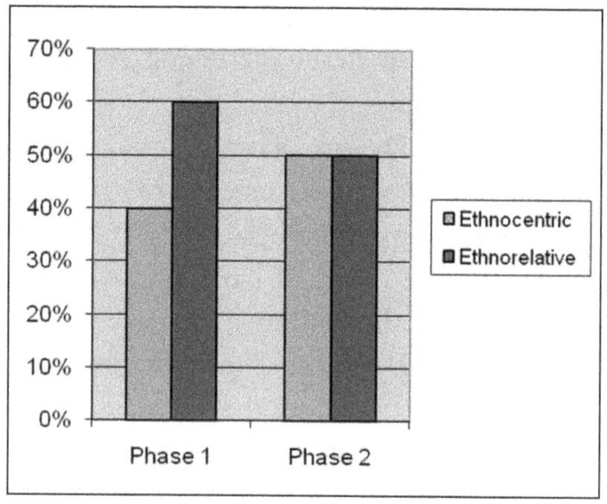

why she would have considered the PACS over a marriage, had it existed prior to her own marriage. The other French informants' judgmental thinking was perpetuated among many students, and a slight shift occurred from ethnorelative to ethnocentric thinking (see Figure 1).

Half of the 16 postings (8/16) reflected the ethnocentric defense perspectives afforded by three of the four French informants who stated that the PACS were lesser of a union than a marriage and/or that the PACS is primarily being abused for social gain. The other half of the postings (8/16) still reflected the ethnorelative thinking (2 Acceptance, 5 Adaptation, 1 Integration) that dominated Phase 1 of the discussion. Examples of comments for each DMIS stage found in Phase 2 are demonstrated below.

Example of Ethnocentric Perspective Statements from Phase 2 of Discussion 3

Example 6: Realizing now the stigma that must come with doing a PACS, I can understand why none of the interviewees really agreed with it. The abuse of the PACS reminds me of the abuse of the welfare system here, so that's not surprising. (Defense Stage)

Examples of Ethnorelative Perspective Statements from Phase 2 of Discussion 3

Example 7: I thought it was interesting that Thomas and Florence said that the PACS were originally for gay couples. I agree when Florence said that it is time to move on from that thinking to include more couples and situations. (Acceptance Stage)

Example 8: I guess I was a little surprised that he (Thomas) said marriage is for people in love, and PACS are a lesser of a union, but I think it has much to do with tradition (Adaptation Stage)

Example 9: Similarly, I don't understand why so many people in the US are against letting gay couples enter a legal contract, since that's basically all that marriage is, at least in terms of the law (like getting health insurance, cosigning a loan, filing your taxes, etc.). As Florence tells us, there's still a place for religious weddings in French society. (Integration Stage)

Half of the participants either appropriated the negative, judgmental perspectives of the three French informants who claimed that the PACS was being abused (Example 6) or the participants critiqued French culture in general due to perceived hypocrisies between the acceptance of the PACS in the authentic texts compared to the predominately judgmental French perspectives in the French informant videos. For example, one of the participants assessed in the Defense Stage expressed her disappointment in the conflicting French perspectives presented stating; "the seemingly not so positive view of PACS in France is a bit of a paradox considering the image of progress France portrays to the United States." Another participant alluded to feeling duped for initially accepting the French perspectives in the authentic texts, and wrote "despite France's air of progress [...] obviously there is more progress to be made." The "air of progress" to which the participant may be referring was found in the authentic text which stated the number of people doing the PACS continued to increase every year since its creation in 1999 with close to 50% of the population choosing the PACS over a wedding in 2008.

The other half of the comments made in Phase 2 of the discussion reflected ethnorelative thinking. The ethnorelative comments either reflected the perspective of the sole French participant who did not pass judgment on the PACS (Examples 7 and 9) or put into question the other three French informants' opinions as misrepresentation of French culture (Example 8). Therefore, in response to the research question concerning the factors in the discussions that influence collective shifts in learners' intercultural sensitivity, the French informant videos appeared to influence a slight collective shift in learners' thinking as reflected in the increase in ethnocentric statements citing three of the four French informants in Phase 2. However, contrary to previous research, the authentic texts were not ignored in this discussion. In fact, the authentic texts appeared to foster several learners' ethnorelative thinking in Phase 2 of the discussion, despite contradicting statements made by the majority of French informants. In fact, many of the ethnorelative statements noted that the French informants' perspectives did not seem to align with the overall societal norm, drawing from the information presented in the authentic texts.

DISCUSSION

Findings from this study modify previous claims (Garrett-Rucks, 2013) of an optimal design for computer-mediated cultural instruction to promote intercultural sensitivity in online discussions. In the present study, the same learners from Garrett-Rucks' (2013) previous study participated in an additional five week discussion about French family practices. What differed was that the OLI culture learning website in the present study contained no explicit cultural instruction, only an outdated authentic text. Additionally, the French informants in Phase 2 of the present study emphasized personal views that conflicted with those presented as societal norms in the authentic texts. Also, the French informants in Discussion 3 could not compare French and US PACS practices because it does not exist in US culture.

Findings from this study corroborate previous research (Garrett-Rucks, 2013) that found the medium of delivery for the cultural instruction—the use of French informant videos—to be persuasive in perpetuating NS perspectives, only here those perspectives perpetuated ethnocentric thinking. For example, in the Phase 2 Defense Stage example above, a student appropriated French informants' perspectives that there is a stigma with doing the PACS in France, and subsequently the learner shifted from an ethnorelative to ethnocentric evaluation. None-the-less, the unfortunate shift away from predominate ethnorelative thinking toward the PACS in Phase 1 of the discussion to more ethnocentric thinking in Phase 2 in the current study provides valuable insight to the design of optimal computer-mediated cultural instruction currently found in the literature (Garrett-Rucks, 2013) around three major points: (1) the use of French informant videos; (2) the use of authentic texts; (3) the inclusion of French perspectives about US cultural practices.

Contrary to previous research findings where collective shifts away from learners' ethnocentric thinking were detected after exposure to French informant perspectives in Phase 2, the video-recorded interviews here perpetuated ethnocentric thinking. Following previous suggestions for optimal cultural instruction, the French informants in this study were deliberately selected to represent diverse perspectives within French culture. As noted by Kramsch (1993), exposure to diverse target-culture members' perspectives is necessary to break monolithic L2 learners' stereotypes, or imagined images of the target culture. Accordingly, the four French informants differed in age (20-60), gender, and level of education (no high school degree to pursuing a Ph.D.), each with differing levels of familiarity with the United States (see Appendix A for French informant profiles). However, contrary to previous research that found that the perspectives provided by the diverse French informants in the videos afforded learners an opportunity to personally relate to an alternate perspective which they may not have previously considered (Garrett-Rucks, 2013), nearly all of the French informants (three of the four) in this study shared a common judgmental perspective toward the alternate marital practice in their society, the PACS. The learners assessed at ethnocentric levels of thinking either appropriated the defensive voices of the judgmental French informants, or commented on the prior misrepresentation of French culture in the authentic texts, as they expressed their belief that the majority of French people are opposed to the PACS based solely on the perspectives provided by the French informants. This phenomenon corroborates Garrett-Rucks' (2013) previous findings, that the French informant perspectives from the YouTube videos are influential on learners' thinking. Yet in the present study, the French informants' perspectives conflicted with the cultural norm, as stated in the authentic texts. Despite attention to selecting a diverse group of French informants, the collective lack of approval of the PACS—a minority perspective in French culture as stated in the authentic texts based on national surveys—emerged. This anomaly brings attention to the fact that selecting diverse French informants does not suffice, rather close attention needs to be paid to the representative L2 perspectives to assure a more accurate depiction of the target-culture norm.

The contradictions between the French perspectives reported by the informants and the authentic texts appeared to frustrate and anger some of the learners as represented in the findings. The Defense Stage postings revealed these learners' tendency to rely more on the perspectives represented in the videos than the authentic texts. On the contrary, the postings that reflected ethnorelative thinking commonly either (1) appropriated the words from the sole French informant who accepted the PACS as an equal union or (2) contained a critique of the validity of the other three French informants' perspectives as representative of the cultural norm based on the contradictory information in the authentic texts that stated nearly 50% of the population was choosing the PACS over a marriage. Contrary to previous research where the authentic texts were ignored when explicit cultural information also existed in Phase 1, the French perspectives in the authentic texts in the current study were influential on learners' thinking.

In addition to inaccurately representing the general French opinion of PACS, the French informants in this study did not address similar US cultural practices during their interviews unlike the previous study. Because the PACS does not exist in US culture, the informants were not asked to discuss this topic. However, French perspectives toward a similar alternate cultural practice, such as common-law marriage, could possibly have been helpful in fostering learners' intercultural sensitivity. It is possible that hearing an outsider's perspective toward one's own cultural practice was needed to create the distance necessary for learners to step back and look at their own culture through the eyes of the other, thus fostering their intercultural sensitivity. Over twenty years ago, Byrnes (1991) suggested an emphasis on the subjective component of culture, serving as a precursor to current pedagogical approaches of intercultural learning. In this same vein Kramsch (1993) described the need for cultural reflection to take place in a negotiated space, which she refers to as a third place, the location between the learners' first culture and the target culture, where all behavior (both that of others and that of oneself) is seen as being grounded in a particular cultural context and a space of intellectual comparison, critique and distance. Findings from this study suggest that there is a danger in perpetuating ethnocentric thinking when outsider perspectives of one's own cultural practices are not emphasized in cultural instruction, a notion not currently reflected in the *Cultures Standards.*

LIMITATIONS AND DIRECTIONS FOR FUTURE RESEARCH

The authentic texts in this study appeared to be more influential on learners' perspectives than in previous research where they were mostly ignored in the presence of explicit cultural instruction. None-the-less, the majority of participants relied more on the French informant videos to inform their worldviews as reflected in the postings on the classroom discussion board. Similar to previous research findings, the French informant videos were found to be persuasive on learners' worldviews of alternate cultural practices. However, it is important to keep in mind that these French informants may have been more credible for learners than the anonymous French perspectives presented in the authentic texts due to the fact that somebody who the learners knew personally, the researcher who presented the study the first day of class, was conducting the YouTube interviews. The personal connection and the credibility of the French perspectives may have been influenced by the perceived proximity of the French informants to many of the participants. In addition, a study on the use of videos in YouTube format versus traditional DVDs that commonly accompany modern textbooks is needed to investigate if learners are more sensitive to the medium of the video representation, than solely to video formats. It is possible that YouTube, a site commonly used among today's youth, may have made the French informants appear more personable. Rendering French informant videos personal to learners may be an important element to consider in future research of the optimal design of computer-mediated cultural instruction. Future research investigating the multiple affective dimensions of target-culture informant videos, particularly the influence of target-culture perspectives of one's own culture, is needed to fully understand the potential of video use in computer-mediated cultural instruction.

There is great value in maximizing the understanding of effective uses of L2 informant videos in FL instruction. It is often difficult for FL instructors to coordinate groups of representatives from the TL to come into a FL course due to their availability during the instructor's class time. In addition, the curriculum does not always permit time for guest speakers during classroom instruction. The use of videos of pre-recorded target culture informant interviews not only allows the instructor more freedom in time management for integrating the interviews into the curriculum, but it also allows the instructor more control of the type of information the informants are disseminating to the learners. If indeed videos are a powerful tool for promoting cross-cultural understanding, as a profession we should attempt to identify which aspects of informant video-recordings render videos most useful.

Previous research on intercultural exchanges in discussion forums report positive findings when learners had the opportunity for exchanges of perspectives, opinions and views with members of the target culture (Furstenberg, Levet, English, & Maillet, 2001; Hanna & de Nooy, 2003; Wade, 2005). This study contributes to the paucity of studies looking at *intracultural* discussions, peer classroom discussions, rather than intercultural discussions. This is of utmost importance because TL use FL classrooms are not always conducive to the type of deep reflection necessary to promote intercultural learning, particularly in beginning courses where learners' have little mastery over TL use. The use of online classroom discussions outside of the classroom in learners' L1 can provide an option for instructors to maintain the use of the TL in beginning level FL courses while promoting intercultural learning outside of the classroom. However, findings from this study revealed the need to closely consider the design of computer-mediated cultural discussions, particularly when considering the input, or cultural instruction that learners will discuss. In particular, this study brings attention to the usefulness of authentic texts rather than providing explicit cultural lessons and the need to pay close attention to French informant perspectives in cultural instruction to assure a more accurate depiction of the target-culture norms. In addition, findings from this study suggest there is a strong need for US learners to have exposure to French informant perspectives of US culture in order to see their own culture through the eyes of "the other," a consideration currently neglected in the *Cultures Standards.*

Today's language teachers face distinct challenges and opportunities to help learners understand languages and cultures other than their own in the increasingly multicultural nature of globalized societies. This chapter explored the effectiveness of pedagogical practices intended to foster learners' development of intercultural sensitivity outside of the classroom while preserving L2 use inside the classroom. The call for the need to help our students learn to "see the world through others' eyes" through the study of another language is prevalent, yet the profession still remains divided on how to integrate cultural instruction in the classroom. There is a strong need in our field for additional discussion and research on ways to integrate meaningful cultural reflection into the beginning FL curriculum while maintaining TL use in the classroom. I hope that this chapter provides the impetus for further research in the ways in which online discussions about cultural practices can help foster learners' intercultural sensitivity. It is time to search for ways to facilitate FL students' understanding of cultures around the world at all levels of instruction as intercultural sensitivity will no doubt be one of the most important skills graduates everywhere will need to possess in this century.

REFERENCES

Abrahms, Z. (2006). From theory to practice: Intracultural CMC use in the L2 classroom. In L. Ducate, & N. Arnold (Eds.), *Calling on CALL: From theory and research to new directions in foreign language teaching* (pp. 181–210). San Marcos, TX: CALICO.

Belz, J. (2002). Social dimensions of telecollaborative foreign language study. *Language Learning & Technology*, *6*(1), 60–81.

Belz, J. (2005). Intercultural questioning, discovery and tension in internet-mediated language learning partnerships. *Language and Intercultural Communication*, *5*, 3–37. doi:10.1080/14708470508668881

Belz, J., & Müller–Hartmann, A. (2003). Teachers as intercultural learners: Negotiating German–American telecollaboration along the institutional fault line. *Modern Language Journal*, *87*(1), 71–89. doi:10.1111/1540-4781.00179

Bennett, J. M. (1993). Toward ethnorelativism: A developmental model of intercultural sensitivity. In R. M. Paige (Ed.), *Education for the intercultural experience* (pp. 21–71). Yarmouth, ME: Intercultural Press.

Bennett, M. J. (1997). How not to be a fluent fool: Understanding the cultural dimension of language. In A. Fantini (Ed.), *New ways in teaching culture* (pp. 16–21). Alexandria, VA: TESOL Inc.

Byrnes, H. (1991). Reflections on the development of cross-cultural communicative competence in the foreign language classroom. In B. Freed (Ed.), *Foreign language acquisition research* (pp. 205–218). Lexington, VA: D. C. Heath and Company.

Charmaz, K. (2006). *Constructing grounded theory: A practical guide through qualitative analysis*. London, CA: Sage.

Cutshall, S. (2012). More than a decade of Standards: Integrating cultures in your language instruction. *Language and Education*, *7*, 32–37.

Darhower, M. (2002). Interactional features of synchronous computer-mediated communication in the intermediate L2 class: A sociocultural case study. *CALICO Journal*, *19*(2), 249–277.

Fantini, A. (2011). Language: An essential component of intercultural communicative competence. In J. Jackson (Ed.), *Routledge handbook of language and intercultural communication* (pp. 263–278). London: Routledge.

Fox, R., & Diaz-Greenberg, R. (2006). Culture, multiculturalism, and foreign/ world language standards in US teacher preparation programs: Toward a discourse of dissonance. *European Journal of Teacher Education*, *29*(3), 401–422. doi:10.1080/02619760600795270

Furstenberg, G., Levet, S., English, K., & Maillet, K. (2001). Giving a virtual voice to the silent language of culture: The CULTURA Project. *Language Learning & Technology*, *5*(1), 55–102.

Garrett-Rucks, P. (2013). Maximizing cross-cultural understanding, minimizing stereotypes: Three case studies. *French Review (Deddington)*, *86*(5), 14–33.

Hanna, B., & de Nooy, J. (2003). A funny thing happened on the way to the forum: Electronic discussion and foreign language learning. *Language Learning & Technology*, *7*(1), 71–85.

Kern, R. (1995). Restructuring classroom interaction with networked computers: Effects on quantity and characteristics of language production. *Modern Language Journal*, *79*(4), 457–476. doi:10.1111/j.1540-4781.1995.tb05445.x

Kern, R., Ware, P., & Warschauer, M. (2004). Crossing frontiers: New directions in online pedagogy and research. *Annual Review of Applied Linguistics*, *24*, 243–260. doi:10.1017/S0267190504000091

Kinginger, C. (2004). Communicative foreign language teaching through tele-collaboration. In O. St. John, K. van Esch, & E. Schalkwijk (Eds.), *New insights into foreign language learning and teaching* (pp. 101–113). Frankfurt: Peter Lang.

Kramsch, C. (1993). *Context and culture in language teaching*. Oxford: Oxford University Press.

Kramsch, C., & Thorne, S. (2002). Foreign language learning as global communicative practice. In D. Block, & D. Cameron (Eds.), *Globalization and language teaching* (pp. 83–100). London: Routledge.

Kumaravadivelu, B. (2003). *Beyond methods: Macrostrategies for language teaching*. New Haven, CT: Yale University Press.

Lomicka, L. (2006). Understanding the other: Intercultural exchange and CMC. In L. Ducate, & N. Arnold (Eds.), *Calling on CALL: From theory and research to new directions in foreign language teaching* (pp. 211–236). San Marcos, TX: CALICO.

McBride, K., & Wildner-Basset, M. (2008). Interpersonal and intercultural understanding in a blended second culture classroom. In S. Sieloff Magnan (Ed.), *Mediating discourse online* (pp. 93–124). Philadelphia, PN: John Benjamins. doi:10.1075/aals.3.08mcb

Meunier, L. (1998). Personality and motivational factors in computer-mediated foreign language communication. In J. A. Muyskens (Ed.), *New ways of learning and teaching: Focus on technology and FL education* (pp. 145–197). Boston, MA: Heinle & Heinle.

Müller-Hartmann, A. (2000). The role of tasks in promoting intercultural learning in electronic learning networks. *Language Learning & Technology*, *4*(2), 129–147.

National Standards in Foreign Language Education Project. (1996). *Standards for foreign language learning in the 21st century*. Yonkers, NY: Allen Press.

National Standards in Foreign Language Education Project. (1999). *Standards for foreign language learning in the 21st century*. Yonkers, NY: Allen Press.

National Standards in Foreign Language Education Project. (2006). *Standards for foreign language learning in the 21st century*. Lawrence, KS: Allen Press.

O'Dowd, R. (2003). Understanding the 'other side': Intercultural learning a Spanish-English e-mail exchange. *Language Learning & Technology*, *7*(2), 118–144.

Phillips, J., & Abbott, M. (2011). A decade of standards: Impact, influence, and future directions. Available from, http://www.actfl.org/sites/default/files/pdfs/public/national-standards-2011.pdf

Thorne, S. (2003). Artifacts and cultures-of-use in intercultural communication. *Language Learning & Technology*, *7*(2), 38–67.

Wade, E. (2005). *Enhancing German language learners' intercultural communicative competence through the on-line exchange project ICE*. (Doctoral dissertation). University of California, Santa Barbara, CA.

Ware, P. (2005). 'Missed' communication in online communication: Tensions in a German-American telecollaboration. *Language Learning & Technology*, *9*(2), 64–89.

Ware, P., & Kramsch, C. (2005). Toward an intercultural stance: Teaching German and English through telecollaboration. *Modern Language Journal*, *89*(2), 190–205. doi:10.1111/j.1540-4781.2005.00274.x

Warschauer, M. (1996). Comparing face-to-face and electronic discussion in the second language classroom. *CALICO Journal*, *13*, 7–25.

Warschauer, M., Shetzer, H., & Meloni, C. (2000). *Internet for English teaching*. Alexandria, VA: TESOL Publications.

ADDITIONAL READING

Garrett-Rucks, P. (2012). Byram versus Bennett: Assessment discrepancies in learners' IC development. *Proceedings of Intercultural Competence Conference*. Vol 2, 11–33.

Garrett-Rucks, P. (2013). Demystifying the *Cultures Standards*: A review of projects and assessments in the professional literature. *Foreign Language Association of Georgia Journal (Fall)*, 7–14.

Garrett-Rucks, P. (2013). A discussion-based online approach to fostering deep cultural inquiry in an introductory language course. *Foreign Language Annals*, *46*(2), 191–212.

Garrett-Rucks, P. (in press). Measuring instructed language learners' IC development: Discrepancies between assessment models by Byram and Bennett. *International Journal of Intercultural Relations*. doi: doi:10.1016/j.ijintrel.2013.12.009

KEY TERMS AND DEFINITIONS

Cultural Instruction: The teaching of culture.

Computer-mediated Discourse: The communication produced when human beings interact with one another by transmitting messages via networked computer.

Cross-cultural Understanding: An awareness of the perspectives found in target cultures, both towards their own culture as well as the learners.

Intercultural Competence: The ability to communicate effectively and appropriately with people of other cultures.

APPENDIX A: FRENCH INFORMANT PROFILES

French Informant	Gender/Age	Region in France	Familiarity with life in the United States
Thomas	M/20	Grenoble	Arrived in the United States 2 days prior to interview for a year- long university exchange program
Sophie	F/25	Mostly the south of France, 2 years in Tahiti (her Dad was in the French navy)	Starting her second year of a French literature Master's program in the United States.
Florence	F/31	Orleans	Starting her 6th year in the United States in a French literature Ph.D. program. She's been married to an American for 5 years.
Aunt Anne	F/ 60	Bordeaux	Aunt Anne has never been to the United States. Her niece married an American and has been residing in the United States for 7 years.

APPENDIX B: FRENCH INFORMANT INTERVIEW PROTOCOL

(5 to 7 minutes per discussion)

- Do you know many people who have done the PACS? Would you consider doing it? What do you think influences one's decision to either get married or do a PACS?
- Does it seem to you that people are getting married later in life? If so, what do you think influences this decision?
- Have you noticed more people deciding to not have children, or to have smaller families? What do you think influences ones decision on family planning?
- Do you perceive differences between how the French perceive the value of "the family" to the way Americans view "the family?"

APPENDIX C: DISCUSSION 3 PROMPTS

Module 4: Leçon 10 La vie quotidienne- famille*: (Chapter 10: les différentes définitions de la famille en France)/*

Part One: Reaction to OLI lesson and Text

Posting 1: Initial Reaction to the OLI Lesson and Texts

Respond to the following discussion prompts below (with a minimum of 50 words)

- Discuss your thoughts and reactions to the information about the different definitions of family presented in the OLI lesson and the text provided. For example, state what surprised you in the OLI lesson and text or how the text you read provided a different perspective from the OLI lesson and why you think this might be. Please be sure to state the source, either the OLI lesson or the text when describing your reactions.

- Please also discuss why you think there might be similar or different perspectives towards "the family" in French culture compared to American culture? (Please feel free to share your personal experiences and views)

Posting 2: First Peer Response Postings (Minimum of Two Postings Required)

- Respond to at least two of your classmates' postings explaining to them why you agree or disagree with statements or opinions made in their postings.
- Do NOT respond to any of the posting until after the due date for the first posting so all students have an opportunity to express their opinions.

Part Two: Reaction to Interviews (recorded in the fall of 2008)

Posting 3: Initial Posting

- First access video of interviews with French citizens (Available under course documents on Blackboard) discussing their perspectives about the different definitions of the French family.
- After viewing the interviews with French citizens, use a minimum of 50 words to discuss the perspectives about the French definitions of family from the interviews compared to what you read in the OLI lesson, text, and discussion board.

Posting 4: Second Peer Response Postings (Minimum of Two Postings Required)

- Respond to at least two of your classmates' postings explaining to them why you agree or disagree with statements or opinions made in their postings.
- Do NOT respond to any of the posting until after the due date for the first posting so all students have an opportunity to express their opinions.

Posting 5: Last Posting for Discussion 1

Use a minimum of 50 words, describing your final impressions about the French definitions of family relating your opinions to previous remarks made on the discussion board and the interviews with the French citizens.

Chapter 6
Offline Peer Dialogue in Asynchronous Computer-Mediated Communication Activities for L2 Teacher Development

Keiko Kitade
Ritsumeikan University, Japan

ABSTRACT

Recent studies in second language (L2) teacher education (L2TE) emphasize the sociohistorical and contextual dimensions of teachers' professional development. In practice, however, teaching practice opportunities, which can help pre-service teachers experience these dimensions, are limited. Innovative technological applications can help address this issue. This chapter proposes a combination of offline and online activities in which pre-service language teachers can engage L2 learners online while augmenting their own learning through offline peer dialogues. Rooted in the sociocultural approach to learning, this chapter presents a case study analyzing the Critical Learning Episodes (CLEs; Kiely & Davis, 2010) found in the peer dialogues of pre-service teachers during their online engagement with L2 learners abroad. The findings suggest that offline peer dialogue serves as an advanced type of reflection-in-practice (Schön, 1983, 1987), utilizing text mediation, a method that assists student teachers to co-construct the situated knowledge and skills that are holistic in nature (thus requiring multiple perspectives) and purportedly crucial for L2 teaching.

INTRODUCTION

Studies on second language teacher education (L2TE) from a sociocultural perspective indicate that it is crucial for teachers' professional development that they engage in active negotiation with the social aspects of their teaching practice (e.g., Johnson, 2009; Kanno & Stuart, 2011). To promote active learning by student teachers, they need to engage in actual teaching practice that also incorporates reflective practice in order to become aware of the context of their teaching. However,

DOI: 10.4018/978-1-4666-6174-5.ch006

most studies on teacher development have focused on the conditions of student teachers' learning in the workplace, as pointed out by Miller (2009). Few studies approach the issue of how to provide the social and cognitive scaffolding needed in the L2TE program in order for pre-service teachers to be able to prepare themselves to participate more fully in their future teaching contexts.

This study attempts to utilize *computer-mediated communication* (CMC) to provide pre-service teachers of Japanese with the opportunity to engage in online tutoring practice with L2 learners of Japanese, combined with an innovative reflective practice, namely offline peer dialogue. By investigating the effectiveness of online tutoring practice incorporating this unique type of reflective practice — offline peer dialogue — this study will explore ways to enhance L2 teachers' professional development through online engagement with L2 learners.

Online Engagement in L2TE: A Sociocultural Perspective

Web 2.0 is comprised of advanced Internet technology and applications including blogs, wikis, rich site summary [RSS], and social bookmarking. One of Web 2.0's crucial advantages for L2 learning and L2 teacher education (L2TE) is the increased possibilities it offers teachers and learners to engage with other people worldwide (e.g., Wang & Vasquez, 2012; Warschauer & Grimes, 2007). A rich research tradition has explored the beneficial aspects of CMC for L2 teacher development and L2 learning by connecting learners and teachers cross-institutionally. Some studies in L2TE have investigated the effects of authentic experience in online engagement with L2 learners and collaboration among teachers (including pre-service teachers) on the development of the teachers' electronic media literacy and autonomy (Fuchs, Hauck, & Müller-Hartmann, 2012) and intercultural competence (Müller-Hartmann, 2006). Another extensive research tradition in cross-institutional collaboration among L2 learners and teachers has examined the social advantages offered by new technology, using a sociocultural theory (SCT) approach (e.g., Lantolf & Thorne, 2006; Thorne & Tasker, 2011).

Studies of SCT (e.g., Thorne, 2003; Warschauer, 1997) have understood CMC to be a computer-mediated tool for human activity and development. According to this perspective, language is a semiotic tool that mediates actions and higher-order mental functions (Vygotsky, 1978). Thus, any social interaction, such as collaborative dialogue or teaching practice, is considered a mediating tool with tremendous impact on human development. Additionally, studies in L2TE based on SCT emphasize the significance of the contextual and social aspects of teaching and teacher training (e.g., Freeman, 2002; Johnson, 2009).

Alongside the mediated roles of CMC media in teaching and learning practices, certain key elements of CMC can further improve and optimize online practice in L2TE. One such key element is the opportunity it presents for pre-service L2 teachers to engage with distance learners. Some student teachers in preparation programs may have the chance to participate in a teaching practicum or an internship abroad (especially in the case of native-speaking teachers of sociopolitically powerful languages like English, where there is some job demand even for inexperienced teachers). However, because of locational, temporal, and financial constraints, as well as the difficulty of finding cooperative institutions abroad with teachers available to mentor practicum students, the opportunities are still quite limited for these pre-service L2 teachers to communicate with or teach learners who live abroad (Richards, 2008). Nevertheless, it is crucial that student teachers become aware of the socially and historically various learning environments of learners abroad before the completion of their program of study. Through actual engagement with L2 learners in a new context, L2 teachers interacting with students abroad face challenges to their initial beliefs, values, and knowledge, which they must then reconstruct to reflect their new understanding (Johnson, 2006; 2009; Kanno & Stuart, 2011). Online interactions with L2 learners offer learning-in-practice opportunities for pre-service teachers to become fully-fledged teachers through direct engagement with L2 learners (Kitade, 2014).

The other important element in CMC for L2TE is the enhancement of teachers' reflective process. The L2TE based on SCT emphasizes *transformative teacher education*, that is, teachers are expected to be active agents in their own training and teaching (Freeman, 2002; Richards, 2008), instead of being reactive learners of general pedagogical knowledge (as offered through traditional education). To enhance active learning, various types of reflective practice, such as peer dialogue and self-reflection, have been proposed (e.g., Freeman, 2002; Miller, 2007; Richards, 1996). Reflective practice is defined as "active, persistent, and careful consideration of any belief or practice in light of the reasons that support it and the further consequences to which it leads" (Dewey, 1933, p. 118). It is believed to enhance the ability of teachers to integrate new discoveries and knowledge while negotiating previous identities and discourses and transforming themselves in the process (Miller, 2007). In particular, researchers have opined that asynchronous CMC (ACMC) is an effective tool for reflective interaction because of its time flexibility, allowing abundant time to complete tasks and thus amplifying the advantages of text mediation for higher mental development in learners (Lamy & Goodfellow, 1999; Lapadat, 2002). Time flexibility and accessibility of previous texts allow users to monitor, analyze, and reflect on interactions with their teachers and peers, thus also monitoring their own learning process. Further, teachers who teach through ACMC may be able to use the extra time afforded them by the technology to compose more carefully considered responses to their students (Hall & Knox, 2009).

Recent studies on L2 teachers' technology-mediated learning suggest that L2 or pre-service teachers engaged in online practitioner communities are able to develop their reflective skills effectively (Lord & Lomicka, 2007). The discussion that takes place in these communities deepens the teachers' pedagogical knowledge and understanding of technology, both of which can be applied to their teaching practice (e.g., Arnold & Ducate, 2006; Arnold, Ducate, Lomicka, & Lord, 2009). Lord and Lomicka (2007) examined the types and amount of reflection involved in different journaling practices and found that social journaling practice (face-to-face or in online groups) yielded a greater amount of journaling output and more in-depth reflection compared with individual journaling. These results also indicate that electronic media, social presence, and format of practice can jointly impact the quantity and quality of reflection by teachers.

An increasing number of studies have explored the collaboration among teachers or between teachers and L2 learners in discussions, as mentioned earlier; however, only a limited number of studies in L2TE have investigated ways of connecting L2 teachers and learners online for actual teaching or tutoring practice, with careful pedagogical consideration of the potential and restrictions of new technology. Because mediating tools such as technology and language, when employed in any human activity (e.g., learning), play a crucial role in the outcome of that activity (Engeström, 1999; Leontiev, 1981), attentive pedagogical innovation is necessary to optimize the new opportunities brought about by advanced technology. Thus, the goal of this chapter is to explore the use and effects of an innovative reflective practice on L2 learning and the development of L2 teachers, as grounded in the principles of SCT. The specific practice is offline peer dialogue conducted through cross-institutional ACMC activity. The next section will discuss the potential role of offline peer dialogue on CMC activities for L2TE.

Offline Peer Dialogue in ACMC Activities as Reflective Practice

To promote active learning among teachers (e.g., Freeman, 2002; Richards, 2008), reflective practice has been emphasized in L2TE. Through reflection, teachers are able to critique their own teaching, resolve problems, and find more effective teaching methods (Burton, 2009). In terms of professional development, such practices help teachers critically observe their own beliefs and teaching styles and challenge themselves to incorporate new aspects into their teaching practice.

Various types of reflection, namely, oral (e.g., stimulated recall and discussion groups) or written (e.g., narratives and journaling) and collaborative (e.g., with experts and peers) or individual, can be practiced to promote teacher learning. To encourage meaningful reflection, its environment as well as the task of reflection itself should be carefully considered (Gustafson & Bennett, 2002). In proposing offline peer dialogue in asynchronous CMC as an innovative practice to promote active learning among teachers, there are some aspects of the theoretical background that support the practice, taking into account the unique features of new media and the collaborative aspect of learning suggested by SCT.

As mentioned above, the unique features of text-based ACMC afford time and text-mediation for the deepening of one's reflective process. However, the interval between interactions in ACMC leads to a lack of immediate feedback and interactivity, resulting in fewer opportunities for collaborative learning (Kitade, 2006). In fact, Lord and Lomicka (2008) explored cross-institutional collaborative learning among L2 teachers across different types of media and found that the use of an online discussion board is less preferred than synchronous discussion (i.e., face-to-face interaction or Internet chat) for the creation of a collaborative learning community.

To exploit the merits of ACMC and compensate for its shortcomings, certain researchers have suggested a hybrid practice incorporating offline dialogue with peers along with online engagement. In the context of L2 learning, Kitade (2008) examined offline metalinguistic conversation among peers in hybrid practice and suggested that these learners can co-construct knowledge with their classmates by monitoring their language use and understanding of their online partners' messages while simultaneously focusing on task content in online interaction with their partners. Figure 1 illustrates the proposed online-offline hybrid learning practice for L2 teacher learning in this study. This practice is modified based on the L2 learning model suggested by Kitade (2008). With this practice, L2 teachers are able to engage in actual teaching and tutoring practice with distance learners online (as illustrated in the upper part of Figure 1) while participating in collaborative dialogue with their peers (as shown in the lower part of Figure 1). In this hybrid process, the L2 teachers are able to use the abundant time offered between online exchanges to discuss with their peers how to respond to their online L2 learners.

Collaborative Peer Dialogue

The peer dialogue process of talk about text has been shown to be effective for children's learning (Wells, 1999). Through this collaborative activity, learners can receive assistance from their partners and engage in reflective thinking via text-based communication (e.g., de Guerrero & Villamil, 2000). This joint activity is supported by a Vygotskian perspective of learning (Vygotsky, 1978), in which knowledge and meaning are first constructed socially and then internalized. According to this view, cognitive development occurs as a result of collaborative dialogue between learners and helpers or partners, whose assistance allows the learners to bridge the gap between the level of development they are capable of attaining independently and what they are capable of achieving with guidance or assistance (the zone of proximal development or ZPD). Through

Figure 1. Combination of online and offline interaction in asynchronous computer-mediated communication (ACMC) activity. Note. L2Ls: L2 distance learners, On: online interaction

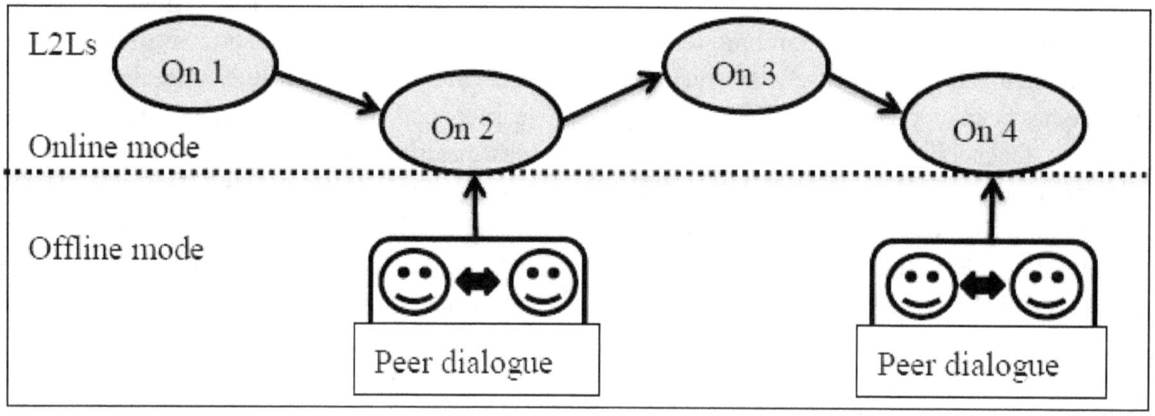

collaborative dialogue, learners use language as a mediated tool to solve problems, to share and construct knowledge, and to complete ideas (Swain, 2000; Swain, Lapkin, Knouzzi, Suzuki, & Brooks, 2009).

In this chapter, collaborative peer dialogue refers to practices where learners are able to expand their own knowledge and extend the development of their peers' knowledge through collaborative interaction (working together) to achieve a common goal. Offline peer dialogue is an innovative version of collaborative peer dialogue and it takes advantage of the time affordance between exchanges in ACMC to allow student teachers to engage in collaborative peer dialogue to discuss the meta-aspects of their teaching practice.

Bailey (1996) investigated the role of collaborative dialogue in L2TE and reported that student teachers were able to challenge their own conceptions of the topics they taught, to learn to perceive their classmates as resources for one another, and to realize the power of collaborative learning through personal experience. Similarly, Lord and Lomicka (2007) found dialogic journaling activity in L2TE to be more effective than individual journaling because the former better enables teachers to share ideas, provide advice, and offer suggestions to each other.

Besides being an effective pedagogical practice, joint activity plays a crucial role as a research method, as shown by previous studies revealing the mental processes of L2 learners engaged in ACMC activities. Specifically, Swain and Lapkin (1998) proposed that verbalization in a collaborative situation not only assists the knowledge-construction process but also makes learning observable because "in a joint problem-solving activity, what normally remains hidden in individually internalized thought may manifest itself in dialogue" (1998, p. 321). Although Swain and Lapkin make this statement regarding L2 learning rather than L2TE, an examination of the collaborative dialogue of L2 teachers should also shed light on their learning processes as engaged through their online engagement with L2 learners.

The offline peer dialogue proposed in this study offers a unique practice for the promotion of active learning among teachers, distinguishable from conventional reflective practices, which are typically carried out after completing a teaching session. Schön (1983, 1987) outlines a distinction between *reflection-in-action* and *reflection-on-action*: the former describes teachers' decision-making behaviors during their teaching practice, whereas the latter describes the process of reflection that takes place after teaching sessions. In reflection-in-action, teachers are in front of learners and under time constraints to reflect and act immediately; thus, the knowledge on which they can draw to make decisions is restricted to what they currently possess based on their previous experience. Taking advantage of the interactional features of ACMC, offline peer dialogue in ACMC activities may allow teachers to surpass the limitations of reflective practice such as these.

This chapter describes a case study that addresses the enhancement in the learning of student L2 teachers potentially achievable through online engagement with L2 learners abroad and investigates the role of offline peer dialogue among these teachers during the implementation of asynchronous online tutoring practices. I address the following questions:

1. In what ways does offline peer dialogue among student teachers during (online) ACMC teaching practice enhance their learning process?
2. How do the features of ACMC assist the learning process?

METHOD

Participants

The 17 participants in the study were third-year undergraduate students enrolled in a seminar class as part of a Japanese-language teacher-education program at a private Japanese university. Three of the participants were men and the rest were women; all were native Japanese-speakers aged 20 to 22 years at the time of the study. Five of the participants had had experience studying abroad for short periods (about three weeks), and one had been an exchange student in the United States for one year. None of them had had prior experience in teaching or tutoring L2 Japanese; however, some of them had joined a volunteer group to assist exchange students on campus.

The seminar in which the online and offline hybrid activities discussed in the present study were carried out as an undergraduate course taken during the third year of study, after the students had taken coursework in Japanese linguistics, general pedagogy, and curriculum development. In their fourth year, the students usually take an optional teaching practicum, start working on their theses and job-hunting. Thus, the two main objectives of the class are to bridge the gap between theoretical knowledge and the competence required in actual teaching practice, and to allow students to settle on individual thesis topics. The class is designed to encourage active learning among students by allowing them to engage with Japanese-language learners of various ability levels and backgrounds and also by the institution of reflective practice. The course includes three different online activities, each conducted online with a different Japanese class abroad. An overview of the course is provided in Figure 2.

Tasks

As mentioned above, after reading and presenting on texts in the research field of Japanese language or Japanese-language teaching, the student teachers interacted with L2 Japanese learners enrolled in three different college-level courses abroad. The first activity was with a beginner-level class in the United States, the second with an advanced-level class in China, and the third with a beginner-level class in South Korea. The online exchanges of each activity contained an average of approximately four communicative postings in Japanese (two each for the student teacher and the L2 learner) posted over a three-week period. The student teachers and learners engaged in interaction through a wiki page created on Wikispaces.com by the instructor (who is also the present researcher) (see Appendix One).

Figure 2. Content of the Japanese-language teacher-education seminar

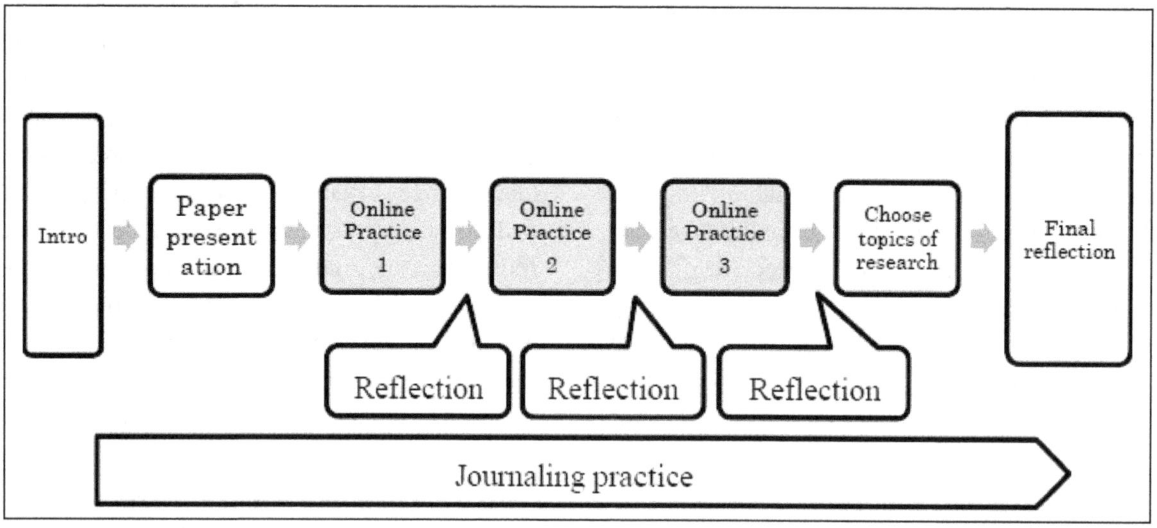

The online projects were carried out in groups of two or three student teachers and two or three learners, randomly assigned by the teachers of the L2 classes and of the student teacher seminar. The total number of groups for each online project was around 9 to 11, and new groups of student teachers were created for each project. The student teachers were instructed to work collaboratively offline in their groups/pairs to read and respond to the learners' posts. Most of the student teachers knew one another to a certain extent, since they had the same major and had taken similar courses during their first and second years in college. Each group sat together at a workstation to work on feedback practice. Their peer conversations were recorded using an integrated circuit (IC) recorder placed between each pair of interlocutors.

The student teachers were asked to post responses to the tasks for each project (for each class of learners) and to write feedback on the content of and the Japanese grammar and usage in their online partners' posts. The instructors of the Japanese L2 classes selected the tasks for each online project. The first project was to write a description of a memorable gift; the second project was to develop a self-promotion piece (called Self–Public Relations in Japanese) intended to help the writer prepare for job hunting in Japanese and in Japanese companies, and the third involved a description of a favorite meal.

To promote the student teachers' awareness of the learning they were expected to experience through online engagement with the L2 learners, individual journaling practice was assigned to each student teacher (or to each group of student teachers) starting on the first day of class. The student teachers were asked to start their journals by writing down their ideal teaching methods and learning practices and the reasons why they considered those methods and practices ideal. They were then asked to write down their new discoveries, questions, and difficulties regarding online practice on a weekly basis and to turn in their journals every week. At the end of the course, they were encouraged to re-read their own reflections in preparation for writing their final reflective papers.

Data Collection and Analysis

Data were collected from two different sources. The main data were from offline peer conversations among the student teachers while they were working on responses to learners' posts. The recordings were made by five volunteer pairs/groups for each of the first and second class projects (for a total of ten recordings); they lasted an average of 35.2 minutes for the first project and an average of 38.5 minutes for the second project. Due to difficulty scheduling the third project during class time, this project was carried out mainly outside regular class time, and the peer interactions in it were not recorded. All the recordings were transcribed by two research assistants based on the transcription system suggested by Szatrowski (1993) (see Appendix Two), designed to capture the details of participants' behaviors to capture crucial aspects of interactions such as pauses, overlaps, and tone of voice.

The other data source was the posts of L2 learners and student teachers on the wiki page of each group; these written data were analyzed with reference to the offline dialogue of student teachers. The advanced tools available on Wikispaces enabled the members of the wiki (i.e., the student teachers and L2 learners) and the instructors to trace the revision process of the participants' personalized pages in the wiki environment, showing when, how, and by whom the pages were revised. The (researcher)instructor took notes during and after the classroom observations. The instructor attempted to observe the activities of each group as well as the whole class; the observation of the non-verbal behaviors of each group was thus limited to the capacity of one observer. The data collected provided information on participants' non-verbal behaviors (e.g., how the student teachers placed themselves in the classroom and used the computer and/or other resources to carry out tasks).

The transcribed data from the offline dialogues were then analyzed to identify critical learning episodes (CLEs) (Kiely & Davis, 2010), which is defined as segments of interaction in the classroom that share three attributes: (1) boundaries, because it has an observable opening and closing; (2) a theme (for each conversational interaction, or hereafter, episode), and (3) significance, such as the resolution of a problem, a relevant realization, or new ideas that develop in relation to teacher learning. The concept of CLEs was developed from that of language-related episodes (LREs) in L2 learning research (e.g., Swain; 2006; Swain & Lapkin, 1998), which may serve as a type of protocol data (Gass & Mackey, 2000) revealing learners' cognitive processes during learning activities. To explore and capture the effects of an innovative pedagogical practice, as suggested by the perspective of action research (Burns, 2009; Kemmis & McTaggart, 1988), this study employs an inductive approach to documenting the learning aspects evidenced by the CLEs. In this study, the researcher identified 51 CLEs; then, the research assistant on the project (a graduate student in the Japanese language teacher program) was invited to independently identify CLEs. Two out of 51 initially identified CLEs were ultimately determined to be better viewed as parts of related episodes and re-classified as such. Thus, the total number of independent CLEs were 49.

RESULTS

Knowledge Constructed through Offline Peer Dialogue

Research question one asked, "How does offline peer dialogue among student teachers during (online) ACMC teaching practice enhance their learning process?" Overall, the results showed that the pre-service teachers encountered various types of decision-making opportunities while engaging in online feedback practice with their distance L2 learners. The content of the offline peer dialogues illustrate that the teachers analyzed the learners' language use, shared their thoughts, and participated in discussions aimed at discovering better tactics for providing feedback that was more appropriate to the needs of their online partners. The CLEs found in the data showed that the student teachers engaged in crucial discussions during the micro-process of giving feedback. These discussions involve setting criteria for learners' language use and emotional concerns, on which the teachers will base their feedback; determining how to correct learners' language usage; establishing effective ways of providing feedback; and identifying reasons for incorrect language usage on the part of the learners. In this section, representative samples of the data are discussed to demonstrate the process of collaborative knowledge construction among peers and the role of text-based ACMC media in this process. The first excerpt presents a typical example of participant discussions to identify reasons behind the Japanese learners' incorrect language use; the second excerpt presents the continuation of the same discussion, capturing student teachers' cognitive progress in searching for the effective way to correct learners' incorrect language usage and the moment when such an approach is found. The excerpts below clearly illustrate the process of realization of new knowledge that the pre-service teachers underwent as they engaged in peer dialogue. Through this collaborative dialogue, the student teachers came to better understand the reasons behind the learners' mistakes and to incorporate the multiple perspectives required in practicing feedback activity.

The CLE depicted in Excerpt 1 illustrates an instance of collaborative learning among the student teachers as they analyzed their student's language usage and provided feedback. Double slashes indicate places where a student teacher began speaking in the middle of his or her colleague's utterance. The transcription symbols used in the data are defined in Appendix Two. It shows how teachers co-constructed knowledge as they tried to figure out why a sentence posted by a L2 learner was incorrect. Student teachers Atsushi, Misa, and Chie (all are pseudo names) discussed how to provide useful feedback to their online partner in the U.S. These student teachers examined their online partner's attempt at a self-introduction paragraph, posted on the wiki page, in order to identify the incorrect parts and figure out how to provide the most useful feedback on them.

Excerpt 1: Dialogue between student teachers during ACMC activity with a Japanese-language class in the United States

215 Atsushi 確かになんでこれ気持ち悪く感じるのかな. "みささんがアカペラやってるってうらやましい"
[Truly, I wonder why we feel that this construction is awkward: "I am jealous that Ms. Misa practices *a capella [singing].]"*

→216 Misa (0.7)あの日本語って主語なくていいやん
[(0.7) *Well, You don't need subjects in Japanese sentences, you know.*]

→217 Chie えっとー多分これちゃう?例えばここが{画面の「さん」の部分を指で消す}
[Uh, it may be this? How about this: {covers up "Ms." on the screen}.]

218 Atsushi (2.2)あ、あ、//そっか.
[(2.2) *Oh, oh,//I got it.*]

219 Misa あー//そういうことか.
[Ohh//I see.]

→220 Atsushi なんかあのきが、気軽な感じと//丁寧な
[Somehow, well, the informal and//formal [tones]…]

221 Misa あっと//丁寧な
[Oh//formal [tone]…]

222 Chie 丁寧な差が//多分
[The formality gap is//possibly…]

223 Atsushi 混在してて
[[the tone] is mixed up and…]

224 Misa だから気持ち悪いんか.
[I see—that's why it sounds awkward.]

225 Atsushi (1.6) なるほど.
[(1.6) *I see.*]

226 Chie これでなんとか、なんかその
[With this, somehow, well, uh…]

227 Misa なんかぽいもん.
[Somehow, it sounds right.]
228 Atsushi うん.
[Yeah.]

In the first line (215), Atsushi asked the group why they had found the construction of the learner's sentence to be awkward. The student teachers had discussed this sentence earlier while reading through the online partner's new post for the first time; the group agreed that they needed to provide some kind of corrective feedback on that sentence. Misa, in line 216, attempted to answer the question posed by Atsushi; she pointed out that the sentence has a subject, which is not always necessary in Japanese sentences. Then, Chie provided another potential reason for the awkward construction by using her finger to cover up the word さん (*-san*), which is a title of respect (similar to *Mr.*, *Ms.*, or *Mrs.*). Chie's verbal and non-verbal actions demonstrated to Atsushi and Misa that the sentence sounded strange because the speech registers used in it were inconsistent (i.e., it mixed formal and informal registers). The distinction between formal and informal register in Japanese is expressed not only through word choice, but also through grammatical forms, and speakers need to pay special attention to choosing an appropriate form (e.g., word choice in general, terms of address in particular, and sentence-/clause-final copulas or verb suffixes) depending on the context. When Japanese native speakers produce an utterance, they have to choose a sentence/clause-final speech register—either formal/polite (with polite-form suffix ます (*-masu*) attached to a verb or polite-form copula です (*-desu*) attached to a predicate) or informal/non-polite—and make it consistent within the utterance (Kitade, 2013). As shown in this excerpt, Atsushi and Misa understood the reason the learner had produced the awkward construction thanks to the point made by Chie. Interestingly, Atsushi, not Chie or Misa, is the one who first verbalized the concept of speech register as being *informal* and *formal*, and all three colleagues repeated the key word formal in lines 220 to 222 as they realized the grammatical reason for the learner's error. This excerpt demonstrates how teachers sought, offered, and constructed ideas in order to solve problems jointly.

After identifying the critical parts of the learner's sentence in Excerpt 1, the student teachers moved on to discuss how they could correct the sentence in such a way that the learner would best understand the reason for the correction and learn from it. Excerpt 2 shows the interaction that followed Excerpt 1. Here, the group of teachers tried to figure out how they could correct the learner's production, which used both polite and informal speech types (that is, さん (*-san*) is a formal title attached to a name, while the adjective うらやましい (*urayamashii*) 'jealous' uses the informal style).

Excerpt 2: Student teacher discussion around online activity with a Japanese learner in the United States

→229 Misa (1.8)でも多分この「さん」は抜かしたらあかんのやろな-{ふふ}
[(1.8) *But I guess we can't delete this "Ms.," right? {laughter}*]
230 Chie どうやろいいん//かな.
[Not sure—I wonder if it may // be okay.]
→231 Atsushi でもなんか確かに向こうの方からしたらさー、なんか「さん」をつけるものやって思ってるからさー、意味が分からへんよな、なんで消されたのか.
[But actually, from the learners' viewpoint, somehow they think that they need to attach [the title] "Ms." and would not understand why it is [supposed to be] deleted, you know.]
232 Chie (そうかー)
[(I see)]
233 Misa あ、たしかに.
[Oh, that's true.]

234 Misa な、なんでって(なる).丁寧に言ったのに.
[She will ask (us) Wh—Why? For the sake of being polite.]
→235 Atsushi こっちに「です」をつける.
[*Attach* desu *here*.]
236 Chie ここに「です」つけて敬語のなんか//をそろえるというか.
[*Attach* desu *here and make it consistent somehow//with polite expression or…*]
237 Atsushi そやね.
[I agree.]
238 Misa うん.
[Yeah.]

Earlier, in Excerpt 1, Chie had noted that さん (*-san*) (which is formal) is problematic; however, in line 229 here, Misa observed that it would be problematic to simply delete さん (*-san*) so as to make the sentence consistent with the informal register. Atsushi supported Misa's idea that, generally, Japanese-language learners are taught to use さん (*-san*) to address people in Japanese across most or all circumstances. Thus, Atsushi suggested in line 235 that an alternative way to correct the sentence would be to add the formal copula です (*-desu*) to the adjective うらやましい (*urayamashii*) 'jealous' to render the speech consistently formal. The learner's original sentence was not consistent, as it ended without the formal copula as うらやましい (*urayamashii*) 'jealous' alone, but started with the formal address term みささん (*Misa-san*) 'Ms. Misa'. Thus, Atsushi proposed to place the sentence consistently in the formal register by inserting the formal copula following the adjective. In lines 236 through 238, Misa and Chie expressed their agreement with this alternative. Thus, encouraged by Atsushi's ideas, the other student teachers found a way to incorporate the learner's perspective and to predict how she will react to the corrective feedback.

As shown in Excerpt 2, the student teachers shared their thoughts, compared possible choices, and came up with the best feedback to assist the learner's understanding of Japanese language. The other CLEs were similarly to this one in that the student teachers engaged in critical discussion when deciding to what extent they should correct learners' Japanese. Through such discussions, the student teachers realized the multiple aspects requiring consideration in giving feedback, the difficulty inherent in identifying what constitutes correct language usage, and the importance of the teacher's role in helping learners maintain the motivation to master Japanese. Unlike teacher discussion surrounding regular lecture-style pedagogical classes, teachers engaging in offline dialogue while providing online feedback are practicing teaching at that moment; thus, they are under immediate pressure to make the best choices to assist their online partners, who eagerly await their feedback.

The Role of Technological Mediation in the Development of Teachers' Knowledge

Research question two asked how the features of ACMC assist the learning process. The data revealed the crucial role of online text-sharing in fostering simultaneous offline peer dialogue, which, in turn, enabled the student teachers to engage in a unique form of reflective practice. Excerpt 3 illustrates how online text-sharing can mediate teachers' construction of knowledge. Student teachers Ami and Yuko had read all the posts put up by their Chinese partner and had chosen several parts upon which to provide corrective feedback. Then, they tried to correct the following sentence, which contains some grammatical mistakes: これから、これについて交流してほしいこと、また本を推薦してもらいたいことを楽しみにしています (*korekara, kore ni tsuite kooryuu *<u>shite hoshii</u> koto, mata hon o suisen shite *<u>moraitai koto o tanoshimi</u> ni shiteimasu*). Literally, this means 'In the future, I look forward to *<u>wanting to</u> exchange ideas with you <u>*for me</u> and to having some books recommended <u>*for me</u>'.

In the following excerpt, Yuko is typing up the correct sentence on the wiki while discussing it with Ami, sitting next to her.

Excerpt 3: Offline dialogue during online activity with a Japanese-language class in China

227 Yuko また本を推薦して{タイピング}、も、らいたい、です.{タイピング}楽しみにしています.ん?
[And I want you to recommend {typing} some books. {typing} I look forward to it. Huh?]

→228 Ami あ、う-ん.何か、多分,
[Oh, ahh. Something like probably,]

229 Yuko 何かさ、言いたいことは多分2つあるんやな.
[Somehow, there are two things she wants to say, I suspect.]

230 Ami なんか、//楽しみで
[Somehow,//She looks forward to…]

231 Yuko 全部楽しみ//なんやな.
[She looks forward to all of them//I suspect.]

232 Ami {笑} 楽しみで
[{laughs} She is looking forward [to something] and…]

233 Yuko 全部楽しみで、本について交流するのも楽しみやし、本を推薦してもらうのも楽しみなんやんな.
[Looking forward to all of them and she is looking forward to exchanging ideas about the books and also looking forward to having the books be recommended, right?]

234 Ami うん.
[Yeah…]

→235 Yuko じゃ、それを全部ひとつの文章にしちゃったから.え.できるんか?やろうと思ったら
[Well, because she failed to put [these ideas] into one sentence… Oh. Would it be possible [to convey her ideas in a single sentence]? If we try…]

236 Ami ん~
[Uh…]

237 Yuko (0.2)え~これから本について交流すること!また、本を
[(0.2) *Uh, exchanging ideas about books in the future! And having the books…*]

→238 Ami あ~、なんか、これから本について、なんかみんなと交流して、本を推薦してもらえることを楽しみにしています、かな
[Ahh, somehow, "I look forward to exchanging ideas about the books with everyone in the future and being able to have books recommended to me," I suspect.]

239 Yuko あ~、それか!
[Ohh, that's it!]

240 Ami うん、「もらえること」が
[Yeah, "being able to"…]

241 Yuko これから{タイピング}、本につい//て{タイピング}
[In the future {typing}…about the books// {typing}]

242 Ami ついて交流し、し//て{タイピング}
[*Exchange ideas about //and { typing}*]

243 Yuko して、「また」いらん?本を、推薦して、も、ら、え、る、ことを?{タイピング}
[And, "also" is not necessary? Being a-b-le to have the books recommended [to her]? {typing}]

244 Ami かな?(0.2) やったら分かる.
[*I suspect?* (0.2) *Then [it's] understandable.*]

245 Yuko やったら分かる.
[Then [it's] understandable.]

In line 227, Yuko was typing and verbalizing the corrected sentence on which she and Ami had agreed. However, by typing and re-verbalizing their attempt at a corrected sentence, Ami and Yuko realized, in lines 228 through 233, that their original attempt did not exactly express what their Chinese partner (the L2 learner) was trying to convey. They noticed that what their partner was looking forward to was not limited to book recommendations, but also included further discussion about the books. Yuko wondered in line 235 whether the meaning of their partner could be conveyed in a single sentence, and her colleague tried to compose such a sentence. Then, in line 238, Ami suggested the final, single-sentence version that they ultimately provided as a correction. Yuko's exclamation in line 239, "Oh, that's it!" shows that she was not able to come up with a sentence by herself and that Ami's suggestion helped her find a solution. As Yuko typed the corrected sentence, Ami assisted her, and Yuko asked Ami for confirmation.

In this offline peer dialogue, the student teachers used the online text to build intersubjectivity (i.e., a shared understanding among them) (Rogoff, 1990), on the basis of which they confirmed and developed a socially constructed understanding. By visualizing and verbalizing their intersubjectivity from moment to moment, huddled around the computer screen, they were able to point out the problem, and develop an optimal correction. Interestingly, Ami's utterances in lines 242 and 244 did not start until Yuko's typing sounds stopped, despite the fact that Yuko had already stopped speaking. Apparently, Ami perceived that Yuko's speech turn was continuing as Yuko typed the sentence on the screen. In other words, the text being typed by Yuko mediated the intersubjectivity between Yuko and Ami at that moment. Although a more accurate and nuanced overall picture of the activity should become possible with the use of video-recording, the data still suggest that text-mediation helped the student teachers indicate and confirm the accuracy of their understanding, which encouraged the construction of knowledge among them.

In summary, the findings of this study demonstrate that offline peer dialogue during the provision of online feedback for L2 distance learners enables teachers to engage jointly in reflection-in-action. The students and teachers engaged in reflection-in-practice through the hybrid activity (as presented in full in Figure 1). In the offline mode, teachers can optimize the time interval between online exchanges by engaging in peer dialogue to identify and to understand the problematic parts of students' L2 communication and then to seek the best way to provide feedback. At each stage, teachers can share their thoughts, compare potential solutions, and determine the optimal solution by relying on the online text and verbal discussion. This hybrid activity suggests a new kind of reflective practice, which can enable teachers to engage in peer-reflective dialogue during their situated practice of teaching.

DISCUSSION

The findings presented above suggest that teachers who engage in offline dialogue as part of hybrid-feedback practice can solve teaching problems actively and jointly. When they practice offline dialogue, teachers are required to verbalize, type, or otherwise share their thoughts; this assists their development of a fresh understanding that they may not be able to attain alone. The present findings suggest that the proposed method has both pedagogical and research-methodological advantages.

Offline peer dialogue functions as a site for reflection-in-action, but differently from the conventional reflection-in-action process, in which teachers are under time constraints and are less likely to have access to each other's knowledge in making decisions. Some scholars have criticized this kind of reflection-in-action conducted in a restricted time frame, saying that "when time is extremely short, decisions have to be rapid and the scope for reflection is extremely limited" (Eraut, 1994, p. 145). Thus, reflection-in-practice is sometimes referred to as *intuition in action* (Johansson & Kroksmark, 2004) due to the lack of psychological elaboration of the idea or feedback on one's decisions (Munby & Russell, 1989).

Offline dialogue in hybrid-feedback activity is different from conventional reflection-in-action thanks to the medium-specific affordances of ACMC. The time flexibility and text-mediatedness of ACMC as a means of peer collaboration in feedback practice enable teachers to approach learners' efforts holistically. Schön (1987) refers to this as professional artistry: teachers' professional competence is holistic in nature, and experienced teachers automatically make decisions with consideration given to multiple perspectives (Szesztay, 2005). Compared to these experienced teachers, who may be able to draw on rich situated knowledge derived from previous experiences, the perspectives and knowledge pre-service teachers need to rely on to make decisions are extremely limited. Thus, peer collaboration for on-the-spot decision-making may be particularly effective in helping pre-service teachers understand the holistic nature of teaching practice. Such situated practical knowledge and skills have been identified as one of the most important but most neglected aspects of teacher learning, and the pedagogical innovations needed to promote such competences in teacher preparation programs have been a crucial part of the research agenda (e.g., Freeman, 2002; Freeman & Johnson, 1998; Johnson, 2009).

In the offline peer dialogues, the student teachers were able to utilize the time affordance to make decisions and compose responses for their learners on the basis of discussions that brought out different perspectives that they may not have become aware of by themselves. The data indicate that moments of realization of new knowledge or understanding, triggered by their peers, helped the student teachers identify errors, understand the reasons for them, and judge and evaluate possible corrections while establishing rapport with their learners, and maintaining the learners' motivation to learn the Japanese language. Unlike reflection on practice (e.g., journal writing, peer coaching, and expert supervision), peer student teachers in offline dialogue stand together *on the spot* of decision-making, where they are capable of maintaining high intersubjectivity and co-constructing new knowledge.

Offline peer dialogue also served to capture the teachers' process of development of situated knowledge and skills. The development of this aspect of competence is prompted by teachers' awareness gained through reflective practice (Prawat, 1991). Unlike retrospective approaches such as journal writing or interviews, offline peer dialogue—similar to the think-aloud protocol (e.g., Cotton & Gresty, 2006)—captured teachers' entire collaborative practice without filtering or possible application of subjective memory. In fact, most of the student teachers' journal entries identified realizations they had made on the abstract level, related to their self-evaluation as professionals. Examples of such realizations include realization of their lack of grammatical knowledge; realization of their (in)ability to address learners' current Japanese levels and needs; and increased awareness of the complex nature of language and culture (Kitade, 2014). In contrast, participants did not often directly mention micro-level incidents such as the CLEs captured in the offline dialogue. Thus, offline peer dialogue may have the advantage of precisely illustrating the process of reflection-in-practice that triggers situated knowledge development in student teachers. However, because no approach is perfect on its own, further research adopting various approaches is expected to shed light on new aspects of situated knowledge development in student teachers.

Pedagogical Considerations

The study presented in this chapter proposed an innovative type of reflective practice implemented as part of teaching practice with the new focus of knowledge afforded by participating student L2 teachers' peers. To optimize these teachers' cognitive development by providing them the opportunity to engage with L2 learners abroad through the Internet, teacher educators implementing reflective practice using student teachers' offline peer dialogue need to consider several pedagogical aspects.

The offline dialogues should be perceived as a reflective practice that can or should be implemented alongside other types of reflective practice, such as individual reflection. As mentioned above, journal entries rarely address the kind of micro-level realizations gained through practice; instead, realizations mentioned in the journals tend to be more abstract and to deal with student teachers' impression of their learners' language use and their self-evaluations as teaching professionals. To promote deeper reflection among teachers and foster their ability to incorporate realizations from peer dialogue (a micro-level activity) into their broader professional competence, including aspects of their theoretical framework such as linguistic and pedagogical knowledge, a combination of other types of reflective practice may be effective. By carefully designing and appropriately combining varied types of reflective practice, pre-service teachers' opportunities for engagement with L2 learners should be maximized.

CONCLUSION, LIMITATIONS, AND FUTURE RESEARCH

This study took an emic rather than etic approach to documenting the learning experiences of student teachers during the innovative activity of integrating online and offline modes in teaching/learning practice. Future studies using a wider variety of data (e.g., interviews and video-recorded data) or adopting an experimental design with pre- and post-practice components may also suggest other significant aspects of offline dialogue and hybrid activity.

In addition, as suggested by the findings of previous studies in L2 collaborative learning (Kitade, 2008; Storch, 2002), the quality and quantity of CLEs vary widely depending on the pairing of learners (i.e., in this case, student teachers). Irrespective of the instructor's intentions, the actual way in which a task is accomplished may vary greatly depending on how learners perceive and construct the task (Coughlan & Duff, 1994). Thus, more qualitative analysis to address the operationalization of the feedback task for each relevant process and collaboration pattern should be incorporated in future research. Furthermore, one challenging question in reflective practice is how to encourage a deeper level of reflection. The level and type(s) of reflection (Lord & Lomicka, 2007) promoted in offline dialogue should be explored in future studies.

Lastly and most importantly, the findings documented in the present study suggest the student teachers' realization and awareness of new aspects of teaching and new and different perspectives on factors relevant to feedback decision-making (e.g., the reasons behind an error, the linguistic features of Japanese, or the consideration of the learners' mental and cognitive status required to provide feedback). These new aspects can promote professional transformation on the part of the (teacher) learners, as expressed in theories of reflective practice (Kiely & Davis, 2010). The findings reported in this study need to be followed up in long-term research addressing in particular the issue of whether or how participants' realizations relate to professional transformations in their future careers. A study collecting longitudinal data will be required to identify evidence of transformation caused by newfound awareness as discussed.

This study explored the innovative practice of offline peer dialogue, which was designed to accompany cross-institutional ACMC activity for L2 teacher development. The results showed that offline practice enhanced student teachers' active learning by enabling them to engage in peer-based reflective practice. In contrast to conventional reflection-in-action, offline dialogue made possible through new technologies provides two advantages. First, teachers can engage with L2 distance learners in the context of their actual teaching practice, even if they are still student teachers in classes on campus. Second, teachers are able to engage in peer reflection and reap the benefits of text mediation, a method that assists them to co-construct the situated knowledge and skills, which are crucial but neglected in teacher education (e.g., Freeman, 2002; Freeman & Johnson, 1998; Johnson, 2009).

The opportunities that online media brings for L2TE should not be restricted to the task of acquiring electronic literacy skills, which has been examined (or investigated) in previous studies (e.g., Fuchs, Hauck, & Müller-Hartmann, 2012). Rather, online media should also be exploited to optimize teachers' learning in actual engagement with learners online. Such opportunities to engage with learners promote active learning among pre-service teachers and encourage professional transformation on their part. Future research should explore and examine this innovative practice for teacher learning, giving careful attention to pedagogical affordances and needs to maximize the potential gains achievable using new electronic media in education.

ACKNOWLEDGMENT

This research is supported by Japan Society for the Promotion of Science Grant-in-Aid for Scientific Research (C) number 24520592. I would like to thank the editors and reviewers for their insightful comments on an earlier version on this manuscript, as well as the research assistants for helping me with the transcription and analysis of the data.

REFERENCES

Arnold, N., & Ducate, L. (2006). Future foreign language teachers' social and cognitive collaboration in an online environment. *Language Learning & Technology*, *10*(1), 42–66.

Arnold, N., Ducate, L., Lomicka, L., & Lord, G. (2009). Assessing online collaboration among language teachers: A cross-institutional wiki case study. *Journal of Technology and Teacher Education*, *8*(2), 121–139.

Bailey, F. (1996). The role of collaborative dialogue in teacher education. In D. Freeman, & J. Richards (Eds.), *Teacher learning in language teaching* (pp. 260–280). Cambridge: Cambridge University Press.

Burns, A. (2009). Action research in second language teacher education. In A. Burns, & J. C. Richards (Eds.), *Cambridge guide to second language teacher education* (pp. 289–297). Cambridge: Cambridge University Press.

Burton, J. (2009). Reflective practice. In A. Burns, & J. C. Richards (Eds.), *Cambridge guide to second language teacher education* (pp. 298–307). Cambridge: Cambridge University Press.

Cotton, D., & Gresty, K. (2006). Reflecting on the think-aloud method for evaluating e-learning. *British Journal of Educational Technology*, *37*(1), 45–54. doi:10.1111/j.1467-8535.2005.00521.x

Coughlan, P., & Duff, P. (1994). Same task, different activities: Analysis of a second language acquisition task from an activity theory perspective. In J. P. Lantolf, & G. Appel (Eds.), *Vygotskian approaches to second language research* (pp. 183–193). Norwood, NJ: Ablex.

De Guerrero, M., & Villamil, O. S. (2000). Activating the ZPD: Mutual scaffolding in L2 peer revision. *Modern Language Journal*, *84*(1), 51–68. doi:10.1111/0026-7902.00052

Dewey, J. (1933). *How we think*. Chicago: Henry Regnery.

Engeström, Y. (1999). Activity theory and individual and social transformation. In Y. Engeström, R. Miettinen, & R.-L. Punamaki-Gitai (Eds.), *Perspectives on activity theory: Learning in doing* (pp. 19–38). Cambridge: Cambridge University Press. doi:10.1017/CBO9780511812774.003

Eraut, M. (1994). *Developing professional knowledge and competence*. London: Falmer Press.

Freeman, D. (2002). The hidden side of the work: Teacher knowledge and learning to teach. *Language Teaching*, *31*, 1–13.

Freeman, D., & Johnson, K. E. (1998). Reconceptualizing the knowledge-base of language teacher education. *TESOL Quarterly*, *32*, 397–418. doi:10.2307/3588114

Fuchs, C., Hauck, M., & Müller-Hartmann, A. (2012). Promoting learner autonomy through multiliteracy skills development in cross-institutional exchanges. *Language Learning & Technology*, *16*(3), 82–102.

Gass, S. M., & Mackey, A. (2000). *Stimulated recall methodology in second language research*. Mahwah, NJ: Erlbaum.

Gustafson, K., & Bennett, W. (2002). *Promoting learner reflection: Issues and difficulties emerging from a three-year study*. Available from, http://www.dtic.mil/cgi-bin/GetTRDoc?Location=U2&doc=GetTRDoc.pdf&AD=ADA472616

Hall, D. R., & Knox, J. (2009). Issues in the education of TESOL teachers by distance education. *Distance Education*, *30*(1), 63–85. doi:10.1080/01587910902845964

Johansson, T., & Kroksmark, T. (2004). Teachers' intuition-in-action: How teachers experience action. *Reflective Practice*, *5*(3), 357–381. doi:10.1080/1462394042000270673

Johnson, K. E. (2006). The sociocultural turn and its challenges for second language teacher education. *TESOL Quarterly*, *40*, 235–257. doi:10.2307/40264518

Johnson, K. E. (2009). Second language teacher education: A sociocultural perspective. New York: Routledge.

Kanno, Y., & Stuart, C. (2011). Learning to become a second language teacher: Identities-in-practice. *Modern Language Journal*, *95*(2), 236–252. doi:10.1111/j.1540-4781.2011.01178.x

Kemmis, S., & McTaggart, R. (1988). *The action research planner* (3rd ed.). Geelong: Deakin University Press.

Kiely, R., & Davis, M. (2010). From transmission to transformation: Teachers learning in English for speakers of other language. *Language Teaching Research*, *14*(3), 277–295. doi:10.1177/1362168810365241

Kitade, K. (2006). The negotiation model in asynchronous computer-mediated communication. *CALICO Journal*, *23*(2), 319–348.

Kitade, K. (2008). The role of offline metalanguage talk in asynchronous computer-mediated communication. *Language Learning & Technology*, *12*(1), 64–84.

Kitade, K. (2013). Analyzing the reframing process from a language socialization perspective. In E. Voss, S.-J. D. Tai, & Z. Li (Eds.), *Selected Proceedings of the 2011 Second Language Research Forum: Converging Theory and Practice* (pp. 29–43). Somerville, MA: Cascadilla Proceedings Project.

Kitade, K. (2014). Second language teachers' identity development through online collaboration with L2 learners. *CALICO Journal*, *31*(1), 83–103. doi:10.11139/cj.31.1.57-77

Lamy, M., & Goodfellow, R. (1999). "Reflective conversation" in the virtual language classroom. *Language Learning & Technology*, *2*(2), 43–61.

Lantolf, J., & Thorne, S. L. (Eds.). (2006). *Sociocultural theory and the genesis of second language development*. Oxford: Oxford University Press.

Lapadat, J. C. (2002). Written interaction: A key component in online learning. *Journal of Computer-Mediated Communication*, *7*(4). Available from http://onlinelibrary.wiley.com/doi/10.1111/j.1083-6101.2002.tb00158.x/full

Leontiev, A. N. (1981). The problem of activity in psychology. In J. V. Wertsch Trans. & Ed. *The concept of activity in Soviet psychology* (pp. 37–71). New York: M. E. Sharpe.

Lord, G., & Lomicka, L. (2007). Foreign language teacher preparation and asynchronous CMC: Promoting reflective teaching. *Journal of Technology and Teacher Education*, *15*(4), 513–532.

Lord, G., & Lomicka, L. (2008). Blended learning in teacher education: An investigation of classroom community across media. *Contemporary Issues in Technology & Teacher Education*, *8*(2), 158–174.

Miller, J. M. (2007). Identity in the ESL classroom. In Z. Hua, P. Seedhouse, L. Wei, & V. Cook (Eds.), *Language learning and teaching as social interaction* (pp. 148–162). Basingstoke: Palgrave Macmillan.

Müller-Hartmann, A. (2006). Learning how to teach intercultural communicative competence via telecollaboration: a model for language teacher education. In J. Belz, & S. Thorne (Eds.), *Internet-mediated intercultural foreign language education* (pp. 63–84). Boston: Heinle & Heinle.

Munby, H., & Russell, T. (1989). Educating the reflective teacher: An essay review of two books by Donald Schön. *Journal of Curriculum Studies*, *21*(7), 71–80. doi:10.1080/0022027890210106

Prawat, R. (1991). Conversations with self and settings: a framework for thinking about teacher empowerment. *American Educational Research Journal*, *28*(4), 737–757. doi:10.3102/00028312028004737

Richards, J. C. (1996). Teachers' maxims in language teaching. *TESOL Quarterly*, *30*(2), 281–296. doi:10.2307/3588144

Richards, J. C. (2008). Second language teacher education today. *RELC Journal*, *39*, 158–177. doi:10.1177/0033688208092182

Rogoff, B. (1990). *Apprenticeship in thinking: Cognitive development in social context*. Cambridge: Cambridge University Press.

Schön, D. (1983). *The reflective practitioner*. New York: Oxford University Press.

Schön, D. (1987). *Educating the reflective practitioner*. New York: Basic Books.

Storch, N. (2002). Patterns of interaction in ESL pair work. *Language Learning*, *52*(1), 119–158. doi:10.1111/1467-9922.00179

Swain, M. (2000). The output hypothesis and beyond: Mediating acquisition through collaborative dialogue. In J. Lantolf (Ed.), *Sociocultural theory and second language learning* (pp. 97–114). Oxford: Oxford University Press.

Swain, M. (2006). Verbal protocols: What does it mean for research to use speaking as a data collection tool? In M. Chalhoub-Deville, C. Chappelle, & P. Duff (Eds.), *Inference and generalizability in applied linguistics: Multiple perspectives* (pp. 97–113). Amsterdam: John Benjamins. doi:10.1075/lllt.12.07swa

Swain, M., & Lapkin, S. (1998). Interaction and second language learning: Two adolescent French immersion students working together. *Modern Language Journal*, *82*(3), 320–337. doi:10.1111/j.1540-4781.1998.tb01209.x

Swain, M., Lapkin, S., Knouzzi, I., Suzuki, W., & Brooks, L. (2009). Languaging: University students learn the grammatical concept of voice in French. *Modern Language Journal*, *93*, 5–27. doi:10.1111/j.1540-4781.2009.00825.x

Szatrowski, P. (1993). *Nihongo no danwa no kouzou bunseki: Kanyu no sutorateji no kousatsu* [Structural analysis of Japanese discourse: A study of the strategy for invitation]. Tokyo: Kuroshio Publishers.

Szesztay, M. (2005). Teachers' ways of knowing. *ELT Journal*, *58*(2), 129–136. doi:10.1093/elt/58.2.129

Thorne, S. L. (2003). Artifacts and culture-of-use in intercultural communication. *Language Learning & Technology*, *7*(2), 38–67.

Thorne, S. L., & Tasker, T. (2011). Sociocultural and cultural-historical theories of language development. In J. Simpson (Ed.), *Routledge handbook of applied linguistics* (pp. 487–500). New York: Routledge.

Vygotsky, L. S. (1978). *Mind in society*. Cambridge, MA: Harvard University Press.

Wang, S., & Vasquez, C. (2012). Web 2.0 and second language learning: What does the research tell us? *CALICO Journal*, *29*(3), 412–430. doi:10.11139/cj.29.3.412-430

Warschauer, M. (1997). Computer-mediated collaborative learning: Theory and practice. *Modern Language Journal*, *81*(4), 470–481. doi:10.1111/j.1540-4781.1997.tb05514.x

Warschauer, M., & Grimes, D. (2007). Audience, authorship, and artifact: The emergent semiotics of Web 2.0. *Annual Review of Applied Linguistics*, *27*, 1–23. doi:10.1017/S0267190508070013

Wells, G. (1999). *Dialogic inquiry: Toward a sociocultural practice and theory of education*. Cambridge, UK: Cambridge University Press. doi:10.1017/CBO9780511605895

ADDITIONAL READING

Belz, J. A., & Thorne, S. L. (Eds.). (2005). *Internet-mediated intercultural foreign language education*. Boston: Heinle & Heinle.

Borg, S. (2006). *Teacher cognition and language education: Research and practice*. London: Continuum.

Burns, A., & Richards, J. C. (Eds.). (2009). *The Cambridge guide to second language teacher education*. New York: Cambridge University Press.

Cross, R. (2010). Language teaching as sociocultural activity: Rethinking language teacher practice. *Modern Language Journal*, *94*, 434–452. doi:10.1111/j.1540-4781.2010.01058.x

Donato, R. (1994). Collective scaffolding in second language learning. In J. P. Lantolf, & G. Appel (Eds.), *Vygotskian approaches to second language research* (pp. 33–56). Norwood, NJ: Ablex.

Farrell, T. (2007). *Reflective language teaching: From research to practice*. London: Continuum.

Freeman, D., & Richards, J. C. (Eds.). (1996). *Teacher learning in language teaching*. Cambridge: Cambridge University Press.

Hatton, N., & Smith, D. (1995). Reflection in teacher education: Towards definition and implementation. *Teaching and Teacher Education*, *11*(1), 33–49. doi:10.1016/0742-051X(94)00012-U

Herring, S. C. (2001). Computer-mediated discourse. In D. Schiffrin, D. Tannen, & H. Hamilton (Eds.), *The Handbook of Discourse Analysis* (pp. 612–634). Oxford: Blackwell.

Kiely, R., Davis, M., & Wheeler, E. (2010). *Investigating critical learning episodes: A practical guide for continuing professional development*. CfBT Education Trust. Available from, http://cdn.cfbt.com/~/media/cfbtcorporate/files/research/2010/r-investigating-critical-learning-episodes-2010.pdf

Kramsch, C., & Thorne, S. L. (2002). Foreign language learning as global communicative practice. In D. Block, & D. Cameron (Eds.), *Globalization and language teaching* (pp. 83–100). London: Routledge.

Lantolf, J. P., & Appel, G. (Eds.). (1994). *Vygotskian approaches to second language research*. Norwood, NJ: Ablex.

Lantolf, J. P., & Thorne, S. L. (2006). *Sociocultural theory and the genesis of second language development*. Oxford: Oxford University Press.

Lave, J., & Wenger, E. (1991). *Situated learning: Legitimate peripheral participation*. Cambridge: Cambridge University Press. doi:10.1017/CBO9780511815355

Lomicka, L., & Lord, G. (Eds.). (2009). *The next generation: social networking and online collaboration in foreign language learning*. San Marcos, TX: CALICO Publications.

Magnan, S. S. (Ed.). (2008). *Mediating discourse online*. Amsterdam: John Benjamins. doi:10.1075/aals.3

Murray, D. E. (2013). *A case for online English language teacher education*. The International Research Foundation. Available from, http://rossier.usc.edu/files/2013/04/A-Case-for-Online-English-Language-Teacher-Education-2013.pdf

Richards, J. C., & Lockhart, C. (1994). *Reflective teaching in second language classrooms*. Cambridge: Cambridge University Press. doi:10.1017/CBO9780511667169

Thorne, S. L. (2009). "Community," semiotic flows, and mediated contribution to activity. *Language Teaching*, *42*(1), 81–94. doi:10.1017/S0261444808005429

Thorne, S. L., & Payne, J. S. (Eds.). (2005). Special issue on computer-mediated communication and foreign language learning: Context, research, and practice. *CALICO Journal*, *22*(3).

Tsui, A. B. M. (2011). Teacher education and teacher development. In E. Hinkel (Ed.), *Handbook of research in second language teaching and learning* (Vol. II, pp. 21–39). New York, London: Routledge.

Van Lier, L. (2007). Action-based teaching, autonomy and identity. *Innovation in Language Learning and Teaching*, *1*(1), 46–65. doi:10.2167/illt42.0

Warschauer, M., & Grimes, D. (2007). Audience, authorship, and artifact: The emergent semiotics of Web 2.0. *Annual Review of Applied Linguistics*, *27*, 1–23. doi:10.1017/S0267190508070013

Wertsch, J. (1991). *Voices of the mind: A sociocultural approach to mediated action*. Cambridge, MA: Harvard University Press.

Wertsch, J., del Rio, P., & Alvarez, A. (Eds.). (1995). *Sociocultural studies of mind*. Cambridge: Cambridge University Press. doi:10.1017/CBO9781139174299

KEY TERMS AND DEFINITIONS

Activity Theory: Activity theory is rooted in Vygotsky's (1978) claim that cultural artifacts mediate human activity. This notion has been extended to conceptualize activity as a social system, wherein interrelated elements affect the outcome of an activity. On this basis, recent studies using this approach suggest analyzing any human activity, including teaching and learning, holistically.

Asynchronous Computer-Mediated Communication: Computer-mediated communication (CMC) refers to any form of communication in which people interact with one other via the Internet. In contrast to synchronous communication, asynchronous CMC takes place when interlocutors are not online simultaneously.

Collaborative Peer Dialogue: The sociocultural theory (SCT) perspective (e.g., Lantolf & Thorne, 2006; Thorne & Tasker, 2011) considers that learners are able to expand their own knowledge and extend the development of their peers through interaction and activity to achieve a common goal.

Offline Peer Dialogue: Taking advantage of the time affordance available between exchanges in ACMC, teachers or learners engage in collaborative peer dialogue to discuss the meta-level aspects of their teaching or learning practice. As a result of online interaction, both teachers and L2 learners can improve their awareness and develop their understanding offline.

Reflective Practice: Reflective practice has been suggested to promote teachers' active learning by providing teachers the opportunity to observe, analyze, and evaluate their teaching practice and their personal beliefs about teaching and learning. These actions are believed to help the teachers understand their particular teaching context and aid in their professional development.

Sociocultural Perspective: Extending the approach to learning inspired by the works of Lev Vygotsky, the sociocultural perspective on L2 learning and L2TE suggests that human mental development is essentially accomplished through engagement with social practices, artifacts, and environments.

Teacher Development: As distinguished from traditional teacher training, this concept suggests that teachers themselves have a responsibility to pursue active learning. By doing so and by overcoming critical incidents during their teaching practice, teachers can reframe their perspectives towards teaching and learning and transform their practice.

APPENDIX A: SAMPLE WIKI PAGE FOR A GORUP IN THE SECOND ONLINE PROJECT

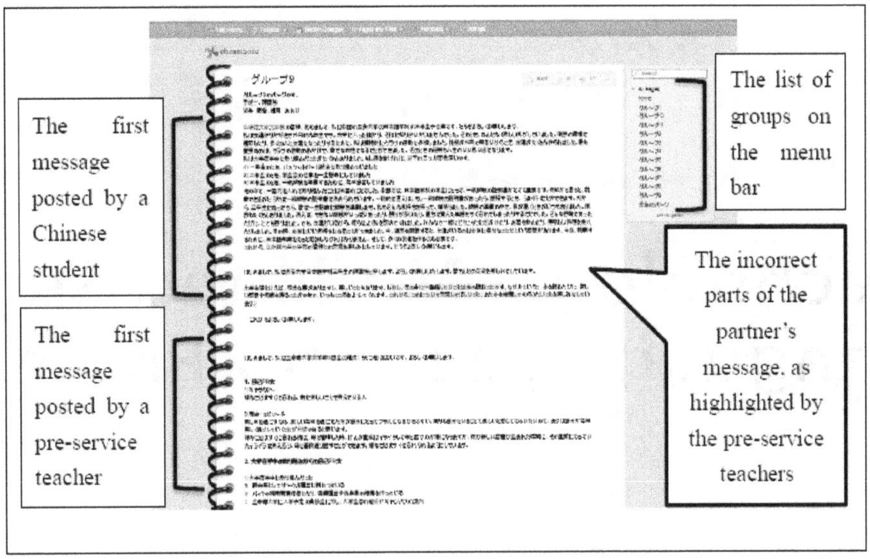

APPENDIX B: TRANSCRIPTION CONVENTIONS

Transcription symbols used in the data are as follows (Szatrowski, 1993):

, short pause between words, phrases, or sentences
. ending with falling tone
() whispered sound
(0.9) exactly timed pauses
// parts following // overlapping with the next-turn utterance
{ } non-verbal behavior
? rising tone

Section 3

Technology-Mediated Second Language Learning Processes

Chapter 7
Pragmatic Development through Blogs:
A Longitudinal Study of Telecollaboration and Language Socialization

Noriko Ishihara
Hosei University, Japan

Yumi Takamiya
Gettysburg College, USA

ABSTRACT

In the acquisition of pragmatic competence, technology-mediated telecollaboration can be a crucial advantage as learners can be socialized into the pragmatic strategies of expert language users in a dynamic interactive context. This chapter focuses on the pragmatic development of three foreign language learners of Japanese over 16-21 months as they blogged with Japanese learners of English in Japan before and after studying in Japan. The blog-mediated learning was provided in conjunction with face-to-face instruction, and the learners' sense of community expanded through the study abroad experience as well as the blog-based telecollaboration. The learners' pragmatic development observable in their blog posts included their use of address terms, gendered sentence-final particles, a regional dialect, emoticons, and style shifting between the clause-final desu/masu and plain forms. The findings indicate that learners' pragmatic language choices can be interpreted in relation to their language socialization and agentive negotiation of emerging multiple identities.

INTRODUCTION

As an increasing body of research in Computer Assisted Language Learning demonstrates, technology can create authentic intercultural contexts and has the potential to enhance language learning, especially in foreign language (FL) contexts (Belz, 2007; Blake, 2011; Kinginger & Belz, 2005). While opportunities to interact with target language (TL) speakers tend to be scarce in the traditional FL classroom, technology-mediated telecollaboration can connect electronically learn-

DOI: 10.4018/978-1-4666-6174-5.ch007

ers to expert speakers of the TL and stimulate the learners' motivation to communicate with them in a meaningful manner. This can be a crucial advantage in the acquisition of pragmatic competence, which is understood here to mean knowledge of appropriate and effective norms of verbal and non-verbal behavior situated at the intersection of language and culture. Following Belz (2007), Taguchi and Sykes (2013), and Thorne, Black, and Sykes (2009), we argue that learners can be socialized into the pragmatic strategies of expert language users in a dynamic interactive context mediated by telecollaboration. In such online interactions, learners' pragmatic choices can bring about real-life consequences (such as offending others) through which both learners and their interlocutors negotiate their relationships.

One platform that can support learners' technology-assisted interactions is blogging technology. Being asynchronous reflective and interactive tools, blogs can facilitate introspective and metacognitive activities such as reading and writing, reflecting, and analyzing on the one hand, as well as written interactions between the authors and multiple blog readers on the other. In addition, since blog posts are direct records of these individual and interactive activities, blogs can afford researchers, educators, and learners themselves opportunities to study and assess or self-reflect on authentic language behavior, an added value for enhanced credibility in research and pedagogy. Given this, this study makes a unique contribution to the current literature by focusing on the potential role of blogs in promoting the development of pragmatic competence and language socialization of learners of Japanese as an FL. More specifically, taking advantage of authentic written data, we investigate the pragmatic development over 16-21 months of the learners as they used blogs as part of their FL courses in the United States (U.S.) before and after they studied in Japan for a period of six to 12 months. Specifically, we explore in depth the pragmatic and metapragmatic awareness and language use of the three focal learners in an attempt to understand the complex processes underlying their language socialization.

BACKGROUND

Computer-mediated communication (CMC) is increasingly viewed as an influential resource with which to facilitate various aspects of language learning. Peer interaction through CMC can facilitate the negotiation of meaning, stimulate learner motivation, enhance autonomy, and promote the construction of bilingual identities (Freiermuth & Huang, 2012; Lam, 2004; Lee, 2011; Smith & Craig, 2013). As opposed to the traditional view of learning that positions learners as passive recipients of knowledge, CMC can construct learners as knowledge creators in the process of social learning (de Andrés Martínez, 2012; Guarda, 2012).

Language and Cultural Learning through Blogs

Blogs (a.k.a. weblogs) are online journals typically consisting of a title, text, images, and links to other webpages. Blogs are increasingly recognized as an interactive virtual medium ranging from a journalistic online resource of a public nature to personal and private reflective websites connected to social networking services (Carney, 2009; Ducate & Lomicka, 2005; Murray, Hourigan, & Jeanneau, 2007; Swanson & Early, 2009). To encourage reader participation, space for comments is often provided after each blog post, which can facilitate multi-directional interactions. As the creation and development of a blog requires no technical knowledge of web programming or web authoring software (Swanson & Early, 2009) and is often free of charge to bloggers, this digital medium is being increasingly adopted in L2 instruction (de Andrés Martínez, 2012; Lee, 2011). Blogs can thus be considered an asynchronous means of self-expression and self-reflection as well as a tool for interactive and collaborative learning (Lee, 2011). Compared to other CMC formats such as forums and wikis, a blog is an individually-oriented, more author-controlled expressive medium that focuses on process rather than product (Miyazoe & Anderson, 2010).

In the past few years, several studies have emerged in the field of language learning investigating the instructional value of blogging. Many of these studies employ blogs for the development of (academic) ESL/EFL writing skills in university contexts (e.g., Arslan & Şahin-Kizil, 2010; Bloch, 2007; Dos & Demir 2013; Miyazoe & Anderson, 2010; Murray et al., 2007; Rivens Mompean, 2010). Typically, blogs are used as mediational tools for writing, self-reflection, and peer editing or feedback, sometimes in conjunction with face-to-face instruction. Positive effects of blog-mediated instruction include improvement in L2 writing in the areas of content and organization (Arslan & Şahin-Kizil, 2010), development of rhetorical strategies (Bloch, 2007), and progress in the learners' abilities to differentiate English writing styles (Miyazoe & Anderson, 2010). Furthermore, the potential of blogs as self-reflective tools is perceived by the learners themselves (Murray et al., 2007).

Not only do blogs provide learners with opportunities to practice writing, publish, and distribute their work online, but they can also facilitate peer interaction and meaningful communication in the L2 with enhanced audience awareness and a heightened sense of voice and ownership of learning (Arslan & Şahin-Kızıl, 2010; Ducate & Lomicka, 2005; Sun, 2009; Warschauer, 2010). In order to maximize the instructional potential of blog technology for language learning, researchers have pointed out the importance of, for example, appropriateness of task types in the instructional context, teacher's moderation and facilitation of blogging interactions, technological readiness among blog users, and the availability of network connections (Miceli, Murray, & Kennedy, 2010; Lee, 2011; Swanson & Early, 2009).

Along with writing development, blogs have also been adopted to enhance learners' intercultural competence (Carney, 2007; Elola & Oskoz, 2008; Lee, 2011; Takamiya, 2009; Yang, 2011). In Elola and Oskoz's research, 23 study abroad students in Spain and 15 at-home students in the U.S., all intermediate learners of Spanish, blogged over the course of a semester, sharing their observations of the U.S. and various Spanish-speaking cultures in their first language and reflecting upon them. Their blogs as well as their responses to questionnaires demonstrated evidence of intercultural competence for both study-abroad and at-home students.

Likewise, Lee's (2011) research on learners of Spanish studying in Spain showed intercultural learning as well as enhanced learner autonomy via blogs. Over the study abroad semester, learners used ethnographic interviews of TL speakers to obtain emic (insider) perspectives of the culture and reported these in blogs. Although the learners often required teacher's guidance for critical reflections, the author argues that the blogs supported self-regulated learning through independent work and reflection on intercultural differences. (See de Andrés Martínez, 2012, for more on learner autonomy and ownership of learning.)

The aforementioned studies focused on the role and effects of blogging in L2 learning, with an emphasis on the development of specific language skills, namely writing and intercultural competence. However, very few studies have investigated the development of pragmatic competence, with the exception of Takamiya and Ishihara (2013), which is part of the larger study from which this chapter is derived. As pragmatic competence is inevitably intertwined with the way in which learners become socialized into the practices of the target culture (Li, 2010; Thorne et al., 2009), in the following section we discuss language socialization and in particular its interface with pragmatic development.

Second Language Socialization, Pragmatic Competence, and Technology

In the framework of language socialization (Schieffelin & Ochs, 1986; Zuengler & Cole, 2005), language learning is viewed as social practice in which learners or novice members of a community gradually become competent members as they acquire culturally organized local practices. Novice community members are exposed to the knowledge, orientations, and social practices of the community, often through activities mediated by language. Increasing knowledge of linguistic patterns and discursive practices gradually turns learners into expert members and moves them from a peripheral position to the center of the community (Lave & Wenger, 1991). Simultaneously, community members, including novice members, do not always reproduce and maintain local sociocultural practice. Rather, they sometimes actively and selectively challenge, resist, and co-construct community practices and the outcomes of interactions (Bayley & Schecter, 2003; Garrett & Baquedano-López, 2002; Ishihara, 2006, 2010; Ochs, 1993; Schieffelin & Ochs, 1986; Watson-Gegeo & Nielsen, 2003). Therefore, language socialization should be seen a multi-directional, dynamic process constantly negotiated among members of the community.

The link between L2 learning and socialization into certain social roles, cultural routines, and discourse structures has been studied from sociocultural, interactional, and pragmatic perspectives (Cook, 2008, 2010; DuFon, 2008; Ishihara, 2006, 2010; Li, 2000, 2010). For example, focusing on workplace language socialization, Li (2000) documented how an immigrant woman in Canada internalized local practices by analyzing her use of requests over 18 months. Her dual socialization into both the workplace and the new language and culture occurred through exposure to and participation in social interactions with scaffolding provided by more competent members of the community.

In L2 Japanese, style shifting between the plain (non-honorific) and *desu/masu* (addressee-honorific) forms is a challenging discourse feature into which learners need to be socialized. These forms serve as clause-final markers of epistemic stance and are obligatory morphological choices except in incomplete or rhetorical sentences. The choice of form indexes the speaker's dynamic stance in relation to the co-participants in the interaction. Unlike the simplistic distinction commonly drawn between these forms in instructional materials, the *desu/masu* form is multi-functional and used to negotiate identities in dynamic discourse (Cook, 2008; Ishida, 2009). Besides the standard assumption that the *desu/masu* form occurs in polite and formal conversation with interlocutors in distant relationships (as in a *soto,* or 'out-group,' as opposed to an *uchi*, or 'in-group' context) or when addressing an interlocutor of higher in status (Cook, 2008; Ishida, 2009), the unmarked choice of the *desu/masu* form appears in, but is not limited to:

1. Self-presentational stance (i.e., "the self which presents an on-stage display of a positive social role to the addressee" (Cook, 2008, p. 46), enacting identities, for example, as an authority figure, a knowledgeable party, and a "good child" (Cook, 2008, pp. 45-64);
2. Quoting others and establishing out-group identities (Cook, 2008);
3. Impersonalizing (defocusing) the speaker (Geyer, 2008); and
4. Indicating a topic shift as an official frame (Geyer, 2008).

In contrast, the plain form is typically used in:

1. Expressing solidarity (Geyer, 2008);
2. Providing mitigation (Geyer, 2008);
3. Embedding a subspace to support the other speaker's floor (Ikuta, 2008); and

4. Expressing internal thoughts self-reflectively, including most self-addressed utterances and monologues (Maynard, 1991).

Although L2 learners' awareness and production of these forms can be explicitly taught and improved in formal FL instruction (Ishida, 2009), learners may also acquire the social meanings of style shifting through socialization into the community in study abroad. Cook (2008) traced the development of style shifting strategies of nine learners of Japanese during their one-year study abroad in Japan. The recordings of their dinner time conversations with host families showed learners' socialization into the use of the *desu/masu* form in the self-presentational style in appropriate contexts.

Similarly, Iwasaki's participants demonstrated an understanding of social meanings of the speech styles in pre- and post-study-abroad oral proficiency interviews (2010) and ethnographic interviews (2011). While three of the learners largely selected the *desu/masu* form after study abroad, as community members typically do, it is notable that two used the plain form in a unique and sometimes divergent manner. For example, they shifted into the plain form to express self-directed thoughts and emotions, subordinate information, or summaries, to avoid sounding distant, and to construct their uniquely-situated identities. Rather than simply characterizing this phenomenon as a regression, Iwasaki (2010, 2011) views it as an aspect of language socialization in which the learners became active agents as they index their complex social identities through style shifting in the target community.

In FL contexts, where exposure to the TL is in general extremely limited, technology, and in particular CMC, can provide an alternative bridge, integrating authentic interaction with TL speakers into the everyday context of language learning. In the area of L2 pragmatics, learners' pragmatic development facilitated through CMC has been documented in terms of addressivity in Spanish (González-Lloret, 2008) and in German and French (Kinginger & Belz, 2005), conversational closing strategies in Spanish (Gonzales, 2013), and strategies and sociopragmatic awareness of refusals in Japanese (Takamiya & Ishihara, 2013).

In a virtual online community, the practices of the community are reproduced and negotiated through participation by community members in technology-mediated activities (e.g., Lam, 2004, 2010; Thorne, Black, & Sykes, 2009). For instance, in Lam's (2004) study of two Chinese immigrants in the U.S., the virtual community of the Chinese-English bilingual chat room provided a new context for language socialization into a mixed-code variety of English within a monolingual U.S. context. In alignment with the framework of second language socialization, we view L2 learners' blogging not as just individual cognitive activity but rather as learners' socialization into and participation in the immediate virtual community as well as in the larger imagined community of TL speakers. We therefore propose to explore how learners acquire the textual and visual practices of blogging through socialization into the TL community, in our case, the virtual community of blogs authored and read mostly by peer university students as well as the real-world community of TL speakers while the learners studied abroad.

The research question addressed in this study is: How does the pragmatic competence of the L2 Japanese learners emerge and develop in blogs in which they were engaged before and after studying abroad?

METHOD

In this section, we describe the technological medium we adopted, the participants, and the language learning context over the 16-21 month period.

Table 1. Participants' profiles

Participants	Age, gender	Level of L2 proficiency	Blogging before study abroad	Period of study abroad	Blogging after study abroad	Total time in L2 culture
Whitley	20, female	Intermediate-Mid	Fall 2009	Spring/Fall 2010	Spring 2011	12 months
Katherine	20, female	Intermediate-Mid	Fall 2009	Spring 2010	Fall 2010, Spring 2011	6 months
Daniel	20, male	Intermediate-Low	Fall 2009	Spring 2010	Fall 2010	6 months

Participants

In the fall of 2009, eight intermediate and three advanced learners of Japanese in two classes in a private university in the eastern part of the U. S. were combined for a blog project and interacted with 23 learners of English enrolled in a large private university in Tokyo. All 11 participants were native speakers of American English majoring in Japanese. Their proficiency levels varied from intermediate-low to advanced-high on the ACTFL Oral Proficiency Guidelines, as estimated by the instructor. In assessing the students' proficiency levels, the instructor took into consideration their performance on achievement tests over the previous semesters as the students did not take a standardized test specifically for this research. Three of the intermediate learners, Whitley, Katherine, and Daniel (all pseudonyms), served as the focal participants in this research. All had studied in Japan for six to 12 months. Before study abroad, all of them took an intermediate Japanese course in which they engaged in the first phase of this blog project. Upon returning to the U.S., they took advanced courses including "advance reading, composition, and conversation," and "contemporary issues in Japanese society," during which they participated in the second phase of the blog project. The backgrounds of the three learners are given in Table 1.

Technology and the Instructional Context

In their intermediate and advanced Japanese courses, the learners kept blog entries using *WordPress*, a blog publishing application made available with support from the Center for Advanced Language Proficiency Education and Research at Pennsylvania State University. Advantages of *WordPress* include the fact that it saves the blog on its own server, maintains it, and provides ample space for data storage, with the option of downloading the free platform onto a local server (Swanson & Early, 2009). Through the blogs, the learners interacted with their peer readers in their own FL classroom as well as with distant expert users of the TL living in Japan. Combined with the learners' intercultural experiences in Japan, these interactions spanned a period of 16-21 months, continuously exposing them to the pragmatic norms and discourse practices of the target community and providing them with opportunities to become socialized into these practices.

In the face-to-face component of the instruction, learners became familiar with key concepts in pragmatics and intercultural communication and were encouraged to develop the metapragmatic awareness with which to analyze their own interactions in Japanese. The authors were, respectively, instructors of Japanese as an FL in the U.S. and of English as an FL in Japan, teaching pragmatics explicitly in face-to-face instruction in their respective courses and promoting interactions among each other's students through blogs for pragmatic and intercultural learning.

The learners of Japanese wrote their blog entries and received feedback in the TL but responded to the Japanese students' blogs in those learners' TL English. In the Japanese courses, the learners were required to post a self-introduction at the beginning of the course, a diary entry every week, and a reflective summary at the conclusion of the course. While these entries were unedited, three additional compositions were assigned and edited in a three-stage process before online posting. The learners' first drafts of these compositions were self-edited once after a one-on-one writing conference with the instructor, edited again by the learners themselves after a whole-class group conference, and edited a third time by the instructor.

Data Collection and Analysis

The data consisted of:

1. Learners' blog entries and responses to and from blog readers;
2. Research papers written by the learners at the end of each semester;
3. Video-recordings and *PowerPoint* slides of the learners' presentations of their research every semester;
4. Video-recordings of writing conferences with the instructor each semester;
5. Video-recordings and *PowerPoint* slides of the focal learners' joint presentation about the blog project at a faculty luncheon in the spring of 2011;
6. Responses to a background survey at the start of each semester; and
7. Responses to a post-instructional questionnaire about the blog project at the conclusion of each semester.

All data were collected during the semesters in the U.S. before and after the study abroad period. Moreover, additional data derived from Whitley's research during her study abroad, including her audio-recordings of two dinner table conversations with her host families at two different times, her poster from a presentation, a video-recording of that presentation, and her final research paper. Audio- and video-recordings were transcribed for analysis in part by Whitley for her own study, and the remainder by the second author for the present study.

To answer the research question, the data were initially analyzed inductively to identify patterns of learner development across the written and spoken data. Using a constant comparative method (Merriam, 1998), we looked for patterns and themes in the data by closely investigating each potential case of pragmatic development within each data type as well as across them, then within each learner as well as across them. Through this cross-case triangulation, similar patterns of development emerged as themes, while each participant' unique experiences or perspectives was also further noted and examined. In doing so, we adopted the framework of language socialization to examine the changes in learners' textual and visual practices in blog posts. Below, we report representative examples of the pragmatic learning of the three focal participants. In particular, we occasionally describe the interactions in which their peer students, the instructor, and expert Japanese speakers engaged with them as they may have collectively influenced the learners' pragmatic development through blogging, in their in-class and faculty luncheon presentations, and during the study abroad period.

RESULTS

In this section, we report on three salient features of the three participants' pragmatic development as demonstrated through the analysis of their blogs written before and after the study abroad period: (1) sophisticated analysis of the Japanese language, pragmatics, and culture, (2) a broadened pragmatic repertoire for expressing a range of pragmatic nuances, and (3) style shifting as negotiation of emerging identities. Below, we describe the learners' blog-based interactions for each of these features.

Sophisticated Analysis of the Japanese Language, Pragmatics, and Culture

Prior to studying abroad, the topics the learners addressed in nine composition blog posts included many pragmatics-related topics such as: *ritual refusal* (Chen, Ye, & Zhang,1995) of the offer of a drink (i.e., an unintended ostensible refusal as a precursor to an acceptance) (Katherine, Whitley), dialects within Japan (Katherine), literal and intended meanings of double negative constructions (Katherine), non-verbal behavior associated with greetings (Whitley), cross-gender friendship (Whitley), linguistic form and non-verbal aspects of requests in the workplace and during home-stay (Whitley), self-introductions (Daniel), and e-mail and letter writing conventions (Daniel).

Figure 1 is a screenshot from Daniel's blog entry regarding e-mail and letter writing conventions (posted on December 6, 2009). Daniel opened the post by explaining that he was going to study in Japan and would need to write emails to his professors in Japanese, which was why he selected this topic. He compared letter writing in English and Japanese and asked why a discussion of the weather and a query regarding the reader's health are required components in Japanese letters. All blog posts reported in this paper were originally written in Japanese. For the purpose of presentation in this paper, cited data were translated into English by two bilingual speakers of English and Japanese through the back translation technique.

...日本語の手紙には...ほかの違いもあります。例えば、いつも最初に、天気のコメントをしていますね。てがみのメインポイントを書く前に、いつも"いいお天気ですね"とか"ひどいあめですね"を書くそうです。それから、いつも"お元気ですか"を聞きます。なぜ"お元気ですか"と"いいお天気ですね"を書くことがすごく大事ですか。

... there are other differences in letters written in Japanese. For example, the writer always comments on the weather first. I've heard that before getting to the main point, the writer always says "the weather is nice, isn't it" or "there has been a terrible rain, hasn't there." Also, the writer always asks "how are you?" Why is it so important to write "how are you" and "the weather is nice, isn't it"?

Daniel then explained that in the U.S., letters went straight to the point to save time and that the reader's health was not inquired about. However, he added that it was better to include a line such as "How are you feeling?" or "Get well soon" when addressing someone sick. In the second paragraph, he brought up the topic of honorifics and asked when formal honorific openings (i.e., お元気でいらっしゃいますか 'How are you (honorific)') and its informal counterpart (お元気ですか 'How are you (non-honorific)') were used in letters and what differences existed between letters and emails in Japanese. He also mentioned that polite language was not used very much in English letters and emails and that generally speaking, letters were longer and more polite than emails. In the final paragraph, he compared formulaic openings in English and Japanese and asked for informal equivalents of "How yah been?" and "Whats up?" [*sic*].

Daniel's post elicited eight comments: four from peers and four from Japanese students respectively. The Japanese students pointed out that they would ask someone older or of higher status how they are but not usually their friends and that they themselves were not accustomed to writing formal letters that would start with a discussion of the weather. These responses highlighted contextual differences, challenging the stereotype Daniel may

Figure 1. Daniel's blog entry regarding e-mail and letter writing conventions

have held whereby letters and emails written in Japanese were invariably formal.

In weekly unedited blog posts, the learners were free to nominate topics of interest to them. Their choices revealed that they were often uncertain of social norms of behavior in Japan, expressed concern about those issues in authentic interactions during study abroad, and sought advice from expert speakers and peers. Indeed, pragmatic issues emerged frequently as a major source of anxiety in the learners' composition blogs before study abroad as they wished to avoid offending their interlocutors in Japan, whom they perceived as polite.

Whereas the nature of blogging interactions before study abroad was primarily informational, the posts the learners made after study abroad were better informed and showed more sophisticated or more critical analysis of social issues in Japan, pragmatic language use, and cultural stereotypes. Here, blogs may have served as a reflective tool, facilitating in-depth retrospection and observation of their previous knowledge and experience. After study abroad, the learners' social topics included: acceptance and refusal of immigrant workers and educational problems of immigrant children (Whitley), urgent medical care (Katherine), declining birth rate (Katherine), pension crisis (Katherine), and public and personal means of transportation (Daniel). Besides the social issues the learners were required to write about as part of the course, pragmatics remained a regular topic, including use of honorifics (Katherine), children's manners (Daniel), and nuances and distributions of onomatopoeia (definitions immediately below) (Daniel).

In the post about onomatopoeia written after study abroad on December 19, 2010 shown below (Figure 2), Daniel defined the concept with examples and stated that there is great variety in Japanese onomatopoeia, citing his textbook and a blog article. He asked about the frequency of use of onomatopoeia by Japanese speakers as well as pragmatic nuances and gender differences in the use of onomatopoeia in Japanese:

...このブログを読んでいる日本人のみなさんは...毎日擬音語か擬態語を使いますか。友だちは、よく使いますか。よく使ったら、子供っぽいですか。擬音語と擬態語とどちらのほうが多いと思いますか。英語では、擬音語は擬態語より、多いのではないでしょうか。アメリカでは、話をする時、もっと生き生きさせるために、*Smack*とか*Boom*のような言葉をたくさん使うことが普通です。日本では、同じですか。せいべつによって違うと思いますか。女の人と男の人と、どちらのほうが擬態語と擬音語を使いますか。...

...do you, the Japanese readers of this blog, use giongo [phonomimes, onomatopoeia representing words that simulate sounds] or gitaigo [phenomimes/psychomimes, describing states and feelings] every day? Do your friends use them often? If you use them frequently, do you sound childish? Which do you think there is more of, giongo or gitaigo? There is more giongo than gitaigo in English, isn't there? In the U.S., it is common to use words like smack or boom to make your story come alive. Is this the same in Japan? Are there any gender differences? Who of women or men use gitaigo and giongo more?...

Curiously, this post elicited no response, even though Daniel's posts usually received a number of comments from the Japanese students. The metapragmatic questions Daniel asked here may have been beyond his readers' explicit linguistic and pragmatic knowledge. The native-speaking Japanese students may not have been aware of when and how they use onomatopoeia themselves, and especially of the potentially distinctive use of *giongo* and *gitaigo*, nor of any gender differences. Because onomatopoeia is frequently used and not necessarily associated with the childishness Daniel inquired about here, Japanese students may not have truly understood his questions.

The other post study abroad diary posts included topics such as: folk beliefs and discrimination

Figure 2. Daniel's blog entry regarding onomatopoeia

Home About

← 日記6－音楽

擬音語と擬態語とアメリカのOnomatopoeiaについてのブログ

Posted on December 19, 2010 by ダニエル

日本人は、擬音語と擬態語をよく使うって聞きました。擬態語と擬音語の違いは知っていますか。擬態語の例は、"きりきり"とか、"のろりくろり"とか、"しくしく"です。その言葉は、痛みのあらわしかたの言葉です。でも、擬音語は、ちょっと違います。擬音語は、音のような言葉です。例えば、わんわん（犬のなきごえ）とかにゃーお（猫のなきごえ）は本当の音のようですから、擬音語です。私の日本語の授業の"Intermediate Japanese"という教科書やこのブログの下の記事によると、日本語では、擬態語と擬音語がとっても多いです。でも、たくさんあると言っても、擬音語と擬態語を使うことはあまり普通じゃないほど、子供っぽいです。それは、本当ですか。擬音語と擬態語は、英語でOnomatopoeiaと言います。難しい単語ですね。アメリカでは、擬音語と擬態語を使うことが普通なのではないでしょうか。本当に、私の場合は、毎日のように使います。たぶん時々ちょっと子供っぽくて、うるさいですが、私の変な話し方のせいで、使うより仕方がありません。Onomatopoeiaが好きです。使いすぎるほど使います。もちろん、よく使うことは、使いますが、アメリカ人のみなさんもよく使うとは限りません。

このブログを読んでいる日本人のみなさんは、どう思いますか。毎日擬音語か擬態語を使いますか。友だちは、よく使いますか。よく使ったら、子供っぽいですか。擬音語と擬態語とどちらのほうが多いと思いますか。英語では、擬音語は擬態語より、多いのではないでしょうか。アメリカでは、話をする時、もっと生き生きさせるために、SmackとかBoomのような言葉をたくさん使うことが普通です。日本では、同じですか。せいべつによって違うと思いますか。女の人と男の人と、どちらのほうが擬態語と擬音語を使いますか。Xamuel.comというウェブサイトは擬態語と擬音語の長いリストがあります。英訳もあります！興味があったら、見てみて下さい。

http://www.yourdictionary.com/library/japonoma.html

http://www.xamuel.com/examples-of-japanese-onomatopoeia/

http://www.nihongoresources.com/dictionaries/onomatopoeia.html

An Integrated Approach to Intermediate Japanese

Search

Recent Posts

- 擬音語と擬態語とアメリカのOnomatopoeiaについてのブログ
- 日記6－音楽
- 日本とアメリカの国内旅行についてのブログ
- 日記4－私の家
- 日記3－ドイツ語

Recent Comments

- ルーカス on 日本とアメリカの国内旅行についてのブログ
- スミス on 日本とアメリカの国内旅行についてのブログ
- Rina on 日本とアメリカの国内旅行についてのブログ
- Rei on 日本とアメリカの国内旅行についてのブログ
- はな on 日本とアメリカの国内旅行についてのブログ

Archives

- December 2010
- October 2010
- September 2010

クラスのブログ

- JPN 303 Blog Café
- JPN301 Blog Café

Meta

- Log in
- Entries RSS
- Comments RSS
- WordPress.org

Figure 3. Katherine's response to a Japanese student, Yuna

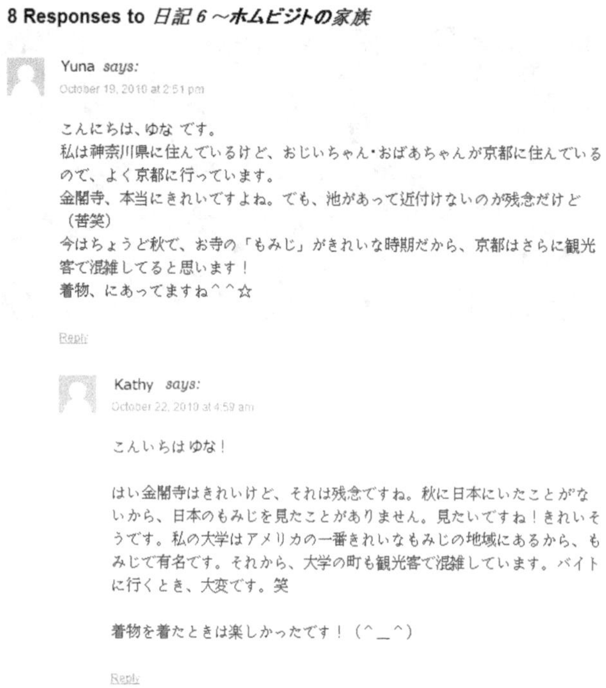

based on blood type, cross-cultural difference in the use of make-up among female college students and the cosmetic business, art and fashion in Japan, and expatriate status in Japan. Japanese students and peer's responses to these post-study abroad posts were in general rather marginal. In most cases, the blog readers merely agreed or provided peripheral information or no responses.

As seen from the learner-selected topics reported above and emerging in learners' composition blog entries, pragmatics remained a major area of interest to the learners before and after study abroad. Before departure, the nature of the blogging interactions was informational and affective as learners gained both useful advice and emotional support for their upcoming study abroad. However, upon return, the learners' observations showed greater sophistication, possibly beyond the level of the pragmatic awareness of the TL speakers.

A Broadened Pragmatic Repertoire

A comparison of the learners' pre- and post-study abroad blog responses and weekly diary posts, all of which consisted of unedited spontaneous writing, revealed apparent differences in the following pragmatics-related areas: addressivity, the use of a regional dialect, the expression of gendered identity through the use of sentence-final particles, the use of emoticons, and style shifting between *desu/masu* and plain forms (see the next section for details of style shifting).

Among the three participants, Katherine showed the most substantial changes after the study abroad experience and appeared to broaden her pragmatic repertoire most extensively. Before study abroad, she referred to herself as *watashi* ('I (formal)'), while upon return, she also used *atashi* ('I (informal, female)') as well as friendly or playful nicknames in addressing close friends (e.g., *uitto, uitto-chama* for Whitley). She also employed the friendly, normative address of

Figure 4. Katherine's response to a Japanese student, Nacchan

2 Responses to ***日記 8 ～ジェットプログラム***

Nacchan *says:*
November 17, 2010 at 4:27 am

こんにちは、キャシー （^　^）☆

ジェット・プログラムの教師かはわかりませんが、
小学校、中学校、高校には、英語の授業のアシスタントとして
外国の講師が来ていましたよ！
どの方も愉快な方々で、とても楽しい授業でした♪

Reply

Kathy *says:*
November 18, 2010 at 6:05 am

こんにちは、なっちゃん　~

そうですか。いいですね！大学の日本語の一年生のときの授業で、日本人の講師が来ていました。その講師は愉快な講師だったから、講師のおかげで授業は楽しかった。そのような教師になりたいから、ジェット・プログラムをしたいです。だから、日本人は外国人の先生は楽しいと思うのはいいと思います。\(^o^)/　そのアシスタントとして外国の講師の授業で、何をしましたか。

Reply

"first name-*san*" for Japanese students before study abroad. Departing from that practice upon return, she used first names only without *–san,* as typically done in English, or the nicknames the Japanese students themselves used. (See Figure 3 for a sample of Katherine's response to a Japanese student's comment, October 22, 2010.)

After study abroad, Katherine and Whitley demonstrated a style shifting skill when handling addressivity in speaking. All three participants had an opportunity to present their experience of blog-mediated language learning telecollaboration in English at a faculty luncheon. Although in informal blog posts written in Japanese, they addressed each other as *kyashii* 'Kathy' and *uitto* 'Whit' as they might do in English, at this rather formal presentation, when they switched to Japanese, they addressed each other as *sumisu-san* 'Smith-san' and *uittolei-san* 'Whitley-san' as typically done in Japanese in such a context.

Furthermore, intensifiers from a Western Japanese dialect (e.g., *honmani* 'really (regional),' *meccha* 'super (informal, regional)') appeared in Katherine's post-study abroad data. While she frequently used the female sentence-final particle *wane* before departure, her use of it was much less frequent after her return. In addition, although she used Japanese-style emoticons moderately before study abroad (e.g., ^_^, ^^, =}, ☆★), she used a greater variety of them with increased frequency after returning (e.g., \(^o^)/, ^_^). Some of these features appear in Figure 4 below, posted on November 18, 2010.

Whitley's pragmatic language use also shifted before and after study abroad in a manner that is not necessarily identical to Katherine's. Prior to study abroad, Whitley usually addressed her classmates using the "last name-*san*" style, a generic gender-free style indexing formality or distance. An exception was made for very close friends, whom she addressed by their first names. When

Japanese students addressed her as *uiitolee,* thus expressing psychological closeness, she did not reciprocate in the same style. Instead, she used their first names and added *–san* (e.g., *keita-san*), a less formal style than the form of address she used before study abroad. After study abroad, she often omitted addressing others in her blog comments but occasionally used *–san* with the first or last names the writers used for self-identification. Moreover, Whitley expressed her concern regarding the obligatory gendered choice between what she perceived as male or female language. In response to her English-speaking peers, she stated that neither Japanese nor American English was gender-free and that choosing gendered language was a difficult issue. In fact, she did not use what is typically considered female language at all before study abroad, whereas she occasionally used some (e.g., …*kashira* 'I wonder (female)') after returning to the U.S. Like Katherine, Whitley also used Japanese-style emoticons more frequently after study abroad.

Of the three focal learners, Daniel exhibited the fewest changes over time in the language he used in spontaneous blog comments. He used *watashi* 'I (formal)' to refer to himself and addressed others using the formal "last name-*san*" style regardless of the relationship both before and after study abroad. The only major observable change (other than style shifting, which is discussed below) was that he started using some Japanese emoticons (such as 笑!'laughter!,' and ^^) after returning home, while he preferred to use American emoticons (e.g.,:(,:p) before going abroad.

In sum, all three learners appeared to have expanded their pragmatic repertoire (e.g., addressivity, the use of a regional dialect and emoticons, the expression of gendered identity), which allowed them to become better able to express pragmatic nuances. It is notable that the learners showed similar patterns of development in certain aspects of pragmatic development (e.g., addressing each other) but not in others (e.g., the use of gendered language and addressivity used for TL speakers).

Style Shifting as Negotiation of Emerging Identities

As stated above, the choice of clause-final particles between the addressee-honorific *desu/masu* and non-honorific plain forms is obligatory in principle in Japanese, and style shifting between these forms indexes the speaker's dynamic epistemic stance, positioning, and identities in a complex manner. Before study abroad, Daniel and Katherine consistently used the *desu/masu* form across contexts. After study abroad, although they continued to use this style in the composition of formal blog entries (e.g., アメリカでは、遠く国内旅行することがとても不便です 'In America, it is inconvenient to travel domestically over long distances (*desu/masu* form),' Daniel, October 27, 2010), they began to use the plain form in informal diary posts directed to their close classmates and to Japanese students of own their age (e.g., 今年の夏、留学した後で、兄の家に引っ越した 'This summer I moved into my brother's house after studying abroad (plain form),' Daniel, October 4, 2010). Such a style shifting pattern was not observed in their pre-study abroad writing.

Unlike Katherine and Daniel, who learned to switch between the two forms largely through exposure to the target culture, Whitley selected style shifting and addressivity as the topics of her own independent project, which was funded by an external private foundation. She researched this complex phenomenon by collecting naturally occurring data while studying abroad. After returning home, she transcribed the audio-taped data, analyzed these using findings from current literature, and wrote up a research paper. Possibly due to such extensive metapragmatic analysis, her style shifting strategies were clearly distinguishable from Katherine and Daniel's in terms of her sensitivity to the genre of the written content (see below).

Whitley stated in her pre-study abroad blog posts that she initially became interested in style shifting while discussing the topic on her blog.

Whitley acknowledged that choosing between the two forms is difficult even for native speakers of Japanese, and she raised the question of how exchange students should deal with this challenge. She mentioned that although she should continue to use the *desu/masu* form when speaking to her professors even after a first encounter, the choice between the *desu/masu* and plain forms is somewhat optional when speaking to age peers at subsequent encounters. She suggested that exchange students could perhaps wait to switch to the plain form until their peers do so first. A peer student responded that it is important to use the plain form to appear friendly in cultivating friendships, but that it is in general safe to start with the *desu/masu* form when meeting someone for the first time. She agreed with Whitley's suggestion about waiting to switch to the plain form until the relationship develops and their interlocutor's style shifts.

Much later, based on the two audio-recordings of the dinner-table conversation Whitley made during study abroad, she offered some observations in her research about the style shifting strategies of her host family members. She found that the father and both daughters (aged 10 and 13) were using a local Western Japanese dialect and the plain form exclusively. The mother primarily adopted the dialect and plain form but occasionally sprinkled her utterances with the *desu/masu* form. In her research paper, which she also presented as a poster talk at an annual student-led cross-disciplinary conference on campus, Whitley explained the self-presentational stance as follows:

...the speaker has become more aware of the addressee and feels as though he or she is on a stage of sorts. This happens when the speaker is assuming the role of a teacher, ... quoting the speech of a socially high-status person, or performing a role-playing scenario ... (Cook, 2008, pp. 112-115)...

Whitley then showed several examples from her naturally-occurring data to demonstrate the *desu/masu* form as a marker of self-presentational stance indexing the identity of: a "knowledgeable party (#1 below), an authority figure in serving a meal (#2), and a teacher of Japanese culinary culture (#3), as shown below (with Whitley's own translations):

1. Mother: *Kore wa iro ga chanto tsuitara aji ga shunderu tte iu shouko* ***desu***. 'This is a type of food in which the taste [of the broth] has penetrated the vegetables if the color has changed.'
2. Mother: *Udon ni shi**mashou**ka*. 'Shall we go with the *udon* noodles?'
3. Mother: *Kore wa totemo bitamin ga houfu* ***desu***. 'This is very rich in vitamins.'

In the video-taped presentation of her research, Whitley also illustrated children's' naturally-occurring use of the unmarked *desu/masu* form in the presentational stance. When her two young host sisters invited Whitley into their room, which they called a "wonderland," and told her to use her "magic power" in a role-play, they gave the instructions in the *desu/masu* form. She concluded in her research paper that style shifting between the *desu/masu* and plain forms was undertaken exactly in accordance with Cook's framework.

Thus, it is important to consider Whitley's style shifting in blog posts in the context of her metapragmatic research. Similar to Daniel and Katherine, most of the spontaneous blog comments Whitley made before study abroad were written in the *desu/masu* form. Even when Japanese students commented using the plain style, Whitley usually responded in the polite form except for the formulaic expression, *arigatou* 'thank you,' in the plain style. Likewise, the language she used in the composition of her more formal blog entries was almost exclusively written in the *desu/masu* form before study abroad.

However, upon returning, she sometimes used the plain form in writing to her English-speaking classmates in spontaneous responses (e.g., うん、

日本語の勉強を続けるつもりだよ 'yeah, I'm planning on continuing to study Japanese (plain form),' March 22, 2011), although her use of the *desu/masu* form was still predominant. While Whitley used the plain form approximately on only 10% of occasions before study abroad, upon returning her use of the plain form increased to 27%. Moreover, in contrast to Katherine and Daniel, who selected the *desu/masu* form in their formal academic compositions, Whitley employed the plain form exclusively in these posts (e.g., 今、ラテンアメリカの移民は36万6千人ぐらい日本に住んでいる 'Nowadays 366,000 Latin American immigrants live in Japan (plain form),' April 7, 2011).

After study abroad, Whitley also used the *desu/masu* form in less formal writing such as diary blog posts (e.g., ですから、多くの食べものは輸入されています 'so (*desu/masu* form), many foods are imported (*desu/masu* form),' May 16, 2011) and in responses to Japanese students as well as in a popular social network service, *Mixi*. Yet, she sometimes switched to the plain form when commenting to her close classmates, as mentioned above (e.g., これはあくまでも推測だが… 'This is only my inference but…' (plain form), March 18, 2011).

Although our main purpose is to investigate the learners' pragmatic development demonstrated through their blog posts, let us also consider their written stylistic choices in light of the style shifting strategies they employed in spoken Japanese. In the in-class presentation after study abroad, the learners predominantly used the *desu/masu* form. This can be viewed as an unmarked style for this type of formal academic speech. Only rarely was the plain style mixed during the talk. Similarly, in asking a close friend (Katherine) a question following the presentation, Whitley employed the *desu/masu* form (as well as the formal address form *sumisu-san* 'Smith-san,' as mentioned above) even though she typically used the plain form and casual language with Katherine in informal situations. Whitley's stylistic choice demonstrates her awareness of the unmarked *desu/masu* form typically used between close interlocutors in the presence of an audience consisting largely of more distant relationships.

On the other hand, inconsistency was found between Whitley's stylistic choice in writing and speech. Before and after study abroad, students had three individual writing conferences with the instructor each semester as well as with peers in class. The conferences were conducted primarily in English, with a few exceptional moments in which the students spoke in Japanese. Before study abroad, Whitley consistently used the *desu/masu* form regardless of whether she was speaking to her instructor or to a close classmate. However, upon return, she frequently switched to the plain form during one-on-one conferences with the instructor (e.g., ほかのへんなところはある? 'Are there any other awkward places? (plain form)' (March 24, 2011), a casual speech style she did not used to employ before study abroad. This choice could be quite face-threatening; in fact, her instructor perceived her speech style as atypical.

In this section, we reported on the change in learners' style shifting strategies over time. While Katherine and Daniel learned to switch between the *desu/masu* and plain forms largely through exposure to the target culture, Whitley's style shifting in blogging operated based on her research on this topic and was reflective of her metapragmatic awareness of the genre. In the following discussion, we will revisit the findings with a view to analyzing the learners' pragmatic development as revealed through their blog posts in relation to their language socialization and negotiation of identities.

DISCUSSION

Although our primary data consist of the learners' blog posts uploaded before and after studying abroad and from which their pragmatic development can be extrapolated, we now take into consideration the learners' experience during study abroad, which may have assisted in shaping their sense of community and identity construction.

Before study abroad, much of the participants' language learning probably occurred within the classroom walls. Communicating with Japanese students through blogs and watching online Japanese videos recommended in face-to-face instruction certainly exposed them to authentic language use and connected them to the TL community outside of the classroom. Yet, their membership in that community is unlikely to have been fully developed in that context. It seems that it was only when the learners anticipated becoming novice members of that community that they began to be more concerned about successful communication. Immediately before study abroad, pragmatic issues emerged frequently as a major source of anxiety in the learners' composition blogs. Blog responses from experienced peers and expert Japanese speakers provided useful information and affective support, which helped the learners feel more secure or at least less anxious. In fact, Daniel reflected much later in the presentation for the faculty luncheon that blogging helped him reduce anxiety. At this stage, more experienced peers and experts appeared to have guided the learners and eased their socialization into the practices of the community through explicit discussion of the pragmatic norms and social conventions.

During study abroad, the learners were immersed in community practices and most likely used Japanese in negotiating their position within the community. As they were concerned about how to present themselves and how they would be perceived in the target community, pragmatic issues may have been their immediate concern. While using the TL, the learners seemed to have been constantly reconstructing their sociocultural being (Pavlenko & Lantolf, 2000), identifying themselves according to the immediate context as an exchange student, a friendly person, a member of a Western-Japanese community, a woman, a young person, or at other times a competent Japanese language user. After study abroad, these (re) constructed identities appear to have manifested themselves in their blog posts through their pragmatic use of Japanese, as in the use of informal personal pronouns and terms of address, the partial adoption of a Western Japanese dialect, gendered sentence-final particles, Japanese emoticons, and style shifting in addressivity markers and clause-final particles.

While negotiating their identities in Japanese, the learners may have been required to make pragmatic choices as to whether to participate in the perceived community norms or resist them to position themselves uniquely within the community, which, in accordance with language socialization theory, can lead to continuity or change in community practices (Garrett & Baquedano-López, 2002). For example, Katherine diversified her pragmatic repertoire by sometimes adopting an informal first-person pronoun, playful nicknames, a Western Japanese dialect, and Japanese emoticons. Notably, she used fewer gendered sentence-final particles after study abroad, possibly due to her deliberate avoidance of sounding too feminine. Although she used normative addressivity with Japanese students before study abroad, she opted to use American-style addressivity after her return, constructing her bilingual identity in the blog community with bilingual American and Japanese students. This departure from conventional language use may seem on the surface to be a regression in a traditional view of language learning. However, we view this as their agentive negotiation of identity, or the deliberate pragmatic choice through which they elect to construct their unique sociocultural being in a target community, a phenomenon that was also demonstrated by Iwasaki (2010, 2011). Instead of choosing between an American speaking English and a Japanese individual speaking Japanese as in a typical monolingual community, Katherine may have perceived her community, both online and in the classroom, as bilingual.

Moreover, all three learners demonstrated the development of effective style shifting strategies. Daniel's and Katherine's stylistic choice between the *desu/masu* and plain forms were similar to each other's, distinguishing the formally written composition blogs, in which the *desu/masu* form was used, from informally written spontaneous posts, in which the plain form was preferred. For their part, Katherine and Whitley were observed to style shift effectively in formal presentations, employing both formal terms of address and the *desu/masu* form.

However, Whitley appeared to be more sensitive to genre-specific style shifting than Katherine and Daniel, perhaps due to the highly developed metapragmatic awareness she achieved through her own pragmatics-focused research. While style shifting strategies in blogs vary under the influence of the content of the blog (Matsumura & Miura, 2005), Whitley's choice appears to conform to the style often employed in professionally written blog entries, newspaper articles, and editorials, which can be viewed as a sign of her language socialization. She may have observed that the plain form was often used in these genres in reading online or studying in Japan. In fact, she was exposed to various online articles in different genres in face-to-face instruction in the Japanese language courses being described in this study, and she may have paid attention to stylistic choices made in relation to the genre in question. Although she did not directly explain her style shifting choices, she appears to have been making a distinction between the two styles in her blog writing in a systematic manner, as often practiced in the online TL community.

Analyzing the naturally-occurring data she collected and citing a well-known researcher of second language acquisition, Whitley's sense of community may have expanded to include not only native-speaking non-expert Japanese speakers but also expert researchers of second language acquisition. Her non-standard use of the plain form employed when addressing her instructor may be viewed as offensive, face-threatening, or divergent from community practice. However, through this unique pragmatic choice, which also falls within the tenets of language socialization, she may have been exercising agency in a creative, non-conventional manner. After study abroad, she may have felt psychologically and socially close to the particular instructor she had known for two years and may have been constructing a form of psychological familiarity with her. It may also be that she was simultaneously claiming her emerging identities as both a competent language user and a researcher, possibly on an equal footing with the instructor, who had by then begun to use more plain forms in speaking to her.

Similarly, Daniel also appears to have successfully constructed himself as a competent language user. His post-study-abroad blog post quoted above indicates that he was meta-pragmatically aware of the use of onomatopoeia in English and Japanese and asked sophisticated questions regarding the pragmatic nuances associated with their use in Japanese. Daniel's metapragmatic awareness seems to have been more advanced than that of less pragmatically-informed Japanese students, who were unable to provide him with any comments. This post appears to have established him as an expert language user, or at least as a pragmatically sophisticated learner.

Stepping back in order to situate this study within current research on technology and language learning, several unique characteristics of this study make a contribution to the broader literature. Among the vast investigation into the impact of technology-mediated language learning, only a handful of studies have examined pragmatic development, especially in Japanese as an FL promoted through blogging, as we did in this study (Taguchi & Sykes, 2013; Takamiya & Ishihara, 2013). This study is also unique in its longitudinal approach to instructed pragmatic development. The learners' pragmatic competence was observed and triangulated across multiple data sources during the semester in which pragmatics were explicitly taught. Moreover, the participants' development during and after study abroad was also traced in relation to their language socialization spanning a period of 16-21 months. An added ingredient in this longitudinal approach is the record of one of the learners' metapragmatic awareness, which was refined through her undergraduate research on the pragmatics of style shifting in Japanese.

It may also be illuminating to acknowledge the pedagogical and analytical role of the medium of blog technology, which we believe facilitated both the learners' pragmatic development and our examination of that development in this study. Unlike more individualized email communication, blogging necessarily implies multi-directionality and appears to have facilitated the formation of the sense of community among the learners and expert speakers of the TL. With the expert speakers in mind, the learners may have developed enhanced audience awareness as they went beyond the transmission of general knowledge about the target culture to include their in-depth critical reflections on researched information. Moreover, the theme-based organization facilitated by the blog format appears to have promoted extended discussions of the issues addressed involving multiple readers. In-depth reflections and dialogue that can occur as a result may thus be viewed as strengths of the blog medium as a pedagogical tool, generating educational effects that may not be readily achieved through other social media such as *Facebook* or *Skype*. Simultaneously, blogs also allowed us access to authentic data, enabling in-depth assessment of learner development over time across learners with enhanced credibility.

CONCLUSION AND FUTURE RESEARCH DIRECTIONS

In this chapter, we examined our focal learners' longitudinal development of pragmatic competence. Close analysis of their pragmatic language use before and after study abroad revealed their development in the areas of: addressivity, gendered language, regional dialect, emoticons, and style shifting between the *desu/masu* and plain clause-final forms. As their sense of community expanded through study abroad and blog-mediated telecollaboration, so did their pragmatic repertoire and identities. Because they were sharing similar backgrounds, their development showed some common features (e.g., increased frequency of emoticons, style shifting for the presentational stance, and use of informal address terms). Meanwhile, these learners also followed unique trajectories in negotiating their own emerging identities (e.g., Daniel as an expert language user, Katherine as a bilingual speaker and a member of a Western-Japan community, and Whitley as a competent researcher).

Accordingly, the role played by blog technology in language development may have differed at various stages in the learning process. Before study abroad, blogs provided the learners with opportunities to use language meaningfully with TL speakers situated remotely. This initial exposure to target community and authentic language use appears to have promoted the learners' socialization and alleviated their anxiety. Upon return, the learners appears to have negotiated their multiple identities more powerfully, sometimes constructing themselves as expert language users or bilingual speakers. They were observed to be not only reproducing community norms but sometimes actively negotiating such norms to use them in a unique manner. The blogging technology and the online interactions it facilitates can therefore be the medium through which such developments occur and can be studied.

As blogs are a relatively new technology, the pragmatic and discursive norms of this online medium may still be in flux. One of the challenges encountered in this study was to identify community practices, such as normative style shifting between the *desu/masu* and plain forms in relation to the genres used in the blog. Future studies investigating technology-assisted language learning should therefore be conducted in a manner sensitive to the influence of the medium, the genre, and the language register, and the complex interactions among them.

Pedagogically, although we were unable to track the participants' development during study abroad in this research, learners can note down in their blogs surprises, shocks, puzzlements, linguistic observations, intercultural misunderstandings, pragmatic errors, discrepancies with previous instruction, sociocultural conventions they feel resistant to conforming to, queries about the underlying cultural meaning of specific community practices, and so forth. Blogs allow learners to keep record of their fresh impressions as well as revisit and analyze these retrospectively with the support of face-to-face instruction, as in this study. In addition, by initiating interaction on the topics of their choice, learners can engage expert and peer speakers of the TL in metacognitive and metapragmatic dialogue, as discussed earlier. Thus, blogs have the potential to facilitate such an autonomous process of language learning and encourage language socialization into the pragmatic and discursive practices of the target community, with the learners being guided with specific instruction. Future research into this language socialization can reveal the process in greater depth, which can in turn propel innovation in devising effective pedagogies for blog-mediated telecollaboration.

REFERENCES

Arslan, R. Ş., & Şahin-Kizil, A. (2010). How can the use of blog software facilitate the writing process of English language learners? *Computer Assisted Language Learning*, *23*(3), 183–197. doi:10.1080/09588221.2010.486575

Bayley, R., & Schecter, S. R. (2003). *Language socialization in bilingual and multilingual societies*. Clevedon, UK: Multilingual Matters.

Belz, J. A. (2007). The role of computer mediation in the instruction and development of L2 pragmatic competence. *Annual Review of Applied Linguistics*, *27*, 45–75. doi:10.1017/S0267190508070037

Blake, R. J. (2011). Current trends in online language learning. *Annual Review of Applied Linguistics*, *31*, 19–35. doi:10.1017/S026719051100002X

Bloch, J. (2007). Abdullah's blogging: A generation 1.5 student enters the blogosphere. *Language Learning & Technology*, *11*(2), 128–141.

Carney, N. (2007). *Language study through blog exchanges*. Paper presented at the Wireless Ready Symposium: Podcasting Education and Mobile Assisted Language Learning, NUCB Graduate School. Nagoya, Japan. Available from, http://wirelessready.nucba.ac.jp/Carney.pdf

Carney, N. (2009). Blogging in foreign language education. In M. Thomas (Ed.), *Handbook of research on Web 2.0 and second language learning* (pp. 292–312). Hershey, PA: IGI Global. doi:10.4018/978-1-60566-190-2.ch016

Chen, X., Ye, L., & Zhang, Y. (1995). Refusing in Chinese. In G. Kasper (Ed.), *Pragmatics of Chinese as a native and target language (Tech. Rep. No. 5)* (pp. 119–163). Honolulu, HI: University of Hawai'i, Second Language Teaching & Curriculum Center.

Cook, H. M. (2008). *Socializing identities through speech style: Learners of Japanese as a foreign language*. Clevedon, UK: Multilingual Matters.

Cook, H. M. (2010). Language socialization in Japanese. In P. A. Duff & N. H. Hornberger (Eds.), Encyclopedia of language and education (2nd ed., vol. 8, pp. 313-326). New York: Springer Science+Business Media LLC.

de Andrés Martínez, C. (2012). Developing metacognition at a distance: Sharing students' learning strategies on a reflective blog. *Computer Assisted Language Learning*, *25*(2), 199–212. doi:10.1080/09588221.2011.636056

Dos, B., & Demir, S. (2013). The analysis of the blogs created in a blended course through the reflective thinking perspective. *Educational Sciences: Theory and Practice*, *13*(2), 1335–1344.

Ducate, L. C., & Lomicka, L. L. (2005). Exploring the blogosphere: Use of web lobs in the foreign language classroom. *Foreign Language Annals*, *38*(3), 410–421. doi:10.1111/j.1944-9720.2005.tb02227.x

DuFon, M. A. (2008). Language socialization theory and the acquisition of pragmatics in the foreign language classroom. In E. S. Alcón, & A. Martínez-Flor (Eds.), *Investigating pragmatics in foreign language learning, teaching, and testing* (pp. 25–44). Bristol, UK: Multilingual Matters.

Elola, I., & Oskoz, A. (2008). Blogging: Fostering intercultural competence development in foreign language and study abroad contexts. *Foreign Language Annals*, *41*(3), 454–477. doi:10.1111/j.1944-9720.2008.tb03307.x

Freiermuth, M. R., & Huang, H. C. (2012). Bringing Japan and Taiwan closer electronically: A look at an intercultural online synchronic chat task and its effect on motivation. *Language Teaching Research*, *16*(1), 61–88. doi:10.1177/1362168811423341

Garrett, P. B., & Baquedano-López, P. (2002). Language socialization: Reproduction and continuity, transformation and change. *Annual Review of Anthropology*, *31*, 339–361. doi:10.1146/annurev.anthro.31.040402.085352

Geyer, N. (2008). Interpersonal functions of style shift: The use of plain and *masu* forms in faculty meetings. In K. Jones, & T. Ono (Eds.), *Style shifting in Japanese* (pp. 39–70). Amsterdam: John Benjamins. doi:10.1075/pbns.180.00int

Gonzales, A. (2013). Development of politeness strategies in participatory online environments: A case study. In N. Taguchi, & J. Sykes (Eds.), *Technology in interlanguage pragmatics research and teaching* (pp. 101–120). Philadelphia, PA: John Benjamins. doi:10.1075/lllt.36.06gon

González-Lloret, M. (2008). Computer-mediated learning of L2 pragmatics. In E. Alcón, & A. Martínez-Flor (Eds.), *Investigating pragmatics in foreign language learning, teaching and testing* (pp. 114–132). Clevedon, UK: Multilingual Matters.

Guarda, M. (2012). Computer-mediated discourse and interaction in second and foreign language learning and teaching. *Journal of E-Learning and Knowledge Society*, *8*(3), 15–27.

Ikuta, S. (2008). Speech style shift as an interactional discourse strategy: The use and non-use of *desu/-masu* in Japanese conversational interviews. In K. Jones, & T. Ono (Eds.), *Style shifting in Japanese* (pp. 71–89). Amsterdam: John Benjamins. doi:10.1075/pbns.180.00speech

Ishida, K. (2009). Indexing stance in interaction with the Japanese desu/masu and plain forms. In N. Taguchi (Ed.), Pragmatic competence (pp. 41-67). Berlin, Germany: Mouton de Gruyter.

Ishihara, N. (2006). *Subjectivity, second/foreign language pragmatic use, and instruction: Evidence of accommodation and resistance.* (Unpublished doctoral dissertation). University of Minnesota, Minneapolis, MN.

Ishihara, N. (2010). Maintaining an optimal distance: Nonnative speakers' pragmatic choice. In A. Mahboob (Ed.), *The NNEST lens: Nonnative English speakers in TESOL* (Vol. 1, pp. 35–53). Newcastle upon Tyne: Cambridge Scholars Press.

Iwasaki, N. (2010). Style shifts among Japanese learners before and after study abroad in Japan: Becoming active social agents in Japanese. *Applied Linguistics*, *31*(1), 45–71. doi:10.1093/applin/amn047

Iwasaki, N. (2011). Learning L2 Japanese "politeness" and "impoliteness": Young American men's dilemmas during study abroad. *Japanese Language and Literature*, *45*(1), 67–106.

Kinginger, C., & Belz, J. A. (2005). Sociocultural perspectives on pragmatic development in foreign language learning: Case studies from telecollaboration and study abroad. *Intercultural Pragmatics*, *2*(4), 369–421. doi:10.1515/iprg.2005.2.4.369

Lam, W. S. E. (2004). Second language socialization in a bilingual chat room. *Language Learning & Technology*, *8*(3), 44–65.

Lam, W. S. E. (2010). Language socialization in online communities. In P. A. Duff & N. H. Hornberger (Eds.), Encyclopedia of language and education (2nd ed., vol. 8, pp. 301-311). New York: Springer Science+Business Media LLC.

Lave, J., & Wenger, E. (1991). *Situated learning: Legitimate peripheral participation*. Cambridge, UK: Cambridge University Press. doi:10.1017/CBO9780511815355

Lee, L. (2011). Blogging: Promoting learner autonomy and intercultural competence through study abroad. *Language Learning & Technology*, *15*(3), 87–109.

Li, D. (2000). The pragmatics of making requests in the L2 workplace: A case study of language socialization. *Canadian Modern Language Review*, *57*(1), 58–87. doi:10.3138/cmlr.57.1.58

Li, D. (2010). Pragmatic socialization. In P. A. Duff & N. H. Hornberger (Eds.), Encyclopedia of language and education (2nd ed., vol. 8, pp. 71-83). New York: Springer Science+Business Media LLC.

Matsumura, N., & Miura, A. (2005). *Buroguni okeru kakiteno itoto modaritii hyougen* [Writers' intentions and modality expressions in weblog articles]. Paper presented at the 19th Annual Conference of the Japanese Society for Artificial Intelligence 2005. Available from, http://www-kasm.nii.ac.jp/jsai2005/schedule/pdf/000133.pdf

Maynard, S. (1991). Pragmatics of discourse modality: A case of *da* and *desu/masu* forms in Japanese. *Journal of Pragmatics*, *15*, 551–582. doi:10.1016/0378-2166(91)90111-A

Merriam, S. B. (1998). *Qualitative research and case study applications in education: Revised and expanded from Case Study Research in Education*. San Francisco, CA: Jossey-Bass Publishers.

Miceli, T., Murray, S. V., & Kennedy, C. (2010). Using an L2 blog to enhance learners' participation and sense of community. *Computer Assisted Language Learning*, *23*(4), 321–341. doi:10.1080/09588221.2010.495321

Miyazoe, T., & Anderson, T. (2010). Learning outcomes and students' perceptions of online writing: Simultaneous implementation of a forum, blog, and wiki in an EFL blended learning setting. *System*, *38*(2), 185–199. doi:10.1016/j.system.2010.03.006

Murray, L., Hourigan, T., & Jeanneau, C. (2007). Blog writing integration for academic language learning purposes: Towards an assessment framework. *IBÉRICA*, *14*, 9–32.

Ochs, E. (1993). Constructing social identity: A language socialization perspective. *Research on Language and Social Interaction*, *26*(3), 287–306. doi:10.1207/s15327973rlsi2603_3

Pavlenko, A., & Lantolf, J. P. (2000). Second language learning as participation and the (re) construction of selves. In A. Pavlenko, & J. P. Lantolf (Eds.), *Sociocultural theory and second language learning* (pp. 155–177). Oxford, UK: Oxford University Press.

Rivens Mompean, A. (2010). The development of meaningful interactions on a blog used for the learning of English as a foreign language. *ReCALL*, *22*(3), 376–395. doi:10.1017/S0958344010000200

Schieffelin, B. B., & Ochs, E. (1986). Language socialization across cultures. Cambridge, UK: Cambridge University Press.

Smith, K., & Craig, H. (2013). Enhancing the autonomous use of CALL: A new curriculum model in EFL. *CALICO Journal*, *30*(2), 252–278. doi:10.11139/cj.30.2.252-278

Sun, Y. C. (2009). Voice blog: An exploratory study of language learning. *Language Learning & Technology*, *13*(2), 88–103.

Swanson, P., & Early, P. (2009). Establish your presence in the blogosphere: A guide to blog development for the foreign language classroom. In C. Wilkerson (Ed.), *Dimension* (pp. 17–28). Valdosta, GA: SCOLT Publications.

Taguchi, N., & Sykes, J. (2013). *Technology in interlanguage pragmatics research and teaching*. Philadelphia, PA: John Benjamins. doi:10.1075/lllt.36

Takamiya, Y. (2009). Rediscovering Japan through blogs: Toward a curriculum that integrates language acquisition and cultural learning. In A. Gabriela (Ed.), *Teacher narratives: CALPER project-based learning and advanced proficiency*. Pennsylvania State University Center for Advanced Language Proficiency Education and Research. Available from, http://calper.la.psu.edu/projectwork/yumi_main.php

Takamiya, Y., & Ishihara, N. (2013). Blogging: Cross-cultural interaction for pragmatic development. In N. Taguchi, & J. Sykes (Eds.), *Technology in interlanguage pragmatics research and teaching* (pp. 185–214). Philadelphia, PA: John Benjamins. doi:10.1075/lllt.36.10tak

Thorne, S. L., Black, R. W., & Sykes, J. M. (2009). Second language use, socialization, and learning in internet interest communities and online gaming. *Modern Language Journal*, *93*, 802–821. doi:10.1111/j.1540-4781.2009.00974.x

Warschauer, M. (2010). New tools for teaching writing. *Language Learning & Technology*, *14*(1), 3–8.

Watson-Gegeo, K. A., & Nielsen, S. (2003). Language socialization in SLA. In C. J. Doughty, & M. H. Long (Eds.), *The handbook of second language acquisition* (pp. 155–177). Malden, MA: Blackwell Publishing. doi:10.1002/9780470756492.ch7

Yang, Y. F. D. (2011). Learner interpretations of shared space in multilateral English blogging. *Language Learning & Technology*, *15*(1), 122–146.

Zuengler, J., & Cole, K. (2005). Language socialization and second language learning. In E. Hinkel (Ed.), *Handbook of research in second language teaching and learning* (pp. 301–316). Mahwah, NJ: Lawrence Erlbaum Associates.

ADDITIONAL READING

Beltran, E. V., Abbott, C., & Jones, J. (2013). *Inclusive language education and digital technology*. Clevedon, UK: Multilingual Matters.

Belz, J., & Vyatkina, N. (2005). Learner corpus analysis and the development of L2 pragmatic competence in networked inter-cultural language study: The case of German modal particles. *Canadian Modern Language Review*, *62*(1), 17–48. doi:10.3138/cmlr.62.1.17

Belz, J. A. (2002). Social dimensions of telecollaborative foreign language study. *Language Learning & Technology*, *6*(1), 60–81.

Cook, H. M. (2006). Japanese politeness as an interactional achievement: Academic consultation sessions in Japanese universities. *Multilingua*, *25*(3), 269–291. doi:10.1515/MULTI.2006.016

Doerr, N., & Sato, S. (2011). The modes of governmentality in language education: Blog activities in a Japanese-as-a-foreign-language classroom. In E. Dunkels, G.-M. Frånberg, & C. Hallgren (Eds.), *Interactive media use and youth: Learning, knowledge exchange and behavior* (pp. 149–167). Hershey, PA: IGI Global. doi:10.4018/978-1-60960-206-2.ch009

Egbert, J. O. Y., Huff, L., McNeil, L., Preuss, C., & Sellen, J. (2009). Pedagogy, process, and classroom context: Integrating teacher voice and experience into research on technology-enhanced language learning. *Modern Language Journal, 93*(s1), 754–768. doi:10.1111/j.1540-4781.2009.00971.x

Gee, J., & Hayes, E. (2011). *Language and learning in the digital age*. New York: Routledge.

Ishihara, N., & Cohen, A. D. (2010). *Teaching and learning pragmatics: Where language and culture meet.* Harlow, UK: Pearson Education.

Jones, K., & Ono, T. (Eds.). (2008). *Style shifting in Japanese*. Amsterdam: John Benjamins. doi:10.1075/pbns.180

Kakegawa, T. (2009). Development of the use of Japanese sentence-final particles through email correspondence. In N. Taguchi (Ed.), *Pragmatic competence: Mouton Series in Pragmatics 5* (pp. 301–333). Berlin, Germany: Mouton de Gruyter.

Pasfield-Neofitou, S. E. (2012). *Online communication in a second language: Social interaction, language use, and learning Japanese*. Bristol, UK: Multilingual Matters.

Shively, R. (2010). From the virtual world to the real world: A model of pragmatic instruction for study abroad. *Foreign Language Annals, 43*(1), 105–137. doi:10.1111/j.1944-9720.2010.01063.x

Siegal, M. (1996). The role of learner subjectivity in second language sociolinguistic competency: Western women learning Japanese. *Applied Linguistics, 17*(3), 356–382. doi:10.1093/applin/17.3.356

Wenger, E. (1998). *Communities of practice: Learning, meaning, and identity*. Cambridge, UK: Cambridge University Press. doi:10.1017/CBO9780511803932

KEY TERMS AND DEFINITIONS

Addressivity: Addressing others while indexing contextual or relational nuances such as a degree of social and psychological familiarity or distance. In Japanese, this is realized by means of a variety of address terms such as *-san, -kun, -chan*, first name only, and last name only.

Blog (Weblog): Online journal typically consisting of a title, text, images, and links to other webpages arranged in reverse chronological order, often with space provided for comments from readers. This can be used as a public resource or as a private personal website and be both a reflective and an interactive medium.

Computer-Mediated Communication (CMC): Distance communication enabled by means of synchronous or asynchronous computer-based technology such as email, forums, wikis, blogs, chat, video conference tools, online gaming, and social networks.

Emoticon: A sequence of keyboard characters often used on the internet to emulate facial expression in an attempt to complement a text message that tends to be scarce in emotional expression in the electronic media (e.g.,:-) 'smile (English),' and (^0^)'laugh (Japanese).'

Gendered Particles in Japanese: Sentence-final morphemes typically perceived as indexing femininity or masculinity, such as *wa* and *no* (female) and *ze* and *zo* (male).

Pragmatic Competence: Verbal and non-verbal ability to understand and use language in a manner socially and culturally preferred in the given interactive context.

(Second) Language Socialization: Process by which novice members of the community gradually become experts as they acquire the knowledge, orientations, and social practices of the community through activities mediated by a (second) language.

Self-Presentational Stance: "On-stage" stance in which the speaker exhibits a positive social role in relation to an addressee(s). In Japanese, an unmarked form of this stance is indexed by the clause-final *desu/masu* form.

Style Shifting in Japanese Between the *Desu/Masu* and Plain Forms: Switching between the addressee-honorific *desu/masu* and non-honorific plain forms, through which the speaker dynamically indexes epistemic stance. The choice of these clause-final forms is obligatory in principle and is influenced by multiple factors beyond the traditional formal-informal or polite-less polite dichotomy.

Telecollaboration: Cooperative on-line interactions sometimes organized for educational purposes and mediated by one or more synchronous and asynchronous media including text or voice chat, audio- or video-conferencing tools, file-, audio- or video-sharing applications, and virtual worlds.

Chapter 8
(Dis)Engagement in Internet Linguistic Practices among Sojourners in China

Wenhao Diao
University of Arizona, USA

ABSTRACT

This chapter reports on a longitudinal study that investigates two American students' engagement in a local Social-Networking Site (SNS), Weibo, at a study abroad program in China. SNSs are often thought to hold great potential for L2 teaching. However, engagement in SNS activities not only requires cultural orientation towards social media but also knowledge about how to communicate on SNSs. Drawing from language socialization and community of practice frameworks, this chapter examines how two American students participated in networking activities on Weibo and to what extent they engaged in the use of Chinese Internet Language (CIL). The findings show that the incorporation of the local SNS in instruction seemed to help the students become aware of CIL, but their participation in Weibo remained peripheral. In addition, compared to the student who did home stay, the student living in the dorm seemed to have more opportunities to be socialized into CIL.

INTRODUCTION

Social networking sites (SNSs) have become increasingly common in our everyday life. As of May 2013, 72% of online adults in the U.S. are SNS users (Duggan & Brenner, 2013). Statistics from China are equally high, with over 90% of its Internet users having accounts on one of the social media sites, such as Sina Weibo and Renren (Chiu, Lin, & Silverman, 2012).

The popularity of social media has drawn attention from scholars in applied linguistics. SNSs are often believed to hold great potential for L2 education (e.g., Mitchell, 2012). Research has shown that some ESL learners in the U.S. develop the ability to participate in English literacy practices by using SNSs (e.g., Chen, 2013; Lam, 2004; Reinhardt & Zander, 2011). Meanwhile, SNSs are also often thought to hinder American students' L2 learning while they are overseas, because they

DOI: 10.4018/978-1-4666-6174-5.ch008

can easily opt out of the local linguistic practices by logging onto U.S.-based sites such as Facebook (Kinginger, 2008).

Such concerns may indeed be the case for study abroad students in many countries where U.S.-based sites are easily accessible and very popular. Yet it remains unknown how these students actually use social media when they are overseas learning other languages. Although American students have been reported to engage in various types of local discourse practices while studying abroad (e.g., Cook, 2008; Shively, 2011), few researchers have explored their participation in SNSs and their experience of learning and using L2 on the Internet during their sojourns. In addition, China has an abundance of popular local SNSs due to its socio-political context, presenting a unique social media landscape (Chiu et al., 2012). The popularity of local SNSs has further engendered a new type of linguistic practices, known as the Chinese Internet Language (CIL). For American students in China, participating in activities on local SNSs and engaging in the corresponding ways of language use can potentially allow such processes of L2 socialization to take place.

This chapter aims to describe how two American students engaged in the use of CIL as well as the activities on local SNS over their semester in China. They were studying at a program where instructors continuously incorporated the use of social media and CIL in the curriculum. Drawing on theories of language socialization (e.g., Duff & Talmy, 2010; Schieffelin & Ochs, 1986) and situated learning (Lave & Wenger, 1991), this study views learning of CIL as a byproduct of their socialization processes with members of China's SNS community – both online and offline (Thorne, Black, & Sykes, 2009). What follows in this chapter outlines the theoretical and methodological frameworks of this project and presents its findings. This chapter concludes with a discussion of implications and future research directions.

BACKGROUND

The Social-Media Landscape in China

With more than 500 million Internet users, China has already surpassed the United States (245 million users) and is currently the country with the largest population online (Chiu et al., 2012). While popular U.S.-based sites such as Facebook are not accessible, local social media sites are becoming increasingly popular among China's urban residents. The focus of this study is Sina Weibo (simply referred to as Weibo below). Weibo is among the most popular SNSs in China. It was reported to have 309 million users by the end of 2012, accounting for 54.7% of all Internet users (including but not limited to users of social media) in China (CNNIC, 2013). Not surprisingly, it was also the SNS selected at the study abroad program under question.

Weibo is a Twitter-like micro-blogging site that allows its users to engage in a variety of sharing and networking activities, including uploading original posts containing texts and/or images, following other users, reading and/or resending their posts, and commenting on other people's posts. Based on what activities one engages in, Chiu et al. (2012) categorized four types of Weibo users, namely, social enthusiasts, resenders, readers, opinionated users, and those who are inactive. Social enthusiasts spend a substantial amount of time online and actively engage in a variety of activities (e.g., uploading, reading, resending, and commenting, etc.). In comparison, resenders, readers, and opinionated users are only participating primarily in a limited number of these activities (Chiu et al., 2012). This categorization can help us conceptualize membership in the Weibo community as being unequal among its users.

China's social media users also demonstrate an interesting demographic pattern. SNS use is particularly common among city dwellers, with over 90% of them having registered on one of the SNSs (Chiu et al., 2012). Furthermore, approximately 80% of China's Internet users are young people between the ages of 10 and 40 living in urban areas (CNNIC, 2013, p. 17). This demographic feature has shaped the nature of the language used on China's social media, which is discussed below

Chinese Internet Language on Social Networking Sites

The medium of Internet provides new resources but also lacks certain conventional contextual cues such as prosody and gesture (Crystal, 2006). Due to the nature of the Internet and its close relationship with the hacker culture (Danet, 2001), language on the Internet tends to embody more innovation, subversiveness and playfulness (Crystal, 2006; Hale & Scanlon, 1999). Furthermore, such modes of language use have entered our face-to-face communication, particularly among the Internet-savvy youth so that they can create "a cool cutting-edge" (Crystal, 2006, p.19).

This phenomenon is also seen in the Sinophone world as the Internet becomes popular. In Chinese the term 网络语言 (*Wǎngluò yǔyán*, "Internet language") refers to the linguistic forms that are created or popularized on the Internet (mostly SNSs, or chat rooms before the creation and popularization of SNSs). Its popularity has led to the establishment of *Hudong*, an encyclopedia site devoted to collecting and defining these emerging expressions of CIL. Although research on CIL is still scarce, some common features of CIL emerge from the existing studies. Below is a summary of three features:

1. **Borrowing:** This is often achieved through using characters that represent sounds in dialects or foreign languages when writing in Mandarin (Gao, 2012; Liu, 2012; Su, 2009; Yan, 2012). For instance, Su (2009) describes the borrowing of Taiwanese Min into Mandarin among Taiwanese Internet users, such as using 帅锅 (*shuàiguō,* "handsome pot") to replace 帅哥 (*shuàigē*, "handsome guy") to create a humorous effect (Su, 2009, p.323). Foreign words can also be borrowed into CIL by using Chinese characters to represent the sounds, such as 恰特 (*qiàtè*, literally "just" and "special," but now used to represent the word "chat") (Gao, 2012). Some English expressions have also entered CIL through literal translation, such as 你懂的 (*nǐ dǒng de*, "you know").
2. **Puns:** Chinese is a homophone-rich language. Puns are often achieved through using homophones to add another semantic (oftentimes humorous) layer to the word (Liu, 2010). For instance, one example identified by Liu (2010) is the recent fad of using 杯具 (bēijù, "cup set") to represent 悲剧 (bēijù, "tragedy"), as in the following example: 人生像茶几,上面摆满了杯具; 人生又像茶杯,本身就是个杯具;人生更像茶叶,终究要被浸泡在杯具之 中。(Life is like a tea table, all covered in cups; life is also like the tea cup, itself also a cup; life is most of all like the tea leaves: in the end, they will all become steeped in the cup set). (Liu, 2010, p. 64). More examples of such punning and wordplays can be found under the categories of "analogy" and "semantic shift" in Gao's (2012) taxonomy.
3. **Contextualization:** Internet users often incorporate audio and visual information as contextual cues through writing (e.g., upper case, smiley icons) (Crystal, 2006). The logographic nature of the Chinese language enables CIL users to draw from the orthography and achieve similar functions (Gao, 2012). For instance, the character 囧 (*jiǒng*) is now used widely as an expression of embarrassment because of its visual resemblance to an awkward face.

As shown above, CIL contains many non-standard features and they tend to fade quickly. Possibly due to its subversive and dynamic nature (Liu, 2010), CIL is often overlooked and sometimes even frowned upon among Chinese linguists and language educators, as evidenced by Pan's book (2008) titled "Chinese under crisis" (c.f., Liu & Tao, 2012). However, CIL is by nature closely linked to the use of the Internet, particularly SNSs. CIL is therefore an important sociolinguistic feature for teachers eager to engage language learners in Chinese SNSs. Meanwhile, it also constitutes an important resource to construct humor in Mandarin communication (Liu, 2010; Su, 2009). As previous research has suggested, study abroad students can and do "learn to be funny" while overseas (Shively, 2013). The absence of CIL instruction in typical language classes in the U.S. then leads one to wonder how Mandarin learners in China can become socialized into such Internet linguistic practices, i.e., the use of CIL both on SNSs and beyond.

Language Socialization, Participation, and Social Networking Sites

Socialization refers to the process by which a child or other novice acquires the "knowledge, orientations, and practices that enable him or her to participate effectively and appropriately in the social life of a particular community" (Garrett & Baquedano-Lopez, 2002, p. 339). Language socialization research examines the dual processes of how novices are socialized through language and how they are socialized into cultural knowledge, orientations and communities (e.g., Ochs & Schieffelin, 1984; Schieffelin & Ochs, 1986). Since the central concern of language socialization research is to analyze how language is used in context within specific cultural communities (Garrett & Baquedano-Lopez, 2002; Schieffelin & Ochs, 1986; Ochs, 1996; Watson-Gegeo, 2004), it is highly compatible with the theory of community of practice (CoP). CoP refers to an aggregate of people who share a common enterprise and ways of doing things (i.e., practices) (Lave & Wenger, 1991). These practices may include ways of talking (Eckert & McConnell-Ginet, 1992). While members of one CoP share understanding concerning these practices (Lave & Wenger, 1991, p. 98), they often do not have the same level of participation and hence their membership statuses differ (Eckert, 2000). Learning, therefore, is defined as the process of moving from legitimate peripheral participation towards central membership (Lave & Wenger, 1991).

The notions of language socialization and CoP have generated a profound impact on the research of computer-mediated communication within the field of applied linguistics. For instance, Lam's (2004) study used these frameworks to examine two ESL learners from Hong Kong and their literacy practices in an online chat room while they were studying overseas. The case study method and the focus on learner's identity and socialization processes in Lam's (2004) study have become a defining feature of research on L2 learning in computer-mediated environments (Block, 2007). In their comprehensive review of research in this line (Thorne, Black, & Sykes, 2009), Thorne and his colleagues further outlined the various online communities (e.g., gaming, fan community) in which L2 learners became socialized into different linguistic and literacy practices. In terms of SNS use, Reinhardt and Zander (2011) and Chen (2013) looked at ESL learners' activities on Facebook while they were in the U.S. However, as Reinhardt and Zander (2011) pointed out, existing research on SNS use and L2 learning has primarily focused on English development in uninstructed contexts and scant attention has been paid to the role of incorporating SNS in formal instruction of other languages.

The current study is informed by the existing research. From the perspectives of language socialization and CoP, learning CIL is a parallel process accompanying one's changing participation in the Weibo community. Similar to the description in Lave and Wenger's work (1991), participation in Weibo activities requires both cultural and linguistic knowledge. The former encompasses familiarity with the functions Weibo offers and the variety of activities one can participate in, and the latter involves knowledge of CIL and the ability to use it both online and offline. Furthermore, the varying levels of participation on Weibo also shape their status in the community. From the perspective of CoP, an inactive user who has registered an account (and is hence legitimate) but does not participate in any of the activities can been defined as a legitimate peripheral participant.

Meanwhile, because adult L2 learners often bring with them their prior cultural orientations when they start to learn another language (Duff, 2008a, p.115; Kramsch, 2009, p. 201), L2 socialization may also result in "ambivalence, defiance, resistance to or rejection of the target language, culture, or community (or aspects thereof)" (Duff, 2012). With regard to the engagement in SNS and use of CIL, we need to consider learners' existing orientations towards such youth cultural and linguistic practices.

Drawing from these frameworks, the overarching goal of this study is to document Mandarin L2 learners' awareness of the emerging linguistic practices on China's social-media landscape and their engagement in the Chinese SNS as their Chinese class incorporates the use of SNS. Specifically the research questions are:

1. To what extent did these American students participate in activities on Weibo?
2. How did their awareness of CIL change over time in China?
3. What opportunities became available for them to engage in the use of CIL outside of class, both within and beyond the Internet space?

METHOD

The Project

This chapter is based on a longitudinal project that was designed to document American students' Mandarin L2 socialization experience while they studied abroad in China (Diao, 2013). The data presented here were collected at a study abroad center in Shanghai during the spring semester of 2012. At the time, four students were selected from 20 volunteers. These students were selected to represent diverse backgrounds as well as different living conditions. Those who were living in the dorm with a Chinese roommate and who were living with a local Chinese family were intentionally included.

The four students were each given an audio-recorder and instructed to record their routine conversations with their tutors, roommates or host family members. They were also interviewed during their second and fifteenth weeks of the program. These semi-structured interviews were intended for me to gain insights into their perspectives (Talmy, 2010) of Mandarin learning experience in China (see sample questions in Appendix A). They were audio-recorded and transcribed into text for further analysis. A short linguistic awareness questionnaire and a background survey were also administered to the participants. The questionnaire was informed by the *Language Awareness Interviews* (LAI) in Kinginger's (2008) study on American students' learning of French sociopragmatic variations while studying in France. Similar to Kinginger's (2008) LAI, I also included a section of ten lexical forms characteristic of CIL (see sample items in Appendix B). Selection of these forms was based on the existing research on CIL (e.g., Liu, 2010; Gao, 2012) and other reference guidebooks or websites for CIL.[1] For each form in this section, the respondent needed to (1) define these lexical items in English (if puns, both meanings) to receive one point, and (2) answer if they used it in their life (another

Table 1. Matrix of research questions, data sources, and analysis

Research Question	Data Source	Data Analysis
1. To what extent did these American students participate in activities on Weibo?	- Field notes - Profiles on Weibo - Postings on Weibo	Thematic analysis
2. How did their awareness of the CIL forms change over their time in China?	- Pre- and post-questionnaires - Interviews	Comparative analysis of questionnaires triangulated with the interview transcriptions.
3. What opportunities became available for them to engage in the use of CIL outside of class, both within and beyond the Internet space?	- Background surveys - Interviews - Field notes - Recordings - Postings on Weibo	Thematic analysis Discourse analysis

point if yes). The questionnaire was administered to all 20 participants in the first week, and again to the focal students during the last week of the program (Week 15). In addition, I observed the focal students' classes and tutorials, and went to a variety of daily activities that they participated in. I also collected their profile information and their postings on Weibo, as well as interviewing the students, their tutors, Chinese roommates, host family members, and their teachers informally.

The data from these multiple sources were analyzed in a triangulated fashion (e.g., Duff, 2008b; Maxwell, 2005) to answer the research questions (see Table 1).

Site

The instructors at the program were urban residents in their mid-twenties with postgraduate level of education. They all frequently used Chinese SNSs such as Weibo and were familiar with CIL. In my informal interviews with them, they considered CIL forms to be an unique advantage for students studying in China and a "fun" experience due to their humorous nature. However, because CIL involves non-standard and creative use of language, only the instructor at the most advanced level was able to continuously incorporate Weibo and CIL into instruction. At the time, such incorporation was implemented at the following three dimensions:

1. Selection of instructional materials that contained CIL items.
2. Inclusion of other CIL lexical items in their instruction. For instance, Figure 1 is a flyer that the teacher used in her teaching. She then hung it in her office.
3. Incorporation of Weibo in class instruction. The teacher introduced Weibo to the students and required all of them to register. She also assigned homework that asked the students to post their responses there, such as expressing their opinions with regard to the specific topics they discussed in class. She also made a special account for the class, reading, resending, and responding to the students' postings.

In addition, the instructors at the program also decorated the hallways in the dorm building with flyers and posters. Many of them contained expressions related to CIL, because they were thought to be funny, playful and popular among the young people. For instance, Figure 2 is a representative picture displaying the pun 杯具 and the visual expression 囧. These CIL forms could also be useful in the dorm because the majority of

Figure 1. Flyer of CIL used in the class and hung in the teacher's office

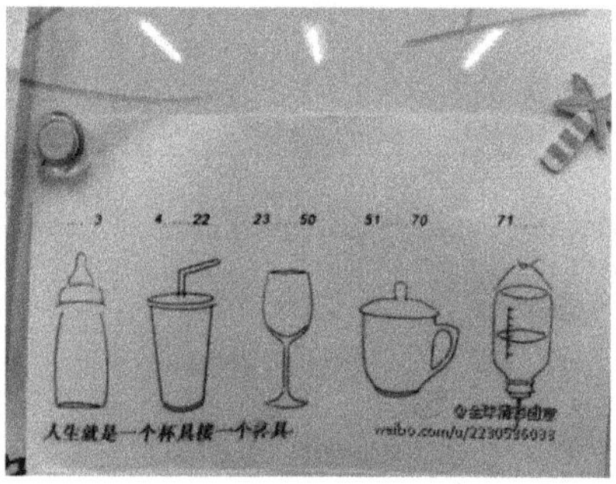

Figure 2. Flyer containing CIL forms in the dorm

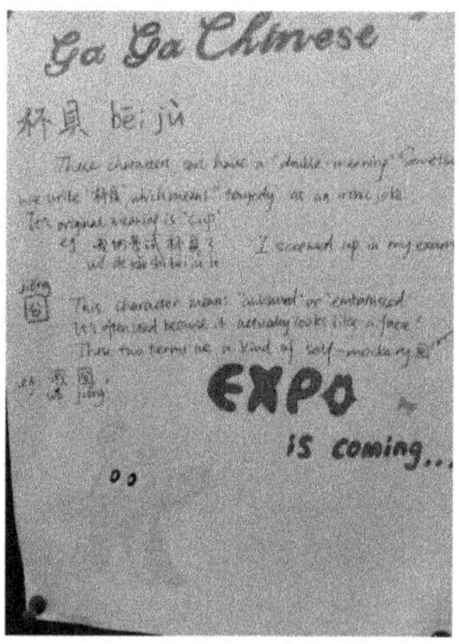

the Chinese roommates were young and educated Internet users who were likely users of CIL too.

These flyers, together with the Chinese college students living in the dorm, shaped the linguistic landscape in the dorm, transforming it into a space where youth linguistic practices were displayed and transmitted.

Participants

The majority of the students had little knowledge about CIL at the beginning of their time in Shanghai. Eighteen of the twenty students received a score of two or lower out of 20 possible points in the linguistic awareness questionnaire in February. Two focal students, Yun and Ellen (both pseudonyms), were selected from the twenty volunteers as the focal cases in this study, as their class was the only one that continuously incorporated the use of Weibo and instruction of CIL items. They were placed into the most advanced Chinese class at the program.[2] However, despite their placement, Ellen and Yun were also within this majority, each receiving two points in the questionnaire in February. Their low scores reveals that knowledge of CIL may not be directly related to one's proficiency in Chinese. Most of these students had very little experience in Chinese social media when they started their time in Shanghai.

Yun and Ellen also had different living conditions. Yun was living with a host family, while Ellen was living with a Chinese roommate in the dorm. Since language socialization defines learning as a mutual process, involving not only the learner but also the expert speaker (e.g., Duff, 2012), Yun's host mother, tutor, and Ellen's Chinese roommate all became participants of the study.

RESULTS

Ellen: "I Would Not Have Learned These in the U.S."

Ellen had taken four semesters of Mandarin at her home institution in Ohio (U.S.) and another semester of intensive Mandarin in northeastern China before coming to Shanghai. She was very committed to learning Mandarin, as her future plan was to teach it to American children.

During her time in China, Ellen's awareness of CIL improved. Her score on the linguistic awareness questionnaire increased from two points in February to seven in May. She was able to define a few more CIL forms, which included those that were not taught in her language classes. She also reportedly used these CIL forms in her everyday life.

Ellen's increasing awareness of CIL might be related to the kind of interactions in which she engaged during her semester in Shanghai. She was particularly interested in interacting with Chinese college students whom she considered to be more "open-minded" (Ellen's pre interview). She feared other Chinese cities would be too conservative for her to discuss certain issues such as gender and sexuality. In her interview, she also expressed concerns that older adults might think she was "too embarrassing" and not take her "seriously" if she brought up these topics. Therefore, she chose to study in Shanghai and opted to live in the dorm because it would allow her "more freedom" and "more opportunity to make friends" (Ellen's background survey).

Ellen did make friends with her roommate, Helen. Helen was a 21-year-old student in her senior year studying Chinese applied linguistics at the hosting university. She was from a medium-sized city in Shanghai's neighboring Jiangsu Province. It was her second time to be a Chinese roommate at the study abroad center. As a typical college student in urban China, Helen had registered on a few Chinese social-media sites, including Weibo. During my site visits, she frequently checked these SNSs on her computer. She also had a mobile device that was connected to these SNSs. Her language frequently contained CIL forms when she spoke to me.

Helen was the person with whom Ellen interacted most frequently in Shanghai. When asked what kind of topics they discussed, Ellen said:

Usually boyfriends, or about finding a boyfriend. Because we are girls. [We] like this topic. Then [we] will also talk about, for example, how is the teacher, how is the homework. […] Sometimes, if I have— if I have an assignment, I would talk to them. We will talk about transportation, social problems. But this [sic: these] are not normal topics. (Ellen, post interview)[3]

Ellen's statement, "because we are girls", reveals the nature of their interactions. In the recordings, their conversations frequently involved informal and non-serious topics such as romantic relationships or their daily schedule such as the schoolwork.

Their language use also reflects this nature of being youthful "girls." For instance, in the excerpt below, Helen and Ellen were involved in a speech event they identified as "gossiping." In this particular excerpt, Helen was recalling with another girl in the program her conversation about a male student:

Excerpt 1: Conversation in the dorm between Helen and Ellen: "*You know*."
(HL=Helen, EL=Ellen, WD=Researcher. 05/17/2012, see Appendix C and D for grammar gloss and transcription conventions)

1. HL 我就讲了(.) 他::>好像<跟别的女孩子啊:: blah blah blah
   [*I just said he seemed to be with another girl. Blah blah blah.*]
2. EL =对. hh. 对. hhh. blah blah.
   [*Right. Right. Blah blah.*]
3. HL hhh. blah blah.
4. EL heh heh heh heh.
5. HL 大家懂就可以了.
   [*It's okay as long as everyone knows.*]
6. EL heh heh heh heh heh heh heh heh heh. hhh. heh heh hhh.
7. 我会开始用这句话,大家懂就可以了. blah blah.
   [*I will begin to use this sentence. It's okay as long as everyone knows. Blah blah.*]
8. 你们懂就可以了.
   [*It's okay as long as you all know.*]
9. HL 对. 我们经常会?(.) ah (.) 你懂的.然后就不说了.
   [*Right. We usually say, "you know," and then just don't say anything more.*]

In the excerpt above, Helen was teaching her the phrase *nǐ dǒng de* ("you know") (lines 5-9) as she told Ellen what she had said about this other male student. The sequence of the four lines appeared to demonstrate some characteristics of interactions between a language teacher and a student (i.e., modeling – repetition – feedback). However, a crucial difference is that, here, the form was contextualized in the event of "gossiping." Therefore specific pragmatic functions such as solidarity building were assigned to it.

The phrase *nǐ dǒng de* ("you know") is one representative CIL item that was originally borrowed from English. It initially emerged in Chinese SNS as a way to comment on sensitive topics and avoid censorship (Hudong, n.d.). Its ambiguous nature has enabled it to become a popular term among young Chinese as a way to create playfulness and solidarity, both on the Internet and in everyday communication offline.

Similar interactions recurred in the recordings. In addition to Helen's use of CIL, the dorm was also decorated with images displaying CIL forms (e.g., the flyer in Figure 2). Not surprisingly, when asked to reflect on the differences between studying in the US and in China, Ellen named learning CIL as one of the advantages of being in China:

This— this— [Things] one will use online. For instance the 囧, 神马 (another pun),and so on. A lot of them. The symbol. I forgot a lot of this [sic: these], but, in the US [I] would not have learned these things. (Ellen. post interview.)

However, despite her exposure to the youth language and her increasing awareness of CIL, Ellen's overall use of CIL was not frequent and the increase was rather limited. As shown in Table 2, she used more CIL forms over the semester in the audio recordings, but the increase was minimal (two in May, one in April, and none in March).

As Table 2 indicates, Ellen's use of CIL decreased over time in her Weibo postings. She used one CIL form in February and none in the following months.

Her actual engagement in Weibo activities may explain this decrease. On her profile, Ellen was only following eight users. Two of them were assigned to all Weibo users by default (e.g., Weibo's official help account). She had merely five followers, all of whom were her instructor and classmates. Although Weibo offers a variety of sharing and networking activities, Ellen only engaged in a limited subset of them. She occasionally uploaded posts and very rarely photos of her traveling. Most of her postings were closely related to topics they discussed in class, which according to her were not typical of her everyday interaction with her roommate in the dorm. For example, below is a posting on her account:

在世界上,中国用最多的木炭,所以关于后代和空气污染,中国政府可能会控制木炭产量。

In the world, China uses the most coal. Therefore concerning [our] offspring and air pollution, the Chinese government may control the production of coal. (Ellen, Weibo posting on 03/05/2012).

Ellen tagged her instructor in ten of her total 14 postings (71.4%), making them have an explicit addressee rather than regular public messages for sharing on a micro-blogging site like Weibo. She stopped posting things on her Weibo in May when the semester ended, and her account has been inactive since then.

Yun: "My Host Mom Would Be Impressed."

Yun began to learn Chinese when she was in high school, and continued to take Chinese classes in her college in the District of Columbia (U.S.). Her score in the linguistic awareness questionnaire also increased, changing from two points in February to five in May. However, when examined closely, the items she was able to answer in the post version overlapped with the CIL items that her language instructor included in class (e.g., two points for "杯具," as in Figure 1 and Appendix B). Her increase in the scores in the questionnaires was also less noticeable than that of Ellen (who received seven points in the post questionnaire).

Table 2. Ellen's use of CIL in the audio recordings and postings on Weibo from February to May

	Recordings		Postings on Weibo	
	Length (min)	CIL tokens	Chinese characters	CIL tokens
Feb	0	-	24	1
Mar	105.5	0	342	0
Apr	116	1	755	0
May	81.5	2	0	0
Total	303	3	1121	1

At her college, Yun built a romantic relationship with a Chinese American student whose family was originally from Shanghai. She chose to study in Shanghai and lived with a local family because she wanted to "learn more about life in Shanghai" (Yun, background survey). In her pre interview, Yun further expressed her interest in interacting with her host family:

I am really interested in talking to my [host] family, just everyone really, just about family structure, um, and community relations. [...] And the sort of ideas of living with your parents. Having your parents live with you. (Yun, pre interview)

At the time, Yun's host family consisted of only two people, the host mother and the grandmother. They were living in an affluent neighborhood near the campus. The host mother treated Yun as her daughter, introducing her to their family visitors as her *gān nǚ'ér* (god-daughter). Yun responded by calling her *m-ma* ("mom" in Shanghainese). The host mother also engaged Yun in activities that she considered as ways to train Yun to become a Shanghai daughter-in-law as her boyfriend's family was originally from Shanghai (see a detailed description in Diao, 2013).

The host mother had an account on Weibo. However, her role on the SNS seemed largely limited to that of a reader, mainly receiving messages and not uploading or resending frequently. Her primary social interaction on the Internet was with her son, for which she used more private networking platforms such as instant video chatting. She also did not use any CIL forms during my observations, which was expected because CIL is considered characteristic of the urban youth.

In their interactions, the host mother encouraged Yun to use formal "good" Chinese that she had learned in school. For instance, their conversations frequently involved the use of *chéngyǔ*, four-syllable idiomatic expressions that came from classical Chinese and are now typically associated with formal communication. As a result, when asked about the advantages of studying in China, Yun named these opportunities for her to use these difficult formal words:

It made me feel like, maybe I would actually learn something today that I could be using, like, NOW. For example, studying the chengyu, I would TRY to use them like so hard. But in the U.S., I study a chengyu and like, this is a pain, because it's harder to study. But it's now something that I would use with my host mom and she'd be impressed. (Yun, post interview)

Besides the host mother, Yun also had a tutor, Ji. They met twice a week for one hour each time. Ji was a sophomore student from Beijing, also majoring in applied linguistics in the hosting institution. It was her first time tutoring American students. She often seemed uneasy during these tutorials, and the tutorials were strictly limited to classroom-like activities such as reading texts and practicing pronunciation.

Table 3. Yun's use of CIL in audio recordings and postings on Weibo from February to May

	Recordings			Postings	
	Length (min) (tutorial)	Length (min) (family)	CIL tokens	Chinese characters	CIL tokens
Feb	-	-	-	67	0
Mar	150	161.5	0	498	0
Apr	119	133	0	0	-
May	98.5	196.5	0	0	-
Total	367.5	491	0	565	0

Probably due to the nature of the conversations between Yun and her host mother and her tutor, she never used any CIL forms throughout the audio recordings (see Table 3). In terms of her activities on Weibo, she posted a total of 5 messages throughout her time in Shanghai, none of which contained any CIL form either.

Yun's profile further reveals her lack of engagement in the use of CIL and her peripheral status on Weibo. She followed only nine users and had seven followers. These numbers were even lower than Ellen's. Moreover, in all of her five postings (100%), her instructor was consistently tagged. She also tagged her classmate (Ellen) in one of the postings. Her Weibo account became inactive even before Ellen's. She stopped posting messages in April, when the instructor no longer assigned her students to do so.

DISCUSSION

To summarize my findings and answer the research questions, first of all, Ellen and Yun both remained as peripheral participants in the Weibo community throughout their time in Shanghai. As their semester in China came to an end, they both completely withdrew from it. In their uploaded posts, they were only interacting with their instructor and classmates, making Weibo nothing but an extension of their classroom. Secondly, with regard to their awareness of CIL, Ellen and Yun did become able to recognize more forms, particularly those that had been taught in class. Despite the improvement, their scores for this section in the post linguistic awareness questionnaires were still rather low. Out of the 20 possible points, Ellen received seven points and Yun only five points in May. This indicates that their knowledge of CIL was still limited.

Thirdly, opportunities for language socialization into SNS-mediated communication did not automatically occur. Their living conditions availed them different types of linguistic practices. Living with a Chinese roommate in a college dorm, Ellen was surrounded physically by artifacts displaying CIL forms and was exposed to these forms in daily communication. She also regarded the acquisition of CIL as a primary advantage of studying abroad in China. In contrast, Yun had little exposure to CIL outside of class due to the family setting she was in. Her living condition facilitated her learning of formal Chinese, but not CIL.

These findings need to be understood in relation to the participants' personal histories and prior cultural orientations (Duff, 2012; Kinginger, 2008). Ellen was more interested in interacting with China's educated urban youth and desired to make friends with them. She lived with a Chinese college student and participated (though quite limitedly) in youth linguistic practices such as using CIL. In comparison, Yun arrived in Shanghai with an interest in the local family life, because of her boyfriend's background. To her, learning CIL was neither a priority nor an advantage of being in China. Their stories demonstrate L2 learners' agency in choosing whether or not to participate in certain cultural and linguistic orientations (e.g., Norton, 2000), including orientations towards Internet activities (Reinhardt & Zander, 2011). The findings also showed engagement in Internet linguistic practices as a mutual process, involving not only language learners but also the people they interact with and the settings they are in. Ellen's dorm was a place where college students resided and signs of CIL were displayed. Her roommate Helen frequently used CIL and actively socialized Ellen into using it too. Yun's host family had no member of the urban youth culture. Using formal words such as *chéngyǔ* was her way to impress the host mother. The linguistic practices in her host home were incongruent with her instructor's promotion of CIL.

Ellen and Yun's disengagement in networking activities on Weibo is consistent with previous research on the potential of introducing technology-mediated communication into L2 education (Reinhardt & Zander, 2011; Stevenson & Liu, 2010). These studies reported similar disengagement in SNS activities among certain L2 learners. Indeed, a user's social network on a social media site can only be expanded to include many individuals after s/he has already developed existing face-to-face networks (boyd & Ellison, 2007). Neither Ellen nor Yun had a face-to-face network with the local people beyond their roommate or host family members. In both living conditions, they had the convenient opportunity to interact with the people face-to-face without actually going online. Hence, there was little need to build up a social network on the SNS. The potential for pedagogically incorporating SNSs in L2 education, therefore, may "lie in first leveraging F2F [face-to-face] class or learner affinity groups into digitally mediated equivalents" (Reinhardt & Zander, 2011, p. 332).

Furthermore, the findings suggest the need to conceptualize what SNSs are and for what purpose we should incorporate them and the Internet language in L2 teaching. In the case presented here, although the instructor enthusiastically incorporated CIL in her instruction and utilized Weibo to maximize her interaction with the students, there were limited pedagogical activities to guide the students into online networking by using the local SNS and actually engaging in using CIL. Weibo became simply an extra course requirement and the CIL forms formed a cosmetic addition to the curriculum. As a result, while the instructors viewed CIL and using Weibo as a "fun" activity and a unique advantage for study abroad students in China, the students on the other hand failed to sustain their participation in the SNS or make use of the CIL forms in daily communication – online or offline. Although Ellen seemed to benefit to some extent from learning and using these CIL forms, there is yet much to consider in order to connect such students' experience with the local youth, the instruction of CIL, and the incorporation of SNS into formal language instruction.

FUTURE RESEARCH DIRECTIONS

The findings presented in this chapter may disappoint many SNS enthusiasts in the field of applied linguistics. However, it is important to note that for the purpose of this exploratory study, data collection was conducted in a primarily observatory manner. The instructor's pedagogical practices of incorporating CIL and Weibo were left intact. The host family and the Chinese roommate were not guided to socialize the students into CIL, either. Future research may consider incorporating interventions so that learners can more effectively engage in the use of SNSs and the corresponding linguistic practices. For instance, for students living with local SNS users such as Ellen, interventional instruction could be carried out so that CIL, SNS, and the living condition can all become connected.

The study also generates methodological implications for future research. While the rise of social media has challenged the application of some conventional research tools, it also enables new ways of analyzing L2 learners' engagement in linguistic and cultural practices. For instance, the SNS in this study, Weibo, provided statistics regarding how the two focal students participated in its activities (e.g., how many people they were following, how many posts on their wall, and with whom they interacted). Many SNSs offer similar analytic services. Future research can utilize these features to understand how L2 learners engage in various activities on different social media sites.

In terms of the selection of a case study approach, a common critique lies in the potential for generalization. However, the findings in this study are *not* intended to be applicable to L2 learners in other contexts. As mentioned in the introduction, China has a unique social media landscape with many popular local SNSs. These findings, therefore, should not and cannot be directly generalized to learners of other languages studying in other countries where U.S.-based SNSs may be easily accessible. However, popularity of different SNSs may still vary across regions and countries. To truly understand how L2 learners can engage in activities on various social media sites and become socialized into different communities online, we need more evidence from a multitude of cultural contexts where SNS use patterns vary.

Finally, Ellen and Yun were also not typical Chinese L2 learners. During the time of this study, they were placed in the most advanced Chinese class with only two other students, while almost all other classes had larger enrollments. However, as the number of advanced Chinese learners is growing and the need to research their learning processes increases (Ke, 2012), such pragmatic features can be an area for further investigation.

REFERENCES

Block, D. (2007). The rise of identity in SLA research, post Firth and Wagner (1997). *Modern Language Journal, 91*(Focus Issue), 863–876. doi:10.1111/j.1540-4781.2007.00674.x

boyd, d. & Ellison, N. (2007). Social network sites: Definition, history, and scholarship. *Journal of Computer-Mediated Communication, 13*(1), 210–230.

Chen, H.-I. (2013). Identity practices of multilingual writers in social networking spaces. *Language Learning & Technology, 17*(2), 143–170.

Chiu, C., Lin, D., & Silverman, A. (2012). China's social-media boom. *McKinsey and Company*. Retrieved from http://www.mckinsey.com/insights/marketing_sales/chinas_social-media_boom

CNNIC. (2013, February 21). *Statistical report on Internet development in China*. China Internet Network Information Center. Retrieved from http://www1.cnnic.cn/IDR/ReportDownloads/201302/P020130221391269963814.pdf

Cook, H. M. (2008). *Socializing identities through speech style: Learners of Japanese as a foreign language*. Bristol, UK: Multilingual Matters.

Crystal, D. (2006). *Language and the Internet* (2nd ed.). Cambridge University Press. doi:10.1017/CBO9780511487002

Danet, B. (2001). *Cyberpl@ y: Communicating online*. Berg.

Diao, W. (2013). *Learning Mandarin and socializing stance through a semester in China*. (Unpublished doctoral thesis). Carnegie Mellon University, Pittsburgh, PA, U.S.A.

Duff, P. (2008a). Language socialization, participation and identity: Ethnographic approaches. In M. Martin-Jones, A-M.de Mejia & N. Hornberger (Eds.), Encyclopedia of language and education (vol. 3, pp. 107–119). New York, NY: Springer.

Duff, P. (2008b). *Case study research in applied linguistics*. New York: Lawrence Erlbaum/Taylor & Francis.

Duff, P. (2012). Second language socialization. In A. Duranti, E. Ochs, & B. Schieffelin (Eds.), *Handbook of language socialization (pp. 564–586)*. New York: Blackwell.

Duff, P., & Talmy, S. (2010). Language socialization approaches to second language acquisition: Social, cultural, and linguistic development in additional languages. In D. Atkinson (Ed.), *Alternative approaches to SLA*. London: Routledge.

Duggan, M., & Brenner, J. (2013, February 14). *The demographics of social media users*. Pew Research Center's Internet & American Life Project. Retrieved from http://pewinternet.org/Reports/2013/Social-media-users.aspx

Eckert, P. (2000). *Linguistic variation as social practice*. Oxford: Blackwell.

Eckert, P., & McConnell-Ginet, S. (1992). Think practically and look locally: Language and gender as community-based practice. *Annual Review of Anthropology*, *21*, 461–490. doi:10.1146/annurev.an.21.100192.002333

Gao, L. (2012). Synchronic variation or diachronic change: A sociolinguistic study of Chinese Internet language. In J. Liu, & H. Tao (Eds.), *Chinese under globalization: Emerging trends in language use in China* (pp. 7–28). Singapore: World Scientific Publishing. doi:10.1142/9789814350709_0002

Garrett, P. B., & Baquedano-Lopez, P. (2002). Language socialization: Reproduction and continuity, transformation and change. *Annual Review of Anthropology*, *31*, 339–361. doi:10.1146/annurev.anthro.31.040402.085352

Hale, C., & Scanlon, J. (1999). *Wired style: Principles of Englishusage in the digital age*. New York: Broadway Books.

Hudong. (n.d.). *In ci* [In words]. Retrieved from http://top.baike.com/

Ke, C. (2012). Research in second language acquisition on Chinese: Where we are, where we are going. *Journal of the Chinese Language Teachers Association*, *47*(3), 43–114.

Kinginger, C. (2008). Language learning in study abroad: Case histories of Americans in France [Monograph]. *Modern Language Journal*, *92*, 1–124. doi:10.1111/j.1540-4781.2008.00821.x

Kramsch, C. (2009). *The multilingual subject*. Oxford, England: Oxford University Press.

Lam, W. (2004). Second language socialization in a bilingual chat room: Global and local considerations. *Language Learning & Technology*, *8*(3), 44–65.

Lave, J., & Wenger, E. (1991). *Situated learning: Legitimate peripheral participation*. Cambridge: Cambridge University Press. doi:10.1017/CBO9780511815355

Liu, J. (2010). Deviant writing and youth identity: Representation of dialects with Chinese characters on the Internet. *Chinese Language and Discourse*, *1*(2), 183–219.

Liu, J. (2012). The use of Chinese dialects on the Internet: Youth language and local youth identity in urban China. In J. Liu, & H. Tao (Eds.), *Chinese under globalization: Emerging trends in language use in China* (pp. 59–78). Singapore: World Scientific Publishing. doi:10.1142/9789814350709_0004

Liu, J., & Tao, H. (Eds.). (2012). *Chinese under globalization: Emerging trends in language use in China*. Singapore: World Scientific Publishing. doi:10.1142/8160

Maxwell, J. A. (2005). *Qualitative research design: An interactive approach* (2nd ed.). Thousand Oaks, CA: SAGE.

Mitchell, K. (2012). A social tool: Why and how ESOL students use Facebook. *CALICO Journal*, *29*(3), 471–493. doi:10.11139/cj.29.3.471-493

Norton, B. (2000). *Identity and language learning: Gender, ethnicity and educational change*. Essex, England: Pearson Education.

Ochs, E. (1996). Linguistic resources for socializing humanity. In J. Gumperz & S. Levinson (Eds.), Rethinking linguistic relativity. Cambridge, UK: Cambridge University Press.

Ochs, E., & Schieffelin, B. (1984). Language acquisition and socialization: Three developmental stories. In R. Shweder, & R. LeVine (Eds.), *Culture theory: Mind, self, and emotion* (pp. 276–320). UK: Cambridge University Press.

Pan, W. G. (2008). *Weiji xia de zhongwen* [Chinese under crisis]. Shenyang, China: Liaoning People's Press.

Reinhardt, J., & Zander, V. (2011). Social networking in an intensive English program classroom: A language socialization perspective. *CALICO Journal*, *28*(2), 326–344. doi:10.11139/cj.28.2.326-344

Schieffelin, B. B., & Ochs, E. (1986). Language socialization. *Annual Review of Anthropology*, *15*, 163–191. doi:10.1146/annurev.an.15.100186.001115

Shively, R. L. (2011). L2 pragmatic development in study abroad: A longitudinal study of Spanish service encounters. *Journal of Pragmatics*, *43*, 1818–1835. doi:10.1016/j.pragma.2010.10.030

Shively, R. L. (2013). Learning to be funny in Spanish during study abroad: L2 humor development. *Modern Language Journal*, *97*(4), 930–946. doi:10.1111/j.1540-4781.2013.12043.x

Stevenson, M., & Liu, M. (2010). Learning a language with Web 2.0: Exploring the use of social networking features of foreign language learning websites. *CALICO Journal*, *27*, 233–259.

Su, H.-Y. (2009). Reconstructing Taiwanese and Taiwan Guoyu on the Taiwan-based Internet: Playfulness, stylization, and politeness. *Journal of Asian Pacific Communication*, *19*(2), 313–335. doi:10.1075/japc.19.2.08su

Talmy, S. (2010). Qualitative interviews in applied linguistics: From research instrument to social practice. *Annual Review of Applied Linguistics*, *30*, 128–148. doi:10.1017/S0267190510000085

Thorne, S. L., Black, R., & Sykes, J. (2009). Second language use, socialization, and learning in Internet interest communities and online games. *Modern Language Journal*, *93*, 802–821. doi:10.1111/j.1540-4781.2009.00974.x

Watson-Gegeo, K. A. (2004). Mind, language, and epistemology: Toward a language socialization paradigm for SLA. *Modern Language Journal*, *88*(3), 331–350. doi:10.1111/j.0026-7902.2004.00233.x

Yan, J. (2012). Writing Cantonese as everyday lifestyle in Guangzhou (Canton city). In J. Liu, & H. Tao (Eds.), *Chinese under globalization: Emerging trends in language use in China* (pp. 171–202). Singapore: World Scientific Publishing. doi:10.1142/9789814350709_0009

ADDITIONAL READING

Crystal, D. (2006). *Language and the Internet* (2nd ed.). Cambridge University Press.

Duff, P. (2008). *Case study research in applied linguistics*. New York: Lawrence Erlbaum/Taylor & Francis.

Duff, P., Anderson, T., Ilnyckyj, R., VanGaya, E., Wang, R., & Yates, E. (2013). *Learning Chinese: Linguistic, sociocultural, and narrative perspectives*. Berlin, New York: Mouton de Gruyter.

Duranti, A., Ochs, E., & Schieffelin, B. (Eds.). (2012). *Handbook of language socialization*. New York: Blackwell.

Ke, C. (2012). Research in second language acquisition on Chinese: Where we are, where we are going. *Journal of the Chinese Language Teachers Association*, *47*(3), 43–114.

Kramsch, C. (2009). *The multilingual subject*. Oxford, England: Oxford University Press.

Lam, W. (2004). Second language socialization in a bilingual chat room: Global and local considerations. *Language Learning & Technology*, *8*(3), 44–65.

Lam, W. (2007). Language socialization in online communities. In P. A., Duff & N. Hornberger (Eds.), Encyclopedia of language and education (Volume 8): Language socialization (pp. 301–311). Boston, MA: Springer.

Lave, J., & Wenger, E. (1991). *Situated learning: Legitimate peripheral participation*. Cambridge: Cambridge University Press.

Liu, J., & Tao, H. (2012). (Eds.) Chinese under globalization: Emerging trends in language use in China. Singapore: World Scientific Publishing.

Magnan, S. (Ed.). (2008). *Mediating discourse online*. Amsterdam: Benjamins.

Reinhardt, J., & Zander, V. (2011). Social networking in an intensive English program classroom: A language socialization perspective. *CALICO Journal*, *28*(2), 326–344.

Thorne, S. L., Black, R., & Sykes, J. (2009). Second language use, socialization, and learning in Internet interest communities and online games. *Modern Language Journal*, *93*, 802–821.

Thorne, S. L., & Payne, J. S. (Eds.). (2005). Computer-mediated Communication and Foreign Language Learning: Context, Research and Practice. Special Issue of CALICO, 22(3).

Warner, C. (2004). It's just a game right?: Types of play in foreign language CMC. *Language Learning & Technology*, *8*(2), 69–87.

Watson-Gegeo, K. A. (2004). Mind, language, and epistemology: Toward a language socialization paradigm for SLA. *Modern Language Journal*, *88*(3), 331–350.

KEY TERMS AND DEFINITIONS

Case Study: Case study is among the five common methods in qualitative research. It allows researchers to contextualize the behaviors under investigation and explore the uniqueness as well as commonalities within and across cases. While the actual ways of selecting focal cases and conducting the research can vary, it typically involves observation, semi-structured interviews, and documentation of case history.

Community of Practice: A community of practice is a community where people come together for a common enterprise and engage in activities together. It posits learning as a process of moving from legitimate peripheral participation towards more central status.

Internet Language: Internet language is the kind of linguistic forms that are created and circulated on the Internet. It has also entered our everyday communication. Chinese Internet Language (CIL) is an example of such linguistic forms in the Chinese-speaking world.

Language Socialization: Language socialization refers to the dual processes of socializing through language and being socialized into the cultural discourses.

Study Abroad: In the applied linguistic literature in North America, study abroad typically refers to the educational experience that takes place in the country where the target language is spoken.

Social Networking Site: A social networking site (SNS) is an online platform where people can build and maintain social relations and networks through participating in activities such as sharing information and expressing opinions.

Weibo: Weibo is a Twitter-like micro-blogging site that is widely popular in the Chinese social media landscape, such as Sina Weibo.

ENDNOTES

1 All forms in this section were typical of CIL, except for one (老外). As a slang term referring to foreigners, it was included because it is also playful language use. It was also a form that these non-Chinese students would encounter most frequently in China.

2 At the time, the class only had four students. Two of them did not volunteer to participate in the research and therefore could not be included.

3 Although my interview questions were in English, Ellen insisted on responding in Mandarin. What is presented here is my English translation of her original response. The translation was made as literal as possible.

APPENDIX A: SAMPLE QUESTIONS FROM THE SEMI-STRUCTURED INTERVIEW PROTOCOL

Pre Interview

1. Why did you decide to study Chinese?
2. How would you describe the Chinese language (what adjectives?)?
3. What challenges have you had as a Chinese learner?
4. Do you use Chinese outside class while in the US? If so, when, where and with whom? Typically how much time (in hours) a week would you estimate that you speak Chinese outside class while in the US?
5. Why did you choose to study abroad in China?
6. Have you been to China before? If so, when, where, and for what purpose?

Post Interview

1. Can you describe to me a typical school day and a weekend of your life in Shanghai? On a typical school day, how much time do you spend speaking Chinese?
2. Whom do you speak Chinese with? Of them, whom do you speak Chinese with most frequently?
3. Have you made any Chinese friends in Shanghai? If so, how did you get to know these friends? What do you usually do together?
4. What kinds of topic do you usually talk about?
5. How would you compare the difference between learning Chinese in China and in the US?
6. Will you continue to study Chinese once you return to the US? Why or why not?

APPENDIX B: SAMPLE QUESTIONS FROM THE LINGUSITIC AWARENESS QUESTIONNAIRE

	I **don't** know the word.	I **know** the word and I can define its "funny" meaning (please provide **definition in English**).	I **use** the word.
杯具 bēijù			
囧 jiǒng			
浮云 fúyún			
坑爹 kēngdiē			

APPENDIX C: GRAMMAR GLOSSARY

CONJ conjunctive adverb
MSR measure word
NEG negation
PERT perfective aspect marker
PRT particles

APPENDIX D: TRANSCRIPTION CONVENTIONS

(.) dot in parenthesis marks pauses shorter than 0.4 second
underline underline marks increased volume of voice
. full stop marks falling intonation
(()) double parentheses contain transcriber's comments
: prolongation of immediately prior sound
[] bracket marks overlapping turns
= latched talk
> < fast speech
hhh laughter

Chapter 9
Using Skype to Focus on Form in Japanese Telecollaboration: Lexical Categories as a New Task Variable

Yuka Akiyama
Georgetown University, USA

ABSTRACT

This chapter examines the effects of lexical categories on Focus on Form (FonF) and the use of multimodal features of Skype for preemptive and reactive Language-Related Episodes (LREs) in a task-based language exchange via Skype (i.e. telecollaboration). Twelve pairs of Japanese-as-a-foreign-language learners and native speakers of Japanese engaged in two decision-making tasks. Each task prompt included target vocabulary of different lexical categories (nouns or onomatopoeia) that participants had to negotiate for task completion. The quantitative analysis of oral interaction revealed a significant effect of lexical categories on the total number and linguistic focus (i.e. morphological, lexical, and phonological items) of preemptive LREs, as well as the correction method, linguistic focus, and the uptake rate of reactive LREs. The analysis of multimodal interaction revealed that participants often used text chat, images, and webcams to carry out telecollaborative interaction and that the lexical categories affected which of these multimodal features of Skype are used for FonF.

INTRODUCTION

Advances in technology, particularly the development of synchronous and asynchronous computer-mediated communication (CMC) tools, have made it possible to break down the classroom wall and connect language learners around the world. Computer-assisted language learning (CALL) researchers postulate that network-based communication can enhance interactional negotiation and thus facilitate language acquisition. A number of studies from the interactionist perspective have revealed abundant evidence of comprehensible input and modified output resulting from CMC-mediated interaction (Blake, 2000; Kitade, 2000; Pellettieri, 2000; Smith, 2003, 2005; Warschauer, 1998).

Language exchanges using CMC tools, also known as telecollaboration or eTandem, have recently gained significant presence in the field as a way

DOI: 10.4018/978-1-4666-6174-5.ch009

to engage foreign language learners in an organized partnership, linking language learners in one part of the world with learners in other parts of the world for reciprocal learning of languages and cultures (Cziko, 2004; Sauro, 2013). Although often used interchangeably, the term telecollaboration refers to international class-to-class partnership within institutionalized settings (Thorne, 2003), while eTandem refers to individual language learning in dyads, spending half the time in learner's first language (L1) and the other half in the target language (Brammerts, 2003; Tian & Wang, 2010). The major two-fold goal of such learning arrangements is the development of second language (L2) proficiency and intercultural competence (Belz, 2003; Zarate, 2003). As such, on the one hand, cognitive-interactionists examine telecollaboration for corrective feedback (Sauro, 2013; Vinagre & Muñoz, 2011; Ware & O'Dowd, 2008; Ware & Pérez-Cañado, 2007), negotiation for meaning (Bower & Kawaguchi, 2011; Kötter, 2003; O'Rourke, 2005), and tasks that elicit negotiated interaction (Hauck & Youngs, 2008). On the other hand, socioculturally-oriented researchers examine telecollaboration as a venue that promotes collaborative scaffolding (Lee, 2008), intercultural competence (Belz, 2003; Belz & Müller-Hartmann, 2003; O'Dowd, 2003, 2006; Thorne, 2003; Ware, 2005; Ware & Kramsch, 2005), creation of online identity (Blake, 2006), and pragmatic competence (Belz, 2007). Whether learning takes place in the brain or in society, social interaction with native-speaking age peers via CMC tools has been shown to broaden the range of available discourse options in comparison to traditional L2 classrooms, to alter and increase the number of epistemic roles that learners may assume, and to create conditions under which learners desire to present and maintain positive face, which, in turn, may result in enhanced L2 performance (Belz, 2003; Belz & Kinginger, 2003; Belz & Vyatkina, 2005; Dussias, 2005; 2006; Kinginger, 2000, 2004; Thorne, 2003; Ware & O'Dowd, 2008).

While such numerous benefits of telecollaboration have been observed, telecollaboration has not been able to demonstrate itself as a way to focus on form (FonF) (Schwienhorst, 2000). The lack of telecollaborative literature on FonF is surprising when we consider learners' desire to improve linguistic accuracy (Akiyama, 2012; Vinagre & Muñoz, 2011; Ware & O'Dowd, 2008). For instance, Schwienhorst (2000) and Ware and O'Dowd (2008) documented a lack of FonF during actual telecollaboration and participants' desire to improve linguistic accuracy. As such, it seems imperative that more studies examine how to promote FonF in telecollaboration in order to meet participants' expectations by creating tasks that spontaneously assist telecollaborators' FonF.

One indicator of learners' FonF is the quantity and quality of language-related episodes (LREs), namely "any part of the discourse where students talk about language they are producing, question their language use, or other- or self-correct their language production" (Swain & Lapkin, 2001, p. 104). Although LREs have been used in many classroom studies (Basterrechea & García Mayo, 2013; Doughty & Williams, 1998; Révész, 2009, 2011), only one study has investigated LREs in eTandem/telecollaborative settings (Ware & O'Dowd, 2008). In a context like eTandem where a native-speaker (NS) functions as a tutor for a non-native speaker (NNS), establishing a reciprocal relationship to promote FonF is essential. In addition, creating tasks that can maximize opportunities to FonF should be investigated.

Along this line of research, the present study examined preemptive and reactive LREs that occur in a task-based language exchange via Skype. The study particularly looked at LREs in relation to tasks that targeted different lexical categories (nouns and onomatopoeia) in order to explore a task variable that could affect telecollaborators' FonF activities. The findings of this study can serve to inform practitioners of ways to promote FonF in Skype-based telecollaboration and contribute to the extensive body of research on task variables that can influence learner interaction.

BACKGROUND

Skype for Language Learning

Skype is a multimodal voice over Internet Protocol (VoIP) that enables video, audio, and text chat. In contrast to text-based online interaction, or written CMC (WCMC), oral computer-mediated communication (OCMC) such as Skype and *Google Hangout* has received much less attention in SLA research because it is not as different from face-to-face communication as WCMC. Most research on OCMC has been conducted in the area of distance language education (Develotte, 2009; Lamy, 2004; Rosell-Aguilar, 2005), and only a few studies (Jepson, 2005; Lee, 2007; Sykes, 2005; Yanguas, 2010) have examined OCMC as a means to develop L2 proficiency.

Yanguas (2010) looked at the effects of communication medium (i.e. audio chat vs. video chat vs. face-to-face chat) on learner interaction. The study looked at how learners of Spanish negotiated meaning when communication breakdowns occurred. Yanguas found that the audio chat group carried out meaning negotiations differently from the video chat group due to the lack of visual contact, but the video chat and face-to-face chat groups did not differ significantly. The study also compared its findings with previous studies on WCMC and concluded that turn-taking patterns were more versatile in OCMC than in WCMC. Another study that compared WCMC and OCMC is Jepson (2005), who looked at EFL (English as a foreign language) learners' repair moves in text chat rooms and voice chat rooms online. Operationalizing repairs as negotiation of meaning and negative feedback (Long, 1983, 1996), the results showed that a significantly higher number of repair moves were made in voice chats than in text chats and that most repair moves in voice chats were pronunciation-related.

In telecollaboration, the medium of communication has mostly been asynchronously and/or synchronously text-based, usually in the form of email exchanges or synchronous chats (Appel & Gilabert, 2002; Belz & Thorne, 2006; Kinginger, 2004; Sotillo, 2005). A few exceptions that reported telecollaborative projects via video chats were O'Dowd (2000), Lee (2007), and Tian and Wang (2010). The first two studies were carried out in a classroom environment with teacher instruction and intervention while the third study was conducted outside the classroom using desktop video chat. O'Dowd (2000), for instance, reported a telecollaboration project between learners of Spanish and EFL students and found a positive effect of such partnership on the development of intercultural competence. Tian and Wang (2010) were the first to examine Skype-based telecollaborative interaction outside the classroom without instructor/researcher's presence. Participants' perception data were collected through surveys and interviews to analyze self-reported gains in linguistic and intercultural competence. The researchers found that telecollaboration via Skype could be a sustainable mode of learning outside the classroom, yet the study did not report any interactional evidence that would facilitate language development. As such, more studies need to investigate the interaction in OCMC and the effect of such interaction on learners' FonF practices for language development.

FonF through LREs

SLA researchers have dedicated a considerable amount of energy to identifying interactional elements that may strengthen the link between interaction and L2 development (see R. Ellis, 2012 for a summary). Initially inspired by the early version of the Interaction Hypothesis (Long, 1983), researchers were mainly concerned about identifying strategies that could promote negotiated interaction such as clarification requests, comprehension checks, and confirmation checks when communication breakdowns occurred. These strategies, also known as negotiation for meaning, are believed to facilitate learners' detection of and attempts for resolving communication problems (R. Ellis, 1985; Long, 1991; Pica, 1994; Swain, 1993, 1995).

More recently, as more acquisitional benefits of conversational interaction are evidenced (Gass, 1997; Long, 1996, 2007; Pica, 1994; Swain, 1995, 2005), the research focus has been extended to discerning task variables that can promote FonF, regardless of communication breakdowns (Révész, 2011). As such, an increasing body of research has been examining language-related episodes (LREs) for occasions in which learners incidentally draw attention to L2 form–meaning connections in the context of meaning-based communication (R. Ellis, Basturkmen, & Loewen, 2001; Loewen, 2005, 2006; Swain & Lapkin, 1998, 2001).

Two types of LREs that have been investigated in meaning-focused communication are reactive and preemptive LREs. Reactive LREs are corrective responses to something problematic on the part of a NNS. They are also known as corrective feedback, and an error is the trigger of such FonF. Studies on corrective feedback to date have explored some important aspects such as feedback types (Lyster & Ranta, 1997), contexts (Lyster & Mori, 2006), and learners' individual differences (Li, 2013; Mackey & Sacks, 2011; Oliver & Mackey, 2003) that can affect the provision and uptake of such negative evidence. Overall, these studies have shown that corrective feedback is frequent in meaning-focused settings; that teachers typically favor indirect, implicit correction rather than direct, explicit correction; that feedback often does not lead to successful uptake; and that individual differences mediate the rate of uptake (Li, 2010).

Uptake is an index that is often used to measure the degree of noticing from receiving different types of corrective feedback and is defined as "a learner's utterance that immediately follows his/her partner's feedback and that constitutes a reaction in some way to the partner's intention to draw attention to some aspect of the learner's initial utterance" (modified fromLyster & Ranta, 1997, p. 49). Considering uptake as a sign of subsequent learning has been highly debated (Goo & Mackey, 2013; Lyster & Izquierdo, 2009; Lyster & Ranta, 2013; Mackey & Philp, 1998), yet successful uptake, or incorporation of linguistic information into production, has been found to be a strong predictor of learning in some studies (Alcón-Soler, 2009; Chen & Eslami, 2013; Shekary & Tahririan, 2006).

Preemptive LREs, on the other hand, are FonF events where a learner initiates attention to form through negotiation of meaning and/or form, even though no actual problem in production has occurred (Loewen, 2005). The following is an excerpt from this study that demonstrates how FonF can arise even without a communication breakdown or erroneous utterance.

Excerpt 1. NNS-initiated preemptive LRE[1]

NNS: period... How do you say period?
[*Period... How do you say period?* ← (preemptive LRE)]
NS: 時代?
[Period? (/jidai/?)]
NNS: はい、その時代に行くと言っていました。
[Yes, so he said we would go to the period. ← (successful uptake)]

Compared to reactive LREs, preemptive LREs have received much less attention in SLA even though preemptive LREs arise as frequently as reactive LREs (R. Ellis, 2001, 2012; R. Ellis, et al., 2001[2]; Zyzik & Polio, 2008). Furthermore, most of the previous studies examined the classroom context, rarely investigating CMC for such incidental FonF events.

Two studies that looked at preemptive LREs as well as reactive LREs in CMC are Shekary and Tahririan (2006) and Chen and Eslami (2013). Shekary and Tahririan (2006) looked at NNS-NNS interaction for LREs that were produced by 16 EFL Persian learners in order to determine the potential of WCMC for promoting noticing. The study used Loewen's (2005) coding scheme to categorize LREs that were produced during dictogloss, jigsaw, and free discussion tasks. Through logistic regression analyses, the study found that successful uptake was the strongest predictor of language gains, which was measured by individually testing linguistic items that have arisen incidentally during interaction. Similarly, Chen and Eslami (2013) looked at NNS-NS interaction in WCMC for LREs that were produced by 16 Taiwanese EFL learners during decision-making and jigsaw tasks. The study also found that one of the three predictors of NNS' accurate recall of LREs was successful uptake. In sum, these two studies have both found that: (1) successful uptake was a major predictor of subsequent learning and that (2) there was no significant difference between RLREs and PLREs. Therefore, it is important to examine both preemptive and reactive LREs.

Studies on FonF in telecollaboration are very few in number (Bower & Kawaguchi, 2011; Kitade, 2006; Kötter, 2003; O'Dowd & Ritter, 2006; Wang, 2003; Ware & O'Dowd, 2008) and only one study (Ware & O'Dowd, 2008) has investigated LREs. Moreover, these studies have investigated synchronous WCMC, and, to the best of the author's knowledge, no previous study has examined LREs produced in Skype-based telecollaborative projects. As such, this study investigated the way telecollaborators FonF via Skype, especially focusing on the task effects of targeting different types of vocabulary. The next section provides a rationale for focusing on lexical categories as one of the task variables.

Types of Lexical Items and Task-Based Interaction

Researchers who investigate task-based communication have identified a number of variables that can affect the quantity and quality of interaction (see R. Ellis, 2003; Samuda & Bygate, 2008 for reviews). However, little empirical research has treated *types* of lexical items (e.g. word class and phonological features) as an independent variable that can affect learners' communication. The lack of research on lexical categories as a task variable is surprising when we consider consistent findings that negotiation for meaning is mostly concerned about lexical items (N. Ellis, 1994; R. Ellis, 1995; Hatch, 1983; Sato, 1986) and that negotiated interaction benefits lexical learning rather than morphosyntactic and phonological learning (Pica, 1994). As such, it is reasonable to extend the current research focus to the types of lexical items that can promote negotiated interaction.

Word class (e.g. nouns, adjectives, adverbs, verbs, and conjunctions) is one way to categorize lexical items. For example, R. Ellis, Tanaka, and Yamazaki (1994) and N. Ellis and Beaton (1993) found that word class is a psycholinguistic variable that can affect vocabulary learning. In their scheme, nouns are the easiest to learn because they easily carry meaning with images, whereas verbs and adverbs are the hardest to learn. Another way to categorize lexical items is by the phonological features (e.g. reduplication, word length, and homophones). For instance, phonologists who study Optimality Theory (Ahn, 2005; Urbanczyk, 2005) have argued that reduplication enhances perceptual distinctiveness of the lexical items.

Japanese is known for owning a unique set of lexical category called *giongo* and *gitaigo*, or onomatopoeic expressions. These expressions are frequently used in everyday conversation and newspaper articles, as well as in various forms of verbal arts from comic books to novels and poems. In fact, Japanese onomatopoeia constitutes a large open class of words, and one mid-sized dictionary lists 1,700 onomatopoeia entries (Atoda & Hoshino, 1995). Japanese onomatopoeia is unique in that it includes not only sound mimetics (such as *nyaa* for cats' meowing) but also words referring to events and states (such as *kiri-kiri* for a sharp stomach ache and *kari-kari* for being irritated) in which sound is not essential (Imai, Kita, Nagumo, & Okada, 2008). Many Japanese onomatopoeic expressions are formed by repeating two syllables (e.g. *niko-niko* for smiling and *gara-gara* for gargling), and those with the voiced initial consonants are associated with larger mass (e.g. *dondon* = pounding) and the voiceless initial consonants are associated with smaller mass (e.g. *tonton* = knocking) (Imai et al, 2008).

Learning onomatopoeia is an arduous task for learners of Japanese because it is difficult to associate such apparently arbitrary phonological system with its meaning. However, to the best of the author's knowledge, there has been no empirical study that specifically investigated LREs surrounding onomatopoeic expressions, let alone in the CMC context. Investigating the effects of target vocabulary type on learners' FonF is important not only to contribute to the task-based learning literature but also to devise an effective model of telecollaboration. For instance, one of the most popular models of telecollaboration, *Cultura* (http://cultura.mit.edu), utilizes word-association as one of the three major steps for its organized e-partnership.

Along this line of investigation, the present study investigates how different types of target vocabulary (nouns and onomatopoeia) affects participants' FonF practices operationalized as LREs. One decision-making task included nouns and the other was seeded with verb/adverb onomatopoeic expressions. If previous findings by N. Ellis (1994) and N. Ellis and Beaton (1993) hold true, onomatopoeia will pose more difficulties to learn, which may affect how telecollaborators FonF. In addition, saliency of onomatopoeic expressions due to their phonological reduplication may raise learners' attention to form. The following five research questions (RQ) guided the study.

Research Questions

1. How do different types of target vocabulary affect telecollaborators' preemptive LREs?
2. How do different types of target vocabulary affect NSs' provision of reactive LREs (RLREs)?
3. How do different types of target vocabulary affect NNSs' uptake of LREs?
4. How does the multimodal nature of Skype facilitate telecollaborators' FonF activities?
5. How do different types of target vocabulary affect the way telecollaborators engaged in multimodal LREs?

METHODS

Participants

The participants were twelve pairs (24 participants) of English (EFL) and Japanese (JFL) learners in Japan and the U.S., respectively. Since this study only looked at the interaction data in Japanese, EFL learners are labeled NSs of Japanese while JFL learners are labeled as NNSs of Japanese. The 12 JFL learners had studied Japanese for a semester before the project started. There were seven males and five females, ranging from 19-26 years of age (*Mdn* = 20.5 years). The Skype project was part of the fast-track, intensive language course that covered three semesters of Japanese in one semester. Most of the participants were officially rated as Intermediate-Low on the ACTFL (American Council on the Teaching of Foreign Languages) Oral Proficiency Interview scale when they completed the course. Eight of the participants were native speakers of English, while the remaining four spoke Spanish, Pakistani, Russian, and Chinese as their first language. The four non-native speakers of English were considered near-native, which was demonstrated by their SAT/TOEFL/GRE scores.

Due to the difference in academic calendar, the EFL learners in Tokyo (NSs of Japanese) were not enrolled in an English course at the time of data collection. They were volunteer language exchange partners (six males and six females; 19-28 of age with a median of 23.50; and four undergraduates, five master's students, and three recent graduates) who took a two-unit English course in the previous semester and who expressed their desire to continue with the project. Although none of these participants were foreign language majors, they were committed to this project and completed all the required assignments on time.

In order to match participants, the researcher asked the participants to fill out a questionnaire. The questionnaire asked such questions as native vs. non-native speaker preference, majors, gender, and personality. In negotiation with participants in the U.S., the instructor/researcher matched participants and made twelve telecollaborative pairs. The instructor/researcher tried to match as many characteristics as possible. Out of concern that telecollaboration can lead to potential online dating, the instructor/researcher matched participants' by the same gender to create six male pairs, five female pairs, and one male-female pair.

Setting

The data came from a larger telecollaboration project (a total of seven biweekly Skype sessions over a semester) between a university in Tokyo and a university on the east coast of the United States. However, for the purpose of this study, the data from two task-based conversations in Japanese (Japanese parts of the 4th and 5th Skype sessions) was analyzed.

This project utilized a number of technologies to connect telecollaborators in Japan and the U.S. First, Skype was used as the main tool in this project. Students also used email to set up a time to Skype over designated weekends. Wikispaces was used as a place for the researcher/instructor to post language resources (e.g. videos and websites), task instructions, and the project schedule. Lastly, participants were instructed to record their conversation using *Audacity* (a free open source digital audio editor and recording software application) and *Vocaroo* (a website to record voice messages).

Regarding project/task sequences, the current project followed a task-based learning model of pre-, main, and post-tasks both at the macro and micro level (see Figure 1). At the macro level, JFL learners prepared for a biweekly Skype session in class (pre-task), Skyped for an hour outside class (main task), and reflected on the Skype session with classmates (post-task). At the micro level, each Skype session started with a one-way information gap task (pre-task) where JFL learners explained a task instruction to their partners. Following the pre-task, the participants engaged in a two-way information gap task and its reporting (main task). For the post-task, telecollaborators were given a task to explore a language structure.

Procedures

Before the two Skype sessions, two surveys (one on nouns and the other on onomatopoeia) were conducted in class to assess JFL learners' existing lexical knowledge and to increase the internal validity of the study (i.e., potential exposure to the targeted items outside and before the Skype sessions). Each survey asked the JFL learners to indicate their familiarity with pre-selected 40 words by checking: "I know the meaning of the word," "I have heard of the word," or "I don't know the word." For "I know the meaning of the word," the participants were also asked to provide a translation of the word in English. All the items (80 items in total for the two surveys - one focusing on nouns and the other focusing on onomatopoeia) had a maximum of four syllables, reflecting N. Ellis and Beaton's finding (1993) that the learn-

Figure 1. Task-based telecollaboration model in this study

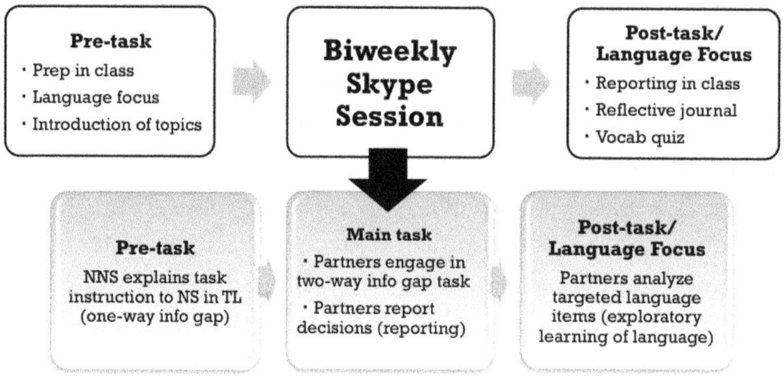

ability of a word decreases after exceeding four syllables. Based on the survey results, 14 words that none of the participants knew/answered correctly were chosen to be included in each Skype task. Of those 14 words, seven were seeded in NSs' task prompt while the other seven were seeded in NNSs' task prompt. The 4th Skype session targeted 14 nouns and the 5th Skype session targeted 14 onomatopoeic expressions (adverbs and verbs). In order to balance the difficulty of the two tasks and reduce the chances of participants' engaging in LREs of non-targeted items, the researcher made sure to include only the words that were previously learned in class for the rest of the language in the task prompts.

The theme of the noun task (4th Skype session) was Doraemon, a popular Japanese manga and anime character who uses futuristic gadgets to save the weak. For the Doraemon task, each telecollaborative pair (NS and NNS) had to go back in history to write a report about the *Edo* period in Japan. In order to go back to the period, the pair borrowed a total of four items from Doraemon that were worth one million yen and weighed less than 10 kilograms. The task prompt was given to both NSs and NNSs, but the specific task instruction was given only to the NNSs, who explained in Japanese the settings, goals, and rules to follow (pre-task) (Appendix A & B). After selecting four gadgets (main task), the telecollaborative pair reported their decision as if they were presenting the decision in front of class. For the post-task, the pair analyzed a grammar structure, ～という… (… *called/named* ～; e.g. a robot called *Doraemon*), which was in accordance with the task content and the course syllabus.

The onomatopoeia task was also a decision making task, but the theme and language focus were different. The task setting was that the pair would go to Europe for a break, for which they had to decide four essential medicines to bring with them. After one-way information gap task (pre-task), each pair chose four types of medicine, whose instruction included target onomatopoeic expressions (main task). For the language focus activity, each pair cooperatively explored phonological rules that accounted for changes in onomatopoeic meanings (post-task).

The telecollaborators were instructed to audio-record their Skype conversations, which were coded for LREs by the researcher. The researcher transcribed the first 18 minutes of participants' conversation in the main task (i.e. gadget selection). Some pairs recorded more than 20 minutes of conversations, but only 18 minutes were transcribed and included in the data analysis so as to follow the task instruction (i.e. 20 minutes for gadget selection). The telecollaborators were also required to email a copy of the text chat history, which the researcher used to analyze multimodal LREs in Skype-based telecollaboration.

Table 1. Coding Scheme in the Present Study (adapted from Loewen, 2005)

Characteristics	Definition	Categories
LRE type	When an LRE is instigated	- Preemptive: NNS-initiated query - Reactive: Error correction (R. Ellis, 2001) - Recasts - Explicit correction - Negotiation
Linguistic focus	Linguistic target	- Grammar - Vocabulary - Pronunciation - N.A. ("not applicable" e.g. meaning)
Modality	How telecollaborators used a multimodal feature of Skype for an LRE	- Audio only - Audio + Text chat - Audio + Images/image links sharing - Audio + Webcam
Uptake incidence	NNS' response to feedback	- Uptake: NNS produces response - No uptake: NNS does not respond - No opportunity: NNS does not have a chance to respond
Uptake quality	Quality of NNS' response to feedback	- Successful uptake: NNS incorporates linguistic information into production - Unsuccessful uptake: NNS does not incorporate linguistic information into production

Data Analysis

This study adapted Loewen's (2005) LRE coding scheme by integrating R. Ellis' taxonomy of incidental FonF (2001), which differentiated four types of incidental FonF based on reactive/preemptive and implicit/explicit contrasts. First, audio transcriptions were coded for LREs, which are then specified using five characteristics (Table 1). Second, LREs were coded by the type of LREs: recasts, negotiation, explicit negative feedback, and preemptive LREs. Third, LREs were coded by the linguistic focus[3]: morphosyntactic, lexical, phonological, and none. Fourth, although the current data were mostly audio-driven, telecollaborators' use of multimodal features of Skype was categorized by four types: audio only, text chat, images, and webcam. Fourth, JFL learner's responses to LREs were coded for the presence of uptake: uptake, no uptake, or no opportunity for uptake. Fifth, uptake was further categorized for the quality: successful uptake or unsuccessful uptake.

In order to measure the potential of noticing, the rate of uptake was calculated by successful uptake ÷ (uptake + no uptake). For statistical analyses to answer RQ1, RQ2, RQ3, and RQ5, this study employed a Wilcoxon Signed-rank test, a non-parametric test that is suitable for frequency data. On the other hand, RQ4 was descriptively analyzed with sample examples.

In order to establish inter-rater reliability, another Japanese instructor coded approximately 20% of the interaction data (4 minutes per conversation x 2 tasks x 12 pairs = approximately 90 minutes). The four minutes to code was taken from the middle section (8-12 minutes) of the 18-minute conversation data. The consistency rate was 93%. For the LREs that were not agreed upon, the two raters discussed and reached a consensus following other examples. The third rater was not employed.

Table 2. The relationship between target vocabulary type and linguistic focus of PLREs

	Frequency and Percentage		Median		Wilcoxon Signed-rank test *p*
	Noun ($N = 188$)	Onomatopoeia ($N = 276$)	Noun	Onomatopoeia	
Morphosyntactic PLREs	24 (12.77%)	17 (6.16%)	2	1.50	.20
Lexical PLREs	159 (84.57%)	251 (90.94%)	12	20.50	.01**
Phonological PLREs	5 (2.66%)	8 (2.90%)	0	.50	NA

* $p < 0.05$; ** $p < 0.01$

RESULTS

Analysis of Audio-Based FonF

RQ1: How do different types of target vocabulary affect telecollaborators' preemptive LREs?

To examine whether target vocabulary type affected the total frequency of preemptive LREs (PLREs), a Wilcoxon Signed-rank test was performed on the total number of PLREs produced during the noun and onomatopoeia tasks. The test revealed a significant effect of target vocabulary type on the total frequency of PLREs, indicating that telecollaborators produced significantly more PLREs in the onomatopoeia task (*Mdn* = 20.50) than in the noun task (*Mdn* = 13.50), $Z = -2.90$, $p < .01$, $r = 0.59$.

Second, to examine whether target vocabulary type affected the linguistic focus of PLREs, three Wilcoxon Signed-rank tests were performed on the raw frequency of morphosyntactic, lexical, and phonological PLREs. The results revealed a significant effect of vocabulary type on the frequency of employing lexical PLREs, indicating that telecollaborators produced significantly more lexical PLREs during the onomatopoeia task (*Mdn* = 20.5) than in the noun task (*Mdn* = 12), $Z = -2.93$, $p < .01$, $r = .60$. However, there was no significant effect of vocabulary type for morphosyntactic PLREs, $Z = -1.27$, $p = .20$. This means that the learners produced more lexical PLREs during the onomatopoeia task than during the noun task, although the number of morphosyntactic PLREs was not affected by vocabulary type. Phonological PLREs could not calculate the Wilcoxon Signed-rank statistic due to the small sample size and many tied values (see Table 2).

RQ2: How do different types of target vocabulary affect NSs' provision of reactive LREs?

First, to find out whether target vocabulary type affected the frequency of reactive LREs (RLREs), a Wilcoxon Signed-rank test was performed on the total number of RLREs (i.e. frequency of recasts, explicit correction, and negotiation combined) that were observed in each task. The test revealed no significant effect of target vocabulary type between noun (*Mdn* =12.60) and onomatopoeia (*Mdn* = 15.17), $Z = -1.38$, $p = .17$. This indicates that target vocabulary type did not affect the overall frequency of RLREs.

To find out whether target vocabulary type affected the linguistic focus of RLREs, three Wilcoxon Signed-rank tests were performed on the raw frequencies of morphosyntactic, lexical, and phonological RLREs, respectively. The tests revealed a significant effect of vocabulary type on phonological RLREs, indicating that NSs of Japanese corrected significantly more phonological errors in the onomatopoeia task (*Mdn* = 5) than

Table 3. The relationship between target vocabulary type and linguistic focus of RLREs

	Frequency and Percentage		Median		Wilcoxon Signed-rank test *p*
	Noun (*N* = 129)	**Onomatopoeia (*N* = 148)**	**Noun**	**Onomatopoeia**	
Morphosyntactic RLREs	44 (34.11%)	52 (35.14%)	4	4	.34
Lexical RLREs	59 (45.74%)	45 (30.41%)	5	2.5	.20
Phonological RLREs	26 (20.16%)	51 (34.46%)	2	5	.01*

* indicates $p < 0.05$; ** indicates $p < 0.01$

in the noun task (*Mdn* = 2), $Z = -2.35$, $p < .05$, $r = .50$. There was no significant difference for lexical or morphosyntactic errors (see Table 3).

Finally, to examine whether target vocabulary type affected the way Japanese NSs provided RLREs, three Wilcoxon Signed-rank tests were performed on the raw frequencies of recasts, explicit correction, and negotiation, respectively. The tests revealed a significant effect of target vocabulary type for recasts, indicating that NSs used more recasts in the onomatopoeia task (*Mdn* = 9.5) than in the noun task (*Mdn* = 6), $Z = -2.59$, $p < .01$, $r = .53$. On the other hand, there was no significant effect of target vocabulary type for explicit correction. Negotiation could not be calculated with the Wilcoxon Signed-rank statistic due to the small sample size and many tied values (see Table 4).

RQ3: How do different types of target vocabulary affect NNSs' uptake of LREs?

To find out whether target vocabulary type affected the rate of JFL learners' uptake, two Wilcoxon Signed-rank tests were performed on the rate at which PLREs and RLREs, respectively, led to successful uptake. The tests revealed a significant effect of vocabulary type on the successful uptake of RLREs, indicating that JFL learners repaired erroneous utterances more successfully during the onomatopoeia task (*Mdn* = 74.76%) than during the noun task (*Mdn* = 66.25%), $Z = -2.27$, $p < .05$, $r = .46$. On the other hand, there was no significant effect of vocabulary type for the uptake of PLREs (Table 6). The table below also shows additional information comparing PLREs and RLREs, indicating that PLREs were successfully repaired at a higher rate than RLREs.

Table 4. Reactive LREs and correction method

	Frequency and Percentage		Median		Wilcoxon Signed-rank test *p*
	Noun (*N* = 129)	**Onomatopoeia (*N* = 148)**	**Noun**	**Onomatopoeia**	
Recasts	79 (61.24%)	111 (86.05%)	6	9.5	.01**
Explicit correction	44 (34.11%)	29 (22.48%)	4	2	.07
Negotiation	6 (4.65%)	8 (6.20%)	0	1	NA

* $p < 0.05$; ** $p < 0.01$

Table 5. Descriptive statistics for the uptake of PLREs and RLREs

	Median		Wilcoxon Signed-rank test *p*
	Noun	Onomatopoeia	
Uptake of PLREs	89.90%	91.00%	.08
Uptake of RLREs	66.25%	74.76%	.02*

* $p < 0.05$; ** $p < 0.01$

In other words, NNS-initiated FonF (i.e., PLREs) resulted in the higher rate of successful uptake than NS-initiated FonF (i.e. PLREs).

Analysis of Skype-Based FonF

To answer RQ 4 and RQ5, the section below first presents examples of how telecollaborators utilized multimodal features of Skype for FonF activities. Second, the interaction data will be analyzed quantitatively, this time focusing on the use of multimodal features of Skype in LREs.

RQ4: How does the multimodal nature of Skype facilitate telecollaborators' FonF activities?

The section below presents examples of how telecollaborators used (1) text chat, (2) images/image links, and (3) webcam to enhance FonF activities. The data demonstrated that telecollaborators often utilized multimodal features of Skype to (a) negotiate meaning, (b) write down *kanji* (i.e. characters borrowed from Chinese to Japanese) so as to clarify *kanji* homophones, (c) provide corrective feedback (RLREs), (d) give visual explanations of linguistic items using images available online, and (e) to demonstrate actions/motions using webcam.

(a) To Negotiate for Meaning

Telecollaborators often used text chat as a way to negotiate for meaning when there was a communication breakdown. In Example 1, the NNS is trying to explain that it will not be a problem to bring a small amount of "Moisture X" (a liquid-type medicine included in the onomatopoeia task prompt) as long as it does not exceed the weight limit set by the customs. After NNS' unclear utterance, the NS asked if he understood the NNS right. NNS, who did not understand NS' confirmation check, kept on repeating himself. Then, the NS, who noticed that the NNS did not understand his previous utterance, wrote down the phrase to help the NNS to understand. In the example below, the focused element is represented by an arrow. This LRE was coded as negotiation (type), N.A. (linguistic focus), text chat (modality), uptake (uptake incidence), and successful (uptake quality).

Example 1.

NNS: でも、more もっとモイスチャーエックスを持っていけません。
[But, we cannot take *more*... more "Moisture X."]
NS: はいはいはい。少しなら大丈夫だけど?
[Oh, OK OK OK. So, you mean a small amount will be fine?]
NNS: 持っていっていけません。持っていってはいけません。
[We cannot take... We cannot take...]
NS: text: 少しなら大丈夫だけど
[text: Just a small amount will be fine.] ←
NNS: はい、少しなら大丈夫だけど。
[Yes, just a small amount will be fine]

(b) To Clarify *Kanji* Homophones

Japanese has a number of homophones that are differentiated by *kanji*. For instance, [*dai*] can be written in dozens of ways using different *kanji*. Even native Japanese speakers often need to negotiate *kanji* by orally explaining which *kanji* they have in mind. As such, telecollaborators used the text chat function to write down *kanji* to clarify *kanji* homophones. In Example 2, the NS asked if the *kanji* he had in mind was correct. The NNS confirmed that that was the *kanji* he meant to use. Then, apart from the previous LRE, the NS explicitly corrected the NNS' word choice in the next LRE. The focused episode (i.e. the first LRE in Example 2) was coded as negotiation (type), phonological (linguistic focus), text chat (modality), uptake (uptake incidence), and unsuccessful (uptake quality).

Example 2.

NNS: *よんだい。
  [Four * /dai/ (machine counter).]
NS: *よんだい?
  [Four * /dai/ (machine counter)?]
NS: text: 四台?
  [text: Four * /dai/ (machine counter)? {typing /dai/ in Chinese characters for clarification}]←
NNS: はい、*よんだい。*よんだいえらびます。
  [Yes, four */dai/. We pick four tools.]
(continued)
NS: 俺だったらよんこを使うけど。
  [I would rather use four /ko/ (small item counter).]
NNS: あ、そうですか。
  [Oh, I see.]

(c) To Provide Corrective Feedback (RLREs)

Telecollaborators also used the text chat to provide corrective feedback, especially in clarifying pronunciation problems. In Example 3, the NNS said *[*kaju*] to mean *weight* , which is actually pronounced as [*kaju:*]. However, since vowel length is contrastive in Japanese, the NS interpreted *[*kaju*] as [*kazu*] (*number* in Japanese) and used the text chat to correct NNS's pronunciation. However, the NNS insisted that he meant to say *[*kaju*] (weight), not [*kazu*] (number). Then, the NS, who realized that NNS meant to say [*kaju:*] with the long vowel, gave the corrective feedback in text in addition to the oral corrective feedback. The following two LREs were both coded as recast (type), phonological (linguistic focus), text chat (modality), uptake (uptake incidence), and successful (uptake quality).

Example 3.

NNS: あと、*かじゅのリミットもあります。
  [Also, there is the */kaju/ limit.]
NS: かずね?
  [/kazu/ (number), right?]
NS: text: かず [text: /kazu/]←
NNS: かず?いえ、かずじゃない。*かじゅです。
  [/Kazu/? No, it's not /kazu/ but */kaju/.]
(continued)
NS: ああ、荷重ね?重さね?荷重。
  [Oh you mean, /kaju:/? Weight, right?]
NNS: 荷重。
  [/Kaju:/]
NS: 荷重。うん、weightね。
  [/Kaju:/. Yeah, *weight*.]
NNS: right。荷重, not かず。
  [*Right*. /Kaju:/, *not* /kazu/.]
NS: text: 荷重
  [text: /kaju:/]←

NNS: はい。荷重のリミットもあります。
[Yes, there is a weight limit.]

(d) To Give Visual Explanations Using Images Available Online

Not only did telecollaborators utilize text chat, they also sent images or image links via Skype to give visual explanations. In Example 4, the NS sent an image of Konjac because the NNS could not verbally explain what the food was like. This is a unique feature of Skype-based language exchange that utilizes immediate access to internet web browsers (e.g. *Google.com*). This episode was coded as negotiation (type), lexical (linguistic focus), image (modality), no chance (uptake incidence), and N.A. (uptake quality).

Example 4.

NNS: コンニャクは何ですか。
[What is Konjac?]
NS: なんか、ゴムみたいな野菜で、なんだろう、なんか、ゼリーみたいな、かたいゼリーのような食べ物です。
[It's like a rubber-like vegetable. How can I say? It's like jelly. It's like hard jelly.]
NNS: うん。。。
[OK…]
NS: ちょっとこれは見たことがないと難しい。これ、コンニャクは。
[It's hard to explain if you've never seen it… Here, this is Konjac.]
NS text: web link for the image of Kanjac
[text: image link for Konjac]←
NNS: おいしいですか。
[Does this taste good?]
NS: あんまり味はついていないです。でも、おいしいですよ。
[Well, it doesn't have much taste, but it's good.]
NNS: ああ、そうですか。
[Huh, I see.]

(e) To Demonstrate Actions/ Motions Using Webcam

Telecollaborators often used webcam to show body movement/actions when verbal explanations did not make sense to one's partner. In Example 5, the NNS asked what [*tsuru tsuru*], (an onomatopoeia for slippery objects) means. Then, the NS explained verbally that it means to *slip*. However, the NNS did not understand the word, which the NS explained using webcam. This episode was coded as preemptive (type), lexical (linguistic focus), webcam (modality), no uptake (uptake incidence), and N.A. (uptake quality).

Example 5.

NNS: ツルツルは何ですか。
[What is /tsuru-tsuru/?]
NS: ツルツルはね、滑ること。わかる?
[/tsuru-tsuru/ means to slip. Get it?]
NNS: 滑る?
[To slip?]
NS: うん。とか、頭に毛が無い人はツルツルって言う。
[Yeah, like, people with no hair are called /tsuru-tsuru/.]
NS webcam: demonstrating slipperiness こんな感じ。
[Like this.]←
NNS: ああ、わかりました。
[Ah, I get it.]

RQ5: How do different types of target vocabulary affect the way telecollaborators engage in multimodal LREs?

As the examples above demonstrated, telecollaborators utilized the multimodal features of Skype to carry out FonF activities effectively. This section presents the quantitative analysis of multimodal LREs.

First, to find out whether target vocabulary type affected the way telecollaborators used multimodal

Table 6. The relationship between target vocabulary type and the use of multimodal features of Skype

	Frequency and Percentage		Median		Wilcoxon Signed-rank test *p*
	Noun (N = 153)	Onomatopoeia (N = 172)	Noun	Onomatopoeia	
Image	31 (20.26%)	11 (6.40%)	2.5	1	.01**
Webcam	13 (8.50%)	61 (35.47%)	1	5	.01**
Text	109 (71.24%)	100 (58.14%)	8.5	8	.59

* $p < 0.05$; ** $p < 0.01$

features of Skype to engage in preemptive FonF activities, three Wilcoxon Signed-rank tests were performed on the raw frequency of text, image, and webcam PLREs, respectively. The tests revealed significant effects of vocabulary type for the use of images, indicating that telecollaborators sent more images during the noun task (*Mdn* = 2.5) than during the onomatopoeia task (*Mdn* = 1), $Z = -2.62, p < .01, r = .53$. The results also showed that telecollaborators resorted to the use of webcam more often during the onomatopoeia task (*Mdn* = 5) than during the noun task (*Mdn* = 1), $Z = -2.80, p < .01, r = .57$. Finally, there was no significant difference for the use of text chat regardless of types of target vocabulary (see Table 6).

Second, in order to examine whether target vocabulary type affected the way Japanese NSs Japanese used multimodal features of Skype to correct their partners' erroneous utterances (RLREs), a Wilcoxon Signed-rank test was performed on the raw frequencies of textually-supported RLREs. The Japanese NSs used textually-supported RLREs 29 and 42 times during noun and onomatopoeia tasks, respectively. The test revealed no significant difference between the noun task (*Mdn* = 2.5) and the onomatopoeia task (*Mdn* = 3), indicating that target vocabulary type did not affect how NSs provided corrective feedback using text chat ($Z = -1.78, p = .08$). There was no instance of using images or webcam to give corrective feedback.

DISCUSSION

This study investigated the effects of target vocabulary type on FonF activities that took place in Skype-based telecollaboration. Regarding RQ1 about the effects of vocabulary type on the use of PLREs, it was found that the total frequency of PLREs was significantly higher and learners produced significantly more lexical LREs during the onomatopoeia task than during the noun task. In contrast, the number of morphosyntactic PLREs was not statistically different. These findings may be attributable to the perceptual saliency of onomatopoeia, which heavily relies on phonological reduplication. As some proponents of Optimality Theory (Miyeon, 2005; Urbanczyk, 2005) have argued, reduplication may have enhanced perceptual distinctiveness of the lexical items, which led JFL learners to initiate LREs on such distinctive lexical category of onomatopoeia. Another reason why telecollaborators engaged in significantly more lexical PLREs during the onomatopoeia task than during the noun task may be related to NNSs' increased perception of NSs as tutors who can provide scaffolding on such perceptually salient and culturally-rich language items. In other words, perceptual saliency of onomatopoeia (due to phonological reduplication) and/or the cultural aspect of learning onomatopoeia (due to its culturally-bounded sound-meaning associations) made it easier for NNSs to construe their partners as language tutors who can respond to NNS-initiated LREs. This aligns with previous research findings that documented the role of identity construction in interaction. For instance, Park (2007) argued that asymmetrical social identities (i.e. NNS as an information "requester" and NS as a "requestee" (p. 343)) led to successful and engaging interaction because participants felt more comfortable when such roles were assigned. Tomita and Spada (2013) also explored the effect of form-focused tasks on identity construction in Japanese EFL learners' peer interaction. They found that designating a grammatical form to use in interaction led to more opportunities to express learners' struggle in using English and consequently resulted in more "investment" in L2 communication (p. 606). As such, the current study also supports the intricate relationship between language and tasks, identity construction, and interaction.

With regard to RQ2 about RLREs, target vocabulary type influenced what errors the NSs focused on correcting and how such correction was provided. Specifically, the NSs corrected more phonological errors and used more recasts during the onomatopoeia task than during the noun task. The finding echoed Lyster (2001) who found that language teachers predominantly used recasts to correct phonological errors. This finding is perhaps attributed to the NSs' focus on phonemes/phonological properties of onomatopoeia (e.g. voicing and vowel quality), which are contrastive in Japanese and change the meanings of onomatopoeia. Example 6 below shows how the NS recasted */gura-gural* (shaky) for */gera-geral* (laughing aloud hard). It shows how a single difference in phonological properties of onomatopoeia (i.e. */u/* vs. */e/*) results in a major meaning change. As such, this finding indicates that creating tasks that focus on one salient linguistic feature (e.g. phonological properties of onomatopoeia) can direct NSs' attention to providing focused feedback. Future studies may examine whether such focused-task can promote FonF and whether the provision of linguistically-focused feedback by NSs in the telecollaborative setting can facilitate language development.

Example 6.

NNS: 次の薬は、えっと、グラグラ、グラグーラ。
[Next we have a medicine */gura-gura/.*]
NS: ぐらぐら、はい。
[*/gura-gural*, OK.]
NNS: はい、グラグーラを飲むと、イライラしている人が笑います。
[Yes, and this is for people who are irritated.]
NS: ゲラゲーラ?
[*/gera-geral*?]
NNS: あ、はい、そうです。ゲラゲーラ。
[Oh, yes. That's right. */gera-geral*.]

With regard to RQ3 on the uptake of LREs through Skype, the rate of successful uptake of RLREs was significantly higher during the onomatopoeia task than during the noun task, although there was no significant difference for PLREs. It was also found that the rate of uptake was higher for PLREs than for RLREs, indicating that NNS-initiated FonF resulted in the higher rate of uptake than NS-initiated FonF. The finding is the first to confirm R. Ellis, et al's (2001) finding in the telecollaborative setting that the uptake rate of PLREs is higher than that of RLREs. Considering telecollaborators' increased FonF during the onomatopoeia task, as was demonstrated by RQ1 and RQ2, it is reasonable to argue that increased FonF resulted in a higher rate of uptake and that target vocabulary type was the trigger of the change in the uptake rate. On the other hand, the reason for the higher rate of uptake for PLREs than for the RLREs is probably due to NNSs' readiness to receive FonF. In other words, it is reasonable to speculate that NNSs paid more attention to form when they initiated LREs and were expecting to receive support from their NS peers.

To answer RQ4, this study first qualitatively analyzed the use of multimodal features of Skype. It was found that telecollaborators frequently combined LREs with some kind of multimodal features of Skype. For instance they used the text chat in giving corrective feedback and, in cases of communication breakdowns, sent images to give visual explanations and used webcams to demonstrate motions. In particular, the use of text chat to support negotiation for meaning and to give corrective feedback should be investigated empirically in the future. Such use of *dual feedback,* namely audio feedback combined with the text chat, may prove to be an effective way to promote FonF and subsequent learning. This study also found that text chat was effective not only to solve *kanji* problems but also to provide learners with opportunities to negotiate *kanji*. Negotiating *kanji* is a regular practice not only for Japanese learners but also for native Japanese speakers. Learning how native Japanese speakers solve *kanji* problems is a language-learning experience as well as an essential cultural practice in Japan. Accordingly, the virtual immersion environment afforded by the telecollaborative partnership has a great potential to bridge the gap between Japanese as a foreign language and Japanese as a second language.

Regarding the effects of target vocabulary type on the use of multimodal LREs (RQ5), it was found that NSs used appropriate multimodal features of Skype in accordance with the nature of the linguistic items. That is, telecollaborators often sent images or image links to solve communication breakdowns during the noun task because nouns carry meaning with images (N. Ellis, 1994; N. Ellis & Beaton, 1993), while demonstrating motions with a webcam during the onomatopoeia task because the targeted onomatopoeic expressions were verbs or adverbs. The findings indicate that vocabulary type can influence how telecollaborators use multimodal features of Skype to FonF. A possible pedagogical implication is that *not* allowing telecollaborators to send image links for noun tasks and *not* allowing them to use webcam for verb/adverb tasks may increase the chance of communication breakdown, which may then lead to more opportunities to FonF. Future studies may investigate such a link between settings (e.g. face-to-face, audio- or video-chat, WCMC, and combination of these), word class, and lexical development as a result of FonF activities.

Lastly, as with any other studies, this study has a number of limitations that need to be addressed in future research. First, because only audio and text chat data were collected and analyzed, it was impossible to know what exactly participants did during the Skype sessions. Although the researcher carefully counted the frequency of webcam use based on the audio data such as "Look," "Like this," followed by "Ah! I see" and followed by silence. It is also possible that telecollaborators engaged in more webcam LREs. It is also possible that some participants used an online dictionary to check word meanings, although they were told not to. The researcher made the decision *not* to video-tape the conversations in consideration for their privacy and for the observer effects, but future studies may consider videotaping the entire conversation to increase the validity of the study. Finally, due to the limited number of uptake instances, the rate of uptake was measured by dividing successful uptake instances by the total frequency of PLREs and RLREs, instead of using more detailed LRE categories and powerful statistical analysis. Future studies may use a more elaborate analysis method and statistics (e.g., regression analysis) to allow integrative analysis of LRE characteristics that lead to successful uptake.

CONCLUSION

The present study examined the effects of lexical categories on FonF and the use of multimodal features of Skype for preemptive and reactive LREs in a task-based language exchange via Skype. The findings indicate that it is possible to prompt telecollaborators to FonF spontaneously by creating tasks that target a specific aspect of language (e.g. vocabulary, phonology, etc.) and that such focused tasks can affect the use of multimodal features of Skype.

Before concluding this chapter, it should be noted that, although this study found numerous benefits of using Skype for telecollaboration, telecollaboration coordinators need be aware of issues that are unique to Skype-based telecollaboration. One potential problem is the technical difficulty of using synchronous video chat, which works well only with powerful Internet connection. In fact, this project encountered several cases where participants had to use text chat temporarily until the Internet connection recovered. Another issue with using Skype or any other synchronous CMC tools is the time and motivational commitment that is required for sustainable telecollaboration. That is, Skype-based telecollaboration can only work if participants/coordinators tackle time differences/scheduling conflicts as well as individual differences such as personality, willingness to communicate, and motivation.

For the further development of telecollaborative projects around the world, more practitioners should realize the great potential of connecting NNSs with NSs online and integrating a telecollaborative component into a language curriculum. To achieve that goal, more studies need to investigate language gains from telecollaboration, the degree of FonF in engaging in different tasks, and the integration of multimodal features afforded by OCMC applications such as Skype. The findings of this study suggest that more studies on Skype-based telecollaboration should be conducted, so practitioners can devise tasks that are appropriate for the specific CMC tool (O'Dowd & Eberbach, 2004; O'Dowd Ware, 2009) and maximize the learning potential of such reciprocal teaching and learning of languages and cultures.

ACKNOWLEDGMENT

I would like to thank the editors and anonymous reviewers for their helpful comments on my manuscripts. I also greatly appreciate Gabby Wallace's and Tracy Alexander's help in editing my original manuscripts.

REFERENCES

Ahn, M. (2005). A phonetically based account of English reduplication. *SNU Working Papers in English Language and Linguistics, 4,* 73-93.

Akiyama, Y. (2012, November). *Potential issues, conditions, and solutions to e-tandem language learning*. Paper presented at American Council on the Teaching of Foreign Languages Conference. Philadelphia, PA.

Alcón-Soler, E. (2009). Focus on form, learner uptake and subsequent lexical gains in learners' oral production. *International Review of Applied Linguistics in Language Teaching*, *47*, 347–365. doi:10.1515/iral.2009.015

Appel, C., & Gilabert, R. (2002). Motivation and task performance in a task-based web-based tandem project. *ReCALL*, *14*, 16–31. doi:10.1017/S0958344002000319

Atoda, T., & Hoshino, K. (1995). *Giongo gitaigo tsukaikata jiten (Usage dictionary of sound/manner mimetics)*. Tokyo: Sotakusha.

Basterrechea, M., & García Mayo, M. (2013). Language-related episodes during collaborative tasks. In K. McDonough, & A. Mackey (Eds.), *Second language interaction in diverse educational contexts* (pp. 25–44). Amsterdam: John Benjamins. doi:10.1075/lllt.34.05ch2

Belz, J. A. (2003). Linguistic perspective on the development of intercultural communicative competence in telecollaboration. *Language Learning & Technology*, *7*(2), 68–117.

Belz, J. A. (2007). The role of computer mediation in the instruction and development of L2 pragmatic competence. *Annual Review of Applied Linguistics, 27*, 45–75. doi:10.1017/S0267190508070037

Belz, J. A., & Kinginger, C. (2003). Discourse options and the development of pragmatic competence by classroom learners of German: The case of address forms. *Language Learning, 53*(4), 591–647. doi:10.1046/j.1467-9922.2003.00238.x

Belz, J. A., & Müller-Hartmann, A. (2003). Teachers as intercultural learners: Negotiating German-American telecollaboration along the institutional fault line. *Modern Language Journal, 87*(1), 71–89. doi:10.1111/1540-4781.00179

Belz, J. A., & Thorne, S. L. (2006). *Computer-mediated intercultural foreign language education*. Boston: Heinle & Heinle.

Belz, J. A., & Vyatkina, N. (2008). The pedagogical mediation of a developmental learner corpus for classroom-based language instruction. *Language Learning & Technology, 12*(3), 33–52.

Blake, R. (2000). Computer-mediated communication: A window on ls Spanish interlanguage. *Language Learning & Technology, 4*(1), 120–136.

Blake, R. (2006). Language, culture, and identity in online fanfiction. *E-learning, 3*, 170–184. doi:10.2304/elea.2006.3.2.170

Bower, J., & Kawaguchi, S. (2011). Negotiation of meaning and corrective feedback in Japanese/English eTandem. *Language Learning & Technology, 15*(1), 41–71.

Brammerts, H. (2003). Autonomous language learning in tandem: The development of a concept. In T. Lewis, & L. Walker (Eds.), *Autonomous Language Learning in Tandem* (pp. 27–36). Sheffield: Academy Electronic Publications.

Chen, W. C., & Eslami, Z. (2013). Focus on form in live chats. *Journal of Educational Technology & Society, 16*(1), 147–158.

Cziko, G. (2004). Electronic tandem language learning (eTandem): A third approach to second language learning for the 21st century. *CALICO Journal, 22*(1), 25–39.

Develotte, C. (2009). From face to face to distance learning: The online learner's emerging identity. In R. Goodfellow & N. M. Lamy (Ed.), Learning Cultures in Online Education (pp. 71–92). London: Continuum Books.

Doughty, C., & Williams, J. (1998). *Focus on form in classroom second language acquisition*. Cambridge, England: Cambridge University Press.

Dussias, P. E. (2005). Telecollaboration and lexical and morphological development in Spanish L2. In J. A. Belz, & S. L. Thorne (Eds.), *Internet-mediated intercultural foreign language education* (pp. 121–146). Boston, MA: Heinle & Heinle.

Dussias, P. E. (2006). Morphological development in Spanish–American telecollaboration. In J. Belz, & S. Thorne (Eds.), *Internet-mediated intercultural foreign language education* (pp. 121–146). Boston, MA: Thomsen & Heinle.

Ellis, N. (1994). Consciousness in second language learning: Psychological perspectives on the role of conscious processes in vocabulary acquisition. *AILA Review, 11*, 37–56.

Ellis, N., & Beaton, A. (1993). Psycholinguistic determinants of foreign language vocabulary learning. *Language Learning, 43*, 559–617. doi:10.1111/j.1467-1770.1993.tb00627.x

Ellis, R. (1985). *Understanding second language acquisition*. Oxford, UK: Oxford University Press.

Ellis, R. (1994). Factors in the incidental acquisition of second language vocabulary from oral input: A review essay. *Applied Language Learning, 5*, 1–32.

Ellis, R. (1995). Modified oral input and the acquisition of word meanings. *Applied Linguistics, 16*, 409–435. doi:10.1093/applin/16.4.409

Ellis, R. (2001). Introduction: Investigating form- focused instruction. *Language Learning, 51. SUPP, 1*, 1–46.

Ellis, R. (2003). *Task-based language learning and teaching*. Oxford, New York: Oxford Applied Linguistics.

Ellis, R. (2012). *Language teaching research and language pedagogy*. Malden, MA: Wiley-Blackwell. doi:10.1002/9781118271643

Ellis, R., Basturkmen, H., & Loewen, S. (2001). Learner uptake in communicative ESL lessons. *Language Learning, 51*, 281–318. doi:10.1111/1467-9922.00156

Ellis, R., Tanaka, Y., & Yamakazi, A. (1994). Classroom interaction, comprehension, and L2 vocabulary acquisition. *Language Learning, 44*, 449–491. doi:10.1111/j.1467-1770.1994.tb01114.x

Gass, S. M. (1997). *Input, interaction and the development of second languages*. Mahwah, NJ: Erlbaum.

Goo, J., & Mackey, A. (2013). The case against the case against recasts. *Studies in Second Language Acquisition, 35*(1), 127–165. doi:10.1017/S0272263112000708

Hatch, E. (1983). Simplified input and second language acquisition. In R. Andersen (Ed.), *Pidginization and creolization in second language acquisition* (pp. 64–86). Rowley, MA: Newbury House.

Hauck, M., & Youngs, B. L. (2008). Telecollaboration in multimodal environments: The impact on task design and learner interaction. *Computer Assisted Language Learning, 21*, 87–124. doi:10.1080/09588220801943510

Imai, M., Kita, S., Nagumo, M., & Okada, H. (2008). Sound symbolism facilitates early verb learning. *Cognition, 109*, 54–65. doi:10.1016/j.cognition.2008.07.015 PMID:18835600

Jepson, K. (2005). Conversations-and negotiated interaction-in text and voice chat rooms. *Language Learning & Technology, 9*(3), 79–98.

Kinginger, C. (2000). Learning the pragmatics of solidarity in the networked foreign language classroom. In J. X. Hall (Ed.), *Second and foreign language learning through classroom interaction*. Mahwah, NJ: Erlbaum.

Kinginger, C. (2004). Communicative foreign language teaching through telecollaboration. In St. John, K. van Esch, & E. Schalkwijk (Eds.), *New insights into foreign language learning and teaching* (pp. 101–113). Frankfurt: Peter Lang.

Kitade, K. (2000). L2 learners' discourse and SLA theories in CMC: Collaborative interaction in internet chat. *Computer Assisted Language Learning, 13*(2), 143–166. doi:10.1076/0958-8221(200004)13:2;1-D;FT143

Kitade, K. (2006). The negotiation model in asynchronous computer-mediated communication (CMC): Negotiation in task-based email exchanges. *CALICO Journal, 23*, 319–348.

Kötter, M. (2003). Negotiation of meaning and codeswitching in online tandems. *Language Learning & Technology, 7*(2), 145–172.

Lamy, M. N. (2004). Oral conversations online: Redefining oral competence in synchronous environment. *ReCALL, 16*(2), 520–538. doi:10.1017/S095834400400182X

Lee, L. (2007). Fostering second language oral communication through constructivist interaction in desktop videoconferencing. *Foreign Language Annals, 40*(4), 635–649. doi:10.1111/j.1944-9720.2007.tb02885.x

Lee, L. (2008). Focus on form through collaborative scaffolding in expert-to-novice online interaction. *Language Learning & Technology, 12*(3), 53–72.

Li, S. (2010). The effectiveness of corrective feedback in SLA: A meta-analysis. *Language Learning*, *60*(2), 309–365. doi:10.1111/j.1467-9922.2010.00561.x

Li, S. (2013). The interactions between the effects of implicit and explicit feedback and individual differences in language analytic ability and working memory. *Modern Language Journal*, *97*(3), 634–654. doi:10.1111/j.1540-4781.2013.12030.x

Loewen, S. (2005). Incidental focus on form and second language learning. *Studies in Second Language Acquisition*, *27*, 361–386. doi:10.1017/S0272263105050163

Loewen, S. (2006). Autonomy and language learning behaviour: The role of student initiation in meaning-focused L2 lessons. In T. Lamb, & H. Reinders (Eds.), *Supporting independent language learning: Issues and options* (pp. 37–53). London: Peter Lang.

Long, M. H. (1983). Native speaker/non-native speaker conversation and the negotiation of comprehensible input. *Applied Linguistics*, *4*, 126–141. doi:10.1093/applin/4.2.126

Long, M. H. (1991). Focus on form: A design feature in language teaching methodology. In K. de Bot, R. Ginsberg, & C. Kramsch (Eds.), *Foreign language research in cross-cultural perspective* (pp. 39–52). Amsterdam: John Benjamins. doi:10.1075/sibil.2.07lon

Long, M. H. (1996). The role of the linguistic environment in second language acquisition. In W. Ritchie, & T. Bhatia (Eds.), *Handbook of second language acquisition* (pp. 413–468). San Diego: Academic Press. doi:10.1016/B978-012589042-7/50015-3

Long, M. H. (2007). *Problems in sla*. Mahwah, NJ: Erlbaum.

Lyster, R. (2001). Negotiation of form, recasts, and explicit correction in relation to error types and learner repair in immersion classrooms. *Language Learning*, *51*, 265–301. doi:10.1111/j.1467-1770.2001.tb00019.x

Lyster, R., & Izquierdo, J. (2009). Prompts versus recasts in dyadic interaction. *Language Learning*, *59*, 453–498. doi:10.1111/j.1467-9922.2009.00512.x

Lyster, R., & Mori, H. (2006). Interactional feedback and instructional counterbalance. *Studies in Second Language Acquisition*, *28*, 269–300. doi:10.1017/S0272263106060128

Lyster, R., & Ranta, L. (1997). Corrective feedback and learner uptake: Negotiation of form in communicative classrooms. *Studies in Second Language Acquisition*, *19*(1), 37–66. doi:10.1017/S0272263197001034

Lyster, R., & Ranta, L. (2013). Counterpoint piece: The case for variety in corrective feedback research. *Studies in Second Language Acquisition*, *1*(35), 167–184. doi:10.1017/S027226311200071X

Mackey, A., & Philp, J. (1998). Conversational interaction and second language development: Recasts, responses, and red herrings? *Modern Language Journal*, *82*, 338–356. doi:10.1111/j.1540-4781.1998.tb01211.x

Mackey, A., & Sachs, R. (2012). Older learners in sla research: A first look at working memory, feedback, and l2 development. *Language Learning*, *62*(3), 704–740. doi:10.1111/j.1467-9922.2011.00649.x

Miyeon, A. (2005). A phonetically based account of English reduplication. *SNU Working Papers in English Language and Linguistics, 4*, 73-93.

O'Dowd, R. (2000). Intercultural learning via videoconferencing: A pilot exchange project. *ReCALL*, *12*(1), 49–63. doi:10.1017/S0958344000000616

O'Dowd, R. (2003). Understanding the "other side": Intercultural learning in a Spanish-English e-mail exchange. *Language Learning & Technology, 7*(2), 118–144.

O'Dowd, R. (2006). *Telecollaboration and the development of intercultural communicative competence*. Munich, Germany: Langenscheidt-Longman.

O'Dowd, R., & Eberbach, K. (2004). Guides on the side? Tasks and challenges for teachers in telecollaborative projects. *ReCALL, 16*(1), 129–144.

O'Dowd, R., & Ritter, M. (2006). Understanding and working with 'failed communication' in telecollaborative exchanges. *CALICO Journal, 23*(3), 623–642.

O'Dowd, R., & Ware, P. (2009). Critical issues in telecollaborative task design. *Computer Assisted Language Learning, 22*(2), 173–188. doi:10.1080/09588220902778369

O'Rourke, B. (2005). Form-focused interaction in online tandem learning. *CALICO Journal, 22*(2), 433–466.

Oliver, R., & Mackey, A. (2003). Interactional context and feedback in child ESL classrooms. *Modern Language Journal, 87*(4), 519–533. doi:10.1111/1540-4781.00205

Park, J. E. (2007). Co-construction of nonnative speaker identity in cross-cultural interaction. *Applied Linguistics, 28*, 339–360. doi:10.1093/applin/amm001

Pellettieri, J. (2000). Negotiation in cyberspace: The role of chatting in the development of grammatical competence. In M. Warschauer, & R. Kern (Eds.), *Network-based language teaching: Concepts and practice* (pp. 59–86). New York: Cambridge University Press. doi:10.1017/CBO9781139524735.006

Pica, T. (1994). Research on negotiation: What does it reveal about second-language learning conditions, processes, and outcomes? *Language Learning, 44*(3), 493–527. doi:10.1111/j.1467-1770.1994.tb01115.x

Révész, A. (2009). Task complexity, focus on form, and second language development. *Studies in Second Language Acquisition, 30*, 437–470. doi:10.1017/S0272263109090366

Révész, A. (2011). Task complexity, focus on L2 constructions, and individual differences: A classroom-based study. *Modern Language Journal, 95*(S1), 162–181. doi:10.1111/j.1540-4781.2011.01241.x

Rosell-Aguilar, F. (2005). Task design for audiographic conferencing: Promoting beginner oral interaction in distance language learning. *Computer Assisted Language Learning, 18*(5), 417–442. doi:10.1080/09588220500442772

Samuda, V., & Bygate, M. (2008). *Tasks in second language learning*. Palgrave MacMillan.

Sato, C. (1986). Conversation and interlanguage development: Rethinking the connection. In R. R. Day (Ed.), *Talking to learn: Conversation in second language acquisition* (pp. 23–45). Rowley, MA: Newbury House.

Sauro, S. (2013). The cyber language exchange: Cross-national computer-mediated interaction. In K. McDonough, & A. Mackey (Eds.), *Second language interaction in diverse educational contexts* (pp. 129–146). Amsterdam: John Benjamins. doi:10.1075/lllt.34.11ch7

Schwienhorst, K. (2000). *Virtual reality and learner autonomy in second language acquisition*. Unpublished manuscript.

Shekary, M., & Tahririan, M. (2006). Negotiation of meaning and noticing in text-based online chat. *Modern Language Journal, 90*(4), 557–573. doi:10.1111/j.1540-4781.2006.00504.x

Smith, B. (2003). Computer-mediated negotiated interaction: An expanded model. *Modern Language Journal*, *87*, 38–57. doi:10.1111/1540-4781.00177

Smith, B. (2005). The relationship between negotiated interaction, learner uptake, and in task-based computer-mediated communication. *TESOL Quarterly*, *39*(1), 33–58. doi:10.2307/3588451

Sotillo, S. M. (2005). Corrective feedback via Instant Messenger learning activities in NS-NNS and NNS-NNS dyads. *CALICO Journal*, *22*(3), 467–496.

Swain, M. (1993). The output hypothesis: Just speaking and writing aren't enough. *Canadian Modern Language Review*, *50*(1), 158–164.

Swain, M. (1995). Three functions of output in second language learning. In G. Cook, & G. Seidhofer (Eds.), *Principles and practice in applied linguistics: Studies in honor of H. G. Widdowson* (pp. 125–144). Oxford, UK: Oxford University Press.

Swain, M. (2005). The output hypothesis: Theory and research. In E. Hinkel (Ed.), *Handbook on research in second language teaching and learning* (pp. 471–484). Mahwah, NJ: Erlbaum.

Swain, M., & Lapkin, S. (1998). Interaction and second language learning: Two adolescent French immersion students working together. *Modern Language Journal*, *82*, 320–337. doi:10.1111/j.1540-4781.1998.tb01209.x

Swain, M., & Lapkin, S. (2001). Focus on form through collaborative dialogue: Exploring task effects. In M. Bygate, P. Skehan, & M. Swain (Eds.), *Researching pedagogic tasks: Second language learning, teaching, and testing* (pp. 99–118). London: Longman.

Sykes, J. (2005). Synchronous CMC and pragmatic development: Effects of oral and written chat. *CALICO Journal*, *22*(3), 399–431.

Thorne, S. (2003). Artifacts and cultures-of-use in intercultural communication. *Language Learning & Technology*, *7*(2), 38–67.

Tian, J., & Wang, Y. (2010). Taking language learning outside the classroom: learners' perspectives of eTandem learning via Skype. *Innovation in Language Learning and Teaching*, *4*(3), 181–197. doi:10.1080/17501229.2010.513443

Tomita, Y., & Spada, N. (2013). Form-focused instruction and learner investment in L2 communication. *Modern Language Journal*, *93*(3), 591–610. doi:10.1111/j.1540-4781.2013.12031.x

Urbanczyk, S. (2005). Enhancing contrast in reduplication. In M. de Gruyter (Ed.), Studies on reduplication (pp. 211-238). Berlin: Walter de Gruyter.

Vinagre, M., & Muñoz, B. (2011). Computer-mediated corrective feedback and language accuracy in telecollaborative exchanges. *Language Learning & Technology*, *15*(1), 72–103.

Wang, Y. (2003). Negotiation of meaning in desktop video-conferencing-supported distance language learning. *ReCALL*, *18*(1), 122–146. doi:10.1017/S0958344006000814

Ware, P. (2005). "Missed communication" in online communication: Tensions in fostering successful online interactions. *Language Learning & Technology*, *9*(2), 64–89.

Ware, P., & Kramsch, C. (2005). Toward an intercultural stance: Teaching German and English through telecollaboration. *Modern Language Journal*, *89*(2), 190–205. doi:10.1111/j.1540-4781.2005.00274.x

Ware, P., & O'Dowd, R. (2008). Peer feedback on language form in telecollaboration. *Language Learning & Technology*, *12*(1), 43–63.

Ware, P., & Pérez-Cañado, L. (2007). Grammar and feedback: Turning to language form in telecollaboration. In R. O'Dowd (Ed.), *Online intercultural exchange: An introduction for foreign language teachers* (pp. 107–126). Clevedon, England: Multilingual Matters.

Warschauer, M. (1998). Interaction, negotiation, and computer-mediated learning. In M. Clay (Ed.), *Practical applications of educational technology in language learning* (pp. 125–136). Lyon, France: National Institute of Applied Sciences.

Yanguas, I. (2010). Oral computer-mediated interaction between l2 learners: It's about time! *Language Learning & Technology*, *14*(3), 72–93.

Zarate, G. (2003). The recognition of intercultural competences: From individual experience to certification. In G. Aired, M. Byram, & M. Fleming (Eds.), *Intercultural experience and education* (pp. 213–224). Clevedon, England: Multilingual Matters.

Zyzik, E., & Polio, C. (2008). Incidental focus on form in university Spanish literature courses. *Modern Language Journal*, *92*(1), 53–70. doi:10.1111/j.1540-4781.2008.00686.x

ADDITIONAL READING

Blake, R. (2005). Bimodal CMC: The glue of language learning at a distance. *CALICO Journal*, *22*(3), 497–511.

Blake, R., & Zyzik, E. (2003). Who's helping whom?: Learner/heritage speakers' networked discussions in Spanish. *Applied Linguistics*, *24*(4), 519–544.

Brammerts, H. (1996). Tandem language learning via the internet and the International E-Mail Tandem Network. In D. Little & H. Brammerts (Eds.), *A guide to language learning in tandem via the internet* (pp. 9-25). CLCS Occasional Paper No. 46, Dublin: Trinity College, Centre for language and Communication Studies.

Cziko, G. A., & Park, S. (2003). Internet audio communication for second language learning: A comparative review of six programs. *Language Learning & Technology*, *7*(1), 15–27.

Fernández-García, M., & Martínez-Arbelaiz, A. (2002). Negotiation of meaning in nonnative speaker-nonnative speaker synchronous discussions. *CALICO Journal*, *19*(2), 279–294.

Guth, S., & Helm, F. (Eds.). (2010). *Telecollaboration 2.0: Language, literacies and intercultural learning in the 21st century*. Bern, Switzerland: Peter Lang AG.

Hauck, M., & Youngs, B. L. (2008). Telecollaboration in multimodal environments: The impact on task design and learner interaction. *Computer Assisted Language Learning*, *21*(2), 87–124.

Iwasaki, J., & Oliver, R. (2003). Chat-line interaction and negative feedback. *Occasional Thematic Issue of the Australian Review of Applied Linguistics*, *17*, 60–73.

Kern, R. (1995). Restructuring classroom interaction with networked computers: Effects on quantity and characteristics of language production. *Modern Language Journal*, *79*(4), 457–476.

Kötter, M. (2001). MOOrituri te salutant? Language learning through MOO-based synchronous exchanges between learner tandems. *Computer Assisted Language Learning*, *14*(3-4), 289–304.

Lee, L. (2004). Learners' perspectives on networked collaborative interaction with native speakers of Spanish in the US. *Language Learning & Technology*, *8*(1), 83–100.

Lee, L. (2006). A study of native and nonnative speakers' feedback and responses in Spanish-American networked collaborative interaction. In J. Belz, & S. Thorne (Eds.), *Internet-mediated intercultural foreign language education* (pp. 147–176). Boston: Thomson Heinle.

Lee, L. (2008). Focus on form through collaborative scaffolding in expert-to-novice online interaction. *Language Learning & Technology*, *12*(3), 53–72.

Little, D., & Brammerts, H. (1996). A guide to language learning in tandem via the Internet. *CLCS Occasional Paper, 46*. Dublin: Trinity College, Centre for Language and Communication Studies.

Nunan, D. (2006). *Task-based language education: From theory to practice*. Cambridge, UK: Cambridge University Press.

O'Dowd, R. (2003). Understanding the 'other side': Intercultural learning in a Spanish-English e-mail exchange. *Language Learning & Technology*, *7*(2), 118–144.

O'Dowd, R. (2007). Evaluating the outcomes of online intercultural exchange. *ELT Journal*, *6*(2), 144–152.

O'Rourke, B. (2008). The other C in CMC: What alternative data sources tell us about text-based synchronous computer mediated communication and language learning. *Computer Assisted Language Learning*, *21*(3), 227–251.

Sauro, S. (2013). The cyber language exchange: Cross-national computer-mediated interaction. In K. McDonough, & A. Mackey (Eds.), *Second language interaction in diverse educational contexts* (pp. 129–146). Amsterdam: John Benjamins.

Schwienhorst, K. (2003). Learner autonomy and tandem learning: Putting principles into practice in synchronous and asynchronous telecommunications environments. *Computer Assisted Language Learning*, *16*(5), 427–443.

Smith, B. (2008). Methodological hurdles in capturing CMC data: The case of the missing self-repair. *Language Learning & Technology*, *12*(1), 85–103.

Sotillo, S. M. (2000). Discourse functions and syntactic complexity in synchronous and asynchronous communication. *Language Learning & Technology*, *4*(1), 82–119.

Ushioda, E. (2000). Tandem language learning via email: From motivation to autonomy. *ReCALL*, *12*(2), 121–128.

Vetter, A., & Chanier, T. (2006). Supporting oral production for professional purpose in synchronous communication with heterogeneous learners. *ReCALL*, *18*(1), 5–23.

Vinagre, M., & Lera, M. (2008). The role of error correction in online exchanges. In F. Zhang, & B. Barber (Eds.), *Handbook of research on computer-enhanced language acquisition and learning* (pp. 326–341). Hershey: IGI Publishing.

Warschauer, M. (1996). Comparing face-to-face and electronic discussion in the second language classroom. *CALICO Journal*, *13*, 7–25.

Warschauer, M. (1997). Computer-mediated collaborative learning: Theory and practice. *Modern Language Journal*, *81*(4), 470–481.

Wooding, J. (1997). Email tandem learning and the communicative curriculum. *ReCALL*, *9*(1), 22–23.

KEY TERMS AND DEFINITIONS

Corrective Feedback: Corrective response to a language learner's non-target-like production that is given either implicitly or explicitly to prompt learners' noticing.

eTandem: Language learning via CMC (computer-mediated communication) tools in NS-NNS dyads, spending half the time in one's first language and the other half in one's target language.

Language-Related Episodes (LREs): Any part of the discourse where students talk about language they are producing, question their language use, or other- or self-correct their language production (Swain & Lapkin, 2001).

Negotiation for Meaning: Modification and restructuring of interaction that occurs when learners and their interlocutors anticipate, perceive, or experience difficulties in message comprehensibility (Pica, 1994).

Onomatopoeia: A group of words whose meanings are indicated by the sounds they mimic. Japanese onomatopoeia also includes words that describe states (*gotaigo*).

Task-Based Language Learning: An approach to language teaching that has grown out of Communicative Language Teaching and that focuses on the use of authentic, meaningful activities. It often consists of a pre-task, a main task, and a post-task, all of which include an aspect of focus on form.

Telecollaboration: Institutionalized language learning via CMC (computer-mediated communication) tools usually in the form of class-to-class partnership.

ENDNOTES

1 Words in italics were spoken in English.

2 R. Ellis et al (2001) considered preemptive LREs both learner- and teacher-initiated

3 In this study, morphosyntactic LREs included (a) tense (i.e. past or non-past), (b) aspect (e.g. progressive, perfective), (c) voice (e.g. passive), (d) predicate conjunctions, (e) particles, (f) formality (i.e. formal vs. casual vs. honorific), and (g) conjunctions. Phonological LREs addressed phonological features that can differentiate meanings. Thus, they included (a) vowel quality including length, (b) consonant quality including *sokuon* (i.e. っ for geminate consonants) and voicing, and (c) word-level pitch (e.g. かみ /kami/ HL for *God* and LH for *hair*). In Japanese, counters/quantifiers are attached after numbers to indicate the nature of objects, actions, and events (e.g. 二匹 /nihiki/ = two small animals, 三個 /mittsu/ = three small items, 四回 /yonkai/ = four times). These counters pose great difficulties to Japanese learners because counters change phonological representations depending on how many entities there are. For instance, 本 /hon/ is a counter for long objects like pens and cucumbers. For number 2, 4, 5, 7, and 9, the default pronunciation /hon/ is used; however, it changes its phonological representation when it follows number 1, 6, 8, and 10 as /pon/ and 3 for /bon/. In this study, a wrong choice of a counter was considered a lexical error while a misrepresentation of the phonological system was coded as a phonological error. If an error was both a wrong choice and a mispronunciation of a counter, the error was counted twice as both lexical and phonological.

APPENDIX A: AMERICAN PARTICIPANTS' (NNS') TASK PROMPT (DORAEMON)

Setting

You are taking a Japanese history class and you need to complete a project about the *Edo* Period. You decided to ask your Japanese partner for help, but your partner had forgotten a lot about Japanese history ☹ So, Doraemon suggested that you and your partner actually visit the *Edo* period using his awesome tools! BUT, the customs in the *Edo* Period impose strict restrictions as follows:

1. Each of you can bring up to 2 of the 5 items from the list below
2. Together you can bring a total of 4 items that are no more than one million yen and weigh less than 10kg
3. In order to get an A on the history report, you need to:
    a. Analyze the customs of both local citizens (farmers, merchants, etc.) and the *Shogun* family in the *Edo* Period
    b. Include personal accounts by conducting interviews/surveys to the locals who speak classical Japanese
    c. Include some kind of visual aids (map like Google Earth) in your report

Pre-Task (5-8 Minutes)

Your partner doesn't have the task instruction above. S/he only has a list of 5 items. In Japanese, explain to your partner **(1) the settings** and **(2) what you are supposed to do.**

Main Task (20 + 5 Minutes)

1. First, with your partner, **decide which 4 items** you will bring to the past. Remember the restrictions on what you can bring and the criteria to get an A on the report. (20 minutes)
2. **Report your decision to Akiyama-sensei as if you were presenting your decision in class** (5 minutes). Take turns presenting. In your report, state (a) what you decided to bring, (b) why you came to the conclusion, and (c) alternatives to the decision (if any).

Your Items (Images Deleted)

- タイムマシン: ひきだしを通(とお)って、タイムマシンに乗ると、過去(かこ)や未来(みらい)に行ける。
  500,000円 / 3kg
- 本物3Dメガネ: このメガネをかけてテレビを見ると、見た物が現実(げんじつ)になる。
  80,000円 / 500g
- タイムふろしき: これを使うと、新しいものを古くしたり、古いものを新しくしたりできる。
  120,000円 / 150g

- まあまあ棒: これをおこっている人の口にあてて、「まあ、まあ」と言うと、その人が急にやさしくなる。
  60,000円 / 1.5kg
- 立体コピー機(き): これを使うと、どんな物でも縮小(しゅくしょう)コピーして、3Dにできる。
  10,000円 / 900g

Post-Task (15 Minutes)

1. During the main task, you probably heard ～という multiple times. Below are examples of "～というNoun". With your partner, discuss when it is appropriate to use "～というNoun" and when it is not. Can you find a general pattern? (5 minutes)
   - ◦ BICというカメラを買いました。 × TOYOTAという会社
   - ◦ 田中さんという人から電話がありました。 × オバマ大統領という人
   - ◦ ガボンという国に行ったことがありますか。 × 中国という国
2. Your partner will ask a question. Discuss the topic for 10 minutes.

APPENDIX B: JAPANESE PARTICIPANTS' (NS'S) TASK PROMPT (DORAEMON)

Pre-Task (5-8 Minutes) & Main Task (20 + 5 Minutes)

Your partner will explain what you are suppposed to do for the main task. Feel free to ask questions.

Your Items (Images Deleted)

- 翻訳こんにゃく: これを食べると、どんなことばでもわかるようになる。
  100,000円 / 300g
- 暗記パン: 暗記(あんき)したい物をパンに書いて食べると、それが覚(おぼ)えられる。
  350,000円 / 100g
- タケコプター: タケコプターを頭(あたま)につけると、空をとべる。
  280,000円 / 800g
- どこでもドア: 行きたい場所を思って、ドアを通ると、その場所に行ける。でも、過去や未来には行けない。
  380,000円 / 4.8kg
- 人生やり直し機: これを使うと、もう一度人生をやり直(なお)せる。もどりたい年齢(ねんれい)にもどれる。
  80,000円 / 6.5kg

Post-Task (15 Minutes)

1. During the main task, you probably heard ～という multiple times. Below are examples of "～という Noun." With your partner, discuss when it is appropriate to use "～という Noun" and when it is not. Can you find a general pattern? (5 minutes)

◦ BICというカメラを買いました。	× TOYOTAという会社
◦ 田中さんという人から電話がありました。	× オバマ大統領という人
◦ ガボンという国に行ったことがありますか。	× 中国という国

2. [Discussion Question] もしタイムマシンを使って、日本かアメリカの昔の時代に行けたら、どの時代に行きたいですか。どうしてですか。パートナーと話し合ってください。(10 Minutes)
(Translation: If you could go back in history to Japan or the U.S. using a time machine, which era would you go and why? Discuss your opinion with your partner.)

Chapter 10
Innovative Wiki Ways:
Engaging Students in Collaborative Writing Processes

Mimi Li
Marshall University, USA

Julie Dell-Jones
University of South Florida, USA

ABSTRACT

Wiki-based collaborative writing has been increasingly implemented in second language classes. This chapter illustrates two small group writing projects conducted via Wikispaces (http://www.wikispaces.com/) and explicates how the distinctive wiki functions (i.e., "Discussion," "Comments," "Edit," and "History") mediate collaborative writing processes in the EFL and ESL contexts. The results reveal that wiki "Discussion" and "Comments" enabled the students to engage in the negotiation of writing tasks, as reflected in content discussion, task management, technical communication, language negotiation, and social talk. Transparency of wiki "History" records motivates students to be actively involved with recursive writing processes through multiple rounds of writing and revising using "Edit," namely addition, deletion, reordering, rephrasing, and correction. The affordances of other wiki modules such as "Projects" and "Writing resources" are reported. The results within the EFL and ESL settings are also briefly compared to illustrate how the wiki tool is used by particular groups of English language learners. This chapter supports wiki small group writing as an innovative way to engage students in collaboration and learning during collaborative writing tasks in both EFL and ESL learning contexts.

INTRODUCTION

Collaborative writing, the shared and negotiated process where multiple authors are responsible for producing a single text (Storch, 2012, 2013), is gaining attention in the second and foreign language learning contexts. The increase in implementation of collaborative writing follows a shift toward more communicative activities, a greater support for writing development, and an awareness of the multiple affordances of collaborative tasks (Bruffee, 1993; Donato, 1994; Lee, 2010;

DOI: 10.4018/978-1-4666-6174-5.ch010

Storch, 2005). Informed by sociocultural theory, collaborative writing is supported by the view of writing as a social activity, which builds on the collective group knowledge through scaffolded negotiation and problem solving. Thus, the primary benefit of collaborative writing draws from the pooled knowledge of many writers to contribute and co-construct a new text that transcends the capabilities of any one writer working alone.

The wiki, a Web 2.0 medium for collaborative writing, facilitates a convergence of the benefits through computer-mediated communication (CMC) and takes advantage of the social participation and interaction in an online learning environment (Kessler & Bikowski, 2010; Li & Zhu, 2011; Storch, 2013). Previous research (e.g., Lee, 2010; Lundin, 2008) posited that the affordance of wikis eases the collaborative process, facilitates interactions, and supports student writing development; however, little is known about the nature of wiki collaboration, and the collaborative process in wiki-mediated writing leaves a wide area for exploration (Storch, 2013).

This chapter illustrates two projects on wiki-based collaborative writing and examines the affordances of wikis for collaborative writing in two different learning contexts—ESL and EFL. In particular, this chapter explicates how the ESL/EFL students apply multiple wiki functions to negotiate writing tasks and co-construct academic essays throughout writing processes.

Theoretical Underpinning: Writing as a Social Activity

Collaborative writing is supported by the sociocultural approach that emphasizes the social construction of knowledge and acknowledges writing as a social process (Ede & Lunsford, 1990). Research on collaborative writing as a problem-solving task in second language contexts often focuses on the discussion of scaffolding between peers engaging in small group or pair work (Anton & DiCamilla, 1998; Donato, 1994; Ohta, 2000; Swain & Lapkin, 1998). A prominent example from Donato (1994) illustrated how learning took place via peer interaction manifested in collective scaffolding. As Donato (1994) noted, "the speakers are at the same time individually novices and collectively experts, sources of new orientations for each other and guides through this complex linguistic problem solving''(p. 46). The "collective orientation to jointly constructed activity" (Donato, 2004, p. 287) enables students to create a written work of higher caliber than the work any single co-writer may have produced independently.

Collaborative writing allows students to step into various roles such as tutor, sounding board, and critical reader (Weissberg, 2006). Collaborative writing also enhances students' awareness of writing for an audience due to the availability of feedback during the process of co-constructing a text (Storch, 2011, 2013). With a specific focus on discussion about linguistic choices, students are engaged in languaging and collaborative dialogue reflected in Language-Related Episodes (LREs) while interacting with peers during collaborative writing tasks. The process of writing collaboratively forces language learners to express themselves aloud and through written text involving both speaking and writing to create an explicit organization of ideas (Storch, 2013). Unlike the spontaneity of speech, the element of time intrinsic to writing creates opportunities for languaging and reflective thinking about the writing process.

Given the development of CMC technologies, collaborative writing in the online modes such as wikis has been increasingly conducted in second and foreign language contexts. As Kessler and Bikowski (2010) posited, ''the evolution of collaborative writing may be intrinsically connected with the iterations of technology since new developments provide new opportunities for collaboration'' (p. 43). Recently, researchers have begun to examine how wikis' collaborative and interactive nature mediates students' joint writing process and facilitates the co-production of writing (e.g., Li, 2013; Lund, 2008).

Wiki-Mediated Collaborative Writing

The benefits of collaborative writing are found to be transferred to the CMC context and are even augmented with the use of wikis (e.g., Chao & Lo, 2009; Lee, 2010; Mak & Coniam, 2008; Storch, 2013). Wiki as an asynchronous tool supports the social aspect of writing and is naturally suited for online group writing projects (Goodwin-Jones, 2003). Wiki is a collaborative website that allows users to freely create and edit the contents of the web pages without the need to be tied to a particular shared time or space. As Ware and Warschauer (2006) stated, "Asynchronous discussion formats, in particular, are believed to combine the interactive aspect of written conversations with the reflective nature of composing" (p. 11). While collaborative writing promotes attention to grammar, lexis, and discourse (DiCamilla & Anton, 1997; Swain & Lapkin, 1998), the asynchronous nature of wiki collaborative writing provides an extra opportunity for students to reflect on the written text and identify writing problems (Storch, 2013).

The wiki functions "Edit," "History," "Discussion," and "Comments" can lead to distinct features which accentuate content development, language deliberation, and social negotiation. As explained in Li (2012a), "Edit" enables the users to write as well as revise the writing on the wiki pages; "History" documents each change that has been made using a color system to reveal deleted and inserted text, and also allows for comparison of different page versions and the freedom to revert to any previous version if needed. "Discussion" allows users to communicate and negotiate the progress of writing tasks via asynchronous messages. "Comments" enables users to pose questions or provide feedback on specific texts at their own pace.

Research on the incorporation of wikis in both second and foreign language learning contexts explored, to some extent, the affordances of collaborative writing combined with CMC and the interactions during wiki communications (e.g., Bradley, Linstrom, & Rystedt, 2010; Li, 2013; Lundin, 2008; Mak & Coniam, 2008). Wikis offer a unique opportunity for exploring the process of collaborative writing. Specifically, the wiki functions' static documentation detailing action over time and space gives researchers a glimpse into the writing and revision process (Arnold, Ducate, & Kost, 2012; Kessler & Bilowski, 2010; Li, 2013; Mak & Coniam, 2008). For instance, Mak and Coniam (2008) delved into the specifics of writing change functions, noting actions such as adding ideas, expanding ideas, reorganizing ideas, and correcting errors while students jointly produced a brochure in a secondary education ESL class. Their findings suggested a tendency for students to pay less attention to error correction and instead focus on adding new ideas. Another study (Kessler & Bilowski, 2010) discussed the writing behaviors of pre-service teachers as they attempted to synthesize course content regarding culture. In this large class wiki project, researchers examined language acts categorized as new information, deleted information, clarification/elaboration of information, synthesis of information, and web links. Also, adding to the lexicon for research on the process of wiki collaborative writing, Kost (2011) found a frequency of meaning-related changes (content issues) over the instances of formal changes (linguistic issues) in a collegiate German as a Foreign Language context. Collectively, these studies revealed valuable potential in understanding the co-construction, negotiation, and scaffolding process during collaborative writing activities.

A large gap still remains in the literature on how multiple wiki functions mediate students' collaborative writing processes. Also rare are studies that elucidate comprehensive collaborative writing processes at multiple writing stages in either EFL or ESL context. This study contributes to filling the research gap through a careful investigation of the multiple functions inherent to the wiki tool via Wikispaces sites. The objective of this study is to examine how ESL/ EFL students in small groups use distinctive wiki functions to negotiate writing tasks and co-construct academic essays throughout the writing processes. This study addresses the following two research questions:

1. How do small groups of ESL/EFL students discuss their writing tasks using wiki "Discussion"/"Comments"?
2. How do small groups of ESL/EFL students use wiki "Edit" to co-construct joint writing products, as revealed in wiki "History"?

METHOD

We adopted a multiple-case study approach (Duff, 2008; Yin, 2009) to explore ESL/EFL students' small group writing processes based on two wiki-mediated collaborative writing projects. In this study, collaborative writing is defined as an activity where small groups of students negotiate and co-construct academic essays at multiple writing stages. The cases in this study are the interactions of multiple small groups (Johnson, 1992) within two wiki writing projects, with each interaction as a bounded system (Stake, 1995). As Creswell (2007) posited, multiple cases illustrate various perspectives on the issue under investigation. Collectively, the two projects reveal student engagements in collaborative writing processes through the use of multiple distinctive wiki functions. In the following section, we describe both the wiki writing projects and illustrate the Wikispaces sites used for this study.

Contexts and Wiki Sites

Chinese EFL Context: "Three Heads are Better than One"

The first project (Project 1) we draw on for this study, "Three heads are better than one," was conducted at a southwestern comprehensive university in China in the summer of 2010. As this university offered no formal courses during the summer, 15 Chinese EFL students volunteered to participate in small group writing in the Wikispaces site in their spare time. These participants had seven to eight years of EFL learning experience, including one or two years of learning in College English, a compulsory course for non-English majors in Chinese universities. Their English proficiency levels are generally intermediate, measured by College English Test (CET), the national English as a Foreign Language test in the People's Republic of China. The fifteen participants formed five self-selected small groups, and shared a Wikispaces site to work collaboratively on three academic writing tasks, i.e., narration, exposition, and argumentation, in their designated group wiki space. Four tabs were set up in the Wikispaces site: tutorials, writing tasks, writing groups, and writing resources. "Wiki tutorials" included official web-based video tours and a PowerPoint tutorial on the use of wikis for the collaborative writing project. "Writing tasks" hosted the details of the three required writing tasks to be worked on in small groups. "Writing resources" hosted useful writing resources such as links to web pages with writing tips. "Writing groups" consisted of the tabs for all five small writing groups. In order to co-work on collaborative writing tasks, members of each small group clicked on their respective writing group tabs and entered the group writing space. Figure 1 shows a sample platform of wiki writing space. As illustrated in Figure 1, three defining wiki modules, i.e., "Edit," "Discussion," and "History," were accessible to the participants during their joint construction of texts in relation to three academic writing tasks.

As noted earlier, the wiki "Edit" allowed the participants to edit the texts with different fonts or colors and insert hyperlinks or files when necessary. The "Discussion" enabled the participants to make posts asynchronously in the form of threads, as displayed in Figure 2. The "History"

Figure 1. Screenshot of sample group wiki site

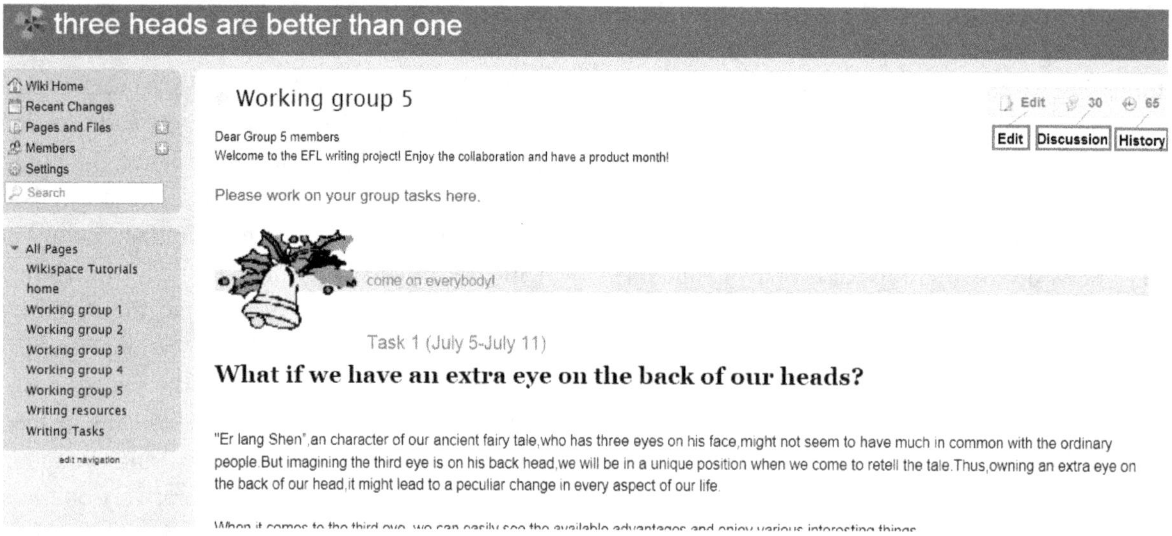

Figure 2. Sample wiki "discussion" threads

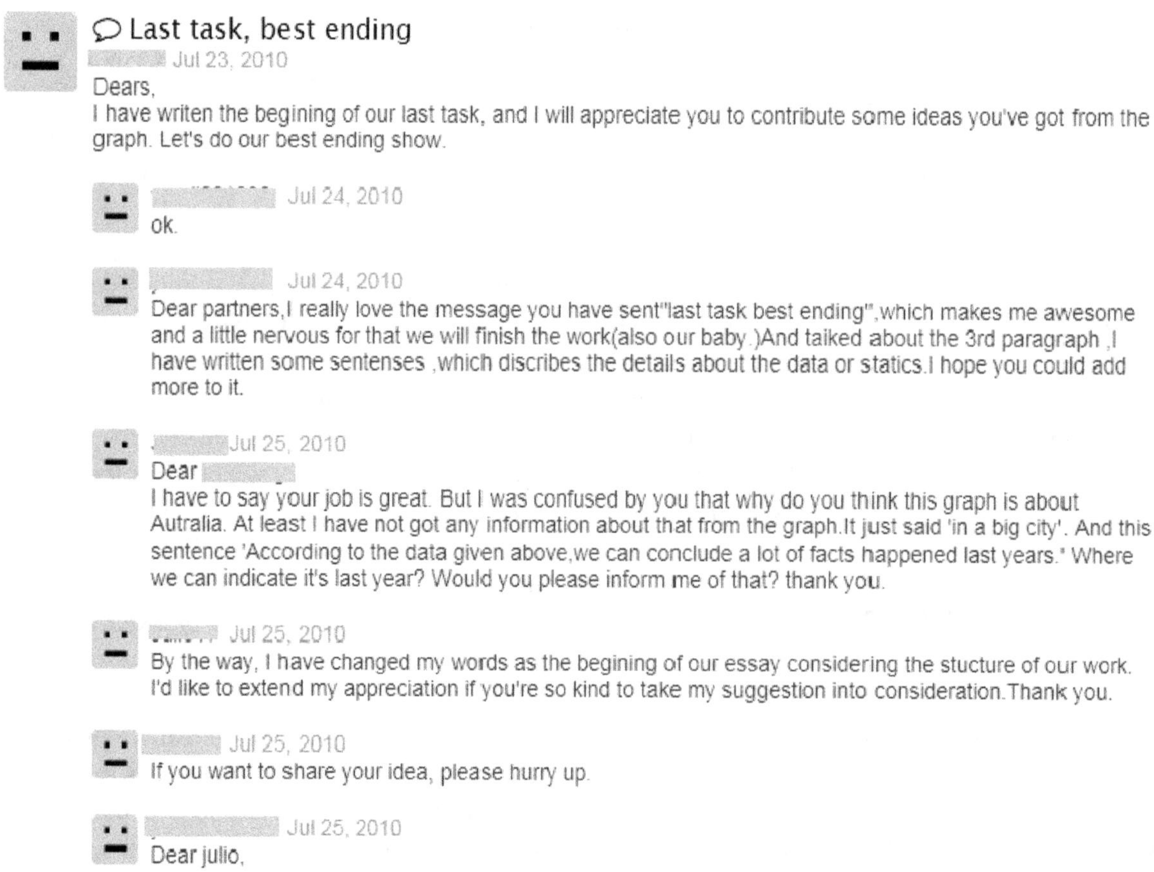

Figure 3. Sample wiki "history" records

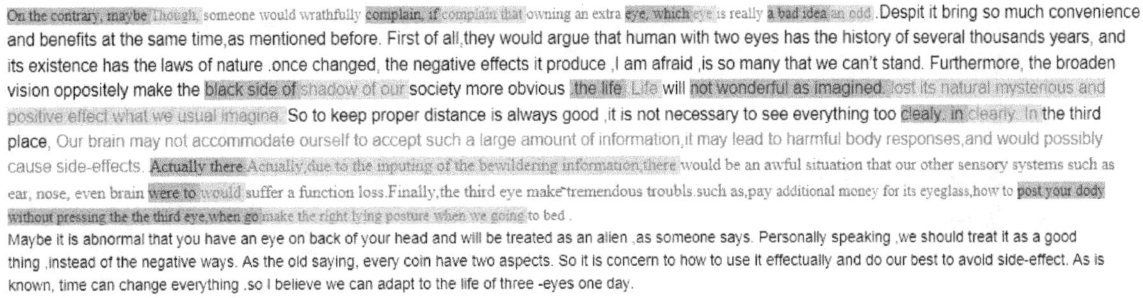
On the contrary, maybe Though, someone would wrathfully complain, if complain that owning an extra eye, which eye is really a bad idea an odd .Despit it bring so much convenience and benefits at the same time,as mentioned before. First of all,they would argue that human with two eyes has the history of several thousands years, and its existence has the laws of nature .once changed, the negative effects it produce ,I am afraid ,is so many that we can't stand. Furthermore, the broaden vision oppositely make the black side of shadow of our society more obvious .the life. Life will not wonderful as imagined. lost its natural mysterious and positive effect what we usual imagine. So to keep proper distance is always good ,it is not necessary to see everything too clealy. in clearly. In the third place, Our brain may not accommodate ourself to accept such a large amount of information,it may lead to harmful body responses,and would possibly cause side-effects. Actually there Actually,due to the inputing of the bewildering information,there would be an awful situation that our other sensory systems such as ear, nose, even brain were to would suffer a function loss.Finally,the third eye make tremendous troubls.such as,pay additional money for its eyeglass,how to post your dody without pressing the the third eye,when go make the right lying posture when we going to bed .

Maybe it is abnormal that you have an eye on back of your head and will be treated as an alien ,as someone says. Personally speaking ,we should treat it as a good thing ,instead of the negative ways. As the old saying, every coin have two aspects. So it is concern to how to use it effectually and do our best to avoid side-effect. As is known, time can change everything .so I believe we can adapt to the life of three -eyes one day.

revealed all the changes of the page with the color coding of inserted and deleted texts. Figure 3 is a screenshot of sample "History" archives.

ESL Context in the U.S: "EAP-Our Wiki Space"

Based on the previous project conducted in China, the second project (Project 2) was implemented in two class sections of an English for Academic Purposes (EAP) course taught by the same instructor in an English Language Institute at a large public university in the southeastern U.S. in the spring of 2013. Out of the 29 ESL graduate-student participants, the majority came from China, and only a few came from other countries such as Iraq, Saudi Arabia, and Russia. Most of the students majored in finance and engineering and had English proficiency levels ranging from intermediate to intermediate-high according to the course curriculum. They formed nine small groups of three or four students each to work on two academic writing tasks using wikis, namely an annotated bibliography and a research proposal.

Similar to Project 1, four tabs, i.e., tutorials, writing groups, writing resources, and writing tasks, were created. Differently, however, per the course instructor's request that the small groups work independently, with no access to other groups' sites, the new wiki feature of "Projects" was adopted. Specifically, the students joined the Wikispaces site and entered their respective writing group links (i.e., Group A, Group B, Group C …) under two projects, namely "Annotated Bibliography" and "Research Proposal." In their group writing space, students used multiple wiki functions: "Edit," "Discussion," "Comments," and "History" throughout the writing processes. Figure 4 illustrates how the small groups jointly worked on the collaborative academic writing assignments using the wiki "Project."

Worthy of note, the participants in Project 2 were trained to use the new feature "Comments," which is embedded in the "Edit" module. As demonstrated in Figure 5, "Comments" allowed the students to provide feedback/comments or raise questions regarding the specific texts, which is difficult to perform via discussion posts.

Procedures

Project 1 lasted for five weeks, with Week 1 as an orientation period. The students were introduced to the project and wiki technology, and those who volunteered to participate in the study signed the informed consent form and provided their basic background information. From Week 2 through Week 4, the fifteen participants in five small groups of three each discussed and co-constructed academic writing for three writing tasks, i.e., narration, argumentation and exposition. They completed one task each week following the pre-

Figure 4. Screenshot of sample "project"

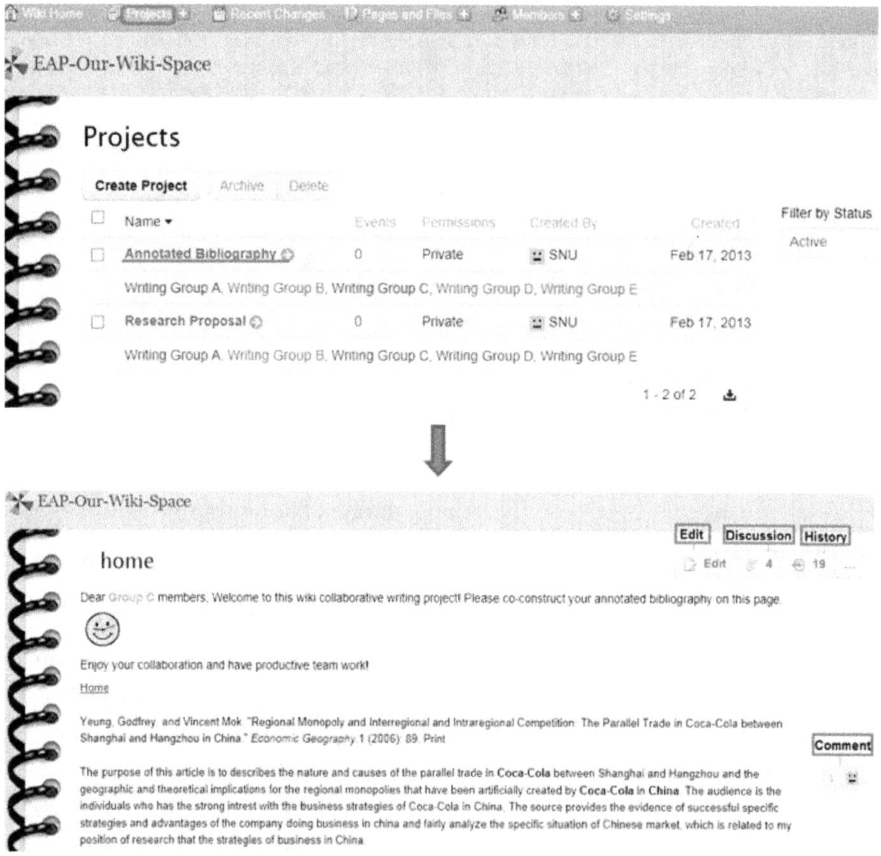

Figure 5. Sample wiki "comments" records

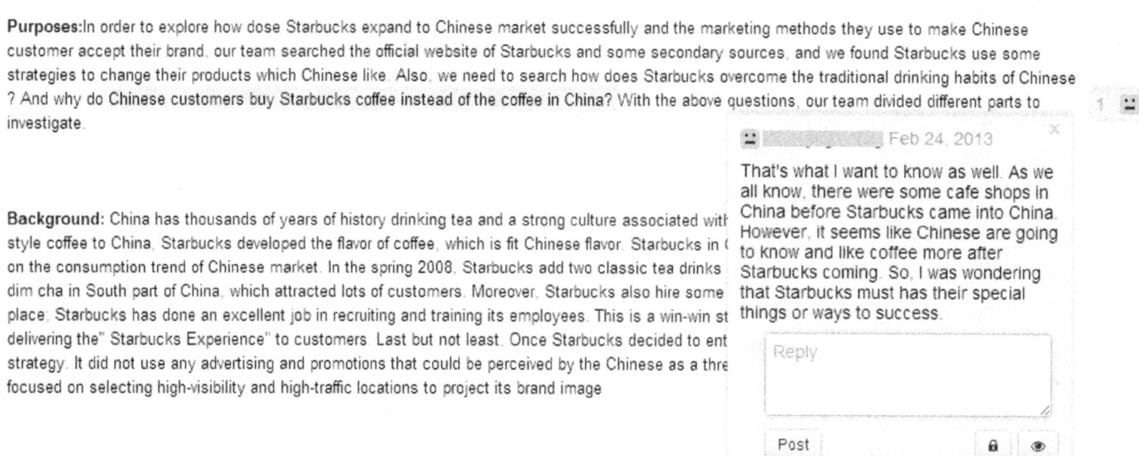

viously specified order. The entire discussion and writing processes were automatically recorded in the wiki site. The collaborative writing was done asynchronously outside of class, taking advantage of the flexible communication options intrinsic to wikis. Participants were allowed to use and share exterior resources such as online dictionaries and other web resources. They also received writing feedback from the first author of this chapter after completing each collaborative writing task. In Week 5, semi-structured individual interviews were conducted with seven participants, who shared their perceptions of the wiki use and their group interaction. Four participants were individually interviewed in a teacher's office by the first author of this chapter. Each interview lasted for about 25 minutes. The interviews were recorded by using the software "Audacity" (http://audacity.sourceforge.net/). At the request of the remaining three students, their interviews were conducted asynchronously via email communication.

Project 2 lasted for nine weeks. It began with an orientation including the introduction to wiki technology for the two sections of an EAP course. The EAP students learned how to join the Wikispaces site, and how to use the "Edit," "Discussion," "Comments," and "History" modules under their group link for the collaborative writing activity. In Week 2, twenty-nine students agreed to participate in the study. They signed the informed consent forms, completed a pre-task questionnaire concerning their demographic information, and then were assigned to small groups. In Week 3, the participants used wikis to work jointly on the research proposal within their small groups. During Week 4 and Week 5, they jointly constructed the annotated bibliography. Again, all the discussion and writing records were automatically archived in the wiki site. Upon completion of the two wiki writing tasks, twelve participants (from four focal groups) received individual post-task semi-structured interviews addressing their perceptions about the purpose of the wiki-based collaborative writing activity, affordances of wikis for collaborative writing, their group interaction/work in the wiki, and their suggestions on the wiki project to be implemented in future classes. Other types of data were also collected in the following three weeks (Weeks 6-8) and member-checking was conducted in Week 9. In member-checking, five participants from the four focal groups provided feedback on the researchers' written reports interpreting the writing process and interaction of their own small groups. The member-checking provided an additional opportunity to discuss and clarify any remaining ambiguities in data analysis and interpretation.

Delimiting the Data Set and Data Analysis

This study mainly addressed how small groups of students used distinctive wiki functions to negotiate writing tasks and co-construct academic essays throughout writing processes in two learning contexts—EFL and ESL. We focused on examining the data of four small groups, two (Groups A and B) from Project 1 and two (Groups C and D) from Project 2. These four groups were purposefully selected because these groups made full use of multiple wiki functions during their collaborative writing processes, and frequent occurrences of peer scaffolding were identified within these groups. Interestingly, both Group A and Group C demonstrated a collective approach to writing tasks, in which group members made joint contribution to task negotiation and mutually supported each other in text construction. Both Group B and Group D exhibited an expert/novice pattern, in which an expert member took more control over writing directions and a novice member was responsive to the expert's ideas and behaviors. Table 1 shows the profiles of the four groups.

Table 1. Profile of four small groups

	Group	Pseudo Name	Gender	Country	English Proficiency	Group Member Familiarity
Project 1	Group A	Li Chen Zhang	Female Female Female	China China China	Intermediate high Intermediate Intermediate	They have been classmates for two years.
	Group B	Wang Lin Zhao	Male Female Female	China China China	Intermediate high Intermediate Intermediate	Lin and Zhao have been classmates for two years, but they are unfamiliar with Wang
Project 2	Group C	Dong Feng Abdul	Male Male Male	China China Saudi Arabia	Intermediate Intermediate-high Intermediate	Dong and Feng have been classmates for half a year, but they are unfamiliar with Abdul.
	Group D	Hai Xia Ali	Male Female Male	China China Iraq	Intermediate -high Intermediate-high Intermediate	Hai and Xia have been classmates for one year, but they are unfamiliar with Ali

As the participants' discussion and writing processes were automatically recorded in group wiki modules, the primary data sources were archived wiki "Discussion"/"Comments" and "History" records under the four group tabs. Wiki "Discussion"/"Comments" revealed how group members negotiated collaborative writing tasks at pre-writing, writing, and revising stages. Wiki "History" reflected how group members engaged with each other's writing efforts and co-produced the essays during both writing and revising stages. Interview transcripts provided additional insight about the small groups' collaborative writing processes.

To analyze the participants' task negotiation for the first research question, we expanded wiki

Table 2. Wiki discussion categories (adapted from Li, 2013, p.756)

Categories	Definitions and Examples
Content discussion	Group members discuss ideas about content development. e.g., We can shelter it [the extra eye] in daily life, and use it at special time, for example, searching for thieves on bus.
Social talk	Group members talk socially to maintain a friendly co-working environment by greeting, acknowledging, and encouraging, etc. e.g., What you say is so funny that I can't help laughing.
Task management	Group members handle the process toward completing writing tasks together. e.g., Let's discuss the purpose of the art roughly.
Technical communication	Group members communicate technical problems and solutions. e.g., --I wonder whether you can view messages on these pages in time online? I have to refresh my page. -- Me too, just refresh. Or kick the button "Discussion".
Language negotiation	Group members negotiate language points such as grammar and word choice, as reflected in language-related episodes (LREs). e.g., If we do not add "we", what is the subject of "go to bed"?
Rhetorical move/ structure discussion	Group members discuss a particular rhetorical pattern or structure that is conventionally found in a certain genre type. e.g., Our proposal structure will be divided into topic, resources, method and problems. How you think about that?

discussion categories identified in Li (2013) and developed the taxonomy as displayed in Table 2. Four of the thematic categories emerging from wiki "Discussion" posts in Project 1, as reported in Li (2013), i.e., content discussion, social talk, task management, and language negotiation, were also found to be applicable to the analyses of "Discussion" and "Comments" records in Project 2. In addition, another category "rhetorical structure discussion" emerged from Project 2. Regarding Project 1, the first author and a doctoral student independently co-coded the wiki "Discussion" records according to the taxonomy; the inter-rater agreement ratio was 92.9% and differences between the two coders were discussed and resolved (Li, 2013). For Project 2, the two authors of the chapter co-coded all the Wiki "Discussion" and "Comments" data; the inter-rater agreement ratio was 88.8% and consensus was reached via discussion.

To analyze the participants' text co-construction behaviors for the second research question, we adapted the taxonomy of writing change functions reported in Li (2013). Each writing change was coded in terms of five categories: addition, deletion, rephrasing, reordering and correction. Writing changes of the five categories were further divided into two levels: global (i.e., paragraph and sentence) and local (i.e., clause, bulletin points, phrase, and word) to explicate the degree of students' writing and revising efforts. Furthermore, writing changes made to self-constructed texts and those made to other-constructed texts were distinguished so as to reveal students' mutual engagement with each other's texts. Both the first author and a doctoral student coded 25% of the whole data, and the inter-coder reliability reached 88.2% (Li, 2013) in Project 1 and 89.4% in Project 2. The differences were resolved through discussion between the two coders; the first author then coded the remaining data following the same steps. Table 3 shows the coding scheme of writing change functions.

Table 3. Coding scheme of writing change functions (adapted from Li, 2013, p.757)

Types of Writing Change Functions	
Addition	Contributing new content and adding language forms
Deletion	Removing existing content and language forms
Rephrasing	Stating the same ideas/meaning in a different way
Reordering	Moving around /reorganizing texts
Correction	Attempting to fix grammatical, spelling, or formatting mistakes
Levels of Writing Change Functions	
Global	Paragraph and sentence
Local	Clause, phrases, words, and spelling
Engagement of Writing Change Functions	
Self	Writing changes made to the texts composed by the member himself/herself
Other	Writing changes made to the texts composed by other group members

RESULTS AND DISCUSSION

To address each research question, we first present an overall picture of participants' wiki discussion/text co-construction behaviors using numerical data, and then illuminate the research findings by explaining some illustrative wiki excerpts. In particular, we highlight how wikis engage small groups of students in collaborative writing processes, particularly in task negotiation and text co-construction, with the use of different wiki functions at multiple writing stages. Afterwards, we compare findings from Project 1 and Project 2 and discuss the salient features distinctive to each learning context, EFL and ESL. A small portion of interview data is discussed to assist in the interpretation of the results.

Task Negotiation

Regarding the first research question, the participants were actively engaged with different types of communication during their negotiation of writing tasks using wiki "Discussion" (and "Comments"),

Table 4. Wiki discussion behaviors performed by group A

	Li		Chen		Zhang		Total
	INIT	RESP	INIT	RESP	INIT	RESP	
Content discussion	4	1	1	1	2	2	11 (26%)
Social talk	1	2	1	1	3	0	8 (19%)
Task management	0	2	3	1	1	1	8 (19%)
Technical communication	0	2	0	0	1	1	4 (10%)
Language negotiation	2	4	1	1	0	3	11 (26%)
Total	18		10		14		42 (100%)

Note. INIT=initiating, RESP=responding.

Table 5. Wiki discussion behaviors performed by group B

	Wang		Lin		Zhao		Total
	INIT	RESP	INIT	RESP	INIT	RESP	
Content discussion	3	0	1	0	0	0	4 (10%)
Social talk	6	2	5	3	1	2	19 (46%)
Task management	7	1	2	0	0	0	10 (24%)
Technical communication	0	1	0	0	1	0	2 (5%)
Language negotiation	2	1	0	1	2	0	6 (15%)
Total	23		12		6		41 (100%)

Note. INIT=initiating, RESP=responding.

including content discussion, language negotiation, task management, technical communication, and social talk at multiple writing stages. Below we discuss the results from Project 1, followed by Project 2.

Project 1: EFL Context in China

Small groups in Project 1 conducted language functions of five categories, namely, content discussion, social talk, task management, technical communication, and language negotiation. Table 4 and Table 5 display the task negotiation behaviors of Group A and Group B, respectively.

As Table 4 and Table 5 depict, both groups were actively engaged with writing discussions in terms of the five aspects: content discussion, social talk, task management, technical communication, and language negotiation. For Group A that demonstrated a pattern of collectively contributing/mutually supportive (Li, 2013; Li & Zhu, 2013), the three members had roughly equal contributions. They were found to perform mostly the instances of content discussion (26%) and language negotiation (26%). For Group B that demonstrated an authoritative/responsive pattern (Li, 2012b; 2013; Li & Zhu, 2013), the expert Wang took most control over writing tasks and fully engaged with his group partners' contribution. This group conducted the most frequent instances of social talk (46%). As Li (2012b) stated, the group members completed wiki collaborative writing smoothly while negotiating writing tasks as well as co-constructing the social interaction.

Below we present specific wiki "Discussion" excerpts from Group A and Group B as a collective to illuminate the group members' wiki interactions during the process of task negotiation. Note that pseudonyms were used and language errors were not removed in the wiki excerpts. In Group A, many instances of content discussion were evident as the students responded to the essay prompt about an imagined extra eye in the back of one's head. Excerpt 1 is an example.

Excerpt 1: Content Discussion (Group A)

Li: *I think it's a imaginative idea. An eye on the back of our heads, if so, will expand our sight largely* [...]

Zhang: *we can shelter it [an extra eye] in daily life, and use it at special time, for example, searching for thieves on bus.*

Li initiated the general idea that an extra eye would expand people's horizon. Her group partners Chen and Zhang actively built on this idea. As shown in Excerpt 1, Zhang supplied a creative supporting example, stating that an extra eye would be helpful in identifying thieves on the bus. The members of Group A joyfully discussed the topic and content development of their writing tasks.

The EFL students also discussed language use at the revising stage via wiki "Discussion." Excerpt 2, as reported in Li (2013), is an example of group members' negotiation of language forms in Group A.

Excerpt 2: Language Negotiation (Group A)

Li: *If we do not add "we", what is the subject of "going to bed".*

Zhang: *I ignored the subject just now. We cannot use "doing" after "we", so it should be corrected into "when we go to bed".*

Li: *yes, you are right.*

The question posed by Li in Excerpt 2 followed Zhang's changing the texts "how to make the right lying posture when we going to bed" to "how to make the right lying posture when going to bed." Li addressed the missing sentence subject "we" in terms of Zhang's modification. Zhang reconsidered this sentence later and corrected it into "how to make the right lying posture when we go to bed." This excerpt confirms that the time gap between wiki postings enables students to develop considered responses to others' posts (Storch, 2012, 2013) so that jointly- constructed peer assistance is more likely to occur. Also, the wiki extends opportunities to develop accuracy through instances of language production that illuminate gaps in the learner's knowledge (Storch, 2013).

Excerpt 3, as reported in Li (2012b), is yet another example demonstrating group members' social negotiation via wiki "Discussion."

Excerpt 3: Social Talk (Group B)

Lin: *Dear partners, I really love the message you have sent "last task best ending", which makes me awesome and a little nervous for that we will finish the work (also our baby).*

The above texts occurred after Wang, the authoritative member (Li & Zhu, 2013), posted the title of "last task best ending" in a wiki "Discussion" thread when this group started the third writing task. In this excerpt, Lin conveyed her strong emotions in a mixture of excitement and concern. She referred to her group members as "dear partners" and addressed their group product as their "baby" to achieve group solidarity and "affective support" (Lee, 2010, p. 269). Such social talk helped build rapport between the members and enabled the collaborative writing tasks to be performed smoothly.

The authoritative person in this group, Wang, was also found to be actively engaged in task management using wiki "Discussion," as illustrated in Excerpt 4. With the due date approaching, Wang pointed out the problem of overall flow in their texts and he strived to lead group members in completing the group assignment successfully.

Excerpt 4: Task Management (Group B)

Wang: *Hi everyone, In my opinion, our have-done jobs seem just like a patchwork, not a real essay. Each part is too independent. So I would like to integrate they into a formal article. Do you mind my editing? Please reply me immediately! Time is running out. Thank you...*

In addition, the EFL students used wiki "Discussion" to communicate about the wiki technology. Excerpt 5, as explained in Li (2013), is an illustrative example.

Excerpt 5: Technical Communication (Group A)

Zhang: *i wonder whether you can view messages on these pages in time online [synchronously]? thus i have to refresh my page.*
Li: *Me too, just refresh*
Li: *Or kick the button "Discussion".*

Excerpt 5 indicates that Zhang inquired about a synchronous use of the wiki at the revising stage, as she saw a necessity of synchronous communication due to the approaching due date. In response to Zhang, Li suggested that she continually "kick" (click) on the button of "Discussion," thus solving the technical problem together.

Project 2: ESL Context in the U.S.

In Project 2, the ESL students performed identical language functions as the EFL students did, including content discussion, social talk, task management, and language negotiation. The additional language function category, rhetorical move discussion, emerged due to the nature of the research-based writing tasks. Specifically, Group C performed most instances of content discussion (40%) and did not have language negotiation, while Group D frequently performed the act of social talk (46%) and had one post addressing the language point. Tables 6 and 7 summarize the findings of task negotiation regarding Group C and Group D, respectively.

Excerpts occurring in Groups C and D below show how the ESL students performed multiple types of discussion in the wiki during task negotiation processes. Wiki "Comments" was found to be particularly helpful when students attempted to comment on specific texts composed by their group partners in Project 2. Excerpt 6 shows how the two ESL students Ali and Hai discussed the contents constructed by the third member Xia using wiki "Comments."

Table 6. Wiki discussion behaviors performed by group C

	Dong		Feng		Abdul		
	INIT	RESP	INIT	RESP	INIT	RESP	Total
Content discussion	3	0	0	2	0	1	6 (40%)
Social talk	0	1	1	2	0	1	5 (34%)
Task management	0	0	1	0	1	0	2 (13%)
Language negotiation	0	0	0	0	0	0	0 (0%)
Rhetorical move discussion	1	0	0	1	0	0	2 (13%)
Total	6		6		3		15 (100%)

Note. INIT=initiating, RESP=responding.*00aker*

Table 7. Wiki discussion behaviors performed by group D

	Hai		Xia		Ali		Total
	INIT	RESP	INIT	RESP	INIT	RESP	
Content discussion	2	1	0	0	2	0	5 (21%)
Social talk	2	1	1	1	0	6	11 (46%)
Task management	2	0	1	0	1	1	5 (21%)
Language negotiation	1	0	0	0	0	0	1 (4%)
Rhetorical move discussion	0	1	0	0	1	0	2 (8%)
Total	10		3		11		24 (100%)

Note. INIT=initiating, RESP=responding.

Excerpt 6: Content Discussion (Group D)

Ali: *Thanks it's great. Are there any criticism against any Disney production??*
Hai: *Maybe it has. But we will not focus on this point.*
Ali: *Okay.*

After Xia wrote "Disney's target market is children. They make a lot of money from children through their products, movies and Disneyland," Ali questioned the benefits of Disney production and thus highlighted Xia's texts and left a comment, inquiring about criticism against Disney production. His group member Hai later addressed his concern and indicated that they would not focus on negative aspects of Disney for this research proposal. This discussion, through wiki "Comments," reveals how multiple co-authors were able to discuss particular aspects of the text at different times, each contributing to the final product.

The ESL students in Group D also addressed specific language points via the wiki "Comments." Regarding Xia's texts "maybe our conceptions came from cartoons another word [world] for us," Hai questioned the attributive clause, so he highlighted "which they" and posted the comment "It's suppose to be 'by which Disney...'. " This example shows that wiki "Comments" affords more opportunities for students to discuss language forms without directly changing others' texts, especially when students feel reluctant to correct others' language forms.

The ESL groups conducted several instances of task management. Group D is an example where each of the three group members was actively involved with the task management. At the beginning of the pre-writing stage, Hai posted on the wiki "Page," "Let's discuss on the discussion post!" In the middle of the wiki project, Xia also asked whether Ali had completed their group worksheet. The novice Ali had little knowledge about the research topic of Disney, but he was willing to learn from his group partners. He posted in the wiki "Discussion," "because you have more information about Disney you should explain more for me so then I will be able to research about better," and his partner Hai responded to his request quickly and provided contingent scaffolding for him.

Moreover, the ESL groups, much like the EFL groups, also talked socially in the wiki to maintain a friendly co-working environment, as displayed in Excerpt 7.

Excerpt 7: *Social Talk (Group C)*

Xia: *Ali, thank you for your sharing such a wonderful information!*
Hai: *Nice job*

As Ali was a novice on the topic of Disney, his group partners encouraged him to explore information on Disney using online resources. After Ali posted a summary of the Disney company's background for the group's research proposal, both Xia and Hai conveyed their acknowledgments of Ali's efforts, which in turn motivated Ali to engage increasingly in the group work.

In addition, the ESL students explicitly discussed the rhetorical moves that they would be including in their research paper. Excerpt 8 illustrates an example of rhetorical move discussion.

Excerpt 8: Rhetorical Move Discussion (Group C)

Dong: *Our proposal structure will be divided into topic, resources, method and problems. How you think about that?*

Feng: *Sure, and rhetorical stance should be presented, and explain the significance of the research. we need a timeline for investigating the topic, possible sources for investigation.*

As Excerpt 8 indicates, Dong initiated a discussion of rhetorical structures that their research proposal would cover. Later, Feng responded and extended Dong's ideas by adding more rhetorical moves. Consequently, Dong composed texts involving the topic and sources, Abdul attended to methods, and Feng added texts regarding significance and the timeline in the wiki "Page."

Taken together, wikis engage the students in task negotiation via different types of communication by using wiki "Discussion" (and "Comments") during collaborative writing processes. Comparing the results from Projects 1 and 2, we detected quite a few similarities in student interactions despite the different learning contexts. Both ESL and EFL students were actively involved with the acts of content discussion, task management and social talk. Both Group B in Project 1 and Group D in Project 2 conducted the most instances of social talk so as to negotiate nicely the social relationship and co-work on the wiki collaborative writing task in a harmonious way. This observation was consistent with the common pattern of interaction that both groups demonstrated: expert/novice. Likewise, both Group A in Project 1 and Group C in Project 2 frequently discussed the topic and content development of their writing tasks. The collective approach that these two groups adopted engaged the group members to attend to coherent flow of their thoughts in developing writing contents.

We also identified several differences in students' task negotiation processes. The ESL groups performed the unique instance of rhetorical move discussion. This finding was largely connected with the nature of the wiki tasks. In Project 2, the ESL groups worked on a research proposal and an annotated bibliography, both of which entailed a logical sequence of rhetorical moves. The nature of these tasks may also have influenced the students' focus on language forms. The writing tasks in Project 2 emphasized practicing new genres and directed less attention to language. Therefore, the ESL students were seldom involved with language negotiation. However, more instances of language negotiation were identified among small groups in Project 1. The Chinese EFL students more frequently discussed grammar and language points, which may relate to the writing requirements that focus on content, organization and language and also their class tradition of focusing on language accuracy. All the findings echoed the interaction between the tools and tasks (Lund & Rasmussen, 2008). It seems inappropriate to argue that students seldom changed language forms because of the informality of the wiki tool. Instead, students' attention to language was largely related to the writing tasks and requirements. Furthermore, the ESL students in Project 2 had another wiki function to use — "Comments." We identified obvious benefits of the "Comments" module: it can be useful for content discussion and language negotiation. In particular, when students are reluctant to change others' texts directly or have doubt about certain ideas, they leave comments and elicit responses from group partners. In addition, the Chinese EFL students were involved with more technical communication partly due to a lesser degree of familiarity with Web 2.0 tools. The ESL students posed few technical questions. The interview with Xia in Project 2 revealed some students' transferring the skill from the use of Google docs to the use of wiki, which shows the role of technology skill as a mediating factor.

Text Co-Construction

Regarding the second research question, we discuss how the ESL and EFL students in small groups co-constructed joint writing products, as evidenced in the "History" records. Due to the space limit, we focus on the four small groups' text co-construction processes when they worked on one wiki writing task, i.e., the task of an essay construction with the writing prompt: ''What if we have an extra eye on the back of our heads?'' in Project 1 and the task of annotated bibliography in Project 2. In this section, we provide a big picture of each group's text co-construction behaviors in a table and discuss illustrative examples from group wiki "History" modules to explain how the group members actively performed multiple writing change functions in the wiki. Below we present the results of Project 1 and Project 2, sequentially.

Project 1: EFL Context in China

Results revealed that the EFL students were engaged in text co-construction via five different types of writing change functions, namely: addition, deletion, reordering, rephrasing and correction, as displayed in Tables 8 and 9. In Group A, three group members were all engaged with text construction, making writing changes to both their own texts and others' texts. In Group B, however, Wang contributed the most to text construction and also took control over the writing direction. The other two group members also made efforts to collaborate on the wiki writing task, though contributing less than Wang. For both groups, correction and addition are the most frequently performed writing change functions.

We further illustrate the findings by discussing the following illuminating excerpts. As Excerpt 9 depicts, the EFL students were involved with several instances of addition and rephrasing when co-producing the wiki essay. This observation indicates that wikis allow the students to deliberate about language points at the revising stage.

Table 8. Writing change functions performed by Group A

	Addition				Deletion				Rephrasing				Reordering				Correction				Total
	G	L	S	O	G	L	S	O	G	L	S	O	G	L	S	O	G	L	S	O	
Li	4	3	6	1	0	1	0	1	1	8	1	8	0	0	0	0	1	4	3	2	22
	(7)				(1)				(9)				(0)				(5)				
Chen	4	4	5	3	2	0	1	1		1	1	02	7	0	2	5	0	1	0	1	20
	(8)				(2)				(2)				(7)				(1)				
Zhang	2	5	2	5	0	2	0	2		0	1	01	0	0	0	0	0	16	3	13	26
	(7)				(2)				(1)				(0)				(16)				
Total	22 (32%)				5 (7%)				12 (18%)				7 (11%)				22 (32%)				68 (100%)

Note. G=global level of change, L=local level of change, S=change to self-constructed texts, O=change to other-constructed texts; (N)= the subtotal of each type of writing change functions produced by each member

Table 9. Writing change functions performed by Group B

	Addition				Deletion				Rephrasing				Reordering				Correction				Total
	G	L	S	O	G	L	S	O	G	L	S	O	G	L	S	O	G	L	S	O	
Wang	1	3	1	3	1	4	1	4	0	2	0	2	4	0	0	4	0	5	2	3	20
	(4)				(5)				(2)				(4)				(5)				
Lin	2	0	2	0	0	0	0	0		0	0	00	0	0	0	0	0	2	0	2	4
	(2)				(0)				(0)				(0)				(2)				
Zhao	0	0	0	0	0	0	0	0		0	0	00	0	0	0	0	0	8	0	8	8
	(0)				(0)				(0)				(0)				(8)				
Total	6 (19%)				5 (16%)				2 (6%)				4 (13%)				15 (46%)				32 (100%)

Note. G=global level of change, L=local level of change, S=change to self-constructed texts, O=change to other-constructed texts; (N)= the subtotal of each type of writing change functions produced by each member.

Excerpt 9: Addition and Rephrasing (Group B)

1. (it [the extra eye] may bring you something sad because it can help you see something you never care about before. (*Lin: addition, self, global*)
2. **Under this circumstance**, it may bring you something ~~sad~~ **unpleasant** because it can ~~help you~~ **force you to** see something you never care about before. **For example, humans often complain about others on their back. The eye on their back make they dare not to speak out, even it is just a whisper.** (*Wang: addition, other, local/ global; rephrasing, other, local*)

Lin added a sub-thesis about the disadvantage of having an extra eye on the back of the head. In the second round, Wang made both local and global levels of addition to Lin's texts. He added a transition phrase, "under this circumstance," to enhance cohesiveness. He also supplied an example to support the topic sentence. Meanwhile, he rephrased "sad" with "unpleasant," and substituted "force" for "help," to enhance the accuracy and complexity of their texts.

In Group B, Wang also deleted quite a few trivial texts that did not contribute to meaning composed by himself or his group partners, such as "In the beginning I say," and "it should start with two perspectives." Also interestingly, in both Group A and Group B, one group member (i.e., Chen in Group A and Wang in Group B) was fully engaged in reordering the texts according to the essay structure advantages plus disadvantages. Excerpt 10 is an illustrative example.

Excerpt 10: Reordering (Group B)

The major change, as having eyes on the back of head brings about, is a more spacious and flexible vision scope. [...] (*Wang: reordering, other, global)*

As Excerpt 10 shows, Wang moved Lin's texts regarding a general advantage of an extra eye to the former part of the essay, functioning as a topic sentence of a paragraph. Moreover, the EFL students paid sufficient attention to the accuracy of language forms, and they performed quite a few correcting acts. For instance, in Group B, Zhao focused on correcting grammar and spelling mistakes in their group writing, such as correcting "piont" to "point," correcting the verb form in the clause " the eye on the back make (corrected to 'makes')...," and "they could teach students while look (corrected to 'looking') at the blackboard."

Of particular note, the results confirm that wikis encourage collaboration and continual revision (Purdy, 2009), as revealed by several rounds of revisions the small groups collectively performed in the wiki projects. Excerpt 11 below, also discussed in Li (2013), illustrates how the EFL students performed multiple acts of addition, rephrasing and correction to their group partner's texts, ultimately producing the joint texts of better quality.

Excerpt 11: Five rounds of writing/revision (Group A)

1. On the contrary, maybe one would wrathfully complain, if owning an extra eye, which is really a bad idea (*Zhang: addition, self, global*)
2. On the contrary, maybe one would wrathfully complain, if owning an extra eye, which is really a bad idea, **although it also bring so much convenience and benefits at the same time**. (*Chen: addition, other, local*)
3. On the contrary, maybe **someone** would wrathfully complain, if owning an extra eye, which is really a bad idea, although it also bring so much convenience and benefits at the same time. (*Chen: rephrasing, other, local*)
4. **Though**, maybe someone would wrathfully complain that owing an extra eye is really an odd, **despite** it bring so much convenience and benefits at the same time. (*Li: rephrasing, other, local*)
5. Though, maybe someone would wrathfully complain that owing an extra eye is really an odd **adventure**, despite it **brings** so much convenience and benefits at the same time. (*Li: correction, other, local*)

Project 2: ESL Context in the U.S.

Table 10 and Table 11 summarize the ESL small groups' text co-construction processes reflected in writing change functions. Group C performed writing change acts of addition, rephrasing, deleting, and correction. Dong and Feng had almost equal contribution to the writing task, and they also engaged with other group members' writing efforts, reflected by revisions made to others' texts. In Group D, Hai, being the "expert," made the greatest contribution in the wiki group writing. The writing changes the group members made included addition, rephrasing, reordering, deleting, and correction. The ESL students in both groups predominantly performed the acts of global addition. The following excerpts illustrate how the ESL students co-constructed the group writing of the annotated bibliography.

Table 10. Writing change functions performed by Group C

	Addition				Rephrasing				Deleting				Correction				
	G	L	S	O	G	L	S	O	G	L	S	O	G	L	S	O	Total
Dong	3	1	4	0	0	1	1	0	0	0	0	0	0	2	0	2	7
	(4)				(1)				(0)				(2)				
Feng	6	1	7	3	0	1	1	0	0	1	1	0	0	0	0	0	9
	(7)				(1)				(1)				(0)				
Abdul	1	0	1	0	0	0	0	0	0	0	0	0	0	0	0	0	1
	(1)				(0)				(0)				(0)				
Total	12 (70%)				2 (12%)				1 (6%)				2 (12%)				17 (100%)

Note. G=global level of change, L=local level of change, S=change to self-constructed texts, O=change to other-constructed texts; (N.)= the subtotal of each type of writing change functions produced by each member

Table 11. Writing change functions performed by Group D

	Addition				Rephrasing				Reordering				Deleting				Correction				Total
	G	L	S	O	G	L	S	O	G	L	S	O	G	L	S	O	G	L	S	O	
Hai	4	1	4	1	1	1	0	2	2	1	1	2	0	4	0	4	0	5	1	4	19
	(5)				(2)				(3)				(4)				(5)				
Xia	3	1	3	1	0	0	0	0	0	0	0	0	0	0	0	0	0	0	0	0	4
	(4)				(0)				(0)				(0)				(0)				
Ali	3	1	4	0	0	0	0	0	0	0	0	0	0	0	0	0	0	0	0	0	4
	(4)				(0)				(0)				(0)				(0)				
Total	13 (48%)				2 (7%)				3 (11%)				4 (15%)				5 (19%)				27 (100%)

Note. G=global level of change, L=local level of change, S=change to self-constructed texts, O=change to other-constructed texts; (N.)= the subtotal of each type of writing change functions produced by each member.

The most notable observation is that the ESL students frequently performed the addition acts; on most occasions, they added to their own texts. The most frequent instance of *self* addition was, to a large degree, related to the nature of the annotated bibliography task that required a combination of each individual member's contribution (e.g., each member composed the annotations of thee sources). Moreover, the students made a few writing change acts of rephrasing. Excerpt 12 illustrates the adding and rephrasing functions.

Excerpt 12: Addition and Rephrasing (Group C)

1. This article describes the nature and causes of the parallel trade in Coca - Cola between Shanghai and Hangzhou and the geographic and theoretical implications for the regional monopolies that have been artificially created by Coca-Cola in China. The source provides the evidence of successful specific strategies and advantages of the company doing business in china and fairly analyze the specific situation of Chinese market. (*Dong: Adding, global, self*)
2. **The purpose of this article is to** describe (*Dong: Rephrasing, local, self*) the nature and causes of the parallel trade in Coca – Cola between Shanghai and Hangzhou and the geographic and theoretical implications for the regional monopolies that have been artificially created by Coca – Cola in China. **The audience is the individuals who has the strong intrest with the business strategies of Coca-Cola in China.** [...] (*Dong: Adding, global, self*) The source provides the evidence of successful specific strategies and advantages of the company doing business in china and fairly analyze the specific situation of Chinese market, **which is related to my position of research that the strategies of business in China**. (*Dong: Adding, local, self*)

Excerpt 12 displays the process of students' learning a new genre by applying what they newly learned (Hirvela, 1999). To meet such task requirements of including rhetorical moves as to the purpose of the work, for what type of audience the work is written, and its relevance to the research topic, Dong rephrased "this article describes [...]" by stating explicitly "the purpose of this article is to describe [...]." He also added to the description of this annotation by including a sentence addressing the audience of this article and a clause which indicated its relevance to their research topic. Dong's wiki writing behavior confirmed that wikis support recursive writing and revision. However, Dong did not attend to language accuracy and quite a few linguistic errors were not removed from the texts.

Moreover, the ESL students attended to text structure and were engaged with reordering and deletion during text co-construction processes. Excerpt 13 is an illustrative example.

Excerpt 13: Reordering and Deletion (Group D)

1. How Disney Magic and the Corporate Media Shape Youth Identity in the Digital Age. Note: This article mainly illustrated that in digital times, how does disney use media to influence youth's identity, including multi-cultures, their living styles, etc. Through this way, Disney's target market is children. They make a lot of money from children through their products, movies and Disneyland ~~Credibility Rating:~~ This article absolutely is that what I am looking for. Since it topic relevant our topic, at the same time it include many statistics and examples which our team can explain it. Link: http://www.truth-out.org/opinion/item/2808:how-disney-magic-and-the-corporate-media- shape-youth-identity-in-the-digital-age (*Xia: addition, self, global*)
2. **Giroux, A. Henry**. "How Disney Magic and the Corporate Media Shape Youth Identity in the Digital Age" Truthout. **Web. 21 August 2011. Link:** http://www.truth-out.org/opinion/item/2808:how-disney-magic-and-the-corporate-media-shape-youth-identity-in-the-digital-age (*Hai: addition, other, local; reordering, other, local)* This article mainly illustrated [...] They make a lot of money from children through their products, movies and Disneyland. Credibility Rating: This article absolutely is that what I am looking for. Since it topic relevant our topic, at the same time it include many statistics and examples which our team can explain it. (*Hai: deletion, local, other*)

As revealed in Excerpt 13, Hai improved the annotation that Xia had composed according to the task requirements, including MLA style, combination of reference and annotation, and description in the paragraph format. Specifically, he modified the citation following the MLA style by adding the author, the retrieving date, and re-ordering the web link of the article. To meet the requirement of the paragraph format, he also deleted the bullet point "credibility rating." Thus, their joint texts better met the course requirements.

In addition, the ESL students conducted a few instances of correction, mostly on formats based on the MLA style. For instance, Dong was found to revise twice the formats of the texts that his group partners constructed where he saw inappropriateness, such as indentation.

This section clearly showed that wiki "History" makes each version of wiki documents transparent to co-writers and this transparency encourages continual refining of the shared writing. Small groups of ESL/EFL students were engaged in recursive writing process via multiple writing change functions at both global and local levels with regards to either their own texts or their partners' texts. Wikis' transparency, asynchronous communication, and collaborative nature enable the students to engage with collaborative writing processes in an innovative and effective way. While not all groups in both projects took full advantage of the affordances, which may be due to factors such as motive, agency, group formation, and group interactional patterns, there were many instances where wikis encouraged recursive writing and continual revision.

Comparing the EFL and ESL population, the former groups aimed to compose coherent and accurate writing. They attended to four aspects of writing: content, organization, language and grammar, which are reinforced in the EFL writing instruction. To produce academic writing guided by the course instruction, the EFL students were found to perform the unique instances of rephrasing, such as substituting simple words with more complicated words, instances of adding transitions and hedges, and deleting redundant texts. They were also found to conduct many instances of correction, particularly in spelling. This observation was related to the EFL students' focus on language accuracy as well as the tendency that they made mechanical mistakes easily due to their unfamiliarity with online writing. In contrast, as ESL students in the U.S. were exposed to the target language and were more familiar with online writing, they did not make many spelling mistakes. The ESL students focused on learning to write two new genre types: a research proposal and an annotated bibliography. Guided by the writing rubrics attaching the predominant importance to task-related skills, the ESL students attended to rhetorical moves and MLA style when co-producing their group writing in the wiki. Thus the instances of rephrasing, deletion, and language correction were much less obvious in the ESL groups. In addition, the EFL students at times reverted to their common first language (L1), Chinese, which may have helped in the negotiation of specific language choices, allowing nuanced differences to be discussed with precision and not dependent upon their ability to address these issues solely in the target language, English. Thus, the important differences between EFL and ESL, namely, the exposure to the target language and the similarity/diversity of the L1, surfaced even in this brief EFL/ESL comparison of wiki collaborations.

CONCLUSION

This study draws on two relevant wiki-based collaborative writing projects and explores how ESL and EFL students in small groups negotiated writing tasks and co-constructed academic essays by making use of distinctive wiki functions, i.e., "Discussion," "Comments" and "History" in the Wikispaces site. Although some differences of their use of wikis within the two projects were identified in this study, the students in both projects made good use of the wiki tool for collaborative writing. "Discussion" allowed the students to communicate writing tasks and meanings asynchronously at their own pace. As in previous studies, the students were able to take advantage of the time- and space-independent characteristic of wikis (Arnold, Ducate, & Kost, 2012; Goodwin-Jones, 2003) in order to continuously communicate via the wiki tools, making the text construction a social activity. "Comments", on the other hand, offered the students opportunities to leave comments or raise questions concerning their group members' specific texts. The "Comments" function would be particularly useful when students felt reluctant to correct others' language forms as reported in previous research (e.g., Kessler & Bikowski, 2010; Mak & Coniam, 2008). The students were found to be actively engaged in content discussion, task management, language negotiation, social talk and technical communication throughout the writing processes. The multiple social negotiations throughout the collaborative writing support Storch's (2005) suggestion that the collaboration is not solely found in one area, but begins even in the idea-generating stage. Also, wiki "History" revealed that the ESL and EFL students collectively made revisions to their joint essay involving multiple levels of texts, ranging from spelling, words, and bullet points to clauses, sentences and paragraphs. They scaffolded each other's efforts on writing development, and co-constructed written texts via different writing change functions, i.e., addition, deletion, rephrasing, reordering, and correction. The abundant use of addition in the ESL context mirrors findings by Mak and Coniam (2008), yet more research is needed to understand why and to further explore the comparisons made here that reveal a focus on grammar in the EFL context. A few students in Project 2 also reported in the post-task interview that the writing samples posted under "Wiki resources" scaffolded their writing processes.

This study contributes to the current body of literature on computer (wiki)-mediated collaborative writing. For the first time, the study includes rich examples to illustrate and clarify how the wiki technology can afford small group writing in both ESL and EFL contexts and how "wiki collaborations guide learners to co-construct texts" (Storch, 2012, p.122). Importantly, it compares the use of wikis by two distinct groups of English language learners (i.e., EFL and ESL), and elucidates the factors that may account for the differences identified among the ESL and EFL populations. Moreover, the coding schemes of wiki discussion and text co-construction developed in this study can be used for analyses of computer-based collaborative writing processes in future research.

With its "intensely collaborative" nature (Godwin-Jones, 2003, p15), the wiki can be a great medium for collaborative writing tasks in second/ foreign language classes. To help facilitate the smooth collaboration process, instructors need to train students in using multiple functions of wiki technology (e.g., "Edit," "Comments," "Discussion," and "History") through lecturing and a collaborative writing practice activity. In particular, the pedagogical use of wiki "Discussion" and "Comments" functions needs more attention since these functions enable students to deliberate on both writing contents and language forms at their own pace. Also, "Projects" as a new feature in Wikispaces can afford group collaboration on multiple projects, but whether or not to construct private "projects" will need to be carefully considered. In this study, a few ESL students in Project 2 expressed in the post-task interview their wish to see other groups' writing products. Moreover, instructors need not only to encourage scaffolding among group members but also to post writing resources as artifact scaffolds in the wiki site. Given recent developments in CMC technology, the use of collaborative writing tasks in online writing contexts will grow in the future (Kessler, Bikowski, & Boggs, 2012). As the wiki technology can open up great possibilities for small group academic writing in the second/ foreign language learning contexts, it is necessary for language instructors to integrate Web 2.0 tools such as wikis in collaborative writing tasks to engage students to the fullest. It would be a worthwhile endeavor for both ESL and EFL learners to wade into the wiki space and Web 2.0 world.

REFERENCES

Anton, M., & DiCamilla, F. (1998). Socio-cognitive functions of L1 collaborative interaction in the L2 classroom. *Canadian Modern Language Review, 54*, 314–342. doi:10.3138/cmlr.54.3.314

Arnold, N., Ducate, L., & Kost, C. (2012). Collaboration or cooperation? Analyzing group dynamics and revision process in wikis. *CALICO Journal, 29*(3), 431–448. doi:10.11139/cj.29.3.431-448

Bradley, L., Linstrom, B., & Rystedt, H. (2010). Rationalities of collaboration for language learning on a wiki. *ReCALL, 22*(2), 247–265. doi:10.1017/S0958344010000108

Bruffee, K. (1993). *Collaborative learning: Higher education, interdependence, and the authority of knowledge*. Baltimore, MD: Johns Hopkins University Press.

Chao, Y., & Lo, H. (2009). Students' perceptions of wiki-based collaborative writing for learners of English as a foreign language. *Interactive Learning Environments*.

Creswell, J. W. (2007). *Qualitative inquiry and research design: Choosing among five approaches* (2nd ed.). Thousand Oaks, CA: Sage Publications.

DiCamilla, F., & Anton, M. (1997). The function of repetition in the collaborative discourse of L2 learners. *Canadian Modern Language Review, 53*, 609–633.

Donato, R. (1994). Collective scaffolding in second language learning. In J. P. Lantolf, & G. Appel (Eds.), *Vygotskian approaches to second language research* (pp. 33–56). Norwood, NJ: Ablex.

Duff, P. (2008). *Case study research in applied linguistics*. New York, NY: Lawrence Erlbaum Associates.

Ede, L., & Lunsford, A. (1990). *Singular texts/plural authors*. Carbondale, IL: Southern Illinois University Press.

Godwin-Jones, B. (2003). Blogs and wikis: Environments for on-line collaboration. *Language Learning & Technology*, *7*(2), 12–16.

Hirvela, A. (1999). Collaborative writing instruction and communities of readers and writers. *TESOL Quarterly*, *8*(2), 7–12.

Johnson, D. (1992). *Approaches to research in second language learning*. New York, NY: Longman.

Kessler, G., & Bikowski, D. (2010). Developing collaborative autonomous learning abilities in computer mediated language learning: Attention to meaning among students in wiki space. *Computer Assisted Language Learning*, *23*(1), 41–58. doi:10.1080/09588220903467335

Kessler, G., Bikowski, D., & Boggs, J. (2012). Collaborative writing among second language learners in academic web-based projects. *Language Learning & Technology*, *16*(1), 91–109. Retrieved April 18, 2012

Kost, C. (2011). Investigating writing strategies and revision behavior in collaborative wiki projects. *CALICO Journal*, *28*(3), 606–620. doi:10.11139/cj.28.3.606-620

Lee, L. (2010). Exploring wiki-mediated collaborative writing: A case study in an elementary Spanish course. *CALICO Journal*, *27*(2), 260–276.

Li, M. (2012a). Use of wikis in second/foreign language classes: A literature review. *CALL-EJ*, *13*(1), 17–35.

Li, M. (2012b). Politeness strategies in wiki-mediated communication of EFL collaborative writing tasks. *IALLT Journal*, *42*(2), 1–26.

Li, M. (2013). Individual novices and collective experts: Collective scaffolding in wiki-based small group writing. *System*, *41*(3), 752–769. doi:10.1016/j.system.2013.07.021

Li, M., & Zhu, W. (2013). Patterns of computer-mediated interaction in EFL collaborative writing groups using wikis. *Computer Assisted Language Learning*, *26*(1), 61–82. doi:10.1080/09588221.2011.631142

Lund, A. (2008). Wikis: A collective approach to language production. *ReCALL*, *20*(1), 35–54. doi:10.1017/S0958344008000414

Lund, A., & Rasmussen, I. (2008). The right tool for the wrong task? Match and mismatch between first and second stimulus in double stimulation. *Computer-Supported Collaborative Learning*, *3*, 387–412. doi:10.1007/s11412-008-9050-8

Lundin, R. W. (2008). Teaching with wikis: Toward a networked pedagogy. *Computers and Composition*, *25*, 432–448. doi:10.1016/j.compcom.2008.06.001

Mak, B., & Coniam, D. (2008). Using wikis to enhance and develop writing skills among secondary school students in Hong Kong. *System*, *36*, 437–455. doi:10.1016/j.system.2008.02.004

Ohta, A. S. (2000). Re-thinking interaction in SLA: Developmentally appropriate assistance in the zone of proximal development and the acquisition of L2 grammar. In J. P. Lantolf (Ed.), *Sociocultural theory and second language learning* (pp. 51–78). Oxford, UK: Oxford University Press.

Purdy, J. P. (2009). When the tenets of composition go public: A study of writing in Wikipedia. *College Composition and Communication, 61*(2), 351–373.

Stake, R. E. (1995). *The art of case study research*. Thousand Oaks, CA: Sage Publications.

Storch, N. (2005). Collaborative writing: Product, process, and students' reflections. *Journal of Second Language Writing, 14*, 153–173. doi:10.1016/j.jslw.2005.05.002

Storch, N. (2011). Collaborative writing in L2 contexts: Processes, outcomes, and future directions. *Annual Review of Applied Linguistics, 31*, 275–288. doi:10.1017/S0267190511000079

Storch, N. (2012). Collaborative writing as a site for L2 learning in face-to-face and online modes. In G. Kessler, A. Oskoz, & I. Elola (Eds.), Technology across writing contexts and tasks (pp. 113–129). Texas State University.

Storch, N. (2013). *Collaborative writing in L2 classrooms*. Bristol, UK: Multilingual Matters.

Swain, M. (2000). The output hypothesis and beyond: Mediating acquisition through collaborative dialogue. In J. P. Lantolf (Ed.), *Sociocultural theory and second language learning* (pp. 97–114). Oxford, England: Oxford University Press.

Swain, M., & Lapkin, S. (1998). Interaction and second language learning: Two adolescent French immersion students working together. *Modern Language Journal, 82*, 320–337. doi:10.1111/j.1540-4781.1998.tb01209.x

Ware, P., & Warschauer, M. (2006). Electronic feedback and second language writing. In K. Hyland, & F. Hyland (Eds.), *Feedback in ESL writing: Context and issues* (pp. 105–122). NY: Cambridge University Press. doi:10.1017/CBO9781139524742.008

Weissberg, R. (2006). *Connecting speaking and writing*. Ann Arbor, MI: University of Michigan Press.

Yin, R. K. (2009). *Case study research design and methods* (4th ed.). Thousand Oaks, CA: Sage Publications.

ADDITIONAL READING

Arnold, N., Ducate, L., & Kost, C. R. (2009). Collaborative writing in wikis: Insights from culture projects in German classes. In L. Lomicka, & G. Lord (Eds.), *The next generation: Social networking and online collaboration in foreign language learning* (pp. 115–144). San Marcos, TX: CALICO.

Castañeda, D., & Cho, M. (2013). The role of wiki writing in learning Spanish grammar. *Computer Assisted Language Learning, 26*(4), 334–349. doi:10.1080/09588221.2012.670648

Cole, M. (2009). Using Wiki technology to support student engagement: Lessons from the trenches. *Computers & Education, 52*(1), 141–146. doi:10.1016/j.compedu.2008.07.003

Cummings, R. E., & Barton, M. (Eds.). (2008). *Wiki writing: collaborative learning in the college classroom Wiki collaborative writing?* Ann Arbor, MI: University of Michigan Press.

Donato, R. (2004). Aspects of collaboration in pedagogical discourse. *Annual Review of Applied Linguistics, 24*, 284–302. doi:10.1017/S026719050400011X

Ducate, L., Anderson, L., & Moreno, N. (2011). Wading through the world of wikis: An analysis of three wiki projects. *Foreign Language Annals, 44*(3), 495–524. doi:10.1111/j.1944-9720.2011.01144.x

Elola, I., & Oskoz, A. (2010). Collaborative writing: Fostering foreign language and writing conventions development. *Language Learning & Technology, 14*(3), 51–71. Retrieved May 20, 2010, from http:// llt.msu.edu/vol14num3/elolaoskoz.pdf

Elola, I., & Oskoz, A. (2011). Writing between the lines: Acquiring the presentational mode through social tools. In N. Arnold, & L. Ducate (Eds.), *Present and future promises of CALL: From theory and research to new directions in language teaching* (pp. 171–210). San Marcos, TX: CALICO.

Hampel, R. (2014, in press). Making meaning online: Computer-mediated communication for language learning. In A. Peti-Stantić, &M. Stanojević (Eds.), *Language as Information Proceedings from the CALS Conference 2012*. Frankfurt am Main: Peter Lang.

Judd, T., Kennedy, G., & Cropper, S. (2010). Using wikis for collaborative learning: Assessing collaboration through contribution. *Australasian Journal of Educational Technology, 26*(3), 341–354.

Kennedy, C., & Miceli, T. (2013). In piazza online: Exploring the use of wikis with beginner foreign language learners. *Computer Assisted Language Learning, 26*(5), 389–411. doi:10.1080/09588221.2013.770035

Kessler, G. (2009). Student-initiated attention to form in wiki-based collaborative writing. *Language Learning & Technology, 13*(1), 79–95.

Kuteeva, M. (2011). Wikis and academic writing: Changing the writer-reader relationship. *English for Specific Purposes, 30*, 44–57. doi:10.1016/j.esp.2010.04.007

Lee, H., & Wang, P. (2013). Discussing the factors contributing to students' involvement in an EFL collaborative wiki project. *ReCALL, 25*(2), 233–249. doi:10.1017/S0958344013000025

Li, X., Chu, S., Ki, W., & Woo, M. (2012). Using a wiki-based collaborative process writing pedagogy to facilitate collaborative writing among Chinese primary school students. *Australasian Journal of Educational Technology, 28*(1), 159–181.

Martinsen, R. A., & Miller, A. (2012). Collaboration through wiki and paper compositions in foreign language classes. *The IALLT Journal, 42*, 72–95.

Miyazoe, T., & Anderson, T. (2010). Learning outcomes and students' perceptions of online writing: Simultaneous implementation of a forum, blog, and wiki in an EFL blended learning setting. *System, 38*, 185–199. doi:10.1016/j.system.2010.03.006

Oskoz, A., & Elola, I. (2010). Meeting at the wiki: The new arena for collaborative writing in foreign language courses. In M. Lee, & C. McLaughlin (Eds.), *Web 2.0-based E-learning: Applying social informatics for tertiary teaching* (pp. 209–227). Hershey, PA: IGI Global. doi:10.4018/978-1-60566-294-7.ch011

Parker, K., & Chao, J. (2007). Wiki as a teaching tool. *Interdisciplinary Journal of Knowledge and Learning Objects, 3*, 57–70.

Rott, S., & Weber, E. D. (2013). Preparing Students to Use Wiki Software as a Collaborative Learning Tool. *CALICO Journal, 30*(2), 179–203. doi:10.11139/cj.30.2.179-203

Stoddart, A., Chan, J. Y. Y., & Liu, G. Z. (2013). Enhancing successful outcomes of wiki-based collaborative writing: a state-of-the-art review of facilitation frameworks. *Interactive Learning Environments*, (ahead-of-print), 1-16. doi:10.1080/10494820.2013.825810

Sykes, J., Oskoz, A., & Thorne, S. (2008). Web 2.0, Synthetic Immersive Environments, and Mobile Resources for Language Education. *CALICO Journal, 25*(3), 528–546.

Trentin, G. (2009). Using a wiki to evaluate individual contribution to a collaborative learning project. *Journal of Computer Assisted Learning*, *25*(1), 43–55. doi:10.1111/j.1365-2729.2008.00276.x

Warschauer, M. (1997). Computer-mediated collaborative learning: Theory and practice. *Modern Language Journal*, *81*(4), 470–481. doi:10.1111/j.1540-4781.1997.tb05514.x

Warschauer, M., & Grimes, D. (2007). Audience, authorship, and artifact: The emergent semiotics of Web 2.0. *Annual Review of Applied Linguistics*, *27*, 1–23. doi:10.1017/S0267190508070013

Wheeler, S., Yeomans, P., & Wheeler, D. (2008). The good, the bad and the wiki: Evaluating student-generated content for collaborative learning. *British Journal of Educational Technology*, *39*(6), 987–995. doi:10.1111/j.1467-8535.2007.00799.x

Woo, M., Chu, S., Ho, A., & Li, X. (2011). Using a wiki to scaffold primary-school students' collaborative writing. *Journal of Educational Technology & Society*, *14*(1), 43–54.

KEY TERMS AND DEFINITIONS

Collaborative Writing: Writing involving multiple writers co-producing the written texts, termed as a singular text/plural authors approach (Ede & Lunsford, 1990). In this study, collaborative writing refers to "the joint production or the co-authoring of a text" (Storch, 2011, p.275) by three or four writers in relation to academic writing tasks in the EFL/ESL contexts.

Comments: A new feature of Wikispaces. Users can comment on specific texts using the "Comments" icon in the editor toolbar to open and post in the comment boxes.

Discussion: The wiki "Discussion" allows users to start new topics, pose questions, or add to others' comments via asynchronous posting.

English as a Foreign Language (EFL): The study of English by non-native speakers in a non-English speaking country (such as China in this study).

English as a Second Language (ESL): The study of English by non-native speakers in an English-speaking environment.

History: The wiki "History" allows users to see who has edited the page and when. Users can also compare versions of a page and revert to any previous version of the page if they have accidentally made unwanted changes.

Wiki: Developed approximately in 1995 as a part of Web 2.0 –the read/write web, the wiki is a piece of software that allows users to freely create and edit the content of web pages (Leuf & Cunningham, 2001). It is a collaborative web site where users can write, post pictures and insert hyperlinks anywhere on the wiki pages.

Wikispaces: One of the largest free wiki applications, competing with PBworks, Wetpaint and Wikia. The site can be set to Private (only members of the wiki can view and edit pages), Protected (it is visible to the public, but only wiki members can edit pages), or Public (all people can view and edit pages). Wikispaces has been widely used in higher education as well as K-12 settings.

Writing Change Functions: This term, used in Mak and Coniam (2008), refers to the ways in which students co-produce the joint texts in wikis, such as adding, expanding, reorganizing, and correcting. The writing change functions in this study are categorized as addition, deletion, reordering, rephrasing and correction.

Writing Engagements: Students' participation and interaction in writing. In this study, writing engagements specifically refer to the group member's communication and interaction in wiki "Discussion"/"Comments" module and their text co-construction behaviors revealed in wiki "History" module under the designated group link.

Section 4

Beliefs and Attitudes toward Technology Integration

Chapter 11
Teachers' Perceptions and Use of Information and Communication Technologies (ICTs) in Chinese Language Education

Dongbo Zhang
Michigan State University, USA

Shouhui Zhao
University of Bergen, Norway

Li Li
Nanyang Technological University, Singapore

ABSTRACT

This chapter reports on a mixed-methods study that examined how factors intrinsic and extrinsic to teachers influence their pedagogical use of modern Information and Communication Technologies (ICTs) in Chinese Language (CL) education. Three-hundred-eleven primary school CL teachers in Singapore participated in an online questionnaire survey that addressed four ICT-related variables: competence to use ICT, availability of resources and support, perceived usefulness of ICT, and pedagogical use of ICT. The results show that the four variables were significantly correlated, and teachers' pedagogical use of ICT was predicted significantly by all the other three variables. To supplement the questionnaire survey, Focus Group Discussions (FGD) were conducted on a randomly selected sample of the teachers who participated in the survey. Teachers reported local (e.g., ICT facilities and resources) as well as global (e.g., national high-stake examinations) factors that determined how ICT-mediated pedagogy was strategically blended with non-ICT-mediated traditional pedagogies. In conclusion, the authors argue that achieving the desired effects of learning through ICT integration necessitates consideration of factors intrinsic to teachers as well as those extrinsic to them that often shape the teacher-intrinsic factors.

DOI: 10.4018/978-1-4666-6174-5.ch011

BACKGROUND

Teachers and ICT Integration in Language Programs

The unprecedented growth of modern Information and Communication Technologies (ICTs), including more recent Web 2.0 and cloud computing technologies, has brought about tremendous opportunities for learning and is redefining what we need to learn and how we learn in the 21st Century. On the one hand, ICT literacy has now arguably been necessitated as a component of our knowledge base in coping with the fast-changing world where the abundance of technologies has transformed almost every aspect of our everyday experience (New London Group, 1996; Warschauer, 2001); on the other hand, modern ICTs of various forms serve as learning tools and provide learning environments to enhance the acquisition of knowledge and skills mandated in traditional school curriculums, such as science and math (Oldknow, Taylor, & Tetlow, 2010). The affordances of ICT for second/foreign language teaching and learning, with no exception, have also been widely endorsed (Blake, 2007; Evans, 2009; Thomas, 2009).

Addressing the challenges brought about by ICT advancements to learning necessitates pedagogical integration of ICT in school education. It is often a pedagogical requirement across curricula that teachers integrate ICT into their instructional design and use ICT to support students' learning and achieve maximal effects of learning (International Society for Technology in Education, 2007). However, a discrepancy is not uncommon between policy or curriculum mandates and actual practice with regard to pedagogical integration of ICT; pedagogical translation of ICT can often be very limited, and its effect on learning can be far from the level of satisfaction that policy makers and curriculum developers expected to achieve (Cuban, 2001).

ICT integrations come under conditions (Ertmer, 1999, 2005; Zhao & Frank, 2003; Zhao, Pugh, Sheldon, & Byers, 2002). A myriad of factors have been reported that may affect ICT integration in education. Ertmer and associates (Ertmer, 1999, 2005; Ertmer, Ottenbreit-Leftwich, & York, 2006) created a two-tier framework to discuss factors that are barriers to or enablers of pedagogical integration of ICT. The first-order factors are extrinsic to teachers. Studies on teachers' pedagogical life revealed that what teachers do and do not do are shaped by many social and institutional factors that do not pertain to teachers themselves (Borg, 2006). These factors can be global and include educational system (e.g., high-stake standardized testing), policy initiatives, curriculum mandates, as well as local that include school policies (e.g., heavy workloads or lack of time for innovation), leadership, availability of facilities and instructional resources, and technical, administrative, and peer support (e.g., Egbert, Paulus, & Nakamichi, 2002; Lam, 2000; Lim & Chai, 2008; Lim & Khine, 2006; Zhao & Frank, 2003; Zhao et al., 2002). Egbert et al. (2002), for example, conducted a questionnaire survey on 20 in-service teachers who were teaching English as a Second Language (ESL) learners at diverse educational levels and had previously taken a graduate course in Computer Assisted Language Learning (CALL). Some teachers reported that they barely used or were unable to integrate CALL activities in their teaching. Time, resources, support, and training were indicated as top factors. One teacher, for example, specifically mentioned that the computer labs in his/her school were too crowded to have a time scheduled for students to work in them. Lim and Khine (2006), based on their interviews with teachers, ICT heads-of-department and school principals, identified a set of strategies that would promote ICT integration, which included, for instance, appointing technical support staff, giving sufficient time for teachers to prepare for ICT-mediated lessons, and school leaders providing support in addressing teachers' ICT concerns.

In addition to teacher-extrinsic or contextual factors, teachers' practice can also be directly influenced by their cognitive system, or factors that reflect teachers' *mental lives* (Borg, 2006, p. 1). Those factors are intrinsic to teachers that constitute Ertmer and associates' (e.g., Ertmer, 1999, 2005; Ertmer et al., 2006) second-order barriers to change or enablers that facilitate change in technology integration. As Ertmer, Addison, Lane, Ross, and Woods (1999) noted,

when educators and researchers look for reasons why teachers are struggling to use ICTs effectively, it may be important to look at what they have (in terms of beliefs and practices) in addition to what they do not have (in terms of equipment). (p. 68)

Second-order or teacher-intrinsic factors pertain to the knowledge, beliefs, and thoughts of teachers with respect to ICT and its pedagogical applications. What teachers know and think about ICT in education and how they perceive the usefulness of ICT have a clear influence on their practice.

Sometimes teachers may not be equipped with adequate skills in ICT and the application of ICT in instructional practice, which can be attributed to inadequate ICT preparation within teacher education programs or in-service professional development opportunities to address their knowledge/skill gap in pedagogical use of ICT (Egbert et al., 2002; Lam, 2000; Peters, 2006). Correlation-based studies show that the extent to which teachers command knowledge and skills to use ICT, or how confident they believe they are in handling ICT (i.e., perceived easiness of ICT use), have a direct influence on their practice of ICT-mediated pedagogy (e.g., Teo, 2011; Teo & Noyes, 2011). As Lam (2000) noted, that classroom computer use is often very scare is not because, as some suggested, teachers are technophobes, but rather because they lack confidence in using computer technology due to the inadequate training and support they have received or could receive from their previous training programs, their schools, and other sources.

In addition to knowledge or competence, what teachers think and believe, or their philosophies about technology in teaching and learning, also have a clear influence on what they do and how they enact a curriculum and integrate ICT in language programs (Egbert, Huff, McNeil, Preuss, & Sellen, 2009). Many studies have revealed that positive attitudes toward ICT and perceptions of or beliefs about the usefulness of ICT for teaching and learning promote, or a lack of them hinders, pedagogical integration of ICT (Lam, 2000; Teo, 2011; Teo & Noyes, 2011).

The above factors, teacher-extrinsic and teacher-intrinsic, work together in determining teachers' pedagogical decision making with regard to the use of ICT. As Borg (2009) comments, understanding of what teachers do, and do not do, requires reference not only to what they think, know, and believe, but also to the context in which teachers' knowledge, thoughts, and beliefs are formed and their practices unfold. Examining ICT integration necessitates consideration of both teacher-extrinsic and teacher-intrinsic factors and their inter-play.

ICT in Chinese Language Education in Singapore

In Singapore, an island country in Southeast Asia with impoverished natural resources, the government has determined that people are the greatest resource of the country, and the government's effort has never been abated in building a strong technological infrastructure and integrating technology in educating its people (Ng, 2008; Toh & So, 2011). It is the Singapore government's policy that school education should not only develop ICT literacy among students for them to deal with challenges in the 21st Century, but also use ICT across curricula to transform students' ways of learning. Under such a policy, it is also a curriculum mandate that ICT be integrated to facilitate teachers' teaching and students' learning of Chinese Language (CL), one of the three designated mother tongue languages of the three major ethnic groups in Singapore (the other two are Malay and Tamil) and a core school subject of Chinese Singaporean students (Singapore Ministry of Education, 2007).

In the bilingual education system in Singapore, CL, though the mother tongue of ethnic Chinese, is designated as the second language of Chinese students in governmental discourse. Such a designation, on one hand, is based on the relative importance ascribed to Chinese in comparison to English, which is the medium of instruction in schools and the designated first language of all Singaporean students. On the other hand, it reflects the *status quo* of the language proficiency of Chinese students in the country. Because of the strong global influence of English and its status as the medium of instruction in Singapore, intergenerational language shift has been increasingly observed in the Chinese community in the country. Reports from the Singapore Ministry of Education and other research reports have revealed that a majority of Chinese families use English as their dominant home language; many Chinese students grow up speaking English as their first language and learning Chinese as their second language in school, and their interest in learning Chinese and willingness to communicate in Chinese tend to be low (Li, Zhang, & Zhao, 2013).

Such a change in the sociolinguistic milieu and linguistic landscape in Singapore schools has created a lot of challenges for CL educational policy makers as well as practitioners. One of their major concerns is how to refine CL curriculum and pedagogy to address the diverse needs of students from different home language backgrounds, particularly the increasing population of students that have had little exposure to CL before entering primary school. One initiative is to use modern ICT to increase pedagogical efficiency, boost students' interest in CL learning, and ultimately increase their CL proficiency (CLCPRC, 2004; MTLRC, 2011). Such an initiative is reflected not only in the explicit mandates of ICT use in curriculum documents (Singapore Ministry of Education, 2007), but also in the efforts taken by different divisions of the Singapore Ministry of Education to develop online teaching and learning resources for teachers and students. A few examples of those efforts are *Xuele*, *10'C Chinese*, and *Chinese Language Word Games* developed by the CL branches of the Ministry of Education's Curriculum Planning and Development Division and Educational Technology Division[1].

However, pedagogical implementation of ICT in CL education has not been satisfactory. A few classroom observation studies revealed that despite the government's heightened investment in ICT in education, and the Ministry of Education's effort to promote ICT in CL education, teachers' use of ICT in CL classes in Singapore tended to be limited. Liu, Goh, and Zhang (2006) found that CL teachers in Singapore mostly used PowerPoint to support their instruction, and multimedia instructional packages or instructional resources from the Internet were yet to be incorporated by CL teachers in their classroom instruction. Such a gap between what is promoted and what is implemented or between what is mandated and what is enacted did not pertain only to ICT in CL education in Singapore. As we reviewed earlier, a myriad of factors extrinsic and intrinsic to teachers could have impacts on pedagogical use of ICT. It is possible that the gap identified in the case of CL education in Singapore could be explained by those factors that were largely identified in studies conducted in other educational contexts. No efforts, however, have been taken to test such a possibility empirically. While a small number of previous studies conducted in Singapore appeared to lend some support for such a possibility (e.g., Lim & Chai, 2008; Lim & Khine, 2006), none had specifically focused on CL teachers and ICT integration in CL education. To fill the research gap, we conducted the present study. Specifically, we aimed to address two questions:

1. How do CL teachers perceive ICT in CL education in Singapore?
2. How do their ICT-related perceptions relate to their pedagogical use of ICT?

METHODS

Addressing the complexity of the various factors that impact teachers' pedagogical decision-making calls for a combination of research methods (Borg, 2009). In the present study, we adopted a mixed-methods design to explore how CL teachers' pedagogical use of ICT was influenced by various factors intrinsic and extrinsic to them in Singapore. The quantitative data came from an online questionnaire survey in which teachers were asked to indicate their level of agreement on various statements related to ICT in CL education. The qualitative data came from focus group discussions (FGDs) where teachers were invited to discuss further in groups issues of ICT in CL education.

Questionnaire Survey

With support from Ministry of Education collaborators and assistance from heads of Mother Tongue Languages Departments, all primary school CL teachers in Singapore were invited to participate in an online questionnaire survey developed by the researchers. Eventually, 311 teachers voluntarily participated. They came from 100 primary schools and included 262 females and 45 males (three with missing information of gender). The distribution of their age was: 20-25 years (N = 36), 26-30 (N = 80), 31-35 (N = 73), 36-40 (N = 48), 41-45 (N = 46), and above 50 (N = 27) with one with missing data. The distribution of their years of teaching CL in Singapore was 0-5 years (N = 176), 6-10 (N = 61), 11-15 (N = 28), 16-20 (N = 20), 21-25 (N = 2), and over 25 years (N = 22) with two with missing data.

The online questionnaire, in addition to items eliciting teachers' background (e.g., age, gender, years of teaching), included 26 bilingual statements in Chinese as well as English that asked teachers to indicate their level of agreement on a 5-point Likert scale (1 = strongly disagree, 2 = disagree, 3 = neutral, 4 = agree, 5 = strongly agree). The statements covered variables that were related to teachers' perceptions of their competence for pedagogical use of ICT (number of items or n = 3; e.g., *I am good at using ICT to support students' CL learning*; Cronbach's α = 0.757), availability of resources and support (n = 5; e.g., *I can get suggestions and help on using ICT from my colleagues*; α = 0.804), usefulness of ICT to CL learning (n = 5; e.g., *ICT can increase students' CL learning interests*) and teaching (n = 6; *ICT can make my CL teaching engaging*) (α = 0.822), and teacher's use of ICT in CL instructional design and teaching (n = 4; e.g., *I often use ICT in my classroom instruction*) and supporting students' CL learning (n = 3; e.g., *I ask my students to use ICT to present their homework*) (α = 0.763).

Focus Group Discussion

To supplement the questionnaire survey, parallel sessions of FGDs were conducted among a sample of 128 teachers randomly selected from those who had participated in the online survey. Those teachers were randomly divided into 14 FGD groups, each group with 8-10 teachers. An experienced research assistant moderated the discussion in each group where teachers were asked semi-structured as well as open-ended questions concerning their perceptions of ICT in CL education and their pedagogical use of ICT. All FGDs were conducted in Chinese. They were audio-recorded and later transcribed in Chinese.

RESULTS

Questionnaire Survey

Table 1 shows the means and standard deviations of teachers' responses to the questionnaire. Overall, teachers' perceptions of their competence for ICT use and the usefulness of ICT and their reported pedagogical use of ICT were high, $M = 3.77$, $M = 3.79$, and $M = 3.68$ (all close to 4 = agree), respectively. Teachers' perception of availability of resources and support for ICT use was lower, $M = 2.94$ (a little below 3 = neutral). *T*-tests revealed no significant difference between female and male teachers in all four ICT variables.

Table 2 shows the correlations between all four ICT-related variables. None of the correlations of teachers' age and years of teaching CL with the ICT variables (not included in the correlation table) was significant. With regard to the significant correlations, teachers' perceived availability of resources and support significantly correlated with their perceived competence for ICT use, perceived usefulness of ICT, as well as the their reported pedagogical use of ICT, $r = .17$ ($p < .01$), $r = .26$ ($p < .001$), and $r = .18$ ($p < .001$), respectively. Teachers' perceived competence for ICT use was also significantly correlated with their perceived usefulness of ICT ($r = .50$), as well as their reported pedagogical use of ICT ($r = .57$), both *ps* $< .001$. Finally, teachers' perceived usefulness of ICT significantly correlated with their reported use of ICT, $r = .50$, $p < .001$.

To further examine how teachers' pedagogical use of ICT was related to the perception variables, a series of regression analyses was conducted with pedagogical use of ICT as the criterion variable and the other three variables as predictors. To examine which variable had the largest effect on pedagogical use of ICT, we manipulated the orders of these variables' entry into regression equations. As shown in Table 3, availability of resources and support ($R^2 = .03$), perceived usefulness of ICT ($R^2 = .26$), and competence to use ICT ($R^2 = .34$), as the first variable in their respective regression equation, all significantly predicted pedagogical

Table 1. Comparison between male and female teachers on different ICT variables

	Mean (SD) (N=311)	Male	Female		
		Mean (SD)	Mean (SD)	t	p
Competence for ICT Use	3.77(0.61)	3.91(0.62)	3.75(0.59)	1.635	.103
Resources and Support	2.94(0.56)	2.82(0.48)	2.96(0.57)	-1.607	.109
Usefulness of ICT	3.79(0.41)	3.85(0.36)	3.78(0.41)	1.582	.115
Pedagogical Use of ICT	3.68(0.49)	3.79(0.51)	3.66(0.49)	1.060	.290

Table 2. Correlations between ICT-related variables

		1	2	3	4
1	Competence for ICT Use	–			
2	Resources and Support	.17**	–		
3	Usefulness of ICT	.50***	.26***	–	
4	Pedagogical Use of ICT	.57***	.18***	.50***	–

Note. ** $p < .01$ *** $p < .001$

Table 3. Hierarchical Regression Analysis Predicting Pedagogical Use of ICT

Step	Predictor	R^2	Adjusted R^2	R^2 change	F change
1	Resources and Support	.03	.03	.03	11.62***
2	Competence for ICT Use	.34	.34	.31	147.2***
3	Usefulness of ICT	.40	.39	.05	29.33***
1	Usefulness of ICT	.26	.26	.26	111.4***
2	Resources and Support	.26	.26	.00	1.49
3	Competence for ICT Use	.40	.39	.13	70.19***
1	Competence for ICT Use	.34	.33	.34	159.0***
2	Usefulness of ICT	.40	.39	.06	32.64***
3	Resources and Support	.40	.39	.00	.841

*** $p < .001$

use of ICT (all p values < .001). These three predictors together explained about 40.5% of the variance in the criterion variable. However, not all of them had a significant, unique contribution to pedagogical use of ICT. Specifically, as shown in Table 3, over and above resources and support and competence for ICT use, perceived usefulness made a unique contribution to pedagogical use of ICT and explained about 5.7% of its variance ($\Delta F = 29.33$, $p < .001$). After controlling for perceived usefulness and resources and support, competence also significantly and uniquely contributed to ICT use; it explained about 13.6% of its variance ($\Delta F = 70.19$, $p < .001$). Such a unique effect, however, failed to surface for resources and support. As Table 3 shows, after the effects of perceived usefulness and competence were partialed out, the unique effect of resources and support was not significant; it only explained about 0.2% unique proportion of variance in ICT use ($\Delta F = .84$, $p = .36$).

Focus Group Discussion

The FGDs produced informative sharing by teachers of their perceptions of ICT and use of ICT over and beyond the summative, quantitative data yielded by the questionnaire survey. In what follows, we report some converging findings across the FGD sessions. The FGDs were conducted and transcribed in Chinese. Given space limit, we only provide English translations of exemplary excerpts (T = Teacher; R = Research Assistant).

Usefulness of ICT and Strategic Use of ICT

The FGDs revealed positive attitudes among teachers toward ICT in CL education, and many teachers voiced the legitimacy of using ICT particularly in relation to its positive effect on arousing students' interests and engaging students in class, particularly younger children. In Excerpt 1, teachers reported students' strong interests in and excitement about having a class in the computer lab; Excerpt 2 shows how teachers believed that the resources they had used successfully engaged children (T10).

Excerpt 1 [FGD Group 2]:

T10: Students were so happy when they were told that you were going to take them to the computer lab. Sometimes you did not have a plan to conduct a class in the computer lab, but they would come to you asking if they could have their class there today or in the following week.

Excerpt 2 [FGD Group 12]:

T9: They liked it, especially the function of changing a text into a song.
T10: They liked activities for which they could move around. They did not like sitting there listening quietly to their teacher. They wanted to participate in activities.

While acknowledging the usefulness of ICT in engaging students, some teachers also cautioned that it might not always achieve the effects desired and students might lose their interest if ICT were to be used too frequently. In Except 3, T7 cautioned that it might not be wise to use ICT in every class, and suggested that there would need to be some changes. This idea was agreed upon by both T8 and T9. Similar observations were also made by teachers in FGD Group 10 who pointed out that too much use of the computer might not have a sustained effect on attracting students as they might get blasé, threatening the original intent of using ICT. As shown in Excerpt 4, T1 described how her Grade 3 students' interests gradually disappeared after a whole year of everyday use of the computer in class.

Excerpt 3 [FGD Group 9]:

R: Do you think those ICT tools could help increase your students' learning interests?
T7: Can't be used too frequently. If ICT were used too often, students would be like, "this again!" They would be uninterested. I think there should be some change.
R: That means you'd better not use it in every class.
T8: Every class...
T9: The same.... It does not seem much fun. I sometimes use ICT, sometimes don't.

Excerpt 4 [FGD Group 10]:

R: Do you think ICT can have an impact on students' Chinese learning interests?
T1: I think it could have an impact at the beginning, but later students might lose their interests. They have had too much and would no longer feel it was something special. Like the Grade 3 class I am teaching, we use the computer every day, and now they have lost their interests. This instructional method did not tend to be engaging to them. I didn't see they were very interested anymore. At the very beginning, they were very interested. Every day they asked me, "teacher, can we use the computer to have our class?" They were very interested in what they were asked to do, like typing. But now, a year later, they all were too used to that to keep their interest.

In addition to arousing students' interest, some teachers also commented on the direct effect that ICT might have on students' CL learning. Opinions from different perspectives were given. For example, T1 in Excerpt 5 pointed out that ICT could be particularly helpful to CL learning among immigrant children from non-Chinese speaking countries or with no CL exposure at home. T6 in Excerpt 6 shared that *iFlash* books in the computer lab and access to online resources developed by her school were particularly helpful to weaker students by giving them additional practice opportunities and opportunities to consolidate what they had learned.

Excerpt 5 [FGD Group 8]:

T2: We are using *iFlash* books. I think the resources are quite helpful to my students.
T1: I agree with her. I think *iFlash* books are very good to foreigners, like those from the Philippines. Because our country attracts many foreign immigrants, and some speak only English, those ICT resources can help them overcome difficulties in learning Chinese.

Excerpt 6 [FGD Group 3]:

T6: I have a Grade 3 class. It is the worst of all. But, sometimes after we finish a lesson, to consolidate what they have learned, I take them to the computer lab where they can use *iFlash* books, or browse the E-Knowledge website. Our school develops learning materials and makes them accessible there. My students can have more practice of Chinese or have an opportunity to consolidate what they have learned.

However, not all teachers showed agreement on the kind of observations above. A few teachers contended that while ICT-assisted teaching could increase students' interest, it might not necessarily have a direct effect on or bring a greater benefit to teaching and learning than could traditional, non-ICT-mediated pedagogies. It was implied that to achieve its best effect on CL learning, ICT would need to be combined with traditional, non-ICT-based methods. For example, T10 in Excerpt 7 was supportive of the idea that ICT can raise students' interest; however, their interest might be rather aroused by the animations in computer-presented *iFlash* books than in CL learning *per se*. In other words, the effect of using *iFlash* books may only stay at the level of making children curious, because "students like seeing the picture moving;" "whether or not they could recognize characters is a concern." (T10 in Excerpt 7) T3 and T5, in Excerpt 8, raised a similar concern. T3 was concerned that presenting Chinese characters with pictures that represent their meanings electronically, such as on PowerPoint, which could arouse students' interest and attract their attention, might not achieve an effect as good as one that could be obtained with the use of the traditional pedagogy where stroke by stroke demonstration of character structure is made on whiteboard. According to both T3 and T5, students may focus on the pictures presented instead of the characters to be learned – they bypass orthographic processing of the target characters and choose to map sounds (e.g., *yùmǐ*, corn) with meaning by looking only at the picture of corn. Consequently, they would have no idea what 玉米 (*yùmǐ*, corn) meant when the picture was removed.

Excerpt 7 [FGD Group 11]:

R: Do you think ICT, like *Xuele* or *iFlash* books, can arouse students' learning interests?

T10: They can raise their interests, but those interests may not be relevant to Chinese, because I think they are only interested in the animated presentation of a text. The texts in their textbooks cannot move. The teacher clicks on the picture that illustrates a text on the computer, and the picture moves. Students like seeing the picture moving, but whether or not they could recognize characters is a concern.

Excerpt 8 [FGD Group 10]:

T3: Because I don't use the computer very often, my students still keep their interests. When ICT is used in class, they are certainly very excited. However, they tend to forget (authors' note: the characters they have been exposed to) very soon. The traditional method seems to be better in that we demonstrate stroke-by-stoke the structure of a character and students would know how to write that character. If you show a character on a PPT, they would say, *yùmǐ, yùmǐ*. The picture is there showing corn. But after the picture is removed, what? They don't know.

R: So, their interest can be there, but the effect on CL learning is not very good.

T5: You have cute pictures on your PPT. They are paying attention to the pictures, not the characters.

Challenges or Barriers

We presented above some teachers' reservations about using ICT in CL education. These include concerns about whether ICT can have a direct effect on CL learning, whether students can have a sustained interest in ICT-mediated instruction, and whether students are interested in picture animations or CL *per se*, etc. While those concerns certainly have had some implicit influence on teachers' pedagogical decision-making as to the use of ICT, in what follows, we focus on some explicit challenges or barriers to implementing ICT-mediated instruction.

(1) Instructional Resources

One dominant challenge that emerged from the discussions across FGD groups was the lack of instructional resources. Many teachers mentioned that *Xuele*, the website with digital materials accompanying textbooks and the primary ICT resource that is made freely available to schools by the Ministry of Education, was under-developed over and beyond Grades 1 and 2. As shown in both excerpts below, teachers agreed that the resources on *Xuele* for Grades 1 and 2 were rich and developed under careful curricular and instructional considerations. However, they all pointed out that the resources for higher grades were barely useful, because available on *Xuele* for those grades was only a digitized version of the texts in textbooks with their read-alouds, which were uninteresting and could be easily replaced by students looking at their textbook and teachers reading a text aloud to them.

Excerpt 9 [FGD Group 1]:

T3: I think the resources (on *Xuele*) for Grades 1 and 2 are adequate. Those for upper primary grades are barely useful.

T4: From Grade 3 onward, there is little for listening and speaking. Games are very few.

T6: So, teachers would question themselves if there is really a need to use *Xuele* for Grades 3 to 6. The resources for Grades 1 and 2 are fairly good, but after Grade 3, there is little that is useful. The teacher can read aloud a text to students instead of playing the audio file on *Xuele*.

Excerpt 10 [FGD Group 11]:

T6: I think the resources for Grades 1 and 2 were selected and designed with some careful considerations. However, from Grades 3 and 4, the resources online are only audio recordings of texts, nothing else. Frankly, we don't use *Xuele* anymore for Grades 5 and 6 at all. What is good of using the resources there? It would certainly be nice if they could be like those for Grades 1 and 2, but unfortunately they are not.

(2) Time Investment

Another challenge reported by teachers was the large amount of time that they often devoted in designing for ICT-mediated classes. In Excerpt 11, teachers are discussing their use of a computer-based CL teaching and learning opportunity (i.e., *10'C Chinese*) made available to their schools by the Educational Technology Division (ETD) of the Singapore Ministry of Education. One of the objectives of *10'C Chinese* is to improve students' reading skills by making extended reading materials accessible to them[2]. According to T2, T4, and T5, to use the *10'C Chinese* learning platform, teachers would need to spend a lot of time developing reading materials for students as well as preparing lessons that would involve making decisions about selecting appropriate texts as well as designing learning activities for students. In Excerpt 12, T8 shared her experience of using digital devices to record Grade 1 students' Chinese pronunciations and playing their pronunciations on the computer to make them aware of their pronunciation errors and tone differences. While acknowledging the advantage of that pedagogy in raising students' interest, she also complained how technically time-consuming it was.

Excerpt 11 [FGD Group 1]:

T3: Teachers need to work with ETD. They need to select reading materials and put them online. Some editing work is also needed.
R: Teachers also need to edit the materials?
T2: That's right. After we select and edit the materials, we collect them and put them online so that everybody will have access to them.
T4: Teachers need to spend time designing those materials. It often takes a lot of time.
R: But you can do that well in advance, right?
T5: Selecting and editing materials can be done much earlier, but of course you also need to prepare your lessons where you are going to use those materials.

Except 12 [FGD Group 3]:

T8: For the Grade 1 class I previous taught, I mostly focused on oral communication and Pinyin at the beginning of their school year. At that stage, they were not able to operate the computer; so computer-mediated instruction was mostly done using the computer in our regular classroom instead of in a computer lab. I often used digital devices to record my students' pronunciations, and then played the recordings back to them. They then would know which syllable was mispronounced, and how the second and the third tones were different. It was fascinating to them to hear their own pronunciations. Technically, however, it was very time-consuming to design lessons in that way.

(3) Lack of Facilities and Technical Inconvenience

Some teachers also mentioned lack of ICT facilities and technical inconvenience as barriers to their application of ICT. In Excerpt 13, when sharing her thought about the use of online resources provided by the Ministry of Education, T5 indicated that teachers would need time to download them[3], and suggested that a disk with those resources directly provided to teachers. Teachers also complained that the wireless connection in their classrooms was unreliable, not all regular classrooms had a computer, and not all computers in those classrooms were functioning well. Consequently, teachers would need to bring their own laptop to the classroom, which, according to T5, would create a lot of technical inconveniences. T1 in Excerpt 14 also pointed out that ICT use in regular classrooms was often teacher-centric, and students barely had an opportunity to interact or have hands-on practice with the computer. Though she believed that teaching in a computer lab could be very appealing to students, logistically the need was seldom accommodated, due to the very small number of computer labs in her school.

Excerpt 13 [FGD Group 12]:

R: The Ministry of Education provides a variety of instructional materials. I remember those materials are online, right?
T5: But do you know we have to download them? We don't have enough time. There are many problems. I think it would be great if a disk or CD with all those materials could be directly provided to us. I feel it is quite a bother to bring your own laptop to the classroom. Not every classroom has a computer ready for use. Sometimes, the computer runs very slowly. I would then need to bring my own and make it connected. It was quite a hassle.
T6: Wireless connection is there, but you may not be able to get online.

T7: Agree. The reception can be very poor and dicey. In some classrooms, you are able to access the Internet; in others, you are not.

Excerpt 14 [FGD Group 9]:

T1: In our school, I think instructional resources are adequate, but still there are problems. The teacher is operating the computer all the time; students are watching and listening. I tell you, if they could be given opportunities to operate the computer by themselves, they would be very interested. But, time does not allow this to happen. There are usually 3-4 computer labs in a school. How could you make sure all children have opportunities to use them?

(4) High-Stake Examinations

Teachers also pointed out how pressure from preparing students for high-stake examinations had created a barrier to their ICT use, despite their knowledge of the usefulness of ICT and their willingness to use ICT-mediated pedagogies. This is particularly evident in T6's argumentation in Excerpt 15 on the clash between teachers' intentions of pedagogical innovation and the realistic goal of completing the syllabus within a stipulated period of time and preparing students for the Primary School Leaving Examination (PSLE), the score of which determines the prestige of the secondary school where a student can be enrolled. Obviously, the pressure from helping students to score well, and a teaching-to-test culture developed out of such pressure in Singapore constrained teachers' pedagogical space and reduced their efficiency and flexibility of pedagogical use of ICT in CL education. T3 in Excerpt 16 provided an observation similar to what T6 made in Excerpt 15. T5's observation is particularly interesting. According to her, the inadequacy of ICT resources for mid to upper primary grades (Grades 3-6) on *Xuele* seemed to be an outcome of purposeful design by the curriculum officers in the Ministry of Education, rather than an issue of under-development that could and would be resolved by the Ministry of Education. In other words, it was the Ministry of Education's decision that the focus of *Xuele* resources for Grades 3-6 be put on listening and reading comprehension, instead of animated activities like those for Grades 1 and 2, so as to meet the realistic goal of preparing students for the PSLE.

Excerpt 15 [FGD Group 2]:

T6: Frankly, you can organize some interesting activities in Grades 1 and 2. Singing, dancing, everybody is happy. In Grades 3-6, it can't be possible anymore, because teachers need to face the reality of producing good grades. Students need a good score on the PSLE. The teaching methods we just talked about are all useful, but they can't be used in every class. Students learn for examinations. Teachers teach for what is tested. It would be useless to talk about how wonderful the methods are if national examinations like the PSLS were not reformed.

T7: Parents only look at their child's grades.

Excerpt 16 [FGD Group 5]:

T3: I think the resources (on *Xuele*) for Grades 1-3 are fairly good. But they are definitely inadequate for Grades 4-6… To be frank, at the stage of Grades 4-6, you won't have much time to foster students' interests. Instead, you prepare them for examinations.

T5: The syllabus has a lot more for Grades 4-6. I think we don't need to use the computer. It (*Xuele*) is actually very realistic. There is little interesting there. It is always reading comprehension whenever you click on resources there. That's what the Ministry of Education has given us. We play games in Grades 1 and 2, but they all disappear

> in Grades 3-6. Everything is reading, or listening, and after reading or listening, you answer questions.

DISCUSSION

Questionnaire Survey

To understand teachers' perceptions and use of ICT in CL education, we conducted this mixed-methods study on primary school CL teachers in Singapore. Two research questions were addressed, that is, how do CL teachers perceive ICT in CL education in Singapore, and how do their ICT-related perceptions relate to their pedagogical use of ICT? Our online questionnaire survey revealed that the teachers' perceptions of ICT in CL education were overall positive, with means of responses to questionnaire items close to 4 (*agree*). These included their perceived usefulness of ICT and competence for pedagogical use of ICT. The teachers were also positive about their actual pedagogical use of ICT. These findings corroborate those of previous research conducted in Singapore on non-CL teachers. Teo's (2008) survey, for example, found that pre-service teachers in a postgraduate education program in Singapore produced the mean scores of 3.5 and above on all the subscales of a 5-point computer attitude scale. The only ICT variable that did not seem to get clear support from teachers in the present study was resources and support. This finding seems surprising at the first sight, given the Singapore government's heavy investments on ICT infrastructure building and the Ministry of Education's huge efforts to develop ICT instructional resources and make those resources available to teachers (Ng, 2008). A reference to what was revealed through the FGDs, however, may help explain this discrepancy. That is, although the ICT resources have been there (e.g., *Xuele*), they might not, at least as the teachers perceived them qualitatively, be effective in engaging students and bringing about the kind of learning that teachers desired. We will return to this issue when we discuss the findings from the FGDs.

We found that male and female teachers did not differ significantly in perceived usefulness of ICT, competence for ICT use, availability of resources and support, as well as reported pedagogical use of ICT. In addition, we did not find significant correlations of age and years of teaching with any ICT variable. Our correlational analysis, however, revealed that teachers' perceptions of ICT all had significant correlations with their pedagogical use of ICT.

Regression analysis with ICT use as the criterion variable further found that after controlling for the other two of the three predictors, perceived usefulness and competence, but not resources and support, were unique predictors and made a direct contribution to ICT use. Given the close relationship of resources and support with competence and perceived usefulness on one hand, and that of competence and usefulness with ICT use on the other hand, statistically, it might be possible that resources and support could influence ICT use indirectly. Logically this also makes sense, because teachers who believed that there were more resources and support might be more confident in using ICT and thus tended to perceive ICT as more useful (i.e., resources and support as an enabling factor for perceiving ICT to be useful), and consequently, they tended to use ICT more frequently. These findings on in-service CL teachers also corroborate the finding of Teo, Lee, and Chai (2008), which focused on non-CL, pre-service teachers enrolled in several types of preparation programs in the National Institute of Education in Singapore where the CL teachers in the present study received their pre-service training. Teo et al. (2008) found that teachers' perceived usefulness of ICT had the greatest effect on their computer attitude, followed by perceived ease of use, which is close to our measure of teachers' self-perceived competence in dealing with ICT. While facilitating condition, which was defined by

Teo et al. (2008) as a variety of factors including, for example, external support and availability of resource, significantly predicted perceived ease of ICT use – a similar finding emerged in the present study – it failed to predict computer attitude significantly after controlling for perceived usefulness and perceived ease of use. Teo et al. (2008) did not provide an explanation as to why facilitation condition, like the resource and support variable in the current study, failed to uniquely predict computer attitude or intention to use ICT. Instead of claiming that resource and support is not an important factor predictive of ICT use, we would argue that it might be because of the nature of the variable itself. Our conjecture is that facilitating condition is like an enabling factor, which has to be there for teachers either to perceive ICT as useful or eventually to use it in pedagogical practice. However, once it has passed a certain threshold level, how teachers believe about their competence to handle ICT (i.e., perceived ease of using ICT) and the extent to which they think ICT is useful would matter more in determining their pedagogical choice of using ICT.

Focus Group Discussion

To get a more intimate understanding of teachers' perceptions of ICT in CL education, particularly as to why they perceived ICT in the way they did, and why they chose to use, or not to use ICT in their pedagogical practice, we supplemented the questionnaire survey with FGDs with a selected sample of teachers. Some interesting findings emerged.

First, no teacher mentioned that they had never used ICT in CL teaching. This is likely due to the Singapore government's heightened investment in ICT infrastructure building for education and promotion of ICT integration in education (Ng, 2008; Toh & So, 2011). The Singapore Ministry of Education, in particular, has taken great efforts to develop ICT resources for and make them available to teachers, and requires teachers to use those resources through curriculum mandates. In a highly centralized education system like Singapore where educational policies and mandates are made top-down from the Ministry of Education, it is naturally expected that teachers adopt ICT in their pedagogical practice, even though on both quantitative and qualitative dimensions there are variations across teachers' practices.

Second, no teacher from any FGD group indicated competence as a factor that had influenced their perceptions of the usefulness of ICT and their pedagogical use of ICT. Instead of arguing, based on this finding, that competence or knowledge about ICT does not influence ICT use, which would be against the quantitative relationship we established through the questionnaire data, we would like to contend that this lack of mention of ICT competence might be attributed to the possibility that teachers had rarely encountered any difficulty in their pedagogical implementation of ICT. Previous observations of pedagogical practice in Singapore CL classrooms revealed that teachers' use of technology remained at the level of traditional tools, such as PowerPoint and overhead projector (e.g., Liu et al., 2006), which did not seem to require sophisticated skills to operate. In a sense, teachers' comfortable use of those tools at their own choice did not prompt them to report on any possible lack of competence or skills in our FGDs. This, of course, would in no way suggest that Chinese teachers in Singapore are all indeed sophisticated ICT users and are adequately competent to deal with any ICT tool in CL instruction. In the current project, we did not aim to match teachers' perceptions of ICT with their actual classroom use of ICT by observing classroom teaching of a selected sample of teachers. Future research should pursue this line so that an understanding could be obtained about how perceived competence may be related to what teachers actually do in class.

Third, teachers largely quoted ICT's usefulness in engaging students' interests in learning Chinese as the most important reason for their use of ICT, with some pointing out its potential to be particularly useful in addressing the learning needs of low achievers and children with little CL exposure at home. Teachers' decision making on ICT use was largely strategized. For example, a few teachers indicated that it might not be wise to use ICT very frequently, as it would not be able to sustain children's interest; consequently, they chose not to use ICT every day. Others mentioned that ICT might not be able to bring a larger benefit for CL learning than would more traditional pedagogies (see Excerpts 7 and 8 on learning Chinese characters). Thus, their verbal report showed a tendency to blend ICT-mediated pedagogies with traditional pedagogies to achieve maximal effects on student learning. This qualitative evidence shows clear alignment with the quantitative results discussed above: teacher's perceptions and beliefs about ICT influenced their ICT use. Such a finding is not unique to CL teachers in Singapore. Previous studies on teachers in various contexts and cultures revealed that teachers make decisions with an aim to achieve optimal instructional effect on students' learning. Instead of being linearly subjected to mandates at different levels, they adopt stratagems to fine-tune their pedagogy according to their beliefs or on the basis of their everyday diagnosis of students' learning needs and progress (Borg, 2006; Condie & Livingston, 2007).

The variations documented among teachers in ICT use, in addition to being a result of teacher-intrinsic belief and perception factors as discussed above (e.g., voluntarily controlling the frequency of ICT use to sustain students' interests in ICT), could also reflect the influence from teacher-extrinsic factors. This brings us to the discussion of the major challenges or barriers teachers reported that constrained their pedagogical space as to the use of ICT.

The first group of challenges was largely related to resources and support. A variety of factors were reported. For example, there were not enough computer labs, computers in regular classrooms sometimes did not work, the ICT resources provided by the Ministry of Education were not able to engage students in mid to upper primary grades (i.e., qualitatively insufficient) and consequently, teachers sometimes needed to design their own ICT-mediated classes, which consumed a substantial amount of time on top of the already hectic teaching schedule. Those reported challenges echo the findings of some previous studies (Egbert et al., 2002; Lam, 2000; Lim & Khine, 2006). Egbert et al.'s (2002) study on in-service ESL teachers , for example, revealed that teachers reported time, resources, and support as top factors to explain why they barely used or were unable to integrate CALL activities in their teaching. Teachers in Lim and Khine's (2006) study also reported that they needed a large amount of time to prepare ICT-mediated lessons, and they often had difficulty in finishing required curriculum contents within a stipulated number of lessons – sometimes due to failures of ICT equipment, which was often not the case when traditional chalk-and-talk methods were used.

The second major challenge was related to the pressure resulting from meeting the needs of high-stake examinations. Because the participants in the current study were primary school teachers, they reported how the PSLE, the performance on which effectively determines the type of secondary school to which a student can go, constrained their pedagogical space or flexibilities as to using ICT in teaching CL, a core subject area to be tested with other subjects in the PSLE. As shown in Excerpts 15 and 16, teachers were aware of the misalignment between ICT-mediated pedagogy and high-stake examinations that take the traditional paper-and-pencil forms, which, coupled with the pressure to finish mandated curriculum contents within a prescribed period of time, led teachers to control their use of ICT or resort completely to traditional pedagogies. Meeting the need of the PSLE seemed to have an overriding effect on ICT use at the higher grades, which interestingly, according to one teacher, led the Ministry of Education to "manipulate" the form of the ICT-related activities – primarily text-based and comprehension-oriented for upper primary grades – in the online ICT resources provided to teachers.

That teachers' pressure from preparing students for high-stake examinations had an impact on their pedagogical decision-making is not a unique finding of the present study. Hogan et al.'s (2013) study on Secondary School Math and English teachers in Singapore clearly pointed to how the national high-stakes assessment system in the country shaped teachers' instructional practice – traditional teacher-fronted, direct instruction often prevailed in comparison to an instructional strategy of teaching for understanding. The impact of the teaching-to-test culture on ICT adoption by teachers has also been previously reported. Lim and Chai (2008) observed six primary school teachers' computer-mediated teaching and also interviewed those teachers. The study revealed a mismatch between teachers' reported preference of constructivist teaching with ICT and their observed teacher-centric teaching that focused more on information acquisition and regurgitation. A primary reason the teacher provided to explain that inconsistency was their pressure to complete the syllabi within stipulated periods of time so that their students could acquire what was needed for examinations.

CONCLUSION

Teachers are not passive curriculum transmitters; they are active decision makers that develop, define, and reinterpret a curriculum; they are agents of pedagogical change (Clandinin & Connelly, 1992; Shawer, 2010). What teachers do at the classroom level is influenced by what they know, think, and believe. At the same time, their beliefs and perceptions are subjected to the influence of various contextual factors that can be local as well as global (Borg, 2006). Our study on primary school CL teachers in Singapore lends clear support to the need to consider both first-order and second-order factors (Ertmer, 1999, 2005) for addressing pedagogical integration of ICT. With quantitative data from an online questionnaire survey and qualitative data from teachers' FGDs, we revealed that from curriculum mandates of ICT to pedagogical use or non-use of ICT, various factors intrinsic and extrinsic to teachers came into play. It is the inter-play of those factors that determines how and to what extent ICT is pedagogically used. If it is to be acknowledged what teachers do at the level of the classroom shapes the kind of knowledge that students acquire and leads to educational change, achieving the desired effects of learning through ICT integration necessitates consideration of teachers' attitudes and beliefs and the contextual factors that shape them.

ACKNOWLEDGMENT

The data reported in this chapter were drawn from a research project (OER 52/08 ZSH) funded by the Singapore Ministry of Education through its Educational Research Fund Program established with the Office of Education Research at National Institute of Education, to which we would like to express our thanks. We also thank the generous support from the teachers who participated in this study and the hard work of many research assistants. Views expressed in this paper are our own.

REFERENCES

Blake, R. J. (2007). New trends in using technology in the language curriculum. *Annual Review of Applied Linguistics*, *27*, 76–97. doi:10.1017/S0267190508070049

Borg, S. (2006). *Teacher cognition and language education: Research and practice*. London: Continuum.

Borg, S. (2009). Language teacher cognition. In A. Burns, & J. C. Richards (Eds.), *The Cambridge guide to Second Language teacher education* (pp. 163–171). Cambridge: Cambridge University Press.

Clandinin, D. J., & Connelly, F. M. (1992). Teacher as curriculum maker. In P. W. Jackson (Ed.), *Handbook of research on curriculum* (pp. 363–401). New York: Macmillan.

CLCPRC. (2004). *Report of the Chinese Language Curriculum and Pedagogy Review Committee*. Singapore: Singapore Ministry of Education.

Condie, M. E., & Livingston, K. (2007). Blending online learning with traditional approaches: Changing practices. *British Journal of Educational Technology*, *38*, 337–348. doi:10.1111/j.1467-8535.2006.00630.x

Cuban, L. (2001). *Oversold and underused: Computers in the classroom*. Cambridge, MA: Harvard University Press.

Egbert, J., Huff, L., McNeil, L., Preuss, C., & Sellen, J. (2009). Pedagogy, process, and classroom context: Integrating teacher voice and experience into research on technology-enhanced language learning. *Modern Language Journal*, *93*, 754–768. doi:10.1111/j.1540-4781.2009.00971.x

Egbert, J., Paulus, T. M., & Nakamichi, Y. (2002). The impact of CALL instruction on classroom computer use: A foundation for rethinking technology in teacher education. *Language Learning & Technology*, *6*, 108–126.

Ertmer, P., Addison, P., Lane, M., Ross, E., & Woods, D. (1999). Examining teachers' beliefs about the role of technology in the elementary classroom. *Journal of Research on Computing in Education*, *32*, 54–72.

Ertmer, P. A. (1999). Addressing first- and second-order barriers to change: Strategies for technology integration. *Educational Technology Research and Development*, *47*, 47–61. doi:10.1007/BF02299597

Ertmer, P. A. (2005). Teacher pedagogical beliefs: The final frontier in our quest for technology integration? *Educational Technology Research and Development*, *53*, 25–39. doi:10.1007/BF02504683

Ertmer, P. A., Ottenbreit-Leftwich, A., & York, C. (2006). Exemplary technology-using teachers: Perceptions of factors influencing success. *Journal of Computing in Teacher Education*, *23*, 55–61.

Evans, M. J. (2009) (Ed.), Foreign language learning with digital technology. London: Continuum.

Hogan, D., Chan, M., Rahim, R., Kwek, D., Aye, K. M., & Loo, S. C. et al. (2013). Assessment and the logic of instructional practice in Secondary 3 English and mathematics classrooms in Singapore. *Review of Education*, *1*, 57–106. doi:10.1002/rev3.3002

International Society for Technology in Education. (2007). *National educational technology standards for students*. Washington, DC: International Society for Technology in Education.

Lam, Y. (2000). Technophilia vs. technophobia: A preliminary look at why second-language teachers do or do not use technology in their classrooms. *Canadian Modern Language Review*, *56*, 390–420. doi:10.3138/cmlr.56.3.389

Li, L., Zhang, D., & Zhao, S. (2013). Willingness to communicate among Singaporean Chinese children. *Huawen Jiaoxue Yu Yanjiu, 2*, 57-63.

Lim, C. P., & Chai, C. S. (2008). Teachers' pedagogical beliefs and their planning and conduct of computer-mediated classroom lessons. *British Journal of Educational Technology*, *39*, 807–828. doi:10.1111/j.1467-8535.2007.00774.x

Lim, C. P., & Khine, M. S. (2006). Managing teachers' barriers to ICT integration in Singapore schools. *Journal of Technology and Teacher Education*, *14*, 97–125.

Liu, Y., Goh, H. H., & Zhang, D. (2006). A preliminary description of Singapore Chinese Language classrooms. *Shijie Hanyu Jiaoxue, 19*, 97–105.

MTLRC. (2011). *Nurturing active learners and proficient users: Report of the Mother Tongue Languages Review Committee*. Singapore: Ministry of Education.

New London Group. (1996). A pedagogy of multiliteracies: Designing social futures. *Harvard Educational Review, 66*, 60–93.

Ng, E. H. (2008). *Opening address at the International Conference on Teaching and Learning with Technology*. Available from http://www.moe.gov.sg/media/speeches/2008/08/05/opening-address-by-dr-ng-eng-h-1.php

Oldknow, A., Taylor, R., & Tetlow, L. (2010). *Teaching mathematics using ICT*. London: Continuum.

Peters, M. (2006). Developing computer competencies for pre-service language teachers: Is one course enough? In P. Hubbard, & M. Levy (Eds.), *Teacher education in CALL* (pp. 153–165). Philadelphia, PA: John Benjamins. doi:10.1075/lllt.14.14pet

Shawer, S. (2010). Classroom-level curriculum development: EFL teachers as curriculum-developers, curriculum-makers and curriculum-transmitters. *Teaching and Teacher Education, 26*, 173–184. doi:10.1016/j.tate.2009.03.015

Singapore Ministry of Education. (2007). *Chinese Language (Primary) Syllabus*. Singapore: Curriculum Planning and Development Division, Ministry of Education.

Teo, T. (2008). Pre-service teachers' attitudes towards computer use: A Singapore survey. *Australasian Journal of Educational Technology, 24*, 413–424.

Teo, T. (2011). Factors influencing teachers' intention to use technology: Model development and test. *Computers & Education, 57*, 2432–2440. doi:10.1016/j.compedu.2011.06.008

Teo, T., Lee, C. B., & Chai, C. S. (2008). Understanding pre-service teachers' computer attitudes: Applying and extending the technology acceptance model. *Journal of Computer Assisted Learning, 24*, 128–143. doi:10.1111/j.1365-2729.2007.00247.x

Teo, T., & Noyes, J. (2011). An assessment of the influence of perceived enjoyment and attitude on the intention to use technology among pre-service teachers: A structural equation modeling approach. *Computers & Education, 57*, 1645–1653. doi:10.1016/j.compedu.2011.03.002

Thomas, M. (Ed.). (2009). *Handbook of research on Web 2.0 and second language learning*. Hershey, PA: Information Science Reference. doi:10.4018/978-1-60566-190-2

Toh, Y., & So, H. J. (2011). ICT reform initiatives in Singapore schools: A complexity theory perspective. *Asia Pacific Education Review, 12*, 345–357. doi:10.1007/s12564-010-9130-0

Warschauer, M. (2001). Millennialism and media: Language, literacy, and technology in the 21st century. *AILA Review, 14*, 49–59.

Zhao, Y., & Frank, K. (2003). Technology uses in schools: An ecological perspective. *American Educational Research Journal, 40*, 807–840. doi:10.3102/00028312040004807

Zhao, Y., Puge, K., Sheldon, S., & Byers, J. L. (2002). Conditions for classroom technology innovations. *Teachers College Record, 104*, 482–515. doi:10.1111/1467-9620.00170

ADDITIONAL READING

Borg, S. (2006). *Teacher cognition and language education: Research and practice*. London: Continuum.

Cuban, L. (2001). *Oversold and underused: Computers in the classroom*. Cambridge, MA: Harvard University Press.

Egbert, J., Huff, L., McNeil, L., Preuss, C., & Sellen, J. (2009). Pedagogy, process, and classroom context: Integrating teacher voice and experience into research on technology-enhanced language learning. *Modern Language Journal*, *93*, 754–768.

Egbert, J., Paulus, T. M., & Nakamichi, Y. (2002). The impact of CALL instruction on classroom computer use: A foundation for rethinking technology in teacher education. *Language Learning & Technology*, *6*, 108–126.

Ertmer, P. A. (1999). Addressing first- and second-order barriers to change: Strategies for technology integration. *Educational Technology Research and Development*, *47*, 47–61.

Ertmer, P. A. (2005). Teacher pedagogical beliefs: The final frontier in our quest for technology integration? *Educational Technology Research and Development*, *53*, 25–39.

Hubbard, P., & Levy, M. (2006) (Eds.) Teacher education in CALL. Philadelphia, PA: John Benjamins.

Kassen, M. A., Lavine, R. Z., Murphy-Judy, K., & Peters, M. (2007). (Eds.) Preparing and developing technology-proficiency L2 teachers. CALICO Monograph Series Volume 6. San Marcos, TX: CALICO.

Lam, Y. (2000). Technophilia vs. technophobia: A preliminary look at why second-language teachers do or do not use technology in their classrooms. *Canadian Modern Language Review*, *56*, 390–420.

Lim, C. P., & Khine, M. S. (2006). Managing teachers' barriers to ICT integration in Singapore schools. *Journal of Technology and Teacher Education*, *14*, 97–125.

Teo, T. (2011). Factors influencing teachers' intention to use technology: Model development and test. *Computers & Education*, *57*, 2432–2440.

Vrasidas, C., & Glass, G. V. (2005). (Eds.). Current Perspectives on Applied Information Technologies: Preparing Teachers to Teach with Technology. Greenwich, CT: Information Age Publishing.

Yamamoto, J., Kush, J. C., Lombard, R., & Hertzog, C. J. (2010). (Eds.). Technology implementation and teacher education: Reflective models. Hershey, PA: Information Science Reference.

Zhao, Y., & Frank, K. (2003). Technology uses in schools: An ecological perspective. *American Educational Research Journal*, *40*, 807–840.

Zhao, Y., Puge, K., Sheldon, S., & Byers, J. L. (2002). Conditions for classroom technology innovations. *Teachers College Record*, *104*, 482–515.

KEY TERMS AND DEFINITIONS

Chinese as a Second Language: Chinese learned as an additional, non-primary language. In Singapore, due to the status ascribed to English as the medium of school instruction, a majority of Chinese students nowadays speak English, instead of Chinese, their ethnic language at home, and they learn Chinese as a Second Language in school.

First-Order Factor: A term that refers to social and institutional factors that shape what teachers do and do not do with regard to technological integration, such as policy initiatives, curriculum mandates, school leadership, availability of facilities and instructional resources, etc.

Focus Group Discussion: a qualitative research method in which people work in a group to share and discuss their perceptions, beliefs, and attitudes toward something, often under the facilitation of the researcher.

Primary School Leaving Examination (PSLE): a high-stake examination in Singapore that all sixth graders need to take. PSLE score has a great impact on the type of secondary school in which a student can be enrolled. The PSLE has been reported to lead to a prevalence of teacher-centered and didactic pedagogies in primary schools, especially at upper primary grades, in Singapore.

Second-Order Factor: a term used to refer to factors intrinsic to teachers that create barriers to change or enablers that facilitate change in technology integration, such as teachers' knowledge, beliefs, and attitudes.

ENDNOTES

1 Refer to the Singapore Ministry of Education's website for a list of the ICT resources developed for Chinese Language: http://www.moe.gov.sg/resources.

2 For more information about 10'C Chinese, please visit its website: http://10c.sg/cos/o.x?c=/etd_cep/user&func=login

3 It was *Xuele* that was under discussion there. Some resources on *Xuele* can but do not have to be downloaded; all resources can be directly accessible with Internet connection. Based on the discussion that followed T5, we predicted that she might have had the problem of poor wireless connection in classrooms, as did T6 and T7. That was probably why she mentioned the need to download *Xuele* resources and use her laptop computer to present the resources to students.

Chapter 12
Use of Computer Technology for Writing Consultations:
Tutors' Opinions and Implications

Cynthia Lee
University of Hong Kong, Hong Kong

ABSTRACT

This chapter investigates the use of computer technology for writing consultations from the tutors' perspective. Tutors' opinions of the hybrid (i.e., a combination of face-to-face and virtual consultations) and the virtual consultation modes in an English writing enhancement service in a university in Hong Kong were collected. Questionnaires were administered to 10 tutors who had used the two consultation modes. It was found that the majority of the tutors were in favor of the two modes, and that they appreciated the benefits of online writing consultations and the text-only consultation platform design. However, they also expressed reservations about replacing the traditional face-to-face writing consultations with computers, because they could not see much increase in tutee-tutor interactions via the two consultation modes. In light of their opinions, recommendations are made to improve the text-only consultation platform and to develop tutors' professional knowledge and pedagogies for online writing consultations.

INTRODUCTION

Computers are a useful and effective teaching and learning tool in education, mainly because they provide convenient information access, effective communication, synchronous and asynchronous learning (Sife, Lwoga, & Sanga, 2007), and increased learning motivation (Son, 2007; Warschauer, 1997). Computer Technology (CT) has been enthusiastically used by language teachers to promote language skills in the classroom.

In spite of computers' versatility and teachers' enthusiastic use of CT in the classroom, research on the use of computers for instructional purposes beyond the classroom, one aspect of which involves writing consultations, is scarce. This chapter focuses on the use of CT for English writing consultations in the context of higher education. First, the author describes the design of an online English writing consultation system in a university in Hong Kong. Then, she reports on 10 writing tutors' opinions of two online writing consulta-

DOI: 10.4018/978-1-4666-6174-5.ch012

tion modes — namely, the virtual and the hybrid modes — offered via the Internet. With reference to the collected opinions, the author recommends some areas for improvement in the text-only consultation platform, and in the related social and pedagogical skills for online writing tutors.

BACKGROUND

Using CT in Language Teaching and Writing Consultations: Teachers' Attitudes and Potential Problems

With the advent of the computer and the Internet in the 20th century, teachers are increasingly using ICT, including, but not limited to, videos, blogs, message boards, and computer games to optimize teaching and learning in education. In language education, interactive computer software and learning websites have been developed to help second/foreign language (L2) learners to better acquire the target language (Lee, Wong, Lee, & Cheung, 2009). Research studies have reported the success of using computers to learn oral and listening skills (AbuSeileck, 2007; Chiu, Liou, & Yeh, 2007; Romeo, 2008), writing skills (Braine, 2004; Colby & Colby, 2008; Lee et al., 2009, 2013; Yeh, Liou, & Li, 2007), vocabulary (Li, 2010), independent learning skills (Groß & Wolff, 2001), and distance language-learning skills (Comas-Quinn, Arcos, & Mardomingo, 2012). The success of the new instructional technique, to a certain extent, rests on language teachers' beliefs and perceptions (Abdullah, Abidin, Wong, Majid, & Atan, 2006).

Many surveys and interviews on in-service English teachers' attitudes and perceptions toward the use of computers have been conducted (Abdullah et al., 2006; Alshumaimeri, 2008; Krish, 2008; Park & Son, 2009). Findings showed that the majority of English school teachers and university professors in Asia had a positive attitude toward such CT use, and that they felt that computers were a useful teaching tool. There were many online materials, and they were willing to integrate and implement computers into their classrooms. Despite the positive and proactive attitudes, the results also pointed to some potential internal and external barriers, such as lack of time, financial, and administrative support from the school or government (Alshumaimeri, 2008; Lee, 2000; Park & Son, 2009), as well as students' communication preferences and readiness to use online technology for learning (Towndrow, 2004). The wealth of online materials and language teachers' enthusiasm, however, may not guarantee success in the use of CT for writing consultations.

Writing consultation plays a role in L2 learning because writing is a demanding task for L2 learners who are required to use the target language to perform academic communication. Writing consultation is important for L2 learners because they can acquire knowledge about writing and talk about their own problems with tutors (Harris, 1995). A large number of writing consultation studies concentrate on face-to-face tutorials, identifying sequential organization (Lee, 2012), writing tutors' behaviors and tutorial features (Ewert, 2009; Lee, 2000; Thonus, 1999, 2004; Waring, 2005). There has been discussion about the development and operation of online writing labs (Rilling, 2005), the different features of face-to-face and text-only online consultation environment (Fitze, 2006), and online tutor training frameworks (Hewett, 2010; Hubbard & Levy, 2006). Some notable online consultation features reported by various researchers include the asynchronicity of communication, lack of verbal clues and body language in online communication, language tutors' technical knowledge to manage online oral and written communication (Hampel & Stickler, 2005), longer average length of online tutoring sessions and specific techniques to manage teacher-student interactions in the electronic space (Breuch & Racine, 2000), and the direct feedback giving strategies (Hewett, 2010). Research on the use of CT for writing consultation is, however, relatively scarce (Lee, 2011).

Online Writing Consultations: A Hong Kong Context

Face-to-face writing consultation or support services are provided in local institutions. A new English writing service which aimed to re-energize its traditional, face-to-face writing service for L2 undergraduates and postgraduates in a university in Hong Kong was initiated in 2009. The new writing service has been reported previously (Lee, 2011). For the purpose of completeness, a brief description of the service and the three consultation modes is provided below.

The new writing service consisted of three consultation modes, namely (1) face-to-face consultation mode, (2) virtual consultation mode (only online consultations are provided via the text-based consultation platform – the Message Board), and (3) hybrid consultation mode (a combination of face-to-face and online consultation sessions where online sessions are conducted via the Message Board). The new writing service allows students to choose and register online for only one type of consultation mode in each semester. Each mode provides a maximum of five consultation sessions for a registered undergraduate student in one semester and a maximum of eight sessions for a registered postgraduate student in one academic year. When a student registers online, the computer system of the writing service asks him/her to fill in his/her available timeslots for consultations and the reason for joining the service for tutors' reference. Then the system automatically matches a student's available schedule provided by him/her with tutors' available timeslots, assigns a tutor for the five or eight consultation sessions, and arranges the first session. Before meeting the assigned tutor, each student is required to submit a written text for diagnostic purpose and is encouraged to indicate some areas of concern on the system (Figure 1). The tutor will discuss the text in the first consultation session and will address the student's concerns in the subsequent sessions.

Students who have chosen the face-to-face mode will meet the assigned tutors at their offices according to the given schedule. Students who have chosen the virtual consultation will interact with tutors online via the Message Board (see Figure 1). Students who have chosen the hybrid consultation mode will meet tutors and agree on the number of face-to-face and online consultation sessions (e.g., two face-to-face + one online + two face-to-face consultation sessions). The online consultation sessions of the hybrid mode are also conducted through the Message Board. The Message Board allows students to submit writings in text files, receive written feedback, post questions, and discuss with their tutors through the writing spaces. Both tutors and students can either write to each other simultaneously at an agreed upon time or write to each other according to their availability. The former type of communication – synchronous text-based communication – requires tutors' and students' special effort to schedule the consultation and finish it in the writing spaces in a short period of time. The latter type – asynchronous communication – is done flexibly and one consultation may spread across a period of time, say from a few hours to one week. The Message Board also provides links to other self-access language resources such as the online reading, speaking, writing and listening websites for independent learning, and the institution's language enquiry forum. No matter what type of communication tutors and students have selected for online consultations, both parties enjoy flexibility in discussions and experience an alternative teaching and learning method by means of CT.

When a tutor finishes one session of the face-to-face, hybrid or virtual consultation, s/he completes an online report provided on the teacher interface for official recording purposes. The online report requests the tutor to (1) indicate the student's weakness(es) in the areas of vocabulary, grammar, organization, and content in the appropriate

Figure 1. A screenshot of the text-only consultation platform – Message Board for tutor-tutee interactions in the virtual consultation mode and the online consultation sessions of the hybrid consultation mode

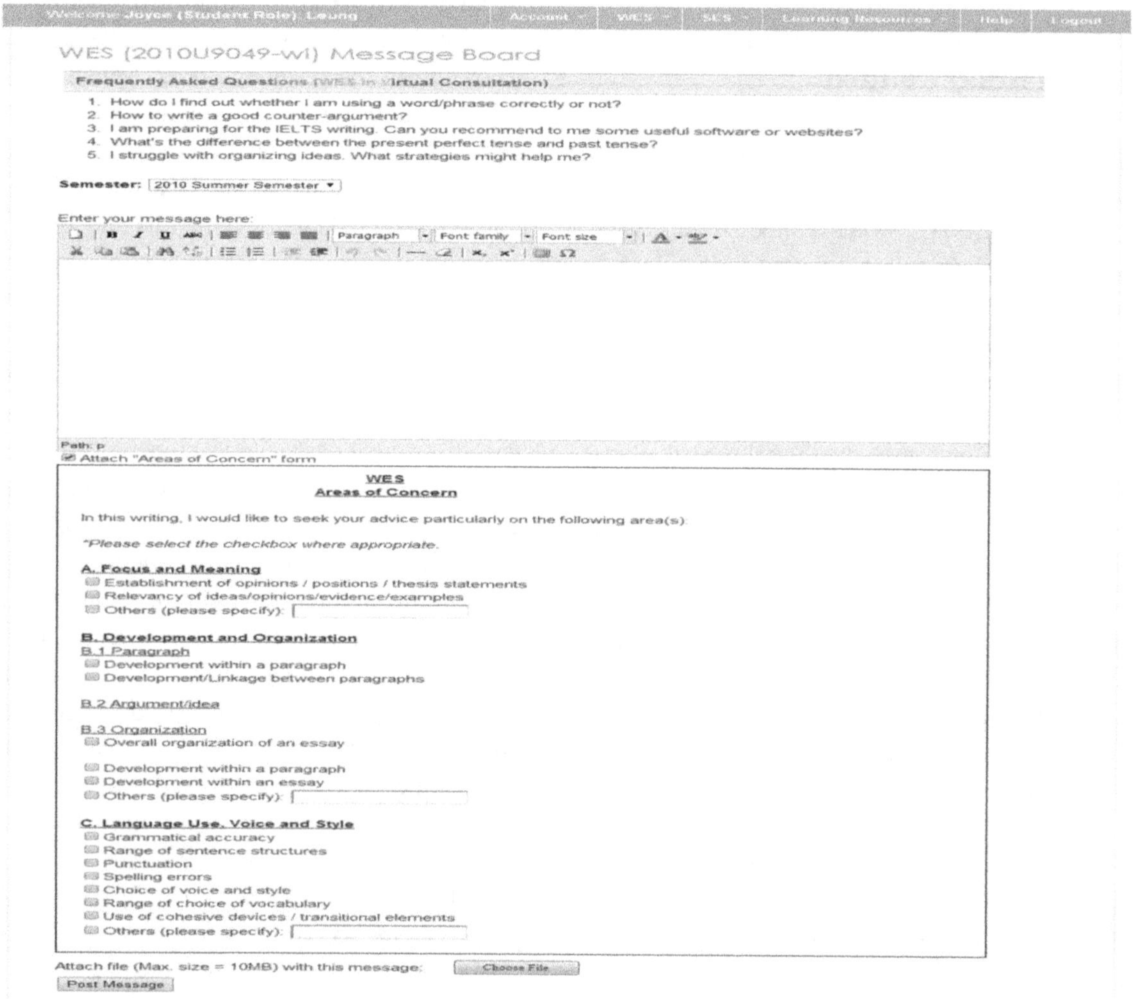

box(es) (e.g., word form for vocabulary); (2) write some comments that can be viewed by students when they access the report (obligatory); and (3) write specific comments for the tutor's reference (optional).

The new online registration and consultation system took approximately one year to develop and pilot. The two new consultation modes, together with the traditional face-to-face mode, were finally launched in fall 2010. The hybrid mode gained its popularity gradually. Table 1 summarizes the total number of undergraduate and postgraduate students who registered for the three modes from AY2010-2011 to AY2012-2013.

The registration rate of the virtual mode was comparatively lower than that of the face-to-face and the hybrid mode. Lee (2011) suggested that the lower registration rate of the virtual mode might be due to the students' previous teacher-centered learning experiences, and the sense of security they could obtain from face-to-face tutor-tutee interactions. Additionally, she explored the students' views and accounts of their preferred modes, followed by some discussions

Table 1. Total number of students and percentage of students who used the three consultation modes in each academic year since inception

	AY2010–2011		AY2011–2012		AY2012–2013	
	N	%	N	%	N	%
Face-to-face consultation mode	76	59%	41	46%	33	46%
Hybrid consultation mode	42	33%	44	49%	49	55%
Virtual consultation mode	11	8%	5	5%	7	8%

and evaluations of their learning behaviors and online learning culture. The increase in usage rate of the hybrid consultation was an indication of the success in integrating online consultation into traditional writing consultation. The increase reflected students' willingness to experience the new consultation mode and a gradual shift of their learning method. In an attempt to expand understanding from the tutors' perspective, the following research questions guided this research:

1. What are the writing tutors' opinions on the hybrid and the virtual consultation modes and the text-only consultation platform (i.e., Message Board)?
2. What are the writing tutors' opinions on the use of computers for writing consultations?

METHODS

Participants' Profiles

The survey questionnaires (Appendix A) were administered to 10 English writing tutors who had used the hybrid and the virtual writing consultation modes in addition to the face-to-face consultation mode in AY2012-2013. The tutors are full-time teaching staff whose responsibilities are to teach regular credit-bearing English proficiency courses and perform other assigned teaching-related duties, one of which is writing consultations. The 10 tutors, three males and seven females, completed and returned the survey questionnaires. As reported by them in the first part of the questionnaires, five of them had one to five years of teaching experience, whereas five had more than 10 years of teaching experience. Six tutors had one to five years of consultation experience while four had more than 10 years of consultation experience. Nine tutors had extensive experience in using computers for language learning and teaching.

Among the 10 tutors, five had used the hybrid consultation mode before. Four of those five tutors had used the mode for at least two years and one had less than one year of experience. Three of tutors provided one to five hours of consultation, one provided six to 10 hours and one provided 16 to 20 hours in a semester. With respect to virtual instruction, five tutors had used the virtual consultation mode before. Three had one year of virtual consultation mode experience and provided one to five hours of consultation in a semester, whereas two had two and three years of experience and provided six to 10 hours of consultation in a semester. All tutors were allowed to choose any type(s) of consultation mode(s) according to their preference and availability. To help tutors to familiarize themselves with the service or to update them on the logistics of the writing service, a brief introduction about the Message Board, appointment procedure, and online report was usually given to writing tutors, particularly novice or newly joined tutors, at the beginning of each semester.

Survey Questionnaire

A survey questionnaire was developed to collect opinions from the tutors who have used the hybrid and virtual consultation modes. The questionnaire was divided into five parts (see Appendix A). The first part involved some personal background information, such as gender, teaching and consultation experiences, and computer knowledge. The second part concerned the tutors' teaching beliefs, philosophies, and interests in using computers to assist language learning and teaching. The third part invited the tutors to rate the functions and importance of the hybrid and the virtual consultation modes on a five-point Likert scale from 1 (*least agree*) to 5 (*strongly agree*), commented on the use of each mode for writing consultation, and stated the necessary skills for tutors for effective online consultation. The fourth part asked the tutors to rate the degree of user-friendliness of the Message Board and the online report on a five-point Likert scale from 1 (*least user-friendly*) to 5 (*very user-friendly*). The last part solicited their opinions on the possibility of replacing face-to-face consultations with computer interactions.

To answer the two research questions, the frequency rate of each survey question was calculated. The tutors' written comments were compiled, analyzed and quoted for illustrations whenever necessary.

RESULTS

Opinions of the Use of the Hybrid and the Virtual Consultation Modes and the Text-Only Consultation Platform (i.e., Message Board)

All of the tutors believed that computers were a teaching tool and that computers complemented classroom instruction in language teaching. Seven of 10 tutors believed that computers were an aid for communication. One tutor felt that computers could be seen as a pathway to new modes of teaching. The tutors began to express an interest in computer-assisted language learning and teaching during their undergraduate studies or teaching. They highly valued communicative language teaching, task-based learning, and collaborative learning. Two tutors stated that they still adopted the direct and audio-lingual methods, and formal grammar instruction. Regarding their expectations of online writing consultations, three tutors preferred tutees to take the initiative to ask and interact with teachers, and expected them to be independent in their learning. Two believed that tutees should have learning incentives. One tutor stated that he attempted to engage tutees in meaningful dialogues and specific task-based writing assignments to make the writing process more beneficial to the tutees involved. Nevertheless, three tutors felt that their language-teaching methods were limited by online writing consultations, as the text-based online consultation process did not seem to favor too much collaboration or interaction. They found face-to-face consultations more effective than online consultations, as the latter only worked well on highly motivated tutees. The following are two tutors' comments that show how their teaching philosophies affect the way in which they handle online consultations.

Since I emphasize interactions and collaborations, I expect my students to take the initiative to raise questions and interact with me. Questions should not be raised by me only. They should have learning incentives. (Tutor 1)

I prefer communicative and task-based teaching. Thus I prefer face-to-face consultation. To me, the online mode is less effective. (Tutor 2)

Eight of the 10 hybrid- and virtual-mode tutors reported being satisfied (rating = 4) or very

Table 2. Participants' degree of satisfaction toward the use of the hybrid and virtual consultation modes

	Least Agree				Strongly Agree
	1	2	3	4	5
Hybrid consultation mode	0%	20%	0%	60%	20%
Virtual consultation mode	20%	0%	0%	40%	40%

satisfied (rating = 5) with the use of the two consultation modes (see Table 2).

Four of five tutors from each mode agreed (rating = 4) and strongly agreed (rating = 5) that the mode encouraged tutees and tutors to seek and provide consultations, and to experience an alternative learning and consultation mode (see Tables 3 and 4). Two hybrid-mode and four virtual-mode tutors agreed (rating = 4) and strongly agreed (rating = 5) that the mode complemented face-to-face learning. However, when they were asked about interactions between tutors and tutees, only two hybrid-mode and one virtual-mode tutors agreed and strongly agreed that the new modes enabled/encouraged tutees to interact more frequently with their tutors. The others remained either neutral or disagreed. Nevertheless, three virtual-mode tutors agreed that tutors were encouraged to interact more frequently with tutees.

Two hybrid-mode teachers, who rated the functions of the mode as a 1 or a 2, stated that tutees did not respond to their questions. They did not bother to ask questions, answer questions, or to seek clarifications. One virtual-mode teacher tutees noted that some tutees did not access the platform frequently. The tutors, to some extent, were discouraged by tutees' low levels of commitment to online consultations.

As seen in the tutors' written comments, two tutors felt that the virtual consultation mode was convenient, efficient, and beneficial to tutees because they could approach each other according to their own schedules. However, four tutors stated that such freedom and flexibility also made consultation less personal. Few virtual consultation-mode tutees would finish the five or eight consultations provided by the service. The others stopped submitting writings after one to two times of consultations. They suspected that it took longer for tutees to understand their major problems, particularly when tutors commented on organization or paragraph coherence. Sometimes tutees could not understand the tutors' feedback and could not improve the essay.

In spite of the challenges, one tutor felt that the introduction of the virtual and the hybrid consultation modes alerted her to think of some ways to increase the frequency rate of tutor–tutee online interactions and to stimulate tutees' responses. In contrast, another tutor stated that an online writing tutor became a resource person or an editor, and that existing student–teacher relationships grew worse. There was little that a tutor could do through computers when a student was not motivated or willing to participate.

The tutor's role has been alerted, I believe. In the face-to-face and the hybrid modes, the tutor is more of a teacher, providing instruction in improving writing. In the online mode, the tutor's role seems to lessen, and instead, the tutor becomes more of a resource, like a librarian or an editing service. Part of the student–teacher relationship that existed previously seems reduced. (Tutor 10)

A tutor made a further suggestion in a follow-up email. She suggested allowing an intervention of face-to-face discussion once if a tutee had serious writing problems or if a tutor felt that the arrangement would be most beneficial to his/her tutee. Some tutors mentioned a number of skills and knowledge that were required to provide effective

Table 3. Participants' level of agreement regarding the functions of the hybrid consultation mode

The hybrid consultation mode enables/encourages tutees to:					
	Least Agree				Strongly Agree
	1	2	3	4	5
a. Seek consultations according to their learning agendas, schedules, and pace.	0%	0%	20%	60%	20%
b. Experience an alternative learning and consultation mode.	0%	0%	20%	60%	20%
c. Complement face-to-face learning.	20%	0%	20%	20%	40%
d. Interact more frequently with their tutors.	0%	20%	40%	20%	20%
The hybrid consultation mode enables/encourages tutors to:					
	Least Agree				Strongly Agree
	1	2	3	4	5
a. Provide consultations according to their schedules and pace.	0%	0%	20%	60%	20%
b. Experience an alternative learning and consultation mode.	0%	0%	20%	60%	20%
c. Complement face-to-face learning.	20%	0%	20%	20%	40%
d. Interact more frequently with their tutees.	0%	20%	40%	20%	20%

Table 4. Participants' level of agreement regarding the functions of the virtual consultation mode

The virtual consultation mode enables/encourages tutees to:					
	Least Agree				Strongly Agree
	1	2	3	4	5
a. Seek consultations according to their learning agendas, schedules, and pace.	0%	0%	0%	20%	80
b. Experience an alternative learning and consultation mode.	0%	0%	20%	0%	80
c. Complement face-to-face learning.	0%	0%	20%	20%	60
d. Interact more frequently with their tutors.	20%	20%	40%	20%	0
The virtual consultation mode enables/ encourages tutors to:					
	Least Agree				Strongly Agree
	1	2	3	4	5
a. Provide consultations according to their schedules and pace.	0%	0%	20%	40%	40%
b. Experience an alternative learning and consultation mode.	0%	0%	20%	0%	80%
c. Complement face-to-face learning.	20%	20%	0%	60%	0%
d. Interact more frequently with their tutees.	20%	20%	0%	60%	0%

Table 5. Participants' ratings regarding the user-friendliness of the message board

	Least User-Friendly				Very User-Friendly
	1	2	3	4	5
To what extent do you think the online tutor–tutee platform is user-friendly?	0%	0%	40%	50%	10%
To what extent do you think the online report is useful to tutors?	0%	10%	20%	60%	10%

online writing consultations. The suggested skills and knowledge could be broadly categorized into three areas; namely, technical knowledge, pedagogical skills, and essential personal qualities of an online writing tutor. Technical knowledge included (1) basic IT skills such as the use of track changes, and (2) familiarity with the institution's online consultation system and operation. Pedagogical skills referred to the skills to motivate students to respond to tutors' messages. Finally, tutors felt that having the patience and discipline to write comments clearly were important aspects. A tutor also noticed that there were some differences between online communication and commentary skills and face-to-face skills. However, she was not sure what the differences were.

Seven writing tutors thought that the Message Board and the online report were user-friendly as shown in Table 5.

Opinions on the Use of Computers for Writing Consultations

In spite of their positive evaluations, six tutors believed that CT could not replace face-to-face consultations, three adopted a neutral stance, and only one was optimistic. In summary, the tutors felt that computers were a useful teaching tool for language teaching and communication, and they had a positive attitude toward the use of CT in teaching. They highly valued interactions with students and their belief shaped their expectations on tutor-student interactions when they interacted via the Message Board. Eight of 10 tutors were satisfied with the hybrid and the virtual consultation modes, and they welcomed the new experience. However, they found that students did not fully utilize the new learning opportunity through the Message Board, and online consultations did not seem to complement face-to-face instructions. Therefore, six of the 10 tutors did not think that online consultations could replace face-to-face consultations.

DISCUSSION

The tutors' opinions seemed to indicate their reservations about the use of CT for writing consultations. Their reservations may have been caused by multiple factors such as the design of the Message Board and online consultation pedagogy. In the remainder of this chapter, the author discusses the multiple factors in relation to the previous studies on the use of CT for language learning. Suggestions to review and improve the text-only consultation platform design, and consider initial and continuing tutor training to better understand the differences between face-to-face and online consultations are made.

Reservations about Using CT for Writing Consultations

The surveyed writing tutors generally agreed that online writing consultations via either the hybrid or the virtual consultation mode were beneficial to tutors and tutees due to their flexibility and convenience. These two consultation modes complemented face-to-face learning and were a new experience (see Tables 3 and 4). As seven of the 10 tutors had extensive experience in using computers for language learning and teaching, and when considering their beliefs in communicative language teaching, collaborative, and task-based learning, it is reasonable to assume that they were enthusiastic and eager to interact with tutees online, and had the same positive perceptions towards the use of computers for language teaching as many English language teachers do in the literature (Abdullah et al., 2006; Alshumaimeri, 2008; Krish, 2008; Lee, 2000; Park & Son, 2009).

Nevertheless, the survey results showed that the majority of the hybrid and virtual consultation mode tutors did not feel that the two new consultation modes encouraged tutees to interact more frequently with their tutors through the Message Board. Instead, tutors interacted more frequently with their tutees (see Tables 3 and 4). Their ratings were consistent with their written comments. The tutors' reservations appear to be related to the tutees' inactive learning behaviors. Such behavior contradicted many tutors' expectations, which, in return, made online consultations become passive. As stated by the writing tutors, some tutees did not access the Message Board, and some seldom took the initiative to ask any questions in writing when they received their tutors' written feedback. This one-way, short and inactive communication can make it difficult for tutors to continue, and can reduce the effectiveness of online consultations. Tutors' initiation will fail if tutees do not write back. Tutees' low motivation is seen to have weakened the tutor's role and has affected the tutor's confidence in using online consultations. In addition, writing feedback clearly is very time consuming for tutors and asking questions by tutees who are weak in writing is a very demanding task. Perhaps these explain why synchronous written communication was not mentioned in the returned questionnaires. In view of all these factors, six tutors were not optimistic and three adopted a neutral stance regarding the replacement of face-to-face consultations entirely by online consultations.

The tutees' inactive learning behavior with regard to tutors' comments may be caused by the lack of verbal clues and body language in online communication – one of the online communication features reported in the CT literature (Hampel & Stickler, 2005). Without any or frequent face-to-face interactions with tutors, tutees may tend to delay responses, resulting in longer length for each online consultation session and lowering the effectiveness of online consultations. Although many tutors have some experience in using computers for classroom teaching and face-to-face consultations and have attended the introductory session, there is still a need to familiarize them with online tutoring techniques because the techniques to manage tutor-tutee interactions and feedback giving strategies in the electronic space have been shown to be specific and different from those in traditional face-to-face consultations (Breuch & Racine, 2000; Hewett, 2010). The tutors have indeed noticed some differences between online and face-to-face consultations and online tutoring problems, such as spending a lot of time on writing clear written feedback on language, content and organization. To better prepare tutors for online consultations, two recommendations that address both technical and tutor training issues are made. The first recommendation is to improve the text-only consultation platform - Message Board to make consultation more interactive and personal. The second one is to develop training for online writing tutors so they may better understand the tutor–tutee online discourse and interaction patterns, and the differences between face-to-face and online consultations. It is this that we turn to next.

PRACTICAL IMPLICATIONS

Improving the Text-Only Consultation Platform: Message Board

As shown in the survey results, a great majority of the tutors were in favor of the communicative teaching or interactive approach. Their preferred language-teaching method has lent some support to the use of computers for writing consultations, as computers provide convenient access and synchronous communication. Nevertheless, the Message Board which provides only writing spaces did not seem to attract tutors and tutees to use the synchronous type of communication. Moreover, tutees' infrequent access to the Message Board and inactive learning behavior further limits the effectiveness of online writing consultations. In view of this, a tutor suggested installing an instant-messaging system such as webcams, live voice, or video chat to the existing text-only platform. The installation can certainly encourage both tutors and tutees to speak and hear each other in real time conversations. It can allow tutors to explain their feedback and answers tutees' quick questions while at their computers. More importantly, tutees who have difficulty articulating their questions in a text-only consultation platform can ask via the Web. Although the greatest challenge between both parties is to find a common time at which to complete a consultation, the instant-messaging system can provide an additional choice for both parties, save on their writing time, and make consultations more interactive and individualized. In this light, online consultations will not become an editing or proofreading service for tutees, and this will be a felicitous experience for tutors who prefer to have discussions with tutees.

Providing Initial and On-Going Tutor Training

Online consultations are found to be challenging to the experienced writing tutors, particularly in managing online written feedback and communication with students. It may be an even more difficult task for new or novice writing tutors who have little or no writing consultation experience. Thus, researchers have called for tutor training specific to online writing spaces. Their recommendations include helping tutors to understand their role (Breuch & Racine, 2000), enrich their technical and pedagogical CALL knowledge and skills (Hubbard & Levy, 2006) and interpersonal social skills (Hampel & Stickler, 2005), and write direct and focused written feedback (Hewett, 2010) so that tutors can develop a personal teaching style. In this light, appropriate guidance and training for both new/ novice and experienced writing tutors are deemed necessary. Based on the researchers' recommendations and the findings, initial workshops are recommended for new/ novice writing tutors, whereas on-going workshops would be arranged for both new/novice and experienced writing tutors throughout the academic year.

Initial workshops can help new tutors to (1) familiarize themselves with the institution's online consultation platform and (2) understand the benefits and constraints of different consultation modes such as students' reticence and online behavior. All of these assist tutors in projecting realistic and appropriate expectations onto online writing consultations, and enable them to understand their roles better. In the on-going workshops, writing tutors would be encouraged to share and discuss the successful and unsuccessful encounters in encouraging tutees to write to tutors, respond to tutors' feedback and continue online consultations, as well as addressing some potential factors affecting success and failure for online writing consultations. With the initial and on-going training workshops/sessions, discussion, and sharing, it is hoped that each online writing tutor will develop a personal consultation style (Hampel & Stickler, 2005) and better understand their role (Breuch & Racine, 2000), and that the online consultation culture will flourish.

CONCLUSION AND DIRECTIONS FOR FURTHER RESEARCH

Online consultation via the hybrid and the virtual modes is a new route. The number of students who registered and used the two modes, particularly the hybrid mode, has soared over the past three years. As shown in the survey, both consultation modes allow for flexibility in teaching and learning via the Message Board. The extent of the effectiveness of online consultations, however, is partly restricted by the text-only consultation platform – Message Board, and is partly caused by the tutees' motivation to pursue learning and respond to their tutors' written feedback. Tutors feel that their role in online consultations has become a passive one. Therefore, the majority of them do not think that online consultations can replace face-to-face consultations. Installing an instant-messaging mechanism seems to be a way to improve the Message Board design and address the tutors' concerns. The installation would make online consultations resemble face-to-face consultations and become more personal and convenient. To train new or novice tutors and provide additional guidance for in-service writing tutors to use CT for writing consultations in the long run, both groups of tutors should be familiar with tutees' behaviors, understand the strengths and weaknesses of various consultation modes and their roles, and determine the pedagogy that they find effective. Initial training is recommended for new/novice writing tutors, and on-going training and development would allow both new/novice and experienced writing tutors to discuss their problems, share good practices, and develop individual online teaching styles and consultation pedagogies.

Although the study was conducted on a small scale in a university, it successfully identified the tutors' concerns over the use of CT for writing consultations, discussed the potential relationship between online communication features and students' inactive learning behavior, and affirmed the significance of tutor training for online writing consultation in face of the new challenges. The findings and recommendations can be considered by other curriculum developers when they develop similar types of writing consultation services in their own contexts. More importantly, the study has added some knowledge to the use of CT from the language classroom context to writing consultations, an area that is not adequately explored in the literature. Further research could focus on the analysis of tutors' and tutees' online interaction patterns or tutors' online commentaries, and on the identification and effectiveness of good practices and online consultation pedagogies. With improvements in system design, and adequate preparation for both new and experienced writing tutors in online consultations, it is hoped that individual teaching pedagogies and an online consultation culture will be gradually cultivated, and will thus benefit L2 teaching and learning.

ACKNOWLEDGMENT

The service was a Strategic Development Project funded by the Hong Kong Baptist University while I was teaching there. I am greatly indebted to Professor K. Ahrens, Head of Language Centre for her unfailing support during the project period. I am grateful to my former colleagues for their contribution to the design and implementation of the hybrid and the virtual consultation modes, as well as the support staff for providing the statistical data and images. My thanks should also go to the 10 anonymous writing tutors who completed the questionnaires.

REFERENCES

Abdullah, N. A., Abidin, M. J. Z., Wong, S. L., Majid, O., & Atan, H. (2006). The attitude and motivation of English language teachers towards the use of computers. *Malaysian Online Journal of Instructional Technology*, *3*(1), 57–67.

AbuSeileck, A. F. (2007). Cooperative vs. individual learning of oral skills in a CALL environment. *Computer Assisted Language Learning*, *20*(5), 493–514. doi:10.1080/09588220701746054

Alshumaimeri, Y. A. (2008). Perceptions and attitudes toward using CALL in English classrooms among Saudi Secondary EFL teachers. *The JALT CALL Journal*, *4*(2), 29–46.

Braine, G. (2004). Teaching second and foreign language writing on LANs. In S. Fotos, & C. Browne (Eds.), *New perspectives on CALL for second language classrooms* (pp. 93–108). Mahwah, New Jersey, London: Lawrence Erlbaum Associates.

Breuch, L. M. K., & Racine, S. J. (2000). Developing sound tutor training for online writing centers: Creating productive peer reviewers. *Computers and Composition*, *17*, 245–263. doi:10.1016/S8755-4615(00)00034-7

Chiu, T. L., Liou, H. C., & Yeh, Y. L. (2007). A study of web-based oral activities enhanced by automatic speech recognition for EFL college learning. *Computer Assisted Language Learning*, *20*(3), 209–233. doi:10.1080/09588220701489374

Colby, R. S., & Colby, R. (2008). A pedagogy of play: Integrating computer games into the writing classroom. *Computers and Composition*, *25*(3), 300–312. doi:10.1016/j.compcom.2008.04.005

Comas-Quinn, A., Arcos, B., & Mardomingo, R. (2012). Virtual learning environments for distance language learning: Shifting tutor roles in a contested space for interactions. *Computer Assisted Language Learning*, *25*(2), 129–143. doi:10.1080/09588221.2011.636055

Ewert, D. E. (2009). L2 writing conferences: Investigating teacher talk. *Journal of Second Language Writing*, *18*, 251–269. doi:10.1016/j.jslw.2009.06.002

Fitze, M. (2006). Discourse and participation in ESL face-to-face and written electronic conferences. *Language Learning & Technology*, *10*(1), 67–86.

Groß, A., & Wolff, D. (2001). A multimedia tool to develop learner autonomy. *Computer Assisted Language Learning*, *14*(3), 233–249. doi:10.1076/call.14.3.233.5794

Hampel, R., & Stickler, U. (2005). New skills for new classrooms: Training tutors to teach languages online. *Computer Assisted Language Learning*, *18*(4), 311–326. doi:10.1080/09588220500335455

Harris, M. (1995). Talking in the middle: Why writers need writing tutors. *College English*, *51*(1), 27–42. doi:10.2307/378348

Hewett, B. L. (2010). *The online writing conference: A guide for teachers and tutors*. Portsmouth, NH: Boynton/ Cook Heinemann.

Hubbard, P., & Levy, M. (2006). The scope of CALL education. In P. Hubbard, & M. Levy (Eds.), *Teacher education in call* (pp. 3–20). Amsterdam, Philadelphia: John Benjamins. doi:10.1075/lllt.14.04hub

Krish, P. (2008). Language learning in the virtual world: Instructors' voices. *The International Journal of Pedagogies and Learning*, *4*(4), 113–129. doi:10.5172/ijpl.4.4.113

Lee, C. (2011). Tertiary students' perceptions and use of information computer technology for language consultation. *Teaching in Higher Education*, *17*(3), 323–339. doi:10.1080/13562517.2011.641007

Lee, C. (2012). The pragmatics of non-compliance by tertiary Cantonese learners of English in writing tutorials. In A. S. Yeung, E. L. Brown, & C. Lee (Eds.), *Communication and language: Surmounting barriers to cross-cultural understanding* (pp. 325–350). Charlotte, N.C.: Information Age Publishing.

Lee, C., Cheung, W. K. W., Wong, K. C. K., & Lee, F. S. L. (2013). Immediate web-based essay critiquing system feedback and teacher follow up feedback on young second language learners' writings: An experimental study in a Hong Kong secondary school. *Computer Assisted Language Learning*, *26*(1), 39–60. doi:10.1080/09588221.2011.630672

Lee, C., Wong, K. C. K., Lee, F. S. L., & Cheung, W. K. W. (2009). Web-based essay critiquing system and EFL students' writing: A quantitative and qualitative investigation. *Computer Assisted Language Learning*, *22*(1), 57–72. doi:10.1080/09588220802613807

Lee, K. W. (2000). English teachers' barriers to the use of computer-assisted language learning. *The Internet TESL Journal*, *6* (12). Available from, http://iteslj.org/Articles/Lee-CALLbarriers.html

Li, J. (2010). Learning vocabulary via computer-assisted scaffolding for text processing. *Computer Assisted Language Learning*, *23*(3), 253–275. doi:10.1080/09588221.2010.483678

Park, C. N., & Son, J. B. (2009). Implementing computer-assisted language learning in the EFL classroom: Teachers' perceptions and perspectives. *The International Journal of Pedagogies and Learning*, *5*(2), 80–101. doi:10.5172/ijpl.5.2.80

Rilling, S. (2005). The development of an ESL OWL or learning how to tutor writing online. *Computers and Composition*, *22*(3), 357–374. doi:10.1016/j.compcom.2005.05.006

Romeo, K. (2008). A web-based listening methodology for studying relative clause acquisition. *Computer Assisted Language Learning*, *21*(1), 51–66. doi:10.1080/09588220701865508

Sife, A. S., Lwoga, E. T., & Sanga, C. (2007). New technologies for teaching and learning: Challenges for higher learning institutions in developing countries. *International Journal of Education and Development Using ICT*, *3*(2), 57–67.

Son, J. (2007). Learner experiences in web-based language learning. *Computer Assisted Language Learning*, *20*(1), 21–36. doi:10.1080/09588220601118495

Thonus, T. (1999). Dominance in academic writing tutorials: gender, language proficiency, and the offering of suggestions. *Discourse & Society*, *10*(2), 225–248. doi:10.1177/0957926599010002005

Thonus, T. (2004). What are the differences? Tutor interactions with first- and second-language writers. *Journal of Second Language Writing*, *13*, 227–242. doi:10.1016/j.jslw.2004.04.012

Towndrow, P. (2004). Reflections of an on-line tutor. *ELT Journal*, *58*(2), 174–182. doi:10.1093/elt/58.2.174

Waring, H. Z. (2005). Peer tutoring in a graduate writing centre: Identity, expertise, and advice resisting. *Applied Linguistics*, *26*(2), 141–168. doi:10.1093/applin/amh041

Warschauer, M. (1997). Computer-mediated collaborative learning: Theory and practice. *Modern Language Journal*, *81*(4), 470–481. doi:10.1111/j.1540-4781.1997.tb05514.x

Yeh, Y. L., Liou, H. C., & Li, Y. H. (2007). Online synonym materials and concordancing for EFL college writing. *Computer Assisted Language Learning*, *20*(2), 131–152. doi:10.1080/09588220701331451

ADDITIONAL READING

Bach, S., Haynes, P., & Smith, J. L. (2007). *Online learning and teaching in higher education*. Berkshire, England: Open University Press.

Boettcher, J. V. (2010). *The online teaching survival guide: Simple and practical pedagogical tips*. San Francisco, CA: Jossey-Bass.

Braine, G. (1998). Teaching writing on local area networks. In C. S. Ward, & W. A. Renandya (Eds.), *Computers and language learning* (pp. 63–76). Singapore: SEAMEO Regional Language Centre.

Buck, A. M. (2008). The invisible interface: MS Word in the writing center. *Computers and Composition*, *25*, 396–415. doi:10.1016/j.compcom.2008.05.003

Chapelle, C. A. (2001). *Computer applications in second language acquisition: Foundations for teaching, testing and research*. Cambridge: Cambridge University Press. doi:10.1017/CBO9781139524681

Cheung, W. K., Mørch, A. I., Wong, K. C., Lee, C., Liu, J., & Lam, M. H. (2007). Grounding collaborative learning in semantics-based critiquing. *International Journal of Distance Education Technologies*, *5*(2), 40–55. doi:10.4018/jdet.2007040104

Crystal, D. (2001). *Language and the internet*. Cambridge, UK; New York: Cambridge University Press. doi:10.1017/CBO9781139164771

Daud, N. M. (1998). Teaching writing using computers. In C. S. Ward, & W. A. Renandya (Eds.), *Computers and Language Learning* (pp. 140–150). Singapore: SEAMEO Regional Language Centre.

Dietz-Uhler, B., & Hurn, J. E. (2013). Strategies for engagement in online courses: Engaging with the content, instructor, and other students. *Journal of Teaching and Learning with Technology*, *2*(1), 62–65.

Futász, R., & Timár, E. (2006). Academic writing: Teaching on line and face to face – EATAW Conference 2005. *Journal of Second Language Writing*, *15*, 147–149. doi:10.1016/j.jslw.2006.05.002

Gupta, R. (1998). Writing with a different tool. In C. S. Ward, & W. A. Renandya (Eds.), *Computers and Language Learning* (pp. 97–120). Singapore: SEAMEO Regional Language Centre.

Hewett, B. L. (2010). *The online writing conference: A guide for teachers and tutors*. Portsmouth, NH: Boynton/ Cook.

Hyland, K. (2002). *Teaching and researching writing*. Harlow, UK: Longman.

Hyland, K. (2003). *Second language writing*. New York: Cambridge University Press. doi:10.1017/CBO9780511667251

Jones, R. H., Garralda, A., Li, D. C. S., & Lock, G. (2006). Interactional dynamics in on-line and face-to-face peer-tutoring sessions for second language writers. *Journal of Second Language Writing*, *15*, 1–23. doi:10.1016/j.jslw.2005.12.001

Joyner, F. (2012). Increasing student interaction and the development of critical thinking in asynchronous threaded discussions. *Journal of Teaching and Learning with Technology*, *1*(1), 35–41.

Joyner, F. (2012). Increasing student interaction and the development of critical thinking in asynchronous threaded discussions. *Journal of Teaching and Learning with Technology*, *1*(1), 35–41.

Lamy, M. N., & Hampel, R. (2007). *Online communication in language learning and teaching*. Basingstoke, New York: Palgrave Macmillan. doi:10.1057/9780230592681

Levy, M. (1997). *Computer-assisted language learning: Context and conceptualization*. Oxford: Oxford University Press.

Pennington, M. C. (2003). The impact of the computer in second language writing. In B. Kroll (Ed.), *Exploring the dynamics of second language writing* (pp. 287–310). Cambridge: Cambridge University Press. doi:10.1017/CBO9781139524810.019

Rilling, S. (2005). The development of an ESL owl, or learning how to tutor writing online. *Computers and Composition*, *22*, 357–374. doi:10.1016/j.compcom.2005.05.006

Wong, K. C., Cheung, W. K. W., Lee, F. S. L., & Lee, C. F. K. (2008). On corpus preparation and deployment of a web-based critiquing system for English essay writing enhancement. In J. Fong, R. Kwan, & F. L. Wang (Eds.), *Hybrid learning: A new frontier* (pp. 43–54). Hong Kong: City University of Hong Kong.

KEY WORDS AND DEFINITIONS

Audio-Lingual Method: A teaching method based on the behaviorist theory. It emphasizes mechanical drills in the use of grammar, and provides positive and negative reinforcement whenever necessary.

Hybrid Consultation Mode: The hybrid consultation mode consists of two components: face-face-to and virtual modes. Tutors and tutees can agree on the ratio of the two parts.

Message Board: The Message Board is an online platform designed for tutors and tutees to write and/or upload text files exclusively for consultation. Tutors can upload the marked essay and write written comments on the Message Board. Similarly, tutees can upload their assignments to the Message Board for submission.

Online Consultation: An online consultation is provided through computers via the Internet. In this paper, it particularly refers to the online component of the hybrid consultation mode and the virtual consultation mode.

Task-Based Learning: Task-based learning emphasizes the use of tasks to use the target language in a meaningful context. A task that promotes communication in the language classroom is called a communicative task. Nunan (1989) categorized communicative tasks as pedagogical tasks that are practiced in the classroom only, and real world tasks as those that are used for the purpose of rehearsing future needs.

Virtual Consultation Mode: A virtual consultation is provided through computers only.

APPENDIX A: A SURVEY ON THE USE OF COMPUTER TECNOLOGY FOR WRITING CONSULTATIONS

Table 6.

Part I: Background information		
1. Gender	☐ M	☐ F
2. Years of tertiary teaching experience	☐ 1-5	☐ 6-10
	☐ 11-15	☐ 16-20
	☐ 21-25	☐ 26-30
	☐ over 30	
3. Years of writing consultation experience	☐ 1-5	☐ 6-10
	☐ 11-15	☐ 16-20
	☐ 21-25	☐ 26-30
	☐ over 30	
4. Please indicate the extent of your experience in using computers for language learning and teaching, from 1 (*very limited*) to 5 (*extensive*).	Very limited --------------Extensive ☐1 ☐2 ☐3 ☐4 ☐5	
Part II: Beliefs 1. Choose the terms that best refer(s) to your notion of the role of computers in language teaching, especially in the context of writing tutorials. You may select more than one. ☐ A teaching tool (e.g., link to other online teaching materials/resources) ☐ An expert system ☐ A complement to classroom instruction ☐ An aid for communication ☐ A surrogate teacher ☐ Others, please specify ____________________ 2. Below is a list of language-teaching philosophies, methods, and approaches. Please tick the box(es) that best describe your own. You may select more than one. ☐ Audio-lingual ☐ Communicative language teaching ☐ Cognitive load learning ☐ Direct method ☐ Formal grammar instruction ☐ Grammar translation ☐ Task-based learning ☐ Collaborative learning ☐ Others (please specify) ____________________ 3. How does your philosophy of language teaching affect the way in which you handle hybrid and/or online consultation modes for writing tutorials? ____________________ 4. As far as you can remember, when and under what circumstances did you begin to be interested in computer-assisted language learning/teaching? ____________________		
Part III: Opinions on the hybrid and/or virtual consultation modes for writing consultations 1. What type(s) of WES consultation mode have you used or provided for your students before? You can tick ( ) more than one answer. A. ☐ Face-to-face mode ** If your answer is A only, please answer Part III - Questions 8 and 9 and Part V only. B. ☐ Hybrid mode How long have you used the **hybrid** consultation mode? ☐ less than 1 year ☐ 1 year ☐ 2 years ☐ 3 years ☐ more than 3 years		

continued on following page

Table 6. Continued

How often do you provide the **hybrid** consultation mode in a semester?

☐ 1-5 hrs/ semester

☐ 6-10 hrs/ semester

☐ 11-15 hrs/ semester

☐ 16-20 hrs/ semester

☐ more than 20 hrs/ semester

** If your answer is B only, please answer Part III - Questions 2, 3,4,8,9, Parts IV and V.
** If your answers are A and B, please answer Part III – Questions 2,3,4,8,9, Parts IV and V.

C. ☐ Online mode

How long have you used the **virtual** consultation mode?

☐ less than 1 year

☐ 1 year

☐ 2 years

☐ 3 years

☐ more than 3 years

How often do you provide the **virtual** consultation mode in a semester?

☐ 1-5 hrs/ semester

☐ 6-10 hrs/ semester

☐ 11-15 hrs/ semester

☐ 16-20 hrs/ semester

☐ more than 20 hrs/ semester

** If your answer is C only, please answer Part III – Questions 5,6,7,8,9, Parts IV and V.
** If your answers are A and C, please answer Part III - Questions 5,6,7,8,9, Parts IV and V.
** If your answers are A, B and C, please answer all answers in Parts III, IV and V.

2. To what extent do you agree with the following statements about the functions/ importance of the hybrid consultation mode? Please rate them from 1 (*least agree*) to 5 (*strongly agree*).

The **hybrid** consultation mode enables/encourages **tutees** to:	Least agree------Strongly agree
A. Seek consultations according to their learning agendas, schedules, and pace.	☐1 ☐2 ☐3 ☐4 ☐5
B. Experience an alternative learning and consultation mode.	☐1 ☐2 ☐3 ☐4 ☐5
C. Complement face-to-face learning.	☐1 ☐2 ☐3 ☐4 ☐5
D. Interact more frequently with their tutors.	☐1 ☐2 ☐3 ☐4 ☐5
E. Others, please state. _______________	

The **hybrid** consultation mode enables/encourages **tutors** to:	Least agree -----Strongly agree
A. Provide consultations according to their schedules and pace.	☐1 ☐2 ☐3 ☐4 ☐5
B. Experience an alternative teaching and consultation mode.	☐1 ☐2 ☐3 ☐4 ☐5
D. Complement face-to-face instruction.	☐1 ☐2 ☐3 ☐4 ☐5
D. Interact more frequently with their tutees.	☐1 ☐2 ☐3 ☐4 ☐5
E. Others, please state. _______________________	

3. To what extent are you satisfied with the use of the **hybrid** consultation mode for writing consultations? Please rate the degree of satisfaction from 1 (*least satisfactory*) to 5 (*very satisfactory*).	Least---------Very satisfactory ☐1 ☐2 ☐3 ☐4 ☐5

If your rating is below 3, can you give the reasons? ____________________

4. What is your opinion on the use of the **hybrid** consultation mode for writing tutorials? ____________________

continued on following page

Table 6. Continued

5. To what extent do you agree with the following statements about the function and/or importance of the **online** consultation mode? Please rate them from 1 (*least agree*) to 5 (*strongly agree*).	
The **online** consultation mode enables/encourages **tutees** to:	Least agree ---- Strongly agree
A. Seek consultations according to their learning agendas, schedules, and pace.	□1 □2 □3 □4 □5
B. Experience an alternative learning and consultation mode.	□1 □2 □3 □4 □5
C. Interact more frequently with their tutors.	□1 □2 □3 □4 □5
D. Others, please state. ____________________	
The **virtual** consultation mode enables/encourages **tutors** to:	Least agree -----Strongly agree
A. Provide consultations according to their schedules and pace.	□1 □2 □3 □4 □5
B. Experience an alternative teaching and consultation mode.	□1 □2 □3 □4 □5
C. Interact more frequently with their tutees.	□1 □2 □3 □4 □5
D. Others, please state. ____________________	
6. To what extent are you satisfied with the use of the **virtual** consultation mode for writing consultation? Please rate the degree of satisfaction from 1 (*least satisfactory*) to 5 (*very satisfactory*).	Least ----------Very satisfactory □1 □2 □3 □4 □5
If your rating is below 3, can you give the reasons? ____	
7. What is your opinion on the use of the **virtual** consultation mode for writing consultations?	
8. Do you think the introduction of the online component (in **hybrid** and **virtual** consultation modes) has modified the tutor's role in language teaching? If so, in what way?	
9. In your opinion, what are the key skills writing tutors need to possess so as to provide effective consultations via the Internet?	
Part IV: Opinions on the writing consultation platform	Least --------Very user-friendly
1. To what extent do you think the **online consultation platform** (i.e., Message Board) is user-friendly? Please indicate the degree from 1 (*least*) to 5 (*very*).	□1 □2 □3 □4 □5
2. To what extent do you think the **online report** is useful to tutors? Please indicate the degree from 1 (*least*) to 5 (*very*).	□1 □2 □3 □4 □5
Part V: Opinions on the use of computers for writing consultations	Least extent -------Large extent
1. Overall, to what extent do you think that face-to-face consultations can be replaced by computers (i.e., online?) Please rate the extent from 1 (*least*) to 5 (*large*).	□1 □2 □3 □4 □5

Chapter 13
Theory and Practice in Computer-Assisted Vocabulary Learning: A Case Study

Peter Prince
University of Aix-Marseille, France

ABSTRACT

This chapter presents an account of the ongoing development of a vocabulary learning resource, VocPAL (Vocabulary: Progressive Autonomous Learning), for French learners of English in a university context. The chapter describes the background to the resource, its theoretical underpinnings, and its presentation features. These include pictures, sound, an association test, and context sentences forming a story. A questionnaire was administered to college students (N = 115) to assess reactions to VocPAL in an online learning environment. Further insights were gained from interviews with users of the resource. Both questionnaire and interview data suggest that, while the resource is judged favourably overall, improvements can be made to make the story more appealing and to add more interactivity. Results are discussed in terms of future development options, limitations to the study, and some broader issues regarding computer-assisted vocabulary learning.

INTRODUCTION

For any second language (L2) learner, vocabulary represents a huge challenge. Depending on the learner's goal, the number of words to be learnt may vary, but in the case of vast numbers of students around the world who are required to learn English in order to read texts related to their field of study, the figure will run to several thousand. Estimates differ as to the number of words one needs to know in order to be comfortable reading texts, but it has been suggested that a minimum of 6,000 word families is necessary (Nation, 2006).

Many students, in France and elsewhere, do not reach this level of vocabulary knowledge (Arnaud, Béjoint & Thoiron, 1985; Schmitt, 2008). One reason for this is that when reading a text, learners may pay only minimal attention to unfa-

DOI: 10.4018/978-1-4666-6174-5.ch013

miliar words (Fraser, 1999). Incidental learning of vocabulary through extensive reading may thus be effective only if learners are exposed to large quantities of text. While incidental vocabulary learning may occur in the first language (L1, Nagy, Herman & Anderson, 1985), it is rarely the case in the L2 (Laufer, 2005). Even when texts are simplified to reduce the number of unfamiliar words, as is the case with graded readers, words are not encountered often enough to ensure effective vocabulary acquisition (Cobb, 2007). It has, therefore, been argued that some form of decontextualised encounter that encourages more elaborative processing is necessary (Laufer & Rozovski-Roitblat, 2011).

The initial aim of such processing is twofold: the first is to set up a mental representation of the word form and then to link the form to the word's meaning. However, as soon as the number of words increases, this double requirement becomes in itself a challenge. Thus, it may be helpful to break down the process, focusing first on form before engaging in semantic elaboration (Barcroft, 2002). Subsequent encounters with the word then help to consolidate the form in memory and enrich the representation of its syntactic and semantic properties.

Because there is not enough classroom time for teachers to present the large number of words to be learnt, it has been suggested that beyond the first two or three thousand most frequent words, learners need to adopt an active commitment to the task (Schmitt, 2008). With the development of computer assisted vocabulary learning (CAVL), learners are given the opportunity to handle the task independently outside of the classroom (Arispe, 2011; Cobb & Horst, 2011; Groot, 2000; Ma & Kelly, 2006; Stockwell, 2007, 2010; Tozcu & Coady, 2004). This, of course, is not exclusive to CAVL – motivated learners make use of many resources to improve their L2 proficiency. However, a well-designed CAVL application can go a long way towards meeting the five criteria of stimulus appraisal that, according to Schumann (1998) are likely to enhance motivation: novelty, pleasantness, coping potential (i.e. the learner's appraisal of how well he or she can cope with the stimulus demands), goal significance, and compatibility with self and social image.

To meet all these criteria fully nonetheless remains a challenge. While pleasantness can be enhanced by the use of pictures or video, the repetitiveness of vocabulary learning means that novelty can quickly wear off. In order to comply with the coping potential criterion, a resource needs to provide a manageable workload and also be user-friendly. Goal significance implies that the learner not only sees vocabulary learning as important but also perceives the CAVL resource as an effective means to reach that goal. One attraction of CAVL applications is that, by means of spaced repetition, they can offer personalised reviewing of individual items based on the learner's previous responses within an expanded rehearsal framework, a feature likely to enhance goal significance. However, as Godwin-Jones (2010) points out, such programmes will work best with already motivated learners who work on a regular basis. Indeed, intrinsic motivation and learner autonomy are connected (Ushioda, 1996), but many learners are not sufficiently motivated to develop their capacity for autonomy. In sum, while CAVL certainly opens up possibilities, it by no means guarantees that the vocabulary learning challenge will be met. Whilst making no claims to provide such a guarantee, Vocabulary: Progressive Autonomous Learning (VocPAL), a CALL project reported and examined in this chapter, is an attempt to combine certain features in such a way as to ease the burden of vocabulary learning for students.

VocPAL can be considered as a dedicated CAVL programme as defined by Ma (2013) in that it adopts a comprehensive and systematic approach. That is, it seeks first, to ensure that words are presented both in context and decontextualized and second, to provide a sufficient number of encounters for the establishing of solid lexical representations in memory (i.e., form-meaning mappings). However, in the sum of activities, the balance is weighted towards reading words in context, with little in the way of form-focused activity. This is compensated by the careful and systematic recycling of target words. The next section describes VocPAL in more detail.

PRESENTATION OF VOCPAL

VocPAL emerged from a written vocabulary learning activity based on the following three-part sequence: (1) presentation of a target word in an invented context sentence, (2) a binary semantic judgment in the form of an association test, (3) feedback in the form of a second context sentence, also invented, in which both the target word and the correct answer to the association test appear. This sequence remains at the core of VocPAL, which is still in development and which in its current form incorporates the following features.

First, it focuses on a specific set of words ranging in frequency from rank 1,805 to 6,260 in Kilgariff's (1995) lemmatised British National Corpus list. Because it is intended for students who have, for the most part, been studying English for seven years or more, higher frequency words are assumed to be already known. French-English cognates were excluded as they call for a different mode of presentation that concentrates on their auditory form. This left roughly 2,500 words, of which VocPAL to date covers the first 400 most frequent, split into five units of 80 words each. Of these 400 words, there are 196 nouns, 114 verbs, 69 adjectives, 14 adverbs, three prepositions, two pronouns, one determiner and one conjunction. They range in frequency from 52 per million to 28.2 ($M = 38.4$). The ultimate goal is to provide a lexical base of frequent words that will allow students to read English texts more easily.

Second, VocPAL presents words in an enriched context combining sound, pictures, context sentences, translations and a story. Each of these elements finds support in the literature. A combination of auditory and visual presentations has been shown to be effective as regards individual word retention (Nassaji, 2004) and also helps to set up a phonological representation that will be needed in aural comprehension. Presenting a target word along with a pictorial representation has been shown to help L2 vocabulary learning in adults (Barcroft, 2009; Omaggio, 1979) and children (Tonzar & Lotto, 2009), while glosses containing pictures are known to help retention in memory (Chun & Plass, 1996; Jones & Plass, 2002; Yoshii, 2006). Context sentences allow learners to gain knowledge of how words are used and as such are a vital part of vocabulary presentation (Nation, 2001). Furthermore, a sentence-level context, as opposed to a larger text, encourages greater focus on the target word (Laufer & Shmueli, 1997). However, a drawback of relying on context sentences for inferring the meaning of target word is that it does not always provide a clear indication of a word's meaning, such that guessing from context is an unreliable process (Kaivanpanah & Alavi, 2008; Webb, 2008). Therefore, as a supplement to context, L1 (i.e., French) translations are provided. It has long been established that a large number of L2 words can be learnt relatively easily with their L1 translations (Lotto & de Groot, 1998; Webb, 1962). Furthermore, translations give an immediate access to meaning, thus lightening the initial learning load and allowing learners to concentrate on word forms (Barcroft, 2002; Schmitt, 2008).

A recent addition to VocPal, further enriching the presentation context, is that the initial context sentences containing the target words (i.e. the sentences in the first part of the three-part sequence) are organised to form a narrative, i.e., the sentences are related to each other insofar as they refer to characters and events evolving in a specific setting. Each unit of 80 sentences comprises a separate story. There is evidence that a learner-generated story can be a powerful aid to retention of words in memory (Bower & Clark, 1969), but a story can also be beneficial when provided by a teacher or software designer. Prince (2012) found that at an immediate post-test, French learners of L2 English recalled significantly more target words seen in sentences forming a story than in sentences that were unrelated to each other. This is likely because stories can provide an extra level of organisation in memory which learners can call upon to aid recall (Bolger & Zapata, 2011; Graesser, Singer & Trabasso, 1994; Laurillard, Stratfold, Luckin, Plowman, & Taylor, 2000). A further advantage of stories is motivational: the description of situated events inherent to narrative strikes a fundamental chord with human cognition and emotions (McLean, Pasupathi, & Pals, 2007), a potential that can be put to good effect in the language classroom, whether through learners sharing their personal stories (Nicholas, Rossiter, & Abbott, 2011) or engaging with them in graded readers (Poulshock, 2010).

Third, VocPAL incorporates a degree of elaborative processing. This is defined by Tulving & Madigan (1970, p.462), as "the storage of additional non-redundant information with the verbal unit to be remembered." In their levels of processing framework, Craik and Lockhart (1972) postulated that deeper or more elaborate processing leads to a more persistent memory trace. Because depth of processing is difficult to operationalize, Hulstijn and Laufer's (2001) involvement load hypothesis seeks to do this in its *evaluation* component, which involves assessment of a word's meaning. This might take the form of deciding which of a word's different meanings best fits a given context, or choosing one of several options in a gap-fill exercise. In VocPAL, this evaluation of a target word's meaning takes the form of an association test in which learners are asked to choose which of two words presented on the screen is more closely related semantically to the target word. In order to ensure the feasibility of the test, the two words are either French-English cognates, (which are not themselves covered in VocPAL) or of higher frequency than the target word. The test is administered to the learners after a target word is read in context (i.e., the invented context sentence intended to make apparent the word's meaning) but before the L1 translation is provided. While such a procedure encourages a certain degree of semantic processing, this is kept deliberately limited. The choice is binary rather than multiple and the correct answer is relatively easy to identify. The reason is to ensure, first, that the learner's progression through the different target word sequences remains fluid, and second, that the evaluation of the target word's meaning entailed by the association test does not distract too much attention from the target word form (Barcroft, 2002). While multiple choice may foster greater mental effort, the demands on attention it entails can lead to less effective learning (Yoshii, 2013). The aim in VocPAL, therefore, is for form and meaning to receive similar levels of attention such that a mapping between the two will be established and access to the resulting lexical representation will be facilitated on subsequent encounters with the word.

A further major feature of VocPAL is the recycling of target words. As words are encountered in descending order of frequency, the more frequent words are encountered again in the context sentences for less frequent target words. Estimates of the number of times a word needs to be seen in order to be learnt vary, but a minimum of six encounters is no doubt necessary (Zahar, Cobb, & Spada, 2001). As the number of target words encountered increases, however, it clearly becomes impossible to continue recycling all the previous target words. Therefore, after a number of encounters ranging from six to twelve, these words are considered to be known and are no longer expressly recycled within VocPAL (although they may reoccur fortuitously). Table 1 indicates how the 400 target words so far covered in VocPAL are recycled within the first five units. For example, aside from their initial presentation in the three-part sequence, the 80 target words introduced in Unit 1 appear 612 times in total in the five units,

Table 1. Mean frequency of recycling of 400 words within the first five units (80 words each) of VocPAL

First Appearance	Mean
Unit 1	7.65
Unit 2	7.15
Unit 3	5.15
Unit 4	3.90
Unit 5	1.20

giving a mean recycling rate of 7.65 for each target word. Recycling rates for words introduced in the subsequent units are lower, since more units need to be added to allow them to be recycled. Once all the words targeted for inclusion in VocPAL have been covered, further units will be added in which no new words are introduced but previous target words are recycled.

Not all words are recycled to the same extent. Words are introduced in order of descending frequency, but as far as recycling is concerned, the more difficult words need to be recycled more often, i.e. a minimum of 12 times as opposed to a minimum of six for easier words. Several criteria enter into the assessment of difficulty. Clear polysemy is one. For example, the Unit 1 word *appeal* (verb) has two main meanings (*request* and *attract*) and it is therefore recycled 13 times (7 times with meaning 1 and 6 times with meaning 2). Similarly, the Unit 3 verb *bother* (*annoy* or *make an effort*) is recycled 10 (5 times with meaning 1 and 5 times with meaning 2). Note that the figures in Table 1 refer to the recycling of word forms, not to the different form-meaning mappings that may exist. Polysemy being a very slippery concept, any precise figure about the recycling of different meanings is bound to be open to question. While the different meanings of *appeal* and *bother* are reasonably easy to distinguish, those of *cross* or *prospect*, for example, are harder. The first can be the Christian symbol or the letter X; the second can refer to the expectation of a future event or the chances of being successful. In both cases, the two meanings are given separate entries in Collins Cobuild dictionary (Sinclair, 2006), but it could be argued that the two meanings share enough semantic features to be considered the same, especially as they both have one main translation in French (*croix* and *perspective* respectively). On the other hand, polysemy shades into near-synonymy, and even when a word has an identifiable core meaning, its collocational behaviour can make it a candidate for recycling.

Thus, the Unit 1 verb *release*, with its different collocations (a person, a product, an emotion), is recycled 9 times. A word's syntactic properties can also create difficulty. For example, the Unit 1 verb *benefit* is recycled 8 times due to the complexity of its argument structure: *to benefit* can be both transitive (e.g. *The measure will benefit everyone*) or transitive indirect (*Everyone will benefit from the measure*). Words of similar frequency but less syntactic complexity (e.g. *shoe*, *wash* or *wheel*) are recycled less often (5, 3 and 5 times respectively). Another criterion is learners' level of familiarity with words: for example *false* (recycled 4 times), having been encountered often at school, is familiar to learners, but *corporate* (recycled 12 times) and *device* (recycled 11 times) are less familiar. Lastly, L1 interference can pose a problem: the French *compréhensif* means *understanding*; the Unit 3 word *comprehensive* is therefore recycled 10 times. In sum, while there is no rigid adherence to a predefined scale, all words deemed difficult for the various reasons cited are candidates for more extensive recycling, i.e. a minimum of 12 times, with further reminders occurring fortuitously thereafter. Thus, of the examples given, *appeal* and *corporate* may reoccur fortuitously, but *bother*, *benefit*, *release*, *device* and *comprehensive* are considered to require further recycling. The words selected for extended recycling were determined by the present author in collaboration with two native English speakers with experience of teaching English in France.

Overall, excluding their initial presentation, target words and their repetitions represent 11.2%

of the running words in the first five units. That is to say, there are 17,887 words altogether, of which 2,006 are target words and their repetitions. To date, then, the first 400 words of VocPAL are recycled on average just over 5 times each; however, on the one hand, this figure is set to increase as more units are added, and on the other hand, the average figure can mask considerable differences between individual words.

Target words are presented on slides that are strung together to form films covering 40 target words (i.e., each story, composed of the 80 context sentences in which the target words first appear, is split into two halves). Each film lasts for roughly 13 minutes. Within the films, chapter headings are inserted after every eight target words, such that each story is composed of ten series of eight context sentences each, with one new target word appearing per sentence. The stories range in length from 1,074 words to 1,954 words (M = 1,389). For every target word there are three slides: (1) the target word highlighted at the top with an indication of its grammatical category, one context sentence, one picture or assemblage of pictures (often including speech bubbles, i.e., characters' comments visible as in comic strips), and audio recording of the context sentence; (2) an association test; and (3) feedback (new context sentence and L1 translation). The context sentences in the first slide are those that comprise the story. The complete sequence of three slides lasts approximately 20 seconds (eight seconds for Slide One, four seconds for Slide Two, and eight seconds for Slide Three), though learners can click the pause button if they want to study a slide for longer. Figures 1 to 3 illustrate the complete sequence for the Unit 1 target word *switch* (verb). Figure 4 illustrates an example of the recycling of *switch* as well as of *alter* and *gift* along with the introduction of a new target word from Unit 3, *shirt*.

The learning process is broken down as follows. First, the learner sees the slide in which the target word is initially presented in a context sentence

Figure 1. Presentation of Switch © 2007, Gehel. Used with permission

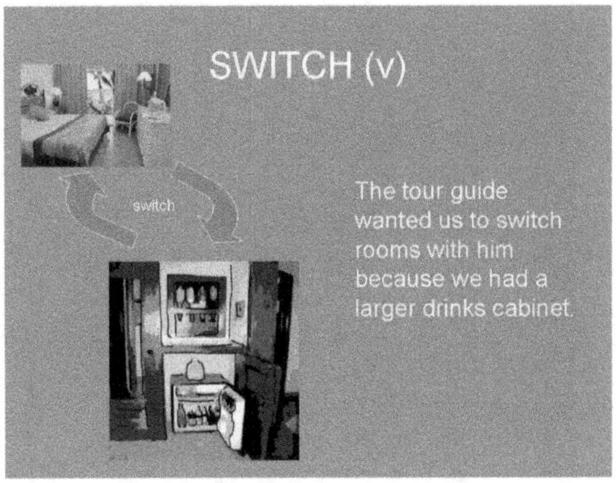

Figure 2. Association test

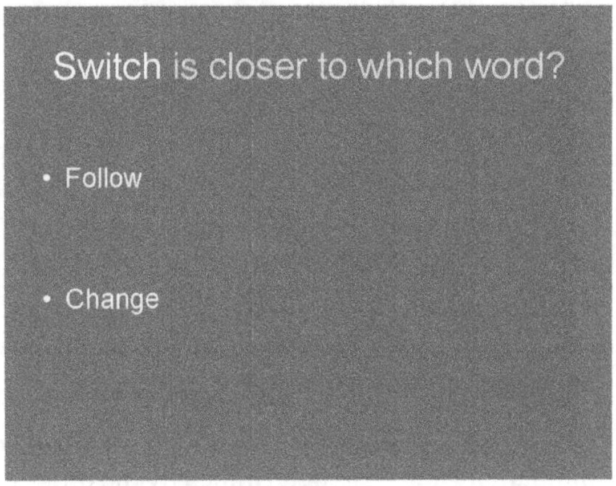

Figure 3. Feedback

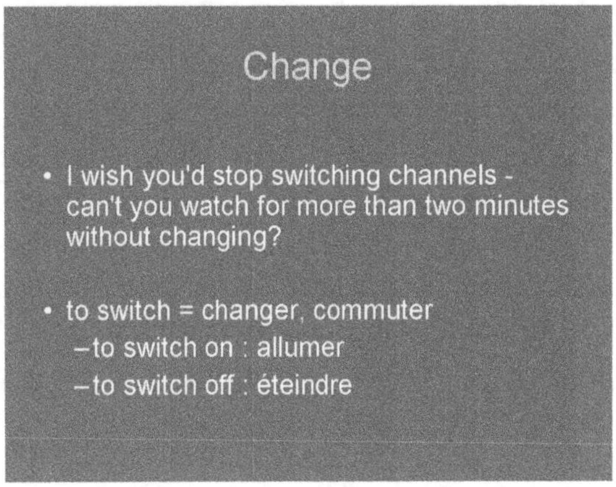

Figure 4. Presentation of Shirt © 2010, Phanlop88, FreeDigitalPhotos.net. Used with permission.

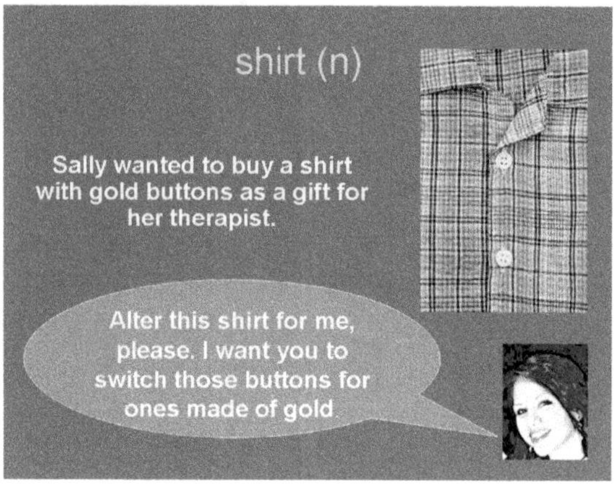

along with a picture; these two elements are designed to give a clear idea of the word's meaning. In the case of concrete words, the picture provides a clear illustration of the target word itself, but for more abstract words, the picture is related to the meaning of the sentence. The context sentence is part of the story, which in the example given here (i.e. Figure 1, illustrating the target word *switch*) is about a holiday on a tropical island with an unreliable tour guide. In the case of words with multiple meanings, the initial presentation focuses wherever possible on the more frequent or dominant meaning, as determined by the order in which the meanings appear in the Collins Cobuild dictionary (Sinclair, 2006). Second, the learner performs the association test by choosing the word most closely related to the target word (Figure 2). This is performed mentally without any physical response such as clicking on the answer. Third, the learner receives feedback in the form of a new context sentence that includes both the target word and the correct answer to the association test. The new context sentence is not part of the story. The third slide also provides the translation(s) of the target word. The complete sequence of three slides constitutes the initial presentation of a target word. Target words are subsequently recycled in different context sentences, either later in the same unit or in subsequent units (Figure 4), in order to consolidate their form and meaning in memory.

The design principles of VocPAL were tested in a series of studies that established the usefulness of the binary association test with feedback, the positive effect of images and the benefit of including L1 translations (Prince, 2006). However, these features were studied in isolation in controlled experiments and with the recent addition of the story, it was important to start examining learners' perceptions of VocPAL in a more natural environment. Whilst a controlled experiment can provide useful information about which features are likely to influence learning outcomes, participants' behaviours may be different from what they would do in a real-world learning environment. What learners expect or seek to achieve in a real-world learning environment depends on a complex combination of factors, including their own motivational profile (e.g. whether they are intrinsically motivated by the field of study or the subject matter), and their ongoing perceptions of the specific activity proposed. Learners' perceptions of the usefulness of activities undertaken in class are known to influence learning outcomes (Brown, 2008) and perceptions of particular resources such as video captions may affect the way learners use them (Montero Perez, Peters, & Desmet, 2014). While assessments of the effectiveness of a CALL resource need to go beyond subjective impressions (Felix, 2005), learners' perceptions can provide a valuable insight when deciding what improvements are to be made. As the full combination of features comprising VocPAL had not yet been tested in ecologically valid conditions, assessing learners' perceptions of it in a real-world learning environment was an important step in its development. Therefore, in order to understand better the interaction between learners and VocPAL, learners engaging with an on-screen version of VocPAL were asked to comment on its design and their reactions to it. The goal is to assess reactions to it in order to incorporate any modifications deemed necessary before developing it further. A questionnaire relating to its use was therefore submitted to students and follow up interviews were conducted. The study focused on three main research questions:

1. How do students perceive VocPAL globally?
2. How do students engage with the methodological aspects of VocPAL?
3. How do students perceive the specific features (i.e., the story, the association test, the pictures, the translations, the recycling of words and the frequency-based selection of target words) that VocPAL incorporates?

METHOD

Participants and Procedure

VocPAL was made available to first year college students in a class named Applied Foreign Languages on a learning platform (the University's adaptation of Moodle), along with a questionnaire devised to assess their perceptions of VocPAL. A brief description of VocPAL, including instructions for its use, was also provided. As Unit 5 was not quite complete, students completed the first four units of VocPAL at their own pace on a voluntary basis. Out of 268 students enrolled in the platform, 124 returned the questionnaire. Only responses from French native speakers were used for the study, leading to the exclusion of five questionnaires for data analysis. Four incomplete questionnaires were discarded. Of the remaining 115 respondents, there were 79 female students and 36 male. Their average age was 19.0 years and they had been studying English for an average of 8.1 years. The students indicated their degree of agreement on a 4-point scale (I agree: 1 = Not at All, 2 = A Little, 3 = Fairly, 4 = Totally) to 30 items developed by the present researcher (author of VocPAL) and a colleague in the University's self-access centre. Corresponding to the three research questions, the items covered three broad categories: global satisfaction, methodology and specific features of VocPAL. These categories were not intended to correspond to putative underlying factors, but rather to serve as a guide for devising the questionnaire, with a view to obtaining opinions on a broad array of questions, both general and specific. Of the 30 items, twelve were negatively worded, i.e. expressed a dissatisfactory aspect of the resource. The complete list of questions along with the scores for each appears in Appendix A.

All participants who returned the questionnaire also indicated their level of proficiency on a 6-point self-assessment scale, with 1 indicating a beginner level and 6 indicating a high degree of proficiency. The wording for the scale was adapted and condensed from the 6-point scale used in the Common European Framework of Reference for Languages (CEFRL). The overall mean on the 6-point scale for self-assessed proficiency was 3.88, equating to slightly below B2 on the CEFRL.

Global satisfaction (14 items) refers to overall perceptions of the resource (e.g. *VocPAL is attractive* or *VocPAL is effective*). Methodology (six items) refers to students' willingness to engage with certain cognitive and strategic dimensions of VocPAL. These were the recycling of words (*Seeing words I know already is a waste of time*), the semantic processing required (*The association test consolidates my knowledge of the words; I try to guess the meaning of the words from the context; It would be better to see the translations straightaway*) and active commitment to the task (*I note down the words I don't know; I click on pause if I want to spend more time on a slide*). Specific features (nine items) relate to students' perceptions of the helpfulness or attractiveness of a specific feature. Three items were devoted to the story (*The story is a motivating element; The stories are uninteresting; It would be better to present the words without a story);* two items related to the association test *(The association test is unnecessary; The association test gets in the way of the story);* one item related to the translations

(The translations are useful); one item related to the pictures (*The pictures help me understand the meanings of the words*); one item related to the recycling of words (*I recognise the words which reoccur more easily*); one item related to the frequency-based criterion for the selection of target words (*The number of unknown words increases with each unit*). One remaining item (*To me, vocabulary is less important than grammar*) applied to vocabulary learning in general. The questionnaire contained no terms unfamiliar to participants, the meaning of a more technical term such as association test being apparent from the description of VocPAL provided as well as from its use.

In order to elucidate and complement the questionnaire data, interviews were conducted with a sub-group of the participants. Of the 115 respondents whose questionnaire data remained for final analysis, 66 indicated willingness to reply to further questions orally. Of these, 24 were selected for follow-up interviews. The interviewees were selected on the basis of their replies to the questionnaire, with 16 chosen amongst those respondents who were least satisfied with VocPAL and eight amongst those who responded more positively. These two groups were determined by the means of respondents' scores to the Global Appreciation category of questionnaire items. Out of a maximum of 4.0, these scores ranged from 2.0 to 2.92 (M = 2.69) for the least satisfied and from 3.25 to 3.75 (M = 3.47) for the most satisfied. The interviews, recorded with the participants' consent, were conducted individually in French, over a three-week period following collection and analysis of the questionnaires. Each interview lasted for about 10 minutes. The initial questions were the same for everyone: *What was your overall impression of VocPAL? What, in your opinion, were the most positive aspects of VocPAL? What were the most negative aspects?* The concluding question was also the same for everyone: *How, in your opinion, can VocPAL be improved?* The other questions were adapted according to the students' questionnaire profiles, i.e. they were asked to explain why they gave scores of 1 or 4, indicating total disagreement or agreement, to individual items.

RESULTS

Questionnaire Data

Figure 5 provides the overall results for each of the three categories (i.e., Global Appreciation, Methodological Engagement and Specific Features). To obtain approval ratings, scores for negatively worded items were reversed. For each questionnaire statement, the number of students agreeing *not at all* or *a little* on the one hand, and *fairly* or *totally* on the other hand, were summed and expressed in percentage terms.

Research question one was *How do students perceive VocPAL globally?* The mean percentage of students responding positively, i.e. 3 or 4, put the global level of satisfaction with VocPAL at 69.2% (column 1, Figure 5). This figure masks large differences between the 8.7% who said it was boring (item 3 in Appendix A) and the 61.7% who wanted greater interactivity (item 9). Assessments of its attractiveness (73.9%, item 1) and effectiveness (84.3%, item 4) suggest that there is room for improvement but also a solid base to work from.

Figure 5. Questionnaire results (percentages)

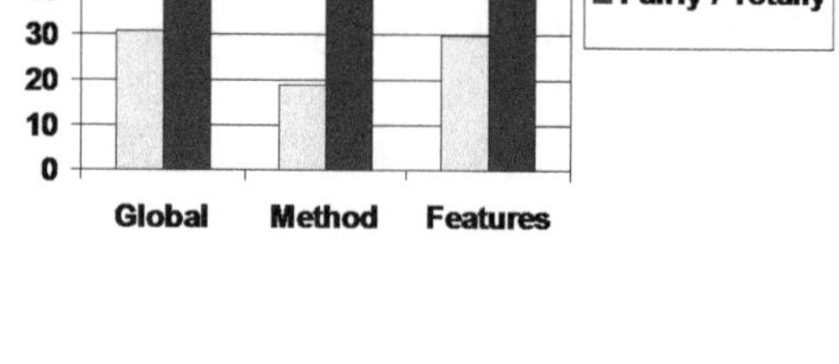

Amongst the factors affecting global appreciation of VocPAL, learners' proficiency level had an impact. There was, indeed, a negative correlation between self-assessed proficiency and global appreciation of the resource ($r = -.47$, $p < .001$). This included a highly significant, if unsurprising, correlation ($r = .49$, $p < .001$) between the means of the self-assessed proficiency scores and scores for item 2, *VocPAL is too easy for me*. Similarly, there was a negative correlation between self-assessed proficiency and item 7, *I learnt new vocabulary with VocPAL* ($r = -.47$, $p < .001$). Of greater interest are the significant correlations between self-assessed proficiency and items 6, *VocPAL is unnecessary for me as I already have my own method* ($r = .47$, $p < .001$), and 8, *I prefer to learn vocabulary with a dictionary* ($r = .23$, $p = .01$). Although only a small minority agreed with these statements, the probable reason for the correlations is that the more proficient learners have thought more about vocabulary learning and adopted strategies of their own. The question of proficiency level is important because an activity perceived as too easy will not provide a challenging enough task to be motivating (Locke, 1996). In the case of VocPAL, a solution would be to incorporate a brief placement test (e.g., Nation & Beglar, 2007), on the basis of which learners could be directed towards a recommended entry level unit.

Research question two was: *How do students engage with the methodological aspects of VocPAL?* Overall, students reported a satisfactory level of methodological engagement with the resource (81.2%, column 2, Figure 5). That this population of learners was ready to engage with new ways of vocabulary learning was attested by their answer regarding the relative importance of vocabulary and grammar (item 30), where only 3.5% considered the former as less important. Despite the recognised importance of vocabulary, however, those who considered VocPAL unnecessary because they already had a vocabulary learning method of their own were in a minority (14.8%, item 6), as were those who preferred to learn words by means of a dictionary (11.3%, item 8).

Research question three was *How do students perceive the specific features that VocPAL incorporates?* The level of satisfaction with the features VocPAL incorporates was less pronounced (70.3%, column 3, Figure 5). The association test was considered useful (90.4%, item 26) as were the translations (86.9%, item 29) and, to a lesser extent, the pictures (57.4%, item 27). As regards the story, the number judging that it would be better not to present the words in a story (7%, item 23) or that the VocPAL stories were uninteresting (20%, item 21) was substantially fewer than those who thought the stories were not very motivating (43.5%, item 24). This figure can be related to the 75.7% who responded negatively to item 12, *After the first half of each film, I want to know what comes next*. Clearly, while the idea of a story *per se* was appealing, there were elements to it which need to be addressed.

Interview Data

The eight students selected for interviews who responded most positively to VocPAL all stressed that they saw vocabulary learning as a necessary chore, but they had no systematic method of their own and in fact rarely set aside time to engage in it. The mean of the self-assessed proficiency score for these eight students was 3.06 compared to the overall mean of 3.88. Five of the students said they underlined unknown words in a text, but only two wrote words, along with their translations, in a notebook. None undertook regular revision of words and none used word frequency as a criterion for selecting words to be learnt. The following excerpt (all interview excerpts have been translated from French), is typical of the positive reactions to VocPAL:

I'd just never thought about how to learn vocabulary before. Even if I try to learn words, I just end up forgetting them and that makes it really difficult

[...] I mean, I see words in texts and I know I've seen them before but I can't remember what they mean. So this makes it more worthwhile, I don't feel as if I'm wasting my time. [...] It's much more motivating, it's not like making a lot of effort for nothing.

The dimension emphasised here, in Schumann's (1997) classification, is goal significance: the input is seen as an effective means towards achieving a goal the learner considers important. Furthermore, all eight students stressed the pleasantness dimension:

It's much better than just a list of words to learn, (with) the pictures and the sound, it's more stimulating, you don't get bored so quickly. [...] In the end you learn more because it's more attractive so you don't have to force yourself quite so much.

Whilst such comments lend support to the general design of the resource, for purposes of improvement it is more instructive to focus on the negative reactions. In the questionnaire data, the story emerged as the feature that, whilst intended to be innovative and motivating, in fact held the least appeal overall. Amongst the 16 respondents least satisfied with VocPAL, several shed light on the reasons for this:

The stories aren't that exciting. They're not boring, but it's not as if you're really caught up with the characters. There's not a lot of action." This idea was expressed several times: "They're not real stories." "Nothing much happens." "They're just characters in a situation, there's no plot.

While the respondents were quick to point out this weakness, 11 of the 16 did not see it as a problem. Rather, they lauded the instructional value of VocPAL, which they saw as taking precedence over the entertainment which was lacking. "It's not like reading an actual story or watching a film. It's just a way of learning vocabulary. It's much better than lists, it's more attractive, but compared to a real film, well, it's completely different." Three students commented more explicitly on the difference: "With VocPAL, I know I'm learning words, I write them down. When I watch a film in English, I think I learn words but I'm more interested in the film. The words just come with it." This remark highlights the distinction between intentional and incidental learning, which the following also refers to:

We have to learn vocabulary, it's part of why we're here. So anything that makes it easier is welcome. But in the end, that's what it's about, not watching films. It would be great if all the vocabulary and grammar came by just watching films but I don't think it happens that way.

Five students nonetheless felt that if the stories were improved, the resource would also be more effective, for example:

It would be good to keep the stories. But maybe have the same characters throughout, like a TV series. Because the words are repeated, so you end up knowing them if you see them several times, but the way it is, you're just thrust into a different story each time so you have to make that effort of starting all over again with different characters.

The opposite viewpoint was also expressed, however, though with a similar appreciation of the recycling feature:

After a while I realised the words were coming back in different contexts and I think that really helps. And having different stories is good, it's not boring. [...] The films are too long, though, 15 minutes without much happening, so the stories would have to be more interesting to make it really work.

The other major point of contention was the lack of interactivity, with ten respondents commenting on the passive nature of the experience:

We watch the pictures go past and read the sentences but we don't actually do anything. If it's on a computer, you expect it to be interactive, it's not like TV. I got a bit impatient, I couldn't intervene to choose different things or go where I wanted.

The interview data overall corroborated the main findings to emerge from the questionnaire results, both negative and positive, and yielded insights into the reasons for those results. On the negative side, the lack of interactivity was a major source of discontent, and the story, though not unanimously decried, came in for criticism as feeble compared to commercial entertainment. The correlation between self-assessed proficiency and a less positive judgement of VocPAL was confirmed in the interviews. Of the 16 least satisfied students, 12 considered that VocPAL was too easy for them, and 8 that the time spent on it was too long compared to what they had learnt. On the positive side, all interview participants pointed to the attractiveness and novelty value of VocPAL, with only one student saying she preferred to learn words with a dictionary. Regarding the improvements that could be made, 19 students suggested greater interactivity, 14 said the films should be shorter and 10 suggested a more personalised approach should be adopted, i.e. a system allowing learners to select words for further revision.

DISCUSSION

Taken as a whole, reactions to VocPAL indicate that the answer to research question one (*How do students perceive VocPAL globally?*) is positive. As Schumann (1998) posits, a learner's appraisal of any learning activity is a composite and fluctuating blend of reactions in which various criteria come together. Amongst the most important are pleasantness (*Am I enjoying this?*) and goal significance (*Is this serving my current goal?*). In this respect, the global perception of VocPAL as both attractive and effective validates the broad approach adopted. Looking closer, though, the positive appreciation is lessened by two aspects which aroused negative reactions amongst a majority of respondents: the poor appeal of the films (item 12) and the lack of interactivity (item 9).

As regards the films, for three quarters of respondents, the first half of each film did not make them curious to see the second half. This can be related partly to a lack of appeal of the story, but more generally to a lassitude that sets in when the series of stimuli comprising a specific input becomes repetitive. In other words, the novelty dimension of Schumann's appraisal criteria fades as the input progresses. Whilst a resource may initially be seen as novel compared to other methods, such as learning words in lists, learners' willingness to persist with it beyond a few minutes will depend in part upon the novelty of each individual stimulus. Although in VocPAL the words and pictures change with each sequence of slides, the activity itself (read the first slide, binary judgement on the second, read the third) soon sets into a pattern where the novelty wears off. As one interviewee put it, "The story would have to be really good to make me forget I'm actually just seeing a list of words." Because vocabulary learning by nature runs the risk of becoming repetitive, the need to maintain novelty in the input is important. The introduction of greater interactivity, whereby the learner is involved more actively, is one way of doing so.

Given the plethora of computer-based activities, whether for learning or entertainment, or a combination of the two, the call for greater interactivity was to be expected. Currently, VocPAL is low in interactivity, consisting as it does of slides assembled into a film. An obvious improvement would be for learners to choose when to move from one slide to the next. Other relatively simple options are for learners to call up translations and collocational information if they wish by clicking on a link, or for the written and spoken text of characters' speech bubbles to be similarly accessed. A more sophisticated feature would allow learners to choose words they are less sure of to be set aside for further elaborative processing. These expedients would lessen learners' impression of submitting passively to the input. In general, however, although interactivity is desirable, it needs to be introduced with care and parsimony in order to avoid an extraneous cognitive load that could be detrimental to learning (De Haan, Reed, & Kuwada, 2010).

The results regarding the second research question (*How do students engage with the methodological aspects of VocPAL?*) were encouraging. The students appeared to understand and approve of the rationale behind certain choices made when conceiving VocPAL, notably the presentation order of context sentence, association test and translation. Students showed willingness to engage in the mental effort this presentation order was intended to encourage. First, they tried to guess the meaning of the words from the context (86.1%, item 16); second, they saw the association test as consolidating their knowledge of the words (77.4%, item 17); finally, they agreed that the translations are better seen at the end (91.3%, item 20). Furthermore, a majority were prepared to engage in further effort by spending more time on a slide if needed (76.5%, item 18) or by noting down words they didn't know (72.2%, item 19). Overall, these results indicate that learners appreciate that vocabulary learning, as suggested by Schmitt (2008), involves a partnership: on the one hand, teachers, researchers and materials writers must combine to offer well-designed activities, but on the other hand learners themselves must be prepared to take an active approach to the task. The results suggest that the participants in the present study at least are indeed willing to take up their role in the partnership.

The third question (*How do students perceive the specific features that VocPAL incorporates?*) gave rise to mixed results. Whilst the association test and the translations were both received positively, the response to the pictures was less favourable, with just 57.4% judging them helpful (item 27). In the interviews, however, all students said the pictures should be kept as they contributed to VocPAL's attractiveness. The issue, then, is whether, despite being attractive, pictures can in some cases actually be detrimental to understanding the target words. For obvious reasons, studies examining the effect of pictures on vocabulary learning have used them in conjunction with concrete words (e.g. Barcroft, 2009; Omaggio, 1979; Tonzar & Lotto, 2009). However, as noted by Oxford and Scarcella (1994), some abstract words, such as *evil*, can be rendered more concrete by the use of a picture. There is a need for more research on the use of pictures with abstract words, and in the case of VocPAL, this should involve a close examination of the effect of the pictures used with the least imageable words, such as *scope* or *breach*. The pictures that accompany the context sentences for these words are, respectively, of a landscape at sunset and a crack in a concrete surface; though related to the story, these pictures are likely to be of little help in conveying the meanings of the words.

The other feature which requires consideration is the story. The questionnaire data clearly point to its potential advantage from a motivational point of view. Indeed, only 7% of respondents considered that it would be better to present the words without a story. However, both questionnaire and interview data suggest that in order to hold learners' interest more fully, it needs a more powerful appeal. Indeed, it is questionable whether the current VocPAL input constitutes a story in the normal sense of the word. This is because, although each unit contains a setting, identifiable characters, a causal chain of events and an outcome, many of the 80 context sentences do not contribute directly to driving the narrative forward, and may therefore weaken the pace and undermine learners' interest.

What makes a good story? In a study of how readers perceive the quality of a story, Baron and Bluck (2011) found that the best stories are seen as entertaining, emotional, memorable, original, rich in imagery and engaging. The stories in that study were in the participants' L1, but given that L2 learners experience stories first in their L1, they are likely to use the same criteria when judging stories in L2. The difference is that to the storyteller targeting L2 learners, an extra challenge applies, namely packing all these qualities into a text adapted to learners' proficiency level. In a study of graded readers, Claridge (2012) mentions that L2 readers' enjoyment of a book comes from being submerged in the world the story creates, an experience which the qualities cited by Baron and Bluck (2011) no doubt help to bring about. Conversely, Claridge (2012) found that reasons for not enjoying a book were "difficulty" and "boredom", the two aspects being linked since a book perceived as difficult soon gives rise to boredom. Whilst most respondents clearly saw VocPAL as an attractive alternative to learning words in a list, perceiving it as neither boring nor difficult, greater attention to the qualities cited by Baron and Bluck (2011) would undoubtedly increase its appeal. Certainly, during its conception, the quest to invent context sentences that were not only conducive to an understanding of the current target word, but also recycled previous words, took precedence over the construction of an engaging story. Today's learners, though, are also discerning, demanding consumers of multiple forms of audio-visual entertainment, and any attempt to increase the novelty and pleasantness of a learning resource will need to take that into account. However, such an aim is not unattainable, and because the motivational dimension of the input is of prime importance for any resource intended for autonomous use, the results of the present study indicate that increasing the appeal of the stories must be the next major goal in the development of VocPAL.

Whilst increasing the attractiveness of a resource is desirable, care needs to be taken to ensure that learners are not so entertained by it that they no longer pay attention to the material to be learnt (Mayer & Johnson, 2010). Indeed, the embedding of material to be learnt within an engaging narrative has been shown in some circumstances to be counter-productive (Mayer, Griffith, Naftaly, & Rothman, 2008). However, the material in such cases typically consists of scientific concepts to which the narrative is extraneous, whereas in the case of language learning, the target material is by definition central to the story being told. The challenge is to ensure that learners, whilst processing the narrative, nonetheless attend explicitly to the target words. Fortunately, as evidenced by comments in the interviews, learners are able to draw a distinction between instruction and entertainment, and in the present study, the number noting down unfamiliar words points to an intention to learn which is commendable – even if regular revision of words noted appears to be seldom undertaken. However, learners can also attend explicitly to material without engaging in intentional learning (Hulstijn, 2001). Through the association test, in which target words are briefly decontextualised and made more salient, it is precisely this form of processing that VocPAL encourages. From this perspective, the story serves as the contextual backdrop which makes the target words more meaningful in that they serve a narrative purpose. However, the establishment and consolidation of lexical representations is likely to stem from other features such as the association test and the recycling.

LIMITATIONS

The major limitation of the study reported here is that it does not address actual learning outcomes. Whilst a majority of respondents (70.4%, item 7) felt they had both learned new words and reactivated their knowledge of words they had forgotten, these subjective impressions need to be supplemented with more precise data on learning gains. Amongst studies which have done this are Cobb and Horst (2011) who reported significant gains amongst learners using *Word Coach* over a four month period and Toczu and Coady (2004) who reported similar results for a CALL tutorial programme, *New Lexis*. In order to support the claim that VocPAL is effective, a similar study needs to be undertaken to compare learning outcomes following its use with those obtained without it. A stringent test here would consist in using a control group engaged in activities that include a specific vocabulary focus. And since a strong point of CALL applications is that they can be used outside of class, a more valid form of comparison may be between use of the vocabulary resource and other forms of personal assignments that include a vocabulary component. Indeed, given the need for learners to adopt a proactive approach to vocabulary learning (Schmitt, 2008), future research could usefully investigate the extent to which learners engage voluntarily with the various resources available to them outside of class in order to achieve this aim. It is likely that time spent on any well-designed activity that focuses on vocabulary will lead to words being learnt, and the ultimate test of a resource is therefore less to be found in this learning outcome than in the motivational aspect reflected in the learners' readiness to use the resource.

Related to the previous point, another limitation in this study was the profile of the learners involved. Ease of access to them via the University's learning platform ensured that a reasonably high level of participation could be expected, but their choice of course, Applied Foreign Languages, means no doubt that they are at a higher level of proficiency than students on courses where English is less central, though generally still compulsory, (i.e. non-specialists). The beginning units of VocPAL that were tested here would therefore be better suited to such non-specialist students, who are less likely to perceive them as too easy. On the other hand, these students are also typically less motivated and given that VocPAL seeks to appeal to them, future studies should also include groups from that population.

Beyond the present study itself, there are also limitations to VocPAL as it stands. The main points to emerge from the study concerned interactivity and the story, but there is also an issue related to personalised learning. In his review of flashcard vocabulary learning programmes, Nakata (2011) notes that an ideal program should have both a presentation mode and a retrieval mode. This is not the case for VocPAL, which for the moment focuses solely on the presentation of items, not on their subsequent testing or retrieval. The emphasis has been on devising a presentation context intended to maximise learners' chances of establishing and consolidating lexical representations on the one hand, and their willingness to engage with the resource on the other. As noted by Godwin-Jones (2010), there is no lack of programs which allow for spaced repetition (e.g. Anki, FullRecall or iKnow), a feature which can guarantee a sufficient number of encounters at intervals calculated to promote effective learning. As indeed was mentioned by 10 students during the interviews, a personalised learning feature would therefore be a welcome addition.

Whilst it may ultimately be desirable, though, spaced repetition is not currently a priority in the development of VocPAL. Unlike flashcard programmes, VocPAL goes beyond paired associate learning or single sentence contexts by presenting words in stories in which the careful recycling of words largely obviates the need for a spaced repetition algorithm as a core feature of the resource. Indeed one aim of VocPAL is to reach out to learners who may lack the motivation to explore new software or create their own flashcards by presenting pre-established sets of words based on frequency. The disadvantage here, as mentioned by Godwin-Jones (2010) with regard to the vocabulary component of Rosetta Stone, is that by imposing a set input, there is a risk that some learners will consider the presentation of words they already know as superfluous to their needs. Although they were in a minority (16.5%, item 15) in the present study, these learners may prefer to adopt a separate approach to the two goals, fluency development through reading or listening on the one hand, and the learning of new words through decontextualised encounters on the other. VocPAL currently takes a hybrid approach by placing learners in both a story reading mode, with its emphasis on increasing automaticity of word recognition, and a more intentional word learning mode. Given that a sizeable minority of respondents (26.2%, item 28) found that the association test gets in the way of the story, it might indeed be judicious to separate the two more clearly.

CONCLUSION

This chapter has presented an account of the ongoing development of a CAVL resource, VocPAL, intended to lighten the burden of vocabulary learning for French learners of English. Whilst this account has inevitably entailed a close consideration of its design features, the aim is not to highlight VocPAL itself but to provide an illustration of a research and development approach to CAVL that incorporates certain established principles relating to L2 vocabulary learning. The research side has not only involved measuring learning outcomes in different experimental conditions (Prince, 2006; 2012) but also, as here, assessing learners' perceptions and reactions. This is a vital stage before committing to a more definitive version. Choices, once made, are difficult to retract after time and money have been invested in them. VocPAL is still at a stage where a degree of flexibility in development options is possible and while the quest for improvement will continue, there are currently no plans to commit to a specific format in a commercially available package.

Far from promoting a product, therefore, the aim here has been to describe one way in which certain design features, based on theoretical and empirical research, can be combined, notably the use of stories in which target words are systematically recycled. This controlled exposure to unknown or partially known vocabulary of gradually decreasing frequency is one way of resolving the "lexical paradox" pointed out by Cobb (2007), namely that learners are often expected to rely on reading in order to acquire the vocabulary they need to be able to read effectively. As pointed out by Cobb (2007), though, an approach that relies on carefully scripting material to ensure the controlled exposure required to increase lexical knowledge is difficult and time-consuming. Other approaches to resolving the paradox have been described by Ghadirian (2002) and Cobb (2007), using dedicated software to modify and sequence texts so as to ensure a gradual progression in lexical knowledge. There are thus several ways of tackling the problem and embedding the controlled exposure within stories, as opposed to more academic texts or indeed unrelated sentences and flashcards, is just one of them. While a dedicated programme like VocPAL invites learners to engage with the stories it proposes, CALL also lends itself to learner-generated stories via computer mediated communication (CMC), which has been shown to be conducive to learner interaction focusing on vocabulary (Blake, 2002). Thus, specific sets of target words can be combined in short stories which can then be improved collaboratively in CMC.

Ever more rapid technological progress means that new ways of providing language input are constantly being developed. While this is both positive and exciting, the L2 vocabulary learning challenge is still problematic for vast numbers of learners. Any way of raising both teachers' and learners' awareness of the importance of vocabulary learning is thus welcome, even more so if done in a manner that is motivating, systematic and based on sound principles. Through the description of one attempt to develop such a resource, it is hoped that this chapter contributes, however slightly, to the endeavour.

REFERENCES

Arispe, K. (2011, November). *L2 vocabulary development as mediated through an ICALL tool, LangBot*. Paper presented at The Fourth International Ubiquitous Learning Conference. Berkeley, CA.

Arnaud, P. J. L., Béjoint, H., & Thoiron, P. (1985). A quoi sert le programme lexical? *Les Langues Modernes*, *79*(3/4), 72–85.

Barcroft, J. (2002). Semantic and structural elaboration in L2 lexical acquisition. *Language Learning*, *52*(2), 323–363. doi:10.1111/0023-8333.00186

Barcroft, J. (2009). Strategies and performance in intentional L2 vocabulary learning. *Language Awareness*, *18*(1), 74–89. doi:10.1080/09658410802557535

Blake, R. (2000). Computer mediated communication: A window on L2 Spanish interlanguage. *Language Learning & Technology*, *4*(1), 120–136.

Bolger, P., & Zapata, G. (2011). Semantic categories and context in L2 vocabulary learning. *Language Learning*, *61*(2), 614–646. doi:10.1111/j.1467-9922.2010.00624.x

Bower, G. H., & Clark, M. C. (1969). Narrative stories as mediators for serial learning. *Psychonomic Science*, *14*, 181–182. doi:10.3758/BF03332778

Brown, A. V. (2009). Students' and teachers' perceptions of effective foreign language teaching: A comparison of ideals. *Modern Language Journal*, *93*, 46–60. doi:10.1111/j.1540-4781.2009.00827.x

Chun, D. M., & Plass, J. L. (1996). Effects of multimedia annotations on vocabulary acquisition. *Modern Language Journal*, *80*(2), 183–198. doi:10.1111/j.1540-4781.1996.tb01159.x

Claridge, G. (2012). Graded readers: How the publishers make the grade. *Reading in a Foreign Language*, *24*(1), 106–119.

Cobb, T. (2007). Computing the vocabulary demands of L2 reading. *Language Learning & Technology*, *11*(3), 38–63.

Cobb, T., & Horst, M. (2011). Does word coach coach words? *CALICO Journal*, *28*(3), 639–661. doi:10.11139/cj.28.3.639-661

Craik, F. I. M., & Lockhart, R. S. (1972). Levels of processing: A framework for memory research. *Journal of Verbal Learning and Verbal Behavior*, *11*, 671–684. doi:10.1016/S0022-5371(72)80001-X

De Haan, J., Reed, W. M., & Kuwada, K. (2010). The effect of interactivity with a music video game on second language vocabulary recall. *Language Learning & Technology*, *14*(2), 74–94.

Felix, U. (2005). Analysing recent CALL effectiveness research – towards a common agenda. *Computer Assisted Language Learning*, *18*(1-2), 1–32. doi:10.1080/09588220500132274

Fraser, C. A. (1999). Lexical processing strategy use and vocabulary learning through reading. *Studies in Second Language Acquisition*, *21*, 225–241. doi:10.1017/S0272263199002041

Ghadirian, S. (2002). Providing controlled exposure to target vocabulary through the screening and arranging of texts. *Language Learning & Technology*, *6*(1), 147–164.

Godwin-Jones, R. (2010). From memory palaces to spacing algorithms: Approaches to second-language vocabulary learning. *Language Learning & Technology*, *14*(2), 4–11.

Graesser, A. C., Singer, M., & Trabasso, T. (1994). Constructing inferences during narrative text comprehension. *Psychological Review*, *101*, 371–395. doi:10.1037/0033-295X.101.3.371 PMID:7938337

Groot, P. J. (2000). Computer assisted second language vocabulary acquisition. *Language Learning & Technology*, *4*(1), 60–81.

Hulstijn, J., & Laufer, B. (2001). Some empirical evidence for the involvement load hypothesis in vocabulary acquisition. *Language Learning*, *51*(3), 539–558. doi:10.1111/0023-8333.00164

Hulstijn, J. H. (2001). Intentional and incidental second–language vocabulary learning: A reappraisal of elaboration, rehearsal and automaticity. In P. Robinson (Ed.), *Cognition and second language instruction* (pp. 258–286). Cambridge: Cambridge University Press. doi:10.1017/CBO9781139524780.011

Jones, L., & Plass, J. (2002). Supporting listening comprehension with multimedia annotations. *Modern Language Journal*, *86*(4), 546–561. doi:10.1111/1540-4781.00160

Kaivanpanah, S., & Alavi, M. (2008). Deriving unknown word meaning from context: Is it reliable? *RELC Journal*, *39*(1), 77–95. doi:10.1177/0033688208091141

Kilgariff, A. (1995). A lemmatised frequency list for the 6,318 words with more than 800 occurrences in the British national corpus. Available from http://www.kilgarriff.co.uk/bnc-readme.html#lemmatised

Laufer, B. (2005). Instructed second language vocabulary learning: The fault in the 'default hypothesis. In A. Housen, & M. Pierrard (Eds.), *Investigations in instructed second language acquisition* (pp. 286–303). Mouton de Gruyter. doi:10.1515/9783110197372.2.311

Laufer, B., & Rozovski-Roitblat, B. (2011). Incidental vocabulary acquisition: The effects of task type, word occurrence and their combination. *Language Teaching Research*, *15*(4), 391–411. doi:10.1177/1362168811412019

Laufer, B., & Shmueli, K. (1997). Memorizing new words: does teaching have anything to do with it? *RELC Journal*, *28*(1), 89–108. doi:10.1177/003368829702800106

Laurillard, D., Stratfold, M., Luckin, R., Plowman, L., & Taylor, J. (2000). Affordances for learning in a non-linear narrative medium. *Journal of Interactive Media in Education*. Available from, http://jime.open.ac.uk/article/2000-2/51

Locke, E. (1996). Motivation through conscious goal setting. *Applied & Preventive Psychology*, *5*, 117–123. doi:10.1016/S0962-1849(96)80005-9

Lotto, L., & de Groot, A. M. B. (1998). Effects of learning method and word type on acquiring vocabulary in an unfamiliar language. *Language Learning*, *48*(1), 31–69. doi:10.1111/1467-9922.00032

Ma, Q. (2013). Computer assisted vocabulary learning: Framework and tracking users' data. *CALICO Journal*, 230–243.

Ma, Q., & Kelly, P. (2006). Computer-assisted vocabulary learning: Design and evaluation. *Computer Assisted Language Learning*, *19*(1), 15–46. doi:10.1080/09588220600803998

Mayer, R. E., Griffith, E., Naftaly, I., & Rothman, D. (2008). Increased interestingness of extraneous details leads to decreased learning. *Journal of Experimental Psychology. Applied*, *14*, 329–339. doi:10.1037/a0013835 PMID:19102616

Mayer, R. E., & Johnson, C. I. (2010). Adding instructional features that promote learning in a game-like environment. *Journal of Educational Computing Research*, *42*(3), 241–265. doi:10.2190/EC.42.3.a

McLean, K. C., Pasupathi, M., & Pals, J. L. (2007). Selves creating stories creating selves: A process model of self-development. *Personality and Social Psychology Review*, *11*(3), 262–278. doi:10.1177/1088868307301034 PMID:18453464

Montero Perez, M., Peters, E., & Desmet, P. (2014). Is less more? Effectiveness and perceived usefulness of keyword and full captioned video for L2 listening comprehension. *ReCALL*, 1–23.

Nagy, W. E., Herman, P. A., & Anderson, P. C. (1985). Learning words from context. *Reading Research Quarterly*, *20*, 233–253. doi:10.2307/747758

Nakata, T. (2011). Computer-assisted second language vocabulary learning in a paired-associate paradigm: A critical investigation of flashcard software. *Computer Assisted Language Learning*, *24*(1), 17–38. doi:10.1080/09588221.2010.520675

Nassaji, H. (2004). Input modality and remembering name-referent associations in vocabulary learning. *Canadian Journal of Applied Linguistics*, *7*, 39–55.

Nation, I. S. P. (2001). *Learning vocabulary in another language*. Cambridge: Cambridge University Press. doi:10.1017/CBO9781139524759

Nation, I. S. P. (2006). How large a vocabulary is needed for reading and listening? *Canadian Modern Language Review*, *63*(1), 59–82. doi:10.3138/cmlr.63.1.59

Nation, P., & Beglar, D. (2007). A vocabulary size test. *Language Teaching*, *31*(7), 9–13.

Nicholas, B. J., Rossiter, M. J., & Abbott, M. L. (2011). The power of story in the ESL classroom. *Canadian Modern Language Review*, *67*(2), 247–268. doi:10.3138/cmlr.67.2.247

Omaggio, A. C. (1979). Pictures and second language comprehension: Do they help? *Foreign Language Annals*, *12*, 107–116. doi:10.1111/j.1944-9720.1979.tb00153.x

Oxford, R. L., & Scarcella, R. C. (1994). Second language vocabulary learning among adults: State of the art in vocabulary instruction. *System*, *22*(2), 231–243. doi:10.1016/0346-251X(94)90059-0

Poulshock, J. (2010). Extensive graded reading in the liberal arts and sciences. *Reading in a Foreign Language*, *22*(2), 2.

Prince, P. (2006). L'Apprentissage des mots: Présentation d'un dispositif basé sur le jugement sémantique. *Cahiers de l'Apliut*, *24*(2), 112–128.

Prince, P. (2012). Second language vocabulary learning: Can a story help? *Language Learning & Technology*, *16*(3), 103–120.

Schmitt, N. (2008). Instructed second language *vocabulary* learning. *Language Teaching Research*, *12*(3), 329–363. doi:10.1177/1362168808089921

Schumann, J. H. (1998). The neurobiology of affect in language. A supplement to "language learning.". *Language Learning*, *48*(Supplement 1), 1–36.

Sinclair, J. (Ed.). (2006). *Collins COBUILD advanced English dictionary* (5th ed.). London: Collins.

Stockwell, G. (2007). Vocabulary on the move: Investigating an intelligent mobile phone-based vocabulary tutor. *Computer Assisted Language Learning*, *20*(4), 365–383. doi:10.1080/09588220701745817

Stockwell, G. (2010). Using mobile phones for vocabulary activities: Examining the effect of the platform. *Language Learning & Technology*, *14*(2), 95–110.

Tonzar, C., Lotto, L., & Job, R. (2009). L2 vocabulary acquisition in children: Effects of learning method and cognate status. *Language Learning*, *59*, 623–646. doi:10.1111/j.1467-9922.2009.00519.x

Tozcu, A., & Coady, J. (2004). Successful learning of frequent vocabulary through CALL also benefits reading comprehension and speed. *Computer Assisted Language Learning*, *17*(5), 473–495. doi:10.1080/0958822042000319674

Tulving, E., & Madigan, S. A. (1970). Memory and verbal learning. *Annual Review of Psychology, 21*(1), 437–484. doi:10.1146/annurev.ps.21.020170.002253

Ushioda, E. (1996). *Learner autonomy 5: The role of motivation*. Dublin: Authentik.

Webb, S. (2008). The effects of context on incidental vocabulary learning. *Reading in a Foreign Language, 20*, 232–245.

Webb, W. B. (1962). The effects of prolonged learning on learning. *Journal of Verbal Learning and Verbal Behavior, 1*, 173–182. doi:10.1016/S0022-5371(62)80026-7

Yoshii, M. (2006). L1 and l2 glosses: Their effects on incidental vocabulary learning. *Language Learning & Technology, 10*(3), 85–101.

Yoshii, M. (2013). Effects of gloss types on vocabulary learning through reading: Comparison of single and multiple gloss types. *CALICO Journal*, 203–229.

Zahar, R., Cobb, T., & Spada, N. (2001). Acquiring vocabulary through reading: Effects of frequency and contextual richness. *Canadian Modern Language Review, 57*(4), 541–572. doi:10.3138/cmlr.57.4.541

ADDITIONAL READING

Carpenter, S. K., Sachs, R. E., Martin, B., Schmidt, K., & Looft, R. (2012). Learning new vocabulary in German: The effects of inferring word meanings, type of feedback, and time of test. *Psychonomic Bulletin & Review, 19*(1), 81–86.

Chiu, Y. H. (2013). Computer-assisted second language vocabulary instruction: A meta-analysis. *British Journal of Educational Technology, 44*(2), E52–E56.

Choo, L. E. E., Lin, D. T., & Pandian, A. (2012). Language learning approaches: A review of research on explicit and implicit learning in vocabulary acquisition. *Procedia: Social and Behavioral Sciences, 55*, 852–860.

Franciosi, S. (2011). A comparison of computer game and language learning task design using flow theory. *CALL-EJ, 12*(1), 11–25.

Horst, M. (2014). Mainstreaming second language vocabulary acquisition. *Canadian Journal of Applied Linguistics, 16*(1), 171–188.

Huang, H. T., & Liou, H. C. (2007). Vocabulary learning in an automated graded reading program. *Language Learning & Technology, 11*(3), 64–82.

Huang, Y. M., Huang, Y. M., Huang, S. H., & Lin, Y. T. (2012). A ubiquitous English vocabulary learning system: Evidence of active/passive attitudes vs. usefulness/ease-of-use. *Computers & Education, 58*(1), 273–282.

Li, J. (2009). The evolution of vocabulary learning strategies in a computer-mediated reading environment. *CALICO Journal, 27*(1), 118–146.

Loucky, J. P. (2010). Constructing a roadmap to more systematic and successful online reading and vocabulary acquisition. *Literary and Linguistic Computing, 25*(2), 225–241.

Nation, P., & Ming-Tzu, K. W. (1999). Graded readers and vocabulary. *Reading in a Foreign Language, 12*(2), 355–380.

Neville, D. O., Shelton, B. E., & McInnis, B. (2009). Cybertextredux: Using digital game-based learning to teach L2 vocabulary, reading, and culture. *Computer Assisted Language Learning, 22*(5), 409–424.

Oberg, A. (2011). Comparison of the effectiveness of a CALL-based approach and a card-based approach to vocabulary acquisition and retention. *CALICO Journal, 29*(1), 118–144.

Peters, E. (2012). The differential effects of two vocabulary instruction methods on EFL word learning: A study into task effectiveness. *International Review of Applied Linguistics in Language Teaching*, *50*(3), 213–238.

Pustejovsky, J., & Boguraev, B. (1997). *Lexical Semantics: The Problem of Polysemy*. Oxford: Oxford University Press.

Smith, G. G., Li, M., Drobisz, J., Park, H. R., Kim, D., & Smith, S. D. (2013). Play games or study? Computer games in eBooks to learn English vocabulary. *Computers & Education*, *69*, 274–286.

Sommers, M. S., & Barcroft, J. (2013). Effects of Referent Token Variability on L2 Vocabulary Learning. *Language Learning*, *63*(2), 186–210.

Uzun, L. (2009). An evaluative checklist for computer games used for foreign language vocabulary learning and practice: Vocaword sample. *Novitas-ROYAL*, *3*(1), 45–59.

Yip, F. W., & Kwan, A. C. (2006). Online vocabulary games as a tool for teaching and learning English vocabulary. *Educational Media International*, *43*(3), 233–249.

KEY TERMS AND DEFINITIONS

Autonomous Learning: This does not mean learning on one's own but the capacity to take control of one's learning, i.e. to plan, monitor and evaluate it. It is linked to motivation: a fully autonomous learner has the intrinsic motivation needed to develop metacognitive knowledge, itself helpful in judging the usefulness of a learning activity or resource.

Frequency: The effect of frequency is ubiquitous in language, with words that occur more frequently being accessed more easily both in comprehension and production. A large percentage of text is covered by the most frequent words of a language, which are therefore the most useful words to know for any learner of that language. L2 words need to be encountered several times for frequency effects to be observed, hence the importance of recycling all words which a teacher or materials designer deems to be important.

Intentional Learning: This is when material is studied with a view to committing it to memory. It can be contrasted with incidental learning, in which material is learnt without any conscious intention to do so. The distinction between the two is not clear-cut as a learner can explicitly attend to material without intending to learn it. Intentional learning can be operationalised through informing learners that they will be tested on the material afterwards. But even in the absence of such information, learning can be more or less intentional depending on the learner's goals and the situation.

Learner Perceptions: Information initially perceived through the senses is interpreted and appraised according to the learner's current long–term and short-term goals. Learners' perceptions of an activity are the result of this appraisal, involving affective and cognitive dimensions, relating to the pleasantness and usefulness of the activity.

Presentation Context: In its broadest sense, this refers to all information accompanying the perception of a given stimulus. With regard to target words to be learnt, context can refer more narrowly to the linguistic context in which the word is embedded. This can be restricted to a single sentence or extended to a paragraph or whole text. A contextualised encounter with a word can be contrasted with a decontextualized encounter in which the word is isolated from the sentence and presented, for example, with its translation or with other words for purposes of comparison.

APPENDIX

Questionnaire (translated from French). Items denoting a dissatisfactory aspect are signalled (-). Categories: 1 = Global Appreciation, 2 = Methodological Engagement, 3 = Specific Features.

	Item	Category	Disagree	Agree
1	VocPAL is an attractive method	1	26.10	73.90
2	It is too easy for me (-)	1	53.90	46.10
3	It is boring (-)	1	91.30	8.70
4	It is an effective method	1	15.70	84.30
5	The films are too long (-)	1	68.70	31.30
6	It is unnecessary for me as I already have my own method (-)	1	85.20	14.80
7	I learnt new vocabulary with VocPAL	1	29.60	70.40
8	I prefer to learn vocabulary with a dictionary (-)	1	88.70	11.30
9	There should be more interactivity (-)	1	38.30	61.70
10	It is useful because it reminds me of words I had forgotten	1	29.60	70.40
11	I would like to continue with the following units	1	37.40	62.60
12	After the first half of each film, I want to know what comes next	1	75.70	24.30
13	My reading comprehension has improved	1	49.60	50.40
14	My listening comprehension has improved	1	39.10	60.90
15	Seeing words I already know is a waste of time (-)	2	83.50	16.50
16	I try to guess the meaning of the words from the context	2	13.90	86.10
17	The association test consolidates my knowledge of the words	2	22.60	77.40
18	I click on 'pause' if I want to spend more time on a slide	2	23.50	76.50
19	I note down the words I don't know	2	27.80	72.20
20	It would be better to see the translations straightaway (-)	2	91.30	8.70
21	The stories are uninteresting (-)	3	80.00	20.00
22	The number of unknown words increases with each unit	3	37.40	62.60
23	It would be better to present the words without a story (-)	3	93.00	7.00
24	The story is a motivating element	3	43.50	56.50
25	I recognise the words which reoccur more easily	3	13.90	86.10
26	The association test is unnecessary (-)	3	90.40	9.60
27	The pictures help me understand the meanings of the words	3	42.60	57.40
28	The association test gets in the way of the story (-)	3	73.40	26.60
29	The translations are useful	3	13.10	86.90
30	To me vocabulary is less important than grammar		3.50	96.50

Section 5

Systematic Review of CALL Research

Chapter 14 Vocabulary CALL for Young ESL/EFL Learners: A Systematic Review of the Research Evidence

Zöe Handley
York University, UK

ABSTRACT

This chapter presents a systematic review of empirical research on vocabulary CALL for primary and secondary learners of English as a foreign or second language published between 2004 and 2013. Twenty-two studies were identified, the majority of which focused on the use of multimedia to communicate the meaning of lexical items and mobile devices to provide "anytime anywhere" vocabulary training, and found a beneficial impact of the use of technology on vocabulary learning. However, while some of the studies provided a theoretically grounded rationale for their choice of technology, the design of some of the studies was found to limit their usefulness in terms of furthering our understanding of Second Language Acquisition (SLA) and building up an evidence base to inform the design of future vocabulary CALL. The chapter concludes by highlighting examples of studies that were found to contribute to furthering our understanding of CALL and SLA.

INTRODUCTION

With government initiatives all over the world introducing technology in schools (Macaro, Handley, & Walter, 2012) and the introduction of technology into the language curriculum (ibid.), technology is now a concern of primary and secondary school language teachers as well as university language tutors. Research on the use of technology in language teaching has, however, until recently focused on the tertiary sector (Bax, 2003). In response to this need, Macaro, Handley, and Walter (2012) recently undertook a systematic review of evidence for the effectiveness of new technologies in primary and secondary language learning – a systematic review involves an exhaustive literature search guided by focused review questions and synthesis of all high quality primary research identified in relation to those questions (EPPI-Centre, March 2007). Reflecting the im-

DOI: 10.4018/978-1-4666-6174-5.ch014

portance that has long been seen in devoting time to vocabulary in language programmes (Wilkins, 1972) and recent research that supports Wilkin's claim that it is more important for learners to acquire vocabulary than learn grammatical rules (Barcroft, 2007a), Macaro et al. (2012) found that vocabulary has long been a focus of research in Computer-Assisted Language Learning (CALL). In this chapter, I present a more in-depth examination of the literature on the use of technology in vocabulary learning and teaching identified in Macro et al.'s (2012) systematic review and an update to it.

Following Pederson (1987), I believe that if CALL is to progress, researchers need to build a body of evidence upon which to base future CALL software design. In order to achieve this, researchers need to move away from atheoretical CALL versus non-CALL comparisons that provide little, if any, insight into what feature of a particular technology or piece software makes it effective and begin to focus on researching the differential impact of coding elements, specifically those features of a technology that might have a differential impact on learning within the framework of second language acquisition (SLA) theory and research. Relating CALL research to SLA theory and research is important because it helps researchers find possible explanations for the success or failure of CALL interventions and make appropriate adjustments to their design. Further, a number of CALL researchers have noted the potential for CALL to make significant contributions to the development of our understanding of SLA, by providing an environment that can be used to operationalize SLA theory and conveniently make sufficient observations of learners' behaviours to shed light on the complex process of language acquisition (Doughty, 1987; Goodfellow, 1995). Reviews of the CALL literature, however, suggest that little CALL research draws on and contributes to theory (Hubbard, 2008; Levy & Stockwell, 2006), and, where it does, it most often draws on SLA to inform the design of a piece of software or an intervention and rarely exploits CALL to operationalize and test SLA theory (Chapelle, 2009; Hubbard, 2008; Levy &Stockwell, 2006). With a view to establishing an evidence base upon which future vocabulary CALL can be developed, I, therefore, elaborate on Macaro et al.'s (2012) analysis of vocabulary studies and situate them within the broader body of research in the field of SLA and consider the degree to which the research has the potential to inform the design of future CALL software and help us better understand SLA.

BACKGROUND

It has long been acknowledged that mastering the vocabulary of a language plays an important role in SLA. Not only has vocabulary knowledge been shown to be more important than grammar (Barcroft, 2007a), but it has also been shown to correlate strongly with a range of measures of language proficiency including grammar, reading, listening and writing, and account for 37-62% of the variance in measures of language proficiency (Alderson, 2005). Further, vocabulary acquisition is an enormous task. It is estimated that in order to engage in daily communicative activities, learners need to know 6,000 to 7,000 word families and in order to read novels and newspapers, 8,000 to 9,000 word families (Nation, 2006). Estimates of the number of words that learners need to master in order to achieve native-like proficiency rise to 16,000 to 20,000 word families (Schmitt, 2010a), where a word family "consists of a headword, its inflected forms, and its closely related derived forms" (Nation, 2001, p. 8). Moreover, there is considerably more to knowing a word and being able to use it than knowing the form-meaning mapping (Nation, 2001). From the perspective of reception, Nation notes that knowing a word involves knowing what the word looks and sounds like, and recognising its parts, knowing its meaning, the intension and extension of its meaning, and its connotations, and knowing the syntactic patterns, collocations, and contexts in which it can be expected to occur. On the other hand, Nation finds that productive knowledge of a word includes knowing how to write and pronounce it, what word parts are needed to express its meaning, what meanings it might be used to express, in what contexts it might be used, and what syntax and collocations are appropriate. It is therefore not surprising that vocabulary learning and teaching has attracted a lot of attention from CALL researchers. According to Jung's (2005) bibliometric study of research published between 1980 and 2004, vocabulary teaching and learning, unlike other areas of linguistic knowledge and skill, has consistently attracted interest from researchers over the history of CALL, and vocabulary was found to be the most frequently investigated of the three areas of linguistic knowledge (vocabulary, grammar and pronunciation) and the four language skills (reading, writing, speaking, and listening) in Stockwell's (2007) systematic review of CALL research.

As mentioned in the introduction, following Pederson (1987), I believe that the goal of CALL research should be to establish an evidence base that can be used to inform the design of future CALL software, and that in order to achieve that goal CALL researchers must investigate the impact of the individual coding elements or features of the various technologies that might be exploited in CALL and draw on SLA theory and research to make sense of their findings. Further, following Doughty (1987) and Garrett (1987), permitting the operationalization of SLA theory and providing functions that facilitate data collection I believe that CALL has the potential to contribute to the development of SLA theory. Before considering vocabulary CALL, I will therefore review the state of the art of our understanding of vocabulary learning and teaching from the perspective of the field of SLA.

Like other areas of knowledge and skills, drawing on the time-on-task principle (Cunningham & Stanovich, 1991), Nation (2007, 2011) argues that learners should receive a balanced curriculum of vocabulary instruction including opportunities for meaning-focused input, meaning-focused output, language-focused learning, and fluency development. The first two strands are motivated by Krashen's (1985) input hypothesis and Swain's (1985) output hypothesis, respectively. The language-focused learning strand is grounded in research that has demonstrated the complementarity of intentional and incidental vocabulary learning – while research suggests that incidental learning has a role to play in consolidating existing vocabulary knowledge and increasing depth of vocabulary knowledge, intentional learning has been found to be far more efficient with respect to the development of the breadth, or size, of a learner's vocabulary (Schmitt, 2010b). The final strand, fluency development, is motivated by research that has found that providing fluency practice (e.g., repetitive perception and production) and timed practice promotes the development of fluency (Nation, 2007).

With respect to the contribution of CALL to vocabulary learning and teaching, an early review of the literature found that the first generation of vocabulary CALL was characterised by computerised versions of word games that focused on testing learners' vocabulary rather than engaging them in processes which promote vocabulary acquisition (Goodfellow, 1995). As discussed below, since then, however, vocabulary CALL has developed and its potential to provide opportunities for language-focused learning and engagement with meaning-focused input has been recognised.

Language-focused learning—learning through deliberate attention to vocabulary (Nation, 2007, 2011)—is the traditional approach to vocabulary learning and has long been the subject of SLA research. Research on direct vocabulary instruction has focused on investigating different ways of communicating the meaning of lexical items and the role of repetition in vocabulary learning. The most common way of providing direct vocabulary instruction is to provide a list of second language (L2) words and their first language (L1) translation or a definition. However, a robust finding in SLA research is that communicating meaning in two modes, verbally and visually, enhances recall (Paivio & Desrochers, 1981). In CALL, multimedia has, therefore, long been seen to have affordances for vocabulary learning (Siegelt & Misselt, 1984).

Another well-established finding in the field of SLA related to language-focused learning is that the common practice of repeatedly copying out a list of vocabulary items and their translations is not adequate. Rather learners need to engage in repeated retrieval (Barcroft, 2007b; Royer, 1973) "perceiving the form and having to retrieve its meaning when the word is met in listening or reading" (Nation, 2001, p. 67) or "wishing to communicate the meaning of the words and have to retrieve its spoken or written form as in speaking or writing" (p. 67). And, to be most effective, repetitions need to be spaced over time, with the distance between repetitions gradually increasing over time (Bloom & Schuell, 1981; Dempster, 1987). That is, learners should be provided the opportunity to engage in spaced retrieval or *expanded rehearsal.* This is another area in which digital technologies have long been seen to have affordances. As early as 1975, Atkinson and Raugh (cited in Goodfellow, 1995) developed computer-based sequencing algorithms that implemented expanded rehearsal. Interest in this area continues, with more recent research investigating the nature of optimal corrective feedback in this context (Nakata, 2006). Nakata's study that compared the effectiveness of structural feedback — feedback in which students were asked to type the correct target word in addition to looking at it — with simply showing students' the target word found no differences between the two types of feedback. Students, however, made fewer errors during training.

Learning vocabulary through meaning-focused input, learning vocabulary through reading and listening activities during which the learner's focus is on comprehension (Nation, 2007, 2011), has also attracted a lot of attention from SLA and CALL researchers. Reflecting SLA research more broadly, and the noticing (Schmidt, 1990) and input hypotheses (Krashen, 1985), the main findings of this line of research that has focused primarily on the acquisition of vocabulary through extensive reading are that learners need to be provided (1) opportunities to notice new vocabulary, (2) support in understanding the meaning of new vocabulary, and (3) repeated opportunities to meet new vocabulary in new contexts (Nation, 2001). In traditional classrooms opportunities to notice new vocabulary are typically provided through graded readers. Graded readers are series of books, typically novels, which are divided into levels each of which is prepared using a strictly limited vocabulary. Consequently, learners should be familiar with around 95% of the vocabulary which they encounter. Unknown vocabulary provides opportunities for noticing and learning from context. Examples of early CALL software which might also provide opportunities for noticing are total text reconstruction programs such as *Storyboard* from *Wida* and *Fun with Texts* from *Camsoft* (Goodfellow, 1995).

In total text reconstruction programs, learners are typically provided with the title of a text and then asked to reconstruct it from scratch. Alternatively, learners may be asked to read or listen to a text and reconstruct it entirely from memory. Filling in the last content words in a total text reconstruction activity may raise learners' awareness of new or less well-mastered vocabulary items. As far as it is possible to establish, the potential of text reconstruction to promote noticing has not been investigated. With respect to understanding the meaning of new vocabulary items, in traditional classrooms, meaning may be communicated directly by providing access to dictionaries and glosses, and through inferring from context. Similarly the potential of hypermedia to provide access to multimedia glosses has been long recognised in CALL (Gillespie & Gay, 1992).

The same is true of the possibility to provide links to online dictionaries and other lexical information, including synonyms and antonyms (Widdig & Esser, 1998), other semantically associated words (Hayet, 1994), word parts (Sussex, 1994), and contexts of use found in corpus extracts (Johns, 1991). Further, text reconstruction activities, as discussed above, provide plentiful opportunities for inferring meaning from context. Of these approaches, in the traditional classroom, glosses have been found to be the most effective (Hulstijn, Hollander, & Greidanus, 1996). Research suggests that learners are poor at guessing (Bensoussan & Laufer, 1984; Nassaji, 2003), and the effectiveness of the use of dictionaries is debatable (see Hulstijn, 1993, and Knight, 1994).

SLA researchers have, therefore, suggested that learners would benefit from strategy instruction (Schmitt, 2010b). Text reconstruction activities might also help learners to develop their learning strategies and consequently their vocabulary because they require learners to develop strategies for guessing the words which might fit the context of the text. However, as far as it is possible to establish, this affordance of text reconstruction activities has not been investigated. Finally, with respect to repeated opportunities to meet vocabulary in new contexts, also referred to as generative use (Nation, 2001), research suggests that developing depth of knowledge of vocabulary items is incremental and that learners need to encounter items at least five times (Horst, Cobb, & Meara, 1998) and sometimes more than 20 in order to acquire them (Pigada & Schmitt, 2006). In the traditional classroom graded readers also provide opportunities for repeated encounters with new vocabulary items in new contexts. Other techniques employed in the traditional classroom to provide repeated encounters with new vocabulary items include, retelling the same story a number of times, serialising a long story and summarising the last instalment before continuing, requiring the use of vocabulary met through reading activities in follow-up speaking activities, and so on (Nation, 2001). *Textladder* (Ghadirian, 2002) is an example of CALL software that has been developed to grade authentic texts in such a way as to ensure that in each text new vocabulary constitutes no more than 5% of the whole text and there are sufficient repeated encounters with new vocabulary items.

On the other hand, research on the acquisition of vocabulary through extensive listening is only in its infancy. The few SLA studies that have been conducted so far suggest that support in the understanding of new vocabulary is beneficial. Providing brief definitions of new vocabulary during listening has been shown to double the amount of vocabulary acquired through listening (Elley, 1989), and modified interaction has been shown to lead to durable vocabulary acquisition (Ellis, 1995; Joe, 1998). With respect to the potential use of CALL to provide extensive listening practice, research by Jones has investigated the impact of multimedia glossing and engaging in computer-mediated collaboration on vocabulary learning. Jones' findings with respect to the impact of multimedia glossing on vocabulary recognition conflict, with one study finding a beneficial impact of dual-mode glosses (i.e. L1 translation and picture) over single-mode glosses (i.e. L1 translation only or picture only; Jones, 2003; Jones & Plass, 2002) and another study finding no differences between dual- and single-mode glosses (Jones, 2004). The provision of an L1 translation was, however, found to have a beneficial impact on retrieval, i.e., the ability to provide an L1 translation. Engaging in computer-mediated collaboration, on the other hand, was not found to have a beneficial impact on vocabulary learning (Jones, 2006; Xu, 2010).

Incidental learning also includes learning through meaning-focused output, the learning of vocabulary through activities in which the learner's focus is on communicating meaning through writing or speech (Nation, 2007, 2011). Despite research which finds learners' productive vocabularies to be significantly smaller than their receptive vocabularies (Laufer, 2005) and that learners only use a relatively small percentage of newly introduced vocabulary in follow-up productive tasks (Lee & Muncie, 2006), few SLA studies have investigated activities that focus on communicating meaning through writing or speech. One exception is de la Fuente's (2006) investigation of the impact of Task-Based Language Teaching (TBLT) and Presentation Practice Production (PPP) on lexical retrieval. More specifically, de la Fuente compared PPP with two forms of TBLT, one involving explicit focus on forms and one without explicit focus on forms. While no differences were observed between the conditions at post-test, learners in the TBLT groups performed better than those in the PPP group at delayed post-test, and the productions of the learners who received TBLT involving explicit focus on forms were more accurate than those of the learners in the other TBLT condition. These results suggest that opportunities to engage in negotiation of meaning, production, and retrieval are important for developing productive vocabulary knowledge, and focus on form has a beneficial impact on productive knowledge of the syntactic patterns which a word selects. While Computer-Mediated Communication (CMC) and Web 2.0 technologies respectively provide opportunities to engage with native speakers and engage in written and spoken production, previous CALL reviews (Goodfellow, 1995; Levy, 2009) have not identified any research focusing on meaning-focused activities for vocabulary development.

Similarly, a survey of the literature suggests that little attention has been paid to fluency development, activities in which the learner's focus is on developing automaticity in the recognition and production of known vocabulary (Nation, 2007, 2011). These studies have found a beneficial impact of repeated exposure to known lexical items through intentional learning, specifically training involving sentence completion, detection and correction of semantic anomalies, and word translation (Snellings, van Gelderen, & de Glopper, 2002, 2004) and intensive reading (Al-Homoud & Schmitt, 2009), and incidental learning, specifically extensive reading (Al-Homoud & Schmitt, 2009). While it is often said that digital technologies might be used to develop untiring language tutors (e.g. Handley, 2009), previous CALL reviews (Goodfellow, 1995; Levy, 2009) report no studies focusing on fluency development.

In summary, previous reviews find that only two strands of a balanced vocabulary curriculum have been addressed in CALL research to date. Given the developments in technology since the reviews cited above, including the advent of Web 2.0 and Smartphones, it might be anticipated that the potential affordances of digital technologies for vocabulary learning and teaching have expanded. It is, therefore, timely to conduct another review of the literature in this area.

Previous CALL research tended to focus on college students (Bax, 2003). Further, in light of the expectations placed on teachers to use technology in primary and secondary language classes and the many ways in which young language learners differ from adult language learners, including at a linguistic and broader cognitive level (Cameron, 2001; Pinter, 2006), a review focusing on primary and secondary school students' use of vocabulary CALL would seem appropriate. The review presented in this chapter is an update to part of a larger review of research on the use technology in primary and secondary EFL and ESL, namely Macaro et al. (2012). This study was guided by the following review questions:

1. What empirical research has been undertaken on the use of digital technology in vocabulary learning and teaching with learners of English as a foreign or second language in

primary and secondary schools between 2004 and 2013?
2. What reasons do researchers provide for their choice of technology?
3. What evidence is there that digital technologies facilitate the acquisition of vocabulary in EFL/ESL?
4. What (pedagogical) insights can be gleaned regarding the use of digital technology technologies in the teaching of vocabulary in EFL/ESL?

Questions 3 and 4 are the main review questions. To clarify, the focus of Question 3 is the effectiveness or 'impact' of digital technologies, and the focus of Question 4 is pedagogical insights, including students' attitudes, motivation and behaviours when using vocabulary CALL.

In this update, the review period was restricted to 2004 to 2013. 2004 was selected as the start date because it corresponds with the peak in interest in a new generation of technology little discussed in previous CALL reviews, namely Web 2.0 and user-generated content (Myers, 2010). This period is also interesting because it saw the introduction of Smartphones which, with their numerous apps, have significantly increased the potential of Mobile-Assisted Language Learning (Godwin-Jones, 2011).

METHOD

Systematic reviews attempt to reduce the subjective bias characteristic of many traditional literature reviews through the use of a transparent and explicit protocol, exhaustive database searches, explicit inclusion/exclusion criteria, and quality assurance measures described shortly (EPPI-Centre, 2007). The search strategy, inclusion/exclusion criteria, review procedure, and synthesis procedure for this review are presented in the following sections.

Search Strategy

As mentioned above, this review is an extension to part of a broader review of research on the use CALL with primary and secondary EFL and ESL students (Macaro et al., 2012). The *Language and Linguistics Behavior Abstracts*, *Education Resources Information Center*, *PsycINFO*, and *INSPEC* electronic databases were searched. The initial searches were conducted in autumn 2009, and the update was conducted in summer 2013. The precise search strategy for each database was slightly different depending on how the articles are keyworded and the search facilities available. Generally, the search strategy involved combining synonyms and hyponyms for the following terms: language, learning and technology.

Inclusion/Exclusion Criteria

The studies identified through the searches were then screened against the following inclusion criteria: only studies published between 2004 and 2013 (inclusive) in peer-reviewed English language journals which reported original empirical studies on the use of technology in vocabulary learning and teaching[1] with primary and secondary school students of English as a foreign or second language were included.

Mapping the Research

All 22 studies that met the inclusion criteria were keyworded according to: technology, country, phase of education, first language, second language, gender, theoretical underpinnings, method (quantitative, qualitative, mixed), and sample size. And, the resulting map (see Appendix A) was explored for trends.

Reviewing the Research

All studies that met the inclusion criteria were reviewed and assessed according to the four quality criteria presented below on a three-point scale (low, mid, high). Over 80% of the studies which met the inclusion criteria were double blind reviewed by the author and another member of their research group. Having reviewed the studies independently, the authors met to discuss and agree on an assessment. If they could not come to an agreement, a third reviewer would have been invited to arbitrate. This was, however, not necessary for any of these articles. The remainder, specifically the studies identified in the update to the review were only assessed by the author. Further, in order to ensure that all studies were treated equally, for each article a grid detailing the main features of the study (rationale, research questions, methodology, sampling, design, analysis, validity and reliability, results, conclusions, and implications) was completed. The four quality criteria that were used in the in-depth reviews were:

1. *Relevance* of the focus of the study to the review questions;
2. *Appropriateness* of the study's research design for addressing the review questions;
3. *Trustworthiness* of the study's overall methodology;
4. *Contribution* of the study (median of 1-3) to the review questions.

The papers were assessed twice, once in relation to each of the main research questions. The results for relevance and contribution for the two main research questions that focus on impact and insights can be seen in Appendix B. There it can be seen that of the studies which met the inclusion criteria, Li (2009) did not meet the criterion of relevance. This was because it did not examine the development of vocabulary learning strategies through use of the reading tutor developed as promised in the abstract of the article, and therefore did not address either of the main review questions (see above). Investigating both the impact of interactive whiteboards, podcasts and digital storytelling on vocabulary acquisition and students' perceptions of the use of those technologies, Hur and Suh (2012), on the other hand, received a high rating for relevance to both of the main review questions. It, however, received a low rating for its contribution to answering the question of the effectiveness of digital technologies because it involved a pre-experiment without control group and the appropriateness of the design of the study was considered to be low. It also received a low rating for its contribution to insights into the use of digital technologies because the data were not analysed in sufficient depth, i.e. appropriateness of the methods was low – perceptions were simply classified into two categories positive and negative. The trustworthiness of the results was also considered to be low due by the omission of second coding and measure of inter-rater reliability. Similarly, Jia, Chen, Ding and Ruan (2011) investigated both the effectiveness and perceptions of blended learning and hence received a high rating for relevance to both of the main review questions. However, the contribution to answering the question of the effectiveness of digital technologies for vocabulary learning was considered to be low. This was mainly due to inadequacies in the reporting which compromised the trustworthiness of the findings. Overall the method was not clear and in particular details of the instrument for the main outcome measure were not provided. Similarly, the contribution to insights was also considered to be low, because the trustworthiness of the findings was compromised by a lack of clarity in the reporting of the methodology.

Synthesizing the Research

Studies were rated on a three-point scale (low, medium, high) according to the aforementioned criteria, and only the findings of those which achieved a rating of medium or high for their contribution to answering at least one of the two main review questions were synthesized.

RESULTS

What Research Has Been Undertaken on the Use of Digital Technologies in Vocabulary Learning and Teaching in Primary and Secondary EFL/ESL?

Twenty-two studies met the inclusion criteria for this review. These articles are marked with a † in Appendix A. The identified studies were either conducted in East Asia (*n* = 13 studies) or Canada and the United States (3 and 6 studies, respectively). More studies were conducted in secondary (*n* = 13) than in primary (*n* = 9) schools. The majority of these studies focused solely on vocabulary (*n* = 14), with the majority of the remaining studies focusing on reading in addition to vocabulary (*n* = 6). The most popular technologies were multimedia (*n* = 7) and mobile technologies (*n* = 5). The former was more frequently investigated with primary (*n* = 6) than secondary (*n* = 1) language learners, while the latter was more frequently investigated with secondary (*n* = 4) than with primary (*n* = 1) language learners.

In addition to multimedia and mobile technologies, the 16 studies reviewed in-depth also investigated the use of researcher-designed CALL software (*n* = 1), electronic dictionaries (*n* = 2), games (*n* = 1), hypermedia (*n* = 2), CMC (*n* = 2) including e-mail (*n* = 1) and discussion forums (*n* = 1), and Natural Language Processing (NLP; *n* = 4), including parsers (*n* = 1) and Text-To-Speech (TTS; *n* = 4) synthesis.

Of these 22 studies, 15 were assessed to make a medium or high contribution to answering the main review questions, Questions 3 and 4 above, these articles are marked with a ‡ in Appendix B and were reviewed in depth and will be synthesized below.

What Reasons Do Researchers Provide for Their Choice of Technology?

Following Chapelle (1998), when selecting digital technologies for use in language learning and teaching, I believe that it is important to consider the extent to which they have the potential to provide ideal conditions for SLA. Further, as mentioned in the introduction, and following Pederson (1987), I believe that if CALL is to make progress, it is necessary for CALL research to draw links with SLA. In this section, I therefore begin by considering whether the choice of technology in the studies identified was motivated by SLA theory and research.

Only six out of the 16 studies relied on SLA theory and research to justify their choice of technology. The two main theories associated with vocabulary learning that were evoked were dual coding theory and the theory of spaced learning. For example, Kim and Gilman (2008) in their investigation of the differential impact of different combinations of modes (e.g., visual text only, visual text and spoken text, visual text and graphics) of introducing vocabulary alluded to Mayer's (Mayer & Moreno, 2002) cognitive theory of multimedia learning, which combines dual coding theory (Paivio, 1986) with cognitive load theory (Sweller, Van Merrienboer, & Pass, 1998). Kim and Gilman (2008) posit that communicating meaning through two modes, verbally and visually, enhances recall, but acknowledge that there are constraints on the amount of information that learners can process in each modality at a single point in time. Grounding their research on the use of video clips for vocabulary learning in dual coding theory (Paivio, 1986) and theory of synergy (Neuman, 1997), Silverman and Hines suggest that the use of multimedia supports vocabulary learning by providing learners additional tools to process information and multiple modes of presentation to draw on during recall.

Spaced learning was evoked in two studies. In Nakata (2008), it was suggested that computer-based sequencing algorithms might be used to implement expanded rehearsal, and in Lu (2008) it was suggested that mobile technologies which permit *anytime, anywhere* learning might be used promote the engagement in such spaced practice.

Two other SLA theories which were drawn to provide a rationale for the use of technology include socio-cultural theory (Lantolf, 2006) and theories of reading. Drawing on socio-cultural theory, Sasaki and Takeuchi (2010) suggest that e-mail might support the vocabulary learning by providing learners opportunities to interact with, and in particular imitate, native speakers of English. In relation to the teaching of vocabulary through extensive reading, Proctor, Dalton, and Grisham (2007) and Dalton, Proctor, Uccelli, Mo, and Snow (2011), alluding to theories of reading (bottom-up, top-down, and interactive), suggest that technology may support a number of the processes involved in reading. Specifically, they suggest that Text-To-Speech (TTS) synthesis supports decoding and hyperlinks support comprehension through the possibility to provide learners with glosses.

Other reasons, not linked to SLA theory and research, cited for the use of mobile technologies included the possibility to use Global Positioning System and Wireless Local Area Network to provide learners contextually appropriate vocabulary lessons (Chen & Li, 2010; Hwang & Chen, 2013), and the possibility to use the voice recording and playback, and communication features available on Personal Digital Assistants (PDAs) to provide listening and speaking practice, and permit students to interact with one another face-to-face and at distance (Hwang & Chen, 2013).

The potential to use the record-keeping capacity of the computer to support the monitoring of learning was also highlighted by Nakata (2008) in his study exploring spaced learning, as was research suggesting that technology has a positive impact on students' levels of motivation. The latter was also mentioned by Kim and Gilman (2008). The popularity of technology with children and in particular digital games was also mentioned by Cobb and Horst (2011), who investigated the use of word games.

As mentioned above, the remaining four studies (Fehr, Davison, Graves, Sales, Seipel & Sekhram-Sharma, 2012; Li, 2010; Yun, Miller, Baek, Jung, & Ko, 2008; Zhang, Gao, Ring, & Zhang, 2007) did not provide concrete reasons for their choice of digital technology.

In summary, the main benefits that were seen in the use of digital technologies in vocabulary teaching and learning were the possibility (1) to enhance vocabulary recall by representing meaning in different modalities through the use of multimedia, (2) to implement spaced practice through the use of computer algorithms and mobile technologies, and (3) to increase students' levels of motivation.

What Evidence Is There That Digital Technologies Facilitate Vocabulary Acquisition?

When reviewing research on the effectiveness of any educational intervention, it is important to consider not only the results of the studies, but also the quality of the evidence, namely the research methods employed. In this section, I begin by considering an important aspect of the design of the studies identified, namely the measures of vocabulary acquisition employed to determine the effectiveness of the technologies evaluated.

As mentioned above, according to researchers in the field of SLA, there is more to knowing a word than knowing the mapping between form (written or spoken) and meaning. Consequently, the potential for digital technologies to facilitate the full range of forms of vocabulary knowledge ought to be assessed in CALL evaluations. Despite this, the majority of studies reviewed only assessed learners' ability to map form to meaning receptively (Dalton et al., 2011; Fehr et al., 2012; Li,

2010; Lu, 2008; Proctor et al., 2007; Silverman & Hines, 2009), and frequently using a test developed for the specific purposes of the study in question (Fehr et al., 2012; Li, 2010; Lu, 2008). Standard measures of receptive vocabulary that were used in the studies included: the Vocabulary Levels Test (Li, 2010; see Schmitt, Schmitt, & Clapham, 2001 for details of the test), the Vocabulary Size Test, a revision of the Vocabulary Levels Test (Cobb & Horst, 2011; see Nation & Beglar, 2007 for details of the test), the Vocabulary sub-test of the Gates-MacGintie Reading Test (Dalton et al., 2011; Proctor et al., 2007; see MacGintie, MacGintie, Maria & Dreyer, 2002 for details of the test), the Peabody Picture Vocabulary Test (Silverman & Hines, 2009; see Dunn & Dunn, 1981 for details of the test).

Form-meaning was also assessed productively by asking students to provide the English translation of an L1 word (Nakata, 2008). Pronunciation of vocabulary items was also assessed in one study (Hwang & Chen, 2013). Breadth of vocabulary knowledge was presumably measured by assessing the completeness of index cards learners were asked to produce for target words (O'Hara & Pritchard, 2008). Productive use was measured by asking learners to write a sentence using the word (Yun et al., 2008), presence of target words in e-mail interactions (Sasaki & Takeuchi, 2010), and presence of new vocabulary in a picture description task (Cobb & Horst, 2011). Further, lexical access was measured by calculating the number of words correctly pronounced in one minute using UNESCO's standard literacy test (Cobb & Horst, 2011). In the remaining studies, the aspect of lexical knowledge tested was unclear (Chen & Li, 2010; Kim & Kim, 2012; Zhang et al., 2007). In summary, despite the depth of knowledge that is involved in mastering a word, the majority of research focused on learners' ability to recognise L2 words and map them to their L1 equivalent. The evidence for the effectiveness of vocabulary CALL is therefore limited. Further, non-standard tests were often used to measure outcomes limiting the possibility to make comparisons with the findings of SLA research and hence the potential of the research to further our understanding of vocabulary acquisition.

The interventions in the majority of the studies involved language-focused learning (n = 9), with just five involving meaning-focused input, four involving meaning-focused output, and none involving fluency development[2].

With respect to the ideal psychological conditions for vocabulary acquisition discussed in the background to this study, the studies that involved language-focused learning investigated the use of the following:

1. Multimedia to enhance the recall of lexical items by communicating their meaning through different modalities (Kim & Gilman, 2008);
2. The computer to implement training which requires recall of vocabulary knowledge (Yun et al., 2008);
3. Computer-based sequencing algorithms (Nakata, 2008) to implement expanded rehearsal;
4. Mobile devices to provide access to learning anytime anywhere (Lu, 2008) and promote expanded rehearsal;
5. Mobile devices to enhance the meaningfulness of learning by adapting the content delivered to the learners' current context (Chen & Li, 2010; Hwang & Chen, 2013).

Furthermore, drawing together the findings of SLA research, Cobb and Horst (2011) investigated the benefits of engaging in a vocabulary game, namely *Word Coach*, based on established principles of vocabulary learning, including recycling, focus on form, focus on receptive and productive learning, and focus on lexical access, alongside normal classroom instruction.

Examining the studies in more depth, Kim and Gilman (2008) specifically compared the use of a number of different combinations of multimedia for the presentation of vocabulary and their analysis of post-test results found that students who received visual text and graphics scored significantly higher than those who received visual text and spoken text or reduced visual text and spoken text. Similarly, at delayed post-test, they found that students who received visual text, spoken text and graphics scored significantly higher than those who received visual text and spoken text or reduced visual text and spoken text. Further, these results were replicated by Kim and Kim (2009) in their study focusing on the impact of screen size on vocabulary learning (see below). On the basis of these findings, they suggested that not all media are the same in terms of their effect on vocabulary learning, and while graphics support vocabulary learning and should therefore be used to communicate meaning, using a combination of media does not necessarily promote learning and care should be taken not to overload students' working memory with multiple representations. That is, Kim and Gilman found further support for the cognitive theory of multimedia learning (Mayer & Moreno, 2002) in the context of vocabulary learning and teaching.

With respect to expanded rehearsal, Nakata (2008) compared the use of vocabulary lists and flash cards with the use of a computer programme designed to implement expanded rehearsal and adapt to the needs of the individual student, by providing more rehearsal for those items that learners are struggling with and stopping rehearsal of an item when students have mastered it. Significant differences in receptive knowledge of the items taught were observed across the three conditions, with students in the flash card and computer-based conditions scoring significantly higher on the post-test than on students in the list condition. Nakata attributed the lack of differences between the flash card and the computer-based conditions to students' lack of experience learning vocabulary with computers, as demonstrated by their responses to a background questionnaire. Nakata also notes that the multimedia capabilities of the computer were not exploited in the computer-based condition.

In Lu's (2008) study of mobile vocabulary learning, which was also motivated by research demonstrating the effectiveness of expanded rehearsal, he compared traditional pen-and-paper list learning with bite-sized vocabulary lessons delivered by text message twice a day timed to correspond with the students' commute to and from school. Each message in the mobile condition contained a word, its translation and its part of speech. Significant gains in receptive knowledge of the trained vocabulary was observed at post-test for both groups, with the students in the mobile condition improving more than those in the pen-and-paper condition, lending support to the use of mobile phones for the delivery of spaced practice.

As mentioned above, two studies investigated the effectiveness of contextualised, or situated, vocabulary learning delivered via mobile devices. The first, Chen and Li (2010), compared the effectiveness of a personalised context-aware ubiquitous learning system which adapted the content of the vocabulary lessons delivered on a Personal Digital Assistant (PDA) to the learner's proficiency, their location and the time of day with a similar system that did not adapt content to learners' proficiency and context. They found that learners working with the personalised context-aware system performed better those working with the non-adaptive system at post-test.

Hwang and Chen (2013) also observed a beneficial impact of situated learning in their study that compared the delivery of food-related vocabulary via PDAs during lunch time with pen-and-paper completion of the same materials during the students' morning self-study period. And, Yun et al. (2008) observed a beneficial impact of recall over recognition in a study investigating the delivery of web-based vocabulary learning. In Cobb and Horst's (2011) study, game play was found to have a beneficial impact on receptive vocabulary knowledge for students in the experimental group of the second round of this counterbalanced study, but not the first. Further, no differences were observed between the experimental and control groups on the test of productive vocabulary knowledge.

Finally, Kim and Kim (2009) investigated a new issue specific to the delivery of vocabulary learning via mobile devices, namely the size of the screen. Their study compared the delivery of the same multimedia vocabulary instruction on three different sized mobile devices, an iPod (small), a smartphone (medium), and a Kindle (large). It found that learners who used the medium and large devices scored higher on a vocabulary achievement test at post-test and delayed post-test than those who used the small device. Kim and Kim (2009) suggested that the differences might be attributed to the increased cognitive load when working on small devices. Specifically, they suggested that small screens may introduce a number of obstacles to cognitive processing such as distortions to the text and images presented on screen and may not hold their attention in the same way as larger screens due to distractions in their field of vision.

As noted, meaning-focused input was the subject of three of the studies. The first investigated the use of multimedia to support comprehension (Silverman & Hines, 2009). The second investigated direct access to monolingual and bilingual electronic dictionaries to support comprehension (Li, 2010). And, the third investigated the use of pedagogical agents to encourage learners to focus on form and provide support with vocabulary learning strategies and reading strategies (Dalton et al., 2011). These studies found a beneficial impact of multimedia videos over traditional books (Silverman & Hines, 2009), using *e-Lective*, a reading tutor integrating direct access to electronic dictionaries, over similar pen-and-paper activities (Li, 2010), and vocabulary support over reading support (Dalton et al., 2011) on incidental vocabulary acquisition in the reading tutor *ICON*.

Two of the studies in which the intervention involved meaning-focused output investigated the impact of interaction via CMC technologies on vocabulary acquisition (Sasaki & Kakeuchi, 2010; Zhang et al., 2007). While Zhang et al. (2007) did not observe gains in vocabulary in their study focusing on students' interactions in discussion forums, Sasaki and Takeuchi (2010), in their study focusing on e-mail interactions between learners and native speakers, found that the learners imitated 60 of the 193 words that the native speaker used and retained 36 of the words that they imitated. There was also a correlation between frequency of imitation and retention. It should be noted, however, that it is possible that these items were acquired by just one learner because the data was treated as a corpus and the gains made by individual learners were not explored. The remaining study found a beneficial impact of preparing a hyperlinked multimedia PowerPoint report on the vocabulary encountered during a content based project on vocabulary learning over preparing a traditional pen-and-paper report (O'Hara & Pritchard, 2008).

The two remaining studies involved a combination of types of language learning activity. Fehr et al. (2012) evaluated the vocabulary learning software *First 4000 words*, which integrates language-focused learning in the form of pronunciation practice with automated feedback, and meaning-focused input during which a narrator reads aloud a passage containing the target vocabulary to the learners. In their comparison of the impact of using the software with normal classroom instruction on receptive vocabulary they found a beneficial impact of using the software for boys and students in second and third grades, with students in the experimental group making greater gains in receptive vocabulary than those in the control group. No differences were, however, found between the experimental and the control group for girls and students in grade 4. Proctor et al. (2007), on the other hand, evaluated the potential of using a reading tutor to reduce the gap in vocabulary knowledge between native speakers and English Language Learners (ELLs). The tutor that they evaluated integrated language-focused learning in the form of pre-reading activities focusing on *power words*, meaning-focused input in the form of activities during which learners read a text with the support of pedagogical agents that encourage them to create their own glossary and provide them strategy support, and meaning-focused output during which learners retell the story from picture-based prompts. As anticipated, Proctor et al. (2007) found that the software reduced the gap between native speakers and ELLs on the vocabulary test.

In summary, the studies identified in this review provide further support for the following SLA theories associated with vocabulary learning and teaching: the cognitive theory of multimedia learning (Mayer & Moreno, 2002) in the context of vocabulary learning (Kim & Gilman, 2008), and training focusing on retrieval rather than recognition (Yun et al., 2008). In other words, the studies identified suggest that the following promote vocabulary learning in language-focused activities: (a) multimedia, and (b) a focus on the recall of the meaning of items of vocabulary. Further, the studies identified support the use of mobile phones to provide: (a) spaced vocabulary practice (Lu, 2008), and (b) content adapted to the learners' context (Chen & Li, 2010). Multimedia was also found to have a beneficial impact on vocabulary learning in activities involving meaning-focused input, as was access to electronic dictionaries and vocabulary support. Similarly, multimedia was found to support vocabulary learning in activities focusing on meaning-focused output.

What Insights Can Be Gleaned Regarding the Use of Digital Technologies in Vocabulary Teaching in EFL/ESL?

Seven of the studies that met the criteria for synthesis provided further insights into the use of technology in vocabulary learning and teaching with primary and secondary school children. Of these, the majority ($n = 5$) focused on students' perceptions of and attitudes towards the software (Chen & Li, 2010; Fehr et al., 2012; Hwang & Chen, 2013; Lu, 2008; Nakata, 2008).[3] The two remaining studies investigated learners' behaviours, one investigated frequency of game use (Cobb & Horst, 2011) and the other learners' use of the different features of a reading tutor (Proctor et al., 2007). The findings of these studies are summarized below.

Students in all studies that investigated language-focused learning, expressed positive attitudes towards the instruction (Chen & Li, 2010; Hwang & Chen, 2013; Lu, 2008) and preferred it over traditional approaches (Chen & Li, 2010; Nakata, 2008). Similar attitudes were expressed by the students in Fehr et al.'s (2012) investigation of the effectiveness of *The First 4000 Words* which integrates both language- and meaning-focused learning.

More specifically, in Hwang and Chen's (2013) investigation of the use of PDAs to provide situated listening and speaking practice, usefulness of the system was the best predictor of intention to use it, accounting for 83.3% of the variance in intention to use it. The interviews also found that students transferred their learning to the home environment – they used the vocabulary learnt at home over the dinner table. Lu's (2008) investigation of the use of mobile phones to deliver bite-sized vocabulary lessons via text message found evidence of engagement in positive learning strategies. One student constructed sentences using the target vocabulary and sent them back to the teacher for feedback. However, there were also limitations, namely the potential distraction from the entertainment and gaming functions. One student reported getting into the habit of playing games rather than attending to the vocabulary instruction.

With respect to behaviours, Cobb and Horst (2011) found that use of the system differed across proficiency levels, with the least and most proficient students playing the games the least. Conversely, in Proctor et al.'s (2007) study which investigated English language learners' and non-native speakers' use of a reading tutor, they found that the ELLs and less proficient non-native speakers made more use of the scaffolding provided by the tutor and that those students that made more use of the supports made greater gains in vocabulary from pre-test to post-test. When interpreting these contrasting findings, it is important to note that *Word Coach* may have overestimated the learners' proficiency level and hence the difficulty of the content the learners received during the intervention may have had a negative impact on the less proficient students' motivation to play the games.

In summary, the studies identified in this review suggest that students generally have positive attitudes to vocabulary CALL and that to foster such positive attitudes it is important to adapt instruction to students' individual levels of proficiency.

DISCUSSION

My main argument, as presented in the introduction, is that in order to provide software developers an evidence base upon which to design new vocabulary CALL, researchers need to ground their studies in SLA and carry out more narrowly focused studies. That is, they need to identify what features of new technologies according to our current understanding of SLA might promote vocabulary learning and evaluate the impact of those specific features on vocabulary acquisition, rather than conduct broad CALL vs. non-CALL comparisons. The degree to which the studies reviewed achieved this will therefore be the focus of the discussion.

With respect to the degree to which the studies were grounded in SLA, in line with previous research (Stockwell, 2007), many of the studies reviewed in this chapter failed to provide a clear rationale for their choice of technology, while others appealed to the pervasiveness of technology to provide the motivation for their study (Zhang et al., 2007), and consequently their potential to contribute to the evidence base was limited. In contrast, some researchers motivated their choice of technology or coding elements with reference to well-established theories in the field of SLA (Kim & Gilman, 2008; Lu, 2008; Nakata, 2008; Sasaki & Takeuchi, 2010). These theories included dual coding theory, the theory of spaced learning or *expanded rehearsal*, and socio-cultural theory. It might be anticipated that the studies identified made a significant contribution to the development of our understanding of SLA and CALL.

The potential for the studies to contribute to the SLA evidence base was, however, limited by the fact that rather than using standard measures of vocabulary knowledge to measure the effectiveness of vocabulary CALL (see Milton, 2009), many studies employed their own measures and consequently it is difficult to make comparisons with previous research in the broader field of CALL. The studies also only addressed a limited number of dimensions of vocabulary knowledge (see Nation, 2001), with most focusing exclusively on the most basic form of receptive vocabulary knowledge, namely being able to provide an L1 translation for a lexical item in the target language, to the exclusion of other dimensions of receptive and productive vocabulary knowledge including the intension and extension of the meaning of a lexical item, its connotations and how to use it in context. Moreover, a number of studies (Fehr et al., 2012; Li, 2010; O'Hara & Pritchard, 2008) employed CALL versus non-CALL comparisons, which it has long been recognised have limited value in informing the design of future CALL software because the conditions often differ along a number of dimensions and it is difficult to know to which dimension any observed differences ought to be attributed (Chapelle, 2001; Levy, 1997; Pederson, 1987). For example, in O'Hara & Pritchard's (2008) evaluation of the impact of preparing a hyperlinked multimedia PowerPoint report on students' knowledge of target vocabulary items, the experimental condition differed in two ways from the control condition, the medium in which the report was produced (PowerPoint vs. pen-and-paper) and access to resources (online vs. classroom). It is, therefore, impossible to know whether the higher levels of vocabulary knowledge observed in the experimental group should be attributed to the medium in which the report was produced or access to online resources.

In contrast with the broader SLA literature on vocabulary learning and teaching, two studies (Sasaki & Takeuchi, 2010; Zhang et al., 2007) reviewed in depth investigated the impact of meaning-focused output on vocabulary learning. While both studies, which involved the use of discussion forums and e-mail respectively, had significant limitations (the pre-tests and checks on fidelity to condition were absent in Zhang et al.'s study and inter-rater reliability was not reported; participants in Sasaki and Takeuchi's study were treated as a group and consequently the 36 items identified in the analysis could have been learnt by a single student) which is perhaps one area where CALL might make a significant contribution to the broader SLA literature on vocabulary learning and teaching. The logs kept in CMC and Web 2.0 technologies facilitate the tracking of learners' use of vocabulary in productive activities, and hence permit the exploration of whether and how students use new vocabulary in productive activities and the relationship students' use of new vocabulary in productive activities and their acquisition and retention of that vocabulary. Such questions, as illustrated in the background to this research, have been rarely explored in the broader field of SLA to date.

In terms of impact, the studies contribute to the SLA evidence base by providing further support for the cognitive theory of multimedia learning (Mayer & Moreno, 2002) in the context of vocabulary learning (Kim & Gilman, 2008), and practice focusing on retrieval rather than simply recognition of vocabulary items (Yun et al., 2008). Further, they provide preliminary evidence to support the use of mobile phones implement expanded rehearsal (Lu, 2008) adapt content to the learners' context (Chen & Li, 2010). In other words, the studies identified in this review provide further evidence to support the use of multimedia and electronic dictionaries in vocabulary learning. More specifically, Kim and Gilman's (2008) confirmation of Mayer and Moreno's (2002, p. 108) finding that all multimedia messages are not equally effective highlights the importance of considering not only the medium (i.e. technology) but also the method (i.e., how the technology is employed) when selecting digital technologies for use in vocabulary learning and language learning more broadly. As Pederson (1987) stated, "CALL in and of itself, does not result in more and better learning; rather, it is the specific way instruction is coded in CALL software that has the potential of affecting learning positively, for specific learners in specific context" (p. 107). Further, the studies provide preliminary evidence to support the use of a new class of technologies namely mobile. In light of Kim and Gilman's research, we should be cautious to generalise beyond the specific uses of mobile devices for vocabulary learning investigated, namely to provide spaced practice (Lu, 2008) and situated learning (Chen & Li, 2010) and conclude that all mobile devices in and of themselves support vocabulary learning.

In terms of insights, the majority of studies investigated students' motivation and attitudes towards vocabulary CALL and found a positive impact of the technology. These results might, however, be explained by the novelty effect given the short duration of the majority of the interventions, or by students trying to please the teacher/researcher. More informative were studies such as Lu (2008) and Hwang and Chen (2013) that investigated attitudes, motivation and behaviour in greater depth through interviews, and studies which explored the processes that students engage in during the use of digital technology such as Proctor et al. (2007). The unanticipated findings that students were spontaneously engaging in behaviours which are believed to promote language acquisition in Lu's (2008) study and transferring their learning to new environments in Hwang and Chen's (2013) study were particularly interesting. Proctor et al.'s (2007) study that found that the less proficient learners, i.e. ELLs and struggling native speakers, made greater use of the supports available in the reading tutor would, however, have been more informative if a more fine-grained analysis had been carried out in which the frequency of use of the different coding elements, or supports, provided in the reading tutor had been considered separately.

CONCLUSION AND FUTURE DIRECTIONS

In conclusion, 22 studies met the inclusion criteria for this systematic review which focused on empirical studies of vocabulary CALL for primary and secondary learners of English as a foreign or second language published between 2004 and 2013. The majority of these studies focused on the use of multimedia to communicate the meaning of lexical items and mobile devices to provide anytime anywhere vocabulary training. With respect to the broader body of evidence on vocabulary learning and teaching, the majority of these studies involved the use of technology in language-focused learning, i.e. intentional vocabulary learning, and a smaller number involved the use of technology in activities involving meaning-focused input and meaning-focused output. Mainly assessing the impact of these interventions on learners' receptive vocabulary, the majority of the studies observed a beneficial impact of technology, including graphics and video to communicate meaning, computer-based sequencing algorithms and mobile technology to provide expanded rehearsal, mobile technology to provide contextualised learning, vocabulary games, reading tutors integrating electronic dictionaries and vocabulary learning strategy support, and producing hypermedia presentations.

However, while some of the studies were grounded in SLA theory, they failed to provide insights into vocabulary CALL that might inform the design of future interventions and software because they involved CALL versus non-CALL comparisons in which there were often multiple differences between the experimental (i.e. CALL) and control (i.e. non-CALL) conditions. While such CALL versus non-CALL comparisons may have been appropriate when there was a need to justify investment in technology for language learning, in today's digital world in which the use of technology is stipulated in the curriculum the question is rather how best to use computer technology to support language learning. More experiments investigating the differential impact of different coding elements are therefore required, as are more observational studies investigating the relationship between learners' use of the features of the technology investigated and learners' levels of achievement. Kim and Gilman's (2008) investigation of the differential impact of different combinations of multimedia to introduce the form and meaning of vocabulary items and Dalton et al.'s (2011) comparison of different versions of a reading tutor integrating different forms of support are good examples of the former. The latter would resemble Proctor et al.'s (2007) investigation of native speakers' and ELLs use of the *Universal Literacy Environment*, but examine use of each of the supports provided by the tutor separately.

Finally, with respect to insights more studies like those of Lu (2008) and Hwang and Chen (2013) that employ interviews to explore students' attitudes, motivation and behaviours in depth would be beneficial, as would observational studies which explore the processes that learners engage in while using CALL software.

ACKNOWLEDGMENT

I would like to thank Professor Ernesto Macaro and Dr. Catherine Walter, my collaborators on the review upon which this article builds, as well as the rest of the systematic review team in the Department of Education at the University of Oxford and Oxford UniversityPress[4]. Further, I would like to express my gratitude to Oxford University Press for funding this project.

REFERENCES

Al-Homoud, F., & Schmitt, N. (2009). Extensive reading in a challenging environment: A comparison of extensive and intensive reading approaches in Saudi Arabia. *Language Teaching Research*, *13*(4), 383–401. doi:10.1177/1362168809341508

Alderson, J. C. (2005). *Diagnosing foreign language proficiency*. London: Continuum.

Atkinson, R., & Raugh, M. (1975). An application of the mnemonic keyword method to the acquisition of Russian vocabulary. *Journal of Experimental Psychology. Human Learning and Memory*, *104*, 125–133.

Barcroft, J. (2007a). When knowing grammar depends on knowing vocabulary: native-speaker grammaticality judgement of sentences with real and unreal words. *Canadian Modern Language Review*, *63*(3), 313–343. doi:10.3138/R601-H212-5582-0737

Barcroft, J. (2007b). Effects of opportunities for word retrieval during second language vocabulary learning. *Language Learning*, *57*(1), 35–65. doi:10.1111/j.1467-9922.2007.00398.x

Bax, S. (2003). CALL – Past, present and future. *System*, *31*(1), 13–28. doi:10.1016/S0346-251X(02)00071-4

Bensoussan, M., & Laufer, B. (1984). Lexical guessing in context in EFL reading comprehension. *Journal of Research in Reading*, *7*(1), 15–32. doi:10.1111/j.1467-9817.1984.tb00252.x

Blake, R. J. (2008). *Brave new digital classroom: Technology and foreign language learning*. Washington, DC: Georgetown University Press.

Bloom, K. C., & Schuell, T. J. (1981). Effects of massed and distributed practice on the learning and retention of second language vocabulary. *The Journal of Educational Research*, *74*, 245–248.

Cameron, L. (2001). *Teaching languages to young learners*. Cambridge: Cambridge University Press. doi:10.1017/CBO9780511733109

Chapelle, C. (2009). The relationship between second language acquisition theory and computer-assisted language learning. *Modern Language Journal*, *93*(Focus issue), 741–753. doi:10.1111/j.1540-4781.2009.00970.x

Chapelle, C. A. (1998). Multimedia CALL: Lessons to be learned from research on instructed SLA. *Language Learning & Technology*, *2*(1), 22–34.

Chapelle, C. A. (2001). *Computer applications in second language acquisition: Foundations for teaching, testing and research*. Cambridge: Cambridge University Press. doi:10.1017/CBO9781139524681

Chen, C.-M., & Li, Y. L. (2010). Personalised context-aware ubiquitous learning system for supporting effective English vocabulary learning. *Interactive Learning Environments*, *18*(4), 341–364. doi:10.1080/10494820802602329

Cobb, T., & Horst, M. (2011). Does word coach words? *CALICO Journal*, *28*(3), 639–661. doi:10.11139/cj.28.3.639-661

Cunningham, A. E., & Stanovich, K. E. (1991). Tracking the unique effects of print exposure in children: Associations with vocabulary, general knowledge, and spelling. *Journal of Educational Psychology*, *83*(2), 264–274. doi:10.1037/0022-0663.83.2.264

Dalton, B., Proctor, C. P., Uccelli, P., Mo, E., & Snow, C. E. (2011). Designing for diversity: The role of reading strategies and interactive vocabulary in a digital reading environment for fifth-grade monolingual English and bilingual students. *Journal of Literacy Research*, *43*, 68–100. doi:10.1177/1086296X10397872

de la Fuente, M. J. (2006). Classroom L2 vocabulary acquisition: Investigating the role of pedagogical tasks and form-focused instruction. *Language Teaching Research*, *10*(3), 263–295. doi:10.1191/1362168806lr196oa

Dempster, F. N. (1987). Effects of variable encoding and spaced presentation on vocabulary learning. *Journal of Educational Psychology*, *59*, 202–206.

Doughty, C. (1987). Relating second-language acquisition theory to CALL research and application. In W. M. Smith (Ed.), *Modern media in foreign language education: Theory and implementation* (pp. 133–167). Lincolnwood, Illinois: National Textbook Company.

Dunn, L. M., & Dunn, L. M. (1981). *Peabody picture vocabulary test – Revised*. Circle Pines, MN: American Guidance Services.

Elley, W. B. (1989). Vocabulary acquisition from listening to stories. *Reading Research Quarterly*, *24*, 411–427. doi:10.2307/747863

Ellis, N. C. (1995). Vocabulary acquisition: Psychological perspectives and pedagogical implications. *Language Teaching*, *19*, 12–16.

EPPI-Centre. (2007, March). *EPPI-Centre methods for conducting systematic reviews*. London: EPPI-Centre, Social Science Research Unit, Institute of Education, University of London.

Fehr, C. N., Davison, M. L., Graves, M. F., Sales, G.C., Seipel, B., & Sekhram-Sharma, S. (2012). The effects of individualized, online vocabulary instruction on picture vocabulary scores: An efficacy study. *Computer Assisted Language Learning*, *25*(1), 97–102. doi:10.1080/09588221.2011.586640

Ghadirian, S. (2002). Providing controlled exposure to target vocabulary through the screening and arranging of texts. *Language Learning & Technology*, *6*(1), 147–164.

Gillespie, J., & Gray, G. (1992). Hypercard and the development of translation and vocabulary skills. *Computer Assisted Language Learning*, *5*(1–2), 3–11. doi:10.1080/0958822920050102

Godwin-Jones, R. (2011). Emerging technologies: Mobile apps for language learning. *Language Learning & Technology*, *15*(2), 2–11.

Goodfellow, R. (1995). A review of the types of CALL programs for vocabulary instruction. *Computer Assisted Language Learning*, *8*(2–3), 205–226. doi:10.1080/0958822940080206

Handley, Z. (2009). Is text-to-speech synthesis ready for use in computer-assisted language learning? *Speech Communication*, *51*, 906–919. doi:10.1016/j.specom.2008.12.004

Hayet, M. (1994). French learner's workbench. *Computers & Education*, *23*(1–2), 97–106. doi:10.1016/0360-1315(94)90037-X

Heift, T., & Schulze, M. (2009). *Errors and intelligence in Computer-Assisted Language Learning*. London: Routledge.

Hewer, S. (1997). *Text manipulation: Computer-based activities to improve knowledge and use of the target language*. Reading, UK: Centre for Information on Language Teaching and Research.

Horst, M., Cobb, T., & Meara, P. (1998). Beyond A Clockwork Orange: Acquiring second language vocabulary through reading. *Reading in a Foreign Language, 11*, 207–223.

Hsu, C. K., Hwang, G. J., & Chang, C. K. (2013). A personalized recommendation-based mobile learning approach to improving the reading performance of EFL students. *Computers & Education, 63*, 327–336. doi:10.1016/j.compedu.2012.12.004

Hubbard, P. (2008, September). *Characterizing theory in computer-assisted language learning*. Paper presented at CALL 2008, University of Antwerp. Antwerp, Belgium. Available from, http://webh01.ua.ac.be/linguapolis/scuati/proceedings_CALL%202008.pdf

Hulstijn, J. H. (1993). When do foreign language readers look up the meaning of unfamiliar words? The influence of task and learner variables. *Modern Language Journal, 77*, 139–147. doi:10.1111/j.1540-4781.1993.tb01957.x

Hulstijn, J. H., Hollander, M., & Greidanus, T. (1996). Incidental vocabulary learning by advanced foreign language students: The influence of marginal glosses, dictionary use, and reoccurrence of unknown words. *Modern Language Journal, 80*, 327–339. doi:10.1111/j.1540-4781.1996.tb01614.x

Hur, J. W., & Suh, S. (2012). Making learning active with interactive whiteboards, podcasts, and digital storytelling in ELL classrooms. *Computers in the Schools, 29*(4), 320–338. doi:10.1080/07380569.2012.734275

Hwang, W. Y., & Chen, H. S. L. (2013). Users' familiar situational contexts facilitate the practice of EFL in elementary schools with mobile devices. *Computer Assisted Language Learning, 26*(2), 101–125. doi:10.1080/09588221.2011.639783

Jia, J., Chen, Y., Ding, Z., & Ruan, M. (2012). Effects of a vocabulary acquisition and assessment system on students' performance in a blended learning class for English subject. *Computers & Education, 58*(1), 63–76. doi:10.1016/j.compedu.2011.08.002

Joe, A. (1998). What effects do text-based tasks promoting generation have on incidental vocabulary acquisition? *Applied Linguistics, 19*, 357–377. doi:10.1093/applin/19.3.357

Johns, T. (1991). Should you be persuaded – Two examples of data-driven learning. *English Language Research Journal, 4*, 1–13.

Jones, L. C. (2003). Supporting listening comprehension and vocabulary acquisition with multimedia annotations: The student's voice. *CALICO Journal, 21*, 41–65.

Jones, L. C. (2004). Testing L2 vocabulary recognition and recall using pictorial written test items. *Language Learning & Technology, 8*(3), 122–134.

Jones, L. C. (2006). Effects of collaboration and multimedia annotations on vocabulary learning and listening comprehension. *CALICO Journal, 24*, 33–58.

Jones, L. C., & Plass, J. L. (2002). Supporting listening comprehension and vocabulary acquisition in French with multimedia annotations. *Modern Language Journal, 86*, 546–561. doi:10.1111/1540-4781.00160

Jung, U. (2005). CALL: Past, present, and future – A bibliometric approach. *ReCALL, 17*(1), 4–17. doi:10.1017/S0958344005000212

Karpati, A. (2009). Web 2 technologies for net native language learners: A "social CALL". *ReCALL, 21*(2), 139–156. doi:10.1017/S0958344009000160

Kim, D., & Gilman, D. (2008). Effects of text, audio, and graphic aids in multimedia instruction for vocabulary learning. *Journal of Educational Technology & Society, 11*(3), 114–126.

Kim, D., & Kim, D. J. (2012). Effect of screen size on multimedia vocabulary learning. *British Journal of Educational Technology*, *43*(1), 62–70. doi:10.1111/j.1467-8535.2010.01145.x

Knight, S. M. (1994). Dictionary use while reading: The effects on comprehension and vocabulary acquisition for students of different verbal abilities. *Modern Language Journal*, *78*, 285–299. doi:10.1111/j.1540-4781.1994.tb02043.x

Krashen, S. (1985). *The input hypothesis: Issues and implications*. London: Longman.

Lantolf, J. P. (2006). Sociocultural theory and L2: state of the art. *Studies in Second Language Acquisition*, *28*, 67–109. doi:10.1017/S0272263106060037

Lara-Alecio, R., Tong, F., Irby, B. J., Guerrero, C., Huerta, M., & Fan, Y. (2012). The effect of an instructional intervention on middle school English learners' science and English reading achievement. *Journal of Research in Science Teaching*, *48*(8), 987–1011. doi:10.1002/tea.21031

Laufer, B. (2005). Focus on form in second language vocabulary learning. *EUROSLA Yearbook*, *5*, 223–250. doi:10.1075/eurosla.5.11lau

Lee, S. H., & Muncie, J. (2006). From receptive to productive: Improving ESL learners' use of vocabulary in a post reading composition task. *TESOL Quarterly*, *40*(2), 295–320. doi:10.2307/40264524

Levy, M. (1997). *Computer-assisted language learning: Context and conceptualization*. Oxford: Oxford University Press.

Levy, M. (2009). Technologies in use for second language learning. *Modern Language Journal*, *93*(Focus issue), 769–782. doi:10.1111/j.1540-4781.2009.00972.x

Levy, M., & Stockwell, G. (2006). *CALL dimensions: Options and issues in computer-assisted language learning*. London: Lawrence Erlbaum.

Li, J. (2009). The evolution of vocabulary learning strategies in a computer-mediated reading environment. *CALICO Journal*, *27*(1), 118–146.

Li, J. (2010). Learning vocabulary via computer-assisted scaffolding for text processing. *Computer Assisted Language Learning*, *23*(2), 253–275. doi:10.1080/09588221.2010.483678

Lu, M. (2008). Effectiveness of vocabulary learning via mobile phone. *Journal of Computer Assisted Learning*, *24*(6), 515–525. doi:10.1111/j.1365-2729.2008.00289.x

Lwo, L., & Lin, C.-T. M. (2012). The effects of captions in teenagers' multimedia L2 learning. *ReCALL*, *24*(2), 188–208. doi:10.1017/S0958344012000067

Macaro, E., Handley, Z. L., & Walter, C. (2012). A systematic review of CALL in English as a second language: Focus on primary and secondary education. *Language Teaching*, *45*(1), 1–43. doi:10.1017/S0261444811000395

MacGintie, W., MacGintie, R., Maria, K., & Dreyer, L. (2002). *Gates MacGintie reading tests* (4th ed.). Itasca, IL: Riverside.

Mayer, R. E., & Moreno, R. (2002). Aids to computer-based multimedia learning. *Learning and Instruction*, *12*, 107–119. doi:10.1016/S0959-4752(01)00018-4

Milton, J. (2009). *Measuring second language vocabulary acquisition*. Bristol, UK: Multilingual Matters.

Myers, G. (2010). *The discourse of blogs and wikis*. London: Continuum.

Nakata, T. (2006). Implementing optimal spaced learning for English vocabulary learning: Towards improvement of the low-first method derived from the reactivation theory. *JALT CALL Journal*, *2*(2), 19–36.

Nakata, T. (2008). English vocabulary learning with word lists, word cards and computers: Implications from cognitive psychology research for optimal spaced learning. *ReCALL*, *20*(1), 3–20. doi:10.1017/S0958344008000219

Nassaji, H. (2003). L2 vocabulary learning from context: Strategies, knowledge sources, and their relationship with success in L2 lexical inferencing. *TESOL Quarterly*, *37*(4), 645–670. doi:10.2307/3588216

Nation, I. S. P. (2001). *Learning vocabulary in another language*. Cambridge: Cambridge University Press. doi:10.1017/CBO9781139524759

Nation, I. S. P. (2006). How large a vocabulary is needed for reading and listening? *Canadian Modern Language Review*, *63*(1), 59–82. doi:10.3138/cmlr.63.1.59

Nation, I. S. P. (2007). The four strands. *Innovation in Language Teaching and Learning*, *1*, 1–12. doi:10.2167/illt039.0

Nation, I. S. P. (2011). Thinking allowed. Research into practice: Vocabulary. *Language Teaching*, *44*(4), 529–539. doi:10.1017/S0261444811000267

Nation, P., & Beglar, D. (2007). A vocabulary size test. *Language Teaching*, *31*(7), 9–13.

O'Hara, S., & Pritchard, R. (2008). Hypermedia authoring as a vehicle for vocabulary development in middle school English as a second language classrooms. *Clearing House: A Journal of Educational Strategies. Issues and Ideas*, *82*(2), 60–65.

Paivio, A., & Desrochers, A. (1981). Mnemonic techniques in second language learning. *Journal of Educational Psychology*, *73*, 780–795. doi:10.1037/0022-0663.73.6.780

Pederson, K. (1987). Research on CALL. In W. F. Smith (Ed.), *Modern media in foreign language education: Theory and implementation* (pp. 99–131). Lincolnwood, IL: National Textbook Company.

Pigada, M., & Schmitt, N. (2006). Vocabulary acquisition from extensive reading: A case study. *Reading in a Foreign Language*, *18*(1), 1–28.

Pinter, A. (2006). *Teaching young language learners*. Oxford: Oxford University Press.

Proctor, C. P., Dalton, B., & Grisham, D. L. (2007). Scaffolding English language learners and struggling readers in a universal literacy environment with embedded strategy instruction and vocabulary support. *Journal of Literacy Research*, *39*(1), 71–93.

Royer, J. M. (1973). Memory effect for test-like events during acquisition of foreign language vocabulary. *Psychological Reports*, *32*, 195–198. doi:10.2466/pr0.1973.32.1.195

Sasaki, A., & Takeuchi, O. (2010). EFL students' vocabulary learning in NS-NNS e-mail interactions: Do they learn new words by imitation? *ReCALL*, *22*(1), 70–82. doi:10.1017/S0958344009990206

Schmidt, R. W. (1990). The role of consciousness in second language learning. *Applied Linguistics*, *11*(1), 129–158. doi:10.1093/applin/11.2.129

Schmitt, N. (2010a). *Researching vocabulary: A vocabulary research manual*. Basingstoke: Palgrave Macmillan. doi:10.1057/9780230293977

Schmitt, N. (2010b). Review article. Instructed second language vocabulary learning. *Language Teaching Research*, *12*(3), 329–363. doi:10.1177/1362168808089921

Schmitt, N., Schmitt, D., & Clapham, C. (2001). Developing and exploring the behaviour of two new versions of the vocabulary levels test. *Language Testing*, *18*(1), 55–88.

Siegel, M., & Misselt, A. (1984). Adaptive feedback and review paradigm for computer-based drills. *Journal of Educational Psychology, 18*, 294–309.

Silverman, R., & Hines, S. (2009). The effects of multimedia-enhanced instruction on the vocabulary of English-language learners and non-English-language learners in pre-kindergarten through second grade. *Journal of Educational Psychology, 101*(2), 305–314. doi:10.1037/a0014217

Snellings, P., van Gelderen, A., & de Glopper, K. (2002). Lexical retrieval: An aspect of fluent second language production that can be enhanced. *Language Learning, 52*, 723–754. doi:10.1111/1467-9922.00202

Snellings, P., van Gelderen, A., & de Glopper, K. (2004). The effect of enhanced lexical retrieval on second language writing: A classroom experiment. *Applied Psycholinguistics, 25*(2), 175–200. doi:10.1017/S0142716404001092

Stockwell, G. (2007). A review of technology choice for teaching language skills and areas in the CALL literature. *ReCALL, 19*(2), 105–120. doi:10.1017/S0958344007000225

Sun, Y., & Dong, Q. (2004). An experiment on supporting children's English vocabulary learning in multimedia context. *Computer Assisted Language Learning, 17*(2), 131–147. doi:10.1080/0958822042000334217

Sussex, R. (1991). Research in practice and practice on research in CALL. *Computer Assisted Language Learning, 4*(3), 191–206. doi:10.1080/0958822910040307

Swain, M. (1985). Communicative competence: Some roles of comprehensible input and output in its development. In S. Gass, & C. Madden (Eds.), *Input in second language acquisition* (pp. 235–253). Rowley, MA: Newbury House.

Widdig, W., & Esser, R. (1988). New possibilities in computer-assisted learning of foreign language vocabulary using Apple Macintosh. In U. Jung (Ed.), *Computers in applied linguistics and language teaching* (pp. 265–278). Frankfurt: Peter Lang.

Wilkins, D. A. (1972). *Linguistics in language teaching*. London: Edward Arnold.

Wong, L. H., & Looi, C.-K. (2010). Vocabulary learning by mobile-assisted authentic content creation and social meaning-making: Two case studies. *Journal of Computer Assisted Learning, 26*(5), 421–433. doi:10.1111/j.1365-2729.2010.00357.x

Xu, J. (2010). Using multimedia vocabulary annotations in L2 reading and listening activities. *CALICO Journal, 27*(2), 311–327.

Yun, S., Miller, P. C., Baek, Y., Jung, J., & Ko, M. (2008). Improving recall and transfer skills through vocabulary building in web-based second language learning: An examination by item and feedback type. *Journal of Educational Technology & Society, 11*(4), 158–172.

Zhang, T., Gao, T., Ring, G., & Zhang, W. (2007). Using online discussion forums to assist a traditional English class. *International Journal on E-Learning, 6*(4), 623–643.

KEY TERMS AND DEFINITIONS

Computer-Mediated Communication (CMC): "Any program that allows learners to exchange language – through text or audio" (Blake, 2008, p. 152). For example, e-mail, discussion forums, chat.

Fluency Development: Activities in which the learner's focus is on developing automaticity (Nation, 2007, 2011).

Language-Focused Learning: Learning through deliberate attention to forms (Nation, 2007, 2011).

Meaning-Focused Input: Learning through meaning focused input, i.e. reading and listening activities during which the learner's focus in on comprehension (Nation, 2007, 2011).

Meaning-Focused Output: Learning through meaning-focused output, i.e. activities during which the learner's focus is on communicating meaning through writing or speech (Nation, 2007, 2011).

Parser-Based CALL: Also referred to as Intelligent CALL (ICALL), parser-based CALL refers to CALL software which integrates parsing technology to identify errors in learners' responses to open-response questions and provide feedback on those errors, where a parser is a technology which "produces a formal linguistic representation of natural language by identifying the grammatical function of the parts of a sentence" (Heift & Schulze, 2009, p. 2).

Text Reconstruction: Text reconstruction refers to a class of CALL activities in which the learner is required to reconstitute a text from a partial text or a jumbled list of its components. Examples of text reconstruction activities include gap-fill, cloze, total text reconstruction, and text unscrambling (Hewer, 1997).

Text-to-Speech (TTS) Synthesis: TTS synthesis is the process of converting an input text to an acoustic signal.

Web 2.0: Web 2.0 is the ''writable web'' (Karpati, 2009: 140). It encompasses any technology which allows users to publish their own content (user-generated content). Blogs, wikis and podcasts are all examples of Web 2.0 technologies.

ENDNOTES

1 Studies in which the technology was designed to support vocabulary learning, but vocabulary development was not assessed were not included in the review. These included studies focusing on reading such as (Hsu, Hwang & Chang, 2013; Lara-Alecio, Tong, Guerrero, Huerta & Fan, 2012; Macaruso & Rodman, 2011).

2 Note that some of the studies involved a combination of these activity types.

3 While Kim and Gilman (2008) report collecting data on learners' attitudes towards multimedia vocabulary CALL, they do not report their analyses of that data.

4 University of Oxford: Ernesto Macaro, Catherine Walter, Zöe Handley, Mairin Hennebry, Amanda Holmbrook, Yuen Yi Lo, Victoria Murphy, Vivienne Rogers, Robert Woore. English Language Teaching Division, Oxford University Press: Luke Baxter, Julia Bell, Elaine Boyd, Jenny Cammons, Phil Davis, Katherine Goldsmith, Joanna Freer, Catherine Kneafsey, Kate Maciver, Antoinette Meehan, Alex Miller, Sarah Parsons, Gail Pasque, Stephanie Richards, Alison Sharpe, Lynne White, Katherine Wyatt.

APPENDIX A: KEYWORD MAP

Note:
* L1: Where the first language of the participants was not indicted in the paper, either the country/region from which the participants originated or the country/region in which the study was conducted is indicated in capital letters.

Table 1.

Author		Date	Language areas and skills	Technology	Country/ Region	Educational setting	L1	L2
Chen & Li	‡	2010	Vocabulary	Mobile, Context-aware	Taiwan (Chinese Taipei)	Secondary	TAIWAN*	English
Cobb & Horst	‡	2011	Vocabulary	Games, Mobile	Canada	Secondary	French	English
Dalton et al.	‡	2011	Vocabulary, Reading	Multimedia, NLP, TTS,	U.S.	Primary	Various including English	English
Fehr et al.	‡	2012	Vocabulary	Adaptive learning	U.S.	Primary	Various	English
Hur & Suh	†	2012	Vocabulary	Digital storytelling, Podcasting, Interactive whiteboards	U.S.	Primary	Korean	English
Hwang & Chen	‡	2013	Vocabulary, Speaking, Listening	Mobile	Taiwan (Chinese Taipei)	Secondary	TAIWAN*	English
Jia et al.	†	2012	Vocabulary	Bended learning, CALL software,	China	Secondary	CHINA*	English
Kim & Gilman	‡	2008	Vocabulary	Web, Web-based, Multimedia, Graphics, Audio	South Korea	Secondary	Korean	English
Kim & Kim	‡	2012	Vocabulary	Mobile	South Korea	Primary	Korean	English
Li	†	2009	Vocabulary, Reading	Electronic dictionary, Text reconstruction, NLP, TTS, Parser-based CALL	Canada	Secondary	CHINA*	English
Li	‡	2010	Vocabulary, Reading	Electronic dictionary, NLP, TTS	Canada	Secondary	Mandarin	English
Lu	‡	2008	Vocabulary	Mobile, Text messaging	Taiwan (Chinese Taipei)	Secondary	TAIWAN*	English
Lwo & Lin	†	2012	Vocabulary, Reading	Multimedia	Taiwan (Chinese Taipei)	Primary	TAIWAN*	English
Nakata	‡	2008	Vocabulary	Adaptive systems	Japan	Secondary	Japanese	English
O'Hara & Pritchard	‡	2008	Vocabulary, Concepts	Hypermedia	U.S.	Secondary	Spanish	English
Proctor et al.	†	2007	Vocabulary, Reading	Web, Web-based, Web-publishing, Hypermedia, Multimedia, NLP, TTS	U.S.	Primary	Spanish, English	English

continued on following page

Table 1. Continued

Author		Date	Language areas and skills	Technology	Country/ Region	Educational setting	L1	L2
Sasaki & Takeuchi	‡	2010	Vocabulary	CMC, E-mail	Japan	Secondary	Japanese	English
Silverman & Hines	‡	2009	Vocabulary	Multimedia, Video	U.S.	Primary	Various including English	English
Sun & Dong	†	2004	Pronunciation, Vocabulary	Multimedia, Animation	China	Primary	Mandarin	English
Wong & Looi	†	2010	Vocabulary	Multimedia, Animation, CMC, Discussion forums, Web 2.0, Wikis, Mobile, Digital photography	Singapore	Primary	Chinese	English
Yun et al.	‡	2008	Vocabulary	Web, Web-based	South Korea	Secondary	Korean	English
Zhang et al.	‡	2007	Reading, Writing, Grammar, Vocabulary, In-class discussion, Critical thinking	CMC, Discussion forums	China	Secondary	CHINA*	English

APPENDIX B: RESULTS OF QUALITY ASSESSMENT

Note: Impact corresponds to Research Question Three, "What evidence is there that digital technologies facilitate the acquisition of vocabulary in EFL/ESL?" Insights correspond to Research Question Four, "What (pedagogical) insights can be gleaned regarding the use of digital technology technologies in the teaching of vocabulary in EFL/ESL?"

Table 2.

Author		Impact		Insights	
		Relevance	Contribution	Relevance	Contribution
Chen & Li 2010	‡	High	High	Medium	Low
Cobb & Horst 2011	‡	High	Medium	Low	Low
Dalton et al. 2011	‡	High	High	Low	Low
Fehr et al. 2012	‡	High	Medium	Low	Low
Hur & Suh 2012	†	High	Low	High	Low
Hwang & Chen 2013	‡	High	Medium	High	High
Jiaet al. 2012	†	High	Low	High	Low
Kim & Gilman 2008	‡	High	High	Medium	Low
Kim & Kim 2012	‡	High	Medium	Low	Low
Li 2009	†	Low	Low	Medium	Low
Li 2010	‡	High	Medium	Medium	Low
Lu 2008	‡	High	High	High	Medium
Lwo & Lin 2012	†	High	Low	Low	Low
Nakata 2008	‡	High	Medium	Medium	Medium
O'Hara et al. 2008	‡	High	Medium	Medium	Medium
Proctor et al. 2007	†	High	Medium	High	Medium
Sasaki & Takeuchi 2010	‡	High	Medium	High	High
Silverman & Hines 2009	‡	High	High	Low	Low
Sun & Dong 2004	†	Medium	Low	Low	Low
Wong & Looi 2010	†	Medium	Low	Medium	Low
Yun et al. 2008	‡	High	Medium	Low	Low
Zhang et al. 2007	‡	High	Medium	Medium	Medium

Compilation of References

Abasi, A., Akbari, N., & Graves, B. (2006). Discourse appropriation, construction of identities, and the complex issue of plagiarism: ESL students writing in graduate school. *Journal of Second Language Writing*, *15*, 102–117. doi:10.1016/j.jslw.2006.05.001

Abdullah, N. A., Abidin, M. J. Z., Wong, S. L., Majid, O., & Atan, H. (2006). The attitude and motivation of English language teachers towards the use of computers. *Malaysian Online Journal of Instructional Technology*, *3*(1), 57–67.

Abrahms, Z. (2006). From theory to practice: Intracultural CMC use in the L2 classroom. In L. Ducate, & N. Arnold (Eds.), *Calling on CALL: From theory and research to new directions in foreign language teaching* (pp. 181–210). San Marcos, TX: CALICO.

AbuSeileck, A. F. (2007). Cooperative vs. individual learning of oral skills in a CALL environment. *Computer Assisted Language Learning*, *20*(5), 493–514. doi:10.1080/09588220701746054

Ahn, M. (2005). A phonetically based account of English reduplication. *SNU Working Papers in English Language and Linguistics, 4,* 73-93.

Akiyama, Y. (2012, November). *Potential issues, conditions, and solutions to e-tandem language learning*. Paper presented at American Council on the Teaching of Foreign Languages Conference. Philadelphia, PA.

Alcón-Soler, E. (2009). Focus on form, learner uptake and subsequent lexical gains in learners' oral production. *International Review of Applied Linguistics in Language Teaching*, *47*, 347–365. doi:10.1515/iral.2009.015

Alderson, J. C. (2005). *Diagnosing foreign language proficiency*. London: Continuum.

Al-Homoud, F., & Schmitt, N. (2009). Extensive reading in a challenging environment: A comparison of extensive and intensive reading approaches in Saudi Arabia. *Language Teaching Research*, *13*(4), 383–401. doi:10.1177/1362168809341508

Ali, H. I. (2013). Minimizing cyber-plagiarism through Turnitin: Faculty's and students' perspectives. *International Journal of Applied Linguistics & English Literature*, *2*(2), 33–42. doi:10.7575/aiac.ijalel.v.2n.2p.33

Allen, J. R. (2008). Why learning to write Chinese is a waste of time: A modest proposal. *Foreign Language Annals*, *41*(2), 237–251. doi:10.1111/j.1944-9720.2008.tb03291.x

Alshumaimeri, Y. A. (2008). Perceptions and attitudes toward using CALL in English classrooms among Saudi Secondary EFL teachers. *The JALT CALL Journal*, *4*(2), 29–46.

Anderson, J. R. (1993). *Rules of the mind*. Hillsdale, NJ: Erlbaum.

Anderson, J. R., & Corbett, A. T. (1992). Acquisition of LISP Programming Skill. In S. Chipman, & A. Meyrowitz (Eds.), *Foundations of knowledge acquisition: Cognitive models of complex learning* (pp. 1–24). Hingham, MA: Kluwer.

Anderson, J. R., & Matessa, M. (1992). Explorations of an incremental, Bayesian algorithm for categorization. *Machine Learning*, *9*, 275–308. doi:10.1007/BF00994109

Anton, M., & DiCamilla, F. (1998). Socio-cognitive functions of L1 collaborative interaction in the L2 classroom. *Canadian Modern Language Review*, *54*, 314–342. doi:10.3138/cmlr.54.3.314

Aoun, J. (1985). *A Grammar of Anaphora*. Cambridge, MA: MIT Press.

Appel, C., & Gilabert, R. (2002). Motivation and task performance in a task-based web-based tandem project. *ReCALL*, *14*, 16–31. doi:10.1017/S0958344002000319

Arispe, K. (2011, November). *L2 vocabulary development as mediated through an ICALL tool, LangBot*. Paper presented at The Fourth International Ubiquitous Learning Conference. Berkeley, CA.

Arnaud, P. J. L., Béjoint, H., & Thoiron, P. (1985). A quoi sert le programme lexical? *Les Langues Modernes*, *79*(3/4), 72–85.

Arnold, N., & Ducate, L. (2006). Future foreign language teachers' social and cognitive collaboration in an online environment. *Language Learning & Technology*, *10*(1), 42–66.

Arnold, N., Ducate, L., & Kost, C. (2012). Collaboration or cooperation? Analyzing group dynamics and revision process in wikis. *CALICO Journal*, *29*(3), 431–448. doi:10.11139/cj.29.3.431-448

Arnold, N., Ducate, L., Lomicka, L., & Lord, G. (2009). Assessing online collaboration among language teachers: A cross-institutional wiki case study. *Journal of Technology and Teacher Education*, *8*(2), 121–139.

Arslan, R. Ş., & Şahin-Kizil, A. (2010). How can the use of blog software facilitate the writing process of English language learners? *Computer Assisted Language Learning*, *23*(3), 183–197. doi:10.1080/09588221.2010.486575

Atkinson, R., & Raugh, M. (1975). An application of the mnemonic keyword method to the acquisition of Russian vocabulary. *Journal of Experimental Psychology. Human Learning and Memory*, *104*, 125–133.

Atkins, T., & Nelson, G. (2001). Plagiarism and the Internet: Turning the tables. *English Journal*, *90*(4), 101–104. doi:10.2307/821911

Atoda, T., & Hoshino, K. (1995). *Giongo gitaigo tsukaikata jiten (Usage dictionary of sound/manner mimetics)*. Tokyo: Sotakusha.

Bailey, F. (1996). **The role of collaborative dialogue** in teacher education. In D. Freeman, & J. Richards (Eds.), *Teacher learning in language teaching* (pp. 260–280). Cambridge: Cambridge University Press.

Baker, R. S. J. d., Corbett, A. T., Gowda, S. M., Wagner, A. Z., MacLaren, B. M., & Kauffman, L. R. et al. (2010). Contextual slip and prediction of student performance after use of an intelligent tutor. In P. D. Bra, A. Kobsa, & D. Chin (Eds.), *User modeling, adaptation, and personalization* (pp. 52–63). Germany: Springer. doi:10.1007/978-3-642-13470-8_7

Barcroft, J. (2002). Semantic and structural elaboration in L2 lexical acquisition. *Language Learning*, *52*(2), 323–363. doi:10.1111/0023-8333.00186

Barcroft, J. (2007a). When knowing grammar depends on knowing vocabulary: native-speaker grammaticality judgement of sentences with real and unreal words. *Canadian Modern Language Review*, *63*(3), 313–343. doi:10.3138/R601-H212-5582-0737

Barcroft, J. (2007b). Effects of opportunities for word retrieval during second language vocabulary learning. *Language Learning*, *57*(1), 35–65. doi:10.1111/j.1467-9922.2007.00398.x

Barcroft, J. (2009). Strategies and performance in intentional L2 vocabulary learning. *Language Awareness*, *18*(1), 74–89. doi:10.1080/09658410802557535

Barr, D. (2008). Computer-enhanced grammar teaching. In F. Zhang, & B. Barbar (Eds.), *Handbook of research on computer-enhanced language acquisition and learning* (pp. 101–115). Hershey: Information Science Reference. doi:10.4018/978-1-59904-895-6.ch007

Basterrechea, M., & García Mayo, M. (2013). Language-related episodes during collaborative tasks. In K. McDonough, & A. Mackey (Eds.), *Second language interaction in diverse educational contexts* (pp. 25–44). Amsterdam: John Benjamins. doi:10.1075/lllt.34.05ch2

Bates, E., & MacWhinney, B. (1989). Functionalism and the Competition Model. In B. MacWhinney, & E. Bates (Eds.), *The cross-linguistic study of sentence processing* (pp. 3–73). New York: Cambridge University Press.

Bax, S. (2003). CALL – Past, present and future. *System*, *31*(1), 13–28. doi:10.1016/S0346-251X(02)00071-4

Bayley, R., & Schecter, S. R. (2003). *Language socialization in bilingual and multilingual societies*. Clevedon, UK: Multilingual Matters.

Belz, J. (2002). Social dimensions of telecollaborative foreign language study. *Language Learning & Technology*, *6*(1), 60–81.

Belz, J. (2005). Intercultural questioning, discovery and tension in internet-mediated language learning partnerships. *Language and Intercultural Communication*, *5*, 3–37. doi:10.1080/14708470508668881

Belz, J. A. (2003). Linguistic perspective on the development of intercultural communicative competence in telecollaboration. *Language Learning & Technology*, *7*(2), 68–117.

Belz, J. A. (2007). The role of computer mediation in the instruction and development of L2 pragmatic competence. *Annual Review of Applied Linguistics*, *27*, 45–75. doi:10.1017/S0267190508070037

Belz, J. A., & Kinginger, C. (2003). Discourse options and the development of pragmatic competence by classroom learners of German: The case of address forms. *Language Learning*, *53*(4), 591–647. doi:10.1046/j.1467-9922.2003.00238.x

Belz, J. A., & Thorne, S. L. (2006). *Computer-mediated intercultural foreign language education*. Boston: Heinle & Heinle.

Belz, J. A., & Vyatkina, N. (2008). The pedagogical mediation of a developmental learner corpus for classroom-based language instruction. *Language Learning & Technology*, *12*(3), 33–52.

Belz, J., & Müller–Hartmann, A. (2003). Teachers as intercultural learners: Negotiating German–American telecollaboration along the institutional fault line. *Modern Language Journal*, *87*(1), 71–89. doi:10.1111/1540-4781.00179

Bennett, J. M. (1993). Toward ethnorelativism: A developmental model of intercultural sensitivity. In R. M. Paige (Ed.), *Education for the intercultural experience* (pp. 21–71). Yarmouth, ME: Intercultural Press.

Bennett, M. J. (1997). How not to be a fluent fool: Understanding the cultural dimension of language. In A. Fantini (Ed.), *New ways in teaching culture* (pp. 16–21). Alexandria, VA: TESOL Inc.

Bensoussan, M., & Laufer, B. (1984). Lexical guessing in context in EFL reading comprehension. *Journal of Research in Reading*, *7*(1), 15–32. doi:10.1111/j.1467-9817.1984.tb00252.x

Bétrancourt, M. (2005). The animation and interactivity principles in multimedia learning. In R. E. Mayer (Ed.), *The Cambridge handbook of multimedia learning* (pp. 287–296). New York, NY: Cambridge University Press. doi:10.1017/CBO9780511816819.019

Betts, L. R., Bostock, S. J., Elder, T. J., & Trueman, M. (2012). Encouraging good writing practice in first-year psychology students: An intervention using *Turnitin*. *Psychology Teaching Review*, *18*(2), 74–81.

Blake, R. (2000). Computer mediated communication: A window on L2 Spanish interlanguage. *Language Learning & Technology*, *4*(1), 120–136.

Blake, R. (2006). Language, culture, and identity in online fanfiction. *E-learning*, *3*, 170–184. doi:10.2304/elea.2006.3.2.170

Blake, R. J. (2007). New trends in using technology in the language curriculum. *Annual Review of Applied Linguistics*, *27*, 76–97. doi:10.1017/S0267190508070049

Blake, R. J. (2008). *Brave new digital classroom: Technology and foreign language learning*. Washington, DC: Georgetown University Press.

Blake, R. J. (2011). Current trends in online language learning. *Annual Review of Applied Linguistics*, *31*, 19–35. doi:10.1017/S026719051100002X

Bloch, J. (2001). Plagiarism and the ESL student: From printed to electronic texts. In D. Belcher & A. Hirvela (Eds.), Linking Literacies: Perspectives on L2 reading-writing connections (pp. 209–228). Ann Arbor, MI: University of Michigan Press.

Bloch, J. (2007). Abdullah's blogging: A generation 1.5 student enters the blogosphere. *Language Learning & Technology*, *11*(2), 128–141.

Bloch, J. (2012). *Plagiarism, intellectual property and the teaching of L2 writing*. Bristol, UK: Multilingual Matters.

Block, D. (2007). The rise of identity in SLA research, post Firth and Wagner (1997). *Modern Language Journal, 91*(Focus Issue), 863–876. doi:10.1111/j.1540-4781.2007.00674.x

Bloom, K. C., & Schuell, T. J. (1981). Effects of massed and distributed practice on the learning and retention of second language vocabulary. *The Journal of Educational Research, 74*, 245–248.

Bolger, P., & Zapata, G. (2011). Semantic categories and context in L2 vocabulary learning. *Language Learning, 61*(2), 614–646. doi:10.1111/j.1467-9922.2010.00624.x

Borg, S. (2006). *Teacher cognition and language education: Research and practice*. London: Continuum.

Borg, S. (2009). Language teacher cognition. In A. Burns, & J. C. Richards (Eds.), *The Cambridge guide to Second Language teacher education* (pp. 163–171). Cambridge: Cambridge University Press.

Bower, G. H., & Clark, M. C. (1969). Narrative stories as mediators for serial learning. *Psychonomic Science, 14*, 181–182. doi:10.3758/BF03332778

Bower, J., & Kawaguchi, S. (2011). Negotiation of meaning and corrective feedback in Japanese/English eTandem. *Language Learning & Technology, 15*(1), 41–71.

boyd, d. & Ellison, N. (2007). Social network sites: Definition, history, and scholarship. *Journal of Computer-Mediated Communication, 13*(1), 210–230.

Bradley, L., Linstrom, B., & Rystedt, H. (2010). Rationalities of collaboration for language learning on a wiki. *ReCALL, 22*(2), 247–265. doi:10.1017/S0958344010000108

Braine, G. (2004). Teaching second and foreign language writing on LANs. In S. Fotos, & C. Browne (Eds.), *New perspectives on CALL for second language classrooms* (pp. 93–108). Mahwah, New Jersey, London: Lawrence Erlbaum Associates.

Brammerts, H. (2003). Autonomous language learning in tandem: The development of a concept. In T. Lewis, & L. Walker (Eds.), *Autonomous Language Learning in Tandem* (pp. 27–36). Sheffield: Academy Electronic Publications.

Breuch, L. M. K., & Racine, S. J. (2000). Developing sound tutor training for online writing centers: Creating productive peer reviewers. *Computers and Composition, 17*, 245–263. doi:10.1016/S8755-4615(00)00034-7

Brown, A. V. (2009). Students' and teachers' perceptions of effective foreign language teaching: A comparison of ideals. *Modern Language Journal, 93*, 46–60. doi:10.1111/j.1540-4781.2009.00827.x

Bruffee, K. (1993). *Collaborative learning: Higher education, interdependence, and the authority of knowledge*. Baltimore, MD: Johns Hopkins University Press.

Brysbaert, M., & New, B. (2009). Moving beyond Kucera and Francis: A critical evaluation current word frequency norms and the introduction of a new and improved word frequency measure for American English. *Behavior Research Methods, 41*, 488–496. doi:10.3758/BRM.41.4.977 PMID:19897807

Buranen, L. (1999). But I wasn't cheating: Plagiarism and cross-cultural mythology. In L. Buranen, & A. Roy (Eds.), *Perspectives on plagiarism and intellectual property in a postmodern world* (pp. 63–74). Albany, NY: State University of New York Press.

Burns, A. (2009). Action research in second language teacher education. In A. Burns, & J. C. Richards (Eds.), *Cambridge guide to second language teacher education* (pp. 289–297). Cambridge: Cambridge University Press.

Burton, J. (2009). Reflective practice. In A. Burns, & J. C. Richards (Eds.), *Cambridge guide to second language teacher education* (pp. 298–307). Cambridge: Cambridge University Press.

Byrnes, H. (1991). Reflections on the development of cross-cultural communicative competence in the foreign language classroom. In B. Freed (Ed.), *Foreign language acquisition research* (pp. 205–218). Lexington, VA: D. C. Heath and Company.

Cameron, L. (2001). *Teaching languages to young learners*. Cambridge: Cambridge University Press. doi:10.1017/CBO9780511733109

Campus Computing Project. (2011). The 2010 National Survey of Information Technology in U.S. Higher Education. Retrieved from http://www.campuscomputing.net/

Cao, F., Rickles, B., Vu, M., Zhu, Z., Chan, H., & Harris, L. et al. (2013). Early-stage visual processing predicts retention in second language learning. *Journal of Neurolinguistics, 26*, 440–461. doi:10.1016/j.jneuroling.2013.01.003 PMID:23798804

Cao, F., Vu, M., Chan, D. H. L., Lawrence, J. M., Harris, L. N., & Guan, Q. et al. (2013). Writing affects the brain network of reading in Chinese: A functional magnetic resonance imaging study. *Human Brain Mapping, 34*, 1670–1684. doi:10.1002/hbm.22017 PMID:22378588

Carney, N. (2007). *Language study through blog exchanges*. Paper presented at the Wireless Ready Symposium: Podcasting Education and Mobile Assisted Language Learning, NUCB Graduate School. Nagoya, Japan. Available from, http://wirelessready.nucba.ac.jp/Carney.pdf

Carney, N. (2009). Blogging in foreign language education. In M. Thomas (Ed.), *Handbook of research on Web 2.0 and second language learning* (pp. 292–312). Hershey, PA: IGI Global. doi:10.4018/978-1-60566-190-2.ch016

Celce-Murcia, M., & Larsen-Freeman, D. (1999). *The grammar book: An ESL/EFL teacher's course* (2nd ed.). Boston, MA: Heinle & Heinle Publishers.

Cen, H., Koedinger, K., & Junker, B. (2006). A general method for cognitive model evaluation and improvement. *Intelligent Tutoring Systems, 4053*, 164–175. doi:10.1007/11774303_17

Chakrabarti, R. (2012). When essays for sale become contract cheating. *BBC News*. Available from, http://www.bbc.co.uk/news/education-20298237

Chao, Y., & Lo, H. (2009). Students' perceptions of wiki-based collaborative writing for learners of English as a foreign language. *Interactive Learning Environments*.

Chapelle, C. A. (1998). Multimedia CALL: Lessons to be learned from research on instructed SLA. *Language Learning & Technology, 2*(1), 22–34.

Chapelle, C. A. (2001). *Computer applications in second language acquisition: Foundations for teaching, testing and research*. Cambridge: Cambridge University Press. doi:10.1017/CBO9781139524681

Chapelle, C. A. (2009). The Relationship Between Second Language Acquisition Theory and Computer-Assisted Language Learning. *Modern Language Journal, 93*, 741–753. doi:10.1111/j.1540-4781.2009.00970.x

Charmaz, K. (2006). *Constructing grounded theory: A practical guide through qualitative analysis*. London, CA: Sage.

Chase, W. G., & Simon, H. A. (1973). Perception in chess. *Cognitive Psychology, 4*, 55–81. doi:10.1016/0010-0285(73)90004-2

Chen, H. C., Chien, H. Y., & Chang, S. P. (2013). *Chinese radical-based character-family E-learning platform*. Retrieved from http://coolch.sce.ntnu.edu.tw/chinese2

Chen, H. C., Lin, Y. C., Xyue, J. Y., Chang, L. Y., Sung, Y. T., & Chang, K. E. (2011). *Development of Radical-Based Character-Family E-Learning Platform*. Paper presented at The Asia-Pacific Conference on Technology Enhanced Learning. Xi'an, China.

Chen, C.-M., & Li, Y. L. (2010). Personalised context-aware ubiquitous learning system for supporting effective English vocabulary learning. *Interactive Learning Environments, 18*(4), 341–364. doi:10.1080/10494820802602329

Chen, H. C., Chang, L. Y., Chou, Y. S., Sung, Y. T., & Chang, K. E. (2011). Construction of Chinese Orthographic Database for Chinese Character Instruction. *Bulletin of Educational Psychology, 43*, 269–290.

Chen, H. C., Hsu, C. C., Chang, L. Y., Lin, Y. C., Chang, K. E., & Sung, Y. T. (2013). Using a radical-derived character E-learning platform to increase learner knowledge of Chinese characters. *Language Learning & Technology, 17*(1), 89–106.

Chen, H.-I. (2013). Identity practices of multilingual writers in social networking spaces. *Language Learning & Technology, 17*(2), 143–170.

Chen, W. C., & Eslami, Z. (2013). Focus on form in live chats. *Journal of Educational Technology & Society, 16*(1), 147–158.

Chen, X., Ye, L., & Zhang, Y. (1995). Refusing in Chinese. In G. Kasper (Ed.), *Pragmatics of Chinese as a native and target language (Tech. Rep. No. 5)* (pp. 119–163). Honolulu, HI: University of Hawai'i, Second Language Teaching & Curriculum Center.

Chinese radical position frequency dictionary. (1984). Hunan, China: Hunan Institute of Computer Science.

Ching, N., & Ching, E. (1975). Teaching the writing of Chinese characters. *Journal of the Chinese Language Teachers Association*, *10*(1), 20–24.

Chiu, C., Lin, D., & Silverman, A. (2012). China's social-media boom. *McKinsey and Company*. Retrieved from http://www.mckinsey.com/insights/marketing_sales/chinas_social-media_boom

Chiu, T. L., Liou, H. C., & Yeh, Y. L. (2007). A study of web-based oral activities enhanced by automatic speech recognition for EFL college learning. *Computer Assisted Language Learning*, *20*(3), 209–233. doi:10.1080/09588220701489374

Chun, D. (2006). CALL technologies for L2 reading. In L. Ducate, & N. Arnold (Eds.), *Calling on CALL: From Theory and Research to New Directions in Foreign Language Teaching* (pp. 69–88). San Marcos, TX: CALICO.

Chun, D. M., & Plass, J. L. (1996). Effects of multimedia annotations on vocabulary acquisition. *Modern Language Journal*, *80*(2), 183–198. doi:10.1111/j.1540-4781.1996.tb01159.x

Clandinin, D. J., & Connelly, F. M. (1992). Teacher as curriculum maker. In P. W. Jackson (Ed.), *Handbook of research on curriculum* (pp. 363–401). New York: Macmillan.

Claridge, G. (2012). Graded readers: How the publishers make the grade. *Reading in a Foreign Language*, *24*(1), 106–119.

Clarke, R., & Lancaster, T. (2006, June). *Eliminating the successor to plagiarism? Identifying the usage of contract cheating sites*. Paper presented at the meeting of the International Plagiarism Conference. Newcastle upon Tyne, UK.

Clark, J. M., & Paivio, A. (1991). Dual coding theory and education. *Educational Psychology Review*, *3*(3), 149–209. doi:10.1007/BF01320076

CLCPRC. (2004). *Report of the Chinese Language Curriculum and Pedagogy Review Committee*. Singapore: Singapore Ministry of Education.

CNNIC. (2013, February 21). *Statistical report on Internet development in China*. China Internet Network Information Center. Retrieved from http://www1.cnnic.cn/IDR/ReportDownloads/201302/P020130221391269963814.pdf

Cobb, T. (2007). Computing the vocabulary demands of L2 reading. *Language Learning & Technology*, *11*(3), 38–63.

Cobb, T., & Horst, M. (2011). Does word coach coach words? *CALICO Journal*, *28*(3), 639–661. doi:10.11139/cj.28.3.639-661

Cochrane, M. (2006). *Does plagiarism-detection service violate student privacy?*. Available from, http://www.buffalo.edu/ubreporter/archive/vol38/vol38n7/articles/FSEC.html

Colby, R. S., & Colby, R. (2008). A pedagogy of play: Integrating computer games into the writing classroom. *Computers and Composition*, *25*(3), 300–312. doi:10.1016/j.compcom.2008.04.005

Comas-Quinn, A., Arcos, B., & Mardomingo, R. (2012). Virtual learning environments for distance language learning: Shifting tutor roles in a contested space for interactions. *Computer Assisted Language Learning*, *25*(2), 129–143. doi:10.1080/09588221.2011.636055

Comrie, B. (1989). Some general properties of reference-tracking systems. In D. Arnold, M. Atkinson, J. Durand, C. Grover, & L. Sadler (Eds.), *Essays on grammatical theory and universal grammar* (pp. 37–51). Oxford: Clarendon Press.

Condie, M. E., & Livingston, K. (2007). Blending online learning with traditional approaches: Changing practices. *British Journal of Educational Technology*, *38*, 337–348. doi:10.1111/j.1467-8535.2006.00630.x

Conference on College Composition and Communication. (2013). *2013 Resolutions & Sense of the House Motions*. Available from, http://www.ncte.org/cccc

Cook, H. M. (2010). Language socialization in Japanese. In P. A. Duff & N. H. Hornberger (Eds.), Encyclopedia of language and education (2nd ed., vol. 8, pp. 313-326). New York: Springer Science+Business Media LLC.

Cook, H. M. (2008). *Socializing identities through speech style: Learners of Japanese as a foreign language*. Clevedon, UK: Multilingual Matters.

Cook, V. (2004). *The English Writing System*. London: Arnold.

Corbett, A. T., & Anderson, J. R. (1995). Knowledge tracing: Modeling the acquisition of procedural knowledge. *User Modeling and User-Adapted Interaction*, *4*, 253–278. doi:10.1007/BF01099821

Cotton, D., & Gresty, K. (2006). Reflecting on the think-aloud method for evaluating e-learning. *British Journal of Educational Technology*, *37*(1), 45–54. doi:10.1111/j.1467-8535.2005.00521.x

Coughlan, P., & Duff, P. (1994). Same task, different activities: Analysis of a second language acquisition task from an activity theory perspective. In J. P. Lantolf, & G. Appel (Eds.), *Vygotskian approaches to second language research* (pp. 183–193). Norwood, NJ: Ablex.

Craik, F. I. M., & Lockhart, R. S. (1972). Levels of processing: A framework for memory research. *Journal of Verbal Learning and Verbal Behavior*, *11*, 671–684. doi:10.1016/S0022-5371(72)80001-X

Creswell, J. W. (2007). *Qualitative inquiry and research design: Choosing among five approaches* (2nd ed.). Thousand Oaks, CA: Sage Publications.

Crystal, D. (2006). *Language and the Internet* (2nd ed.). Cambridge University Press. doi:10.1017/CBO9780511487002

Cuban, L. (2001). *Oversold and underused: Computers in the classroom*. Cambridge, MA: Harvard University Press.

Cui, S. (2003). 浅谈篇章语法的定义与教学问题 (On the definition of discourse grammar and pedagogy). *JCLTA*, *38*(1), 1–24.

Cunningham, A. E., & Stanovich, K. E. (1991). Tracking the unique effects of print exposure in children: Associations with vocabulary, general knowledge, and spelling. *Journal of Educational Psychology*, *83*(2), 264–274. doi:10.1037/0022-0663.83.2.264

Currie, P. (1998). Staying out of trouble: Apparent plagiarism and academic survival. *Journal of Second Language Writing*, *7*(1), 1–18. doi:10.1016/S1060-3743(98)90003-0

Cutshall, S. (2012). More than a decade of Standards: Integrating cultures in your language instruction. *Language and Education*, *7*, 32–37.

Cziko, G. (2004). Electronic tandem language learning (eTandem): A third approach to second language learning for the 21st century. *CALICO Journal*, *22*(1), 25–39.

Dahl, S. (2007). The student perspective on using plagiarism detection software. *Active Learning in Higher Education*, *8*(2), 173–191. doi:10.1177/1469787407074110

Dalton, B., Proctor, C. P., Uccelli, P., Mo, E., & Snow, C. E. (2011). Designing for diversity: The role of reading strategies and interactive vocabulary in a digital reading environment for fifth-grade monolingual English and bilingual students. *Journal of Literacy Research*, *43*, 68–100. doi:10.1177/1086296X10397872

Danet, B. (2001). *Cyberpl@ y: Communicating online*. Berg.

Darhower, M. (2002). Interactional features of synchronous computer-mediated communication in the intermediate L2 class: A sociocultural case study. *CALICO Journal*, *19*(2), 249–277.

de Andrés Martínez, C. (2012). Developing metacognition at a distance: Sharing students' learning strategies on a reflective blog. *Computer Assisted Language Learning*, *25*(2), 199–212. doi:10.1080/09588221.2011.636056

De Guerrero, M., & Villamil, O. S. (2000). Activating the ZPD: Mutual scaffolding in L2 peer revision. *Modern Language Journal*, *84*(1), 51–68. doi:10.1111/0026-7902.00052

De Haan, J., Reed, W. M., & Kuwada, K. (2010). The effect of interactivity with a music video game on second language vocabulary recall. *Language Learning & Technology*, *14*(2), 74–94.

de la Fuente, M. J. (2006). Classroom L2 vocabulary acquisition: Investigating the role of pedagogical tasks and form-focused instruction. *Language Teaching Research, 10*(3), 263–295. doi:10.1191/1362168806lr196oa

Deckert, G. (1993). Perspectives on plagiarism from EFL students in Hong Kong. *Journal of Second Language Writing, 2*(2), 131–148. doi:10.1016/1060-3743(93)90014-T

DeFrancis, J. (1989). *Visible speech: the diverse oneness of writing systems Honolulu*. HI: University of Hawaii Press.

Dempster, F. N. (1987). Effects of variable encoding and spaced presentation on vocabulary learning. *Journal of Educational Psychology, 59*, 202–206.

Develotte, C. (2009). From face to face to distance learning: The online learner's emerging identity. In R. Goodfellow & N. M. Lamy (Ed.), Learning Cultures in Online Education (pp. 71–92). London: Continuum Books.

DeVoss, D., & Rosati, A. (2002). "It wasn't me, was it?" Plagiarism and the web. *Computers and Composition, 19*(2), 191–203. doi:10.1016/S8755-4615(02)00112-3

Diao, W. (2013). *Learning Mandarin and socializing stance through a semester in China.* (Unpublished doctoral thesis). Carnegie Mellon University, Pittsburgh, PA, U.S.A.

DiCamilla, F., & Anton, M. (1997). The function of repetition in the collaborative discourse of L2 learners. *Canadian Modern Language Review, 53*, 609–633.

Donato, R. (1994). Collective scaffolding in second language learning. In J. P. Lantolf, & G. Appel (Eds.), *Vygotskian approaches to second language research* (pp. 33–56). Norwood, NJ: Ablex.

Dos, B., & Demir, S. (2013). The analysis of the blogs created in a blended course through the reflective thinking perspective. *Educational Sciences: Theory and Practice, 13*(2), 1335–1344.

Doughty, C. (1987). Relating second-language acquisition theory to CALL research and application. In W. M. Smith (Ed.), *Modern media in foreign language education: Theory and implementation* (pp. 133–167). Lincolnwood, Illinois: National Textbook Company.

Doughty, C., & Williams, J. (1998). *Focus on form in classroom second language acquisition.* Cambridge, England: Cambridge University Press.

Dryden, L. M. (1999). A distant mirror or through the looking glass? Plagiarism and intellectual property in Japanese education. In L. Buranen, & A. Roy (Eds.), *Perspectives on plagiarism and intellectual property in a postmodern world* (pp. 75–85). Albany, NY: State University of New York Press.

Ducate, L. C., & Lomicka, L. L. (2005). Exploring the blogosphere: Use of web lobs in the foreign language classroom. *Foreign Language Annals, 38*(3), 410–421. doi:10.1111/j.1944-9720.2005.tb02227.x

Duff, P. (2008a). Language socialization, participation and identity: Ethnographic approaches. In M. Martin-Jones, A-M.de Mejia & N. Hornberger (Eds.), Encyclopedia of language and education (vol. 3, pp. 107–119). New York, NY: Springer.

Duff, P. (2008b). *Case study research in applied linguistics*. New York: Lawrence Erlbaum/Taylor & Francis.

Duff, P. (2012). Second language socialization. In A. Duranti, E. Ochs, & B. Schieffelin (Eds.), *Handbook of language socialization (pp. 564–586).* New York: Blackwell.

Duff, P., & Talmy, S. (2010). Language socialization approaches to second language acquisition: Social, cultural, and linguistic development in additional languages. In D. Atkinson (Ed.), *Alternative approaches to SLA*. London: Routledge.

DuFon, M. A. (2008). Language socialization theory and the acquisition of pragmatics in the foreign language classroom. In E. S. Alcón, & A. Martínez-Flor (Eds.), *Investigating pragmatics in foreign language learning, teaching, and testing* (pp. 25–44). Bristol, UK: Multilingual Matters.

Duggan, M., & Brenner, J. (2013, February 14). *The demographics of social media users*. Pew Research Center's Internet & American Life Project. Retrieved from http://pewinternet.org/Reports/2013/Social-media-users.aspx

Dunn, L. M., & Dunn, L. M. (1981). *Peabody picture vocabulary test – Revised.* Circle Pines, MN: American Guidance Services.

Dussias, P. E. (2005). Telecollaboration and lexical and morphological development in Spanish L2. In J. A. Belz, & S. L. Thorne (Eds.), *Internet-mediated intercultural foreign language education* (pp. 121–146). Boston, MA: Heinle & Heinle.

Dussias, P. E. (2006). Morphological development in Spanish–American telecollaboration. In J. Belz, & S. Thorne (Eds.), *Internet-mediated intercultural foreign language education* (pp. 121–146). Boston, MA: Thomsen & Heinle.

Eckert, P. (2000). *Linguistic variation as social practice*. Oxford: Blackwell.

Eckert, P., & McConnell-Ginet, S. (1992). Think practically and look locally: Language and gender as community-based practice. *Annual Review of Anthropology*, *21*, 461–490. doi:10.1146/annurev.an.21.100192.002333

Ede, L., & Lunsford, A. (1990). *Singular texts/plural authors*. Carbondale, IL: Southern Illinois University Press.

Egbert, J., Huff, L., McNeil, L., Preuss, C., & Sellen, J. (2009). Pedagogy, process, and classroom context: Integrating teacher voice and experience into research on technology-enhanced language learning. *Modern Language Journal*, *93*, 754–768. doi:10.1111/j.1540-4781.2009.00971.x

Egbert, J., Paulus, T. M., & Nakamichi, Y. (2002). The impact of CALL instruction on classroom computer use: A foundation for rethinking technology in teacher education. *Language Learning & Technology*, *6*, 108–126.

Elley, W. B. (1989). Vocabulary acquisition from listening to stories. *Reading Research Quarterly*, *24*, 411–427. doi:10.2307/747863

Ellis, N. (1994). Consciousness in second language learning: Psychological perspectives on the role of conscious processes in vocabulary acquisition. *AILA Review*, *11*, 37–56.

Ellis, N. C. (1995). Vocabulary acquisition: Psychological perspectives and pedagogical implications. *Language Teaching*, *19*, 12–16.

Ellis, N., & Beaton, A. (1993). Psycholinguistic determinants of foreign language vocabulary learning. *Language Learning*, *43*, 559–617. doi:10.1111/j.1467-1770.1993.tb00627.x

Ellis, R. (1985). *Understanding second language acquisition*. Oxford, UK: Oxford University Press.

Ellis, R. (1993). The structural syllabus and second language acquisition. *TESOL Quarterly*, *27*, 91–113. doi:10.2307/3586953

Ellis, R. (1994). Factors in the incidental acquisition of second language vocabulary from oral input: A review essay. *Applied Language Learning*, *5*, 1–32.

Ellis, R. (1995). Modified oral input and the acquisition of word meanings. *Applied Linguistics*, *16*, 409–435. doi:10.1093/applin/16.4.409

Ellis, R. (2001). Introduction: Investigating form-focused instruction. *Language Learning, 51. SUPP*, *1*, 1–46.

Ellis, R. (2003). *Task-based language learning and teaching*. Oxford, New York: Oxford Applied Linguistics.

Ellis, R. (2012). *Language teaching research and language pedagogy*. Malden, MA: Wiley-Blackwell. doi:10.1002/9781118271643

Ellis, R., Basturkmen, H., & Loewen, S. (2001). Learner uptake in communicative ESL lessons. *Language Learning*, *51*, 281–318. doi:10.1111/1467-9922.00156

Ellis, R., Tanaka, Y., & Yamakazi, A. (1994). Classroom interaction, comprehension, and L2 vocabulary acquisition. *Language Learning*, *44*, 449–491. doi:10.1111/j.1467-1770.1994.tb01114.x

Elola, I., & Oskoz, A. (2008). Blogging: Fostering intercultural competence development in foreign language and study abroad contexts. *Foreign Language Annals*, *41*(3), 454–477. doi:10.1111/j.1944-9720.2008.tb03307.x

Emerson, L. (2008). Plagiarism, a *Turnitin* trial, and an experience of cultural disorientation. In C. Eisner, & M. Vicinus (Eds.), *Originality, imitation, and plagiarism: Teaching writing in the digital age* (pp. 183–194). Ann Arbor, MI: University of Michigan Press.

Engeström, Y. (1999). Activity theory and individual and social transformation. In Y. Engeström, R. Miettinen, & R.-L. Punamaki-Gitai (Eds.), *Perspectives on activity theory: Learning in doing* (pp. 19–38). Cambridge: Cambridge University Press. doi:10.1017/CBO9780511812774.003

EPPI-Centre. (2007, March). *EPPI-Centre methods for conducting systematic reviews.* London: EPPI-Centre, Social Science Research Unit, Institute of Education, University of London.

Eraut, M. (1994). *Developing professional knowledge and competence*. London: Falmer Press.

Ertmer, P. A. (1999). Addressing first- and second-order barriers to change: Strategies for technology integration. *Educational Technology Research and Development, 47*, 47–61. doi:10.1007/BF02299597

Ertmer, P. A. (2005). Teacher pedagogical beliefs: The final frontier in our quest for technology integration? *Educational Technology Research and Development, 53*, 25–39. doi:10.1007/BF02504683

Ertmer, P. A., Ottenbreit-Leftwich, A., & York, C. (2006). Exemplary technology-using teachers: Perceptions of factors influencing success. *Journal of Computing in Teacher Education, 23*, 55–61.

Ertmer, P., Addison, P., Lane, M., Ross, E., & Woods, D. (1999). Examining teachers' beliefs about the role of technology in the elementary classroom. *Journal of Research on Computing in Education, 32*, 54–72.

Evans, M. J. (2009) (Ed.), Foreign language learning with digital technology. London: Continuum.

Everson, M. E. (1998). Word Recognition among Learners of Chinese as a Foreign Language: Investigating the Relationship between Naming and Knowing. *Modern Language Journal, 82*(2), 194–204. doi:10.1111/j.1540-4781.1998.tb01192.x

Ewert, D. E. (2009). L2 writing conferences: Investigating teacher talk. *Journal of Second Language Writing, 18*, 251–269. doi:10.1016/j.jslw.2009.06.002

Fantini, A. (2011). Language: An essential component of intercultural communicative competence. In J. Jackson (Ed.), *Routledge handbook of language and intercultural communication* (pp. 263–278). London: Routledge.

Fehr, C. N., Davison, M. L., Graves, M. F., Sales, G.C., Seipel, B., & Sekhram-Sharma, S. (2012). The effects of individualized, online vocabulary instruction on picture vocabulary scores: An efficacy study. *Computer Assisted Language Learning, 25*(1), 97–102. doi:10.1080/09588221.2011.586640

Feldman, L. B., & Siok, W. W. T. (1999). Semantic radicals in phonetic compounds: Implications for visual character recognition in Chinese. In J. Wang, A. W. Inhoff, & H.-C. Chen (Eds.), *Reading Chinese script: A cognitive analysis* (pp. 19–35). Mahwah, NJ: Lawrence Erlbaum Associates.

Felix, U. (2005). Analysing recent CALL effectiveness research – towards a common agenda. *Computer Assisted Language Learning, 18*(1-2), 1–32. doi:10.1080/09588220500132274

Fish, S. (2010). Plagiarism is not a big moral deal. *New York Times.* Available from, http://opinionator.blogs.nytimes.com/2010/08/09/plagiarism-is-not-a-big-moral-deal/

Fitze, M. (2006). Discourse and participation in ESL face-to-face and written electronic conferences. *Language Learning & Technology, 10*(1), 67–86.

Foley, W. A., & Van Valin, R. (1984). *Functional Syntax and Universal Grammar.* Cambridge: Cambridge University Press.

Foster, A. L. (2002). *Plagiarism-detection tool creates legal quandary.* Available from, http://chronicle.com

Fox, B. (1987). *Discourse Structure and Anaphora.* Cambridge: Cambridge University Press. doi:10.1017/CBO9780511627767

Fox, R., & Diaz-Greenberg, R. (2006). Culture, multiculturalism, and foreign/ world language standards in US teacher preparation programs: Toward a discourse of dissonance. *European Journal of Teacher Education, 29*(3), 401–422. doi:10.1080/02619760600795270

Fraser, C. A. (1999). Lexical processing strategy use and vocabulary learning through reading. *Studies in Second Language Acquisition, 21*, 225–241. doi:10.1017/S0272263199002041

Freeman, D. (2002). The hidden side of the work: Teacher knowledge and learning to teach. *Language Teaching, 31*, 1–13.

Freeman, D., & Johnson, K. E. (1998). Reconceptualizing the knowledge-base of language teacher education. *TESOL Quarterly*, *32*, 397–418. doi:10.2307/3588114

Freiermuth, M. R., & Huang, H. C. (2012). Bringing Japan and Taiwan closer electronically: A look at an intercultural online synchronic chat task and its effect on motivation. *Language Teaching Research*, *16*(1), 61–88. doi:10.1177/1362168811423341

Fuchs, C., Hauck, M., & Müller-Hartmann, A. (2012). Promoting learner autonomy through multiliteracy skills development in cross-institutional exchanges. *Language Learning & Technology*, *16*(3), 82–102.

Furstenberg, G., Levet, S., English, K., & Maillet, K. (2001). Giving a virtual voice to the silent language of culture: The CULTURA Project. *Language Learning & Technology*, *5*(1), 55–102.

Gao, L. (2012). Synchronic variation or diachronic change: A sociolinguistic study of Chinese Internet language. In J. Liu, & H. Tao (Eds.), *Chinese under globalization: Emerging trends in language use in China* (pp. 7–28). Singapore: World Scientific Publishing. doi:10.1142/9789814350709_0002

Garrett, N. (1987). A psycholinguistic perspective on grammar and CALL. In W.F. Smith (Ed.), Modern media in foreign language education (pp. 169–196). Lincolnwood: National Textbook.

Garrett, N. (1991). Technology in the service of language learning: Trends and issues. *Modern Language Journal*, *75*, 74–101. doi:10.1111/j.1540-4781.1991.tb01085.x

Garrett, N. (1995). ICALL and second language acquisition. In V. M. Holland, J. D. Kaplan, & M. R. Sams (Eds.), *Intelligent language tutors* (pp. 345–358). Mahwah: Lawrence Erlbaum.

Garrett, P. B., & Baquedano-López, P. (2002). Language socialization: Reproduction and continuity, transformation and change. *Annual Review of Anthropology*, *31*, 339–361. doi:10.1146/annurev.anthro.31.040402.085352

Garrett-Rucks, P. (2013). Maximizing cross-cultural understanding, minimizing stereotypes: Three case studies. *French Review (Deddington)*, *86*(5), 14–33.

Gass, S. M. (1997). *Input, interaction and the development of second languages*. Mahwah, NJ: Erlbaum.

Gass, S. M., & Mackey, A. (2000). *Stimulated recall methodology in second language research*. Mahwah, NJ: Erlbaum.

Gergen, K. (2009). *An invitation to social construction* (2nd ed.). London: Sage.

Geyer, N. (2008). Interpersonal functions of style shift: The use of plain and *masu* forms in faculty meetings. In K. Jones, & T. Ono (Eds.), *Style shifting in Japanese* (pp. 39–70). Amsterdam: John Benjamins. doi:10.1075/pbns.180.00int

Ghadirian, S. (2002). Providing controlled exposure to target vocabulary through the screening and arranging of texts. *Language Learning & Technology*, *6*(1), 147–164.

Gillespie, J., & Gray, G. (1992). Hypercard and the development of translation and vocabulary skills. *Computer Assisted Language Learning*, *5*(1–2), 3–11. doi:10.1080/0958822920050102

Gobet, F., & Lane, P. C. R. (2012). Chunking mechanisms and learning. In Encyclopedia of the Sciences of Learning (pp. 541-544). Springer.

Gobet, F., Lane, P. C. R., Croker, S., Cheng, P. C.-H., Jones, G., Oliver, I., & Pine, J. M. (2001). Chunking mechanisms in human learning. *Trends in Cognitive Sciences*, *5*(6), 236–243. doi:10.1016/S1364-6613(00)01662-4 PMID:11390294

Godwin-Jones, B. (2003). Blogs and wikis: Environments for on-line collaboration. *Language Learning & Technology*, *7*(2), 12–16.

Godwin-Jones, R. (2010). From memory palaces to spacing algorithms: Approaches to second-language vocabulary learning. *Language Learning & Technology*, *14*(2), 4–11.

Godwin-Jones, R. (2011). Emerging technologies: Mobile apps for language learning. *Language Learning & Technology*, *15*(2), 2–11.

Gonzales, A. (2013). Development of politeness strategies in participatory online environments: A case study. In N. Taguchi, & J. Sykes (Eds.), *Technology in interlanguage pragmatics research and teaching* (pp. 101–120). Philadelphia, PA: John Benjamins. doi:10.1075/lllt.36.06gon

González-Lloret, M. (2008). Computer-mediated learning of L2 pragmatics. In E. Alcón, & A. Martínez-Flor (Eds.), *Investigating pragmatics in foreign language learning, teaching and testing* (pp. 114–132). Clevedon, UK: Multilingual Matters.

Goodfellow, R. (1995). A review of the types of CALL programs for vocabulary instruction. *Computer Assisted Language Learning*, *8*(2–3), 205–226. doi:10.1080/0958822940080206

Goo, J., & Mackey, A. (2013). The case against the case against recasts. *Studies in Second Language Acquisition*, *35*(1), 127–165. doi:10.1017/S0272263112000708

Graesser, A. C., Singer, M., & Trabasso, T. (1994). Constructing inferences during narrative text comprehension. *Psychological Review*, *101*, 371–395. doi:10.1037/0033-295X.101.3.371 PMID:7938337

Groark, M., Oblinger, D., & Choa, M. (2001). Term paper mills, anti-plagiarism tools, and academic integrity. *EDUCAUSE Review*, *36*(5), 40–48.

Groot, P. J. (2000). Computer assisted second language vocabulary acquisition. *Language Learning & Technology*, *4*(1), 60–81.

Groß, A., & Wolff, D. (2001). A multimedia tool to develop learner autonomy. *Computer Assisted Language Learning*, *14*(3), 233–249. doi:10.1076/call.14.3.233.5794

Guan, C. Q., Liu, Y., Chan, D. H. L., Ye, F., & Perfetti, C. A. (2011). Writing strengthens orthography and alphabetic-coding strengthens phonology in learning to read Chinese. *Journal of Educational Psychology*, *103*(3), 509–522. doi:10.1037/a0023730

Guarda, M. (2012). Computer-mediated discourse and interaction in second and foreign language learning and teaching. *Journal of E-Learning and Knowledge Society*, *8*(3), 15–27.

Gu, Q., & Brooks, J. (2008). Beyond the accusation of plagiarism. *System*, *36*, 337–352. doi:10.1016/j.system.2008.01.004

Gustafson, K., & Bennett, W. (2002). *Promoting learner reflection: Issues and difficulties emerging from a three-year study*. Available from, http://www.dtic.mil/cgi-bin/GetTRDoc?Location=U2&doc=GetTRDoc.pdf&AD=ADA472616

Hale, C., & Scanlon, J. (1999). *Wired style: Principles of Englishusage in the digital age*. New York: Broadway Books.

Hall, D. R., & Knox, J. (2009). Issues in the education of TESOL teachers by distance education. *Distance Education*, *30*(1), 63–85. doi:10.1080/01587910902845964

Hampel, R., & Stickler, U. (2005). New skills for new classrooms: Training tutors to teach languages online. *Computer Assisted Language Learning*, *18*(4), 311–326. doi:10.1080/09588220500335455

Handley, Z. (2009). Is text-to-speech synthesis ready for use in computer-assisted language learning? *Speech Communication*, *51*, 906–919. doi:10.1016/j.specom.2008.12.004

Hanna, B., & de Nooy, J. (2003). A funny thing happened on the way to the forum: Electronic discussion and foreign language learning. *Language Learning & Technology*, *7*(1), 71–85.

Harris, M. (1995). Talking in the middle: Why writers need writing tutors. *College English*, *51*(1), 27–42. doi:10.2307/378348

Hatch, E. (1983). Simplified input and second language acquisition. In R. Andersen (Ed.), *Pidginization and creolization in second language acquisition* (pp. 64–86). Rowley, MA: Newbury House.

Hauck, M., & Youngs, B. L. (2008). Telecollaboration in multimodal environments: The impact on task design and learner interaction. *Computer Assisted Language Learning*, *21*, 87–124. doi:10.1080/09588220801943510

Hayet, M. (1994). French learner's workbench. *Computers & Education*, *23*(1–2), 97–106. doi:10.1016/0360-1315(94)90037-X

Heather, J. (2010). Turnitoff: identifying and fixing a hole in current plagiarism detection software. *Assessment & Evaluation in Higher Education*, *35*(6), 647–660. doi:10.1080/02602938.2010.486471

Heift, T., & Schulze, M. (2009). *Errors and intelligence in Computer-Assisted Language Learning*. London: Routledge.

Hewer, S. (1997). *Text manipulation: Computer-based activities to improve knowledge and use of the target language*. Reading, UK: Centre for Information on Language Teaching and Research.

Hewett, B. L. (2010). *The online writing conference: A guide for teachers and tutors*. Portsmouth, NH: Boynton/Cook Heinemann.

Hirvela, A. (1999). Collaborative writing instruction and communities of readers and writers. *TESOL Quarterly*, *8*(2), 7–12.

Hogan, D., Chan, M., Rahim, R., Kwek, D., Aye, K. M., & Loo, S. C. et al. (2013). Assessment and the logic of instructional practice in Secondary 3 English and mathematics classrooms in Singapore. *Review of Education*, *1*, 57–106. doi:10.1002/rev3.3002

Horst, M., Cobb, T., & Meara, P. (1998). Beyond A Clockwork Orange: Acquiring second language vocabulary through reading. *Reading in a Foreign Language*, *11*, 207–223.

Howard, R. M., & Davies, L. J. (2009). Plagiarism in the internet age. *Literacy 2.0, 66*(6), 64–67.

Howard, R. M. (1993). A plagiarism pentimento. *Journal of Teaching Writing*, *11*(2), 233–246.

Howard, R. M. (1995). Plagiarisms, authorships, and the academic death penalty. *College English*, *57*(7), 788–806. doi:10.2307/378403

Howard, R. M. (2007). Understanding "internet plagiarism.". *Computers and Composition*, *24*, 3–15. doi:10.1016/j.compcom.2006.12.005

Hsu, C. K., Hwang, G. J., & Chang, C. K. (2013). A personalized recommendation-based mobile learning approach to improving the reading performance of EFL students. *Computers & Education*, *63*, 327–336. doi:10.1016/j.compedu.2012.12.004

Huang, Y. (2003). Switch-reference in Amele and logophoric verbal suffix in Gokana: A generalized neo-Gricean pragmatic analysis. In M. Georgiafentis, E. Haeberli, & S. Varlokosta (Eds.), Reading working papers in linguistics 7 (pp. 53–76). Reading, UK: University of Reading.

Huang, H., & Hanley, R. (1994). Phonological awareness and visual skills in learning to read Chinese and English. *Cognition*, *54*, 73–98. doi:10.1016/0010-0277(94)00641-W PMID:7851080

Hubbard, P. (2008, September). *Characterizing theory in computer-assisted language learning*. Paper presented at CALL 2008, University of Antwerp. Antwerp, Belgium. Available from, http://webh01.ua.ac.be/linguapolis/scuati/proceedings_CALL%202008.pdf

Hubbard, P. (2009). Introduction. In P. Hubbard (Ed.), Computer Assisted Language Learning (vol. 1, pp. 1–20). London: Routledge.

Hubbard, P., & Levy, M. (2006). The scope of CALL education. In P. Hubbard, & M. Levy (Eds.), *Teacher education in call* (pp. 3–20). Amsterdam, Philadelphia: John Benjamins. doi:10.1075/lllt.14.04hub

Hudong. (n.d.). *In ci* [In words]. Retrieved from http://top.baike.com/

Huebner, T. (1983). *A longitudinal analysis of the acquisition of English*. Ann Arbor, MI: Karoma Publishers, Inc.

Hulstijn, J. H. (1993). When do foreign language readers look up the meaning of unfamiliar words? The influence of task and learner variables. *Modern Language Journal*, *77*, 139–147. doi:10.1111/j.1540-4781.1993.tb01957.x

Hulstijn, J. H. (2001). Intentional and incidental second–language vocabulary learning: A reappraisal of elaboration, rehearsal and automaticity. In P. Robinson (Ed.), *Cognition and second language instruction* (pp. 258–286). Cambridge: Cambridge University Press. doi:10.1017/CBO9781139524780.011

Hulstijn, J. H., Hollander, M., & Greidanus, T. (1996). Incidental vocabulary learning by advanced foreign language students: The influence of marginal glosses, dictionary use, and reoccurrence of unknown words. *Modern Language Journal*, *80*, 327–339. doi:10.1111/j.1540-4781.1996.tb01614.x

Hulstijn, J., & Laufer, B. (2001). Some empirical evidence for the involvement load hypothesis in vocabulary acquisition. *Language Learning*, *51*(3), 539–558. doi:10.1111/0023-8333.00164

Hunt, R. (2002). *Four reasons to be happy about Internet plagiarism*. Available from, http://www.stu.ca/~hunt/plagiary.htm

Hur, J. W., & Suh, S. (2012). Making learning active with interactive whiteboards, podcasts, and digital storytelling in ELL classrooms. *Computers in the Schools*, *29*(4), 320–338. doi:10.1080/07380569.2012.734275

Hwang, W. Y., & Chen, H. S. L. (2013). Users' familiar situational contexts facilitate the practice of EFL in elementary schools with mobile devices. *Computer Assisted Language Learning*, *26*(2), 101–125. doi:10.1080/09588221.2011.639783

Hyland, K. (2003). Genre-based pedagogies: A social response to process. *Journal of Second Language Writing*, *12*, 17–29. doi:10.1016/S1060-3743(02)00124-8

Hyland, K. (2006). *English for academic purposes: An advanced resource book*. London: Routledge.

Hyland, K., & Hamp-Lyons, L. (2002). EAP: Issues and directions. *Journal of English for Academic Purposes*, *1*, 1–12. doi:10.1016/S1475-1585(02)00002-4

Ikuta, S. (2008). Speech style shift as an interactional discourse strategy: The use and non-use of *desu/-masu* in Japanese conversational interviews. In K. Jones, & T. Ono (Eds.), *Style shifting in Japanese* (pp. 71–89). Amsterdam: John Benjamins. doi:10.1075/pbns.180.00speech

Imai, M., Kita, S., Nagumo, M., & Okada, H. (2008). Sound symbolism facilitates early verb learning. *Cognition*, *109*, 54–65. doi:10.1016/j.cognition.2008.07.015 PMID:18835600

International Society for Technology in Education. (2007). *National educational technology standards for students*. Washington, DC: International Society for Technology in Education.

Ionin, T., Ko, H., & Wexler, K. (2004). Article semantics in L2-acquisition: the role of specificity. *Language Acquisition*, *12*(1), 3–69. doi:10.1207/s15327817la1201_2

Ishida, K. (2009). Indexing stance in interaction with the Japanese desu/masu and plain forms. In N. Taguchi (Ed.), Pragmatic competence (pp. 41-67). Berlin, Germany: Mouton de Gruyter.

Ishihara, N. (2006). *Subjectivity, second/foreign language pragmatic use, and instruction: Evidence of accommodation and resistance*. (Unpublished doctoral dissertation). University of Minnesota, Minneapolis, MN.

Ishihara, N. (2010). Maintaining an optimal distance: Nonnative speakers' pragmatic choice. In A. Mahboob (Ed.), *The NNEST lens: Nonnative English speakers in TESOL* (Vol. 1, pp. 35–53). Newcastle upon Tyne: Cambridge Scholars Press.

Iwasaki, N. (2010). Style shifts among Japanese learners before and after study abroad in Japan: Becoming active social agents in Japanese. *Applied Linguistics*, *31*(1), 45–71. doi:10.1093/applin/amn047

Iwasaki, N. (2011). Learning l2 Japanese "politeness" and "impoliteness": Young American men's dilemmas during study abroad. *Japanese Language and Literature*, *45*(1), 67–106.

Jenkins, R. (2011, August 14). Toward a rational response to plagiarism. *The Chronicle of Higher Education*. Available from, http://chronicle.com

Jepson, K. (2005). Conversations-and negotiated interaction-in text and voice chat rooms. *Language Learning & Technology*, *9*(3), 79–98.

Jia, J., Chen, Y., Ding, Z., & Ruan, M. (2012). Effects of a vocabulary acquisition and assessment system on students' performance in a blended learning class for English subject. *Computers & Education*, *58*(1), 63–76. doi:10.1016/j.compedu.2011.08.002

Jiang, N. (2012). *Conducting reaction time research in second language studies*. London: Routledge.

Jing-Schmidt, Z. (2011). Zero anaphora in higher level Chinese writings across learner backgrounds. *Teaching Chinese in the World*, *25*(2), 258–267.

Jin, H. (1994). Topic-prominence and subject prominence in L2 acquisition: Evidence of English-to-Chinese typological transfer. *Language Learning*, *44*, 101–121.

Jin, H. G. (2003). Empirical evidence on character recognition in multimedia Chinese tasks. *Concentric: Studies in English Literature and Linguistics*, *29*(2), 36–58.

Joe, A. (1998). What effects do text-based tasks promoting generation have on incidental vocabulary acquisition? *Applied Linguistics*, *19*, 357–377. doi:10.1093/applin/19.3.357

Johansson, T., & Kroksmark, T. (2004). Teachers' intuition-in-action: How teachers experience action. *Reflective Practice*, *5*(3), 357–381. doi:10.1080/1462394042000270673

Johnson, K. E. (2009). Second language teacher education: A sociocultural perspective. New York: Routledge.

Johnson, D. (1992). *Approaches to research in second language learning*. New York, NY: Longman.

Johnson, K. E. (2006). The sociocultural turn and its challenges for second language teacher education. *TESOL Quarterly*, *40*, 235–257. doi:10.2307/40264518

Johns, T. (1991). Should you be persuaded – Two examples of data-driven learning. *English Language Research Journal*, *4*, 1–13.

Jones, L. C. (2003). Supporting listening comprehension and vocabulary acquisition with multimedia annotations: The student's voice. *CALICO Journal*, *21*, 41–65.

Jones, L. C. (2004). Testing L2 vocabulary recognition and recall using pictorial written test items. *Language Learning & Technology*, *8*(3), 122–134.

Jones, L. C. (2006). Effects of collaboration and multimedia annotations on vocabulary learning and listening comprehension. *CALICO Journal*, *24*, 33–58.

Jones, L., & Plass, J. (2002). Supporting listening comprehension with multimedia annotations. *Modern Language Journal*, *86*(4), 546–561. doi:10.1111/1540-4781.00160

Jung, U. (2005). CALL: Past, present, and future – A bibliometric approach. *ReCALL*, *17*(1), 4–17. doi:10.1017/S0958344005000212

Kaivanpanah, S., & Alavi, M. (2008). Deriving unknown word meaning from context: Is it reliable? *RELC Journal*, *39*(1), 77–95. doi:10.1177/0033688208091141

Kanno, Y., & Stuart, C. (2011). Learning to become a second language teacher: Identities-in-practice. *Modern Language Journal*, *95*(2), 236–252. doi:10.1111/j.1540-4781.2011.01178.x

Karpati, A. (2009). Web 2 technologies for net native language learners: A "social CALL". *ReCALL*, *21*(2), 139–156. doi:10.1017/S0958344009000160

Ke, C. (2012). Research in second language acquisition on Chinese: Where we are, where we are going. *Journal of the Chinese Language Teachers Association*, *47*(3), 43–114.

Keck, C. (2006). The use of paraphrase in summary writing: A comparison of L1 and L2 writers. *Journal of Second Language Writing*, *15*, 261–278. doi:10.1016/j.jslw.2006.09.006

Kemmis, S., & McTaggart, R. (1988). *The action research planner* (3rd ed.). Geelong: Deakin University Press.

Kern, R. (1995). Restructuring classroom interaction with networked computers: Effects on quantity and characteristics of language production. *Modern Language Journal*, *79*(4), 457–476. doi:10.1111/j.1540-4781.1995.tb05445.x

Kern, R., Ware, P., & Warschauer, M. (2004). Crossing frontiers: New directions in online pedagogy and research. *Annual Review of Applied Linguistics*, *24*, 243–260. doi:10.1017/S0267190504000091

Kessler, G., & Bikowski, D. (2010). Developing collaborative autonomous learning abilities in computer mediated language learning: Attention to meaning among students in wiki space. *Computer Assisted Language Learning*, *23*(1), 41–58. doi:10.1080/09588220903467335

Kessler, G., Bikowski, D., & Boggs, J. (2012). Collaborative writing among second language learners in academic web-based projects. *Language Learning & Technology*, *16*(1), 91–109. Retrieved April 18, 2012

Ki, W. W., Lam, H. C., Chung, A. L. S., Tse, S. K., Ko, P. Y., Lau, E. C. C., …Lai, S. M. S. (2003). Structural awareness, variation theory and ICT support. *L1-Educational Studies in Language and Literature*, *3*, 53–78.

Kiely, R., & Davis, M. (2010). From transmission to transformation: Teachers learning in English for speakers of other language. *Language Teaching Research*, *14*(3), 277–295. doi:10.1177/1362168810365241

Kilgariff, A. (1995). A lemmatised frequency list for the 6,318 words with more than 800 occurrences in the British national corpus. Available from http://www.kilgarriff.co.uk/bnc-readme.html#lemmatised

Kim, D., & Gilman, D. (2008). Effects of text, audio, and graphic aids in multimedia instruction for vocabulary learning. *Journal of Educational Technology & Society, 11*(3), 114–126.

Kim, D., & Kim, D. J. (2012). Effect of screen size on multimedia vocabulary learning. *British Journal of Educational Technology, 43*(1), 62–70. doi:10.1111/j.1467-8535.2010.01145.x

Kinginger, C. (2000). Learning the pragmatics of solidarity in the networked foreign language classroom. In J. X. Hall (Ed.), *Second and foreign language learning through classroom interaction*. Mahwah, NJ: Erlbaum.

Kinginger, C. (2004). Communicative foreign language teaching through telecollaboration. In St. John, K. van Esch, & E. Schalkwijk (Eds.), *New insights into foreign language learning and teaching* (pp. 101–113). Frankfurt: Peter Lang.

Kinginger, C. (2008). Language learning in study abroad: Case histories of Americans in France[Monograph]. *Modern Language Journal, 92*, 1–124. doi:10.1111/j.1540-4781.2008.00821.x

Kinginger, C., & Belz, J. A. (2005). Sociocultural perspectives on pragmatic development in foreign language learning: Case studies from telecollaboration and study abroad. *Intercultural Pragmatics, 2*(4), 369–421. doi:10.1515/iprg.2005.2.4.369

Kitade, K. (2013). Analyzing the reframing process from a language socialization perspective. In E. Voss, S.-J. D. Tai, & Z. Li (Eds.), *Selected Proceedings of the 2011 Second Language Research Forum: Converging Theory and Practice* (pp. 29–43). Somerville, MA: Cascadilla Proceedings Project.

Kitade, K. (2000). L2 learners' discourse and SLA theories in CMC: Collaborative interaction in internet chat. *Computer Assisted Language Learning, 13*(2), 143–166. doi:10.1076/0958-8221(200004)13:2;1-D;FT143

Kitade, K. (2006). The negotiation model in asynchronous computer-mediated communication (CMC): Negotiation in task-based email exchanges. *CALICO Journal, 23*, 319–348.

Kitade, K. (2008). The role of offline metalanguage talk in asynchronous computer-mediated communication. *Language Learning & Technology, 12*(1), 64–84.

Kitade, K. (2014). Second language teachers' identity development through online collaboration with L2 learners. *CALICO Journal, 31*(1), 83–103. doi:10.11139/cj.31.1.57-77

Kitajima, R. (2001). Enhancing higher order interpretation skills for Japanese reading. *CALICO Journal, 19*, 571–581.

Kitalong, K. (1998). A web of symbolic violence. *Computers and Composition, 15*, 253–263. doi:10.1016/S8755-4615(98)90058-5

Knight, S. M. (1994). Dictionary use while reading: The effects on comprehension and vocabulary acquisition for students of different verbal abilities. *Modern Language Journal, 78*, 285–299. doi:10.1111/j.1540-4781.1994.tb02043.x

Koedinger, K. R., Baker, R. S. J. d., Cunningham, K., Skogsholm, A., Leber, B., & Stamper, J. (2010). A data repository for the edm community: The PSLC DataShop. In C. Romero, S. Ventura, M. Pechenizkiy, & R. S. J. d. Baker (Eds.), *Handbook of educational data mining* (pp. 43–56). Boca Raton, FL: CRC Press. doi:10.1201/b10274-6

Koedinger, K. R., Corbett, A. C., & Perfetti, C. (2012). The knowledge-learning-instruction (kli) framework: Bridging the science-practice chasm to enhance robust student learning. *Cognitive Science, 36*, 757–798. doi:10.1111/j.1551-6709.2012.01245.x PMID:22486653

Koedinger, K. R., & Nathan, M. J. (2004). The real story behind story problems: Effects of representations on quantitative reasoning. *Journal of the Learning Sciences, 13*(2), 129–164. doi:10.1207/s15327809jls1302_1

Kost, C. (2011). Investigating writing strategies and revision behavior in collaborative wiki projects. *CALICO Journal, 28*(3), 606–620. doi:10.11139/cj.28.3.606-620

Kötter, M. (2003). Negotiation of meaning and codeswitching in online tandems. *Language Learning & Technology*, *7*(2), 145–172.

Kramsch, C. (1993). *Context and culture in language teaching*. Oxford: Oxford University Press.

Kramsch, C. (2009). *The multilingual subject*. Oxford, England: Oxford University Press.

Kramsch, C., & Thorne, S. (2002). Foreign language learning as global communicative practice. In D. Block, & D. Cameron (Eds.), *Globalization and language teaching* (pp. 83–100). London: Routledge.

Krashen, S. (1985). *The input hypothesis: Issues and implications*. London: Longman.

Krashen, S. (1996). *Under Attack: The case against bilingual education*. Culver City, CA: Language Education Associates.

Krish, P. (2008). Language learning in the virtual world: Instructors' voices. *The International Journal of Pedagogies and Learning*, *4*(4), 113–129. doi:10.5172/ijpl.4.4.113

Kumaravadivelu, B. (2003). *Beyond methods: Macrostrategies for language teaching*. New Haven, CT: Yale University Press.

Lam, W. S. E. (2010). Language socialization in online communities. In P. A. Duff & N. H. Hornberger (Eds.), Encyclopedia of language and education (2nd ed., vol. 8, pp. 301-311). New York: Springer Science+Business Media LLC.

Lam, H. C., Ki, W. W., Chung, A. L. S., Ko, P. Y., Lai, A. C. Y., & Lai, S. M. S. et al. (2004). Designing learning objects that afford learners the experience of important variations in Chinese characters. *Journal of Computer Assisted Learning*, *20*, 114–123. doi:10.1111/j.1365-2729.2004.00071.x

Lam, H. C., Ki, W. W., Law, N., Chung, A. L. S., Ko, P. Y., Ho, A. H. S., & Pun, S. W. (2001). Designing CALL for learning Chinese characters. *Journal of Computer Assisted Learning*, *17*, 115–128. doi:10.1046/j.1365-2729.2001.00164.x

Lam, W. S. E. (2004). Second language socialization in a bilingual chat room. *Language Learning & Technology*, *8*(3), 44–65.

Lam, Y. (2000). Technophilia vs. technophobia: A preliminary look at why second-language teachers do or do not use technology in their classrooms. *Canadian Modern Language Review*, *56*, 390–420. doi:10.3138/cmlr.56.3.389

Lamy, M. N. (2004). Oral conversations online: Redefining oral competence in synchronous environment. *ReCALL*, *16*(2), 520–538. doi:10.1017/S095834400400182X

Lamy, M., & Goodfellow, R. (1999). "Reflective conversation" in the virtual language classroom. *Language Learning & Technology*, *2*(2), 43–61.

Lantolf, J. (2000). Second language learning as a mediated process. *Language Teaching*, *33*, 79–96. doi:10.1017/S0261444800015329

Lantolf, J. P. (2006). Sociocultural theory and L2: state of the art. *Studies in Second Language Acquisition*, *28*, 67–109. doi:10.1017/S0272263106060037

Lantolf, J. P., & Poehner, M. E. (2011). Dynamic assessment in the classroom: Vygostkian praxis for second language development. *Language Teaching Research*, *15*(1), 11–33. doi:10.1177/1362168810383328

Lantolf, J. P., & Thorne, S. (2006). *Sociocultural theory and the genesis of second language development*. Oxford: Oxford University Press.

Lapadat, J. C. (2002). Written interaction: A key component in online learning. *Journal of Computer-Mediated Communication*, *7*(4). Available from http://onlinelibrary.wiley.com/doi/10.1111/j.1083-6101.2002.tb00158.x/full

LaPolla, R. J. (1990). *Grammatical Relations in Chinese: Synchronic and Diachronic Considerations*. Unpublished doctoral dissertation. University of California, Berkeley, U.S.A.

Lara-Alecio, R., Tong, F., Irby, B. J., Guerrero, C., Huerta, M., & Fan, Y. (2012). The effect of an instructional intervention on middle school English learners' science and English reading achievement. *Journal of Research in Science Teaching*, *48*(8), 987–1011. doi:10.1002/tea.21031

Laufer, B. (2005). Focus on form in second language vocabulary learning. *EUROSLA Yearbook*, *5*, 223–250. doi:10.1075/eurosla.5.11lau

Laufer, B. (2005). Instructed second language vocabulary learning: The fault in the 'default hypothesis. In A. Housen, & M. Pierrard (Eds.), *Investigations in instructed second language acquisition* (pp. 286–303). Mouton de Gruyter. doi:10.1515/9783110197372.2.311

Laufer, B., & Rozovski-Roitblat, B. (2011). Incidental vocabulary acquisition: The effects of task type, word occurrence and their combination. *Language Teaching Research, 15*(4), 391–411. doi:10.1177/1362168811412019

Laufer, B., & Shmueli, K. (1997). Memorizing new words: does teaching have anything to do with it? *RELC Journal, 28*(1), 89–108. doi:10.1177/003368829702800106

Laurillard, D., Stratfold, M., Luckin, R., Plowman, L., & Taylor, J. (2000). Affordances for learning in a non-linear narrative medium. *Journal of Interactive Media in Education.* Available from, http://jime.open.ac.uk/article/2000-2/51

Lave, J., & Wenger, E. (1991). *Situated learning: Legitimate peripheral participation.* Cambridge: Cambridge University Press. doi:10.1017/CBO9780511815355

Law, N., Ki, W. W., Chung, A. L. S., Ko, P. Y., & Lam, H. C. (1998). Children's stroke sequence errors in writing Chinese characters. *Reading and Writing, 10*, 267–292. doi:10.1023/A:1008091730338

Leck, K. J., Weekes, B. S., & Chen, M. J. (1995). Visual and phonological pathways to the lexicon: Evidence from Chinese readers. *Memory & Cognition, 23*, 468–476. doi:10.3758/BF03197248 PMID:7666760

Ledwith, A., & Rísquez, A. (2008). Using anti-plagiarism software to promote academic honesty in the context of peer reviewed assignments. *Studies in Higher Education, 33*(4), 371–384. doi:10.1080/03075070802211562

Lee, K. W. (2000). English teachers' barriers to the use of computer-assisted language learning. *The Internet TESL Journal, 6* (12). Available from, http://iteslj.org/Articles/Lee-CALLbarriers.html

Lee, C. (2011). Tertiary students' perceptions and use of information computer technology for language consultation. *Teaching in Higher Education, 17*(3), 323–339. doi:10.1080/13562517.2011.641007

Lee, C. (2012). The pragmatics of non-compliance by tertiary Cantonese learners of English in writing tutorials. In A. S. Yeung, E. L. Brown, & C. Lee (Eds.), *Communication and language: Surmounting barriers to cross-cultural understanding* (pp. 325–350). Charlotte, N.C.: Information Age Publishing.

Lee, C., Cheung, W. K. W., Wong, K. C. K., & Lee, F. S. L. (2013). Immediate web-based essay critiquing system feedback and teacher follow up feedback on young second language learners' writings: An experimental study in a Hong Kong secondary school. *Computer Assisted Language Learning, 26*(1), 39–60. doi:10.1080/09588221.2011.630672

Lee, C., Wong, K. C. K., Lee, F. S. L., & Cheung, W. K. W. (2009). Web-based essay critiquing system and EFL students' writing: A quantitative and qualitative investigation. *Computer Assisted Language Learning, 22*(1), 57–72. doi:10.1080/09588220802613807

Lee, L. (2007). Fostering second language oral communication through constructivist interaction in desktop videoconferencing. *Foreign Language Annals, 40*(4), 635–649. doi:10.1111/j.1944-9720.2007.tb02885.x

Lee, L. (2008). Focus on form through collaborative scaffolding in expert-to-novice online interaction. *Language Learning & Technology, 12*(3), 53–72.

Lee, L. (2010). Exploring wiki-mediated collaborative writing: A case study in an elementary Spanish course. *CALICO Journal, 27*(2), 260–276.

Lee, L. (2011). Blogging: Promoting learner autonomy and intercultural competence through study abroad. *Language Learning & Technology, 15*(3), 87–109.

Lee, S. H., & Muncie, J. (2006). From receptive to productive: Improving ESL learners' use of vocabulary in a post reading composition task. *TESOL Quarterly, 40*(2), 295–320. doi:10.2307/40264524

Leontiev, A. N. (1981). The problem of activity in psychology. In J. V. Wertsch Trans. & Ed. *The concept of activity in Soviet psychology* (pp. 37–71). New York: M. E. Sharpe.

Levy, M. (1997). *Computer-assisted language learning: Context and conceptualization.* Oxford: Oxford University Press.

Levy, M. (2009). Technologies in use for second language learning. *Modern Language Journal*, *93*(Focus issue), 769–782. doi:10.1111/j.1540-4781.2009.00972.x

Levy, M., & Stockwell, G. (2006). *CALL dimensions: Options and issues in computer-assisted language learning*. London: Lawrence Erlbaum.

Li, D. (2010). Pragmatic socialization. In P. A. Duff & N. H. Hornberger (Eds.), Encyclopedia of language and education (2nd ed., vol. 8, pp. 71-83). New York: Springer Science+Business Media LLC.

Li, L., Zhang, D., & Zhao, S. (2013). Willingness to communicate among Singaporean Chinese children. *Huawen Jiaoxue Yu Yanjiu*, *2*, 57-63.

Li, C., & Thompson, S. A. (1981). *Mandarin Chinese: A functional reference grammar*. Berkeley: University of California Press.

Li, D. (2000). The pragmatics of making requests in the L2 workplace: A case study of language socialization. *Canadian Modern Language Review*, *57*(1), 58–87. doi:10.3138/cmlr.57.1.58

Li, J. (2009). The evolution of vocabulary learning strategies in a computer-mediated reading environment. *CALICO Journal*, *27*(1), 118–146.

Li, J. (2010). Learning vocabulary via computer-assisted scaffolding for text processing. *Computer Assisted Language Learning*, *23*(3), 253–275. doi:10.1080/09588221.2010.483678

Li, M. (2012a). Use of wikis in second/foreign language classes: A literature review. *CALL-EJ*, *13*(1), 17–35.

Li, M. (2012b). Politeness strategies in wiki-mediated communication of EFL collaborative writing tasks. *IALLT Journal*, *42*(2), 1–26.

Li, M. (2013). Individual novices and collective experts: Collective scaffolding in wiki-based small group writing. *System*, *41*(3), 752–769. doi:10.1016/j.system.2013.07.021

Li, M., & Zhu, W. (2013). Patterns of computer-mediated interaction in EFL collaborative writing groups using wikis. *Computer Assisted Language Learning*, *26*(1), 61–82. doi:10.1080/09588221.2011.631142

Lim, C. P., & Chai, C. S. (2008). Teachers' pedagogical beliefs and their planning and conduct of computer-mediated classroom lessons. *British Journal of Educational Technology*, *39*, 807–828. doi:10.1111/j.1467-8535.2007.00774.x

Lim, C. P., & Khine, M. S. (2006). Managing teachers' barriers to ICT integration in Singapore schools. *Journal of Technology and Teacher Education*, *14*, 97–125.

Li, S. (2010). The effectiveness of corrective feedback in SLA: A meta-analysis. *Language Learning*, *60*(2), 309–365. doi:10.1111/j.1467-9922.2010.00561.x

Li, S. (2013). The interactions between the effects of implicit and explicit feedback and individual differences in language analytic ability and working memory. *Modern Language Journal*, *97*(3), 634–654. doi:10.1111/j.1540-4781.2013.12030.x

Liu, J. (2010). Deviant writing and youth identity: Representation of dialects with Chinese characters on the Internet. *Chinese Language and Discourse*, *1*(2), 183–219.

Liu, J. (2012). The use of Chinese dialects on the Internet: Youth language and local youth identity in urban China. In J. Liu, & H. Tao (Eds.), *Chinese under globalization: Emerging trends in language use in China* (pp. 59–78). Singapore: World Scientific Publishing. doi:10.1142/9789814350709_0004

Liu, J., & Tao, H. (Eds.). (2012). *Chinese under globalization: Emerging trends in language use in China*. Singapore: World Scientific Publishing. doi:10.1142/8160

Liu, Y., Goh, H. H., & Zhang, D. (2006). A preliminary description of Singapore Chinese Language classrooms. [Teaching Chinese in the World]. *Shijie Hanyu Jiaoxue*, *19*, 97–105.

Li, W. (2004). The discourse perspective in teaching Chinese grammar. *JCLTA*, *39*(1), 25–44.

Li, Y., & Casanave, C. P. (2012). Two first-year students' strategies for writing from sources: Patchwriting or plagiarism? *Journal of Second Language Writing*, *21*, 165–180. doi:10.1016/j.jslw.2012.03.002

Locke, E. (1996). Motivation through conscious goal setting. *Applied & Preventive Psychology*, *5*, 117–123. doi:10.1016/S0962-1849(96)80005-9

Loewen, S. (2005). Incidental focus on form and second language learning. *Studies in Second Language Acquisition, 27*, 361–386. doi:10.1017/S0272263105050163

Loewen, S. (2006). Autonomy and language learning behaviour: The role of student initiation in meaning-focused L2 lessons. In T. Lamb, & H. Reinders (Eds.), *Supporting independent language learning: Issues and options* (pp. 37–53). London: Peter Lang.

Lomicka, L. (2006). Understanding the other: Intercultural exchange and CMC. In L. Ducate, & N. Arnold (Eds.), *Calling on CALL: From theory and research to new directions in foreign language teaching* (pp. 211–236). San Marcos, TX: CALICO.

Long, M. H. (1983). Native speaker/non-native speaker conversation and the negotiation of comprehensible input. *Applied Linguistics, 4*, 126–141. doi:10.1093/applin/4.2.126

Long, M. H. (1991). Focus on form: A design feature in language teaching methodology. In K. de Bot, R. Ginsberg, & C. Kramsch (Eds.), *Foreign language research in cross-cultural perspective* (pp. 39–52). Amsterdam: John Benjamins. doi:10.1075/sibil.2.07lon

Long, M. H. (1996). The role of the linguistic environment in second language acquisition. In W. Ritchie, & T. Bhatia (Eds.), *Handbook of second language acquisition* (pp. 413–468). San Diego: Academic Press. doi:10.1016/B978-012589042-7/50015-3

Long, M. H. (2007). *Problems in sla.* Mahwah, NJ: Erlbaum.

Lord, G., & Lomicka, L. (2007). Foreign language teacher preparation and asynchronous CMC: Promoting reflective teaching. *Journal of Technology and Teacher Education, 15*(4), 513–532.

Lord, G., & Lomicka, L. (2008). Blended learning in teacher education: An investigation of classroom community across media. *Contemporary Issues in Technology & Teacher Education, 8*(2), 158–174.

Lotto, L., & de Groot, A. M. B. (1998). Effects of learning method and word type on acquiring vocabulary in an unfamiliar language. *Language Learning, 48*(1), 31–69. doi:10.1111/1467-9922.00032

Lu, M. T. P. (2011). *The effect of instructional embodiment designs on Chinese language learning: The use of embodied animation for beginning learners of Chinese characters.* (Doctoral dissertation). Retrieved from ProQuest Dissertations and Theses database.

Lu, M. (2008). Effectiveness of vocabulary learning via mobile phone. *Journal of Computer Assisted Learning, 24*(6), 515–525. doi:10.1111/j.1365-2729.2008.00289.x

Lund, A. (2008). Wikis: A collective approach to language production. *ReCALL, 20*(1), 35–54. doi:10.1017/S0958344008000414

Lund, A., & Rasmussen, I. (2008). The right tool for the wrong task? Match and mismatch between first and second stimulus in double stimulation. *Computer-Supported Collaborative Learning, 3*, 387–412. doi:10.1007/s11412-008-9050-8

Lundin, R. W. (2008). Teaching with wikis: Toward a networked pedagogy. *Computers and Composition, 25*, 432–448. doi:10.1016/j.compcom.2008.06.001

Lwo, L., & Lin, C.-T. M. (2012). The effects of captions in teenagers' multimedia L2 learning. *ReCALL, 24*(2), 188–208. doi:10.1017/S0958344012000067

Lyster, R. (2001). Negotiation of form, recasts, and explicit correction in relation to error types and learner repair in immersion classrooms. *Language Learning, 51*, 265–301. doi:10.1111/j.1467-1770.2001.tb00019.x

Lyster, R., & Izquierdo, J. (2009). Prompts versus recasts in dyadic interaction. *Language Learning, 59*, 453–498. doi:10.1111/j.1467-9922.2009.00512.x

Lyster, R., & Mori, H. (2006). Interactional feedback and instructional counterbalance. *Studies in Second Language Acquisition, 28*, 269–300. doi:10.1017/S0272263106060128

Lyster, R., & Ranta, L. (1997). Corrective feedback and learner uptake: Negotiation of form in communicative classrooms. *Studies in Second Language Acquisition, 19*(1), 37–66. doi:10.1017/S0272263197001034

Lyster, R., & Ranta, L. (2013). Counterpoint piece: The case for variety in corrective feedback research. *Studies in Second Language Acquisition, 1*(35), 167–184. doi:10.1017/S027226311200071X

Macaro, E., Handley, Z. L., & Walter, C. (2012). A systematic review of CALL in English as a second language: Focus on primary and secondary education. *Language Teaching*, *45*(1), 1–43. doi:10.1017/S0261444811000395

Macaruso, P., & Rodman, A. (2011). Benefits of Computer-Assisted Instruction to Support. *Bilingual Research Journal*, *34*(2), 301–315. doi:10.1080/15235882.2011.622829

Macdonald, R., & Carroll, J. (2006). Plagiarism- a complex issue requiring a holistic institutional approach. *Assessment & Evaluation in Higher Education*, *31*(3), 233–245. doi:10.1080/02602930500262536

MacGintie, W., MacGintie, R., Maria, K., & Dreyer, L. (2002). *Gates MacGintie reading tests* (4th ed.). Itasca, IL: Riverside.

Mackey, A., & Philp, J. (1998). Conversational interaction and second language development: Recasts, responses, and red herrings? *Modern Language Journal*, *82*, 338–356. doi:10.1111/j.1540-4781.1998.tb01211.x

Mackey, A., & Sachs, R. (2012). Older learners in sla research: A first look at working memory, feedback, and l2 development. *Language Learning*, *62*(3), 704–740. doi:10.1111/j.1467-9922.2011.00649.x

MacWhinney. (1987). The competition model. In B. MacWhinney (Ed.), *Mechanisms of language acquisition* (pp. 249–308). New York: Psychology Press.

MacWhinney, B. (1995). Evaluating foreign language tutoring systems. In V. M. Holland, J. D. Kaplan, & M. R. Sams (Eds.), *Intelligent language tutors: Theory shaping technology* (pp. 317–326). Mahwah, NJ: Lawrence Erlbaum.

Mak, B., & Coniam, D. (2008). Using wikis to enhance and develop writing skills among secondary school students in Hong Kong. *System*, *36*, 437–455. doi:10.1016/j.system.2008.02.004

Ma, Q. (2013). Computer assisted vocabulary learning: Framework and tracking users' data. *CALICO Journal*, 230–243.

Ma, Q., & Kelly, P. (2006). Computer-assisted vocabulary learning: Design and evaluation. *Computer Assisted Language Learning*, *19*(1), 15–46. doi:10.1080/09588220600803998

Marsh, B. (2004). *Turnitin*.com and the scriptural enterprise of plagiarism detection. *Computers and Composition*, *21*, 427–438. doi:10.1016/j.compcom.2004.08.002

Matsumura, N., & Miura, A. (2005). *Buroguni okeru kakiteno itoto modaritii hyougen* [Writers' intentions and modality expressions in weblog articles]. Paper presented at the 19th Annual Conference of the Japanese Society for Artificial Intelligence 2005. Available from, http://www-kasm.nii.ac.jp/jsai2005/schedule/pdf/000133.pdf

Maxwell, J. A. (2005). *Qualitative research design: An interactive approach* (2nd ed.). Thousand Oaks, CA: SAGE.

Mayer, R. E. (1999). Multimedia aids to problem-solving transfer. *International Journal of Educational Research*, *31*, 611–623. doi:10.1016/S0883-0355(99)00027-0

Mayer, R. E. (2003). The promise of multimedia learning: using the same instructional design methods across different media. *Learning and Instruction*, *13*, 125–139. doi:10.1016/S0959-4752(02)00016-6

Mayer, R. E., Griffith, E., Naftaly, I., & Rothman, D. (2008). Increased interestingness of extraneous details leads to decreased learning. *Journal of Experimental Psychology. Applied*, *14*, 329–339. doi:10.1037/a0013835 PMID:19102616

Mayer, R. E., & Johnson, C. I. (2010). Adding instructional features that promote learning in a game-like environment. *Journal of Educational Computing Research*, *42*(3), 241–265. doi:10.2190/EC.42.3.a

Mayer, R. E., & Moreno, R. (2002). Aids to computer-based multimedia learning. *Learning and Instruction*, *12*, 107–119. doi:10.1016/S0959-4752(01)00018-4

Mayer, R., & Moreno, R. (1998). A split-attention effect in multimedia learning: Evidence for dual processing systems in working memory. *Journal of Educational Psychology*, *90*, 312–320. doi:10.1037/0022-0663.90.2.312

Maynard, S. (1991). Pragmatics of discourse modality: A case of *da* and *desu/masu* forms in Japanese. *Journal of Pragmatics*, *15*, 551–582. doi:10.1016/0378-2166(91)90111-A

McBride, K., & Wildner-Basset, M. (2008). Interpersonal and intercultural understanding in a blended second culture classroom. In S. Sieloff Magnan (Ed.), *Mediating discourse online* (pp. 93–124). Philadelphia, PN: John Benjamins. doi:10.1075/aals.3.08mcb

McCabe, D. L. (2005). Cheating among college and university students: A North American perspective. . *International Journal of Educational Integrity*, *1*(1), 1–11.

McCarthy, C. P. (1999). Reading theory as a microcosm of the four skills. The Internet TESL Journal, 5(2). Retrieved from http://iteslj.org/Articles/McCarthy-Reading.html

McKeever, L. (2006). Online plagiarism detection services- saviour or scourge? *Assessment & Evaluation in Higher Education*, *31*(2), 155–165. doi:10.1080/02602930500262460

McLean, K. C., Pasupathi, M., & Pals, J. L. (2007). Selves creating stories creating selves: A process model of self-development. *Personality and Social Psychology Review*, *11*(3), 262–278. doi:10.1177/1088868307301034 PMID:18453464

Merriam, S. B. (1998). *Qualitative research and case study applications in education: Revised and expanded from Case Study Research in Education*. San Francisco, CA: Jossey-Bass Publishers.

Meunier, L. (1998). Personality and motivational factors in computer-mediated foreign language communication. In J. A. Muyskens (Ed.), *New ways of learning and teaching: Focus on technology and FL education* (pp. 145–197). Boston, MA: Heinle & Heinle.

Miceli, T., Murray, S. V., & Kennedy, C. (2010). Using an L2 blog to enhance learners' participation and sense of community. *Computer Assisted Language Learning*, *23*(4), 321–341. doi:10.1080/09588221.2010.495321

Miller, G. A. (1956). The magical number seven, plus or minus two: Some limits on our capacity for processing information. *Psychological Review*, *63*, 81–97. doi:10.1037/h0043158 PMID:13310704

Miller, J. (1991). Short report: Reaction time analysis with outlier exclusion: Bias varies with sample size. *The Quarterly Journal of Experimental Psychology*, *43*, 907–912. doi:10.1080/14640749108400962 PMID:1775668

Miller, J. M. (2007). Identity in the ESL classroom. In Z. Hua, P. Seedhouse, L. Wei, & V. Cook (Eds.), *Language learning and teaching as social interaction* (pp. 148–162). Basingstoke: Palgrave Macmillan.

Milton, J. (2009). *Measuring second language vocabulary acquisition*. Bristol, UK: Multilingual Matters.

Mitchell, K. (2012). A social tool: Why and how ESOL students use Facebook. *CALICO Journal*, *29*(3), 471–493. doi:10.11139/cj.29.3.471-493

Miyazoe, T., & Anderson, T. (2010). Learning outcomes and students' perceptions of online writing: Simultaneous implementation of a forum, blog, and wiki in an EFL blended learning setting. *System*, *38*(2), 185–199. doi:10.1016/j.system.2010.03.006

Miyeon, A. (2005). A phonetically based account of English reduplication. *SNU Working Papers in English Language and Linguistics, 4*, 73-93.

Montero Perez, M., Peters, E., & Desmet, P. (2014). Is less more? Effectiveness and perceived usefulness of keyword and full captioned video for L2 listening comprehension. *ReCALL*, 1–23.

MTLRC. (2011). *Nurturing active learners and proficient users: Report of the Mother Tongue Languages Review Committee*. Singapore: Ministry of Education.

Müller-Hartmann, A. (2000). The role of tasks in promoting intercultural learning in electronic learning networks. *Language Learning & Technology*, *4*(2), 129–147.

Müller-Hartmann, A. (2006). Learning how to teach intercultural communicative competence via telecollaboration: a model for language teacher education. In J. Belz, & S. Thorne (Eds.), *Internet-mediated intercultural foreign language education* (pp. 63–84). Boston: Heinle & Heinle.

Munby, H., & Russell, T. (1989). Educating the reflective teacher: An essay review of two books by Donald Schön. *Journal of Curriculum Studies*, *21*(7), 71–80. doi:10.1080/0022027890210106

Murray, L., Hourigan, T., & Jeanneau, C. (2007). Blog writing integration for academic language learning purposes: Towards an assessment framework. *IBÉRICA*, *14*, 9–32.

Myers, G. (2010). *The discourse of blogs and wikis*. London: Continuum.

Nagata, N. (1993). Intelligent computer feedback for second language instruction. *Modern Language Journal*, *77*, 330–339. doi:10.1111/j.1540-4781.1993.tb01980.x

Nagy, W. E., Herman, P. A., & Anderson, P. C. (1985). Learning words from context. *Reading Research Quarterly*, *20*, 233–253. doi:10.2307/747758

Nakata, T. (2006). Implementing optimal spaced learning for English vocabulary learning: Towards improvement of the low-first method derived from the reactivation theory. *JALT CALL Journal*, *2*(2), 19–36.

Nakata, T. (2008). English vocabulary learning with word lists, word cards and computers: Implications from cognitive psychology research for optimal spaced learning. *ReCALL*, *20*(1), 3–20. doi:10.1017/S0958344008000219

Nakata, T. (2011). Computer-assisted second language vocabulary learning in a paired-associate paradigm: A critical investigation of flashcard software. *Computer Assisted Language Learning*, *24*(1), 17–38. doi:10.1080/09588221.2010.520675

Nassaji, H. (2003). L2 vocabulary learning from context: Strategies, knowledge sources, and their relationship with success in L2 lexical inferencing. *TESOL Quarterly*, *37*(4), 645–670. doi:10.2307/3588216

Nassaji, H. (2004). Input modality and remembering name-referent associations in vocabulary learning. *Canadian Journal of Applied Linguistics*, *7*, 39–55.

National Standards in Foreign Language Education Project. (1996). *Standards for foreign language learning in the 21st century*. Yonkers, NY: Allen Press.

Nation, I. S. P. (2001). *Learning vocabulary in another language*. Cambridge: Cambridge University Press. doi:10.1017/CBO9781139524759

Nation, I. S. P. (2006). How large a vocabulary is needed for reading and listening? *Canadian Modern Language Review*, *63*(1), 59–82. doi:10.3138/cmlr.63.1.59

Nation, I. S. P. (2007). The four strands. *Innovation in Language Teaching and Learning*, *1*, 1–12. doi:10.2167/illt039.0

Nation, I. S. P. (2011). Thinking allowed. Research into practice: Vocabulary. *Language Teaching*, *44*(4), 529–539. doi:10.1017/S0261444811000267

Nation, P., & Beglar, D. (2007). A vocabulary size test. *Language Teaching*, *31*(7), 9–13.

New London Group. (1996). A pedagogy of multiliteracies: Designing social futures. *Harvard Educational Review*, *66*, 60–93.

Ng, E. H. (2008). *Opening address at the International Conference on Teaching and Learning with Technology*. Available from, http://www.moe.gov.sg/media/speeches/2008/08/05/opening-address-by-dr-ng-eng-h-1.php

Nicholas, B. J., Rossiter, M. J., & Abbott, M. L. (2011). The power of story in the ESL classroom. *Canadian Modern Language Review*, *67*(2), 247–268. doi:10.3138/cmlr.67.2.247

Norton, B. (2000). *Identity and language learning: Gender, ethnicity and educational change*. Essex, England: Pearson Education.

O'Dowd, R. (2003). Understanding the "other side": Intercultural learning in a Spanish-English e-mail exchange. *Language Learning & Technology*, *7*(2), 118–144.

O'Dowd, R., & Eberbach, K. (2004). Guides on the side? Tasks and challenges for teachers in telecollaborative projects. *ReCALL*, *16*(1), 129–144.

O'Dowd, R., & Ritter, M. (2006). Understanding and working with 'failed communication' in telecollaborative exchanges. *CALICO Journal*, *23*(3), 623–642.

O'Dowd, R., & Waire, P. (2009). Critical issues in telecollaborative task design. *Computer Assisted Language Learning*, *22*(2), 173–188. doi:10.1080/09588220902778369

O'Malley, J. M., & Chamot, A. U. (1990). *Learning strategies in second language acquisition*. Cambridge, England: Cambridge University Press. doi:10.1017/CBO9781139524490

O'Rourke, B. (2005). Form-focused interaction in online tandem learning. *CALICO Journal*, *22*(2), 433–466.

Ochs, E. (1996). Linguistic resources for socializing humanity. In J. Gumperz & S. Levinson (Eds.), Rethinking linguistic relativity. Cambridge, UK: Cambridge University Press.

Ochs, E. (1993). Constructing social identity: A language socialization perspective. *Research on Language and Social Interaction*, *26*(3), 287–306. doi:10.1207/s15327973rlsi2603_3

Ochs, E., & Schieffelin, B. (1984). Language acquisition and socialization: Three developmental stories. In R. Shweder, & R. LeVine (Eds.), *Culture theory: Mind, self, and emotion* (pp. 276–320). UK: Cambridge University Press.

O'Dowd, R. (2000). Intercultural learning via videoconferencing: A pilot exchange project. *ReCALL*, *12*(1), 49–63. doi:10.1017/S0958344000000616

O'Dowd, R. (2003). Understanding the 'other side': Intercultural learning a Spanish-English e-mail exchange. *Language Learning & Technology*, *7*(2), 118–144.

O'Dowd, R. (2006). *Telecollaboration and the development of intercultural communicative competence*. Munich, Germany: Langenscheidt-Longman.

O'Hara, S., & Pritchard, R. (2008). Hypermedia authoring as a vehicle for vocabulary development in middle school English as a second language classrooms. *Clearing House: A Journal of Educational Strategies. Issues and Ideas*, *82*(2), 60–65.

Ohta, A. S. (2000). Re-thinking interaction in SLA: Developmentally appropriate assistance in the zone of proximal development and the acquisition of L2 grammar. In J. P. Lantolf (Ed.), *Sociocultural theory and second language learning* (pp. 51–78). Oxford, UK: Oxford University Press.

Oldknow, A., Taylor, R., & Tetlow, L. (2010). *Teaching mathematics using ICT*. London: Continuum.

Oliver, R., & Mackey, A. (2003). Interactional context and feedback in child ESL classrooms. *Modern Language Journal*, *87*(4), 519–533. doi:10.1111/1540-4781.00205

Omaggio, A. C. (1979). Pictures and second language comprehension: Do they help? *Foreign Language Annals*, *12*, 107–116. doi:10.1111/j.1944-9720.1979.tb00153.x

Oxford, R. L. (1990). *Language learning strategies: What every teacher should know*. New York: Newbury House.

Oxford, R. L., & Scarcella, R. C. (1994). Second language vocabulary learning among adults: State of the art in vocabulary instruction. *System*, *22*(2), 231–243. doi:10.1016/0346-251X(94)90059-0

Packard, J., Chen, X., Li, W., Wu, X., Gaffney, J., Li, H., & Anderson, R. C. (2006). Explicit instruction in orthographic structure and word morphology helps Chinese children learn to write characters. *Reading and Writing*, *19*, 457–487. doi:10.1007/s11145-006-9003-4

Paivio, A., & Desrochers, A. (1981). Mnemonic techniques in second language learning. *Journal of Educational Psychology*, *73*, 780–795. doi:10.1037/0022-0663.73.6.780

Pak, A. K. H., Cheng-Lai, A., Tso, I. F., Hua, S., Wenling, L., & Anderson, R. C. (2005). Visual chunking skills of Hong Kong children. *Reading and Writing*, *18*, 437–454. doi:10.1007/s11145-005-6575-3

Pan, W. G. (2008). *Weiji xia de zhongwen* [Chinese under crisis]. Shenyang, China: Liaoning People's Press.

Park, C. (2003). In other (people's) words: Plagiarism by university students--literature and lessons. *Assessment & Evaluation in Higher Education*, *28*(5), 471–489. doi:10.1080/02602930301677

Park, C. N., & Son, J. B. (2009). Implementing computer-assisted language learning in the EFL classroom: Teachers' perceptions and perspectives. *The International Journal of Pedagogies and Learning*, *5*(2), 80–101. doi:10.5172/ijpl.5.2.80

Park, J. E. (2007). Co-construction of nonnative speaker identity in cross-cultural interaction. *Applied Linguistics*, *28*, 339–360. doi:10.1093/applin/amm001

Park, Y., Zheng, B., Lawrence, J., & Warschauer, M. (2013). Technology-enhanced reading environments. In M. Thomas, H. Reinders, & M. Warschauer (Eds.), *Contemporary computer-assisted language learning* (pp. 267–285). London: Continuum.

Pavlenko, A., & Lantolf, J. P. (2000). Second language learning as participation and the (re)construction of selves. In A. Pavlenko, & J. P. Lantolf (Eds.), *Sociocultural theory and second language learning* (pp. 155–177). Oxford, UK: Oxford University Press.

Pavlik, P. I. Jr, & Anderson, J. R. (2005). Practice and forgetting effects on vocabulary memory: An activation-based model of the spacing effect. *Cognitive Science*, *29*, 559–586. doi:10.1207/s15516709cog0000_14 PMID:21702785

Pecorari, D. (2008). *Academic writing and plagiarism: A linguistic analysis*. London: Continuum.

Pecorari, D. (2013). *Teaching to avoid plagiarism: How to promote good source use*. Berkshire, England: Open University Press.

Pederson, K. (1987). Research on CALL. In W. F. Smith (Ed.), *Modern media in foreign language education: Theory and implementation* (pp. 99–131). Lincolnwood, IL: National Textbook Company.

Pellettieri, J. (2000). Negotiation in cyberspace: The role of chatting in the development of grammatical competence. In M. Warschauer, & R. Kern (Eds.), *Network-based language teaching: Concepts and practice* (pp. 59–86). New York: Cambridge University Press. doi:10.1017/CBO9781139524735.006

Peng, D. L., Li, Y. P., & Yang, H. (1997). Orthographic processing in the identification of Chinese characters. In H.-C. Chen (Ed.), *Cognitive processing of Chinese and related Asian languages* (pp. 85–108). Hong Kong: The Chinese University Press.

Pennycook, A. (1996). Borrowing others' words: Text, ownership, memory, and plagiarism. *TESOL Quarterly*, *30*(2), 201–230. doi:10.2307/3588141

Perfetti, C. A., & Tan, L. H. (1998). The time course of graphic, phonological, and semantic activation in Chinese character identification. *Journal of Experimental Psychology. Learning, Memory, and Cognition*, *24*, 101–118. doi:10.1037/0278-7393.24.1.101

Perfetti, C. A., & Tan, L. H. (1999). The constituency model of Chinese word identification. In J. Wang, A. W. Inhoff, & H. C. Chen (Eds.), *Reading Chinese script: A cognitive analysis* (pp. 115–134). Mahwah, NJ: Lawrence Erlbaum Associates, Inc.

Peters, M. (2006). Developing computer competencies for pre-service language teachers: Is one course enough? In P. Hubbard, & M. Levy (Eds.), *Teacher education in CALL* (pp. 153–165). Philadelphia, PA: John Benjamins. doi:10.1075/lllt.14.14pet

Phillips, J., & Abbott, M. (2011). A decade of standards: Impact, influence, and future directions. Available from, http://www.actfl.org/sites/default/files/pdfs/public/national-standards-2011.pdf

Pica, T. (1994). Research on negotiation: What does it reveal about second-language learning conditions, processes, and outcomes? *Language Learning*, *44*(3), 493–527. doi:10.1111/j.1467-1770.1994.tb01115.x

Pigada, M., & Schmitt, N. (2006). Vocabulary acquisition from extensive reading: A case study. *Reading in a Foreign Language*, *18*(1), 1–28.

Pinter, A. (2006). *Teaching young language learners*. Oxford: Oxford University Press.

Poulshock, J. (2010). Extensive graded reading in the liberal arts and sciences. *Reading in a Foreign Language*, *22*(2), 2.

Pousada, A. (2011, November). *Cultivating respect for intellectual property in the English Class*. Paper presented at the meeting of Puerto Rico TESOL. San Juan, Puerto Rico.

Prawat, R. (1991). Conversations with self and settings: a framework for thinking about teacher empowerment. *American Educational Research Journal*, *28*(4), 737–757. doi:10.3102/00028312028004737

Presson, N., Davy, C., & MacWhinney, B. (2013). Experimentalized CALL for adult second language learners. In J. W. Schwieter (Ed.), *Innovative research and practices in second language acquisition and bilingualism* (pp. 139–164). Amsterdam, the Netherlands: John Benjamins. doi:10.1075/lllt.38.10pre

Price, M. (2002). Beyond "gotcha!": Situating plagiarism in policy and pedagogy. *College Composition and Communication*, *54*(1), 88–115. doi:10.2307/1512103

Prince, P. (2006). L'Apprentissage des mots: Présentation d'un dispositif basé sur le jugement sémantique. *Cahiers de l'Apliut*, *24*(2), 112–128.

Prince, P. (2012). Second language vocabulary learning: Can a story help? *Language Learning & Technology*, *16*(3), 103–120.

Proctor, C. P., Dalton, B., & Grisham, D. L. (2007). Scaffolding English language learners and struggling readers in a universal literacy environment with embedded strategy instruction and vocabulary support. *Journal of Literacy Research*, *39*(1), 71–93.

Pu, M.-M. (1997). Zero anaphora and grammatical relations in Mandarin. In T. Givón (Ed.), *Grammatical relations: Typological studies in language 35* (pp. 283–322). Amsterdam: John Benjamins Publishing Company. doi:10.1075/tsl.35.08pu

Purdy, J. (2005). Calling off the hounds: Technology and the visibility of plagiarism. *Pedagogy*, *5*(2), 275–296.

Purdy, J. (2009). Anxiety and the archive: Understanding plagiarism detection services as digital archives. *Computers and Composition*, *26*, 65–77. doi:10.1016/j.compcom.2008.09.002

Purdy, J. P. (2009). When the tenets of composition go public: A study of writing in Wikipedia. *College Composition and Communication*, *61*(2), 351–373.

Rastle, K., Davis, M. H., Marslen-Wilson, W. D., & Tyler, L. K. (2000). Morphological and semantic effects in visual word recognition: A time course study. *Language and Cognitive Processes*, *15*, 507–538. doi:10.1080/01690960050119689

Reinhardt, J., & Zander, V. (2011). Social networking in an intensive English program classroom: A language socialization perspective. *CALICO Journal*, *28*(2), 326–344. doi:10.11139/cj.28.2.326-344

Révész, A. (2009). Task complexity, focus on form, and second language development. *Studies in Second Language Acquisition*, *30*, 437–470. doi:10.1017/S0272263109090366

Révész, A. (2011). Task complexity, focus on L2 constructions, and individual differences: A classroom-based study. *Modern Language Journal*, *95*(S1), 162–181. doi:10.1111/j.1540-4781.2011.01241.x

Richards, J. C. (1996). Teachers' maxims in language teaching. *TESOL Quarterly*, *30*(2), 281–296. doi:10.2307/3588144

Richards, J. C. (2008). Second language teacher education today. *RELC Journal*, *39*, 158–177. doi:10.1177/0033688208092182

Rilling, S. (2005). The development of an ESL OWL or learning how to tutor writing online. *Computers and Composition*, *22*(3), 357–374. doi:10.1016/j.compcom.2005.05.006

Ritter, K. (2005). The economics of authorship: Paper mills, student writers, and first-year composition. *College Composition and Communication*, *56*(4), 601–631.

Rivens Mompean, A. (2010). The development of meaningful interactions on a blog used for the learning of English as a foreign language. *ReCALL*, *22*(3), 376–395. doi:10.1017/S0958344010000200

Robinson, P. (2005). Cognitive complexity and task sequencing: Studies in a componential framework of second language task design. *IRAL*, *43*, 1–32. doi:10.1515/iral.2005.43.1.1

Rogoff, B. (1990). *Apprenticeship in thinking: Cognitive development in social context*. Cambridge: Cambridge University Press.

Rolfe, V. (2011). Can *Turnitin* be used to provide instant formative feedback? *British Journal of Educational Technology*, *42*(4), 701–710. doi:10.1111/j.1467-8535.2010.01091.x

Romeo, K. (2008). A web-based listening methodology for studying relative clause acquisition. *Computer Assisted Language Learning*, *21*(1), 51–66. doi:10.1080/09588220701865508

Rosell-Aguilar, F. (2005). Task design for audiographic conferencing: Promoting beginner oral interaction in distance language learning. *Computer Assisted Language Learning*, *18*(5), 417–442. doi:10.1080/09588220500442772

Royce, J. (2003). Has *Turnitin*.com got it all wrapped up? *Teacher Librarian*, *30*(4), 26–30.

Royer, J. M. (1973). Memory effect for test-like events during acquisition of foreign language vocabulary. *Psychological Reports, 32*, 195–198. doi:10.2466/pr0.1973.32.1.195

Rubin, G. S., & Becker, G. A. (1979). Morphological structure and its effect on visual word recognition. *Journal of Verbal Learning and Verbal Behavior, 18*, 757–767. doi:10.1016/S0022-5371(79)90467-5

Sagarra, N. (2007). From CALL to face-to-face communication: The effect of computer-delivered recasts and working memory on L2 development. In A. Mackey (Ed.), *Conversational interaction in second language acquisition* (pp. 229–248). New York: Oxford University Press.

Samuda, V., & Bygate, M. (2008). *Tasks in second language learning*. Palgrave MacMillan.

Sasaki, A., & Takeuchi, O. (2010). EFL students' vocabulary learning in NS-NNS e-mail interactions: Do they learn new words by imitation? *ReCALL, 22*(1), 70–82. doi:10.1017/S0958344009990206

Sato, C. (1986). Conversation and interlanguage development: Rethinking the connection. In R. R. Day (Ed.), *Talking to learn: Conversation in second language acquisition* (pp. 23–45). Rowley, MA: Newbury House.

Sauro, S. (2009). Computer-mediated corrective feedback and the development of L2 grammar. *Language Learning & Technology, 13*, 96–120.

Sauro, S. (2013). The cyber language exchange: Cross-national computer-mediated interaction. In K. McDonough, & A. Mackey (Eds.), *Second language interaction in diverse educational contexts* (pp. 129–146). Amsterdam: John Benjamins. doi:10.1075/lllt.34.11ch7

Scanlon, P., & Neumann, D. (2002). Internet plagiarism among college students. *Journal of College Student Development, 43*(3), 374–382.

Schieffelin, B. B., & Ochs, E. (1986). Language socialization across cultures. Cambridge, UK: Cambridge University Press.

Schmidt, R. W. (1990). The role of consciousness in second language learning. *Applied Linguistics, 11*(1), 129–158. doi:10.1093/applin/11.2.129

Schmitt, N. (2008). Instructed second language *vocabulary* learning. *Language Teaching Research, 12*(3), 329–363. doi:10.1177/1362168808089921

Schmitt, N. (2010a). *Researching vocabulary: A vocabulary research manual*. Basingstoke: Palgrave Macmillan. doi:10.1057/9780230293977

Schmitt, N., Schmitt, D., & Clapham, C. (2001). Developing and exploring the behaviour of two new versions of the vocabulary levels test. *Language Testing, 18*(1), 55–88.

Schneider, W., Eschman, A., & Zuccolotto, A. (2002). *E-Prime user's guide*. Pittsburgh, PA: Psychology Software Tools, Inc.

Schnotz, W., Böckheler, J., & Grzondziel, H. (1999). Individual and co-operative learning with animated pictures. *European Journal of Psychology of Education, 14*(2), 245–265. doi:10.1007/BF03172968

Schnotz, W., & Rasch, T. (2005). Enabling, facilitating and inhibiting effects of animations in multimedia learning: Why reduction of cognitive load can have negative results on learning. *Educational Technology Research and Development, 53*(3), 47–58. doi:10.1007/BF02504797

Schön, D. (1983). *The reflective practitioner*. New York: Oxford University Press.

Schön, D. (1987). *Educating the reflective practitioner*. New York: Basic Books.

Schumann, J. H. (1998). The neurobiology of affect in language. A supplement to "language learning.". *Language Learning, 48*(Supplement 1), 1–36.

Schwienhorst, K. (2000). *Virtual reality and learner autonomy in second language acquisition*. Unpublished manuscript.

Scollon, R. (1995). Plagiarism and ideology: Identity in intercultural discourse. *Language in Society, 24*(1), 1–8. doi:10.1017/S0047404500018388

Seliger, H. W., & Shohamy, E. (1989). *Second language research methods*. Oxford: Oxford University Press.

Shake, M. C., & Stine-Morrow, E. A. L. (2011). Age Differences in Resolving Anaphoric Expressions During Reading. *Neuropsychology, Development, and Cognition. Section B, Aging, Neuropsychology and Cognition, 18*(6), 678–707. doi:10.1080/13825585.2011.607228 PMID:21995819

Shawer, S. (2010). Classroom-level curriculum development: EFL teachers as curriculum-developers, curriculum-makers and curriculum-transmitters. *Teaching and Teacher Education, 26*, 173–184. doi:10.1016/j.tate.2009.03.015

Shei, C., & Hsieh, H. (2012). Linkit: a CALL system for learning Chinese characters, words, and phrases. *Computer Assisted Language Learning, 25*(4), 319–338. doi:10.1080/09588221.2011.589390

Shekary, M., & Tahririan, M. (2006). Negotiation of meaning and noticing in text-based online chat. *Modern Language Journal, 90*(4), 557–573. doi:10.1111/j.1540-4781.2006.00504.x

Shen, H. H., & Ke, C. (2007). Radical awareness and word acquisition among nonnative learners of Chinese. *Modern Language Journal, 91*, 97–111. doi:10.1111/j.1540-4781.2007.00511.x

Shi, L. (2012). *The effects of a custom-designed animation program on learning Chinese characters*. (Doctoral dissertation). Retrieved from ProQuest Dissertations and Theses database.

Shi, L. (2006). Cultural backgrounds and textual appropriation. *Language Awareness, 15*, 264–282. doi:10.2167/la406.0

Shi, L. (2008). Textual appropriation and citing behaviors of university undergraduates. *Applied Linguistics, 31*(1), 1–24. doi:10.1093/applin/amn045

Shi, L. (2011). Common knowledge, learning, and citation practices in university writing. *Research in the Teaching of English, 45*(3), 308–334.

Shively, R. L. (2011). L2 pragmatic development in study abroad: A longitudinal study of Spanish service encounters. *Journal of Pragmatics, 43*, 1818–1835. doi:10.1016/j.pragma.2010.10.030

Shively, R. L. (2013). Learning to be funny in Spanish during study abroad: L2 humor development. *Modern Language Journal, 97*(4), 930–946. doi:10.1111/j.1540-4781.2013.12043.x

Shu, H., & Anderson, R. C. (1999). Learning to read Chinese: the development of metalinguistic awareness. In J. Wang, A. W. Inhoff, & H.-C. Chen (Eds.), *Reading Chinese script: A cognitive analysis* (pp. 1–18). Mahwah, NJ: Lawrence Erlbaum Associates.

Siegel, M., & Misselt, A. (1984). Adaptive feedback and review paradigm for computer-based drills. *Journal of Educational Psychology, 18*, 294–309.

Sife, A. S., Lwoga, E. T., & Sanga, C. (2007). New technologies for teaching and learning: Challenges for higher learning institutions in developing countries. *International Journal of Education and Development Using ICT, 3*(2), 57–67.

Silverman, R., & Hines, S. (2009). The effects of multimedia-enhanced instruction on the vocabulary of English-language learners and non-English-language learners in pre-kindergarten through second grade. *Journal of Educational Psychology, 101*(2), 305–314. doi:10.1037/a0014217

Sinclair, J. (Ed.). (2006). *Collins COBUILD advanced English dictionary* (5th ed.). London: Collins.

Singapore Ministry of Education. (2007). *Chinese Language (Primary) Syllabus*. Singapore: Curriculum Planning and Development Division, Ministry of Education.

Skinner, E. A., & Belmont, M. J. (1993). Motivation in the classroom: Reciprocal effects of teacher behavior and student engagement across the school year. *Journal of Educational Psychology, 85*, 571–581. doi:10.1037/0022-0663.85.4.571

Smith, B. (2003). Computer-mediated negotiated interaction: An expanded model. *Modern Language Journal, 87*, 38–57. doi:10.1111/1540-4781.00177

Smith, B. (2005). The relationship between negotiated interaction, learner uptake, and in task-based computer-mediated communication. *TESOL Quarterly, 39*(1), 33–58. doi:10.2307/3588451

Smith, K., & Craig, H. (2013). Enhancing the autonomous use of CALL: A new curriculum model in EFL. *CALICO Journal*, *30*(2), 252–278. doi:10.11139/cj.30.2.252-278

Snellings, P., van Gelderen, A., & de Glopper, K. (2002). Lexical retrieval: An aspect of fluent second language production that can be enhanced. *Language Learning*, *52*, 723–754. doi:10.1111/1467-9922.00202

Snellings, P., van Gelderen, A., & de Glopper, K. (2004). The effect of enhanced lexical retrieval on second language writing: A classroom experiment. *Applied Psycholinguistics*, *25*(2), 175–200. doi:10.1017/S0142716404001092

Son, J. (2007). Learner experiences in web-based language learning. *Computer Assisted Language Learning*, *20*(1), 21–36. doi:10.1080/09588220601118495

Sotillo, S. M. (2005). Corrective feedback via Instant Messenger learning activities in NS-NNS and NNS-NNS dyads. *CALICO Journal*, *22*(3), 467–496.

Stake, R. E. (1995). *The art of case study research*. Thousand Oaks, CA: Sage Publications.

Stake, R. E. (2003). Case studies. In N. Denzin, & Y. Lincoln (Eds.), *Strategies of qualitative research* (pp. 134–164). Thousand Oaks, CA: Sage.

Stapleton, P. (2012). Gauging the effectiveness of anti-plagiarism software: An empirical study of second language graduate writers. *Journal of English for Academic Purposes*, *10*, 125–133. doi:10.1016/j.jeap.2011.10.003

Stappenbelt, B., & Rowles, C. (2009, September). *The effectiveness of plagiarism detection software as a learning tool in academic writing education*. Paper presented at the meeting of the Asia Pacific Conference on Educational Integrity. Wollongong, Australia.

Stehle, M. (2009). *The interlanguage development of articles in English as a second language: A longitudinal study*. (Unpublished MA thesis). University of Pittsburgh, Pittsburgh, PA.

Stevenson, M., & Liu, M. (2010). Learning a language with Web 2.0: Exploring the use of social networking features of foreign language learning websites. *CALICO Journal*, *27*, 233–259.

Stockwell, G. (2007). A review of technology choice for teaching language skills and areas in the CALL literature. *ReCALL*, *19*(2), 105–120. doi:10.1017/S0958344007000225

Stockwell, G. (2007). Vocabulary on the move: Investigating an intelligent mobile phone-based vocabulary tutor. *Computer Assisted Language Learning*, *20*(4), 365–383. doi:10.1080/09588220701745817

Stockwell, G. (2010). Using mobile phones for vocabulary activities: Examining the effect of the platform. *Language Learning & Technology*, *14*(2), 95–110.

Storch, N. (2012). Collaborative writing as a site for L2 learning in face-to-face and online modes. In G. Kessler, A. Oskoz, & I. Elola (Eds.), Technology across writing contexts and tasks (pp. 113–129). Texas State University.

Storch, N. (2002). Patterns of interaction in ESL pair work. *Language Learning*, *52*(1), 119–158. doi:10.1111/1467-9922.00179

Storch, N. (2005). Collaborative writing: Product, process, and students' reflections. *Journal of Second Language Writing*, *14*, 153–173. doi:10.1016/j.jslw.2005.05.002

Storch, N. (2011). Collaborative writing in L2 contexts: Processes, outcomes, and future directions. *Annual Review of Applied Linguistics*, *31*, 275–288. doi:10.1017/S0267190511000079

Storch, N. (2013). *Collaborative writing in L2 classrooms*. Bristol, UK: Multilingual Matters.

Su, H.-Y. (2009). Reconstructing Taiwanese and Taiwan Guoyu on the Taiwan-based Internet: Playfulness, stylization, and politeness. *Journal of Asian Pacific Communication*, *19*(2), 313–335. doi:10.1075/japc.19.2.08su

Sun, Y. C. (2009). Voice blog: An exploratory study of language learning. *Language Learning & Technology*, *13*(2), 88–103.

Sun, Y., & Dong, Q. (2004). An experiment on supporting children's English vocabulary learning in multimedia context. *Computer Assisted Language Learning*, *17*(2), 131–147. doi:10.1080/0958822042000334217

Sussex, R. (1991). Research in practice and practice on research in CALL. *Computer Assisted Language Learning*, *4*(3), 191–206. doi:10.1080/0958822910040307

Sutherland-Smith, W., & Carr, R. (2005). *Turnitin*.com: Teachers' perspectives of anti-plagiarism software in raising issues of educational integrity. *Journal of University Teaching and Learning Practice*, *2*(3), 93–101.

Swain, M. (1985). Communicative competence: Some roles of comprehensible input and output in its development. In S. Gass, & C. Madden (Eds.), *Input in second language acquisition* (pp. 235–253). Rowley, MA: Newbury House.

Swain, M. (1993). The output hypothesis: Just speaking and writing aren't enough. *Canadian Modern Language Review*, *50*(1), 158–164.

Swain, M. (1995). Three functions of output in second language learning. In G. Cook, & G. Seidhofer (Eds.), *Principles and practice in applied linguistics: Studies in honor of H. G. Widdowson* (pp. 125–144). Oxford, UK: Oxford University Press.

Swain, M. (2000). The output hypothesis and beyond: Mediating acquisition through collaborative dialogue. In J. Lantolf (Ed.), *Sociocultural theory and second language learning* (pp. 97–114). Oxford: Oxford University Press.

Swain, M. (2005). The output hypothesis: Theory and research. In E. Hinkel (Ed.), *Handbook on research in second language teaching and learning* (pp. 471–484). Mahwah, NJ: Erlbaum.

Swain, M. (2006). Verbal protocols: What does it mean for research to use speaking as a data collection tool? In M. Chalhoub-Deville, C. Chappelle, & P. Duff (Eds.), *Inference and generalizability in applied linguistics: Multiple perspectives* (pp. 97–113). Amsterdam: John Benjamins. doi:10.1075/lllt.12.07swa

Swain, M., & Lapkin, S. (1998). Interaction and second language learning: Two adolescent French immersion students working together. *Modern Language Journal*, *82*(3), 320–337. doi:10.1111/j.1540-4781.1998.tb01209.x

Swain, M., & Lapkin, S. (2001). Focus on form through collaborative dialogue: Exploring task effects. In M. Bygate, P. Skehan, & M. Swain (Eds.), *Researching pedagogic tasks: Second language learning, teaching, and testing* (pp. 99–118). London: Longman.

Swain, M., Lapkin, S., Knouzzi, I., Suzuki, W., & Brooks, L. (2009). Languaging: University students learn the grammatical concept of voice in French. *Modern Language Journal*, *93*, 5–27. doi:10.1111/j.1540-4781.2009.00825.x

Swales, J. M. (1990). *Genre analysis: English in academic and research settings*. Cambridge: Cambridge University Press.

Swanson, P., & Early, P. (2009). Establish your presence in the blogosphere: A guide to blog development for the foreign language classroom. In C. Wilkerson (Ed.), *Dimension* (pp. 17–28). Valdosta, GA: SCOLT Publications.

Sykes, J. (2005). Synchronous CMC and pragmatic development: Effects of oral and written chat. *CALICO Journal*, *22*(3), 399–431.

Szabo, A., & Underwood, J. (2004). Cybercheats: Is information and communication technology fueling academic dishonesty? *Active Learning in Higher Education*, *5*(2), 180–199. doi:10.1177/1469787404043815

Szatrowski, P. (1993). *Nihongo no danwa no kouzou bunseki: Kanyu no sutorateji no kousatsu* [Structural analysis of Japanese discourse: A study of the strategy for invitation]. Tokyo: Kuroshio Publishers.

Szesztay, M. (2005). Teachers' ways of knowing. *ELT Journal*, *58*(2), 129–136. doi:10.1093/elt/58.2.129

Taft, M., & Chung, K. (1999). Using radicals in teaching Chinese characters to second language learners. *Psychologia*, *42*, 234–251.

Taft, M., & Forster, K. I. (1975). Lexical storage and retrieval for pre.xed words. *Journal of Verbal Learning and Verbal Behavior*, *14*, 638–647. doi:10.1016/S0022-5371(75)80051-X

Taft, M., & Zhu, X. (1997). Submorphemic processing in reading Chinese. *Journal of Experimental Psychology. Learning, Memory, and Cognition*, *23*, 761–775. doi:10.1037/0278-7393.23.3.761

Taft, M., Zhu, X., & Peng, D. (1999). Positional specificity of radical in Chinese character recognition. *Journal of Memory and Language*, *40*, 498–519. doi:10.1006/jmla.1998.2625

Taguchi, N., & Sykes, J. (2013). *Technology in interlanguage pragmatics research and teaching*. Philadelphia, PA: John Benjamins. doi:10.1075/lllt.36

Takamiya, Y. (2009). Rediscovering Japan through blogs: Toward a curriculum that integrates language acquisition and cultural learning. In A. Gabriela (Ed.), *Teacher narratives: CALPER project-based learning and advanced proficiency*. Pennsylvania State University Center for Advanced Language Proficiency Education and Research. Available from, http://calper.la.psu.edu/projectwork/yumi_main.php

Takamiya, Y., & Ishihara, N. (2013). Blogging: Cross-cultural interaction for pragmatic development. In N. Taguchi, & J. Sykes (Eds.), *Technology in interlanguage pragmatics research and teaching* (pp. 185–214). Philadelphia, PA: John Benjamins. doi:10.1075/lllt.36.10tak

Talmy, S. (2010). Qualitative interviews in applied linguistics: From research instrument to social practice. *Annual Review of Applied Linguistics*, *30*, 128–148. doi:10.1017/S0267190510000085

Tan, L. H., & Perfetti, C. (1998). Phonological codes as early sources of constraint in Chinese word identification: A review of current discoveries and theoretical accounts. *Reading and Writing*, *10*, 105–200. doi:10.1023/A:1008086231343

Tao, L. (1993). *Zero anaphora in Chinese: Cognitive strategies in discourse processing*. (Unpublished doctoral dissertation). University of Colorado, Boulder, CO.

Tao, L. (1996). Topic discontinuity and zero anaphora in Chinese discourse: Cognitive strategies in discourse processing. In B. Fox (Ed.), *Studies in Anaphora* (pp. 487–513). Amsterdam: John Benjamins Publishing Company. doi:10.1075/tsl.33.15tao

Tao, L. (2001). Switch reference and zero anaphora: Emergent reference in discourse processing. In A. Cienki, B. J. Luka, & M. B. Smith (Eds.), *Conceptual and discourse factors in linguistic structure* (pp. 253–267). Stanford, CA: CSLI Publications.

Tao, L., & Healy, A. F. (1996). Cognitive strategies in discourse processing: A comparison of Chinese and English speakers. *Journal of Psycholinguistic Research*, *25*, 597–616. doi:10.1007/BF01712411

Tao, L., & Healy, A. F. (2005). Zero anaphora: Transfer of reference tracking strategies from Chinese to English. *Journal of Psycholinguistic Research*, *34*, 99–131. doi:10.1007/s10936-005-3634-5 PMID:15991875

Teo, T. (2008). Pre-service teachers' attitudes towards computer use: A Singapore survey. *Australasian Journal of Educational Technology*, *24*, 413–424.

Teo, T. (2011). Factors influencing teachers' intention to use technology: Model development and test. *Computers & Education*, *57*, 2432–2440. doi:10.1016/j.compedu.2011.06.008

Teo, T., Lee, C. B., & Chai, C. S. (2008). Understanding pre-service teachers' computer attitudes: Applying and extending the technology acceptance model. *Journal of Computer Assisted Learning*, *24*, 128–143. doi:10.1111/j.1365-2729.2007.00247.x

Teo, T., & Noyes, J. (2011). An assessment of the influence of perceived enjoyment and attitude on the intention to use technology among pre-service teachers: A structural equation modeling approach. *Computers & Education*, *57*, 1645–1653. doi:10.1016/j.compedu.2011.03.002

Thomas, M. (Ed.). (2009). *Handbook of research on Web 2.0 and second language learning*. Herskey, PA: Information Science Reference. doi:10.4018/978-1-60566-190-2

Thompson, S. V., & Riding, R., J. (1990). The effect of animated diagrams on the understanding of a mathematical demonstration in 11 to 14 years-old pupils. *The British Journal of Educational Psychology*, *60*, 93–98. doi:10.1111/j.2044-8279.1990.tb00925.x PMID:1693087

Thonus, T. (1999). Dominance in academic writing tutorials: gender, language proficiency, and the offering of suggestions. *Discourse & Society*, *10*(2), 225–248. doi:10.1177/0957926599010002005

Thonus, T. (2004). What are the differences? Tutor interactions with first- and second-language writers. *Journal of Second Language Writing*, *13*, 227–242. doi:10.1016/j.jslw.2004.04.012

Thorne, S. (2003). Artifacts and cultures-of-use in intercultural communication. *Language Learning & Technology*, *7*(2), 38–67.

Thorne, S. L., Black, R. W., & Sykes, J. M. (2009). Second language use, socialization, and learning in internet interest communities and online gaming. *Modern Language Journal, 93*, 802–821. doi:10.1111/j.1540-4781.2009.00974.x

Thorne, S. L., & Tasker, T. (2011). Sociocultural and cultural-historical theories of language development. In J. Simpson (Ed.), *Routledge handbook of applied linguistics* (pp. 487–500). New York: Routledge.

Tian, J., & Wang, Y. (2010). Taking language learning outside the classroom: learners' perspectives of eTandem learning via Skype. *Innovation in Language Learning and Teaching, 4*(3), 181–197. doi:10.1080/17501229.2010.513443

Toh, Y., & So, H. J. (2011). ICT reform initiatives in Singapore schools: A complexity theory perspective. *Asia Pacific Education Review, 12*, 345–357. doi:10.1007/s12564-010-9130-0

Tomasello, M. (1998). Introduction: A cognitive-functional perspective on language structure. In M. Tomasello (Ed.), *The new psychology of language: Cognitive and functional approaches to language structure* (pp. vii–xxiii). Mahwah, NJ: Erlbaum.

Tomita, Y., & Spada, N. (2013). Form-focused instruction and learner investment in L2 communication. *Modern Language Journal, 93*(3), 591–610. doi:10.1111/j.1540-4781.2013.12031.x

Tonzar, C., Lotto, L., & Job, R. (2009). L2 vocabulary acquisition in children: Effects of learning method and cognate status. *Language Learning, 59*, 623–646. doi:10.1111/j.1467-9922.2009.00519.x

Towndrow, P. (2004). Reflections of an on-line tutor. *ELT Journal, 58*(2), 174–182. doi:10.1093/elt/58.2.174

Tozcu, A., & Coady, J. (2004). Successful learning of frequent vocabulary through CALL also benefits reading comprehension and speed. *Computer Assisted Language Learning, 17*(5), 473–495. doi:10.1080/0958822042000319674

Tulving, E., & Madigan, S. A. (1970). Memory and verbal learning. *Annual Review of Psychology, 21*(1), 437–484. doi:10.1146/annurev.ps.21.020170.002253

Turnitin. (2014, February 5). *Turnitin study shows impact of plagiarism prevention and online grading at higher education institutions.* Available from, http://turnitin.com/en_us/about-us/press/turnitin-study-shows-impact-of-plagiarism-prevention-and-online-grading-at-higher-education-institutions

Urbanczyk, S. (2005). Enhancing contrast in reduplication. In M. de Gruyter (Ed.), Studies on reduplication (pp. 211-238). Berlin: Walter de Gruyter.

Ushioda, E. (1996). *Learner autonomy 5: The role of motivation.* Dublin: Authentik.

Valentine, K. (2006). Plagiarism as literacy practice: Recognizing and rethinking ethical binaries. *College Composition and Communication, 58*(1), 89–110.

Van Lier, L. (2004). *The ecology and semiotics of language learning*. Dordrecht: Kluwer Academic. doi:10.1007/1-4020-7912-5

Van Sommers, P. (1984). *Drawing and cognition: Descriptive and experimental studies of graphic production processes*. Cambridge: Cambridge University Press. doi:10.1017/CBO9780511897672

Van Valin, R. D., Jr. (1987). Aspects of the interaction of syntax and pragmatics: Discourse coreference mechanisms and the typology of grammatical systems. In *The pragmatic perspective: Selected papers from the 1985 international pragmatics conference 232* (pp. 513–531). Amsterdam: Benjamins Publishing Company.

Vanacker, B. (2011). Returning students' right to access, choice and notice: a proposed code of ethics for instructors using *Turnitin. Ethics and Information Technology, 13*(4), 327–338. doi:10.1007/s10676-011-9277-3

Verity, D. (2005). Vygotskyan Concepts for teacher education. Pan-SIG Conference "Lifelong learning" proceedings. Retrieved from http://jalt.org/pansig/2005/HTML/Verity.htm

Vinagre, M., & Muñoz, B. (2011). Computer-mediated corrective feedback and language accuracy in telecollaborative exchanges. *Language Learning & Technology, 15*(1), 72–103.

Vygotsky, L. S. (1978). *Mind in society*. Cambridge, MA: Harvard University Press.

Wade, E. (2005). *Enhancing German language learners' intercultural communicative competence through the on-line exchange project ICE.* (Doctoral dissertation). University of California, Santa Barbara, CA.

Walker, J. (2010). Measuring plagiarism: researching what students do, not what they say they do. *Studies in Higher Education, 35*, 41–59. doi:10.1080/03075070902912994

Walker, M., & Townley, C. (2012). Contract cheating: a new challenge for academic honesty? *Journal of Academic Ethics, 10*, 27–44. doi:10.1007/s10805-012-9150-y

Wang, S. C. (1998). A study on the learning and teaching of hanzi-Chinese characters. *Working Papers in Educational Linguistics, 14*(1), 69–101.

Wang, M., Perfetti, C. A., & Liu, Y. (2003). Alphabetic readers quickly acquire orthographic structure in learning to read Chinese. *Scientific Studies of Reading, 7*(2), 183–208. doi:10.1207/S1532799XSSR0702_4

Wang, S., & Vasquez, C. (2012). Web 2.0 and second language learning: What does the research tell us? *CALICO Journal, 29*(3), 412–430. doi:10.11139/cj.29.3.412-430

Wang, Y. (2003). Negotiation of meaning in desktop videoconferencing-supported distance language learning. *ReCALL, 18*(1), 122–146. doi:10.1017/S0958344006000814

Ware, P. (2005). "Missed communication" in online communication: Tensions in fostering successful online interactions. *Language Learning & Technology, 9*(2), 64–89.

Ware, P. (2005). 'Missed' communication in online communication: Tensions in a German-American telecollaboration. *Language Learning & Technology, 9*(2), 64–89.

Ware, P., & Kramsch, C. (2005). Toward an intercultural stance: Teaching German and English through telecollaboration. *Modern Language Journal, 89*(2), 190–205. doi:10.1111/j.1540-4781.2005.00274.x

Ware, P., & O'Dowd, R. (2008). Peer feedback on language form in telecollaboration. *Language Learning & Technology, 12*(1), 43–63.

Ware, P., & Pérez-Cañado, L. (2007). Grammar and feedback: Turning to language form in telecollaboration. In R. O'Dowd (Ed.), *Online intercultural exchange: An introduction for foreign language teachers* (pp. 107–126). Clevedon, England: Multilingual Matters.

Ware, P., & Warschauer, M. (2006). Electronic feedback and second language writing. In K. Hyland, & F. Hyland (Eds.), *Feedback in ESL writing: Context and issues* (pp. 105–122). NY: Cambridge University Press. doi:10.1017/CBO9781139524742.008

Waring, H. Z. (2005). Peer tutoring in a graduate writing centre: Identity, expertise, and advice resisting. *Applied Linguistics, 26*(2), 141–168. doi:10.1093/applin/amh041

Warschauer, M. (1995). *E-mail for English teaching: Bringing the Internet and computer learning networks into the language classroom.* Alexandria, Virginia: TESOL Publications.

Warschauer, M. (1996). Comparing face-to-face and electronic discussion in the second language classroom. *CALICO Journal, 13*, 7–25.

Warschauer, M. (1997). Computer-mediated collaborative learning: Theory and practice. *Modern Language Journal, 81*(4), 470–481. doi:10.1111/j.1540-4781.1997.tb05514.x

Warschauer, M. (1998). Interaction, negotiation, and computer-mediated learning. In M. Clay (Ed.), *Practical applications of educational technology in language learning* (pp. 125–136). Lyon, France: National Institute of Applied Sciences.

Warschauer, M. (2001). Millennialism and media: Language, literacy, and technology in the 21st century. *AILA Review, 14*, 49–59.

Warschauer, M. (2010). New tools for teaching writing. *Language Learning & Technology, 14*(1), 3–8.

Warschauer, M., & Grimes, D. (2007). Audience, authorship, and artifact: The emergent semiotics of Web 2.0. *Annual Review of Applied Linguistics, 27*, 1–23. doi:10.1017/S0267190508070013

Warschauer, M., Shetzer, H., & Meloni, C. (2000). *Internet for English teaching*. Alexandria, VA: TESOL Publications.

Watson-Gegeo, K. A. (2004). Mind, language, and epistemology: Toward a language socialization paradigm for SLA. *Modern Language Journal, 88*(3), 331–350. doi:10.1111/j.0026-7902.2004.00233.x

Watson-Gegeo, K. A., & Nielsen, S. (2003). Language socialization in SLA. In C. J. Doughty, & M. H. Long (Eds.), *The handbook of second language acquisition* (pp. 155–177). Malden, MA: Blackwell Publishing. doi:10.1002/9780470756492.ch7

Webb, S. (2008). The effects of context on incidental vocabulary learning. *Reading in a Foreign Language*, *20*, 232–245.

Webb, W. B. (1962). The effects of prolonged learning on learning. *Journal of Verbal Learning and Verbal Behavior*, *1*, 173–182. doi:10.1016/S0022-5371(62)80026-7

Weissberg, R. (2006). *Connecting speaking and writing*. Ann Arbor, MI: University of Michigan Press.

Wells, G. (1999). *Dialogic inquiry: Toward a sociocultural practice and theory of education*. Cambridge, UK: Cambridge University Press. doi:10.1017/CBO9780511605895

Wenden, A., & Rubin, J. (Eds.). (1987). *Learner strategies in language learning*. Cambridge: Prentice-Hall.

Wenger, E. (1998). *Communities of practice: Learning, meaning, and identity*. Cambridge: Cambridge University Press. doi:10.1017/CBO9780511803932

Wette, R. (2010). Evaluating student learning in a university-level EAP unit on writing using sources. *Journal of Second Language Writing*, *19*, 158–177. doi:10.1016/j.jslw.2010.06.002

Widdig, W., & Esser, R. (1988). New possibilities in computer-assisted learning of foreign language vocabulary using Apple Macintosh. In U. Jung (Ed.), *Computers in applied linguistics and language teaching* (pp. 265–278). Frankfurt: Peter Lang.

Wilkins, D. A. (1972). *Linguistics in language teaching*. London: Edward Arnold.

Wolcott, H. F. (1994). *Transforming qualitative data: Description, analysis, and interpretation*. Thousand Oaks, CA: Sage.

Wong, L. H., & Looi, C.-K. (2010). Vocabulary learning by mobile-assisted authentic content creation and social meaning-making: Two case studies. *Journal of Computer Assisted Learning*, *26*(5), 421–433. doi:10.1111/j.1365-2729.2010.00357.x

Xu, J. (2010). Using multimedia vocabulary annotations in L2 reading and listening activities. *CALICO Journal*, *27*(2), 311–327.

Xu, X., & Padilla, A. M. (2013). Using meaningful interpretation and chunking to enhance memory: The case of Chinese character learning. *Foreign Language Annals*, *14*(3), 402–422.

Yang, C. L., Gordon, P. C., Hendrick, R., & Wu, J. T. (1999). Comprehension of referring expressions in Chinese. *Language and Cognitive Processes*, *14*, 715–743. doi:10.1080/016909699386248

Yanguas, I. (2010). Oral computer-mediated interaction between l2 learners: It's about time! *Language Learning & Technology*, *14*(3), 72–93.

Yang, Y. F. D. (2011). Learner interpretations of shared space in multilateral English blogging. *Language Learning & Technology*, *15*(1), 122–146.

Yan, J. (2012). Writing Cantonese as everyday lifestyle in Guangzhou (Canton city). In J. Liu, & H. Tao (Eds.), *Chinese under globalization: Emerging trends in language use in China* (pp. 171–202). Singapore: World Scientific Publishing. doi:10.1142/9789814350709_0009

Yao, T. C. (2009). The Current Status of Chinese CALL in the United States. *Journal of the Chinese Language Teachers Association*, *44*(1), 1–23.

Yeh, Y. L., Liou, H. C., & Li, Y. H. (2007). Online synonym materials and concordancing for EFL college writing. *Computer Assisted Language Learning*, *20*(2), 131–152. doi:10.1080/09588220701331451

Yin, R. K. (2009). *Case study research design and methods* (4th ed.). Thousand Oaks, CA: Sage Publications.

Ymura-Takei, M., Fujiwar, M., & Aizawa, T. (2001). Resolving and generation zero anaphor in Japanese: A language learning aid perspective. In *Proceedings of the 6th Natural Language Proceeding Pacific Rim Symposium* (pp. 557–562). New Delhi: Allied Publisher, Ltd.

Yoshii, M. (2006). L1 and l2 glosses: Their effects on incidental vocabulary learning. *Language Learning & Technology*, *10*(3), 85–101.

Yoshii, M. (2013). Effects of gloss types on vocabulary learning through reading: Comparison of single and multiple gloss types. *CALICO Journal*, 203–229.

Youmans, R. J. (2011). Does the adoption of plagiarism-detection software in higher education reduce plagiarism? *Studies in Higher Education*, *36*(7), 749–761. doi:10.1080/03075079.2010.523457

Yun, S., Miller, P. C., Baek, Y., Jung, J., & Ko, M. (2008). Improving recall and transfer skills through vocabulary building in web-based second language learning: An examination by item and feedback type. *Journal of Educational Technology & Society*, *11*(4), 158–172.

Zahar, R., Cobb, T., & Spada, N. (2001). Acquiring vocabulary through reading: Effects of frequency and contextual richness. *Canadian Modern Language Review*, *57*(4), 541–572. doi:10.3138/cmlr.57.4.541

Zarate, G. (2003). The recognition of intercultural competences: From individual experience to certification. In G. Aired, M. Byram, & M. Fleming (Eds.), *Intercultural experience and education* (pp. 213–224). Clevedon, England: Multilingual Matters.

Zhang, W. W. [章文文] (2012). *A research into the orthographically similar radicals and characters in Chinese as a foreign language education.* (Master's thesis). Retrieved from CNKI database.

Zhang, F., & Barber, B. (2008). *Handbook of research on computer-enhanced language acquisition and learning*. Hershey: Information Science Reference. doi:10.4018/978-1-59904-895-6

Zhang, L. X., & Li, X. X. (2004). A comparative study on learner autonomy between Chinese students and west European students. *Foreign Language World*, *4*, 15–23.

Zhang, T., Gao, T., Ring, G., & Zhang, W. (2007). Using online discussion forums to assist a traditional English class. *International Journal on E-Learning*, *6*(4), 623–643.

Zhang, W. X. (1990). From character chunks to character structure in Chinese as a foreign language teaching. *Teaching Chinese in the World*, *2*, 112–120.

Zhang, Z. (1998). CALL for Chinese – Issues and Practice. *Journal of Chinese Language Teachers Association*, *33*(1), 51–82. Available at http://www.csulb.edu/~txie/learn_online/issues.htm

Zhao, H. (2012). *Explicitness, cue competition, and knowledge tracing: A tutorial system for second language learning of English article usage*. (Unpublished Ph.D. Dissertation). Carnegie Mellon University, Pittsburgh, PA.

Zhao, H., Koedinger, K., & Kowalski, J. (2013). Knowledge tracing and cue contrast: Second language English grammar. In M. Knauff, M. Pauen, N. Sebanz, & I. Wachsmuth (Eds.), *Proceedings of the 35th Annual Conference of the Cognitive Science Society* (pp. 1653–1658). Austin, TX: Cognitive Science Society.

Zhao, Y., & Frank, K. (2003). Technology uses in schools: An ecological perspective. *American Educational Research Journal*, *40*, 807–840. doi:10.3102/00028312040004807

Zhao, Y., Puge, K., Sheldon, S., & Byers, J. L. (2002). Conditions for classroom technology innovations. *Teachers College Record*, *104*, 482–515. doi:10.1111/1467-9620.00170

Zhu, X., & Taft, M. (1994). *Complexity effects in Chinese character processing*. Paper presented to the Asian–Australian Workshop on Cognitive Processing of Asian Languages. Beijing, China.

Zhu, Y., Fung, A. S. L., & Wang, H. Y. (2012). Memorization effects of pronunciation and stroke order animation in digital flashcards. *CALICO Journal*, *29*(3), 563–577. doi:10.11139/cj.29.3.563-577

Zhu, Y., & Hong, W. (2005). Effects of Digital Voiced Pronunciation and Stroke Sequence Animation on Character Memorization of CFL Learners. *Journal of the Chinese Language Teachers Association*, *40*(3), 49–70.

Zuengler, J., & Cole, K. (2005). Language socialization and second language learning. In E. Hinkel (Ed.), *Handbook of research in second language teaching and learning* (pp. 301–316). Mahwah, NJ: Lawrence Erlbaum Associates.

Zyzik, E., & Polio, C. (2008). Incidental focus on form in university Spanish literature courses. *Modern Language Journal*, *92*(1), 53–70. doi:10.1111/j.1540-4781.2008.00686.x

About the Contributors

Shuai Li is an Assistant Professor of Chinese at Georgia State University. He is the director of GSU's Chinese program in the Department of Modern and Classical Languages. His research interests include interlanguage pragmatics, Chinese as a second language acquisition, computer-assisted language teaching and learning, and business Chinese instruction. His research papers have appeared in *Language Learning, Modern Language Journal, Pragmatics and Cognition, Chinese as a Second Language Acquisition Research*, and *Journal of Chinese Language Teachers Association.*

Peter B. Swanson is an Associate Professor of Foreign Language Education at Georgia State University. He is the Director of Graduate Studies in the Department of Modern and Classical Languages and also serves as the Director of the Foreign Language Teacher Preparation Program. His two strands of research focus on (1) the assessment and the integration of technology into instruction and (2) the recruitment and retention of language teachers. He has authored dozens of publications, and his latest book, *Identifying and recruiting language teachers: A research-based approach* advances an empirical approach to determining the personality patterns of language teachers and methods for recruiting such talented individuals into the profession.

***

Yuka Akiyama is a PhD student in Applied Linguistics at the Department of Linguistics, Georgetown University. Her research interests include social interaction, corrective feedback, and task-based language teaching. Her current research agenda is centered on investigating interaction that takes place in telecollaboration/virtual language exchange, a method where language learners teach and learn each other's languages and cultures using technology. Prior to starting her PhD at Georgetown University, she had taught Japanese at American Universities like the Massachusetts Institute of Technology and Boston University. She also coordinated task-based language exchange projects between schools in Japan and the United States and is actively engaged in setting up such exchange programs at Georgetown University. Her previous publications investigated the effect of dynamic written corrective feedback and the use of telecollaboration for faculty development.

Li-Yun Chang is a doctoral candidate in the cognitive psychology program and a graduate student researcher in the Learning Research and Development Center at the University of Pittsburgh. She completed her BEd in 2008 and MEd in 2010 in Educational Psychology and Counseling at National Taiwan Normal University, Taiwan. Her research focuses on the cognitive mechanisms related to second language acquisition, especially word-level processing. One line of her research focuses on Chinese orthography, specifically the probability that a radical appears in a permissible position within a configuration, and how statistical regularities inform Chinese orthographic learning. Another line of her research investigates how the similarities and differences between writing systems (e.g., English and Chinese) affect how adults learn to read in a foreign language. The methodologies she uses to address these issues include corpus linguistics methods, cognitive experimental approaches, and electrophysiology (ERPs).

Julie Dell-Jones is a doctoral candidate in Second Language Acquisition/Instructional Technology at the University of South Florida. Her research interests include multiliteracies, critical literacy, and multicultural education. She draws from a background in visual arts in her approach to interdisciplinary language pedagogy and advocates for both arts-infused education and arts-based research methodologies. Recently, Julie has led creative collaborative projects using photo-elicitation with English language learners and has used digital storytelling and arts-as-inquiry to explore language-learning experiences. She has taught French and English as a foreign language and English as a second language. She currently teaches various ESOL education courses to pre-service and in-service teachers.

Wenhao Diao is an Assistant professor in the Department of East Asian Studies and an affiliated faculty member in the interdisciplinary graduate program of Second Language Acquisition and Teaching (SLAT) at the University of Arizona. Using sociolinguistic and ethnographic approaches, her research examines language socialization processes between study abroad students and local speakers. She is also interested in understanding how gender, nationality, and place are constructed through language in contemporary China. Dr. Diao received her PhD from Carnegie Mellon University in Pittsburgh, Pennsylvania. Some of her recent work has appeared in *Frontiers: The Interdisciplinary Journal of Study Abroad*, *Texas Linguistic Forum*, and the *Journal of International Students*.

Miriam Eisenstein Ebsworth is the director of Doctoral and Post-MA Programs in Multilingual, Multicultural Studies at New York University. She has worked with second language learners from K-adult for over 40 years, has mentored second language teachers and researchers, and has held various leadership positions on a local and national level. In addition to her research in sociolinguistics, L2 writing, and second language pedagogy, Miriam is co-developer (with PI Pat Duffy) of *Action Through Words*, an online course for English learners whose content is how the UN works for peace around the world. She is research editor of *Writing and Pedagogy* and also serves on the editorial boards of the *Bilingual Research Journal* and *The International Journal of Foreign Language Teaching*. Dr. Ebsworth is currently chair of the Research SIG of the National Association for Bilingual Education.

Paula Garrett-Rucks (PhD in Second Language Acquisition with concentration in French) is an active researcher in foreign language instruction and learning and second language learner identity. Recent and forthcoming publications center on the formation of learners' cultural perceptions and stereotypes, the role of affect in second language learning and the use of technology in foreign language instruction. Dr. Garrett-Rucks has presented her papers nationally and internationally at venues such as AAAL, AILA, ACTFL, CERCLL and SLRF in addition to having conducted multiple workshops and presentations at the local and state levels. Dr. Garrett-Rucks also serves as a reviewer for peer-reviewed scholarly journals such as the *Modern Language Journal* and *Foreign Language Annals*.

Zöe Handley is a Lecturer in Language Education in the Department of Education at the University of York. She supervises doctoral students and teaches on the MA in Teaching English to speakers of Other Languages (TESOL) and the MA in Applied Linguistics for English Language Teaching. Her research interests are in computer-mediated task-based language learning and computer-assisted pronunciation training.

Noriko Ishihara holds a PhD in curriculum and instruction from the University of Minnesota and is currently associate professor of EFL/TESOL at Hosei University in Tokyo, Japan. She also advises graduate students at Temple University Japan and leads language teachers' professional development course in instructional pragmatics at the Center for Advanced Research in Language Acquisition (CARLA) at the University of Minnesota. She has designed a web-based curriculum for learning L2 Japanese pragmatics and developed ESOL materials for intercultural communication. Her research interests include instructional pragmatics, identity, technology-mediated language learning/teaching and language teacher development. She has authored or co-authored papers in these areas for *TESOL Quarterly, TESL Canada Journal, Modern Language Journal, TESL-EJ, Teaching and Learning Pragmatics* (2010, book co-authored with Andrew D. Cohen, Pearson/Longman), and *Communication in Context* (2010, Japanese pragmatics textbook co-authored with Magara Maeda, Routledge), among others.

Keiko Kitade (PhD, University of Hawaii at Manoa, and MA, Columbia University) is associate professor of Japanese and Japanese language teacher education at the College of Letters and Graduate School of Education Language and Information Science, Ritsumeikan University, Japan. Her interests are second-language learning, computer-mediated communication, intercultural learning, and teacher development. Her research has appeared in various journals related to Computer-Assisted Language Learning including *Computer-Assisted Language Instruction Consortium Journal, Computer-Assisted Language Learning*, and *Language Learning and Technology.*

Ilka Kostka (PhD, New York University) is a full-time faculty member at Northeastern University, where she teaches courses in academic reading and writing to both undergraduate and graduate ESL students. She has also taught English at the Wuhan University Summer Intensive English Program (WUSIEP) in Wuhan, China. She is currently the Chief Copy Editor of TESL-EJ, and a member of the Book Publications Standing Committee of TESOL International Association.

Cynthia Lee is an Associate Professor at the Centre for Applied English Studies at the University of Hong Kong. She has extensive tertiary teaching and supervision experiences. Her research interests are in the use of computers for second language writing and writing consultations, teaching and learning of pragmatics in the Chinese context, and tutor-tutee interactions in writing consultations. She has published papers in various international referred journals such as *Computer-Assisted Language Learning, Pragmatics, Journal of Pragmatics,* and *Teaching in Higher Education.* She has also authored, co-authored, and co-edited several books with international scholars. Her recent co-edited book is *Communication and Language: Surmounting Barriers to Cross-cultural Understanding* (with Alexander S. Yeung and Elinor L. Brown) published by Information Age Publishing, Inc. in 2012.

Li Li is currently a Research Associate at the Singapore Centre for Chinese Language. Previously, she worked as a Research Associate at the Centre for Research in Pedagogy and Practice at National Institute of Education in Singapore. She earned her master's degree in Engineering in 2006 and PhD in Applied Linguistics in 2009, both from the Communication University of China. She is interested in bilingual education, second language acquisition, teaching Chinese as a second language, and computational linguistics. Her work has appeared in *International Journal of Bilingual Education and Bilingualism*, *Journal of Chinese Language Teaching* and other reputable Chinese journals.

Liu Li is an Assistant professor of Chinese at Ball State University. She holds a Masters Degree in Linguistics from Beijing Normal University in China and a PhD in Second Language Acquisition from Carnegie Mellon University in USA. Broadly, her research interests include Chinese linguistics and teaching/learning Chinese as a second language. Currently, she focuses on second language reading including improving second language literacy through computer-assisted language learning. She has published articles in Chinese discourse analysis, transfer of readings skills from L1 to L2, and learning Chinese as a second language in various contexts. Her goal for research and teaching is to provide students with better opportunities to develop the skills, knowledge, awareness and attitudes necessary to participate in a multicultural society and in an interconnected global landscape.

Mimi Li just received her PhD in Second Language Acquisition/ Instructional Technology from the University of South Florida in the USA. She is a new faculty member in the English Department of Marshall University and teaches in the MA TESOL program. She also taught a range of courses in English as a Foreign Language, ESOL teacher education, and Chinese as a Foreign Language in the past decade. Her research interests include computer-assisted language learning, second language writing, and English for academic/specific purposes. Her articles have appeared in journals such as *Computer Assisted Language Learning*, *System*, *Computers & Education*, *IALLT Journal*, and *Asian ESP Journal*.

Peter Prince is a senior lecturer in Applied Linguistics in Aix-Marseille University, where he set up and ran a self-access centre, coordinating its activities, and developing online courses and materials for non-specialist learners of English. His research interests include second language lexical access and vocabulary acquisition, second language listening comprehension, and motivation and autonomy in second language acquisition. He has been involved in teacher training both in France and abroad, with a particular focus on the motivational aspects of EFL vocabulary acquisition. Keenly interested in fiction, his current focus is on harnessing the potential of stories to enhance vocabulary acquisition.

Yumi Takamiya is an Assistant Professor at Gettysburg College, USA. She gained her PhD in Applied Linguistics from Purdue University, USA, in 2010. She is an experienced Japanese language teacher having worked in Japan and the USA. Her research interests include pragmatics, language pedagogy, technology-mediated language learning, second language acquisition, teacher development, and language assessment. Using a conversation analytic approach, she is currently investigating how second language learners of Japanese develop pragmatic competence. She has worked on a series of research projects focused on classroom interactions and dialogic teaching that rely on a sociocognitive approach, Dynamic Assessment, and Action Research. She is co-editor (with Yuko Saegusa) of *From Japan to the world: Life* *history of Japanese language teachers* (Bunkyo University Press, 2012), and she has authored a number of articles in the journals *Kotoba* [Language] and *Gengo to Bunka* [Language & Culture].

Yi Xu received her PhD degree in Second Language Acquisition and Teaching at the University of Arizona in 2009. Currently, she is an Assistant Professor of Chinese Language and Linguistics and Coordinator of the Chinese Language Program at the University of Pittsburgh. She has taught Chinese as a foreign language courses from beginning to advanced levels, English as a second/foreign language courses, and content courses on second language acquisition and Chinese linguistics. Her research interests are interdisciplinary in nature, and her recent projects focus on Chinese as a foreign language. Those include learner language development at the syntax level, using psycholinguistic methodologies in second language acquisition research, corpus linguistics, computer-assisted language learning, and orthographic and character learning in Chinese.

Dongbo Zhang (PhD, Carnegie Mellon University) is an Assistant professor in the Department of Teacher Education at Michigan State University. Prior to his current appointment, he was a research scientist in the Center for Research in Pedagogy and Practice at National Institute of Education in Singapore. His research interests include second language education, bilingual children's literacy acquisition, and language teacher education. His recent publications have appeared in *Applied Psycholinguistics, International Journal of Bilingualism, Modern Language Journal*, among many other journals. He is the author of *China through the Dynasties: Cultural and historical milestones* published by Cengage Learning (2010, with Shouhui Zhao).

Helen Zhao is an Assistant Professor in the English Department at Chinese University of Hong Kong. She works in the area of second language acquisition with a focus on grammar instruction and computer assisted language learning. She explores methods of teaching grammatical structures (English article, tense and aspect, preposition, verb particle construction, etc.) that have shown to be difficult for advanced and near-native second language learners. She aims at helping these learners to overcome the barriers to ultimate attainment. She designs computer-based language instruction that draws connection with theories and models in cognitive psychology and learning sciences. These instructional tools have been applied in English learning programs in China, Japan, Hong Kong, and Singapore.

Shouhui Zhao is a tenured associate professor at the University of Bergen. He obtained his PhD in linguistics from the University of Sydney. His work has appeared in *Language Policy, Current Issues in Language Planning, Language Problems and Language Planning, Asia-Pacific Education Researcher, International Journal of Bilingual Education and Bilingualism* and numerous Chinese journals. He is the author of *Planning Chinese Characters: Evolution, revolution and reaction* published by Springer (2008, with R.B. Baldauf, Jr.) and *China through the Dynasties: Cultural and historical milestones* published by Cengage Learning (2010, with Dongbo Zhang). A professionally trained language teacher, Dr. Zhao has taught and researched Chinese language and culture at eight universities in six different countries since 1988 upon completion of his MA study at Renmin University of China in Beijing.

Index

www.ingramcontent.com/pod-product-compliance
Lightning Source LLC
LaVergne TN
LVHW060408300926
849162LV00006B/1370